Books and Beyond

Books and Beyond

The Greenwood Encyclopedia of New American Reading

VOLUME 2:   E–M

WITHDRAWN

Edited by

KENNETH WOMACK

GREENWOOD PRESS

Westport, Connecticut • London

Library of Congress Cataloging-in-Publication Data

Books and beyond : the Greenwood encyclopedia of new American reading / edited by Kenneth Womack.
    p. cm.
  Includes bibliographical references and index.
    ISBN: 978-0-313-33738-3 (set : alk. paper) — ISBN: 978-0-313-33737-6 (v. 1 : alk. paper) — ISBN: 978-0-313-33740-6 (v. 2 : alk. paper) — ISBN: 978-0-313-33741-3 (v. 3 : alk. paper) — ISBN: 978-0-313-33742-0 (v. 4 : alk. paper)
    1. Books and reading—United States—Encyclopedias. 2. Reading interests—United States—Encyclopedias. 3. Popular literature—United States—Encyclopedias. 4. Fiction genres—Encyclopedias. 5. American literature—History and criticism. 6. English literature—History and criticism. I. Womack, Kenneth.
Z1003.2B64   2008
028'.9097303—dc22   2008018703

British Library Cataloguing in Publication Data is available.

Library of Congress Catalog Card Number: 2008018703
ISBN: 978–0–313–33738–3 (set)
      978–0–313–33737–6 (vol. 1)
      978–0–313–33740–6 (vol. 2)
      978–0–313–33741–3 (vol. 3)
      978–0–313–33742–0 (vol. 4)

First published in 2008

Greenwood Press, 88 Post Road West, Westport, CT 06881
An imprint of Greenwood Publishing Group, Inc.
www.greenwood.com

Printed in the United States of America

The paper used in this book complies with the
Permanent Paper Standard issued by the National
Information Standards Organization (Z39.48–1984).

10 9 8 7 6 5 4 3 2 1

Contents

E

ECOPOETRY

Definition. Readers use the term *ecopoetry* to describe the most recent development in a longstanding tradition of nature-oriented poetry. Ecopoetry uses language to deepen a sense of nature's presence in our lives, and these invocations of nature's presence—celebratory of the biological fact that we *are* nature—suggest an ecological understanding of nature and its processes. As John Elder explains in the first book-length treatment of the intersections between poetry and ecology, *Imagining the Earth* (1985), the principles of ecology change one's vision of nature as well as the form in which that vision is expressed.

History. As early as 1980, Robert Bly suggested that poets have long imagined something like an ecological worldview. This poetic, cultural, and spiritual orientation to the world is organized around a sense of interrelatedness between the human and the more-than-human world. The erosion of this more holistic worldview appears in the more self-conscious nature writing of late eighteenth-century Romantic poets in Europe as well as the early nineteenth-century writers in America. The work of these writers expresses a troubled separation from nature, as well as a concern with the irreversible industrial, technological, and political events that were shaping new conditions for human life.

"A poem concerned with a larger economy than the human one"—this is Jonathan Bate's summary assessment of John Keats's "To Autumn," an ode that expresses a network of relations between inner and outer ecologies of mind. Bate's *Song of the Earth* (2000) discusses the contexts and legacies of the Romantic tradition through the affinities between the imagination and the biosphere. Wordsworth is the source for the tradition of poems that no longer arise from an *occasion* but rather respond to a *place*. This response to place is most vividly expressed in the poems of two nineteenth-century American writers, Emily Dickinson and Walt Whitman. Their work undermines the religious discourses that determine the place of nature and its value in our lives. In his *Walt Whitman and the Earth: A Study in Ecopoetics* (2004), M. Jimmie Killingsworth turns to Whitman for "a more radical investigation into the possibilities and limits of human creativity" in order to better understand "how we use language to figure out our relationship to the earth" (4). His study of the intersections between environmental rhetoric and ecopoetics demonstrates how "Whitman's poetry embodies the kinds of conflicted experience and language that continually crop up in the discourse of political ecology" (9–10).

This "conflicted experience and language" recurs in nature poetry throughout the twentieth century. Reading William Wordsworth as an ecologically minded naturalist, John Elder traces changing attentiveness to nature and increasingly conflicted attitudes toward tradition from T.S. Eliot and Robinson Jeffers through the intricacies of nature's processes in the poems of Gary Snyder, A.R. Ammons, Robert Pack, and Wendell Berry. The intellectual context for Guy Rotella's 1991 *Reading and Writing Nature* is American nature poetry, from the Puritan poets Anne Bradstreet and Edward Taylor to Emerson and Dickinson. His study traces the broad epistemological and aesthetic implications of this early work in the poetry of Robert Frost, Wallace Stevens, Marianne Moore, and Elizabeth Bishop. These four poets turn to nature to explore the possibilities and limits of language and meaning and to envision poetic forms that are, in Rotella's reading, "at best conditional or 'fictive' consolations, not redemptive truths" (xi). Bernard W. Quetchenbach's *Back from the Far Field: American Nature Poetry in the Late Twentieth Century* (2000) then extends Rotella's study of American nature poetry into the postwar poetry of Robert Bly, Gary Snyder, and Wendell Berry that incorporates the public rhetoric of environmentalism.

Other literary critics who reread modern poetry using the insights and general principles of ecology include Gyorgyi Voros, whose *Notations of the Wild: The Poetry of Wallace Stevens* (1997) describes six familiar aspects of Steven's work that "readily lend themselves to an ecological reading" (83–86). Jane Frazier, in *From Origin to Ecology: Nature and the Poetry of W.S. Merwin* (1999), follows the development of Merwin's ecological worldview. Frost, Stevens, and Moore are read together in Bonnie Costello's *Shifting Ground: Reinventing Landscape in Modern American Poetry* (2003) to demonstrate how landscape serves as both structure and meaning in the later generation of poets. Costello's book, although not explicitly a study of ecopoetics, explores poetic responses to the modern world in Charles Wright, Amy Clampitt, A.R. Ammons, and John Ashbery as they create new representations of the landscape. "In Stevens' work, as in Frost's," Costello explains, "the desire for the real, and for nature, must reckon always with the frame, with landscape" (15). Scott Bryson's *The West Side of Any Mountain: Place, Space, and Ecopoetry* (2005) also turns to poems that "become models for how to approach the landscape surrounding us so that we view it as a meaningful place rather than abstract place" (12), with a focus on the poems of Wendell Berry, Joy Harjo, Mary Oliver, and W.S. Merwin.

Trends and Themes. These critical discussions of the relationship between the human and the nonhuman world—between the language of poetry and the world that surrounds a poem—are a part of the historical development of an ecological perspective. Ernst Haeckel's term *oecologie* suggested to his nineteenth-century contemporaries the potential to reimagine human affairs as a part of the larger economy of nature. As late nineteenth-century and early twentieth-century ecologists studied biological entities as a part of an ecosystem, the discipline of ecology sought standing in the scientific community as a quantitative science. The science of ecology then diverged from the descriptive explanations of nature and the role of humans in the natural world and the spatial metaphors that defined the field. The science of ecology also moved from more general conceptions of ecological processes to more complex, unpredictable, and open natural systems, random events, disequilibrium, and flux.

The concept of the ecosystem, however, offered an abstract but at the same time tangible way to conceive of (and study) the relationship between natural and human environments. Ecosystem ecology, more simply put, offered a new vision that would help people reidentify with the processes of the natural world. In his 1989 book *The End of Nature,* Bill McKibben reviews the underlying habits of mind that need to be rethought: "we tell time badly . . . our sense of scale is awry . . . [and] our more-is-better obsession with 'positive' numbers prevents us from seeing that we have ruptured our link with Nature" (13–14). This critique begins with the ecological imperatives of the environmental crisis. It envisions the necessity of developing ecological values within the political, social, and technological realms—encompassing scientific awareness, a reverence for the living world, and the responsibility of the continuing work of seeking to align social and community systems with the grander systems of life. These ecological precepts are at the center of Robert Dish's *The Ecological Conscience: Values for Survival* (1970)—a collection of essays that includes Aldo Leopold, Barry Commoner, Paul Shepard, Lewis Mumford, Paul Goodman, and R. Buckminster Fuller, as well as an essay by "eco-poet" Gary Snyder, "Poetry and the Primitive: Notes on Poetry as an Ecological Survival Technique." More recently, enthnobotanist Gary Paul Nabhan has reiterated these ecological values in his *Cross-Pollinations: The Marriage of Science and Poetry* (2004). Nabhan provides a case study in mixing the practices of field science with indigenous poetic knowledge (of desert plants, in this case). He moves freely within and across scientific and poetic discourses to discover the possibilities for a more integrated (and more humane) understanding of the natural world.

The development of an ecological perspective in the twentieth century is part of a national and international strain in literary modernism that changed the direction of poetry and art "as a necessary condition for changing the ways in which we think and act as human beings" (Joris and Rothenberg 1995, 2). These poets and artists work from the conviction "that poetry is a part of a struggle to save the wild places—in the world and in the mind." They view "the poem as a wild thing and of poetry and the poet as endangered species" (12).

Literary applications of the term *ecology* have, as these examples suggest, extended the scientific study of interrelationships to the process of the mind, giving rise to the now familiar phrases "ecology of mind" and "environmental imagination."

Ecopoetry uses comparable metaphors for describing the relationship between poetic making and ecology. Snyder writes that the ecologist looks at "population dynamics, plant and animal succession, predator-prey relationships, competition and cooperation, feeding levels, food chains, whole ecosystems, and the flow of energy through ecosystems" (1968, 31). The kind of poem that might draw on these energies in an ecosystem, he goes on to suggest, would be much like developments in fiction that have moved beyond "stock figures and charming plots" to "the inner lives and psyches of our characters, all their obsessions, kinkiness, and secrets" (32).

Context and Issues. Contemporary readers have defined the ecopoet's inclination toward primary, lived experience and the world of the senses through phenomenology. J. Hillis Miller's *Six Poets of Reality* (1965) first suggested to readers of American poetry the theoretical resources of phenomenology—specifically through the writings of the German philosopher Martin Heidegger and the French phenomenologist Maurice Merleau-Ponty. But it was not until Charles Altieri's study of American poetry in the 1960s that readers would begin to explore the relationship between poetry and ecology. *Enlarging the Temple* (1979) explores what Altieri calls *radical presence*, "the insistence that the moment immediately and intensively experienced can restore one to harmony with the world and provide ethical and psychological renewal" (78). Altieri offered a sophisticated reading of Snyder that appreciated the ecological system as central metaphor in his poetry. "Ecology deals not with ideas," Altieri argues in his chapter on Snyder and Robert Duncan, "but with modes of action and with the unity of interrelationships in nature, and its verification is the fullness of the environment it creates" (135). Using this definition, he reads Snyder's incorporation of the mind's process into the natural pattern of relationships in the poems "A Walk" and "Six-Month Song in the Foothills" from the 1968 volume *The Backcountry*. "Six-Month Song in the Foothills," for example, works from a deep sense of connection and responsibility to the earth that, in turn, "prepares a possible meditative mode where one can construct an imaginary space in which particular balances reveal a deeper unity" (137). "Grinding the falling axe/sharp for the summer/a swallow shooting out over/over the river, snow on the low hills/sharpening wedges for splitting" (Snyder 1968, 17). These lines suggest a complex spatial experience by balancing elements in the natural world as well as revealing a mind alive with the exchange of inner and outer life.

Altieri raises significant questions regarding the philosophical adequacy of any poetics of presence in his subsequent discussion of W.S. Merwin's struggles with presence and absence in *The Lice* (1968) and Denise Levertov's attempts to use the aesthetics of presence in her poems in the late 1960s. "Considered as metaphysical or religious meditation," Altieri says, "the poetry of the sixties seems to me highly sophisticated; it takes into account all the obvious secular objections to traditional religious thought and actually continues and extends the inquiries of philosophers as diverse as Heidegger, Whitehead, and Wittgenstein" (1979, 226). Frank O'Hara, Snyder, Robert Creeley, and Merwin all "give resonance and imaginative life to Heideggerean claims that poetry is the taking up of sites in which being, or the numinous familiar, discloses itself and testifies to the powers of the attentive mind" (225). However, this very success, Altieri insists, "makes it disappointing that the poetry fails so miserably in handling social and ethical issues." What is missing is an acknowledgement of the gap between values found in meditating on nature and those values developed through reflection on public themes and problems (236).

Leonard Scigaj argues that this gap is not tenable given the environmental crisis and the need to use language to understand nature's process. "With its emphasis on referential context," he insists, "environmental poetry must contain an activist dimension to foreground particular acts of environmental degradation and degraded planetary ecosystems" (1999, 21). Scigaj's *Sustainable Poetry* (1999) seeks to reorient readers to the referential function of literature and the standpoint of environmentalism. His project, as he succinctly puts it, seeks to "critique poststructuralist language theory and provide an alternative" (xiii). He turns to the phenomenology of Maurice Merleau-Ponty to elucidate the cultural value of writers such as A.R. Ammons, Wendell Berry, Denise Levertov, W.S. Merwin, Gary Snyder, and Adrienne Rich. These poets approach language as "a positive instrument that can promote authentic social and environmental relations between humans and their environment—relations that can lead to emancipatory change" (33). As Scigaj admonishes, "We need a sustainable poetry, a poetry that does not allow the degradation of ecosystems through inattention to the referential base of all language. We need a poetry that treats nature as a separate and equal other and includes respect for nature conceived as a series of ecosystems—dynamic and potentially self-regulating cyclic feedback systems" (5). Scigaj concludes that in the face of environmental crisis, we are no longer able to naturalize these ecosystems "into benign backdrops for human preoccupations" or to "reduce them to nonexistence by an obsessive focus on language" in our literary work.

Jonathan Bate argues, to the contrary, that ecopoetics properly begins "not as a set of assumptions or proposals about particular environmental issues, but as a way of reflecting upon what it might mean to dwell upon the earth" (2000, 266). Killingsworth makes a similar distinction. "I use the term ecopoetics when my readings aim for a primarily phenomenological significance and ecocriticism when they take a sharply political turn, invoking issues on the current environmentalist agenda" (2004, 6). As the literary critic Jed Rasula points out, after all, the poet seeks not to "'change the world'—a futile repetition of the Prometheus complex— but [to] change the mind that conceives, and accedes to, that composition of the real we acknowledge as the world" (2002, 62). Rasula's *This Compost: Ecological Imperatives in American Poetry* (2002) elaborates the ecological dynamics at play in the modern poetics of Charles Olson, Robert Creeley, and Robert Duncan. Rasula has no interest in defining and arguing for the distinctiveness of a select group of poets with common ecological concerns. Rather his subject is poets who call on the imagination "as a resource of ecological understanding" and poetry "in a truly re-creational capacity, one that redefines 'recreation' as original participation" (3). For Rasula, ecopoetry begins with the inadequacy of the self and its anthropocentric preoccupations, and it goes on to envision language and poetry, in the words of Snyder, "as an ecological survival technique" (1969, 117).

Reception. Any poet who writes with an environmental or ecological perspective is implicated in what Bate calls the "ontologically double" nature of the poetic. As Bate describes it, "The poetic is either (both?) a language (*logos*) that restores us to our home (*oikos*) or (and?) a melancholy recognizing that our only home (*oikos*) is language (*logos*)" (2000, 281). Angus Fletcher's *A New Theory for American Poetry: Democracy, the Environment, and the Future of Imagination* (2004) affirms this "ontological doubleness" as the condition of any poetic use of language. John Clare, Walt Whitman, and John Ashberry elaborate "both the powers and the constraints operating upon poetry when it seeks to represent the world around us" (3). Fletcher's argument addresses the question of what happens when the poet's way of being in the world "is defined as an ecological surrounding" (5). To what degree is the environment poem, Fletcher asks, "designed to increase our knowledge, as distinct from our experience, and if the latter, must our increased knowledge be of a factual nature?" (135); is it possible, in the environment poem, to distinguish the widest possible definition of nature "from any locally confined notion of any singular environment, any singular ecosystem?" (136–137). And as ecological discourse continues to permeate human thinking about the natural world, how might poetry contribute not to representing the environment or "saving the earth," but rather to seeing the future world as an ecosystem?

As Fletcher explains, "Unlike most prose discourse, poetry expresses close personal involvements, and hence pertains to the way we humans respond, on our own, to environmental matters." Fletcher elaborates the development of a more democratic and descriptive mode of poetry, the environment poem, that "introduces the experience of an outside that is developed for the reader inside the experience of the work . . . a surrounding that actually has more presence than any state of mind" (2004, 227). Rather than focus on the end of the poem as representing a place (the topographic), Fletcher privileges space (the chorographic). He recognizes the limits of defining space in terms of place or limiting the experience of an environment to a fixed and static state. The chorographic poetry of Clare, Whitman, and Ashberry "names the turbulent surface of the living ground on which or in which every thing is placed, even imprinted, while this sitting or placement remains always shaken and oscillating in the changes of the becoming" (269). The ecopoet, in this definition, uses description to undermine the more accessible comforts of place, "the nostalgia for home that place humanly implies." As Fletcher concludes, the chorographic "questions topos or *place,* by showing turbulent movements within *space."*

Scott Bryson reads the ecopoet's exploration of place and space as working toward "an increased awareness of the ecological interconnection between all the inhabitors of a particular place" and a "healthy space-consciousness . . . inherently humble" and grounded in "the inadequacies in human attempts to control, master, or even fully understand the world around them" (2005, 22). Bryson argues that the ecopoet offers a vision of the world with two interdependent if not paradoxical desires: "to *create place,* making a conscious and concerted effort to know the more-than-human world around us . . . and to *value space,* recognizing the extent to which that very world is unknowable" (8).

While Fletcher's work does not explicitly draw on the critical discourse of ecopoetics, his argument extends Bryson's discussion of poets who seek to both create place and value space—"to know the world and to recognize its ultimate unknowability" (Bryson 2005, 8). In organizing his study around the idea that "environmental sensitivity demands its own new genre of poetry" (Fletcher 2004, 9), however, Fletcher argues that environment poems "are not *about* the environment, whether natural or social, they *are* environments" (103). The question of how a reader enters and becomes subject to the environment poem then becomes a matter of entertaining the possible powers of environmental and ecological identification with a symbolic or semiotic space.

Selected Authors. The primary ecological imperative of poetry, in the words of Gary Snyder, "must be that we try to see whatever current crisis we are in as part of an older larger pattern" (2004, 10). The assimilated "compost of feeling and thinking" that gives rise to a poem is a source, for Snyder, deeper than the individual and more connected. Buddhist philosophy and Native American cultural perspectives and life ways provide additional sources for his distinctive bioregional poetics. Snyder conceives of poetry and scholarship as treating language and memory as part of the natural systems of exchange that inspire human song. He seeks to accomplish this through abandoning the fiction of the self to access a more primary source for understanding, through archaic practices and human values more closely associated with nature. From this point of view, poets have more to do than write poems "about" the environment or "speak for" nature, for their creative work arises out of and informs the complex exchanges between nature and human cultures.

Ecology and biology have informed Snyder's poetics since the 1960s. "As the evolutionary model dominated nineteenth- and twentieth-century thinking, henceforth the ecological model will dominate our model of how the world is—reciprocal and interactive rather than competitive" (130), Snyder proposes in his 1969 collection of journals and essays, *Earth House Hold*. In Snyder's early poetry, reciprocity and interactivity play out in forms of consciousness and metaphor modeled on the continual exchanges of natural energy and form. His poetics incorporate the impulse to think *about* nature in language as he articulates a way of being *within* nature. At the same time that he has elegantly and successfully developed a distinctive poetry, Snyder has established himself as a preeminent spokesperson for living more responsibly on the earth. The poems in *Turtle Island* (1974) celebrate and affirm life at the same time they suggest a broader vision of living.

Ecological succession is a central metaphor in the bioregional focus of the collection of poems *Axe Handles* (1983). As his work develops, moreover, Snyder continues to affirm the deep and intricate relationship between the ancient cultural traditions of art in China and Japan and the ecological worldview of the twentieth century. Snyder sees the world through the prism of language as well as through the impulse of most Chinese and Japanese poetry, of "seeing the world *without* any prism of language, and to bring that seeing *into* language" (1968, 143).

Mountains and Rivers Without End (1996) is a book-length poem that Anthony Hunt calls "a fundamental wisdom text for the modern ecological movement" (272). The sequence of poems explores the present moment (for Snyder the 10,000 years or so of human experience in the Holocene) by moving across cultures and time. The poem explores the history of the North American landscape and its geological and geomorphic processes, while drawing on a long tradition of Chinese art that takes mountains and rivers as the central metaphors for organizing space. *Mountains and Rivers Without End* affirms Bate's conclusion that Snyder is "the most ecologically self-conscious of twentieth century poets" (2000, 246). The ecological corollary to Snyder's observation that nature will always exceed our attempts to define it is precisely the refusal to accept the idea that we are separate from nature. This reminder expresses a complex and highly developed program Snyder has called re-inhabitation, a part of what Snyder has called the practice of the wild. Snyder's ecopoetry in this way suggests a broader role for itself, as a guide to the creation of an ecology of readers and writers. For "what we ultimately need most," writes Snyder, "are human beings who love the world" (1968, 70).

Wendell Berry's agrarian aesthetic parallels Snyder's bioregional poetics. Elder observes that "Berry identifies his life as a farmer and a poet with the cycle of decay and renewal in the soil. This is an analogy for the process of health in art and human life to which Gary Snyder returns" (1996, 52). Both are persuasive writers of nonfiction who are fiercely eloquent on the importance of place, the cultivation of regional economies, and the renewal of place-based, community values. Yet Berry's Christian vision provides a distinctive path for developing a poetry that seeks to redress a radically diminished state of human affairs. His ecological vision casts man in the role of responsible and responsive steward of the land—in his case, the land of his farm in Port Royal, Kentucky. Such stewardship requires a rejection of a modern urban-industrial society organized around "a series of radical disconnections between body and soul, husband and wife, marriage and community, community and the earth" (1991, 64).

Berry explores the possibilities of restoring these broken connections in his first books of poetry. These poems speak directly to the contemporary origins of an increasingly indifferent and destructive attitude toward the natural world. The acute sense of loss and destruction of the human community and its relationship to the land in the twentieth century is as troubling a problem for Berry as the history of indifference to the land and the human community that have been a part of this irresponsible behavior. Much like William Carlos Williams in the 1920s, Berry sees the relationship to the land as inseparable from a more complex ecology that includes human history. "I am forever being crept up on and newly startled by the realization that my people established themselves here by killing or driving out the original possessors, by the awareness that people were once bought and sold here by my people, by the sense of the violence they have done to their own kind and to each other and to the earth, by the persistent failure to serve either the place or their community in it" (1969, 104). The problem lies in the failure to see the affinities between the wild and what he calls the domestic. "The wild and the domestic now often seem isolated values, estranged from one another. And yet these are not exclusive polarities like good and evil. There can be continuity between them, and there must be," Berry insists in *Long-Legged House* (1964, 18).

For Berry, the continuity between the wild and the domestic is sustained through daily labor. Such service, moreover, involves healing. From his first collection *Broken Ground* (1968) Berry seeks to reground his life in the soil of his native Kentucky. Too, he eschews the too-common sense that an understanding of place might be won at little cost. Rather, Berry's poems urge the contemporary reader to see beyond the narrow vision of one individual's relationship to the land and to accept the inherited fate of environmental restoration. As his speaker Nathan Coulter puts it in the poem "Where" from *Farming: A Handbook,* "the idea of making/my lifetime one of the several/it will take to bring back/the possibilities of this place/that used to be here" (93). In his fifth collection of essays, *A Continuous Harmony* (1972), he aligns farming with ecology rather than economy, an argument much like Snyder's in the 1960s that economics, properly understood, would be a sub-branch of ecology. Berry goes on to say that ecology "may well find its proper disciplines in the arts, whose function is to refine and enliven *perception,* for ecological principles, however publicly approved, can be enacted only upon the basis of each man's perception of his relation to the world" (100). In this, Berry calls attention to the necessity of discovering things as they are—rather than the impulse to create and impose human forms on the natural world.

This vision of immersion in the more-than-human world has been difficult for poets to sustain given the heightened environmental and ecological concerns of the late twentieth century. Although Snyder and Berry's work is deeply informed by science, A.R. Ammons has fulfilled Walt Whitman's prophecy in *Democratic Vistas* of a future that would produce a poet "consistent with science." Ammons begins with the scientific view that the planet is ancient and has preceded humans by billions of years. And he rejects the idea of permanence and embraces nature as an intricate, evolving, and adaptive system. The critic Helen Vendler celebrates Ammons's use of scientific language as a distinctive contribution to modern poetry. Ammons is the first American poet, Vendler writes, "to use scientific language with manifest ease and accuracy, as a part of his natural vocabulary" (2005, 215).

Ammons's first book-length poem, *Tape for the Turn of the Year* (1965), is most explicit about his ecological interests: "*ecology* is my word: tag/me with that," writes Ammons, "come in there: you will find yourself/in a firmless country:/centers & peripheries/in motion,/organic, interrelations!" (112). He puts this perspective more directly in his poem "Exotic": "Science outstrips/other modes & reveals more of/the crux of the matter/than we can calmly/handle" (69). Ideas and terminology from science pervade *The Collected Poems 1951–1971*, especially the quatrains of "Extremes and Moderations" and the tercets of "Essay on Poetics" and "Hibernaculum." The poem "Extremes and Moderations" explores the self-regulating laws of nature in what has been called Ammons's most significant ecological testimony. Its primary interest is the precarious relationship between the natural and the artificial. On one level the poem is a romantic paean to those caught in the fixed and constricted environment of the city. However, the poem is more centrally concerned with the question of human purpose in the age of science and technology. The poem cautiously accepts human activity at the same time that it rejects outright the idea that human ingenuity and innovation can control nature. It registers a self-conscious environmental concern with the effects of human activity. Echoing Rachel Carson's response to the excesses of human ambition and arrogance in *Silent Spring* (1962), Ammons takes umbrage at "the rampaging industrialists, the chemical devisors and manipulators," intoxicated with "dollar lust"—the cause, he writes, of the loss of "common air" and "common rain's/losing its heavenly clarity." Ammons's position is a natural consequence of his interest in physics, biology, physical chemistry, and meteorology, his love for the inexhaustible mysteries of the natural world, and his meditations on the philosophical and ethical implications of science.

Ammons revives the romantic correspondence between nature and human perception through a lifelong study of the intricacies of observable phenomena and the networks of energy and material that make up the natural world. His praise for the quotidian, the overlooked and the useless, is therefore compensatory in the face of the dazzling ephemerality of human activity. His love of the particular thing, moreover, is enriched by his relentless exploration of transient forms. His broad and eclectic knowledge of science moves from the intercellular depths of biology to the interstellar heights of astronomy. And his meditative mind is drawn to the abstract philosophical implications of physical things and processes—infused with the multiple actions and energies of the natural world that exist beyond the narrow boundaries of the self.

In his early essay "Literature and Ecology," the critic William Rueckert writes that he knows of no other book of poems "so aware of the biosphere and what human beings have done to destroy it" as W.S. Merwin's book *The Lice* (1967). "Reading this book of poems," Rueckert writes, "requires one to unmake and remake one's mind" (qtd. in Glotfelty and Fromm 1978, 117–118). The poems in *The Lice* hold human culture accountable to the delicate and sustaining web of life, as in the speaker's haunting address to a gray whale in the poem "For a Coming Extinction." Nevertheless, Merwin's devotion to nature is shaped by a profound engagement with the contradictions of human culture—a concern with the contours of human desire and its at times unacceptable costs.

In his more than 15 books of poetry and 4 books of prose, Merwin's theme, especially as it is developed in the later phase of his work, is the postmodern problem of finding language that can offer an adequate and just account of the world. Merwin's poems urge the reader to affirm a more capacious sympathy with the nonhuman world of nature. In *The River Sound* (1999), nature's persistence appears as an anti-dote to human and ecological loss. "The Gardens of Versailles," for example, addresses the human impulse to shape nature; the poem identifies the diminishment of the natural world as the result, moreover, of "form's vast claim/to have been true forever as the law/of a universe in which nothing appears/to change" (8).

However, the final lines of the poem intimate that despite this rage for order, the river goes on, as "the sound of water falling echoes in the dream/the dream of water in which the avenues/all of them are the river on its way." Merwin accepts the difficult and conflicting struggles with language as he seeks to invent distinctive imaginative structures for understanding nature as well as the human place in a more-than-human world. The origin of a poem, Merwin writes in the "Preface" to *The Second Four Books of Poems* (1993), is "a passion for the momentary counte-nance of the unrepeatable world." The destiny of a poem, it might follow, is to awaken in a reader a fuller recognition of the self within the all-too-fragile and quickly passing frame of our lives.

For Merwin, as well as for Mary Oliver, the ecological poem might be said to arise out of what the biologist E.O. Wilson calls the innate "urge to affiliate with other forms of life" (1984, 1). As Vicki Graham elaborates, Oliver's poems register a persistent belief "in the possibility of intimate contact with the non-linguistic world of nature and the confidence in the potential of language to represent that experi-ence" (1994, 1). Despite the fact that language mediates our relationship to nature, Laird Christensen adds in a more recent overview of her ecopoetry, "Oliver clearly believes that poetry can call attention to the fact that we dwell in a world of presences" (2002, 140). However, in a 1995 review essay, the poet and critic Gyorgi Voros disparages Oliver's work for its "peculiar lack of genuine engagement with the natural world," a failure, Voros concludes, that makes Oliver's poetry "ecolog-ically unsound" (231, 238). Voros points to the passion for transcendence in Oliver that "impairs the poet's powers of observation" (235). For Voros, the problem is that despite appearances, Oliver is not "content to perceive and honor *this* world in all its ordinariness"; rather, her adoration of the natural world betrays a "passion for transcendence" that "impairs the poet's powers of observation" (235).

In addition to the two-volume *New and Selected Poems* (1992), Oliver's most recent collections of poetry include *What Do We Know* (2002), *Owls and Other Fantasies* (2003), *Why I Wake Early* (2004), *Blue Iris* (2004), and *Thirst* (2006). In these poems Oliver rejects the limits of the confessional strain in contemporary poetry (and the tendency to reproduce merely individually significant moments in a life). What Voros overlooks is that Oliver's descriptions of individual experiences in nature are working toward an ecological understanding of the self and human agency. Oliver's focus on dramatizing human experiences in nature works to reinforce or alter the way in which we experience the natural world. Her work does not dramatize the commonplace statements that nature is a previously harmonious realm undisturbed by human activity; that nature is a restorative space for human use to recuperate from the excesses of human culture; or that nature would simply reawaken us to a more harmonious or ecological way of being in the world.

Oliver's book-length poem *The Leaf and the Cloud* (2000) may best foreground the limits of what Voros calls "ecologically sound" poetry. One of commonplaces of normative ecology is that we are connected to everything else—a truism, but only in the most trivial sense, for bodily identification with the nonhuman world is, of course, what we already have. One contribution of *The Leaf and the Cloud*, as a book-length poem, is its generic departure from the aesthetics of presence that determine how poems think about the natural world. *The Leaf and the Cloud* is devoted to exploring what Charles Olson once called a poet's "stance toward reality." It is a poem preoccupied with the relationship between the work of the poet and the work of the world. And it is devoted to bringing the reader into its investigation. For instance, in the first of its seven sections, "Flare," Oliver welcomes the reader "to the silly, comforting poem" (1). The immediate concern of the speaker is with what the poem is not. It is not "the sunrise,/which is a red rinse,/which is flaring all over the eastern sky"; nor is it the "trees, or the burrow burrowing into the earth." The 12 numbered parts of section 1 move from Whitman-like questions of a reader ("Therefore, tell me:/what will engage you?") to declarative instructions to the reader ("The poem is not the world./It isn't even the first page of the world," 5).

Calling attention to the poem as a poem is of course nothing new. But the extended and discursive space of the long poem creates a place to record the daily work of the writer who takes as her subject the states of mind that arise in observing the daily unfolding of natural phenomena. In part 2 of the poem, "Work," the poet's work is set alongside what Oliver calls the "work of the world," the "deliberate music" of the ears of corn swelling under their green leaves, the dark stone, the grouse's fan-tail. The refrain throughout the sections of part 2—"this is the world"—calls attention to the plenitude of the surroundings and the poet's surprise and amazement at finding out—most often what one does not know. Oliver then poses the inevitable questions that arise in any sustained inquiry into the music of what is happening. "Would it better to sit in silence?/to think everything, to feel everything, to say nothing?" (12), Oliver asks. After all, she responds, such is the impulse of the river and the stone. Her answer is instructive. She is not willing (or able) to accept the odd human preoccupation with the promise that to abandon cultural and anthropocentric frameworks—of language and symbolic representation, of ideas such as beauty, devotion, and respect—would somehow place one "closer" to the natural world. As she puts it, "the nature of man is not the nature of silence." The nature of man, that is, is wild *and* civilized—utterly alive in the flesh and fiercely obliged to the anthropocentric devotions to beauty, curiosity, and respect.

The Leaf and the Cloud enacts the process of building a response to nature through deliberate self-consciousness. The meaning that Oliver attaches to events or phenomena—whether more descriptive and empirical or more abstract and emblematic—comes from an ability to cultivate one's self, to remain distinct and to live more fully in our language and its capacities to mediate between our conscious bodies and the environment that surrounds us and of which we are always already a part. *The Leaf and the Cloud* is in this way a summation, a generative moment in an evolving ecopoetics.

Gary Snyder, Wendell Berry, W.S. Merwin, A.R. Ammons, and Mary Oliver are representative of a more diverse group of twentieth-century poets whose work has been explicitly shaped by an ecological perspective. In *Green Voices: Understanding Contemporary Nature Poetry* (1995), for instance, Terry Gifford highlights the ecological nature poetry of the British poets Patrick Kavanagh, Sorley MacLean, Seamus Heaney, and Ted Hughes. Environmental and ecological themes also shape the work of a number of other poets, including Adrienne Rich, Robert Pack, Louise Glück, Joy Harjo, Linda Hogan, Charles Wright, Ernesto Cardenal, Jimmy Santiago Baca, Simon J. Ortiz, Arthur Sze, Daphne Marlatt, Derek Walcott, and Margaret

Atwood. This array of voices suggests the expanding focus of ecopoetics as well as its reach beyond the Anglo-American tradition. The tendency to canonize particular authors, and forms of writing about the natural world, according to Jamie M. Killingsworth, is in part a product of the desire to better understand our relationship to the more-than-human world. But, as he explains, "as we come to see 'saving the earth' as one metaphor among many—a metaphor conditioned perhaps by the historical experience of the cold war—our focus can broaden to include a greater diversity of writers" (2004, 11). The study of writers with a wider range of imaginative responses might thereby offer readers new ways of exploring the interdependencies of language, human experience, and the more-than-human world.

If one accepts the idea that poetry is "the place where we save the earth," in the words that bring Bate's *Song of the Earth* to a close, then the term ecopoetry signals a preoccupation with the fate of the planet. While the narrow framework of human lives and the perspective gained through generations of human life register radical geomorphic changes (volcano eruptions, earthquakes, tidal waves, melting icecaps), the earth's processes unfold across a timeline not apparent to the perceptions and actions of human beings. Ecopoetry recognizes these limitations at the same time that it models forms of attention and linguistic acts that might make a difference in human lives and the forms of responsibility that arise in the peculiar human capacity for ethical reflection about forms of life beyond our own.

Bibliography

Ammons, A.R. *Collected Poems, 1951–1971.* New York: Norton, 1972.
———. *Tape for the Turn of the Year.* Ithaca, NY: Cornell University Press, 1965.
Bate, Jonathan. *The Song of the Earth.* Cambridge: Harvard University Press, 2000.
Berry, Wendell. *The Broken Ground.* New York: Harcourt, 1969.
———. *A Continuous Harmony.* New York: Harcourt, 1972.
———. *Farming: A Handbook.* Sand Diego: Harvest, 1970.
———. *The Long-Legged House.* New York: Harcourt, 1964.
———. *Recollected Essays, 1965–1978.* San Francisco: North Point, 1981.
———. *Standing on Earth: Selected Essays.* Ipswich: Golgonooza Press, 1991.
Carson, Rachel. *Silent Spring.* Boston: Houghton, 1962.
Christensen, Laird. "The Pragmatic Mysticism of Mary Oliver." In *Ecopoetry: A Critical Introduction.* J. Scott Bryson, ed. Salt Lake City: University of Utah Press, 2002. 135–152.
Frazier, Jane. *From Origin to Ecology: Nature and the Poetry of W.S. Merwin.* Madison, NJ: Farleigh Dickinson University Press, 1999.
Killingsworth, M. Jimmie. *Walt Whitman and the Earth: A Study in Ecopoetics.* Iowa City: University of Iowa Press, 2004.
Merwin, W.S. *The First Four Books of Poems: A Mask for Janus, The Dancing Bears, Green with Beasts and the Drunk in the Furnace.* Port Townsend, WA: Copper Canyon Press, 2000.
———. *The Lice.* New York: Atheneum, 1967.
———. *The River Sound.* New York: Knopf, 1999.
———. *The Second Four Books of Poems: The Moving Target, the Lice, the Carrier of Ladders, Writings to an Unfinished Accompaniment.* Port Townsend, WA: Copper Canyon, 1993.
———. *Travels.* New York: Knopf, 1993.
Miller, J. Hillis. *Six Poets of Reality.* Cambridge: Harvard University Press, 1965.
Oliver, Mary. *The Leaf and the Cloud.* Cambridge, MA: Da Capo Press, 2000.
———. *New and Selected Poems: Volume One.* Boston: Beacon, 1992.

————. *New and Selected Poems: Volume Two.* Boston: Beacon, 2005.

Scigaj, Leonard. *Sustainable Poetry: Four American Ecopoets.* Lexington: University of Kentucky Press, 1999.

Snyder, Gary. *Axe Handles.* San Francisco: North Point, 1983.

————. *The Back Country.* New York: New Directions, 1968.

————. *Back on the Fire: Essays.* Emeryville, CA: Shoemaker & Hold, 2007.

————. "Ecology, Literature, and the New World Disorder." *ISLE: Interdisciplinary Studies in Literature and the Environment* 11.1 (2004): 1–13.

————. *Earth House Hold: Technical Notes and Queries to Fellow Dharma Revolutionaries.* New York: New Directions, 1969.

————. *Mountains and Rivers Without End.* Washington, D.C.: Counterpoint, 1996.

————. *No Nature: New and Selected Poems.* New York: Pantheon, 1992.

————. *Turtle Island.* New York: New Directions, 1974.

Wilson, E. O. *Biophilia: The Human Bond with Other Species.* Cambridge: Harvard University Press, 1984.

Further Reading

Altieri, Charles. *Enlarging the Temple: New Directions in American Poetry during the 1960s.* Lewisburg, PA: Bucknell University Press, 1979; Bryson, J. Scott, ed. *Ecopoetry: A Critical Introduction.* Salt Lake City: University of Utah Press, 2002; Bryson, J. Scott, ed. *The West Side of Any Mountain: Place, Space, and Ecopoetry.* Iowa City: University of Iowa Press, 2005; Costello, Bonnie. *Shifting Ground: Reinventing Landscape in Modern American Poetry.* Cambridge: Harvard University Press, 2003; Disch, Robert, ed. *The Ecological Conscience: Values for Survival.* Englewood Cliffs, NJ: Prentice Hall, 1970; Elder, John. *Imagining the Earth: Poetry and the Vision of Nature.* 2nd ed. Athens: University of Georgia Press, 1996; Fletcher, Angus. *A New Theory for American Poetry: Democracy, the Environment, and the Future of Imagination.* Cambridge: Harvard University Press, 2004; Gifford, Terry. *Green Voices: Understanding Contemporary Nature Poetry.* New York: St. Martin's Press, 1995; Gilcrest, David W. *Greening the Lyre: Environmental Poetics and Ethics.* Reno: University of Nevada Press, 2002; Graham, Vickie. "'Into the Body of Another': Mary Oliver and the Poetics of Becoming Other." *Papers on Language and Literature* 30.4 (1994): 352–372; Joris, Pierre, and Jerome Rothenberg, eds. *Poems for the Millennium: The University of California Book of Modern and Postmodern Poetry, Volume One: From Fin-de-Siècle to Negritude.* Berkeley: University of California Press, 1995; Joris, Pierre, and Jerome Rothenberg, eds. *Poems for the Millennium: The University of California Book of Modern and Postmodern Poetry, Volume Two: From Postwar to Millennium.* Berkeley: University of California Press, 1998; Nabhan, Gary Paul. *Cross-Pollinations: The Marriage of Science and Poetry.* Minneapolis, MN: Milkweed, 2004; Quetchenbach, Bernard W. *Back from the Far Field: American Nature Poetry in the Late Twentieth Century.* Charlottesville: University Press of Virginia, 2000; Rasula, Jed. *This Compost: Ecological Imperatives in American Poetry.* Athens: University of Georgia Press, 2002; Rueckert, William. "Literature and Ecology: An Experiment in Ecocriticism." *The Ecocriticism Reader: Landmarks in Literary Ecology.* Ed. Cheryll Glotfelty and Harold Fromm. Athens: University of Georgia Press, 1996. 105–123; Vendler, Helen. "A.R. Ammons: Dwelling in the Flow of Shapes." In *The Music of What Happens: Poems, Poets, Critics.* Cambridge: Harvard University Press, 1988, 310–342; Vendler, Helen. "*The Snow Poems* and *Garbage*: Episodes in an Evolving Poetics." In *Complexities of Motion: New Essays on A.R. Ammons's Long Poems.* Rutherford, NJ: Fairleigh Dickinson University Press, 1999, 23–50; Voros, Gyorgyi. "Exquisite Environments." *Parnassus: Poetry in Review* 21.1–2 (Winter 1995): 231–250; Voros, Gyorgyi. *Notations of the Wild: Ecology in the Poetry of Wallace Stevens.* Iowa City: University of Iowa Press, 1997.

MARK C. LONG

EROTIC LITERATURE

Definition. Erotic literature is composed of works in which sex, sexuality, and/or sexual desire has a dominant presence. Literature from almost every genre can be considered erotic literature, including drama, poetry, fiction, and memoirs. Scholars and governments have even classified erotic treatises and sex manuals as erotic literature. However, the inclusion of a sex scene is not the only criteria for erotic literature; instead erotic literature—through the exploration of desire and sexuality—interrogates or calls attention to important cultural, sociological, and philosophical concepts. Often these texts point to a perceived or real disconnect between the body and society, between the sexes, and even between children and adults.

Erotic literature differs from pornography in that society views the former as socially acceptable. Both can also arouse the reader, but erotic literature seeks to engage the reader's mind in an exploration of sexuality, while pornography seeks only to elicit a physical response. Erotic literature, especially erotica, can be pornographic, but pornography rarely (if ever) raises philosophical, cultural, or sociological questions for the reader. At times, the line between erotica and pornography blurs. The ostensible impetus behind their creation, that is, to arouse and titillate a reader, is similar, but erotica, as in erotic literature as a whole, usually manages to transcend the purely sexual.

Erotica also moves across genre lines, intersecting with detective fiction, historical narratives, science fiction and—within the last 10 years—supernatural erotica. Thus, erotica functions like most literary modes in that it is not tied to any specific form or genre.

History. Erotic literature has a rich and varied history that dates back to the ancient Greeks and the ancient civilizations of the Middle East and Asia. This history includes the many attempts of governments to censor many works now considered to be classics.

Erotic prose written by the ancient Greeks dates back to the third century B.C.E., but it peaked during the second and third century CE during the Second Sophistic. According to Dominic Montserrat, the works emphasize "romance, seduction, sexuality, and the erotic development of individuals," and the writers were the first to "make the sexual self a field of enquiry" (2006, 584). Moreover, the government did not consider some of this erotic prose, which included treatises, romantic narratives, and drama, as immoral. In fact, Montserrat notes that some of these works were "praised for their medical benefits, because they could stimulate impotent men" (584). Censure of works with erotic content stemmed from representations of excess and unbalanced behavior, and the Greek government did not target erotic texts.

Trends and Themes. Ancient Greek verse, like prose, explores the erotic but incorporates two basic themes, requited and unrequited love. The Greek poets

In erotica, the narrative focuses on a concrete, explicit sexual act to interrogate notions of taboo in broader cultural context instead of the more abstract notions of sexuality and desire. As Patrick Califia-Rice notes, erotica is "one way to write sexual history—the slang, fashion, community institutions, music, controversies, mores, the signifiers and significance of sexual expression at various points in time and in several different sexual minority communities" (2001, 150). The preferred form is prose, primarily in the shape of short fiction or novels, and occasionally poetry.

wrote on the latter with considerable frequency. Monica Cyrino explains that this unrequited desire is characterized by an "unfulfilled and perhaps even unfulfillable feeling of erotic desire, and is denoted by the absence of the beloved, the lack of satisfaction, and the impossibility of erotic realization;" in this type of verse, "the lover's desire is difficult, painful, and ultimately devastating" (2006, 588). Poets did not hesitate to explore both heterosexual and homosexual love, as well as the effects of erotic desire on the mind and body. Aeschylus, in addition to his tragedies, wrote of the relationship between King Laius of Thebes and his love of the Chrysippus, a young boy, and Anacreon of Teos was so influential that the cult of Anacreonitic verse formed, which covered all poetry in praise of wine and women. Sappho also focused on both the deleterious and beneficial effects of eros on the mind and body.

After the ancient Greeks, writers from Britain and France provide texts that have been perhaps most influential on both American erotic literature and erotica. The traditions and conventions established by the English and the French are apparent in the works of contemporary American authors.

In the seventeenth century, England enjoyed an increase in literacy for both men and women. Paired with this rise in literacy was the increased availability in the number of poems, plays, and books designed to arouse sexual desire. The erotic literature of this time period is marked by a distinct escapist quality, and much was written to shock as well as to arouse. Literature relating to sexual freedom and divorce was quite popular. Other prevalent themes were women's sexual voracity and prostitution. Although many of the writers during this time intended to titillate, their pieces often commented on the political, the religious, and the social.

Although popular tastes dictated the types of erotica that writers were producing, the printing industry itself suffered under tight constraints beyond the control of the reading public. Due to the monopoly on printing rights instigated by James I in 1603, Stationers' Company had a tight hold on the printing industry (Curth 2006, 413). According to Louise Hill Curth, Charles I aided in maintaining this monopoly by "establishing the most repressive system of press censorship since the reign of Elizabeth I" (412). The monopoly eventually collapsed in 1640, and independent printers flourished in London.

The eighteenth century saw the rise of the erotic novel, as well as the emergence of pornography in England. A popular theme in the narratives of this time features the male examination of the female prostitutes' life. Bradford K. Mudge explains that these "[w]hore dialogues," such as John Cleland's *Fanny Hill,* "combined lascivious passages with sex education, anti-ecclesiastical diatribes, and radical philosophy," thus meeting the definition of erotic literature (2006, 416). With the movement of erotic poetry into periodicals, prose became the genre of choice for erotic literature, and Mudge contends that by 1789, "sexual obscenity and the novel were joined at the hip" (418).

Just as erotic literature appeared in England, France saw a surge in the production of erotic texts. In 1635, literary production in France came under the auspices of the French government, which through the Académie Française made it clear that it expected French literature to conform to governmental sanctions. In this repressive atmosphere, erotic literature fell into the hands of a group of writers known as the libertines. These writers produced work that challenged the censors, sometimes by openly bypassing official publishing channels, and at other times through more oblique means. French erotic literature became a battleground where writers fought a sexually repressive regime by showing the hypocrisy government officials practiced, and officials destroyed works that illustrated the link between the political and the religious. Yet the execution of Claude Le Petit in 1662 also made it clear that blasphemous and obscene writing could have deadly consequences.

As in eighteenth century England, the novel became a popular vehicle for erotic literature in France. The novel, as an experimental and radical form, allowed writers to challenge their readers in their exploration of the nuance of the erotic. Fairy tales are an unexpected hotbed of erotic literature, where allegorical elements allow writers to obliquely critique French society. Charles Perrault's "Le Petit chaperone rouge" ("Little Red Riding Hood") is a tale fraught with eroticism, and it serves as a warning to aristocratic young ladies to avoid the "wolves," or rakes, of Louis XIV's court. According to Paul Scott, however, the conventional representation of romantic love in fairy tales "accepts the dominant discourse of sexuality, with its implicit exaltation of patriarchy," reinforcing rather than challenging the mores of the time (2006, 479).

After 1740, French erotic literature flourished, thanks in part to the publication of the best-selling novel *Histoire de D[om Bougre]* and to the flowering of French Enlightenment philosophy. In fact, Natania Meeker notes the important role the "erotic and obscene" played within the "culture of the French Enlightenment, both as a form of literate entertainment and as a vehicle for the development and diffusion of new modes of thought" (2006, 481). She also argues that several of the most prominent philosophers, such as Julien Offray de La Mettrie and Charles-Louis de Secondat, Baron de La Brède et de Montesquieu, delved into the erotic as well.

In the eighteenth century two general categories of the novel—the libertine novel of seduction and the pornographic novel—proved the novel to be one of the most exciting genres of the period. Meeker explains that "[c]ritics have historically been reluctant to associate the frank obscenity of the latter with the elegant suggestiveness of the former, even though the two genres share an Epicurean focus on sensual and sensorial pleasure" (481). Also during this time, the "oriental tale" was highly successful as part of the general interest in the East. Despite a fair amount of exoticism, some of the writers took the change in setting as an opportunity to critique the "morals, fashions and rituals of the court of Louis XV" (Meeker 2006, 481). In its examination and critique of matters of social, political, and moral importance, French erotic literature became increasingly political in tenor in the years leading up to the Revolution. In fact, supporters of the revolution used satirical and scathing erotic literature as a tool against the aristocracy, often depicting them as amoral hedonists. These works were popular in France until long after the collapse of Louis XV's regime.

Censorship and American Erotic Literature. While sexual descriptions have become an integral part of American fiction, our Puritan roots and censorial past ensured that literary sex scenes—explicit or not—have come under careful scrutiny. The Americans were initially less puritanical than their English counterparts, enjoying Latin poetry, Shakespeare, and the more contemporary works of English novelist Henry Fielding (Tom Jones) and Scottish writer Tobias Smollett (Roderick Random) for much of the eighteenth century with relative impunity. According to Felice Lewis, early America had "almost no tradition of indigenous erotic fiction," in part because American literature was "born in the early nineteenth century" at a time when the English writing model was quite sedate (1976, 12). The most popular pieces of American erotic writing were Benjamin Franklin's "Advice to a Young Man on Choosing a Mistress" and "A Letter to the Royal Academy at Brussels," but the manuscripts were available only in limited copies. Though neither was published in the United States by Franklin, the London-based Gentleman's Magazine published "Advice to a Young man on Choosing a Mistress" in 1747 (Loth 1961, 115). Another American erotic work that managed to elude the censors was Mark Twain's Conversation, as it was by the social fireside in the time of the Tudors, or 1601, and like Franklin's letters, Twain's text was not published in the United States in his lifetime. Written in 1876 between Tom Sawyer and Adventures of Huckleberry Finn, 1601 critiques the "elevated reputation of Elizabethan society and its vulgar behavior" (Lee 2006, 1320). Though markedly scatological in nature, 1601 was available only in manuscript and private editions before 1996.

Context and Issues. By the mid-nineteenth century, American writers were beginning to explore the erotic and its moral implications. Nathaniel Hawthorne's *The Scarlet Letter* was an instant success because it handled spiritual and moral issues from a uniquely American point of view. Lewis notes that the novel was originally charged with "perpetrating bad morals," even though Hawthorne "could not have handled the material more carefully," reiterating the sentiment that sexual urges lead to immorality and moral decay (1976, 15). However, because Hawthorne was well established in the New England literary community, his potentially risqué novel was not censored and passed into the realm of appropriate texts. In contrast to *The Scarlet Letter*, Walt Whitman's *Leaves of Grass* bursts with exuberant sensuality, especially the poems "Song of Myself," "Children of Adam," and "Calamus." The first edition was maligned by some critics for being "exceedingly obscene," and in the third edition, the publishers juxtaposed poems with "homosexual overtones." *Leaves of Grass* was criticized and suppressed, but never censored, in part because it was "too abstruse to have wide appeal" (Lewis 1976, 15). These two important early American texts illustrate the already-forming relationship between text, audience size and type, and censorship. Lewis argues the aristocracy's view "of the masses as children who are easily led astray" (16) drove nineteenth century censorship.

In the United States, compulsory education and an increase in literacy created a new market for less than literary erotic literature. David Loth contends that, in order to satisfy these demands, American publishers imported erotic literature from England (1961, 120). John Cleland's *Memoirs of a Lady of Pleasure,* also known as *Fanny Hill,* was one of the first erotic works to find its way to the United States, where it was banned in 1821—almost a century after similar censure in England—when Massachusetts judges convicted Holmes of obscene libel. *Commonwealth vs. Holmes* marked the first time a book and its publisher were prosecuted for lewdness. In 1821, Vermont established the first obscenity statute, followed by Connecticut in 1834 and Massachusetts in 1836 (Loth, 121).

Even though obscenity laws had been on the books since 1821, they were rarely enforced on printed material before 1870, though plays were heavily censored throughout the 1800s. Lewis contends that the "anti-obscenity movement in both England and America begins with Lord Campbell's Act" of 1857, which allowed authorities to seize books and prints that were "in their opinions obscene" (7). The first case tried under Lord Campbell's Act proved more influential than the act itself. In 1868, a magistrate seized copies of Henry Scot's pamphlet titled *The Confessional Unmasked: Shewing the Depravity of the Roman Priesthood, the Iniquity of the Confessional and the Questions put to Females in Confession* (7). Scot appealed and Benjamin Hicklin, the Recorder of London, "ruled in his [Scot's] favor on the basis that his purpose was good, that he had no intention of corrupting public morals"—a decision that was soon overturned by Chief Justice Alexander Cockburn, who stated, "The test of obscenity is whether the tendency of the matter charged as obscenity is to deprave and corrupt those whose minds are open to such immoral influences and into whose hands a publication of this sort may fall" (Lewis, 7–8). Cockburn's definition of obscenity would continue to be cited by American judges well into the twentieth century, providing an extremely broad, subjective definition of obscenity (8).

Anthony Comstock and the New York Society for the Suppression of Vice (NYSSV) were pivotal in the censorship movement. The NYSSV was an outgrowth of the Young Men's Christian Association and was supported by wealthy, influential men (Biesel 1997, 76). Nicola Biesel argues that, while Comstock appealed to the wealthy by citing concern about "youthful corruption in terms of problems that could befall wealthy children," he also appealed to the middle class's concern for their children (76). He accomplished this by linking "the corruption of children by obscene materials to other issues already established as 'social problems,' such as prostitution, abortion, and juvenile delinquency" (76). Comstock and the NYSSV lobbied for a more restrictive law regarding the mailing of obscene items, and in March 1873, President Grant signed the Comstock Law. Comstock was reputed to have banned fictional work, sex manuals, newspaper and magazine articles deemed obscene, and contraceptive manuals. In general, he tended to attack works with little literary merit that were regarded as "unquestionably pornographic in his day," but he also opposed the sale of classics like *The Decameron* and others (Lewis, 12).

The increase in legal actions against "literature of repute" coincided with popularity of the European realistic-naturalistic fiction (Lewis, 12). Writers like Stephen Crane, Theodore Dreiser, and Frank Norris fought against American publishers who were reluctant to publish potentially obscene works. Pulp novels, however, were thriving and increased in availability in the nineteenth century. According to Chris Packard, pulp Westerns produced before 1900 feature an often all-male world where "homoerotic affection holds a favored position," and "affection for women destroys cowboy *comunitas* and produces children, and both are unwanted hindrances to those who wish to ride the range freely" (2005, 3). The cowboy, Packard argues, is a queer figure who "eschews lasting ties with women but embraces rock-solid bonds with same-sex partners; he practices same sex desires" (3). Westerns written after 1900 do not present male affection as freely because of the "modern invention of the 'homosexual' as a social pariah" (3). The same type of homoeroticism extends to other texts written before 1900, including *Adventures of Huckleberry Finn* and *The Leatherstocking Tales,* where the male partnerships are erotic yet unconsummated (4). Even though homoerotic relationships abound in the pulp Westerns of the 1800s, they were situated in the mythical West, and publishers and writers managed to avoid censors.

Censorship reared its head in the middle of the twentieth century with the trials of an unexpurgated edition of D.H. Lawrence's *Lady Chatterley's Lover,* Henry Miller's *Tropic of Cancer* and *Tropic of Capricorn,* and William S. Burroughs's *Naked Lunch.* The novels were eventually deemed not obscene because of their social value and literary merit, and the court rulings were based on precedents set in cases dealing with James Joyce's *Ulysses* and Cleland's *Fanny Hill,* which sanctioned writing about sex that did not intentionally appeal to prurient interests.

Reception. There is a surprising paucity of scholarly criticism on erotica specifically, though there is a fair amount on erotic literature as a whole. Like the pulp

Western, contemporary erotica is rarely censored, and scholars rarely, if ever, write on the themes and issues prevalent in the subgenre. This dearth can possibly be attributed to scholars' dismissal of the genre as smut or to a reluctance to analyze sexually explicit texts. This reluctance on the part of the academy—though not unexpected—has not gone unnoticed by writers of erotica. In an America where "signifiers of sex are everywhere we turn," Simon Sheppard points out that the shame is still with us (2001, 208). Califia-Rice writes that a simplistic discussion of writing erotica as simply smut omits the "lack of serious critical attention (because everyone 'knows' pornography requires no serious literary talent)" (2001, 145).

To this day, contemporary novels containing explicit sexual content or those with homosexual themes are still seen as threat to children and society. Books written by Toni Morrison, Richard Wright, J.D. Salinger, and Lesléa Newman have all been challenged and charged as unacceptable and obscene, but because of their literary merit, they have not been banned.

Selected Authors. Most contemporary American erotica written today is fiction. While there are still single-authored short story collections and novels being published, the vehicle of choice is the anthology. Such collections are popular because they allow editors to feature a cross section of stories centered on a particular theme. Anthologies are also one of the few outlets for emerging writers to get published, a role editors have taken over from print magazines.

Since the mid- to late 1990s, specialized anthologies have exploded onto the market. These anthologies target specific, marginalized groups including (but not limited to) heterosexual women, gays, lesbians, bisexuals, women, African Americans, Latinos, and those in the sadomasochistic communities. Many anthologies target a combination of these groups. Such specificity can be credited to an increased demand from readers to see themselves represented in the fiction, as well as to publishers targeting specific audiences. General anthologies are popular as well, and they tend to include a sampling of erotica meant to appeal to a broad range of tastes. Notably, with the exception of some geographically specific anthologies, like *Best American Erotica*, many of the anthologies being published tend to have an international list of authors, and some, like editor Maxim Jakubowski's *Mammoth Book of Erotica*, and *Mammoth Book of New Erotica*, originate in an international market. This inclusionary trend is a product of literary globalization. Another trend includes the overwhelming presence of first person narratives in erotica, which draw readers directly into the story, immersing them in the narrative.

Coinciding with this international trend of specialization is the abundance of "best of" anthologies. Some, such as *Best American Erotica, Best Lesbian Erotica,* and *Best Gay Erotica,* are annual publications. However, a "best of" anthology generally allows for at least one sequel anthology if the initial volume is successful. These anthologies promise to deliver the best erotica taken from short story collections, novels and novellas, and online and print magazines.

While few print magazines carry erotica exclusively, editors have taken the genre into cyberspace. Online magazines such as *Nerve, Clean Sheets, Libido,* and *Scarlet Letters* are flourishing. These peer-edited, free, online magazines allow the reader to peruse erotic fiction and poetry, rendering erotica more readily accessible.

Gender and Sexual Minorities. Much of the erotica written in the last 10 years explores what mainstream society terms *deviant* sexuality, including sadomasochism, homosexuality, transgender sex, and a number of fetishes. According to Califia-Rice, "most subcultures rely on staying underground to survive. . . . Any work that celebrates a stigmatized way of being in the world cuts two ways. It is both celebratory and revealing, sometimes dangerously so" (2001, 152). Works dealing with sadomasochism do not hesitate to depict both the sadist's and the masochist's points of views. Likewise, homosexual erotica both challenges and upholds stereotypes about the gay and lesbian community, where hetero-normative sexual constructs still exist. Many authors, however, are writing stories that redefine sexuality as a place where men and women negotiate, manipulate, or accept traditional notions of gender and power. Male and female writers are also crossing gender lines, proving it is possible for a man to successfully write women's, and even lesbian, erotica, and vice versa.

Mary Gaitskill's erotic story "A Romantic Weekend" focuses on the characters' desires, and the sex act becomes almost inconsequential to their angst and disappointment with each other. Beth and her unnamed lover falsely present themselves as a sadist and a masochist, respectively. Beth desires to be a masochist, but she misconstrues what masochism requires of her. She tells her partner, "I won't do anything I don't want to do. You have to make me want it" (2000, 192). She wants to be forced, but she does not understand that the key tenets of sadomasochism are trust and surrender. Similarly, her lover wants to dominate her but is unable to overcome her refusal to surrender. The sex scene, although beautifully written, is terse in its rendering of sex while explicitly exploring the failure of desire. Gaitskill writes:

> She put her glass on the coffee table, crossed the floor and dropped to her knees between his legs. She threw her arms around his thighs. She nuzzled his groin with her nose. He tightened. She unzipped his pants. "Stop," he said. "Wait." She took his shoulders—she had a surprisingly strong grip—and pulled him to the carpet. . . . He felt assaulted and invaded. This was not what he had in mind, but to refuse would make him seem somehow less virile than she. Queasily, he stripped off her clothes and put their bodies in a more viable position. He fastened his teeth on her breast and bit her. She made a surprised noise and her body stiffened. He bit her again, harder. She screamed. He wanted to draw blood. Her screams were short and stifled. He could tell that she was trying to like being bitten, but that she did not. He gnawed her breast. She screamed sharply. They screwed. (189)

Rather than Beth yielding to her partner, she makes him yield to her will, leaving them both dissatisfied in the process. Her desire to be dominated "had been completely frustrated" (190). Gaitskill's purpose here is not to titillate the reader or allow the reader to linger on the intimacy of the act. It is written to disconcert. This story does not be qualify as erotica—mainly because the story focuses on unfulfilled desire and its effect on the characters—but it challenges the easy suppositions about who should surrender.

Patrick Califia-Rice's short story "Gender Queer" tackles the complexity of transgender identity, specifically that of female-to-male transgender. Califia-Rice uses sex to talk about important issues because "people are reluctant to think about many of the issues surrounding sex and gender. Or there's a knee-jerk reaction that reflects what 'everybody knows' to be true," but he is also dedicated to questioning the "mores or policies they develop to socialize new members, regulate the conduct of insiders, and handle relationships with outsiders" (2001, 153).

The main character, Carleton, is a female-to-male (FTM) transgender who leads a FTM support group. There we see oblique and explicit references to problems that plague the transgender community. The men in the support group grapple with finding a doctor to perform a mastectomy, as well as with social concerns about attracting the "perfect straight girl" who is unattainable pre-phalloplasty (2006, 80). In effect, once they have completed their transition, most of the FTM transmen will become heterosexual males. Carleton is the only bisexual in the group, and he gets no empathy from his support group concerning his anxiety about going to gay bars downtown. This lack of empathy points to a limited definition of masculinity and the expectation that identifying as male means identifying as a heterosexual male, excluding the full spectrum of masculinity.

The story's central conflict lies in Carleton's relationship with "Moss," a woman who verbally attacked Carleton at a lecture months before because, at the time, she was afraid of her own desire to be male. She wants to know what it would be like to be a man, to:

> stand there without these sandbags strapped to my chest, and feel my body straight and strong and free. I wanted to know how it felt to shave my face and walk out my front door whistling. To have the guy at the gas station call me sir and not have anybody give me a second look. (Califia-Rice 2005, 80)

For Moss, these are the characteristics of masculinity, the things that deserve envy, and she sees Carleton as the embodiment of these traits. It is Carleton who mitigates her fears and validates her desires, and it is he who names her Moss. At this point in the story, Moss's gender pronoun switches from female to male.

Carleton then offers to be her guide, because "[m]aking things easier for new guys was one of the ways Carleton exorcised the pain of his own coming out process" (82). He shows Moss how to bind his chest, applies facial hair, and even gives Moss a haircut. The pre-operation transformation is complete when Carleton gives Moss a "packer," or a silicon mold of a flaccid penis.

In the sex scene, Moss and Carleton must negotiate the disconnect between the male gender they claim and the physical reality of their bodies. Carleton is anxious about his body, making Moss promise that he's "not going to think [Carleton is] a girl" once he is naked (85). Post coitus, Carleton reflects it is "good to be touched by someone who understood that you could be a guy and still have girl parts, but this intimate act reminded him again that his body was not perfectly and entirely male" (88–89).

Califia-Rice's interest in gender construction is indicative of a growing trend in erotica today. Marginalized groups are redefining for themselves how they are represented to and within the dominant culture. Erotica written by and for marginalized groups often presents a more nuanced representation, and these works are in conversation with the stereotype they are consciously working against. This is not to say that all writers of marginalized erotica scrupulously avoid stereotypes or attempt to complicate or react against it. Some writers seem content to write prose that present a marginalized group in a stereotypical fashion without bothering to delve into the politics of being that might surround that group.

Within lesbian erotica, for example, writers are constantly imagining and re-imagining the literary representation of lesbian relationships, including the traditional butch/femme, top/bottom power structures, femme/femme, butch/butch, as well as the interactions between "bois" and "grrls." The re-appropriation and revision of how lesbians are represented is a reaction, in some ways, to the derivative, butch/femme (or femme/femme if the medium is visual), hetero-normative images in popular media. This type of revisionist play is not exclusive to lesbian erotica, and it points to a growing trend of writers unpacking the possibilities of representation. Some black erotica focuses on issues of family and stability. The unfortunately titled "Homecumming" by Cherysse Welcher-Calhoun presents a long-married African American couple that is happy to have a weekend alone. The story turns the stereotype of the black broken home on its head, describing a close-knit family where the father is present and both parents work in the corporate world. The female protagonist comes home from work and is responsible for cleaning the house and taking care of the kids. She occupies both spheres, but seems happy to do so. This type of representation is emblematic of the trend in African American erotica. This story is not particularly radical, but the normative representation of the black family seems in direct conversation with images of the black family.

Sex-Positive Erotica. Patrick Califia-Rice, Susie Bright, Cecilia Tan, Bill Brent, and other erotica writers have written, and continue to write, in the spirit of sex-positive images that allow for power variations in any healthy sexual encounter. Sex-positive writer Carol Queen writes that one of the "crucial cultural functions of erotic literature," specifically sex-positive work, is that it "always serves as a kind of protest literature exploring (and exploding) taboos, gender roles, and socially imposed notions of appropriate sexuality" (2001, 47). Sex-positive feminists and writers are at direct odds with the feminist anti-porn movement that gained prominence in the mid- to late 1970s as a result of and in reaction to the sexual revolution that heralded an increase in number of pornographic magazines and films.

Anti-porn feminists criticize pornography for its representation of women as hyper-sexualized victims and blame the abundance of pornography for the rise in rape and domestic violence rates. According to Lori Saint-Martin, they condemn "both literary erotica and mainstream pornography, which they say deliver the same sexist message," and while they call for women to "develop their own erotic imaginations," they consider the task virtually impossible, given their "patriarchal conditioning" (2006, 456). As a result, the anti-porn feminists' definition of a healthy relationship does not include any form of consensual sadomasochistic sexual relationship, or any sexual relationship in which the power dynamics are not equal.

Members of the sex-positive movement embrace the many manifestations of human sexuality, including the practices of sexual minorities, and believe in sexual freedom for all people. They argue that to consider a woman's engagement in, say, sadomasochistic activities as deviant, or to say it eroticizes power and violence does not take into consideration the consensual nature of such play. The sex-positive movement attracts activists from numerous spheres, including anti-censorship feminists, activists in the LGBT community, pornographers, writers of erotica, and sexual radicals.

Anti-porn feminists view prostitution as yet another site of female subjugation, where women are reduced to objects, victims of male violence. In his introduction to *Macho Sluts,* Califia describes the prostitute as someone potentially beyond the control of men. Unlike housewives who put no price on their time, who have no "demarcation between business and pleasure"—thus leaving them with no space of their own—prostitutes get men to "part with some of their property instead of becoming property themselves. . . . The whore does not sell her body. She sells her time" (1988, 20). This revision of prostitution foregrounds the prostitute's agency.

Queen's story "Best Whore in Hillsboro" takes the reader into the world of high-class prostitutes. Queen admits to "being a sort of Pollyanna of sex writing . . . so sex positive that there's not enough for critics who like that cutting-edge style that wallows in taboo and shame, nouveau de Sade" (2001, 50). Instead of a sordid tale of prostitution and redemption, Queen presents a narrative that moves prostitution out of the margins and presents it as a normal job, a job people can like or hate. Indeed, the main character, Kitty, likes her job. She and fellow prostitute Corrina do not suffer poor working conditions, and they do not have a pimp; they prostitute themselves because they want to. The prostitutes in Queen's story do not conform to stereotypical norms for their profession: Corrina attended law school, and Kitty was in the undergraduate honor society, Phi Beta Kappa. Kitty learned early "that most whores dress up, no down; signaling that your ass is for sale on the night streets of the Tenderloin is one thing, but slipping into the Fairmont to service an out-of-town CEO is quite another, and Kitty's bought more conservative clothes since she began working than she's ever owned in her life" (1999, 235). This is not the traditional representation of prostitutes, but then, it is Queen's assertion that there are women who like sex work.

Corrina is less than happy with her job for several reasons, the first being that she "got caught by the IRS a few years ago and she's still paying off the heavy fines. Pimped by the government, the whores called it" (234). In addition to paying fines, she is jaded, preferring to dominate clients rather than have sex with them (235). The clients she and Kitty are servicing together are an affluent couple who have renewed her enthusiasm for her job.

Instead of condemning prostitution, Queen critiques the institution of marriage. Kitty's view of marriage is particularly cynical. She estimates that 98 percent of her clients are married, and that they do not "tell their wives where they go on those long lunch hours" (236). She is tired of men who "have" to call her because they "think their wives are too pure or too 'frigid'" (236). According to Kitty, her profession is "weird" in that it helps shore "up the illusion that married life is a functional state" (236). It seems more "legitimate" to work for a married couple. Kitty is not oblivious to the class differences, and on meeting Tom and Pam, she realizes they are "creating the near-seamless illusion for Corrina and Kitty that they are all affectionate friends, in the same class, and enjoying the same life circumstances—that they are equals chatting about Christmas and sipping brandy" (237).

Queen also plays on the reader's expectation that Kitty and Corrina are paying Tom and Pam a visit at Tom's request, but it's really Pam, a former prostitute herself, who desires their company the most because she does not quite fit into the high-class society she has married into. She cannot be herself, and, if Kitty's analysis is on target, being "herself" involves having an active sex life.

This movement promotes sexual responsibility, well, and in "Best Whore in Hillsboro," the characters are careful to use plenty of latex. With the AIDS epidemic and the increased spread of STDs, writers working within the sex positive movement are careful about depictions of unprotected sex. When Simon Sheppard co-edited the gay male anthology *Rough Stuff,* he and co-editor M. Christian decided not to accept works that "explicitly eroticized the *unprotected aspect* of the barebacking" (2001, 211)—i.e. the practice of unprotected, gay male sex—and in rejecting stories that sensationalized the dangerous aspects of this act instead of showing the real life repercussions, Sheppard and Christian demonstrate the careful considerations editors must make while still allowing for the creativity of their authors.

IMPORTANT EDITORS IN EROTIC PUBLISHING

In some respects, the editors of erotica anthologies are as influential in shaping modern erotica as the authors they include. Editors like Thomas S. Roche and Cecilia Tan both founded a space for genre erotica, while those like M. Christian and Susie Bright work to expand its the parameters. As the editor of the *Noirotica* series, Roche wanted the "chance to merge cutting-edge writing with crime-noir, and bring the erotic subtext up to the surface of a genre that was always playing with it" (Wharton 2000). Cecilia Tan's publishing company, Circlet Press, routinely publishes sci-fi erotica, and she has edited several sci-fi erotica anthologies.

M. Christian is the author of five books, including the Lambda-nominated *Dirty Words, Speaking Parts, The Bachelor Machine,* and *The Bloody Marys.* His fiction has appeared in more than 200 anthologies, including *Best American Erotica, Best Gay Erotica, Best Lesbian Erotica, Best Transgendered Erotica,* and *Friction.* Christian is the editor of over 20 anthologies, including *S/M Erotica, Love Under Foot* (with Greg Wharton), *Bad Boys* (with Paul Willis), *The Burning Pen, Guilty Pleasures,* and many others. Christian's editorial eye is geared towards stories that are sexually titillating and mentally stimulating.

Susie Bright is arguably one of the most important editors in erotica today. She has edited 18 anthologies and novels. Since 1993, she has been the editor of *Best American Erotica,* published by Simon and Schuster. Bright was also the founding editor of the first women's anthology, *Herotica,* in 1988, and she edited the first three volumes. She co-edited *On Our Backs,* an influential magazine geared toward lesbians, from 1984 to 1991. As series editor of *Best New Erotica,* Bright has managed to expand the boundaries of erotica, including work from well-known writers like Mary Gaitskill, John Updike, and David Sedaris, as well as erotica industry standards like Peggy Munson, Carol Queen, and Skian McGuire. It is clear that Bright subscribes to the notion that erotica has a more important cultural function than glandular stimulation.

Bibliography

Biesel, Nicola Kay. *Imperiled Innocents: Anthony Comstock and Family Reproduction in Victorian America.* Princeton, New Jersey: Princeton University Press, 1997.

Bright, Susie, ed. *Best American Erotica.* New York, New York: Touchstone, 1993–2007.

Burroughs, William S. *Naked Lunch.* New York: Grove Press, 1990.

Califia, Pat. *Macho Sluts.* Los Angeles, California: Alyson Publications, 1988; 20.

Califia-Rice, Patrick. "Gender Queer." In *Best Gay Erotica 2006.* Richard Lambonte, ed. San Francisco, California: Cleis Press, 2005; 76–90.

———. "An Insistent and Indelicate Muse." In *The Burning Pen.* M. Christian, ed. Los Angeles, California: Alyson Publications, 2001; 145–154.

Christian, M., series ed. *Best S/M Erotica: Extreme Stories of Extreme Sex.* Pahoa, Hawaii: Black Books, 2001–2006.

Cleland, John. *Fanny Hill: Or, Memoirs of a Woman of Pleasure.* New York: Penguin Putnam Inc., 1986.

Curth, Louise Hill. "English: United Kingdom, Seventeenth Century." In *Encyclopedia of Erotic Literature.* Gaetan Brulotte and John Phillips, eds. New York: Routledge, Taylor and Francis Group, 2006; 411–415.

Cyrino, Monica. "Greek, Ancient: Verse." In *Encyclopedia or Erotic Literature.* Gaetan Brulotte and John Phillips, eds. New York: Routledge, Taylor and Francis Group, 2006; 588–596.

Gaitskill, Mary. "A Romantic Weekend." In *The Second Gates of Paradise.* Alberto Manguel, ed. Toronto, Canada: Stoddart Publishing Co., 2000; 175–204.

Jakubowski, Maxim, editor. *Mammoth Book of Erotica.* New York: Carroll & Graf, 2000.

Lewis, Felice Flanery. *Literature, Obscenity, and Law.* Carbondale, IL: Southern Illinois University Press, 1976.

Loth, David. *The Erotic in Literature.* New York: Julian Messner, Inc., 1961.

Meeker, Natania. "French: Eighteenth Century." In *Encyclopedia or Erotic Literature.* Gaetan Brulotte and John Phillips, eds. New York: Routledge, Taylor and Francis Group, 2006; 481–488.

Miller, Henry. *Tropic of Cancer.* New York: Grove Press, 1999.

Montserrat, Dominic. "Greek, Ancient: Prose." In *Encyclopedia or Erotic Literature.* Gaetan Brulotte and John Phillips, eds. New York, New York: Routledge, Taylor and Francis Group, 2006; 584–588.

Mudge, Bradford K. "English: United Kingdom, Eighteenth Century." In *Encyclopedia or Erotic Literature.* Gaetan Brulotte and John Phillips, eds. New York, New York: Routledge, Taylor and Francis Group, 2006; 415–420.

Packard, Chris. *Queer Cowboys.* New York, New York: Palgrave Macmillan, 2005.

Queen, Carol. "Best Whore in Hillsboro." In *More Totally Herotica.* Marcy Sheiner, ed. New York, New York: QPBC, 1999; 234–243.

———. "What Do Women Want? We Want to Be Big Slutty Fags, Among Other Things." In *The Burning Pen.* M. Christian, ed. Los Angeles, CA: Alyson Publications, 2001; 44–50.

Roche Thomas S., series ed. *Noirotica.* Pahoa, Haiwaii: Black Books, 1996–2001.

Saint-Martin, Lori. "Feminism: Anti-Porn Movement and Pro-Porn Movement." In *Encyclopedia or Erotic Literature.* Gaetan Brulotte and John Phillips, eds. New York: Routledge, Taylor and Francis Group, 2006; 455–460.

Scott, Paul. "French: Seventeenth Century." In *Encyclopedia or Erotic Literature.* Gaetan Brulotte and John Phillips, eds. New York: Routledge, Taylor and Francis Group, 2006; 476–480.

Taormino, Tristan, ed. *Best Lesbian Erotica.* San Francisco, CA: Cleis Press, 1996–2007.

Welcher-Calhoun, Cherysse. "Homecumming." In *Best Black Women's Erotica.* Blanche Richardson, ed. San Francisco, CA: Cleis Press, 2001; 28–40.

Wharton, Greg. An Interview with Thomas S. Roche. [Online, 2000] Suspect Thoughts: A Journal of Subversive Writing <www.suspectthoughts.com/roche.htm>

Whitman, Walt. *Whitman: Poetry and Prose.* Justin Kaplan, ed. New York: Library of America, 1996.

DONIKA ROSS

F

FANTASY LITERATURE

Definition. Fantasy literature is a genre of literature that has produced much discussion in regard to definition. What is and is not considered fantasy is often reflective of the worldview of the critic, and the definition can habitually be too narrow or general to be considered agreeable. The word *fantasy* itself comes from the Greek *phantasia,* meaning "to make visible." In its most agreed-upon definition, fantasy literature is the genre in which heroic or villainous characters narrate from a setting wholly imagined (i.e., secondary) or amalgamated with existent creations (i.e., those from existing mythological texts), geographically influenced by historical settings and often depicting environments in accordance to their nature (e.g., haunted forests are dark and diseased, while sacred groves are beautiful and potent), and chronologically set during (or having a strong connection with) the past. Stories often involve a conflict between the forces of good and evil in which a war is fought, a quest is embarked on, a life is chronicled, or order must be restored by central characters. Fantasy embodies the development of the past and the evolution of the future; it is an alternate reality, glimpsing into the impossible. Fantasy literature is sharply divided by its subgenres, constructing their own doctrine and considering themselves related only through superficial trappings.

The following subgenres are among the largest in fantasy literature:

High fantasy (also known as epic fantasy) is often written in an ancient or secondary world setting, richly detailed and exhibiting cultures similar to that of reality (such as medieval). Such fantasy tends to be written in an epic-like manner (often narrated over several novels), reminiscent of historical and mythological texts, so as to project a sense of grandeur and significance, and such works often reflect a great deal of research (much like **historical fantasy**). Research can extend to races, language, social customs, and industry. The goal of high fantasy is that of realism, so to depict the unnatural as being normal. Well-known works in this field include David A. Drake's Lord of the Isles series (1997–), David Eddings's Belgariad

FANTASY COMPARED TO MAINSTREAM FICTION

Famed author of fantasy literature Stephen R. Donaldson (best known for his Chronicles of Thomas Covenant, the Unbeliever, series, 1977–), offers a unique school of thought:

> [Compare] fantasy to realistic, mainstream fiction. In realistic fiction, the characters are expressions of their world, whereas in fantasy the world is an expression of the characters. Even if you argue that realistic fiction is about the characters, and that the world they live in is just one tool to express them, it remains true that the details which make up their world come from a recognized body of reality—tables, chairs, jobs, stresses which we all acknowledge as being external and real, forceful on their own terms. In fantasy, however, the ultimate justification for all the external details arises from the characters themselves. The characters confer reality on their surroundings. (Donaldson 1986, 7)

series (1982–1984), Robin Hobb's Farseer trilogy (1995–1997), and Tad Williams's Memory, Sorrow, and Thorn trilogy (1988–1993).

Low fantasy (also known as urban fantasy) primarily takes place in the real world, often relocating fantastical creatures and characters into a natural environment. While such stories can venture into secondary worlds, these are the lesser to the real world because the emphasis of this subgenre is to merge the elements of fantasy with the world of readers. Such fantasy is often dependent on existing mythologies (which it has a tendency to modernize) and visible to characters who believe or seek out the fantastical, which is mostly hidden from the natural world. Books by authors who have excelled in this genre include Emma Bull's *War for the Oaks* (1987), Jonathan Carroll's *The Land of Laughs* (1980), John Crowley's *Little, Big* (1981), and Charles de Lint's *Moonheart* (1984). At times, fairy tales are included in this subgenre, but they are usually set in the past and are often set in a secondary world, such as Wilhelm and Jakob Grimm's three-volume *Kinder-und-Hausmarchen* (1812) and modern anthologies such as editor Jack Zipes's *Spells of Enchantment: The Wondrous Fairy Tales of Western Culture* (1991).

Sword and sorcery fiction (also known as heroic fantasy) is a subgenre named by author Fritz Reuter Leiber Jr. (1910–1992) to identify a type of fantasy he and fellow authors were writing predominantly in the later twentieth century, but that had originated in the 1920s with Robert E. Howard's short story "The Shadow Kingdom" (1929). Sword and sorcery fiction is written in a secondary world setting, in which protagonists are often social or cultural outcasts who live outside the law and possess a love-hate relationship with civilization. Like **adventure fiction**, the subgenre is full of emotionally charged action and adventure that involves magic, monsters, and traditional maidens in distress; however, the latter trend has changed with the growth in warrior women, thanks in part to Jessica Amanda Salmonson (e.g., *Tomoe Gozen*, 1981; rev. *The Disfavored Hero*, 1999). Works that have excelled in this subgenre include Fritz Leiber's Fafhrd and the Gray Mouser series (recently collected in *The First Book of Lankhmar*, 2001, and *The Second Book of Lankhmar*, 2001); Charles R. Saunders's Imaro series (*Imaro*, 1981, rev. 2006; *Imaro: The Quest for Cush*, 1984, rev. 2007; *Imaro: The Trail of Bohu*, 1985, rev. 2008); Karl Edward Wagner's Kane series (*Darkness Weaves*, 1970, restored text 1978; *Bloodstone*, 1975, *Dark Crusade*, 1976, and short story collections *Death*

Angel's Shadow, 1973, and *Night Winds,* 1978); Richard L. Tierney's Simon Magus series (short story collection *Scroll of Thoth: Simon Magus and the Great Old Ones,* 1997, and *The Gardens of Lucullus,* 2001, a collaborative novel with Glenn Rahman); and Darrell Schweitzer's short story collection *We Are All Legends* (1981) and novels *The Shattered Goddess* (1982), *The White Isle* (1990), and *The Mask of the Sorcerer* (1995). This subgenre is not to be confused with dark fantasy, which merges fantastical elements with horror.

Historical fantasy is a subgenre set exclusively in the past, often merging fiction with fact in a display of exhaustive research. Events in history are often retold in an alternative or contemporary manner (e.g., the reign of King Arthur in Marion Zimmer Bradley's Avalon series starting with *Mists of Avalon,* 1979, and the Trojan War in David Gemmell's trilogy of *Troy: Lord of the Silver Bow,* 2005; *Troy: Shield of Thunder,* 2006; and *Troy: Fall of Kings,* 2007) in which familiar figures are changed and their characters are reinterpreted differently (such as the life of Jesus Christ in Michael Moorcock's *Behold the Man,* 1966, rev. 1969) and Dan Brown's *The Da Vinci Code,* 2003). Dan Brown's novels are a prime example of when fictional stories are appended to well-known historical events or figures so to explore a "secret history," which has resulted in readers considering the works as nonfiction. Primarily, historical fantasy does not include supernatural beings and at times seeks to logically explain the elements of mythology (e.g., Michael Crichton's *Eaters of the Dead,* 1976). However, some authors of historical fantasy willingly incorporate the supernatural into their stories but are careful that these elements do not obscure the rich detail of historical events and characters (e.g., Robert E. Howard's historical adventures such as "Marchers of Valhalla," 1932, and "The Dark Man," 1931, among others).

Dark fantasy is a subgenre that can be divided into two types of story. The first is when elements of fantasy are used as the primary source of horror (as exampled in the short stories of Ray Bradbury, Christopher Golden, Joe R. Lansdale, Thomas Ligotti, Michael Mignola, and Clark Ashton Smith), while the second type is when sword and sorcery fiction is overtly embedded with elements of horror, to allow the development and exploration of darker themes. Often, in the latter type of dark fantasy, anti-heroes are the protagonists, and the plot includes more violence, sexuality, or psychological detail (as exampled in the series of Charles R. Gramlich's Kainja, Les Daniels's Don Sebastian de Villenueva, and Karl Edward Wagner's Kane).

It is important to note that public perception as to what constitutes fantasy literature can vary dramatically. Some critics have commented that the trappings of fantasy exist in more genres than most would initially suspect, as all fiction itself is fantasy to begin with, and that even the so-called realistic authors are presenting readers with their own particular, often odd or unusual, perception of reality.

History. An overview of the development of fantasy literature is the grounds for much discussion, but it is relatively easy to determine a foundational work. Ancient mythology, primarily Sumerian epics such as *The Epic of Gilgamesh* (c. 1500 B.C.E.) and Greco-Roman epics such as *The Iliad* (c. 750 B.C.E.), *The Odyssey* (c. 750 B.C.E.), and later *The Argonautica* (c. 250 B.C.E.), are often considered the first forms of fantasy literature because they are ripe with heroes, villains, quests, and supernatural beings (living creatures, deities, and the undead), and the once theological aspects of the stories are no longer considered relative (hence ruling out Jewish, Christian, and later Islamic sacred literature from being labeled early fantasy literature). For untold centuries both the oral tradition and the world's dominant story modes (myths, epics, folktales, legends, and some pseudo-histories) have been fantastic. That fantasy literature can be redefined as modern mythology may not be as difficult to imagine as one may believe, for all literature comes beneath the banner of a unique mythos.

In the United States, it is harder to determine a seminal work. Some commentators accredit the sacred texts of Native Americans with being the first forms of American fantasy literature (written down as early as the nineteenth century by ethnographers working with select tribes), but this opinion is uncommon because the theological belief of these deities and entities still exists. More common is the belief that Washington Irving's stories of dark fantasy, "The Legend of Sleepy Hollow" and "Rip van Winkle" (collected in *The Sketch Book Of Geoffrey Crayon, Gent.*, 1819–1820) are the first true American fantasies, followed by the works of Edgar Allan Poe, Nathaniel Hawthorne, Herman Melville, Mark Twain, and L. Frank Baum, to name but a few American classics of the genre.

During the early twentieth century, the growth of fantasy literature was tremendous. Pulp magazines such as *Weird Tales: The Unique Magazine* (1923–1954), *Unknown* (1939–1943), *Fantastic Adventures* (1939–1953), *Famous Fantastic Mysteries* (1939–1953), *The Magazine of Fantasy and Science Fiction* (1949–), and *Fantastic* (1952–1980) supplied everyday Americans with fantasy literature and published thousands of authors. Several of these magazines have become best sellers. Even when some of these magazines died off because of either financial or production difficulties, small presses such as Arkham House republished many of these pulp magazine authors in handsome hardcover editions, including H.P. Lovecraft, Robert E. Howard, Clark Ashton Smith, Frank Belknap Long, and August Derleth. Slowly but surely, fantasy literature was recapturing the imagination of American readers again, and with the publication of J.R.R. Tolkien's Lord of the Rings trilogy and Robert E. Howard's Conan the Barbarian series in the latter half of the twentieth century, book publishers (such as Sphere, Ace, Bantam, and Del Rey/Ballantine) matched a demand that went into the millions, also publishing the countless imitators and anthologies of fantasy that emerged soon after.

Trends and Themes. Fantasy literature in the twenty-first century continues the same trends and themes that have existed in the genre for millennia, and unlike many other genres, in particular **science fiction** and horror, it is debatable as to whether one can consider national or international events as reflective of successful trends (or sales). For example, events such as the terrorist attacks of September 11, 2001, on America have resulted in new subgenres, and while critics have accredited this to changes in genres such as political thrillers, the theme of terrorism is not new

---

IMPORTANT FANTASY AUTHORS IN THE 2000s

Since 2000, fantasy literature has shown no sign of stopping, with small presses mainly publishing short story collections and mass market publishers manufacturing countless fantasy novels. With the release of several cinematic adaptations of fantasy novels, the genre continues to generate new readers, profitable sales, and the opportunity for new authors such as Jeff Vandermeer, Elizabeth Hand, Jeffrey Ford, Jeffrey Thomas, Michael Cisco, Shelley Jackson, and Michael Chabon to emerge in a professional manner.

and can hardly be seen as redefining an entire genre. Publishing phenomena like J.K. Rowling's Harry Potter series (1997–2007) and Dan Brown's **historical fantasy** *The Da Vinci Code* (2003) are difficult to attribute to a particular event and could not fairly be considered a widespread trend. The only identifiable change in the themes of fantasy literature may be modernization for contemporary audiences (as seen in the works of Neil Gaiman, such as the Sandman series, 1987–1996, and *American Gods*, 2001) so to have the imagined world inherit more of the world's sociological norms, a trend already witnessed in dark fantasy. Reaffirmation of the fantastical is an unusual theme in fantasy literature, particular low fantasy, in which the elements of fantasy are expressed in a manner that indicates they are a natural part of the real world and not imaginary; it is the belief and survival of fantasy in the work that becomes its very theme, such as J.M. Barrie's play *Peter Pan, or, The Boy Who Would Not Grow Up* (1928). It is also possible to identify the growth of more mature and heavily researched work across all subgenres of fantasy literature, such as Susanna Clarke's *Jonathan Strange & Mr. Norrell* (2004) and Elizabeth Kostova's historical fantasy *The Historian* (2005).

The theme of the hero's journey, which one may label as traditional, is among one the largest in fantasy literature. Joseph Campbell's *The Hero with a Thousand Faces* (1949) is divided into three stages: Departure, Initiation, and Return. Departure begins with "The Call to Adventure" and is then followed by "Refusal to the Call," "Supernatural Aid," "Crossing the First Threshold," and then "Belly of the Whale." Initiation begins with "The Road of Trials" and is then followed by "Meeting the Goddess," "Woman as Temptress," "Atonement with the Father," "Apotheosis," and finally "The Ultimate Boon." Finally, Return begins with "Refusal of the Return" and is then followed by "The Magic Flight," "Rescue from Without," "The Crossing of the Return Threshold," "Master of the Two Worlds," and finally "Freedom to Live." The debate over whether most, if even all, fantasy adheres to this formula has long been a discussion among authors and critics of the genre. Campbell's most successful influence was on George Lucas's Star Wars saga (1977–2005), which is a merger of fantasy and science fiction. An alternative is the ongoing series in which short stories compose the main characters' biography over a period of time. Fritz Leiber's Fafhrd and the Gray Mouser sword and sorcery fiction (1939–1988) works are free of set archetypes such as Campbell's, as they choose to explore the identity of their characters and often do not have an ending in sight (irrespective of what sequence in which they were written).

In fantasy literature, particularly high fantasy, the ongoing battle between the forces of good and evil is a natural component of the plot. Michael Moorcock has made explicit use of this in his Multiverse series, in which an "Eternal Champion" (the best known incarnation being Elric, who first appeared in *Elric of Melniboné*, 1972) is directly involved in the battle between the forces of good and evil (which Moorcock retitles Law and Chaos). However this battle is described or presented, while existing in all subgenres of fantasy, it is most prominent in high fantasy because of its epic-like presence. An alternative to this is the restoration of order by a force of good, in a world already ruled by the forces of evil, as in the works of Roger Zelazny (the Chronicles of Amber series, 1970–1991). From this often emerges the theme of power and the responsibility that comes with it, also prominent in fantasy literature. In J.R.R. Tolkien's *Lord of the Rings: The Fellowship of the Ring* (1954), Hobbit Frodo Baggins learns that he will be the one to possess Sauron's One Ring and travel to the volcanoes of Mordor to destroy its evil forever.

In Neil Gaiman's *Books of Magic* (1991), novice magician Timothy Hunter learns that he will inherit great power, but it is yet undetermined whether he will use the power for the force of good or evil. **Christian fiction,** in which elements of fantasy are renowned, also details the battle between good and evil in which Satan (and his demons) battle against God (and his angels) in accordance with their natures as described in the Old and New Testament canons. Christian fantasists such as Karen Hancock (the Guardian-King series, 2003–2007) and Brock Thoene and Bodie Thoene (A.D. Chronicles series, 2003–) are authors who often depict Christian protagonists surviving in a world where the war between God and Satan is ever-present, but they depict this world allegorically (best exampled in C.S. Lewis's Chronicles of Narnia series, 1950–1956). The first three volumes of Orson Scott Card's Alvin Maker series are also worth mentioning (*Seventh Son,* 1987; *Red Prophet,* 1988; *Prentice Alvin,* 1989), as the author's devotion to Mormonism comes through in his writings.

Humorous fantasy is a limited trend in fantasy literature, particularly works written primarily for a young audience. While mostly present in British fantasy literature, there are some notable American authors who merge comedy with fantasy. L. Sprague de Camp and Fletcher Pratt wrote a series about the time-traveling Harold Shea, beginning in *Incompleat Enchanter* (1942); Poul Anderson's novel *Three Hearts and Three Lions* (1961) is often referred to as a work of humor, as is Piers Anthony's *A Spell for Chameleon* (1977). Fritz Leiber's Fafhrd and the Gray Mouser sword and sorcery stories (1939–1988) also contained humorous moments, as did the dark fantasy stories of Robert Bloch.

Fantasy works in which animals are protagonists follow a well-known theme and have existed as far bask as the fables of Aesop (c. 6 B.C.E.) and have remained a cornerstone within British fantasy, as seen in the works of Lewis Carroll, Beatrix Potter, Kenneth Grahame, and Richard Adams. Animals that talk come in two forms: humanoids who talk, eat, and dress like humans or animals that retain their nature but are able to speak the human language. Examples of American authors who have chosen to narrate their stories through animals include Joel Chandler Harris (*Uncle Remus: His Songs and His Sayings,* 1880), Fritz Leiber (*The Green Millennium,* 1953, and the Gummitch short stories in *Gummitch & Friends,* 1992), and Art Spiegelman (*Maus: A Survivor's Tale,* 1992, a retelling of the Holocaust, belonging to the subgenre of historical fantasy).

Contexts and Issues. In regard to the discussion of fantasy literature and how it reflects contemporary issues, in "Why Fantasy and Why Now?" Bakker comments that fantasy is "the primary literary response to what is often called the 'contemporary crisis of meaning' . . . [representing] a privileged locus from which one might understand what is going in [modern] culture." Citing the aftermath of the Enlightenment as an indication of a return to fantasy (and one could argue religion), Bakker rightly decrees the following:

> Fantasy is the celebration of what we no longer are: individuals certain of our meaningfulness in a meaningful world. The wish-fulfillment that distinguishes fantasy from other genres is not to be the all-conquering hero, but to live in a meaningful world. The fact that such worlds are enchanted worlds, worlds steeped in magic, simply demonstrates the severity of our contemporary crisis. "Magic" is a degraded category in our society; if you believe in magic in this world, you are an irrational flake. And yet magic is all we have in our attempt to recover some vicarious sense of meaningfulness. If fantasy primarily

looks back, primarily celebrates those values rendered irrelevant by post-industrial society, it is because our future only holds the promise of a more trenchant nihilism. One may have faith otherwise, but by definition such faith is not rational. Faith, remember, is belief without reasons. (Bakker 2002)

Themes are universal, as are the emotions we share. When reading fantasy literature, this is no different. It is composed of a variety of philosophical elements and structured in an inimitable manner that upholds a particular ideology, connecting it closer to the values and beliefs of the real world. For example, the appeal of a dragon may for one reader simply be the entertainment value derived from a sense of awe at an otherworldly and wondrous beast while for another it might embody and symbolize his or her dream to fly (either literally or metaphorically). The term *escapism* is often applied to fantasy literature, in that fantasy is seen as a means of escaping the realities of contemporary life. While the elements of horror or **science fiction** might be seen as either too confronting or too complex, the worlds of fantasy are often depicted as being far more favorable and welcoming because they are absent of the social and ecological problems of the real world. However, when establishing the weird tale canon, S.T. Joshi includes fantasy but is quick to discard "imaginary-world fantasy" and heroic fantasy; rather, he includes only fantastical elements unnatural to this world in the weird tale canon, for the former types of fantasy seem "to lack a certain metaphysical ramifications present in nearly all other types of weird fiction" (Joshi 1990, 9). This point of view is open to debate.

As a genre, fantasy literature has faced being stereotyped by the works of a single subgenre (for example, all fantasy must include sorcerers, dragons, and knights, as in high fantasy). Formulaic writing is also inherent in some fantasy literature, again in high fantasy and also sword and sorcery fiction. Public perception of fantasy literature has shown people's inability to differentiate its subgenres, and in some instances, it is seen as the same as **science fiction**. Others think of fantasy literature as being the same as **children's literature**, reflective of how fantasy was depicted and presented in the earlier days of the older generation.

Fantasy literature, particularly high fantasy, has often been charged with overwriting, whether in relation to exhausting the genre as a whole (as is often said of the subgenre of vampire fiction in horror), too much detail on inconsequential matter (sometimes considered as self-absorption of research), or the sheer length of a series that does not appear to have an ending in sight (such as Robert Jordan's Wheel of Time series, 1990–). Additionally, some authors have carelessly paid too much respect, admiration, and honor to the work of an earlier, often classic, author. Both J.R.R. Tolkien and Robert E. Howard have been the cause of countless imitators, most of whom are mediocre in comparison to their source of inspiration. Tolkien's imitators include authors such as Terry Brooks, David Eddings, Robert Jordan, and Dennis McKiernan, to name but a few, while Howard's imitators, primarily located in sword and sorcery fiction, include Lin Carter, Gardener Fox, John Jakes, and Roy Thomas. Howard's works, like H.P. Lovecraft's horror stories (resulting in the infamous "Cthulhu Mythos"), have resulted in dozens of pastiches in which established authors (such as L. Sprauge de Camp, Björn Nyberg, and Harry Turtledove) have continued the saga of well-known creations, in this case, Conan of Cimmeria. In stating this issue, paying homage in fantasy literature is not to be seen as a flaw or deemed unworthy of study. A prime example of successful homage is Lovecraft's Dunsanian period of writing between the years 1919 and 1921, when the author's writing reflected the works of Lord Dunsany (1878–1957). Dunsany is known for his mythological worlds and characters and has rightly been considered foundational to fantasy literature. Lovecraft was a great admirer of his work, writing several stories that were Dunsanian in nature, some of the well-known works being "The Doom That Came to Sarnath," "The Cats of Ulthar," and "The White Ship." Lovecraft never truly used a creation by Dunsany, only adopting the feeling and elements present within them.

Another important issue is the lack of literary criticism devoted to the works of authors within fantasy literature. While classic authors of fantasy, often British, have produced volumes of critical studies, studies of the life and works of some American fantasy authors are not as abundant as they should or need to be. That several American fantasy authors have produced a large oeuvre of work and have won countless awards without receiving the serious critical recognition they deserve is an issue of concern (as witnessed in the next section).

Reception. Fantasy literature has attracted incredible interest at the beginning of the twenty-first century as a result of cinematic adaptations. Historical fantasy has been predominant in the last decade, with *Gladiator* (2000), *Troy* (2004), *Alexander* (2004), *Kingdom of Heaven* (2005), the Pirates of the Caribbean trilogy (2003–2007), and others proving to be financially successful. Film adaptations of recent fantasy literature such as Christopher Paolini's *Eragon* (2005) and J.K. Rowling's Harry Potter series (1997–2007) are watched either by young readers who have read the texts and desire to visually experience the story or by younger audiences who are compelled to read the texts after having seen the cinematic adaptation. Film adaptations of classic fantasy literature such J.R.R. Tolkien's Lord of the Rings trilogy and C.S. Lewis's Chronicles of Narnia series (1950–1956), while certainly watched by younger audiences, are predominately watched by an older generation who have read the texts before seeing the adaptations. It would not be unfair to comment that had these movies not been released, the output of fantasy literature in the last decade would have been less productive or, at the very least, less profitable.

Critical studies are often limited to book-length examinations by actual fantasy authors such as Lin Carter's *Imaginary Worlds: The Art of Fantasy* (1973), Ursula K. Le Guin's *The Language of the Night: Essays on Fantasy and Science Fiction* (1979, rev. 1992), and Michael Moorcock's *Wizardry and Wild Romance: A Study of Epic Fantasy* (1987, rev. 2004) or are written by academics, such as Brian Attebery's *The Fantasy Tradition in American Literature* (1980), editor Brian M. Thomsen's *The American Fantasy Tradition* (2002), and David Sandner's *Fantastic Literature: A Critical Reader* (2004). They are published by either academic or small presses (spotlighting a subgenre or a single author). The number of magazines and journals dedicated to the serious study of fantasy literature has shrunk over the years, for only a few noteworthy titles exist today (such as *Studies in Fantasy Literature; Wormwood: Writings about Fantasy, Supernatural and Decadent Literature; Mythlore: A Journal of J.R.R. Tolkien, C.S. Lewis, Charles Williams, and the Genres of Myth and Fantasy Studies; Extrapolation; The Bulletin of the Science Fiction and Fantasy Writers Association; Journal of the Fantastic in the Arts;* and *The New York Review of Science Fiction,* to name a few). Essays on fantasy literature are often found sporadically, either on the Internet (such as webzines, though few are peer reviewed) or in journals of nation-specific literature (such as *Journal of Popular Culture* and *American Literature*). As stated previously, despite the output of some fantasy authors, the critical study of their fiction is despondently dearth.

Selected Authors. The following discussion of four major authors active in fantasy literature includes an analysis of each author's works. The following American-born and raised authors are observed: James Blaylock (1950–), Tim Powers (1952–), Jessica Amanda Salmonson (1950–), and Darrell Schweitzer (1952–).

Author James Blaylock writes both science fiction and fantasy, but it is the latter in which he excels and is most successful artistically. The books in Blaylock's earliest trilogy, *The Elfin Ship* (1982), *The Disappearing Dwarf* (1983), and *The Stone Giant* (1989), are best read as children's literature, merging with high fantasy but lacking a literary depth that would rank them alongside most contemporary authors of the subgenre. Far better is *Land of Dreams* (1987), a dark fantasy for young adults in which children uncover the border between reality and fantasy, resulting in an unsolved murder and the return of a sinister carnival. *The Digging Leviathan* (1984) is more humorous science fiction than fantasy, and while *Homunculus* (1986) and its sequel *Lord Kelvin's Machine* (1992) are somewhat fantastical in their prose and conception, they are better labeled "steampunk," a struggling subgenre within science fiction. It is not until *The Last Coin* (1988) that Blaylock successfully masters the use of fantastical elements in an original and rewarding manner. In a tale set in Southern California, innkeeper Andrew Vanbergen unwillingly becomes the force of good against the traveling Jules Pennyman, who is attempting to collect Judas Iscariot's original 30 pieces of silver because by doing so he will achieve immortality. *The Paper Grail* (1991) is similar in that the Holy Grail is revealed to be an origami cup, which when folded in particular ways can achieve different types of magic. Set in northern California, this book features aging grail guardian Michael Graham, who leaves the Holy Grail to museum curator Howard Barton, beginning an adventurous story in which Barton, unaware of forthcoming dangers and hopelessly in love, must ensure that the holy artifact does not end up in the wrong hands. In *All the Bells on Earth* (1995), small-business owner Walt Stebbins accidentally receives a delivery in the mail, a deceased "Bluebird of Happiness" that makes all his dreams come true. However, the individual who was to receive the artifact, former friend and business partner Robert Argyle, is desperate to retrieve the artifact at all costs because it is the key to repossessing his soul (which he sold to a satanic clergyman decades ago). Blaylock's next novels, *Night Relics* (1994), *Winter Tides* (1997), and *The Rainy Season* (1999), are all contemporary ghost stories, and although they share elements with stories in dark fantasy, they are best considered and studied as horror.

To date there has been no critical study of Blaylock's work, the closest being the author's own Web site (http://www.sybertooth.com/blaylock/index.htm).

Tim Powers is an author of fantasy literature, best known for his works of historical fantasy and occasional dark fantasy (though some of his novels could easily be classified as adventure fiction with supernatural elements). Powers's novels are richly researched and are always multilayered with history, mythology, and the supernatural, and it is often difficult to summarize a novel because of the countless plots it contains. *Epitaph in Rust* (1976) is a science fantasy detailing the life of Brother Thomas, who flees his monastery and finds himself in a future Los Angeles where revolution is afire. *The Drawing of the Dark* (1979) is set in sixteenth-century Europe in which Irishman Brian Duffy, a mercenary, retires and becomes a bouncer at a Viennese inn, brewer of the legendary Herzwesten beer. Soon enough, the inn is visited by figures from Celtic and Norse mythology, and Duffy learns that he is a central figure in protecting western Europe from the encroaching Turkish Ottoman Empire. *The Anubis Gates* (1983), while possessing elements of science fiction, is also a fantasy novel. Scholar Brendan Doyle, who is living in the 1980s, is sent back to nineteenth-century London with a group of students, to work on a biography of (fictional) poet William Ashbless as well as to experience a lecture by Samuel Taylor Coleridge. However, when Doyle is kidnapped by gypsies, who are led by a powerful sorcerer who desires to destroy the British Empire's hold over Egypt, the story take a fantastical turn. The dark fantasy *On Stranger Tides* (1987) is a supernatural pirate story set in the eighteenth century in which Jack Shandy (formerly accountant John Chandagnac) seeks revenge on a family member who financially betrayed his father as well as engaging in battle against the legendary Blackbeard, who is not only a fierce warrior but also a practicing voodoo priest.

The Stress of Her Regard (1989) is a dark fantasy, set in the early nineteenth century, and revolves around Doctor Michael Crawford, who, on the eve of his wedding, places his wedding ring on a town statue for safe keeping. The morning after, the statue has disappeared, and his bride is brutally murdered. Accused by the townspeople and unsure of his actions, he flees and finds solace in the company of Lord Byron, Percy Shelley, and John Keats, where it is revealed that the statue with his ring is, in fact, a vampire. *Last Call* (1992) is centered around tarot magic and card gambling, in which ex-professional card player Scott Crane battles against his father, the current incarnation of the Fisher King, in a game of life and death. *Expiration Date* (1995) is a supernatural fantasy in which 11-year-old Koot Hoomie Parganas becomes possessed by the ghost of Thomas Edison and must evade a horde of "ghost eaters" who wish to devour the power of Edison's ghost.

Earthquake Weather (1997) is the sequel to both *Last Call* and *Expiration Date,* in which the new Fisher King Scott Crane is killed and presided over by Koot, who will either resurrect the chaos awoken since the king's death or will become the Fisher King himself and restore order. *Declare* (2000) is a supernatural **spy thriller**, with fantastical elements thrown in, surrounding recalled spy Andrew Hale. Hale must investigate Mount Ararat, where it is said Noah's Ark resides, before the Russians, who are supernaturally protected during the Cold War. *Three Days to Never* (2006) is a more interesting novel (and like other novels contains elements of science fiction), detailing the life of Albert Einstein's illegitimate daughter (who has superpowers) and her evasion of the Israeli Mossad and the mystical group the Vespers. It is soon revealed the Einstein successfully created and used a time machine, and it is the desire of these groups to possess the machine for their own diabolical use.

Surprisingly, very little literary criticism has been devoted to the works of Tim Powers, the most notable being Arinn Dembo's "Impassion'd Clay: On Tim Powers' *The Stress of Her Regard*" (1991) and Fiona Kelleghan's "Getting a Life: Haunted Spaces in Two Novels by Tim Powers" (1998), both in the *New York Review of Science Fiction,* and the largest unofficial Web site at http://www.theworksoftimpowers.com/.

Jessica Amanda Salmonson is known as an author of both fantasy literature and horror, her books in the latter genre often including elements of dark fantasy, in addition to being a prolific editor and poet. Salmonson is of importance to the genre in that her best-known fantasy works, mostly being sword and sorcery fiction, were upon their publication both unique and original within a genre that is primarily patriarchal and at many times mediocre. Salmonson's edited anthologies *Amazons!*

(1979), *Amazons II* (1982), *Heroic Visions* (1983), and *Heroic Visions II* (1986) were groundbreaking in that they reestablished the warrior woman in fantasy literature in an era when stereotypes were still existent, and this was critically explored further in her exhaustive *The Encyclopedia of Amazons: Women Warriors from Antiquity to the Present Era* (1991) and the forthcoming *Amazonia: Antiquity's Bold Utopian Experiment.* Equally enduring is Salmonson's Tomoe Gozen trilogy (*Tomoe Gozen,* 1981, rev. *The Disfavored Hero,* 1999; *The Golden Naginata,* 1982; *Thousand Shrine Warrior,* 1984), which refreshingly relocated sword and sorcery fiction from a secondary world setting to a twelfth-century Japan in which the supernatural exists. Loosely based on the historical figure, Tomoe Gozen is a masterless female samurai who unwillingly killed her master Shojiro Shigeno as a result of being resurrected by his enemy, the magician Huan. From that point on, her journey is one of redemption and continues in the following novels, in which she must learn to live in a patriarchal world of revenge, betrayal, and obedience.

The Swordswoman (1982) spotlights the life of Erin Wyler, who upon unleashing the power of a magical sword, begins a life full of trials and tribulation. Set in China, *Ou Lu Khen and the Beautiful Madwoman* (1985) is a dark fantasy set exclusively in the past and details the forbidden love of Ou Lu Khen for a beautiful woman who is favored by the gods. Faced with stigma, but overcome with love, Ou Lu Khen follows her, even if it means he too must succumb to madness. *Anthony Shriek, His Doleful Adventures; or, Lovers of Another Realm* (1992) introduces the character of Anthony Shriek, a college student who learns he is a demon from the Nightlands. A dark fantasy, the story explores Shriek's psychological acceptance of his nature as well as his relationship with the enigmatic Emily, who is also a demon. Although Salmonson is currently writing horror stories, many can easily be classified as dark fantasy, as evidenced by the stories in her collections *Mystic Women: Their Ancient Tales & Legends Recounted by a Woman Inmate of the Calcutta Insane Asylum* (1991), *The Goddess Under Siege* (1992), and *Wisewomen & Boggy-Boos: A Dictionary Of Lesbian Fairy Lore* (1992). Particular stories worth citing are "Angel's Exchange," "Madame Enchantia and the Maze Dream," "Mamishka and the Sorcerer," "Eagle-Worm," and "The View from Mount Futuba."

To date there has been no critical study of Salmonson's work, the closest being an analytical interview titled "Jessica Amanda Salmonson: Storyteller" for *Jitterbug Fantasia* (2004) and the author's own Web site at http://www.violetbooks.com/.

Darrell Schweitzer is an author, editor, and critic of fantasy literature, writing in the subgenres of low fantasy, dark fantasy, and sword and sorcery fiction. Former editor of *Isaac Asimov's Science Fiction Magazine* (1977–1982) and *Amazing Stories* (1982–1986) and current coeditor of the modern incarnation of *Weird Tales: The Unique Magazine* (1988–) with George Scithers, Schweitzer is among one of the most important assets to the genre and continues to contribute invaluable works. While *The Shattered Goddess* (1982) is a science fantasy set in the future, it does involve the deception of a witch who replaces her son with the heir to the throne. The royal-blooded child grows up as a sorcerer, and when he learns of his true origins, he must make a decision that will affect the entire world. *Tom O'Bedlam's Night Out, and Other Strange Excursions* (1985) is a collection of whimsical short stories about the legendary figure from English folklore and his amusing exploits. *The White Isle* (1988) is a dark fantasy novella focusing on the attempts by Prince Evnos from the Island of Iankoros to retrieve his beloved bride from the God of Death and is rich in its poetic language and description of an unscrupulous deity.

The Mask of the Sorcerer (1995) is in many ways high fantasy, being an episodic novel set in an alternative Egypt about the travails of the Sekenre (an immortal sorcerer trapped in the body of a child) and his desire to again become a powerful sorcerer, like his father Vashtem, even if it means traveling to the Land of the Dead. *Sekenre: The Book of the Sorcerer* (2004), the former's sequel of sorts, is a collection of short stories exploring the trails and tribulations of the emerging sorcerer, written in first person. *We Are All Legends* (1981) is a collection of short stories involving a wandering crusader called Sir Julian the Apostate, who, because of bedding a witch, is cursed by God and traveling the lands of Europe in search of redemption and a means to reverse his unsavory fate. Schweitzer's works are an amusing exploration of religion by an increasingly popular author and are among the better sword and sorcery fiction of the era. *Transients: And Other Disquieting Stories* (1993) and *Necromancies and Netherworlds: Uncanny Stories* (1999) with Jason van Hollander are both collections of dark fantasy stories, some with a humorous edge and others that are clearly horror. Schweitzer is the editor of important anthologies of literary criticism, such as *Exploring Fantasy Worlds: Essays on Fantastic Literature* (1985), *Discovering Classic Fantasy Fiction: Essays on the Antecedents of Fantastic Literature* (1996), and *The Neil Gaiman Reader* (2006) and is the sole author of the book-length studies *Pathways to Elfland: The Writings of Lord Dunsany* (1989) and *Windows of the Imagination* (1998).

Schweitzer has received very little critical study, despite his popularity and volume of work. Steve Behrends's "Holy Fire: Darrell Schweitzer's Imaginative Fiction," in *Studies in Weird Fiction* (1989), and the analytical interview "The Sorcery of Storytelling: The 'Imaginary Worlds' of Darrell Schweitzer" for *Black Gate Magazine* (Fultz 2006) are all that currently exist.

Bibliography

Anderson, Poul. *Three Hearts and Three Lions*. London: Victor Gollancz, 2003.

Anthony, Piers. *A Spell for Chameleon*. New York: Del Rey/Ballantine, 1977.

Attebery, Brian. *The Fantasy Tradition in American Literature*. Bloomington: Indiana University Press, 1980.

Bakker, Scott R. "Why Fantasy and Why Now?" August 2002. http://www.sffworld.com/authors/b/bakker_scott/articles/whyfantasyandwhynow.html.

Behrends, Steve. "Holy Fire: Darrell Schweitzer's Imaginative Fiction." *Studies in Weird Fiction* 5 (1989): 3–11.

Berlyne, John. *The Works of Tim Powers*. http://www.theworksoftimpowers.com.

Blaylock, James. *All the Bells on Earth*. New York: Ace Books, 1995.

———. *The Disappearing Dwarf*. New York: Del Rey/Ballantine, 1983.

———. *The Elfin Ship*. New York: Del Rey/Ballantine, 1982.

———. *Land of Dreams*. New York: Arbor House, 1987.

———. *The Last Coin*. New York: Ace Books, 1988.

———. *The Paper Grail*. New York: Ace Books, 1991.

———. *The Stone Giant*. New York: Ace Books, 1989.

Bradley, Marion Zimmer. *Mists of Avalon*. New York: Ballantine, 1985.

Brennan, Kristen. "Jessica Amanda Salmonson: Storyteller." Interview. *Jitterbug Fantasia* Summer 2004. http://www.spookybug.com/violet/index.html.

Brown, Dan. *The Da Vinci Code*. New York: Doubleday, 2003.

Bull, Emma. *War for the Oaks*. New York: Ace Books, 1987.

Campbell, Joseph. *The Hero with a Thousand Faces*. Princeton, NJ: Princeton University Press, 1972.

Card, Orson Scott. *Prentice Alvin*. New York: Tor, 1989 [Alvin Maker 3].

———. *Red Prophet*. Alvin Maker series. New York: Tor, 1988 [Alvin Maker 2].

———. *Seventh Son*. New York: Tor, 1987 [Alvin Maker 1].

Carroll, Jonathan. *The Land of Laughs*. New York: Viking Press, 1980.

Carter, Lin. *Imaginary Worlds: The Art of Fantasy*. New York: Ballantine, 1973.

Clarke, Susanna. *Jonathan Strange & Mr. Norrell*. New York: Bloomsbury, 2004.

Crichton, Michael. *Eaters of the Dead*. New York: Ballantine, 1976.

Crowley, John. *Little, Big*. Westminster, MD: Bantam Books, 1981.

de Camp, L. Sprague, and Fletcher Pratt. *Incomplete Enchanter*. London: Sphere, 1979.

de Lint, Charles. *Moonheart*. New York: Ace Books, 1984.

Dembo, Arinn. "Impassion'd Clay: On Tim Powers' *The Stress of Her Regard*." *New York Review of Science Fiction* 37 (1991): 1, 3–7.

Donaldson, Stephen R. *Epic Fantasy in the Modern World: A Few Observations by Stephen R. Donaldson*. Kent, OH: Kent State University Libraries, 1986.

———. *Fatal Revenant*. The Last Chronicles. New York: Putnam, 2007.

———. *The Illearth War*. The First Chronicles. Orlando, FL: Holt, 1977.

———. *Lord Foul's Bane*. The First Chronicles. Orlando, FL: Holt, 1977.

———. *The One Tree*. The Second Chronicles. New York: Del Rey/Ballantine, 1982.

———. *The Power That Preserves*. The First Chronicles. Orlando, FL: Holt, 1977.

———. *The Runes of the Earth*. The Last Chronicles. New York: Putnam, 2004.

———. *White Gold Wielder*. The Second Chronicles. New York: Del Rey/Ballantine, 1983.

———. *The Wounded Land*. The Second Chronicles. New York: Del Rey/Ballantine, 1980.

Drake, David. A. *The Fortress of Glass*. New York: Tor Books, 2006.

———. *Goddess of the Ice Realm*. New York: Tor Books, 2003.

———. *Lord of the Isles*. New York: Tor Books, 1997.

———. *Master of the Cauldron*. New York: Tor Books, 2004.

———. *Mistress of the Catacombs*. New York: Tor Books, 2001.

———. *Queen of Demons*. New York: Tor Books, 1998.

———. *Servant of the Dragon*. New York: Tor Books, 1999.

Eddings, David. *Castle of Wizardry*. New York: Del Rey/Ballantine, 1984.

———. *Enchanters' End Game*. New York: Del Rey/Ballantine, 1984.

———. *Magician's Gambit*. New York: Del Rey/Ballantine, 1983.

———. *Pawn of Prophecy*. New York: Del Rey/Ballantine, 1982.

———. *Queen of Sorcery*. New York: Del Rey/Ballantine, 1982.

Fultz, John R. "The Sorcery of Storytelling: The 'Imaginary Worlds' of Darrell Schweitzer." Interview. *Black Gate: Adventures in Fantasy Literature* 2006. http://www.black-gate.com/articles/schweitzer.htm.

Gaiman, Neil. *American Gods*. London: Headline Book, 2001.

———. *Books of Magic*. New York: Detective Comics, 1991.

Gemmell, David. *Troy: Fall of Kings*. New York: Putnam, 2007.

———. *Troy: Lord of the Silver Bow*. New York: Ballantine, 2005.

———. *Troy: Shield of Thunder*. London: Transworld, 2006.

Hancock, Karen. *The Light of Eidon*. Minneapolis, MN: Bethany House, 2003.

———. *Return of the Guardian-King*. Minneapolis, MN: Bethany House, 2007.

———. *Shadow Over Kiriath*. Minneapolis, MN: Bethany House, 2005.

———. *The Shadow Within*. Minneapolis, MN: Bethany House, 2004.

Harris, Joel Chandler. *Uncle Remus: His Songs and His Sayings*. New York: Penguin, 1982.

Hobb, Robin. *Assassin's Apprentice*. New York: Bantam Books, 1995.

———. *Assassin's Quest*. New York: Bantam Books, 1997.

———. *Royal Assassin*. New York: Bantam Books, 1996.

Irving, Washington. *The Sketch Book Of Geoffrey Crayon, Gent*. New York: Modern Library, 2001.

James P. Blaylock Fantasy and Steampunk Author. http://www.sybertooth.com/blaylock/index.htm.

Joshi, S.T. *The Weird Tale*. Austin: University of Texas Press, 1990.

Kelleghan, Fiona. "Getting a Life: Haunted Spaces in Two Novels by Tim Powers." *New York Review of Science Fiction* 115 (1998): 13–17.

Kostova, Elizabeth. *The Historian*. New York: Little, Brown, 2005.

Le Guin, Ursula K. *The Language of the Night: Essays on Fantasy and Science Fiction*. New York: HarperCollins, 1992.

Leiber, Fritz. *The First Book of Lankhmar*. London: Victor Gollancz, 2001.

———. *The Green Millennium*. New York: Ace, 1969.

———. *Gummitch & Friends*. New Hampshire: Donald M. Grant, 1992.

———. *The Second Book of Lankhmar*. London: Victor Gollancz, 2001.

Lewis, C.S. *The Horse and His Boy*. Grand Rapids, MI: Zondervan, 1994.

———. *The Last Battle*. Zondervan, 1994.

———. *The Lion, the Witch and the Wardrobe*. Grand Rapids, MI: Zondervan, 1994.

———. *The Magician's Nephew*. Grand Rapids, MI: Zondervan, 1994.

———. *Prince Caspian*. Grand Rapids, MI: Zondervan, 1994.

———. *The Silver Chair*. Grand Rapids, MI: Zondervan, 1994.

———. *The Voyage of the "Dawn Treader."* Grand Rapids, MI: Zondervan, 1994.

Moorcock, Michael. *Behold the Man*. London: Mayflower Books, 1973.

———. *Elric of Melniboné*. London: Victor Gollancz, 2001.

———. *Wizardry and Wild Romance: A Study of Epic Fantasy*. Austin, TX: MonkeyBrain Books, 2004.

Paolini, Christopher. *Eragon*. New York: Knopf, 2005.

Powers, Tim. *The Anubis Gates*. London: Victor Gollancz, 2005.

———. *Declare*. Scranton, PA: William Morrow, 2001.

———. *The Drawing of the Dark*. London: Victor Gollancz, 2002.

———. *Earthquake Weather*. New York: Tor, 1997.

———. *Expiration Date*. New York: Tor, 1996.

———. *Last Call*. New York: Avon Books, 1993.

———. *On Stranger Tides*. New York: Putnam Berkley, 1988.

———. *The Stress of Her Regard*. New York: Ace Books, 1991.

———. *Three Days to Never*. Scranton, PA: William Morrow, 2006.

Rowling, J.K. *Harry Potter and the Chamber of Secrets*. London: Bloomsbury, 1997.

———. *Harry Potter and the Goblet of Fire*. London: Bloomsbury, 2000.

———. *Harry Potter and the Half-Blood Prince*. London: Bloomsbury, 2006.

———. *Harry Potter and the Order of the Phoenix*. London: Bloomsbury, 2003.

———. *Harry Potter and the Philosopher's Stone*. London: Bloomsbury, 1997.

———. *Harry Potter and the Prisoner of Azkaban*. London: Bloomsbury, 1999.

Salmonson, Jessica Amanda, ed. *Amazons!* New York: DAW, 1979.

———, ed. *Amazons II*. New York: DAW, 1982.

———. *Anthony Shriek, His Doleful Adventures or, Lovers of Another Realm*. New York: Dell, 1992.

———. *The Disfavored Hero*. Boulder Creek, CA: Pacific Warriors, 1999.

———. *The Encyclopedia of Amazons: Women Warriors from Antiquity to the Present Era*. New York: Paragon House, 1991.

———. *The Golden Naginata*. New York: Ace Books, 1982.

———, ed. *Heroic Visions*. New York: Ace Books, 1983.

———, ed. *Heroic Visions II*. New York: Ace Books, 1986.

———. *Ou Lu Khen and the Beautiful Madwoman*. New York: Ace Books, 1985.

———. *The Swordswoman*. New York: Tor, 1982.

———. *Thousand Shrine Warrior*. New York: Ace Books, 1984.

———. *Violet Books Antiquarian Supernatural Literature, Fantasy & Mysterious Literatures, Vintage Westerns, Swashbucklers, & Juveniles*. http://www.violetbooks.com

Sandner, David. *Fantastic Literature: A Critical Reader*. Westport, CT: Greenwood Press, 2004.

Saunders, Charles R. *Imaro.* Newberg, OR: Night Shade Books, 2006.

————. *Imaro: The Quest for Cush.* Newberg, OR: Night Shade Books, 2007.

Schweitzer, Darrell. *Discovering Classic Fantasy Fiction: Essays on the Antecedents of Fantastic Literature.* Philadelphia, PA: Wildside Press, 1996.

————. *Exploring Fantasy Worlds: Essays on Fantastic Literature.* San Bernardino, CA: Borgo Press, 1985.

————. *The Mask of the Sorcerer.* Doylestown, PA: Wildside Press, 2003.

————. *The Neil Gaiman* Reader, Doylestown, PA: Wildside Press, 2006.

————. *Pathways to Elfland: The Writings of Lord Dunsany.* Philadelphia: Owlswick Press, 1989.

————. *Sekenre: The Book of the Sorcerer.* Doylestown, PA: Wildside Press, 2004.

————. *The Shattered Goddess.* Philadelphia, PA: Wildside Press, 1982.

————. *Tom O'Bedlam's Night Out, and Other Strange Excursions.* Buffalo, NY: W. Paul Ganley, 1985.

————. *We Are All Legends.* Philadelphia, PA: Wildside Press, 1981.

————. *The White Isle.* Philadelphia: Owlswick Press, 1988.

————. *Windows of the Imagination.* Philadelphia, PA: Wildside Press, 1998.

Spiegelman, Art. *Fifth Seal.* Wheaton, Illinois: Tyndale House, 2006.

————. *First Light.* Wheaton, Illinois: Tyndale House, 2003.

————. *Fourth Dawn.* Wheaton, Illinois: Tyndale House, 2005.

————. *Maus: A Survivor's Tale.* New York: Scholastic, 1992.

————. *Second Touch.* Wheaton, Illinois: Tyndale House, 2004.

————. *Third Watch.* Wheaton, Illinois: Tyndale House, 2004.

Thomsen, Brian M., ed. *The American Fantasy Tradition.* New York: Tor Books, 2002.

Tierney, Richard L. *Scroll of Thoth: Simon Magus and the Great Old Ones.* Canada: Chaosium, 1997.

Tierney, Richard L., and Glenn Rahman. *The Gardens of Lucullus.* Minneapolis, MN: Sidecar Preservation Society, 2001.

Tolkien, J.R.R. *Lord of the Rings: The Fellowship of the Ring.* Boston: Houghton Mifflin, 2001.

————. *Lord of the Rings: The Return of the King.* Boston: Houghton Mifflin, 2001.

————. *Lord of the Rings: The Two Towers.* Boston: Houghton Mifflin, 2001.

Wagner, Karl Edward. *Bloodstone.* New York: Warner Books, 1975.

————. *Dark Crusade.* New York: Warner Books, 1976.

————. *Darkness Weaves.* New York: Warner Books, 1978.

————. *Death Angel's Shadow.* New York: Warner Books, 1973.

————. *Night Winds.* New York: Warner Books, 1978.

Williams, Tad. *The Dragonbone Chair.* New York: DAW, 1988.

————. *To Green Angel Tower.* New York: DAW, 1993.

————. *Stone of Farewell.* New York: DAW, 1990.

Zipes, Jack, ed. *Spells of Enchantment: The Wondrous Fairy Tales of Western Culture.* New York: Viking Press, 1991.

Further Reading

Anderson, Douglas A. *The 100 Best Writers of Fantasy & Horror.* New York: Cold Spring Press, 2006; Austin, Alec. "Quality in Epic Fantasy." *Strange Horizons,* June 2002. http://www.strangehorizons.com/2002/20020624/epic_fantasy.shtml; Langford, Michele K., ed. *Contours of the Fantastic.* Westport, CT: Greenwood Press, 1990; Morse, Donald E., ed. *The Fantastic in World Literature and the Arts.* Westport, CT: Greenwood Press, 1987.

BENJAMIN SZUMSKYJ

FILM ADAPTATIONS OF BOOKS

Definition. At its most basic, film adaptation is a translation of a literary text into a cinematic one; though film adaptation can be defined very broadly, as well as more specifically. In fact, one can generalize that many films, despite their lack of any conventional literary source, are innately adaptations of some aspect of human experience. Even horror films can, with their seemingly unrealistic ghouls and monsters, metaphorically depict the fears and anxieties embedded in the human psyche. However, generalizations aside, most scholars agree that a film is considered an adaptation when its primary intention is to reinterpret a novel, short story, or other traditional literary genre. As Dudley Andrew suggests, "the broader notion of the process of adaptation has much in common with interpretation theory, for in a strong sense adaptation is the appropriation of a meaning from a prior text," and subsequently, an interpretation of that previous text (1980, 29). In most cases, film adaptation is a transfer of meaning from one system of signs into another that occurs via a practice of filmic translation. The "distinct feature" of adaptation, Andrew remarks, is "the matching of a cinematic sign system to a prior achievement in some other system" (qtd. in McFarlane 1996, 21). Indeed, much of the material available that takes film adaptation as its primary subject borrows heavily from a variety of established theorists and critics, including Christian Metz, W.J.T. Mitchell, and Roland Barthes, whose work on semiotics has had an immense influence on scholarly discussion of film adaptations as interpretative signs of preceding texts.

Like the novels and stories that films strive to simulate, adaptations are intricately constructed narratives that possess plot, setting, characters, and manner of discourse. The definition of a narrative, as Andrew Horton and Stuart McDougal indicate, is "a perceptual activity that organizes data into a special pattern which represents and explains experience" (1998, 2). Film adaptations fit squarely into this definition because they most certainly involve an extensive degree of "perceptual activity," and they also exhibit a wide range of human encounters and emotions. Just as reading a novel provides the reader with an opportunity for making meaning, viewing a film adaptation allows a similar experience for the filmgoer. "Like reading," Peter Reynolds asserts, "spectating involves a complex interaction between the spectator and the performance in which what has been encoded by the author(s) is decoded by the spectator" (1993, 3). Both versions of narrative—the conventional text as well as its cinematic counterpart—are encoded with meaning that is then decoded by the reader or viewer. However, this meaning-making process is uniquely amended during the viewing of a film adaptation, given that many viewers who are already familiar with the source text are inevitably forced to decode a narrative that they have already seemingly decoded. Yet the film adaptation is, in itself, a new narrative that must be re(de)coded by the viewer. This narratological rereading is utterly exclusive to film adaptations.

Because not all film adaptations are completely loyal to their textual antecedents, some can be seen as critiques, rewritings, or alternate readings of their source texts. A film adaptation of a nineteenth-century novel that utilizes contemporary dress, discourse, and setting is an example of a rewrite or alternate reading of the novel in question. Though the general plot and characters are the same as the novel, the updated costumes and so on make the adaptation explicitly different from its original. Indeed, adaptations can be both very similar to and extensively distinctive from their predecessors. Kamilla Elliott, in her 2003 publication *Rethinking the*

Novel/Film Debate, devises a number of categories into which many adaptations can fit, implying that film adaptations, both overtly and covertly, address, interpret, and imitate their source texts in diverse ways. The psychic film adaptation is essentially a "passing of the spirit of the text" into film (Stam 2005, 49, n. 48). In Elliott's words, "the form changes; the spirit remains constant" (138). Of course, the spirit of any text is generally the spirit of the author, manifested in authorial intent. How does the author want us to feel about his or her work? What are we supposed to get out of the text or film? In many cases, an accomplished film director or screenwriter can alter the content of a text while still remaining true to its supposed essence or theme. The ventriloquist model, unlike the psychic one, writes Elliott, "pays no lip service to authorial spirit: rather, it blatantly empties out the novel's signs and fills them with filmic spirits" (143). In a ventriloquist adaptation, the intent of the original author becomes secondary to that of the text's appointed cinematic author. Most notably, ventriloquist renderings often add to the original text in some way, so that the end result is often heavily altered from its source. The film adaptation, in essence, takes on its own voice, apart from that of the novel.

The genetic concept of adaptation, Elliott's third category, refers to the transfer of "an underlying 'deep' narrative structure [between literature and film] akin to genetic structure" (2003, 150). Elliott insinuates that a film adaptation, as an offspring of some mother-text, will naturally possess many analogous traits to its textual "mother," yet will exist as an innately different entity. The "de(re)composing" concept of adaptation is arguably Elliott's most complex and abstract category. In this model, "the novel and film decompose, merge, and form a new composition at 'underground' levels of reading. The adaptation is a composite of textual and filmic signs merging in audience consciousness together with other cultural narratives and often leads to confusion as to which is novel and which is film" (157).

Any audience disorientation ultimately arises from the total inclusion of any number of accepted "texts" into a specific cultural imagination. For instance, a certain story, so ingrained into popular culture, may be without a designated origin. Thus, the story or content of the adaptation is confusedly understood as "original" when it certainly is not.

Elliott's fourth type of film adaptation, the "incarnational," literally occurs when "word becomes flesh." In many cases, according to Elliott (161), "the word is only a partial expression of a more total representation that requires incarnation for its fulfillment," in which case the production of the film becomes an act of completion. The adapted film realizes its source text in a visual and audible manner, creating a genuine sensorium in which the reader, now viewer, can revel. The internal, imaginative world of reading a novel simply cannot compare with the definitive phenomenological experience of seeing the words incarnated into a pseudo-realistic product. The sixth and final category is that of the "trumping" model of adaptation in which "the film shows its superior capacities to tell the story" (Stam 2000, 49, n. 48). The trumping concept addresses the possibility that the film adaptation can be better than its forerunner. As Elliott notes, "adaptations frequently condemn novels of prior centuries as representationally immature, their values antiquated, irrelevant, and inexplicable to contemporary audiences, and their accounts of history, psychology, and politics inaccurate" (174). Contemporary updates of classic novels and dramas have been very popular in Hollywood for several years, though many of these modernized versions retain the historically accurate mode of discourse. Traditionally, critics and viewers have held the view that the source text is almost always better than its adaptation. However, as Robert Stam postulates, "The clichéd response that 'I thought the book was better' really means that our experience, our phantasy of the book was better than the director's" (15). Elliott believes that adaptations have the ability to be conceived of as superior texts though they are conventionally not, in part because the word still triumphs over the image in contemporary thought, although this sentiment is beginning to change in light of the publication of landmark works on the word–image wars, such as W.J.T. Mitchell's *Iconology* (1987). It is conclusively difficult to discern which is better, book or film, primarily because a film adaptation is automatically different from its source text. Not only does the medium differ, but often the authorial intent and overall content change as well. In the end, however, most directors and screenwriters strive for what Stam calls "equivalency," the ability to find "equivalents in a new medium for the novelist's style or techniques" (18). The decision as to whether the film adaptation is better than its progenitor appears to be mostly subjective given that "everyone who sees films based on novels feels able to comment, at levels ranging from the gossipy to the erudite on the nature and success of the adaptation involved" (McFarlane 1996, 3). Most critics and scholars would agree that every viewer, despite his or her familiarity with the source text, can make a judgment on the achievement of any film adaptation, even from a general perspective.

Subfields of Film Adaptation. The term *film adaptation* can often apply to a variety of subfields that, in many respects, are adaptations, though perhaps not principally. Most notably, the remake and the biopic are types of adaptations that may not be conventionally considered as adaptations, even though at their core they possess many of the same intentions. Remakes are generally updated versions of previous films or, as in recent years, filmic interpretations of celebrated television shows such as Jay Chandrasekhar's 2005 remake of *The Dukes of Hazard* and Nora Ephron's *Bewitched* (also 2005). Remakes have, indeed, become such popular fodder for Hollywood studios in the last few years that many critics have called the craze an epidemic. Like other kinds of adaptations, remakes strive to transform an existing text into something new. In fact, "more obviously than other forms of art," writes Leo Braudy, "the remake—like its close kin . . . the sequel—is a species of inter-pretation" (1998, 327). The remake reinterprets a source text just like any other adaptation and necessarily seeks to add to the spirit of that preceding text.

The biopic is yet another subfield of film adaptation. Simply put, a biopic is a filmic adaptation of a person's life. Biopics are often much more conventional than one may initially think, as many of these adaptations pull material from published sources such as **biographies** or memoirs. Both Julie Taymor's *Frida* (2002) and Ron Howard's *A Beautiful Mind* (2001) are adaptations of acclaimed biographical studies on the films' respective subjects. "The bio-pic," Neil Sinyard observes, "is an awkward hybrid that falls somewhere between fiction and documentary" because one can adapt a biography very rigidly, sticking closely to accepted sources, or he or she can capture what Sinyard calls the "spirit" of a person's life, abandoning certain details about the subject that may not enhance the cinematic portrayal of that particular "spirit" (1986, 143–4). Biopics have also proliferated over the last few decades, which calls to attention the voyeuristic nature of contemporary American society: as viewers of these biopics, we are literally peeking into the subject's personal and professional life.

History. Film adaptations have been in consistent production since the birth of the American film industry. In fact, according to the American Film Institute's Web site, the oldest surviving reel in American archives is a silent film adaptation of Shakespeare's *Richard III* (1912). However, American production companies began adapting popular American literature even before 1912. Early American filmmaker Gene Gauntier adapted Mark Twain's *Tom Sawyer* and Nathaniel Hawthorne's famous novel *The Scarlet Letter* for the screen as early as 1907 and 1908, respectively (Internet Movie Database). "As soon as cinema began to see itself as a narrative entertainment," McFarlane notes, "the idea of remaking the novel—that already established repository of narrative fiction—for source material got underway, and the process has continued more or less unabated [since]" (1996, 6–7). Many American film adaptations are considered "classic," exemplary examples of American filmmaking at its best. At least 17 of the American Film Institute's "100 Greatest American Movies of All Time" are film adaptations, including such genuinely American classics as *The Godfather* (1972), *Gone with the Wind* (1939), *One Flew Over the Cuckoo's Nest* (1975), and *The Grapes of Wrath* (1940). Indeed, as Barbara Tepa Lupack asserts, film, "from its very beginnings, has turned to literature for inspiration and persisted in the practice of translating books into film" (1994, 1). The bulk of early film adaptations produced in the United States pulled their content from traditional literary works such as established nineteenth-century novels, but as the twentieth century wore on, directors and screenwriters began to turn their attentions toward contemporary popular fiction for ideas as well. Hence came the explosion of what were initially (and still are) considered "cult classics" in the 1970s and beyond: Francis Ford Coppola's version of Mario Puzo's *The Godfather* (1972), Milos Forman's 1975 adaptation of Ken Kesey's *One Flew Over the Cuckoo's Nest,* and Stanley Kubrick's take on Stephen King's *The Shining* (1980).

Trends and Themes. Around the turn of the millennium, as technological advancements in filmmaking equipment reached a zenith, films began to reflect a major shift in American culture that had been occurring for several decades: a shift from a very

---

BOOKS MADE INTO MOVIES WIN AWARDS

Adaptations generally fare well in prestigious award circles. Linda Seger speculates that "eighty-five percent of all Academy Award-winning Best Pictures are adaptations, forty-five percent of all television movies-of-the-week are adaptations, yet seventy percent of all Emmy Award winners come from these films, and eighty-three percent of all miniseries are adaptations, out of which ninety-five percent of Emmy award winners are drawn" (1992, xi). Though Seger's book, *The Art of Adaptation,* was published in 1992, the staggering statistics therein have not changed. In 2003 alone, Academy Award nominees in the top six categories (Best Picture, Best Director, Best Actor/Actress, Best Supporting Actor/Supporting Actress) came from 13 films, of which 9 were adaptations (6 of those were American).

The trend to award films adapted from literature continues to hold true, as more and more filmmakers are looking to contemporary novels, plays, and short stories for inspiration. "Today's adaptations," Lupack agrees, "are not restricted to literary classics, and embrace many genres" (1994, 5). Even graphic novels are fair game for adaptations, as the popularity of Sam Mendes's *Road to Perdition* (2002) and Terry Zwigoff's *Ghost World* (2001) certainly indicates. Adaptations have yet to become unpopular or irrelevant in American culture, and with more film adaptations made each year, this rich cultural tradition continues through its appreciation by both filmmakers and filmgoers.

A third filmic trend of recent years involves the securing of production rights for literary works at very early stages of publication and distribution. Popular novels such as Dan Brown's *The Da Vinci Code* (2003, 2006) and Lauren Weisberger's *The Devil Wears Prada* (2003, 2006) are instantly deemed "filmable," and studios clamor for the rights to produce adaptations. Film adaptations are no longer simply cinematic versions of classic literary works, and directors, always after the best story, often seek out very contemporary sources from which to film adaptations.

linear view of history and human experience to a view of the world as multilayered, interdisciplinary, and seemingly ambiguous. The ability to reinsert oneself into the historical record through film was first glimpsed by moviegoers in *Forrest Gump* (1994). Director Robert Zemeckis could place a fictional character (originally created by novelist Winston Groom) in a variety of actual historical milieus to the surprise of many viewers. Forrest Gump (played by Tom Hanks, who, incidentally, captured the 1995 Best Actor Oscar for his portrayal) could now shake hands with Richard Nixon and sit rigidly next to John Lennon during one of his famous interviews with Dick Cavett because of the technological sophistication of computer-generated graphics. Film adaptations became more accurate as a result of this astonishing hi-tech revolution.

Another major trend in film adaptation that has sprung up in the last several years is the increased production of remakes. As mentioned previously, remakes have become so rampant that many film critics argue that Hollywood has simply run out of original material for its films. Of course, whether this is the case or not, remakes have become very popular over the past decade. In many ways, this turn to "remaking" our culture can be seen in other media arenas as well. Reality television, the popular genre that exploded with the premieres of *Survivor* and *Big Brother,* has certainly altered the way that we perceive and understand our immediate realities, a change that has inevitably affected the film industry. We are constantly remaking the terms of "reality"; the millennial remake culture and, specifically, the propagation of cinematic updates certainly confirm this.

Context and Issues. One of the most pressing issues for filmmakers is the fidelity of the adaptation to its source text. "The skeleton of the original can, more or less thoroughly, become the skeleton of a film. More difficult," Andrew concurs, "is the fidelity to the spirit, to the original's tone, values, imagery, and rhythm, for finding equivalents in film for these intangible aspects" (1980, 12). If Andrew is correct, then it would be nearly impossible for any adaptation to be completely accurate because the change in medium, the passing of information from one semiotic system into another, would effectively alter the resulting "spirit." Though the filmic outcome indubitably depends on the source work for its shell, it transforms the static text into a lifelike phantasmagoria of the senses. Adaptations borrow from their predecessors but should be viewed as intersections between word and image rather than true translations of one into the other. "The differences between the novel and film extend from formal considerations to their conditions of production—which themselves have quite distinct meanings attached to them" (Cartmell and Whelehan 1999, 6). Many adaptations, because of issues such as these, are expected to possess some value as stand-alone filmic productions. A film adaptation can still be considered "good" even if it is not totally loyal to its source. Critics of adaptation fidelity ultimately depend on "a notion of the text as having and rendering up to the (intelligent) reader a single, correct 'meaning' which the filmmaker has either adhered to or in some sense violated or tampered with" (McFarlane 1996, 8). For any film adaptation to be absolutely true to its subject, it would have to assume that only a single universal meaning is applicable to that subject, a presumption that seems highly implausible. If every adaptable text has only one meaning, then it would be unreasonable for multiple adaptations to be made. Yet filmmakers consistently return to certain texts in order to portray the multiplicities of their respective spirits. Arguments over film adaptations "arise not only because of disputes concerning the fidelity of adaptations, but also because there is little or no argument on what the adapter's role with respect to the original should be" (Reynolds 1993, 9). How should a filmmaker approach a source text? Without fixed meanings, these texts can be handled in a variety of ways, hence the existence of multiple adaptations of the same text. As McFarlane attests, "discussion of adaptation has been bedeviled by the fidelity issue, no doubt ascribable in part to the novel's coming first, in part to the ingrained sense of literature's greater respectability in traditional critical circles" (8); however, there are many other angles from which the topic can be approached.

Reception. Various theories of film adaptation have been posed by numerous scholars throughout the twentieth century. Many of these theories rely on previous schools of thought, especially the works of structuralist and poststructuralist theorists and semioticians. For example, one expert on film adaptation, Robert Stam, borrows both from Roland Barthes and from the narrative theorist Gerard Genette. In *Literature and Film: A Guide to the Theory and Practice of Adaptation*, Stam describes how Genette's multifarious theories of textuality are applicable to film adaptations. He writes,

> While all of Genette's categories ["intertextuality," "paratextuality," "metatextuality," and "architextuality"] are suggestive, Genette's fifth type, "hypertextuality," is perhaps the type most clearly relevant to adaptation. "Hypertextuality," [*sic*] refers to the relation between one text, which Genette calls "hypertext," to an anterior text or "hypotext," which the former transforms, modifies, elaborates, or extends. Filmic adaptations, in this sense, are hypertexts derived from pre-existing hypotexts that have been transformed by operations of selection, amplification, concretization, and actualization. (2005, 31)

Stam's use of Genette's theories is just one of the ways that critics have theorized film adaptations.

Other critics, apart from philosophizing about the loyalty of any adaptation to its source, also focus on the ways in which adaptations can be both repressive and liberating (Reynolds 1993, 11). In an adaptation, the new author is free to make something that has never been seen yet that is bound to original materials from which it cannot be severed. This situation appears to be the ultimate paradox of film adaptation. Though adaptations strive to be unique, the viewer will always be plagued by his or her ideas about the source text. Another difficulty of transcribing an already established story into film is the transmutation of novelistic linearity into filmic spatiality. Though both novels and films are regularly bound by specific chronologies, film has the ability to transcend time by utilizing space more freely. Films, in a sense, take up (viewing) space and are less devoted to issues of time than the traditional novel. They explode on-screen and envelop the audience in a display of visual and oral splendor. "The movie theatre," David Denby (2006) observes, "is a public space that encourages private pleasures: as we watch, everything we are—our senses, our past, our unconscious—reaches out to the screen. The experience is the opposite of escape; it is more like absolute engagement." Novels, on the other hand, though they do occupy the recesses of human imagination, hardly engage space.

As Deborah Cartmell and Imelda Whelehan (1999) point out, criticism on film adaptation has, since its inception, taken on one of five major theoretical guises: an all-around disdain for adaptations as lowly copies of more superior originals; a narratological approach that examines adaptations, as well as their source texts, as belonging to a narrative system, be it textual or filmic; a film-adaptation-as-nostalgia approach that considers adaptations to be nods to a bygone era; a method of viewing adaptations as an extension of the human inclination toward voyeurism in the cinema; and finally, the "textuality" method, preferred by Stam and others, that contemplates film adaptations in light of recent discussions in critical theory and textual studies. Each approach to film adaptation, despite the inherent differences among them, attempts to analyze the relationship between the initial text and its filmic successor. In nearly every article and book devoted to the subject, attention is focused solely on adaptations of novels, an exception being Horton and McDougal's work on remakes as adaptations, as well as Mireia Aragay's edited volume *Books in Motion* (2006). Nevertheless, very few critics have ventured to investigate the multiplicity of genres from which film adaptations collect their material. The remainder of this article takes into account film adaptations that stem from a variety of genres.

Selected Film Adaptations

Ghost World *(2001)*. **Graphic novels** are only beginning to be taken seriously by critics and scholars in the academic sphere, so naturally film adaptations (read: serious and respected film adaptations) of this innately multimedia genre could not have been possible at any other historical moment. Though film adaptations of comic books have been successful in the past (e.g., *Superman* and the many incarnations of *Batman*), the narratological sophistication of the graphic novel has, up until recently, placed the genre in limbo: stuck between the popular cultural aspects of a **comic book** and the conventional narrative structures and complexities of the novel form. Zwigoff's adaptation of Daniel Clowes's *Ghost World* effectively altered the status of graphic novels, allowing them to be deemed adaptable material.

Director Zwigoff is famous for using the comic world as hardware for his films, having produced *Crumb* (1994), a keen documentary on the legendary Robert Crumb, creator of veritably poignant and bawdy comics that became popular during the late 1960s. In *Ghost World,* Zwigoff turns to the content of the comics themselves, adapting Clowes's cult favorite into a bright, yet existential film that follows the daily proceedings of a cynical teenager lost amid a sea of superficiality. As Roger Ebert (2001) notes, Enid, the 18-year old protagonist (played by Thora Birch), "is so smart, so advanced, and so ironically doubled back upon herself, that most of the people she meets don't get the message. She is second-level satire in a one-level world, and so instead of realizing, for example, that she is mocking the 1970s punk look, stupid video store clerks merely think she's 25 years out of style." The fact that people simply do not "get" Enid's agenda mirrors the customary reception of comics and graphic novels, narrative types that, for a certain period of time, academics bluntly disregarded because they missed the alacrity and authenticity of the dual genres' exposition of real human situations and emotions. In essence, the realness of the genres was below academic critique because the twentieth century was so utterly bogged down with theories that embraced unreality and ambiguity.

Ghost World's appeal has been quickly realized by a number of other directors since its release. In 2002 Sam Mendes and David Self adapted *Road to Perdition* to the screen with the ever-popular Tom Hanks as the film's redemptive central character. The story, originated in graphic novel form by Max Allan Collins and Richard Piers Rayner, follows the seedy employment of family man Michael Sullivan (played by Hanks), whose son (Tyler Hoechlin), after glimpsing one of his father's "jobs," tags along with him as he seeks revenge for a slew of personal and professional mishaps. The darkly envisioned cinematography, made possible by the late Conrad L. Hall, snatched an Academy Award. Indeed, the look of the film captures the crepuscular mien of the original graphic novel, which was composed in black and white. Mendes and Hall successfully translated the dinginess of the graphic novel to a filmic composition that is as inky as its predecessor.

American Splendor (2003) is a double adaptation of sorts that is not only a biopic but also a more conventional adaptation of Harvey Pekar's series of similarly named comics and graphic novels. Shari Springer Berlman and Robert Pulcini direct this film that highlights the near failure of comic artist Harvey Pekar (played by Paul Giamatti), who, in conjunction with Crumb and others, launched a noteworthy chain of comics about an autobiographical everyman. Pekar's character, also called Harvey, encounters a number of realistic, yet sardonically humorous people and situations and struggles to persevere through an increasingly dismal world. Berlman and Pulcini juxtapose straightforward cinematic fiction with live-action comic sequences and impromptu interviews with the real Harvey Pekar, his family, and close friends. The doubleness of this piece can be found in at least two combinations: the film is an adaptation of comics that are adaptations of an actual person's life, and also, the film adapts the life along with the material comics. Other contemporary adaptations will embrace this multilayered approach.

Two other, more recent adaptations of graphic novels, *Sin City* (2005) and *Art School Confidential* (2006), continue the tradition of well-adapted pictorial genres to the screen. Frank Miller and Robert Rodriguez utilize techniques borrowed from film noir in order to capture the grimy landscape and shady society of Miller's classic graphic novel series. Zwigoff's *Art School Confidential* (another Clowes work), like *Ghost World,* is adapted in a more direct manner, though it satisfactorily portrays the vividness of Clowes's style. Each adaptation of a graphic novel is another step toward an acceptance of the genre into mainstream American culture. Whether this transformation is favorable to loyal fans is of little consequence, as the graphic novel and its historical bedfellow, the comic, are swept into the folds of popular literature.

Adaptation *(2002).* Although *Adaptation* is an adaptation of Susan Orlean's *The Orchid Thief,* it also stands as a commentary on the nature of film adaptation in an increasingly commercialized Hollywood. Written by Charlie Kaufman and his pseudo-brother Donald and directed by Spike Jonze, *Adaptation* follows the efforts of "Charlie Kaufman" to adapt Orlean's *Orchid Thief* into an acceptable Hollywood film. However, Charlie must contend with the difficulties of adapting a seemingly plotless tome about the beauty and wonder of orchids—the enigmatic flowers that have, themselves, adapted magnificently into a variety of different species—into another profitable studio blockbuster. "I don't want to cram in sex or guns or car chases [into the adaptation]. You know? Or characters learning profound life lessons" (Kaufman and Kaufman 2002, 5). Charlie also must, amid his adaptational woes, learn to adapt to adulthood and to the demands of being a successful Hollywood screenwriter. In the end, despite Charlie's hopes of protecting his screenplay from the claws of contemporary filmic predictability, *Adaptation* quickly transmogrifies into a plot-driven narrative brimming with sex, drugs, and monstrous explosions. Charlie and Donald (both played by Nicolas Cage), in an attempt to hunt down Susan Orlean (played by Meryl Streep) and to gather the "true" story behind *The Orchid Thief,* end up in a mysterious chase in a swamp where Donald meets his untimely fate. Just like the story of the orchid thief, the final moments of the film declare its purpose as another "study in shape-shifting," given that the process of adaptation is ultimately about the alteration of forms (Orlean 2002, vii). In Orlean's own words, *Adaptation* "is about orchids, about how they adapt to their environment, sometimes resulting in the strangest and most marvelous forms, proving that the answer to everything might indeed be adaptation" (ix). At its core, Charlie's adaptation, as a person and screenwriter, is also our adaptation: the adaptation of *The Orchid Thief,* given to us by the writers and directors, as well as our adaptation as viewers who, unfortunately for Charlie, do indeed learn "a profound life lesson."

Karen Diehl asserts that *Adaptation,* along with a group of other films that draw attention to their authorial intentions, "add[s] narratives to that of [its] source literary text that relocate film and literature as cultural practices determined and shaped by a specific context. These added narratives variously include the narrativization of the process of writing, the process of reading, and the process of adapting to the screen itself" (2005, 103).

Chicago *(2002).* Unlike many adaptations that stem from grandiloquent novels, *Chicago* is a flashy adaptation of the lauded Broadway musical, expertly choreographed by the legendary Bob Fosse in 1975. The musical version of Chicago is itself an adaptation of a play from the 1920s by Maurine Dallas Watkins. The famous Broadway duo John Kander and Fred Ebb added music and lyrics to Watkins's drama about a flapper-wannabe named Roxie Hart (played by Renée Zellweger in

---

ADAPTATION IS AN ADAPTATION

The film *Adaptation* does not rely wholly on Susan Orlean's story, but rather makes up certain storylines, with the help of many foreseeable popular plot twists that are, in turn, added to the adaptation. This dynamic exposes the meta-commentary about authorship that is instinctive to the film. "Reader and spectator alike," Diehl writes, "are thus persuaded not to believe in what they read or see, but to accept it as fictitious," just as the mechanism of film adaptation is, itself, a fictitious enterprise (2005, 102). The culminating events in *Adaptation* are certainly not conceivable, and their utter implausibility, in fact, brandishes the sheer impossibility of accurately adapting any piece of literature in an industry that is obsessed with profit to the exclusion of literary and cinematic nuance. Hence, viewers are left with only the "*illusion* of a dialogue with a literary author" (100). *Adaptation* successfully reveals the flaws of film adaptation using its own medium.

the 2002 update) who dreams of becoming a successful actress and singer like her idol Velma Kelly (played by Catherine Zeta-Jones). However, things go awry when Miss Hart lands in prison after killing her lover. There she meets her idol, convicted of a similar charge, and learns that scandal and celebrity are powerful tools in the media-laden society of what Roger Ebert (2002) calls a "Front Page era." Marshall's 2002 adaptation is a brilliant filmic remake of the original musical that, in some respects, trumps the original in terms of staging and effects. Film, as opposed to staged theatre, possesses a much greater level of flexibility; films can be edited, and special effects can be added after their completion. A live musical, on the other hand, cannot be halted midway so that a scene can be performed again. Additionally, because the stage is the only real setting for the action, a musical is aesthetically limited. Films, however, can have multiple sets and numerous filming locations, lending greater versatility to the story. *Chicago* is an example of how increased filmic flaccidity can bring forth subtle aspects of a source text that are often underplayed onstage.

The film's Jazz Age heroine, Hart, has obviously been affected by the nascent celebrity system of early twentieth-century America in which—because of the rise of Vaudeville, radio, and other cultural phenomenon—many citizens, now lost amid the brightness of the modern era, turned to celebrities of all sorts in order to seek out their own personal identity. Marshall's film splendidly portrays this harsh aspect of past Americana by staging the musical numbers "more or less within Roxie's imagination" (Ebert 2002). Thus the director accomplishes two tasks: he brings out a psychocultural feature of the original that may have been softened because of difficulties in theatrical staging, and he creates a seamless drama that does not annoy audiences with constant musical interruptions. In essence, Marshall finds a perfect cinematic balance between the inceptive musical, with its grand song-and-dance routines, and the filmic adaptation that strives to remain a unified dramatic narrative. As Ebert explains, "*Chicago* is a musical that might have seemed unfilmable . . . because it was assumed it had to be transformed into more conventional terms" and forced into a Hollywood formula. Like *Adaptation, Chicago* overcomes formulaic dispositions about what a film adaptation should be and masterfully "adapts" the standards of filmmaking as it adapts its source material.

Frida (2002). Director Julie Taymor brings the tumultuous life and art of Mexican artist Frida Kahlo to the screen in this moving biopic. Taymor captures Kahlo's life most acutely by utilizing the source of the artist's passion: her art. Not only does Taymor engage the viewer in the sometimes unfortunate details of Kahlo's marriage and other painful life experiences, but she also animates a number of Kahlo's original paintings, canvases that sway back and forth between seething criticisms of bourgeois values and heart-wrenching self-portraits. Kahlo, who became permanently disabled as a result of a bus accident in her youth, channeled her pain and frustration into her unique paintings. Like the vibrant pictures for which Kahlo is renowned, Taymor's film embraces the hues and tones of revolutionary Mexico. This film ultimately succeeds as a biopic because Taymor mixes biography and artistry into a delectable fusion of filmic brilliance. "Biopics of artists," writes Ebert (2002) in his review of the film, "are always difficult, because the connections between life and art always seem too easy and facile. The best ones lead us back to the work itself and inspire us to sympathize with its maker." Indeed, biopics are different from other adaptations because they often tackle a subject that involves living people. In the case of *Frida*, Taymor referenced an established biography on

Kahlo's life by Hayden Herrera in which most of the "characters" are deceased. However, biopics such as Ron Howard's *A Beautiful Mind,* an adaptation of the life of John Nash, a Nobel Prize-winning mathematician who struggles with schizophrenia, employ a subject who is still living. Issues such as these can present problems for the directors, screenwriters, and producers of these projects who are regularly forced to consult with the subject or with his or her family members. The approval of these individuals sometimes inhibits the filmmakers from illuminating the life in full. For instance, when director Christine Jeffs and writer John Browlow wished to adapt the life of Sylvia Plath, they were obliged to confer with Plath's daughter, Frieda Hughes, who bluntly "refused to allow any of her mother's poems to be used in the script and . . . vowed never to see the film" (Milmo 2004). Biopics certainly have their detractors, and in fact, the process of adapting a person's life into a filmic narrative is rather arduous.

In many respects, makers of the biopic must struggle to present their subjects as more than simply images. In a culture that thrives on the continuous elevation of celebrities to idol-like statuses and the incessant circulation of images in the media and elsewhere, it is easy for adapters to fall into the trap of turning their subject into just another metonymy for the actual human life. Rather, the biopic should be an arena in which the filmmaker may topple cultural assumptions about the person in question by seeking to tell the "true" story. The biopic grapples with the same sorts of complexities as does any other adaptation, including matters of fidelity. Does the biopic faithfully render the person's life? Or does the biopic act as an extension or representation of the person's life, artistically removed from actual events? The answers to these questions are extremely pertinent to the overall understanding of biopic production.

Other films in recent years have highlighted the lives and works of famous artists. Julian Schnabel's 1996 adaptation of the life of New York graffiti artist Basquiat, titled *Basquiat,* depicts the street artist's discovery by Andy Warhol (played by David Bowie) and his subsequent popularity. Schnabel, a close friend of the late Basquiat, poignantly captures the instant celebritization of Warhol's protégé and the destructiveness that ensues as a result. As with many misunderstood artists who are thrust reluctantly into the blaring lights of celebrity, Basquiat is unable to overcome his difficulties in the face of stardom and dies of a drug overdose at age 28. Following in the footsteps of *Basquiat, Pollock* (2000) similarly illustrates the life and art of a struggling artist who finds himself coping with the ramifications, personally and professionally, of iconoclasm in twentieth-century American culture. Jackson Pollock, leader of the artistic movement known as Abstract Expressionism, is veritably portrayed by director and leading actor Ed Harris as the sensitive artiste and brash cultural ingénue who exploded onto the New York art scene with his controversial abstract "string" paintings. The film also shows the artist's tempestuous marriage to fellow painter Lee Krasner as well as his numerous extramarital affairs and battles with alcoholism. As with *Frida, Pollock* gives the art its own story, though one that acutely parallels the artist's life.

The Hours *(2002). The Hours* dwells within a category of multilayered adaptations that have distinct textual lineages. Similar to *Chicago,* Stephen Daldry's and David Hare's adaptation of Michael Cunningham's Pulitzer Prize–winning novel is not a singular transformation of novel into film but rather an adaptation of a novel that is, itself, an adaptation of another novel and a biography (in *Chicago,* the historical trajectory extends even further). The celebrated modern British novel from which Cunningham and his adapters draw their inspiration is Virginia Woolf's *Mrs. Dalloway*, a stunning exploration of the relevance of the seemingly mundane, quotidian exploits of a middle-class, middle-aged woman. The novel also examines how the veil of memory often impedes our ability to glimpse what closely surrounds us in the present. Cunningham borrows these thematic elements for his tale about the interconnected lives of three women: Laura Brown (played by Julianne Moore), a young wife and mother grappling with domestic dissatisfaction in postwar suburban America; Virginia Woolf (played by Nicole Kidman), the eminent British novelist who also struggles with an edgy domestic situation, worsened by mental instability, as she begins a new novel, *Mrs. Dalloway*; and Clarissa Vaughn (Cunningham's contemporary Dalloway, played by Meryl Streep), a well-to-do twenty-first-century New Yorker who, like the protagonist of Woolf's *Mrs. Dalloway*, is hosting a party of old friends and colleagues at her apartment for which she is frantically preparing. Scholar Karen Diehl describes the film, and its source text, as interconnecting "strands" of narrative in which one story is dependent on another for its existence (2005, 94–5). Though each of these strands appears to be separate at first, as the film progresses, the viewer is soon clued in to how the three narratives intertwine. We learn that Clarissa's party—for which she has to buy the flowers herself, just like the original Mrs. Dalloway—is, in fact, being thrown for her longtime friend Richard Brown (played by Ed Harris), who has recently won a prestigious award for his own novel. We also learn that Laura Brown, from another strand of the story, is Richard's mother. And of course, in a gesture of mastery, the author Virginia Woolf has, from her historical viewpoint, inaugurated all of these events with the composition and publication of *Mrs. Dalloway*. Woolf's own biography prompts her to write *Mrs. Dalloway*, the book read by the depressed Laura Brown and eventually by her son as well, who, for as long as he can remember, has called Clarissa Vaughn his very own "Mrs. Dalloway." The stories unite in both direct and indirect ways.

Daldry manages this adaptation by using basically three different casts to tell three distinct, yet associated narratives. The characters in this film are generally molded into two opposing groups—victims and survivors—though each can fit into either of the categories at assorted moments in the film. All of the characters fall victim to an author, be it Woolf, Cunningham, or screenwriter Hare, who determines their fate onscreen. They also fall victim to the respective societies and cultures in which they live. Woolf's mental illness and eventual suicide stemmed from multiple factors, not the least of which was her inability to overcome the instances of sexual abuse that she experienced as a child. Laura Brown finds it difficult to withstand the pressures of being a wife and mother in postwar America, and Clarissa Vaughn attempts to please everyone but herself. Additionally, Woolf certainly becomes a victim after her suicide, as does Richard Brown when, like the shell-shocked Septimus Warren-Smith in *Mrs. Dalloway*, he jumps to his death from a second-story window. Laura Brown nearly commits suicide but decides to live instead, thus cementing her status as a survivor. Clarissa Vaughn also survives, appropriately mirroring the outcome of her predetermined fictional equivalent. Those who survive, incidentally, also learn to adapt, much like the characters in *Adaptation*.

Everything Is Illuminated (2005). *Everything Is Illuminated* is a fascinating adaptation of a seemingly unadaptable postmodern novel about the lasting effects of the Holocaust on two distant families—unadaptable because, as Stephanie Zacharek

(2005) notes, the book is made up of "the sort of prose whose wordy digressions and repetitiveness are part of its style (and part of its challenge)." Though based only loosely on its source text, the film manages to convey the same emotional firmament as its predecessor. The novel, written by Jonathan Safran Foer and published in 2002, traces the story of a young Jewish American (also named "Jonathan Safran Foer" and played by Elijah Wood) who travels to Ukraine in order to find information about his family's roots, specifically the whereabouts of the mysterious Augustine, the woman who supposedly saved his grandfather from the Nazi invasion. As with *The Hours* (the originally published version), *Everything Is Illuminated* is composed of more than one story that is combined into a single narrative: the recounting of the search by Alexander Perchov (played by Eugene Hutz), Foer's guide and translator throughout his journey, and also Foer's literary reinterpretation of those events in a more historical context. The stories are connected by a series of letters between the two men that are also included in the novel. Schreiber's adaptation does not attempt to film all of these stories but instead chooses Alex's point of view. The film is separated into chapters, conceivably determined by Alex as he "writes" his account of the journey with Foer.

Jonathan is known as "The Collector" by his family, and by the Perchovs in due time, because wherever he travels, he carries a stock of Ziploc bags in which he collects fragments of the people and experiences with which he comes into contact. In one scene, Jonathan pilfers a container of hand soap from a train's restroom, acting as if his slightly kleptomaniacal act is completely normal. It becomes obvious, however, that his itinerant collecting has a more than superficial purpose. In one of the film's final moments, Jonathan swipes a heap of Ukrainian dust that he eventually takes back to America, after the mystery is solved, and throws onto his grandfather's grave. Jonathan's penchant for collecting can also be understood as a metaphor for the nature of adaptation. When the viewer first glimpses Jonathan clandestinely gathering objects, the method seems random or even quirky. As the film advances, however, we begin to comprehend its true intention. By amassing as large of a collection as he can, Jonathan somehow, at least tangibly, recreates the past and thus reconnects with it. In the end, the collection no longer resembles a piecemeal cluster of various objects but rather a unified material landscape of memory. Similarly, a film adaptation, especially one such as *Everything Is Illuminated,* appears to be a loose assemblage of the "best of" moments from a novel, story, or play. In most cases, because of time and budget constraints, directors, producers, screenwriters, and other industry personnel are forced to make an acceptable adaptation out of these presumably random parts. *Everything Is Illuminated* is a keen example of when a director's "collection" of narrative pieces becomes a clearly distinguished whole.

The core of the film can be found in a few of its final lines, that "everything is illuminated in the light of the past. It is always along the side of us, on the inside, looking out." Though the search for the past illumines the present, the past always remains with us. Film adaptations often disappoint audiences for this very reason; they are beleaguered by the past, that is, by the literary source that stays with them as they watch the adaptation. In order for adaptations to garner success, the spectators are obligated to separate the film from its original and to consider them as two divergent narratives that are to be held at different standards. "It must be tiresome [for filmgoers]," *Slate* reviewer David Edelstein (2005) avers, to read yet another review trumpeting the news that a movie is not as good as the book on which it's based, and that the medium rarely does justice to narrative loop-de-loops or to characters' labyrinthine inner lives. After all, film and literature are different media, a movie ought to be judged on its own merits.

The film version of *Everything Is Illuminated* is a markedly reduced adaptation of Foer's novel and must inevitably be judged on its own terms, despite its apparent disloyalty to its source.

Brokeback Mountain *(2005)*. Perhaps one of the most controversial Hollywood films since the turn of the millennium, Ang Lee's *Brokeback Mountain* is an adaptation by Larry McMurtry and Diana Ossana of E. Annie Proulx's short story of the same name. The story first appeared in *The New Yorker* on October 13, 1997, and was subsequently included in *Close Range: Wyoming Stories,* Proulx's Pulitzer Prize–winning collection. Jenny Shank of *New West* (2005) writes that "when [Proulx] was first approached about turning 'Brokeback Mountain' into a screenplay, she 'was terrified because this wasn't my idea of a story that could be made into a film. It's the sort of thing that Hollywood has been avoiding for a hundred years.'" The tale of two Wyoming ranch hands (played by Heath Ledger and Jake Gyllenhaal) who fall in love during a summer assignment on Brokeback Mountain shocked the Hollywood establishment and many filmgoers because of its blatant inclusion of homosexuality, a topic that the film industry has, indeed, avoided since its beginnings. The filmic treatment of the story is subtle yet breathtaking, and the gay element of the story, so hyped by the media, is subtle as well. One walks away from the film believing that he or she has seen simply a love story, not necessarily a homosexual love story. This type of spotlighting is hardly relevant, as the film ultimately transcended any media controversy that may have surrounded its release.

Proulx has said that she "may be the first writer in America to have a piece of writing make its way to the screen whole and entire" (2005, www.annieproulx.com). In fact, in adapting the piece, McMurtry and Ossana began by transcribing the entire story into a screenplay format. However, "when we first scripted only what was contained in the short story," McMurtry remembers, "those pages only comprised about one-third of the final script for Brokeback—about 35 pages of script. The shooting script was 110 pages long; the other 75 pages were added by us" (qtd. in Shank 2005). That the screenplay contains the story in its entirety is a rare feat for Hollywood film adaptations. Generally, screenwriters are compelled to cut and paste moments of the novel, story, or other source text into the screenplay in order to form a unified film that is also marketable to a wide-ranging audience. To adapt a work completely, covering every event and nuance therein, would result in an extremely lengthy and costly production. "Generally in adaptation, say it's a novel, for example," Ossana attests,

> you really have to cut away and decide what you're going to keep and what you're going to retain. As a general rule, very often you can make a very good movie out of a not-so-good book because you can cut away and then you add things in. It's harder, sometimes, to make a good film out of good prose fiction because the beauty of it is in the actual prose rather than the action. In this particular story, there would be a single sentence and we could take that sentence and write an entire scene about it. It would spark our imaginations and we would just take it and run. (qtd. in Anderson 2005)

In this case, it was necessary for the screenwriters to heavily augment and expand the original story, simply because of its scantiness. *Brokeback Mountain* is an example of a truly incarnational film adaptation, in which the adapters transform the words into a fleshed-out cinematic body.

War of the Worlds *(2005)*. Steven Spielberg's *War of the Worlds* is the apogean *mise-en-abyme* of contemporary film adaptations. Its hypertextual chain extends backward expansively, connected by a series of historical nodes. This expensive adaptation, transformed for the screen by Josh Friedman and David Koepp, is a remake of the 1953 film, directed by Byron Haskin. Haskin's film was, itself, an adaptation of Orson Welles's eerie 1938 radio program, an adaptation of H.G. Wells's lauded 1898 novel. The history of this story certainly runs deep. Wells's earlier novel, a work of **science fiction**, describes an invasion of Earth (nineteenth-century England) by alien creatures from Mars who are equipped with chemical weapons. In one of its endings, the novel finds its narrator and the rest of humanity starting anew after the Martians are destroyed by some viral illness. But Wells apparently provided his readers with an alternate ending in which the Martians triumph over human civilization. The novel has been viewed both as an indictment of British colonial rule and as a treatise in favor of various scientific theories popular during Wells's lifetime, particularly Darwin's philosophy on evolution.

In the 1930s, burgeoning film director Orson Welles staged a Halloween radio performance of Wells's novel that frightened a number of listeners who believed that aliens were actually attacking the planet. The radio play, written by Harold Koch, was a modern retelling of the original, presented as a series of news broadcasts. Though a disclaimer had been communicated at the beginning of the act, those tuning in after the opening credits were naturally shocked by what they understood to be an impending attack. A public outcry arose following the broadcast, partially because of the heightened anxiety of citizens preparing for another world war. The 1953 film, written for the screen by Barré Lyndon, again updates Wells's material for its contemporary film-going audiences and, like Welles's radio version, transplants the action from England to the United States. Spielberg's 2005 version takes its cue from its predecessors, refurbishing the plot and setting for present-day viewers. The protagonist Ray Ferrier, a working class man from New Jersey, is, at the start of the film, estranged from his wife and family. By the close of the film, Ray (played by Tom Cruise) becomes a proverbial working-class hero, saving his daughter Rachel (played by Dakota Fanning) from the alien invaders and surviving the worldwide destruction. Different from previous adaptations, Spielberg's *War* utilizes sophisticated special effects, marks of the current trend in twenty-first century science fiction filmmaking to adopt technologically advanced production techniques, similarly seen in the first three episodes of *Star Wars,* appearing in 1999, 2002, and 2005, respectively. Though David Edelstein of *Slate* (2005) argues that "this *War of the Worlds* does not bear much resemblance to H.G. Wells' novel, or to the Orson Welles '30s radio play," other critics see Spielberg's adaptation as doing the same things, culturally and politically, as its forbears. Both Wells's original novel and Welles's radio adaptation reflect a specific national or international mood. The novel echoed debates over colonial rule as well as scientific evolution, whereas the radio play emulated a sense of interwar distress that plagued the United States in the 1930s. "At one point [in Spielberg's film]," reviewer Stephanie Zacharek (2005) alleges, "the camera scans a wall covered with fliers of missing loved ones (presumably humans who have been abducted or just plain disintegrated by the marauding aliens). [This gesture is] as direct a reference to post-9/11 New York City as you could make." Spielberg's overt cinematic allusion indubitably refers to the current state of affairs in the United States. The very basic themes of his remake mimic the general feelings of terror that Americans now experience on a daily basis in a world wrought with terrorism. Are Spielberg's alien invaders metaphors for the world terrorists who leave devastation in their wake? Several critics of this film seem to agree with this proposition.

The Devil Wears Prada (2006). *The Devil Wears Prada* is director David Frankel's and screenwriter Aline Brosh McKenna's adaptation of Lauren Weisberger's *roman à clef* about a recent college graduate who travels to New York City to become a paid intern at an influential fashion magazine. In the film, Andy Sachs (played by Anne Hathaway) has come to the Big Apple from the Midwest in order to procure a much-coveted position at *Runway,* a *Vogue*-style publication headed by the notoriously strict Miranda Priestly (played by Meryl Streep). The novel, an extension of the chick lit phenomenon—a genre of fiction that combines contemporary postfeminist musings on love and relationships with the world of high-style fashion—differs from the film in a number of ways. Adapters chose to give Andy Midwestern roots, rather than Eastern ones, and many of the characters found in the original novel are lost in the film version. Brosh McKenna took several liberties with the screenplay in order to maintain the novel's casual and comical tone, as well as to create a "happy ending" for Andy and her live-in boyfriend Nate (played by Adrian Grenier). Additionally, the screenwriter chose to downplay two major cultural themes of the novel. In the original, both Andy and Miranda are Jewish Americans, but Miranda changes her name and disguises her heritage more so than Andy. Critics view Weisberger's inclusion of these details in the novel as an important, if brief, examination of Jewish assimilation in the American twenty-first century. Similarly, filmmakers chose to exclude various details about the sexuality of Andy's coworkers, especially that of Nigel, who in the novel is very openly homosexual. Several conclusions can be drawn as to the director's and screenwriter's reasoning for disallowing these more serious thematic elements from entering into the final film. As a buoyant comedy-drama, *The Devil Wears Prada* would appear inconsistent if, all of a sudden, a more formidable thematic undercurrent was launched into the previously jocund plot. Adapters are responsible for making choices about the content of adaptations based on several criteria, and marketability is most certainly at the top of that list. The inclusion of these issues, though assuredly elevating the film to an exceedingly more critical cinematic echelon, would have necessarily been a mistake.

Both the film and the novel are strong examples of a trend in popular entertainment in which young working females and their interpersonal relationships are presented in a humorous or even satiric light. Weisberger's novel stems from her experience as an intern at *Vogue,* a situation that is masked thinly by her fictional account. Indeed, the film reflects an even more widespread drift in twenty-first-century cinema toward lighthearted adaptations of very contemporary novels and stories. *The Devil Wears Prada* was first published in 2003 and was in the hands of producers almost immediately. However, the final draft of the screenplay was not concluded until 2005, when Brosh McKenna signed onto the project. The film's success at the box office, making over $100 million domestically, will further the production of film adaptations within the chick lit genre.

Fast Food Nation *(2006).* Eric Schlosser's 2001 book, *Fast Food Nation,* is a scathing account of the not-so-healthy practices of the American fast-food industry. According to Schlosser, the influx of fast food into American society "has helped to transform not only the American diet, but also our landscape, economy, workforce, and popular culture" (3). The book also exposes how the fast-mood market, as well as its sibling the meat-packing industry, exploits its workers and, like other profit-seeking corporate bodies, rarely considers its ultimately negative effects on global culture. Schlosser's treatise, though a work of nonfiction, has often been compared to the realist novels of the early twentieth century, most specifically to Upton Sinclair's *The Jungle.*

Richard Linklater's 2006 adaptation of Schlosser's documentary-style book is a fictionalized story featuring an ensemble cast in which members of the fast-food industry relay the consequences of their line of employment on public health, the environment, and society as a whole. As Stephanie Zacharek recognizes, "it can't be easy to wrest a work of investigative journalism into narrative form, to take facts, figures and arguments and work them into a structure actors can easily inhabit." The fictionalization of a nonfiction book certainly risks the possibility of turning convincing evidence into mindless filmic plotlines; however, Linklater's movie, complete with clips of bovine slaughtering, resolves to maintain the disturbing facts embedded in Schlosser's premiere volume. In Zacharek's words, the "slaughterhouse climax is bluntly effective; I walked out of the movie feeling wobbly and a little faint." Todd McCarthy (2006) agrees with Zacharek's sentiments:

> Making a shaped, involving film from Schlosser's intensively researched, highly popular exposé of the junk food juggernaut in the United States repped a considerable challenge, and the author and Linklater have made eminently reasonable decisions about where to train their focus.

Critics concede that Linklater's film accomplished its proposed goal: to promote awareness of the methods and practices of the fast-food agglomerate through the lens of fiction.

Adapting fact into fabrication has become an increasingly trendy cultural anomaly. Bennett Miller's *Capote* (2005), starring Academy Award–winner Phillip Seymour Hoffman as the literary artist Truman Capote, is essentially an adaptation of a factual search for the material that eventually formed the framework for Capote's 1965 "nonfiction novel" *In Cold Blood.* The film relates events not only from Capote's life but also from the novel, the plot of which follows the story of two murderers on death row responsible for killing an innocent Kansas family. Capote fictionalizes the murderers and their crimes simply by placing them in his novel. The film picks up where the novel leaves off, continuing to fictionalize those occurrences and adding to them by narrativizing Capote's life during that period. Indeed, the narrative structure of film naturally transforms any work into a kind of fiction given that, according to the *Oxford English Dictionary,* fiction is authentically defined as "the act of fashioning or imitating." *Capote* effortlessly mimics and refashions a legitimate literary historical moment. Perhaps in this light, all film adaptations are, themselves, forms of fiction, each existing as a cinematic imitation of a source text. Some are very loyal to their origins, choosing to represent aspects of the novel, story, or biography rather realistically, while others are merely shells of their predecessors. In either case, the end result is a manufactured cinematic narrative that generates from a desire to represent a specific text in a heterogeneous medium.

Filmography

Adaptation. Directed by Spike Jonze. Columbia Pictures, 2002.

American Splendor. Directed by Shari Springer Berman and Robert Pulcini. FineLine Features, 2003.

Art School Confidential. Directed by Terry Zwigoff. United Artists, 2006.

Brokeback Mountain. Directed by Ang Lee. Focus Features, 2005.

Capote. Directed by Bennett Miller. United Artists, 2005.

Chicago. Directed by Rob Marshall. Miramax Films, 2002.

Crumb. Directed by Terry Zwigoff. Superior Pictures, 1994.

The Devil Wears Prada. Directed by David Frankel. 20th Century Fox, 2006.

Everything Is Illuminated. Directed by Live Schreiber. Warner Independent Pictures, 2005.

Fast Food Nation. Directed by Richard Linklater. BBC Films, 2006.

Frida. Directed by Julie Taymor. Miramax Films, 2002.

Ghost World. Directed by Terry Zwigoff. United Artists, 2001.

The Hours. Directed by Stephen Daldry. Miramax Films, 2002.

Road to Perdition. Directed by Sam Mendes. 20th Century Fox, 2002.

Sin City. Directed by Frank Miller and Robert Rodriguez. Dimension Films, 2005.

War of the Worlds. Directed by Stephen Spielberg. Dreamworks SKG, 2005.

Bibliography

American Film Institute. http://www.afi.com.

Anderson, Matt. "Adapting *Brokeback Mountain:* From Page to Screen." *Movie Habit.* 2005. http://www.moviehabit.com.

Andrew, Dudley. "The Well-Worn Muse: Adaptation in Film History and Theory." In *Narrative Strategies.* Sydney M. Conger and Janice R. Welsh, eds. Macomb: Western Illinois University, 1980, 9–19.

Braudy, Leo. Afterword. In *Play It Again, Sam: Retakes on Remakes.* Andrew Horton and Stuart Y. McDougal, eds. Berkeley, CA: University of California Press, 1998, 327–335.

Cartmell, Deborah, and Imelda Whelehan, eds. *Adaptations: From Text to Screen, Screen to Text.* London: Routledge, 1999.

Clowes, Daniel. *Art School Confidential.* Seattle: Fantagraphics, 2005.

———. *Ghost World.* Seattle: Fantagraphics, 1998.

Collins, Max Allan, and Richard Payner. *Road to Perdition.* New York: Pocket Books, 2002.

Cunningham, Michael. *The Hours.* New York: Farrar, Straus, and Giroux, 1998.

Denby, David. "Big Pictures: Hollywood Looks for a Future." *The New Yorker.* December 2006. http://www.newyorker.com.

Diehl, Karen. "Once Upon an Adaptation: Traces of the Authorial on Film." In *Books in Motion: Adaptation, Intertextuality, Authorship.* Mireia Aragay, ed. Amsterdam: Rodopi, 2005.

Ebert, Roger. "Chicago." *Chicago Sun-Times.* December 2002. http://rogerebert.suntimes.com.

———. "Frida." *Chicago Sun-Times.* November 2002. http://rogerebert.suntimes.com.

———. "Ghost World." *Chicago Sun-Times.* August 2001. http://rogerebert.suntimes.com.

Edelstein, David. "Adapt This: *Everything Is Illuminated* and *Thumbsucker* Are Lost in Translation." *Slate.* September 2005. http://www.slate.com.

———. "They Came From Below: Stephen Spielberg's *War of the Worlds.*" *Slate.* June 2005. http://www.slate.com.

Elliott, Kamilla. *Rethinking the Novel/Film Debate.* Cambridge: Cambridge University Press, 2003.

Foer, Jonathan Safran. *Everything Is Illuminated*. Boston: Houghton Mifflin, 2002.

Herrera, Hayden. *Frida*. New York: Harper & Row, 1983.

Horton, Andrew, and Stuart Y. McDougal, eds. *Play It Again, Sam: Retakes on Remakes*. Berkeley: University of California Press, 1998.

Internet Movie Database. http://www.imdb.com.

Kaufman, Charlie, and Donald Kaufman. *Adaptation*. The Shooting Script. New York: Newmarket Press, 2002.

Lupack, Barbara Tepa. *Take Two: Adapting the Contemporary American Novel to Film*. Bowling Green, OH: Bowling Green University Press, 1994.

McCarthy, Todd. "Fast Food Nation." *Variety*. May 2006. http://www.variety.com.

McFarlane, Brian. *Novel to Film: An Introduction to the Theory of Film Adaptation*. Oxford: Clarendon Press, 1996.

Milmo, Cahal. "Stop Digging Up Mother's Troubled Past, Says Plath's Daughter." *The Independent*. November 2004. http://enjoyment.independent.co.uk.

Nasar, Sylvia. *A Beautiful Mind*. New York: Simon and Schuster, 1998.

Orlean, Susan. Foreword. *Adaptation*. The Shooting Script. New York: Newmarket Press, 2002.

———. *The Orchid Thief*. New York: Random House, 1998.

Oxford English Dictionary. http://www.oed.com.

Pekar, Harvey, et al. *American Splendor: The Life and Times of Harvey Pekar*. New York: Ballantine Books, 2003.

Proulx, E. Annie. *Brokeback Mountain*. New York: Scribner, 2005.

———. "Brokeback Mountain FAQ." *Annie Proulx Online*. December 2005. http://www.annieproulx.com.

Reynolds, Peter, ed. *Novel Images: Literature in Performance*. London: Routledge, 1993.

Seger, Linda. *The Art of Adaptation: Turning Fact and Fiction Into Film*. New York: Henry Holt, 1992.

Schlosser, Eric. *Fast Food Nation*. New York: Harper Perennial, 2005.

Shank, Jenny. "Pulitzer Prize Winner Says the West's 'Got Balls': Proulx, McMurtry, and Ossana Discuss Adapting 'Brokeback Mountain.'" *New West*. November 2005. http://www.newwest.net.

Sinyard, Neil. *Filming Literature: The Art of Screen Adaptation*. London: Croom Helm, 1986.

Stam, Robert. "Beyond Fidelity: The Dialogics of Adaptation." In *Film Adaptation*. James Naremore, ed. New Brunswick, NJ: Rutgers University Press, 2000.

Stam, Robert, and Alessandra Raengo, eds. *Literature and Film: A Guide to the Theory and Practice of Film Adaptation*. Malden, MA: Blackwell, 2005.

Weisberger, Lauren. *The Devil Wears Prada*. New York: Doubleday, 2003.

Zacharek, Stephanie. "Everything Is Illuminated." *Salon*, September 2005. http://dir.salon.com/story/ent/movies/review/2005/09/16/everything_is_illuminated/index.html.

———. "Fast Food Nation." *Salon*, November 2006. http://www.salon.com/ent/movies/review/2006/11/17/fast_food/index.html.

———. "War of the Worlds." *Salon*, June 2005. http://dir.salon.com/story/ent/movies/review/2005/06/29/war/index.html.

Further Reading

Aragay, Mireia, ed. *Books in Motion: Adaptation, Intertextuality, Authorship*. Amsterdam: Rodopi, 2006; Cartmell, Deborah, and Imelda Whelehan, eds. *Adaptations: From Text to Screen, Screen to Text*. London: Routledge, 1999; Chatman, Seymour. *Coming to Terms: The Rhetoric of Narrative in Fiction and Film*. Ithaca, NY: Cornell University Press, 1990; Conger, Sydny M., and Janice R. Welsh. *Narrative Strategies*. Macomb: Western Illinois University, 1980; Desmond, John, and Peter Hawkes. *Adaptation: Studying Film and Literature*. Columbus, OH: McGraw-Hill, 2005; Elliott, Kamilla. *Rethinking the Novel/Film Debate*. Cambridge: Cambridge University Press, 2003; Giddings, Robert, Keith Selby, and Chris Wensley. *Screening the Novel.* New York: St. Martin's, 1990; Horton, Andrew, and Stuart Y. McDougal, eds. *Play It Again, Sam: Retakes on Remakes.* Berkeley: University of California Press, 1998; Lupack, Barbara Tepa. *Take Two: Adapting the Contemporary American Novel to Film.* Bowling Green, OH: Bowling Green University Press, 1994; McFarlane, Brian. *Novel to Film: An Introduction to the Theory of Film Adaptation.* Oxford: Clarendon Press, 1996; Naremore, James. *Film Adaptation.* New Brunswick, NJ: Rutgers University Press, 2000; Reynolds, Peter, ed. *Novel Images: Literature in Performance.* London: Routledge, 1993; Seger, Linda. *The Art of Adaptation: Turning Fact and Fiction Into Film.* New York: Henry Holt, 1992; Sinyard, Neil. *Filming Literature: The Art of Screen Adaptation.* London: Croom Helm, 1986; Stam, Robert. *Literature through Film: Realism, Magic, and the Art of Adaptation.* Malden, MA: Blackwell, 2005; Stam, Robert, and Alessandra Raengo, eds. *Literature and Film: A Guide to the Theory and Practice of Film Adaptation.* Malden, MA: Blackwell, 2005; Stam and Raengo. *A Companion to Literature and Film.* Malden, MA: Blackwell, 2004; Zatlin, Phyllis. *Theatrical Translation and Film Adaptation: A Practitioner's View.* Clevedon: Multilingual Matters, 2005.

AMY MALLORY-KANI

FLASH FICTION

Definition. Many editors and writers today define flash fiction as a story ranging from a few words to not usually over 1,500 to 2,000 words (but more often less than 1,000 words). A traditional short story ranges from 3,000 to 20,000 words, so flash fiction is considerably shorter. However, while length can help identify flash fiction, it is of little use in actually defining it.

The amorphous and protean quality of flash fiction allows for the constant changing of shapes as these stories draw and invent from various genres and traditions to create stand-alone stories that often work on their own terms. Countless writers are involved in writing flash fiction in various ways. Many are involved in following the form's long tradition, and many others are reinventing the form as they continue to experiment with the boundaries and methods of fiction. These shortest of stories are not always diversions for the moment but are often stories that are profound and memorable—as good fiction of longer lengths can be.

Charles Baxter notes in the introduction to *Sudden Fiction International: 60 Short Short Stories* (1989), "this form is not about to be summarized by any one person's ideas about it . . . the stories are on so many various thresholds: they are between poetry and fiction, the story and the sketch, prophecy and reminiscence, the personal and the crowd . . . as a form, they are open, and exist in a state of potential" (25).

FLUSH FICTION?

Flash fiction often travels by several interesting names, depending on what publishers, editors, readers, or writers prefer to call such stories. Some of these names include fictions, short-shorts, sudden fiction (the preceding three usually representing the upper length limits), micro, zip, miniaturist, minimalist, minute, postcard, fast, furious, quick, snap, and skinny fiction. They are also sometimes called palm-of-the hand stories, drabbles, smoke-long stories, and in some cases, prose poetry and American *haibun.* These small stories have also been called "flush fiction" to emphasize the important single-sitting ideal Edgar Allan Poe recommended for short stories.

Some names for flash fiction are chosen to stress brevity, suggesting that such stories can be read or even written in a flash. Other names are chosen to emphasize the way in which the stories affect and enlighten readers. And still other names are chosen for the way in which they cause readers to perform the act of reading, many times forcing them to slow down and read such pieces as slowly and carefully as they would read good poetry.

Even though this type of writing travels by several names, flash fiction has become the most popular label, likely because of its snappy poetic consonance, which makes it easy to hold in memory, and because of its distance from the older, less descriptive term "short-shorts." More and more writers, editors, and readers use "flash fiction" to refer to very short stories.

Some current flash fiction continues to follows the writing strategy of O. Henry by displaying a trick or twist ending. Other flash fiction borrows strategies from the longer short story, and such pieces will often have a traditional beginning, middle, and end. Still other flash fiction pieces tend more toward prose poetry or toward the experimental, and the results are hybrid pieces that push the boundaries of what fiction typically does.

While some flash fiction pieces are to be read quickly as simple entertainment, other types are similar to lyric poetry—condensed, thickly layered, evoking a full range of emotions, and making demands on reader attention and imagination. Many poetically compressed pieces depend on implication, suggestion, voice, or situation for their effects and often devote less attention to traditional fiction concepts such as plot or character development. Characters in some flash fiction pieces are nameless, and instead of having names, characters display an archetypal relationship identification (such as "mother" or "father"). Those pieces without character names often give the impression that the stories are "everyman" or "everywoman" stories. Gitte Mose points out, "Through their testing and tentative art of storytelling, these writers of short-shorts are able to show the world as fickle and immense, a world we cannot fathom but perhaps approach when it is captured at the 'roots' of a kind of fiction that is probing and challenging the capabilities of language." Writers of short-shorts assume "that the world is full of possibilities, that it *can* be examined and told by imposing their artistic form on some small corners of chaos" (2004, 93).

Some of the more unusual types of flash fiction include plotless stories; monologues; language, tone, or mood pieces; list stories (such as using biographical material or a course syllabus to tell a story); the use of unusual second-person point of view or address; and the use of one, two, or three long sentences covering two or three pages. More and more writers use flash fiction to "reveal the hidden, to accentuate the subtle, to highlight the seemingly insignificant, or, as William Blake said in another context, 'to see a world in a grain of sand'" (Fuller and Casto 2001, 30). To do this, protean flash fiction puts many old and new and experimental writing strategies to work.

History. The idea of flash fiction has been around as long as people have been telling stories around campfires and as long as writers have been writing. Brief, potent, and suggestive short-short stories abound in ancient literature and continue to be a strong presence in today's stories. These short stand-alone stories were once generally known as short-shorts, and a history of flash fiction will of necessity parallel a history of short-shorts. But when several popular anthologies were published in the mid-1980s and 1990s, the study of what these brief stories are and what they can do began in earnest. Along with these studies came the search for and use of new and interesting names. However, until recently most flash fiction has managed to slip beneath literary radar.

The name *flash fiction* likely came into widespread acceptance and use with the publication of *Flash Fiction: 72 Very Short Stories*, edited by James Thomas, Denise Thomas, and Tom Hazuka (1992). As the memorable and snappy title spread, especially across the Internet, "flash fiction" became for many a generic catchall name for very short stories (along with "sudden fiction" and other descriptive and memorable names—see this chapter's sidebar).

Some of the early writers of short-shorts who are major influences on present-day flash fiction include O. Henry (1862–1910), master of the surprise ending; Charles Baudelaire (1821–1867), acclaimed for his prose poems; Guy de Maupassant (1850–1910), known for stories from everyday life that often reveal hidden aspects of people; Hector Hugh Munro (Saki) (1870–1916), praised for short-short sardonic and macabre stories; and Ambrose Bierce (1842–1910), acclaimed for his brief stories of the supernatural.

In his dedication for his series of prose poems in *Paris Spleen* (1869) Baudelaire says, "We can cut wherever we please, I my dreaming, you your manuscript, the reader his reading; for I do not keep the reader's restive mind hanging in suspense on the threads of an interminable and superfluous plot. . . . Chop it into numerous pieces and you will see that each one can get along alone" (ix). Some of Baudelaire's pieces are less than a half page long while others run two or three pages in length. That flash fiction can also "get along alone" is one of its main characteristics—each small story, like each of Baudelaire's pieces, is complete in itself.

According to Mildred I. Reid and Delmar E. Bordeaux, editors of *Writers: Try Short Shorts!* (1947), prior to 1926, short-shorts were published daily in McClure's Newspaper Syndicate. Then in 1926 *Colliers Weekly,* who claimed the one-page stories they published were the "greatest innovation in short story publication since O. Henry," ran such stories in 20 issues, and the short-short quickly became a popular form. Some of the authors for *Colliers* were Rupert Hughes, Zona Gale, Sophie Kerr, and Octavus Roy Cohen. *Cosmopolitan* magazine soon followed suit and engaged W. Somerset Maugham and A.J. Cronin to write short-shorts for their pages as well (13). As of 1947, from the "slicks to the pulps," over two hundred magazines and newspapers were publishing short-short stories as regular features. The stories also began appearing on radio where they found other eager audiences (25).

Ernest Hemingway (1899–1961), known for his deceptively simple and spare prose style and for his withholding of information so readers can draw necessary conclusions, is another major influence on modern flash fiction. Some of his flash-length stories include "Hills Like White Elephants," "A Very Short Story," "Cat in the Rain," "A Clean Well-Lighted Place," "Ten Indians," "A Simple Enquiry," and "A Canary For One."

Other early writers whose work is a strong influence on modern flash fiction include Fredrick Brown and Richard Brautigan. The horror stories collected in Fredrick Brown's popular *Nightmares and Geezenstacks* (1961) are all flash-fiction length. Richard Brautigan's only story collection, *Revenge of the Lawn* (1971), influenced interest in stories that blurred genre boundaries. Many of Brautigan's stories are less than a half page long.

Through the years there have been several other acclaimed authors associated with flash fiction–length stories—far too many to explore in the confines of this chapter. Instead this chapter's focus is on some of the major and influential anthologies that have been published. Not all authors in the anthologies are included here, but the names mentioned show the diversity of writers engaged in writing extremely short fiction.

Robert Coover and Kent Dixon edited the *Stone Wall Book of Short Fictions* (1973), a work made possible by a grant from the National Endowment for the Arts. The stories range from the straightforward to the highly experimental. Authors include Joyce Carol Oates, Donald Barthelme, Elie Wiesel, Kent Dixon, Robert Kelly, Richard Brautigan, Robert Coover, Russell Edson, Jorge Luis Borges, Rikki, W.S. Merwin, and others.

Coover, serving as guest coeditor along with editor Elliott Anderson, collected and featured 87 "Minute Stories" in the Winter 1976 issue of *TriQuarterly*. Some of the stories are as brief as an average paragraph, while others are a page long, and others run two or three pages. The authors include W.S. Merwin, Alain Robb-Grillet, Angela Carter, Russell Edson, Michael Benedikt, Jorge Luis Borges, Andrei Codrescu, Annie Dillard, Kent Dixon, Robert Kelly, Richard Brautigan, and others.

Isaac Asimov, Martin H. Greenberg, and Joseph D. Olander published *Microcosmic Tales: 100 Wondrous Science Fiction Short-Short Stories* (1980). All the stories are 2,000 words or fewer with many less than two pages long. Some of the authors are Isaac Asimov, Arthur C. Clark, Harlan Ellison, Mack Reynolds, Alice Laurance, Robert Silverberg, A.E. van Vogt, Fredric Brown, Harry Harrison, Larry Niven, Joanna Russ, Lester del Rey, and Fritz Leiber.

Irving Howe and Ilana Wiener Howe edited *Short-Shorts: Anthology of the Shortest Stories* (1982), which includes masterpieces from around the world. The average length for the stories is 1,500 words. Some of the authors are Leo Tolstoy, Anton Chekhov, Ernest Hemingway, James Joyce, D.H. Lawrence, Luigi Pirandello, Sherwood Anderson, Katherine Anne Porter, Isaac Babel, William Carlos Williams, Doris Lessing, Jorge Luis Borges, Octavio Paz, Grace Paley, Gabriel Garcia Marquez, Augusto Monterroso, Heinrich Boll, and Luisa Valenzuela.

100 Great Fantasy Short Short Stories (1984) was edited by Isaac Asimov, Terry Carr, and Martin H. Greenberg. The stories are 2,000 words or fewer, and many are as short as a half page. Authors include Roger Zelazny, H.P. Lovecraft, Marion Zimmer Bradley, Harlan Ellison, Damon Knight, Bruce Boston, Jane Yolen, Steve Rasnic Tem, Lawrence C. Connolly, Mack Reynolds, Fredric Brown, Barry Malzberg, Edgar Pangborn, Jack Dann, Gene Wolfe, Andre Maurois, and others.

A serious search for a new name for such short stories came with the publication of *Sudden Fiction: American Short-Shorts* (1986), edited by Robert Shapard and James Thomas. The anthology contains good debate and discussion on this type of writing, and the stories featured range from one to five pages long. The editors describe the stories as "highly compressed, highly charged, insidious, protean, sudden, alarming, tantalizing, these short-shorts confer form on small corners of chaos" (xvi). The authors include Robert Coover, Donald Barthelme, John Cheever, Roy Blount, Jr., John Updike, Gordon Lish, Mary Robison, Langston Hughes, Raymond Carver, Tobias Wolff, Ray Bradbury, Tennessee Williams, Pamela Painter, Mark Strand, Joyce Carol Oates, Russell Edson, Stuart Dybek, James B. Hall, Russell Banks, Ron Carlson, Lydia Davis, Jayne Anne Phillips, Bernard Malamud, and others.

4 Minute Fictions: 50 Short-Short Stories from the North American Review (1987) was edited by Robley Wilson Jr. The *North American Review* is the oldest magazine in the United States and has been published since 1815. Wilson includes a brief introduction to the 50 stories that range from 200 to 2,000 words and says, "What's important is that these are excellent pieces of fiction wrought within a limited frame of space and of time. Each works in its own way, on its own terms." He says that like the work in the anthology, "fiction covers everything, is eclectic, clings to no armature of critical fashion" (iii). Among the authors are Barry Lopez, Raymond Carver, T. Coraghessan Boyle, Stephen Dixon, Stuart Dybek, Thomas Farber, Edward Hirsch, Thaisa Frank, Edward Hirsch, W.P. Kinsella, Pamela Painter, and Allen Woodman.

Sudden Fiction International: 60 Short-Short Stories (1989), edited by Robert Shapard and James Thomas, also includes with the various stories an excellent and useful afterword section where various writers, editors, and theorists comment on such things as the popularity of this type of fiction and the characteristics of very short stories. The anthology features notable writers from around the world such as Margaret Atwood, Yasunary Kawabata, Jamaica Kincaid, Colette, R.K. Narayan, Heinrich Boll, Jorge Luis Borges, Slawomir Mrozek, Doris Lessing, Gabriel Garcia Marquez, Peter Handke, Joyce Carol Oates, Richard Brautigan, David Brooks, Krisnan Varma, Isak Dinesen, Panos Ioannides, Hernan Lara Zavala, Rodrigo Rey Rosa, Talat Abbasi, Denis Hirson, Jeanette Winterson, Luisa Valenzuela, Italo Calvino, Ron Carlson, Edla Van Steen, Isaac Babel, Feng Jicai, Nadine Gordimer, Fernando Sorrentino, Daniel Boulanger, Bessie Head, Donald Barthelme, Clarice Lispector, Julio Ortega, Bai Xiao-Yi, and Paul Theroux.

Flash Fiction: 72 Very Short Stories (1992), edited by James Thomas, Denise Thomas, and Tom Hazuka, includes stories 250 to 750 words in length. The editors set out to answer the question "How short can a story be and still truly be a story?" They decide such stories are "short stage presentations or musical pieces that play to the full range of human sensibilities—some evoke mood while other provoke the intellect, some introduce us to people we're interested to meet while others tell us of unusual but understandable phenomena in this world, and some of them do several or all of these things, the things good fiction of any length does" (12). Stories included are by Francine Prose, Raymond Carver, Lon Otto, Bret Lott, Russell Edson, Luisa Valenzuela, Pamela Painter, Don Shea, Carolyn Forche, Richard Brautigan, Jamaica Kincaid, Bruce Holland Rogers, Heinrich Boll, Julio Cortazar, John Updike, Tim O'Brien, Mark Strand, Gordon Lish, Joyce Carol Oates, Margaret Atwood, Ronald Wallace, and others.

Allen Kornblum's Coffee House Press published a series flash fiction collections by individual authors in the early 1990s as part of their Coffee To Go: Short-Short Story series. Author collections include Jessica Treat's *A Robber in the House* (1993), Kenneth Koch's *Hotel Lambosa and Other Stories* (1993), and Barry Silesky's *One Thing That Can Save Us* (1994).

Sudden Fiction (Continued) (1996) was edited by Robert Shapard and James Thomas. The editors point out,

> The spirit of experimentation continues to be most alive these days in the shorter forms. No longer relegated to special sections, they are scattered as regular fare throughout the pages of an even larger number of magazines, including the larger-circulation magazines. But one thing remains constant: each story revels in its own

elements of surprise; each, whether traditional or experimental, proves that a tale told quickly offers pleasure long past its telling. (12)

This collection's authors include Margaret Atwood, Alice Walker, Robin Hemley, Molly Giles, Don DeLillo, Charles Baxter, Milos Macourek, Ursula Hegi, Ron Carlson, Bret Lott, Robert Olen Butler, Andrei Codrescu, Allen Woodman, Pagan Kennedy, Richard Plant, Madison Smartt Bell, and Bruce Holland Rogers.

Micro Fiction: An Anthology of Really Short Stories (1996), edited by Jerome Judson, features a decade of winners and finalists from the annual World's Best Short Short Story Contest, which had been running since 1986. It also includes other writers who took up the challenge of writing such short stories, and all of the stories presented are 300 words or fewer. Stern says, "These short short stories represent work by writers who have found ways to play upon a very small field, and yet to invent their own imaginative and resonant worlds" (19). Writers include Molly Giles, Roberta Allen, Pamela Painter, Kim Addonizio, Virgil Suarez, Fred Chappell, Ron Wallace, Stuart Dybek, Russell Edson, Ron Carlson, Ursula Hegi, Amy Hempel, Antonya Nelson, and Padgett Powell.

Horrors! 365 Scary Stories (1998), edited by Stefan Dziemianowicz, Robert Weinberg, and Martin H. Greenberg, presents readers a story a day for one year's reading. The anthology won the Horror Writer's Association Best Anthology Award and includes over 300 writers whose work on average is less than three pages long. The stories are by Lawrence C. Connolly, Michael Arnzen, Linda J. Dunn, Paula Guran, Brian McNaughton, Adam Niswander, Steve Resnic Tem, Tim Waggoner, William Marden, Brian Hodge, Phyllis Eisenstein, Brian A. Hopkins, Hugh B. Cave, Lisa Morton, Bruce Boston, and others.

Trends and Themes. Short-short stories have undergone various changes through the years. Early popular short-short stories often adhered to the strategies begun by O. Henry and Guy de Maupassant, with use of a surprise or trick ending. Many writers and editors today still stick with this tried-and-true formula. But flash fiction also takes on many other methods of telling a story. As boundaries continued to be pushed and genre lines became blurrier, the results were new and inventive ways of telling stories—less predictable stories that refuse to remain within any strict formulations about them. This trend continued as short-short stories evolved into today's concept of very short fiction, which includes models and strategies from older short-shorts and which takes stories into new, interesting, and inventive directions. Following are some of the directions flash-fiction type stories have taken.

Reid and Bordeaux say that by 1947 short-shorts "began dealing with every variety of emotion" and became committed to "presenting the beauties, the frailties, and the striking nuances of complex human nature" (14). They describe this type of story as "a dramatic narrative whose primary aim is to arouse in its readers a shock of astonishment or surprise" (19). The commonality shared by stories of the time was "dramatic form, or plot," which helps the story "achieve its intended effect." They claim that in the short-short story, "it is not the solution, but the astonishing *nature* of the solution which is depended upon for the chief effect" (17). In these stories the author "presents a character, or a group of characters acting in and through a crisis" (19).

Reid and Bordeaux also say the majority of legitimate short-short stories of the time consisted of eight types: the complication short-short, the character short-short, the decision short-short, the alienation or reconciliation short-short, the psychological short-short, the dilemma short-short, the parallel-action short-short, and the identity short-short.

Whereas stories up until at least 1947 emphasized plot and crisis as essential to the short-short story, Irving Howe and Ilana Wiener Howe (1983) give plot a much less central position of importance and point out that in the stories they collected, character seems to "lose its significance, seems in fact to drop out of sight." Instead, such stories depict "human figures in a momentary flash," in fleeting profile, in "archetypal climaxes which define their mode of existence." In short-shorts, "situation tends to replace character, representative condition to replace individuality" (x).

The average length for stories in the Howes' anthology is 1,500 words (with some stories as long as 2,500 words). The editors say that while a traditional short story has a simple plot "resembling a chain with two or three links," in the short-short "there's only one link." In successful short-short stories "everything depends on intensity, one sweeping blow of perception" (xi). Such stories, like lyric poetry, strive for "a rapid unity of impression, an experience rendered in its wink of immediacy." Writers "stake everything on a stroke of inventiveness" (xii). The four variations in the short-shorts they feature include one thrust of incident, life rolled up, snap-shot or single frame, and like a fable (xiii–xiv).

Mark Mills in *Crafting the Very Short Story: An Anthology of 100 Masterpieces* (2004) says that the primary stylistic features of the stories in the anthology are voice, point of view, and setting. "Character," says Mills, is "only glanced at and plot is a slim shadow of the larger and more important structure" (xv). Such stories "illuminate the human condition by dramatizing universal aspects of human nature," and the results are stories that are "ostensibly simple in appearance, yet complex and precise in detail." The writers, Mills says, "deftly employ the tools of fiction to maximize each story's power while minimizing length" (xiv). The pace of this succinct genre is "swift yet unhurried," and its "uncommon voice [is] supplemented by inventive design" (xv).

In *Sudden Fiction: American Short-Short Stories* (1986), Stephen Minot says short-shorts are rooted in at least five different traditions: the true experience story ("vivid, intense, dramatic" and which seems highly personal), the anecdote (which includes jokes, parables, and fables), the speculative story (often without plot where "character and even plot become subservient to theme"), dream stories (where "mood is stressed more than theme" and "tone is everything"), and poetic stories (rich in auditory effects and where "imagery is more highly valued than narrative structure") (235–237).

As Minot points out, flash pieces often seem highly personal and true. Some flash fiction pieces are read as true stories, and some true stories are read as fictional accounts—one will often pass as the other. This blurring of genre boundaries continues in the publication of three popular anthologies of what can be viewed as flash memoirs or flash creative nonfiction—all related to flash fiction in technique.

Judith Kitchen and Mary Paumier Jones edited *In Short: A Collection of Brief Creative Nonfiction* (1996). The anthology includes work by Stuart Dybek, Maxine Kumin, Terry Tempest Williams, Tobias Wolff, Tim O'Brien, Michael Ondaatje, Joy Harjo, Rita Dove, Lee Gutkind, Charles Simic, Denise Levertov, Andrei Codrescu, Gretel Ehrlich, Donald Hall, Barry Lopez, Diane Ackerman, Albert Goldbarth, Naomi Shihab Nye, and others. The editors point out that such work is similar to flash fiction, but in these stories "the people, the places, the events are real." And like flash fiction, the pieces are complete in themselves (25).

Kitchen and Jones also edited *In Brief: Short Takes on the Personal* (1999). The editors note that these short-shorts "employ many techniques of fiction—narrative, dialogue, descriptive imagery, point of view, interior voice," but they do so "to make something *of* the facts" (19). Included are pieces by Anne Carson, Frank McCourt, Albert Goldbarth, Pattiann Rogers, Bernard Cooper, Edwidge Danticat, Andre Dubus, Charles Baxter, Jamaica Kincaid, Mary Oliver, William Heyen, Robert Shapard, Stuart Dybek, and others.

In 2005 Judith Kitchen edited *Short Takes: Brief Encounters with Contemporary Nonfiction,* and the anthology includes work by Salman Rushdie, Amy Tan, Stephen Dunn, Ron Carlson, Hayden Carruth, Stuart Dybek, Dinty W. Moore, Terry Tempest Williams, Albert Goldbarth, Naomi Shihab Nye, and many others.

Another trend is the creation of author collections of flash fiction. Many acclaimed authors have created and published short story collections that include their shortest pieces (either exclusively or along with longer stories). Some of those writers are Raymond Carver, Barry Yourgrau, Yasunari Kawabata, Amy Hempel, Jayne Anne Phillips, and Bruce Holland Rogers, to name just a few. But another developing trend is the creation of the flash-fiction style novel. Among these unusual novels are Italo Calvino's literary classic *Invisible Cities* (1974), Richard Currey's *Fatal Light* (1988), and Peter Marcus's *Good, Brother* (2006). Roberta Allen notes that Allen Lightman's *Einstein's Dream* and her own novella, *The Daughter,* are composed of linking short-shorts. She also notes that Sandra Cisneros's novel, *The House on Mango Street,* makes use of the form as well (1997, 5).

All the structures and strategies of past flash fiction are still viable for writers and publishers today. And today's writers can continue to push the boundaries of what fiction can do.

Context and Issues. Charles Baxter calls very short stories "tunes for the end of time, for those in an information age who are sick of data" (1986, 226). Baxter also says, "The novel is spatially, like an estate; the very short story is like an efficiency on the twenty-third floor. As it happens, more people these days live in efficiencies than on estates. The result may be that we will start to see a shift in the imperial self of the traditional novel to the *we* and the *they* of communal stories. . . it is as if we ourselves are living in tighter psychic spaces" (1989, 21).

Today's readers have less time available for serious or even pleasurable reading. In many homes both partners have full-time jobs, and families often engage in hectic lifestyles. For convenience people often replace lengthy novels with films and replace short stories with half-hour television shows.

People are also bombarded with information from every direction: from radio, 24-hour television newscasts, news tracks in newscasts, split-screen television news, daily newspapers, cell phones, e-mails, fax machines, pagers, beepers, text messages, billboards, telemarketing, junk mail, and more. As Charles Baxter (2001) points out, a type of "data nausea" can be the result of such an overwhelming amount of information coming from every direction.

Dinty W. Moore, who also teaches flash fiction and serves as editor for *Brevity* online (for short-short creative nonfiction), is often asked to defend such brief writing. He says in *Sudden Stories: The Mammoth Book of Miniscule Fiction* (2003), "People today consume information at a much-accelerated rate. Some of the information they consume is shallow and of little value, certainly, but some is incredibly sophisticated. The best examples of short short fiction fall into the latter category . . . though brief, they are incredibly sophisticated, stuffed to the gills" (16).

Flash fiction fits well with busy lifestyles because it can be read in the small breaks that life provides, such as while waiting for a doctor's appointment, while riding on a subway or bus or as a passenger in a car, while waiting at the barber shop or at the hair salon, while relaxing in the bathtub—any time a few minutes of freedom present themselves. Readers still seek stories that provide a bit of escapism or that provide insights into modern-day people and what it can mean to be human. Readers also still require good literature to help them make some sense of their lives. Flash fiction can satisfy these desires, and these small stories fit well with a rushed and hectic manner of living where there is little time available for prolonged reading.

Recent advances in electronic technology have given flash fiction an even greater boost in readership. Now readers can read flash fiction on the Internet and via e-mail, cell phones, and mobile devices, as well as hear it over podcasts, depending on what electronic devices are available to the reader and the publisher. Through flash fiction and electronic availability, readers can get the benefits of reading good literature without the time commitment longer works require.

Publishing economics enters into this equation as well. Printing costs are expensive, but publishers can give their readers good flash fiction pieces and can publish more stories in each print issue. Because of the high cost of printing and the difficulty of finding funding, many publishers are discontinuing their print publications and are turning instead to Internet publishing.

Reception. After years of mostly escaping literary radar, flash fiction has come into its own. Today it is regularly featured in newspapers, magazines, literary journals, anthologies, and collections. It is an especially popular form of fiction for Internet publications. In addition to being published in these ways, flash fiction has also been published on coffee cans, coffee mugs, public transportation, t-shirts, and beer mats and has even been sold in vending machines.

Currently this type of writing is taught and studied in high school and university courses, taught and studied online, and explored in numberless in-person workshops. As of 1989, Shapard and Thomas's *Sudden Fiction International: 60 Short-Short Stories* anthology was used in courses at over 200 colleges and universities (1989, 15).

A further indication of flash fiction's popularity and reception is the publication of general "how to" books on the subject. Roberta Allen published *Fast Fiction: Creating Fiction in Five Minutes* (1997), which guides writers in crafting such stories, in turning five-minute writing sessions into short-short fiction. The book contains exercises and a good overview of modern-day flash fiction. Allen describes such stories as "intense fictions that use language with power and precision" and as a type of story "that gets quickly to the core and reveals the essence of a situation or moment in a very few words" (40).

Other general how-to books include Harvey Stanbrough's *Writing Realistic Dialogue & Flash Fiction: A Thorough Primer for Writers of Fiction & Essays* (2004), which focuses mainly on dialogue and flash fiction of 100 words or fewer, and Michael Wilson's *Flash Writing: How to Write, Revise and Publish Stories Less Than 1000 Words Long* (2004). Popular writing magazines such as *Writer's Digest, Poets & Writers,* and *The Writer* have also run several feature-length articles on writing flash fiction.

Flash fiction is now receiving more attention from scholars as well. *The Art of Brevity: Excursions in Short Fiction Theory and Analysis* (2004), edited by Per

Winther, Jakob Lothe, and Hans H. Skei, brings together American and Nordic scholars for a close critical look at short-short fiction. Some of the contributors of articles include Charles E. May, Mary Rohrberger, Susan Lohafer, John Gerlach, Hans H. Skei, Andrew K. Kennedy, Per Winther, Stuart Sillars, Gitte Mose, Jakob Lothe, W.H. New, Gerd Bjorhovde, Laura Castor, Jan Nordby Gretlund, Sandra Lee Kleppe, Axel Nissen, and Hans B. Lofgren.

Derek White, editor of *Sleepingfish*, which is almost exclusively devoted to flash fiction, and publisher at Calamari Press, says that with the exception of one poetry collection, all the collections published through Calamari Press have been literary flash fiction collections (see online catalog at http://calamaripress.com/Catalog.htm). These collections have also been widely reviewed in *American Book Review*, *NY Press*, *Bookslut*, and elsewhere (personal e-mail communication, December 24, 2006).

Other Recent Directions. Oprah Winfrey's *O Magazine* published several flash fictions, 300 words and fewer, in its First Ever Summer Reading Issue ("Flash Fictions" 2006). The high-circulation magazine brought flash fiction before the eyes of millions of readers. A description of the stories says, "They're short (and we mean short), intense (imagine a novel crossed with a haiku), and mesmerizing (whether they're illuminating a single moment or a whole life). The result: eight little beauties that leave a wake of wonder and wondering" (168). The authors of the flash fiction stories are A.M. Holmes, Antonya Nelson, Anna Deavere Smith, Dawn Raffel, Mark Leyner, Stuart Dybek, John Edgar Wideman, and Amy Hempel.

Some of the shortest pieces of all appeared in "Very Short Stories" in the November 2006 issue of *Wired* magazine, another publication with a large circulation. The editors invited writers of science fiction, fantasy, and horror to submit stories just six words in length. The resulting collection includes work by such renowned writers as Margaret Atwood, Arthur C. Clark, Ursula Le Guin, Ben Bova, and Orson Scott Card and even a story by actor William Shatner (and several other writers).

Esquire (February 2007) sent out 250 napkins to various well-known writers across the United States, asking them to write a short-short story on them. Nearly 100 writers responded, and the magazine published some of the resulting stories in their print magazine. Those not published in the print version were published in their online version. The writers who created the napkin stories included Madison Smartt Bell, Aimee Bender, Tony Epril, Sheila Heti, Michael Mejia, Rick Moody, Ethan Paquin, Jim Ruland, Erika Kraus, Ron Carlson, and many others.

The Internet has given flash fiction an even bigger boost in writer and reader popularity by bringing it before a larger reading public than ever possible before. Currently there are countless online publications featuring flash fiction and hundreds that feature flash fiction exclusively. There are also countless online critique workshops and dozens of online flash fiction courses. The stories published on the Internet run the gamut from sheer entertainment to literary, thought-provoking stories. The Internet has also helped spread the various newer names for this type of writing.

Some Internet editors also make use of advances in technology to turn flash fiction into multimedia events. Some incorporate music and art into the online presentations. Such productions range from amateur work to highly professional. With the arrival of recent technology, flash fiction is often read on Internet radio as well.

In 2003 podcasts began broadcasting on the Internet. Podcasts are media files that use video images, audio, or both and that make use of syndication feeds for playback on personal computers and mobile devices. Many podcasters use flash fiction in their broadcasts.

Short-short pieces have always been popular on the radio and were a regular staple in the 1930s and 1940s. But now such pieces often travel on the radio under the many newer names for flash fiction. National Public Radio features flash fiction as part of its regular offering.

In January 2007, Symphony Space on Broadway in New York City arranged an evening with the stories in *Sudden Fiction: Short-Short Stories from America and Beyond* (2007). Actors read the stories, and they were taped before an audience. The stories later aired on National Public Radio's "Selected Shorts" (Personal e-mail communication with Robert Shapard, December 28, 2006).

Flash fiction has also made its way into film. Several of Raymond Carver's short-short stories were made into a film titled *Short Cuts* (1993), directed by Robert Altman. The film depicts the way lives intersect among 22 Los Angeles characters and features actors Andie MacDowell, Tom Waits, Mathew Modine, Lily Tomlin, Tim Robbins, Jack Lemmon, Julianne Moore, and Anne Archer. A film reviewer for *Time Out London* wrote, "The marvelous performances bear witness to Altman's iconoclastic good sense, with Tomlin, Waits, Modine, Robbins, MacDowell and the rest lending the film's mostly white, middle-class milieu an authenticity seldom found in American cinema. But the real star is Altman, whose fluid, clean camera style, free-and-easy editing, and effortless organisation of a complex narrative are quite simply the mark of a master." The film also won the Golden Globe Award in 1994 and was nominated for a Special Achievement Award.

Barry Yourgrau's short-short collection *The Sadness of Sex* (1995) was turned into a comedy of modern romance and starred the author himself. The film was composed of 15 short acts showing the many phases of a love affair. Different types of camerawork and various types of music were used to distinguish one story from another (Brennan 2007).

Michael Arnzen's flash fiction collection *100 Jolts: Shockingly Short Stories* (2005) was a finalist for the 2005 Bram Stoker Award for Superior Achievement in a Fiction Collection. Some individual stories in the collection also received honorable mention in *The Year's Best Fantasy and Horror*. Because of *100 Jolts's* popularity, it was reissued in hardcover in 2007. Further, 16 stories from *100 Jolts* have also been released in an audio version titled *Audiovile*. In 2006 about half of the stories in *100 Jolts* were adapted to film in Jim Minton's *Exquisite Corpse: An International Collaboration of Dark Cinema*, an experiment in horror cinema that is an international collaboration of directors, multimedia artists, and animators. The other half of the stories in the film were adapted from Arnzen's poems (personal e-mail communication, January 13, 2007).

Lawrence C. Connolly's flash fiction, "Echoes," was published in over a dozen publications worldwide. It was also twice adapted to film. The first, a film festival production, was filmed in Hollywood by Steve Muscarella. The second adaptation was directed by Rodney Altman and won Best Achievement in Cinematography at the Fusion Film Festival in New York City in March 2004 (personal e-mail communication, January 15, 2007).

Peter Marcus, author of short-short collections *The Singing Fish* (2005) and *Good, Brother* (2006; a reissue of a book that was published through a different press in 2001), saw a short film based on the title story of *Good, Brother* that premiered at the Slamdance Film Festival in 2002 (personal e-mail communication, January 22, 2007).

Selected Authors. There are countless writers involved in writing flash fiction, and the number grows every day. The stories take on a myriad of subjects, themes, strategies, and methods. Following is a brief overview of some of the influential anthologies published since the year 2000, along with the names of some of the authors engaged in writing flash fiction. Not all authors for each anthology are included, but those mentioned give a glimpse of the variety of writers of flash fiction.

Dinty W. Moore edited *Sudden Stories: The Mammoth Book of Miniscule Fiction* (2003). The anthology of stories 350 words or fewer also includes some thoughts on flash or sudden fiction by the writers themselves. The authors are Molly Giles, Michael Arnzen, Josip Novakovich, Robin Hemley, Allen Woodman, Aimee Bender, Denise Duhamel, Jesse Lee Kercheval, Ron Wallace, William Heyen, Virgil Suarez, Jim Heynen, Gail Galloway Adams, Mark Budman, and several others.

Mark Mills's textbook *Crafting the Very Short Story: An Anthology of 100 Masterpieces* (2003) looks at the work of various distinguished authors and includes essays on the short-short written either by scholars or by the writers themselves. The textbook also includes brief writing instructions. Some of the acclaimed writers in this culturally diverse textbook are Sherwood Anderson, Amiri Baraka, Giovanni Boccaccio, Bertolt Brecht, Charles Bukowski, Italo Calvino, Angela Carter, Raymond Carter, Colette, Sandra Cisneros, Charles Dickens, Fyodor Dostoevsky, E.M. Forster, Eduardo Galeno, Graham Greene, James Joyce, Langston Hughes, Shirley Jackson, Pam Houston, Ursula K. Le Guin, Clarice Lispector, Thomas Mann, W. Somerset Maugham, Herman Melville, Alice Munro, Vladimir Nobakov, Anais Nin, Joyce Carol Oates, Frank O'Connor, Dorothy Parker, Petronius, Jayne Anne Phillips, Marcel Proust, Mary Robison, John Steinbeck, James Thurber, Paul Theroux, Jean Toomer, John Updike, Luisa Valenzuela, Voltaire, Alice Walker, Eudora Welty, Dorothy West, Tennessee Williams, Oscar Wilde, Tobias Wolff, Virginia Woolf, and others.

James Thomas and Robert Shapard coedited *Flash Fiction Forward: 80 Very Short Stories* (2006). The anthology includes all new stories that, for the editors, represent the best flash fiction from America in the twenty-first century. Some of the authors are Don Shea, Paul Theroux, Carolyn Forche, Ron Carlson, Robert Coover, Utahna Faith, Barbara Jacksha, Lydia Davis, Lon Otto, Dave Eggers, Donald Hall, Grace Paley, Jim Heynen, John Updike, Mark Budman, Amy Hempel, James Tate, Bruce Holland Rogers, and Pamela Painter. The editors say that the stories, 750 words or fewer, "depend for their success not on their length but on their depth, clarity of vision, and human significance." A good flash fiction "should move the reader emotionally or intellectually" (2006, 11–13).

Peter Connors edited *PP/FF: An Anthology* (2006), which bridges flash fiction and prose poetry. Connors says the anthology "is prose poetry and flash fiction balanced on a makeshift teeter-totter that never lands. Sometimes it is more prose poetry, sometimes more flash fiction, but it is always in motion between the two." Connors says it is "a symbol of a vital and important literary form that is constantly in flux, appropriating, moving and growing" (9). Included are stories by Jessica Treat, Stuart Dybek, Daryl Scroggins, Peter Markus, Mark Tursi, G.C. Waldrep, Brian Clements, Anthony Tognazzini, Lydia Davis, Harold Jaffe, Derek White, Ethan Paquin, Kim Addonizio, and others.

Robert Shapard and James Thomas also coedited *New Sudden Fiction: Short-Short Stories from America and Beyond* (2007). These stories came from both print publications and Internet publications, and the editors consider the stories to be some of the best sudden fiction of the twenty-first century. The editors also point out that none of these new works end with an ironic twist (in the style of O. Henry) but instead are *"suddenly just there,* surprising, unpredictable, hilarious, serious, moving, in only a few pages" (14). Authors include Tobias Wolff, Robert Olen Butler, Sam Shepard, Aimee Bender, Nadine Gordimer, Joyce Carol Oates, Robin Hemley, Ron Carlson, Ursula Hegi, Steve Almond, Elizabeth Berg, Sherrie Flick, Ian Frazier, Barry Gifford, and others.

An anthology titled *You Have Time for This: Contemporary Short-Short Stories* was published by Ooligan Press in 2007. This anthology of flash fiction under 500 words was coedited by Mark Budman, editor of *Vestal Review,* an online publication that specializes in flash fiction only, and Tom Hazuka. Among the authors are Aimee Bender, Bruce Holland Rogers, Steve Almond, Deb Unferth, Katharine Weber, and Pamela Painter (personal communication with Mark Budman, May 6, 2007).

Bibliography

Allen, Roberta. *Fast Fiction: Creating Fiction in Five Minutes.* Cincinnati: Story Press, 1997.

Asimov, Isaac, Terry Carr, and Martin H. Greenberg, eds. *100 Great Fantasy Short Short Stories.* Garden City, NY: Doubleday, 1984.

Asimov, Isaac, Martin H. Greenberg, and Joseph D. Olander, eds. *Microcosmic Tales: 100 Wondrous Science Fiction Short-Short Stories.* New York: Daw Books, 1992.

Baudelaire, Charles. *Paris Spleen.* Trans. Louise Varese. New York: New Directions Publishing, 1970. Originally published in 1869.

Baxter, Charles. Introduction. *Sudden Fiction International: 60 Short Short Stories.* Robert Shapard and James Thomas, eds. New York: Norton, 1989.

———. "Shame and Forgetting in the Information Age." 2001. http://www.giarts.org/library_additional/library_additional_show.htm?doc_id=494628.

———. "The Tradition." *Sudden Fiction: American Short-Short Stories.* Robert Shapard and James Thomas, eds. Layton, Utah: Gibbs Smith, 1986. 229.

Brautigan, Richard. *Revenge of the Lawn/The Abortion/So the Wind Won't Blow It All Away.* Omnibus Edition. Boston: Houghton Mifflin, 1995.

Brennan, Sandra. "All Movie Guide." *New York Times,* May 12, 2007. http://movies2.nytimes.com/gst/movies/movie.html?v_id=135640.

Brown, Fredric. *Nightmares and Geezenstacks.* New York: Bantam, 1961.

Calvino, Italo. *Invisible Cities.* Trans. William Weaver. San Diego, CA: Harcourt Brace, 1974.

Connors, Peter, ed. *PP/FF: An Anthology.* Buffalo: Starcherone Books, 2006.

Coover, Robert, and Kent Dixon, eds. *The Stone Wall Book of Short Fictions.* Iowa City: Stone Wall Press, 1973.

Currey, Richard. *Fatal Light.* Boston: Houghton Mifflin, 1988.

Dziemianowicz, Stefan, Robert Weinberg, and Martin H. Greenberg. *Horrors! 365 Scary Stories.* New York: Metro Books, 1998.

Esquire. "The Napkin Project." February 2007. http://www.esquire.com/fiction/napkin-fiction/napkinproject.

"Flash Fictions." *O: The Oprah Magazine.* July 2006.

Fuller, Geoff, and Pamelyn Casto. "A Short Course in Short-Short Fiction." *Writer's Digest,* February 2001.

Hemingway, Ernest. *The Complete Short Stories of Ernest Hemingway.* The Finca Vigia Edition. New York: Simon & Schuster, 1998.

Howe, Irving, and Ilana Wiener Howe, eds. *Short Shorts: An Anthology of the Shortest Stories* Toronto: Bantam Books, 1983.

Kitchen, Judith. *Short Takes: Brief Encounters with Contemporary Nonfiction*. New York: Norton, 2005.

Kitchen, Judith, and Mary Paumier Jones, eds. *In Short: A Collection of Brief Creative Nonfiction*. New York: Norton, 1996.

———, eds. *In Brief: Short Takes on the Personal*. New York: Norton, 1999.

Mills, Mark, ed. *Crafting the Very Short Story: An Anthology of 100 Masterpieces*. Upper Saddle River, NJ: Prentice Hall, 2003.

Minot, Stephen. "The Tradition." *Sudden Fiction: American Short-Short Stories*. Robert Shapard and James Thomas, eds. Layton, Utah: Gibbs Smith, 1986. 235–237.

"Minute Stories." *TriQuarterly 35* (Winter 1976). Edited by Elliot Anderson and guest coedited by Robert Coover.

Moore, Dinty W., ed. *Sudden Stories: The Mammoth Book of Miniscule Fiction*. Du Bois, PA: Mammoth Press, 2003.

Mose, Gitte. "Danish Short Shorts in the 1990s and the Jena-Romantic Fragments." In *The Art of Brevity: Excursions in Short Fiction Theory and Analysis*. Per Winther, Jakob Lothe, and Hans H. Skei, eds. Columbia: University of South Carolina, 2004.

Reid, Mildred I., and Delmar E. Bordeaux, eds. *Writers Try Short Shorts: All Known Types with Examples*. Rockford, IL: Bellevue Books, 1947.

Shapard, Robert, and James Thomas, eds. *New Sudden Fiction: Short-Short Stories from America and Beyond*. New York: Norton, 2007.

———, eds. *Sudden Fiction: American Short-Short Stories*. Salt Lake City: Peregrine Smith Books, 1986.

———, eds. *Sudden Fiction (Continued): 60 New Short-Short Stories*. New York: Norton, 1996.

———, eds. *Sudden Fiction International: 60 Short Short Stories*. New York: Norton, 1989.

Sleepingfish. http://www.sleepingfish.net.

Stern, Jerome, ed. *Micro Fiction: An Anthology of Really Short Stories*. New York: Norton, 1996.

Thomas, James, and Robert Shapard, eds. *Flash Fiction Forward: 70 Very Short Stories*. New York: Norton, 2006.

Thomas, James, Denise Thomas, and Tom Hazuka, eds. *Flash Fiction: 72 Very Short Stories*. New York: Norton, 1992.

"Time Out Film Guide 13: *Short Cuts*." *Time Out London*. http://www.timeout.com/film/74563.html.

"Very Short Stories." *Wired*. November 2006.

Wilson, Michael. *Flash Writing: How to Write, Revise and Publish Stories Less Than 1000 Words Long*. College Station, TX: Virtualbookworm.com, 2004.

Wilson, Robley, Jr., ed. *4 Minute Fictions: 50 Short-Short Stories from The North American Review*. Flagstaff, AZ: Word Beat Press, 1987.

Winther, Per, Jakob Lothe, and Hans H. Skei, eds. *The Art of Brevity: Excursions in Short Fiction Theory and Analysis*. Columbia: University of South Carolina Press, 2004.

Further Reading

Casto, Pamelyn. "Flashes on the Meridian: Dazzled by Flash Fiction." *Writing World*. http://www.writing-world.com/fiction/casto.shtml; Casto, Pamelyn, and Geoff Fuller. "Give Your Tales a Twist." *Guide to Writing Fiction Today: Writers Yearbook*. A *Writer's Digest* publication, December 2002; Davis, Lydia. *Almost No Memory*. New York: Picador, 2001; Davis, Lydia. *Samuel Johnson Is Indignant*. New York: Picador, 2004; Fuller, Geoff, and Pamelyn Casto. "Simple Complexity: A Course in Short-Short Fiction." *Start Writing Now:*

Your Introduction to the Writing Life: Writer's Yearbook. A *Writer's Digest* publication, January 2002; Fuller, Geoff, and Pamelyn Casto. "Put the Flash into Fiction." *Guide to Writing Fiction Today: Writer's Yearbook.* A *Writer's Digest* publication, Winter 2002; Hempel, Amy. *Reasons to Live.* New York: Harper Perennial, 1985; Kawabata, Yasunari. *Palm-of-the-Hand Stories.* Translated from the Japanese by Lane Dunlop and J. Martin Holman. New York: North Point Press, 1988; Koch, Kenneth. *Hotel Lambosa and Other Stories.* Minneapolis, MN: Coffee House Press, 1993; Phillips, Jayne Anne. *Black Tickets.* New York: Vintage Contemporary Series, 2001; Rogers, Bruce Holland. *The Keyhole Opera.* Wilsonville, OR: Wheatland Press, 2005; Silesky, Barry. *One Thing That Can Save Us.* Minneapolis, MN: Coffee House Press, 1994; Treat, Jessica. *A Robber in the House.* Minneapolis, MN: Coffee House Press, 1993; Yourgrau, Barry. *A Man Jumps Out of an Airplane.* New York: Arcade Publishing, 1999.

PAMELYN CASTO

G

GLBTQ LITERATURE

Definition. Gay, lesbian, bisexual, transgender, and queer (GLBTQ) literature is a challenging category to define and then contain. For the purposes of this chapter, GLBTQ literature encompasses both those works of fiction written by GLBTQ persons as well as those with themes involving GLBTQ persons. However, the term *GLBTQ literature* in itself is hard to define. For example, the Lambda Literary Foundation, the "country's leading organization for LGBT literature" (Lambda Literary Foundation 2006), offers awards in 24 separate categories, with 19 of them potentially or positively linked to fiction. Therefore, because authoring a chapter on GLBTQ literature is quite a daunting task, not all GLBTQ authors who *should* be represented here *can* be.

History. Prior to the Victorian era, there was no description for GLBTQ persons, so all GLBTQ writings prior to this period have been labeled as such after the fact. During the Victorian era, scientists began using the term *homosexual* to label those with same-sex attractions as mentally ill (Forrest, Biddle, and Clift 2006). However, with the negative implications of mental illness tied to this term, the terms *gay* and *lesbian* soon become more popular for those with same-sex attractions.

Following World War II, the homophile movement lobbied politely for social acceptability for GLBTQ persons (Matzner 2004). This continued until 1969, when the Stonewall Riots led to organized activism. The term *gay* was widely adopted as an antonym to *straight*, which then implied respectable sexual behavior. The term *gay* was utilized by both men and women with same-sex attractions throughout this period, but starting with the feminist movement of the 1970s, *lesbian* became more popular for women and the term *gay* became more associated with men (Rich 1980). The groups splintered until the mid-1980s, when the AIDS crisis shifted the focus to solidarity, and bisexuals and transgendered individuals were eventually included. This is how the now-popular acronym of GLBTQ came to exist.

WHAT IS QUEER THEORY?

The Q became commonly attached to GLBTQ with the advent of the queer identity movement (Beemyn and Eliason 1996). This movement was formed around two main premises. First, on the activist front, it was a reclaimed word, one which the GLBTQ community (and its allies) used to revoke its power (Jagose 1996). Second, it became attached to the academic field of queer theory, which called for a broader definition of persons with same-sex attractions than those offered by the rigid GLBTQ categories. The term queer, however, is still one fraught with controversy, for some find it to be an insult, while others find it empowering.

Trends and Themes. Much of the GLBTQ literature prior to Stonewall accepted the negative societal attitudes towards GLBTQ persons, or homophobia, as it existed at the time, and the literature of this period was often limited in printing and difficult to access for those not in urban areas. The homophile movement encouraged a lack of publicity of sexuality by GLBTQ persons, instead insisting that GLBTQ persons conform as much as possible.

The works of E.M. Forster (1879–1970) personify much of this period, for his early work reflects much of his own sexual frustration, while throughout his life a shift is seen as his works begin to more openly fight oppression and social injustice. While many focus on *Maurice* (1971), often cited as the "first modern homosexual novel" (Fone 1998, 351), published posthumously and cementing his role as a GLBTQ author, much of his earlier works still deserve consideration for their reflection of the restraint required of GLBTQ authors in the early twentieth century. These earlier works include *Where Angels Fear to Tread* (1905), *The Longest Journey* (1907), *A Room with a View* (1908), *Howards End* (1910), and *A Passage to India* (1924).

Christopher Isherwood (1904–1986) followed a similar path to Forster, coming to terms with his homosexuality throughout his life and eventually becoming very active in the GLBTQ rights movement. Born in England, he spent time in Berlin in the 1930s, a period of great artistic output, seeking escape from the repression in England. Prior to this escape, he authored *All the Conspirators* (1928), featuring repressed homosexual characters. During his exploratory period in Berlin, he authored *The Memorial* (1933), which portrays homosexual life through the impact of the loss of the protagonist's best friend during World War II. In 1939, Isherwood emigrated to America with his partner W.H. Auden (with whom he engaged in a nonromantic sexual relationship), and there he authored *A Single Man* (1964), his masterpiece reflecting Isherwood's growing concern with gay oppression.

The works of Jean Genet (1910–1986) begin to shift this dialogue from assimilation and portrayals of the "tragic queer" (Woods 1998, 275) to questions of power and identity. Genet is one of the first authors to positively discuss transgendered persons, hence reflecting the French intellectual tradition of deconstructing a topic in order to celebrate it (Fone 1998). Genet's first novel, *Our Lady of the Flowers* (1942), a prison novel (which formed the basis for the majority of his works), was written while he was in prison and graphically and explicitly portrays male prostitution and masturbation. *The Thief's Journal* (1948) portrays the men Genet loves, and *The Miracle of the Rose* (1951) shows the development of a gay man from "feminized" to "masculine." However, Genet's obsession with prison and the subversive side of gay life has often left his works open to criticism, for the revolution he felt he was beginning by personifying gay prison life has often been portrayed as a reinscription of the deviance of homosexuality.

James Baldwin's (1924–1987) *Go Tell It on the Mountain* (1953), a critical piece in the development of African American literature, also tells of the protagonist's sexual evolution. The original manuscript for the book was supposedly much more homosexually oriented, but this draft was rejected and major revisions ensued, tamping down GLBTQ themes. *Giovanni's Room* (1956) dealt much more explicitly with homosexuality, particularly notions of internalized homophobia. Both *Another Country* (1962) and *Tell Me How Long the Train's Been Gone* (1968) offer its protagonists redemptive roles as gay men, once again setting the stage for the upcoming Stonewall Riots of 1969.

Gore Vidal (b. 1925) unabashedly portrayed GLBTQ persons in his works, and "asserts that gay men are not women in disguise nor, indeed, even very special, and sets out to prove that effeminacy and homosexuality do not need to occupy the same conceptual space in novels" (Fone 998, 690). In *The City and the Pillar* (1948), the first coming-out novel emerges. It is in Vidal's work that GLBTQ issues are brought into a normalizing discourse, a critical step between previous views of the traumatized GLBTQ person and the impending Stonewall Riots. However, in the original printing, the editor changed the ending to include a violent death that was not part of the original manuscript, therefore perpetuating the myth of the "tragic queer," which Vidal recanted when he republished the novel in its original version, entitling it *The City and the Pillar Revised* (1968). Pushing the envelope even further (and again setting the stage for the Stonewall Riots of 1969), Vidal published *Myra Breckinridge* (1968), which concerns a transsexual undergoing sexual reassignment surgery.

This very abridged overview of twentieth century pre-Stonewall GLBTQ literature is by no means exhaustive, and it is used here to portray the shift from an acceptance of repression to a need for the normalization of GLBTQ persons. Many other critical works, themes, and activities can be included here, including Oscar Wilde's symbolic status as a pervert, thanks to his sentencing as a sodomite; Herman Melville's homosexual texts of the late nineteenth century, including *Redburn* (1849), *White-Jacket* (1850), *Moby Dick* (1851), and *Billy Budd* (written 1891, published posthumously 1924); Henry James' ambivalent relationship with homosexuality at the turn of the century; Gertrude Stein's many novels, including *Q.E.D.* (1903), *Fernhurst* (1904), *Three Lives* (1909), *Tender Buttons* (1912), *The Making of Americans* (1925), and *The Autobiography of Alice B. Toklas* (1933); Virginia Woolf's portrayals of women's passionate friendships; Jean Cocteau's homoerotic avant-garde texts; Djuna Barnes's *Nightwood* (1936), which disturbs the compulsory heterosexuality imposed by the field of sexology; Mary Renault's initial portrayals of lesbianism and her switch to gay novels; Carson McCullers, the sexually ambiguous author of *The Heart is a Lonely Hunter* (1940); Ann Bannon's lesbian pulp fiction novels of the 1950s; Marguerite Yourcenar's lesbian lifestyle, not reflected in her writings except through gay men; and Truman Capote's development of a homosexual writing style in the 1950s and 1960s.

With the Stonewall Riots of 1969, the concept of *coming out* as a gay person emerged. With this, the development of a political agenda developed in much GLBTQ literature. In the 1970s, the influence of feminism on lesbian literature cannot be understated. As feminism grew and changed, in the 1980s, literature reflected the splintering as distinct categories of people began to emerge, dissatisfied with the portrayal of GLBTQ persons as solely white and middle class. Fiction by GLBTQ people of color began to emerge during this period. However, with the AIDS crisis affecting gay men in the 1980s, this splintering lessened, and the literature began to reflect the entire GLBTQ spectrum. As GLBTQ becomes more common as a unified group and term, queer literature challenges the rigidity of this alphabet soup.

Rita Mae Brown (b. 1944) published the critical feminist lesbian novel *Rubyfruit Jungle* in 1973. The novel "espouses a doctrine of radical individualism" (Kattelman 2002) that challenges the homophobia of the pre-Stonewall era. Brown continues her career as a novelist to this day, publishing works such as *Sudden Death* (1983), inspired by her real-life lesbian relationship with tennis star Martina Navratilova; *Southern Discomfort* (1982); and *High Hearts* (1986); *Bingo* (1988); as well as a series of mystery novels, including *Wish You Were Here* (1990), *Rest in Pieces* (1992), and *Venus Envy* (1993).

Katherine V. Forrest (b. 1939) struggled with the internalized homophobia she learned during the pre-Stonewall years, and it was only in her forties that she began writing. *Curious Wine* (1983), a lesbian romance, established Forrest's place in the lesbian fiction genre. However, it was the publication of *Amateur City* (1984) that marked her as a writer of lesbian mysteries, a developing subgenre of lesbian fiction. She continues to work in this vein today, publishing works such as *The Beverly Malibu* (1989), *Murder by Tradition* (1991), and *Liberty Square* (1996). Simultaneously, she contributed to the establishment of another lesbian subgenre—lesbian science fiction—with the publication of *Daughters of a Coral Dawn* (1984) and *An Emergence of Green* (1986).

Jeannette Winterson (b. 1959) began her career with *Oranges Are Not the Only Fruit* (1985), which challenges the homophobia of Christian fundamentalism by interweaving Old Testament references into the coming-out narrative so present in the 1970s. Her work continues with *The Passion* (1987), which has characters who are not easily identifiably by sexual orientation, androgyny, and bisexuality, which can be viewed as a portal to the changes occurring in GLBTQ literature that was becoming more inclusive of transgendered people, bisexuality, and queer theory. *Sexing the Cherry* (1989) further asserts Winterson's influence in the world of queerness with its disregard for boundaries such as geography, gender, and even time. Her most recent work, *Written on the Body* (1992), also dealing with a protagonist with gender ambiguity, continues her themes of the transience of socially constructed norms.

Michael Cunningham (b. 1952) published his pivotal piece *At Home at the End of the World* in 1990, when gay authors were often writing about the impact of AIDS, with Cunningham's piece being no exception. He weaves a tale laden with alternative families in numerous configurations, which is indicative of the postmodern bent of queer theory emerging in the 1990s. Cunningham continues to write complex novels that challenge societal norms, most recently recognized in *The Hours* (1999).

Again, the post-Stonewall authors listed above are by no means an exhaustive group, but rather a reflection of some of the general themes emerging during this period. Some additional works critical to this time include Isabel Miller's historical lesbian romance *Patience and Sarah* (1971); Andrew Holleran's portrayals of gay life in *Dancer from the Dance* (1978) and *Nights in Aruba* (1983); Paula Monette's moving novels of AIDS, *Afterlife* (1990) and *Halfway Home* (1991); Dorothy Allison's *Bastard Out of Carolina* (1992); David B. Feinberg's examination of the AIDS crisis and gay men, including *Eight-sixed* (1986) and *Spontaneous Combustion* (1991); Randall Kenan's exploration of Southern Black gay men in *A Visitation of Spirits* (1989); and Karin Kallmaker's lesbian romance and erotica.

Contexts and Issues. In the twenty-first century, GLBTQ issues have become a matter of civil rights. These include issues surrounding religion, marriage and adoption, medical and legal rights, transgender rights, and identity politics. This is direct result of the AIDS activism of the 1980s and 1990s, which required GLBTQ persons to work together to fight for rights in the public health crisis (rather than fight separatist battles for lesbians, gay men, bisexuals, and transgendered persons, as in the past).

A landmark moment in civil rights occurred in 2003, when the U.S Supreme Court declared laws against sodomy unconstitutional. In the case of *Lawrence v. Texas,* "two gay men say the state of Texas deprived them of privacy rights and equal protection under law when they were arrested in 1998 for having sex" (*Lawrence and Garner v. State of Texas* 2006). This was granted on the grounds of privacy and equal protection rights, and was pivotal in legitimizing the rights of GLBTQ persons.

Religion has often made headlines when connected with GLBTQ persons. Until recently, issues such as civil rights, same-sex marriage, and protections under the law for GLBTQ persons were often not even discussed in a religious context. Religious texts, particularly the Bible, are often used as the basis for opposition to GLBTQ rights. Recently, some religious groups have come forward in support of GLBTQ rights, often with much controversy. Reform Judaism and the United Church of Christ are accepting of GLBTQ persons. Certain segments of Christianity, including Unitarian Universalists, as well as some Presbyterians and Anglicans, are also supportive. However, the Anglican Church is almost evenly split amongst traditionalists, who view homosexuality as incompatible with scripture, and others viewing same-sex relationships as viable.

Along with religion comes the issues of gay marriage and same-sex parenting. Full marriage rights for same-sex partners would entail equality with heterosexuals in relation to "finances, health care, children, [and] divorce" (Arthur 2004). However, just a few states offering these rights would not help the majority of GLBTQ persons, for the Defense of Marriage Act (DOMA) of 1996 allows states not to recognize same-sex marriages sanctioned as viable in other states; and it also does not allow the federal government to recognize same-sex marriages at all. As of the 2006 elections, one state allowed same-sex marriage, five recognized same-sex unions, 12 states banned recognition of any same-sex union, 26 states amended their constitution to prohibit same-sex marriage, and 20 states enacted their own DOMAs (Defense of Marriage Act 2007). The DOMA has done more harm for the civil rights of GLBTQ persons than almost any other government initiative for, in the public's eye, it has combined issues of religious marriage with civil marriage. Some religions have begun to offer same-sex unions, although it is always the decision of each religious group whether to grant this privilege.

For GLBTQ persons wishing to adopt, the process varies from state to state. Florida, Utah, Mississippi, and Arkansas specifically do not allow same-sex adoptions. Other states make it challenging for same-sex couples to adopt, particularly as home visits by social workers (who may or may not be in favor of same-sex adoption) are often a mandatory part of the adoption process. Another challenge is states not recognizing same-sex couples as legal parents. However, certain states, such as

New Jersey, New York, and Washington, D.C. recognize joint adoptions. The *Lawrence v. Texas* ruling mentioned previously gives credence to same-sex relationships, and is helping more GLBTQ persons adopt (Arthur 2006).

Transgender rights came to the forefront of the GLBTQ rights movement in response to the public health crisis of the AIDS epidemic, when GLBTQ persons came together and formed an inclusive community united by health care inequalities. A series of influential transgender rights groups developed throughout the 1990s, including Transgender Nation, Transsexual Menace, It's Time America, and GenderPAC. The release of the Academy Award winning film *Boys Don't Cry* (2000), showing the violence transgendered persons often face, opened the public's eyes to the problem. Although acknowledgment of the transgender community has been achieved through activism, the road to full equality is still quite long (Meyerowitz 2002).

Queer has emerged, for some, as a unifying term for LGBT (and all its variations), whereas others in the LGBT community take offense to the term. With the traditional definition of queer meaning "different," those using the term see this as a reclamation of the power of the word, but those in opposition view it as an inappropriate word with which to be associated. The term *queer*, when used by those activists who embrace it, acknowledges the fluidity of sexual orientation and gender identity and is therefore the preferred term for the complex issues of these areas. The debate over the usage of the term *queer* continues (Queercore 1992).

As these issues continue into the twenty-first century, the civil rights issues of GLBTQ persons are at the forefront. While GLBTQ persons continue to live productive lives in society, and in some cases gain acceptance by their family, friends, and community, there are still great legislative battles to be fought. All of the issues in some way return to the need for recognition of GLBTQ persons as people with rights. Many of these issues are overtly or covertly portrayed in GLBTQ literature.

Reception. Since Stonewall, there has been an increase in the publishing and distribution of GLBTQ-themed texts. As GLBTQ issues are discussed more openly, younger generations are coming out sooner, and new youth markets for GLBTQ materials are emerging. As online booksellers such as Amazon and Barnes and Noble overtake the marketplace, however, the gay bookstore, a source of pride during so much of the immediate post-Stonewall era, is becoming a thing of the past, and the Internet is taking its place. Internet book clubs with GLBTQ themes, such as InsightOut, are developing to keep pace with the technological demands of GLBTQ persons. Technology is allowing GLBTQ persons from around the world, regardless of proximity to a GLBTQ cultural center, to access resources and materials, while it also separates these communities by changing the need for cultural centers (like gay bookstores).

With the battle for a cure for AIDS raging for over 25 years, activism has decreased in this arena in the GLBTQ community, as new generations of young GLBTQ persons did not witness the horrendous personal impact AIDS had on the GLBTQ community in the 1980s. As a reflection of this, "the number of books dealing primarily with AIDS is down compared to 2,000, which had fewer AIDS titles than the year before. AIDS is more likely to be treated as an incidental fact, not a focus" (Hix 2001) in GLBTQ literature. In contrast, publications regarding transgendered persons and those identifying as queer are becoming more easily available to a mainstream audience.

GLBTQ literary criticism has not always been openly embraced by the larger literary criticism community. It is a newer strand of English that evolved from its relationship to other fields, such as Women's Studies, History, and Philosophy. Indeed,

> queer criticism *is* connected, historically and methodologically, to feminism, cultural materialism, psychoanalytical criticism, and post-colonial studies. Although such approaches are not interchangeable, they share a common scepticism about literary tradition, and they continue to evolve through a process of collective influence. Indeed, it is largely because of their rise that the very notion of unitary disciplines . . . has come into question. (Quinn, 1997)

Literary criticism is not always a field open to non-traditional forms and readings, and the interdisciplinarity of the development of GLBTQ literature, plus its inbred questioning of literary "traditions," has led some to view GLBTQ literary criticism as unimportant. However, the field continues forward, often portrayed as a disruptive form of reading.

Much of the criticism of GLBTQ literature comes from questions of identity and community. In stressing the commonalities of this community, there is a denial of personal identities. Although the term *queer* has attempted to fill this void, by being placed on the end of the GLBTQ alphabet chain, it is simply reinscribing the communal identity it tries to deny. In addition, it is becoming more challenging to label a person as GLBTQ as it becomes more common to label an *act* as GLBTQ. The recent phenomena of men on the DL, or down low, which signifies men who identify as heterosexual but engage in homosexual sexual acts; the lesbian-identified woman who wishes to engage in sexual acts with men; a man who engages in exclusively homosexual acts but does not define himself as gay; a former lesbian-identified woman who is now in an exclusively heterosexual relationship and identifies as straight; a male-to-female (MtF) transgendered person who is involved with a male partner and identifies as gay; and any queer person, all push the boundaries of GLBTQ. By determining a single category to identify lesbians, gay men, bisexuals, transgendered persons, and queers, the literature of this grouping reflects some serious disparities in what GLBTQ "means" (Summers 1993).

In addition, another criticism of GLBTQ literature centers around identifying works that belong in the canon. Should a work written by a non-GLBTQ person, but which has GLBTQ themes and characters, be incorporated? How about when a GLBTQ-identified author writes a book with no inherent GLBTQ content? It is uncertain how to acknowledge this potential disparity. However, it is the gradual recognition of GLBTQ literature as an emerging field that allows us to ask these types of questions.

The emergence of the growing body of GLBTQ literature, and its wider acceptance, is visible in mainstream works that have been adapted for film. There has always been an independent film market featuring GLBTQ themes adapted from literature, with a blossoming in film production occurring post-Stonewall. Some early adaptations of GLBTQ novels include *A Florida Enchantment* (1914), based on the 1891 novel of Fergus Redmond and Archibald Gunter; *Reflections in a Golden Eye* (1967), based on a 1941 novel by Carson McCullers; *Cruising* (1980), novel by Gerald Walker; *The Hotel New Hampshire* (1984), based on John Irving's 1981 novel; *Last Exit to Brooklyn* (1989), adapted from Hubert Selby, Jr.'s novel (1964); *Fried Green Tomatoes* (1991), from Fannie Flagg's *Fried Green Tomatoes at the Whistle Stop Café* (1987); *Love and Death on Long Island* (1997), based on Gilbert Adair's 1990 novel; and *The Object of My Affection* (1998), based on Stephen McCauley's 1987 novel.

Since 2000, there have been some critical film adaptations of LGBT-themed works, many of which garnered international attention and awards. Michael Cunningham's *The Hours* (2002), based on his 1998 novel, earned a Best Actress award for Nicole Kidman, as well as nominations for Best Picture, Best Supporting Actor, Best Supporting Actress, Best Director, Best Adapted Screenplay, and others. The piece features Meryl Streep as a lesbian book editor caring for her friend who is dying from AIDS. However, the entire piece focuses on three generations of women who may be lesbian or bisexual. Cunningham himself states, "were such characters born at later times in different circumstances they would come out as lesbians" (2007).

The Wonder Boys (2000), based on Michael Chabon's 1995 novel of the same name, was a critically acclaimed film success. James Kirkwood Jr.'s 1970 cult classic *P.S. Your Cat is Dead,* a farce involving homosexuality, bisexuality, and bondage, was made into an independent film in 2002. *Under the Tuscan Sun* (2003) chronicles the adventures of two women—one lesbian, one heterosexual—on a gay tour of Italy after both have suffered heartbreak. It is based on Frances Mayes's 1996 novel. Michael Cunningham's *A Home at the End of the World* (1998), a celebration of love in all its forms, was adapted to the screen in 2004.

2005's *Brokeback Mountain,* based on Annie Proulx's short story, opened the general public's eyes to the fluidity of sexuality and the challenges of labels. It won 71 awards and had 52 nominations (Awards for Brokeback Mountain 2007). Much debate ensued over the sexual orientation of the main characters, as to whether they were gay, bisexual, or heterosexual. Some claimed the main characters to be heterosexual men with a deep friendship, which included a sexual component, whereas others embraced the epitome of queerness and sexual ambiguity. A criticism from the GLBTQ community about the film is that neither of the lead actors is GLBTQ identified, although others claims this to be irrelevant, as GLBTQ actors play heterosexuals in film frequently. The Catholic Church praised the film's acting but not its content (White 2005). A limited number of movie theatres refused to show the film. When *Brokeback Mountain* lost its bid for Best Picture, some complained that this was due to homophobic judges. By far, this film brought the most discussion around the definitions of sexual orientation than any other.

Authors and Their Works. We now turn to contemporary American texts (all of which have published since 2000, with the majority of writers publishing quite extensively pre-2000 as well) to exemplify the questions of identity and civil rights for GLBTQ persons in the twenty-first century.

"One of the most prominent and highly acclaimed figures of contemporary gay literature, Edmund White works in many distinct categories of fiction and nonfiction" (Woodland 2004). His career reads like a map of post-Stonewall literature. His first novel, *Forgetting Elena* (1973), was published when he was quite young, and features no GLBTQ content. His second novel, *Nocturnes for the King of Naples* (1978), "the mysterious and lush lament of a young man for his older love" (Zebrun 2004, 28), explores gay themes openly.

In 1982, White authored *A Boy's Own Story,* "widely recognized as a coming-of-age classic, with a hero who holds his own alongside Huck Finn or Holden Caulfield" (Ehrhardt 2006). "The honesty White brought to the narration of gay life made him part of a new wave of gay writers who no longer used euphemisms or tragic language to describe their same-sex desires and experiences" (Lee 2006). In this piece, White traces "the quest for self-identity against the expectations of family and friends" (Ehrhardt 2006). This semiautobiographical novel also led to another, *The Beautiful Room Is Empty* (1988).

The Beautiful Room Is Empty traces the narrator's experiments with desire and romance as he moves through an exclusive prep school, sessions with a psychotherapist, and witnesses the Stonewall riots. The narrator's swings between joyful acceptance and critical self-loathing reflect the emerging national gay consciousness. The events of these novels mirror the shape of White's own early life: growing up in Cincinnati, dealing with a demanding father, and attending the exclusive Cranbrook Academy (Ehrhardt 2006). This led to the final work in his semiautobiographical trilogy, *The Farewell Symphony* (1998).

White also authored *Caracole* (1985), set in the nineteenth century and exploring the sexuality of two lovers, male and female. In 1988, White published, with Adam Mars-Jones, an anthology of stories dealing with the impact of AIDS, *The Darker Proof: Stories from a Crisis*. "As White and Mars-Jones shape it, the greatest challenge posed by the AIDS crisis is the spiritual one: What sustains the soul that is bereft of family, enduring slow death" (Arena 1988)?

White's next highly acclaimed work *The Married Man* (2000), in the words of White, is

> about two people who are really very marginal to gay life—one because he's bisexual and the other because he's too old—and who are very involved in a relationship with each other that isn't primarily sexual but is very much a love story, I didn't need to worry about "doing justice" to gay life. I'm only doing justice to a love story. (White 2000, 26)

In *The Married Man*, White incorporates bisexuality into his work. This piece is an homage to White's lover Hubert, who passed away from AIDS, similar to the character of Julien, who also has AIDS. The story of the couple's last trip together had been told previously in White's 1994 memoir as well as in *The Farewell Symphony*. This beautiful yet unsettling novel recalls "loving a self-absorbed, childlike and ultimately enigmatic bisexual man" (Bahr 2000).

White continues to be a prolific writer. Throughout his career, he has also written highly influential non-fiction (including 1977's *The Joy of Gay Sex)*, biography, memoir, and anthologies (including the highly acclaimed *Fresh Men* (2004)). Since the publication of *The Married Man* in 2000, he has also published *A Fine Excess* (2000), a contemporary literature anthology; *Fanny* (2003), a fictional work; *Arts and Letters* (2004), a work of nonfiction; *My Lives* (2006), a memoir; *Terre Haute* (2006), a play based on Timothy McVeigh; and *Hotel de Dream*, his latest fictional work, due in fall 2007.

Allan Gurganus's four novels range in publication dates from 1989 to 2001. His two most influential pieces are *The Oldest Living Confederate Widow Tells All* (1989), "a comic epic about the history of the South, and *Plays Well With Others* (1997), about the New York Art scene in the 1980s, just as AIDS was emerging" (Kaczorowski 2005). Gurganus's first break as an author came in 1974 when *The New Yorker* accepted his short story "Minor Heroism" (which was submitted by his mentor without Gurganus's knowledge), the first "story the magazine had ever published that featured a gay character" (Kaczorowski 2005).

The Oldest Living Confederate Widow Tells All is the story of the South as told by Lucy, a 99-year-old woman in a nursing home. Gay themes emerge throughout the over 700-page piece, particularly in reference to Lucy's husband, Will, and his relationship to a boyhood friend killed in war, Ned. The piece had appeal to a wide audience, particularly when adapted to television and, less successfully, to stage. *White People* (1991) is a wide-ranging collection of short stories told in first-person voices. Several stories deal with same-sex desire, both openly and covertly.

Plays Well With Others was Gurganus's first novel with openly gay characters, in which the young gay protagonist moves to New York from the rural South to pursue a writing career and finds himself swept up in the burgeoning AIDS epidemic of the 1980s and 1990s. "Gurganus has explained in interviews that the impetus for writing the novel was to celebrate, and commemorate, the 'complicated love we have for friends when we're in our twenties . . . when everybody is a sexual object in one form or another'" (Kaczorowki 2005). As Hartley, the protagonist, notes after a particularly joyous sexual romp in the bathhouses, "The prigs won't tell you how sweet and rollicking the peasant dance was. Before such accurate lightning struck us" (as quoted in Freeman 1998, 48), portraying both the joy of the sexual freedom gay men felt in the early 1980s and the impending doom of the AIDS crisis beginning to emerge in the community. The piece accurately reflects the insights of Charles Krause (1998) about his own move to New York City as a young writer in 1980:

> "And the best part was, there was nothing to be afraid of. In 1980, the clap and crabs were the worst things you could get, and a trip to the clinic or a dousing with Rid could fix you up in no time. No one had yet heard of AIDS. (48)

Plays Well With Others has been critically acclaimed as one of the most important works of AIDS-related fiction. It reflects the innocence of a pre-Stonewall era, and the immigration many young GLBTQ persons were making to urban centers, only to find themselves embroiled in a battle over public health, and dying as a result.

Gurganus has often been praised for his simple and Mark Twain-esque writing style, which, it is often speculated, is why his first novel had such mass market appeal. Gurganus recognized this appeal and felt, since *Plays Well With Others* was published after *Oldest Living Confederate Widow Tells All,* he had the ability to bring mass market interest to gay-themed work (Gurganus 1998). This heralded a change in tone in Gurganus's work:

> Minority fiction usually begins as coded lingo known only to the initiated. To communicate with those beyond the ghetto is seen as mutinous. But after years of in-jokes, of bashing most straight people, we've sobered, noticing a bigger world parenthesizing the Castro and the West Village. (Gurganus 1998)

Gurganus questioned why it was acceptable for GLBTQ persons to come hear his readings in "straight" bookstores, but heterosexuals would not venture into gay bookstores. He chastised his GLBTQ readers that "we do need tellers and askers in this land named 'Don't Ask, Don't Tell'" (Gurganus 1998).

In 2001, Gurganus published *The Practical Heart,* a series of four novellas. He feels the novella is "the perfect genre of our time: a novel with attention deficit disorder" (Jeffreys 2001, 43). The novellas include the title story about a woman who may have sat for a painting by John Singer Sargent; "Preservation News," a newsletter formatted story about a conservationist dying of AIDS; "Saint Monster," in which a boy places Bibles in motel rooms while his mother carries on a torrid affair at home; and "He's One, Too," the story of a man arrested for making sexual advances to a young boy in a bathroom, as told through the point of view of his neighbor who idolized the man as a young boy himself (Jeffreys 2001). More so than any of his earlier works, *The Practical Heart* reaches "across risky barriers of race, sexuality, and class" (Miller 2001).

As can be seen through Gurganus's work, he has moved from covert to overt expression of GLBTQ content in his works, reflecting the societal changes occurring (and demanded) through the AIDS crisis. Gurganus's personal role as a caregiver for many friends dying of AIDS becomes more apparent in each of his works. In his own words,

> In the long run I think my value as a writer and my career will be immeasurably enhanced because I think I can treat gay and straight people fairly. I'm not a gay writer in the sense that I've never written about straight people. I find pathos in both camps (as quoted in Jeffreys 2001, 43–44).

Gurganus is currently at work on a sequel to his first novel.

David Ebershoff published his first novel, *The Danish Girl,* in 2000. This piece of historical fiction, which occurs in early twentieth century Denmark, Paris, and Dresden, is loosely based on the story of the first known transsexual operation. Throughout the piece, we meet Einar and his wife, Greta. As Einar struggles with his own need to cross-dress and, eventually, live his life as Lili, we also witness Greta's transformation as she, too, struggles to fulfill Einar's needs.

> The novel is as much Greta's history as it is Einar's: a record of her rebellion from the confines of her wealthy class and family, of her previous marriage to a young man who died of tuberculosis, and of her need to become as singular and unique as possible. Not that Einar's own curious life isn't brilliantly laid out. . . . Einar emerges inventively, elegantly: The author is uncommonly seductive in presenting the Danish man's passage from an ordinary life into his new life as the extremely pretty—and sexually stimulating—Lili. We are allowed to enter the thoughts and feelings of a man living in a far less information-drenched time than our own, as he begins and then follows through his exploration of what is, after all, a truly deviant psycho-sexuality. (Picano 2000, 60)

Indeed, although *The Danish Girl* handles gender identity issues head on, it also probes into what forms a marriage and a relationship. Greta's "wonder, sorrow, and acceptance lift what could have been a melodrama into a poignant meditation on change and the meaning of loyalty" (Blue 2000, 15). *The Danish Girl* reflects the modern GLBTQ theme of flexibility and changeability, and it analyzes what becomes of such dynamics when others are involved. It is being adapted for film as of this writing.

Ebershoff's first collection of short stories, *The Rose City,* consists of seven short stories that offer "fascinating glimpses into the hearts and minds of extraordinarily ordinary men" (Woelz 2002, 40). "Trespass," one of the stories, revisits the coming-out story, often abandoned after the 1990s, through the eyes of an adolescent boy watching a neighbor's house when he learns his neighbor is gay; and "Regime" "takes us into the mind of an adolescent anorexic who wants desperately to remain pure, a 'special boy' unsullied by hunger" (Wolez 2002, 40). In both stories, Ebershoff looks unflinchingly at the psychological and sexual impacts of coming out on adolescents, sometimes in a manner which is quite disturbing.

Sarah Waters's first novel, *Tipping the Velvet* (1998), is historical fiction set in Victorian England, where Nan, a female, explores her life as a gender-bending male prostitute, eventually to be taken in by a wealthy patron and later discarded.

> *Tipping the Velvet* proves a rollicking reading adventure, not simply because of its Victorian (though not vanilla) flavoring, but also because it offers a fictional rendering of such late twentieth-century lesbian issues as the sex wars, outing, gender performance, and grassroots coalition organizing. (Breen 2002)

The lesbian aspect of the novel is not by any means covert but openly embraced, as is the gender-violating performance of Nan.

> So *Tipping the Velvet* is a special kind of fiction—one that tries to imagine what the largely undocumented lives of lesbians of that era might have been like. Waters not only imagines what the underground lesbian scene might have been like, she even imagines the slang that might have been part of this scene. (Poubelle 2006, 8)

Tipping the Velvet's 2002 BBC adaptation for television also helped bring Waters serious public attention.

After *Tipping the Velvet,* Waters next pens *Affinity* (1999), also set in Victorian England. This novel has been compared to "not only Charlotte Bronte's *Villette,* Elizabeth Barrett Browning's *Aurora Leigh,* and even Wilkie Collins's sensationalist novel *The Woman in White,* but also Terry Castle's 1993 study of lesbian representation, *The Apparitional Lesbian*" (Breen 2002). The heroine, Margaret, attempts to make sense of her own desires for women as she does charitable work in women's prisons. Similar to Cunningham's portrayal of Virginia Woolf in *The Hours,* Margaret has attempted suicide due to her desire for a different kind of life, one in which she is not proprietary to men.

> Nineteenth-century-style novels have been under a cloud since the invention of the remote control, but stepping into *Tipping the Velvet* and *Affinity* is like entering the Best of the BBC. In both novels, Waters guides the reader through the late 1800s London milieu like she grew up there. Better even than Charles Dickens, she summons the era's attitudes and ambiance, projecting them onto the screen of the reader's mind with Dolby wrap-around sound such that you feel you're vacationing on all points between Chelsea and the East End. Not many contemporary writers make novels as sumptuous as a symphony. And what an era Sarah Waters renders! The fact that both novels are richly embroidered period pieces doesn't limit their audience appeal. Waters spellbinds readers with insights into 1870s dance halls and 1880s women's prisons that the History Channel would never provide—notably lesbians set in a historical point of view we're not likely to find on the telly. And how Sarah Waters writes of lesbians! Not simply as characters, but highlighting the context of an overbearing heterosexual environment that necessitates closets; boldfacing the sexism that puts such a stranglehold on all women. (Allegra 2001)

Fingersmith (2002), Waters's third novel, is yet another tale of Victorian entrapment. In this novel, a pickpocket works with a criminal to defraud a lonely heiress of her fortune. An interesting twist is used in *Fingersmith* in that the narrator is changed partway through, and different levels of deceit are revealed. *Fingersmith* was made into a serial for BBC in 2005.

In her latest novel, *The Night Watch* (2006), Waters moves from Victorian England to GLBTQ themes in World War II–era London. She weaves a tale full of sexual "deviance"—from GLBTQ-themed sexual encounters to heterosexual adultery. Waters' latest book reads in reverse chronological order, sometimes causing intentional confusion about relationships or situations, but always in a manner that builds suspense. Although very different from her previous pieces, *The Night Watch* has been called "a splendidly written, engaging novel, by a writer who gets better with every effort" (DeCresenczo 2006).

Although the focus of this chapter has been general GLBTQ literature, it is important to recognize the works of some influential authors in specific categories of literature. In the GLBTQ science fiction arena, Jim Grimsley is winning notice for his works, particularly 2000's *Kirith Kirin* and 2004's *The Ordinary*. John Morgan Wilson contributes to gay men's mysteries with his Benjamin Justice series (*Simple Justice* (1996), *Revision of Justice* (1997), *Justice at Risk* (1999), *The Limits of Justice* (2000), *Blind Eye* (2003), *Moth and Flame* (2004), and *Rhapsody in Blood* (2006)). Steve Kluger is making waves with his gay romance novels, including *Almost Like Being in Love* (2004), *Last Days of Summer* (1999), *Changing Pitches* (1998), *Yank* (1992), and the upcoming *The Year We Grew Up* (2007). Finally, Tristan Taormino's enormous contributions as an author and editor in erotica cannot be underplayed, including *Hot Lesbian Erotica* (2005), *True Lust* (2002), the *Best Lesbian Erotica* series (annually since 1996), and *Ritual Sex* (1996), which have won her many awards.

Bibliography

Allegra, Donna. "Embroidering Life." *Lesbian Review of Books* 7 (2001).

Arena, Joe. "The Darker Proof: Stories from a Crisis." *Washington Monthly* (1988).

Arthur, Mikaila Mariel Lemonik. Adoption. [Online, March 2006]. GLBTQ: An Encyclopedia of Gay, Lesbian, Bisexual, Transgender, and Queer Culture website <www.GLBTQ.com/social-sciences/adoption.html>.

———. Domestic Partnerships. [Online, May 2005]. GLBTQ: An Encyclopedia of Gay, Lesbian, Bisexual, Transgender, and Queer Culture website <www.GLBTQ.com/social-sciences/domestic_partnerships.html>.

"Awards for Brokeback Mountain." [Online, 2007]. Internet Movie Database website <www.imdb.org>.

Bahr, David. "French Lessons." *Advocate* 814 (2000): 137.

Beemyn, Brett and Mickey Eliason, eds. *Queer Studies: A Lesbian, Gay, Bisexual, and Transgender Anthology.* New York: New York University Press, 1996.

Bergman, David. *Gaiety Transfigured: Gay Self-Representation in American Literature.* Madison: University of Wisconsin Press, 1991.

Blue, Daniel. "Changing Places." *Lambda Book Report* 8 (2000): 15–16.

Bredbeck, Gregory W. "Literary Theory: Gay, Lesbian, and Queer." *GLBTQ.* <http://www.glbtq.com/literature/lit_theory.html>.

Breen, Margaret Soenser. Sarah Waters. [Online, December 2002]. GLBTQ: An Encyclopedia of Gay, Lesbian, Bisexual, Transgender, and Queer Culture website <www.GLBTQ.com/social-sciences/waters_s.html>.

Castle, Terry. *The Apparitional Lesbian: Female Homosexuality and Modern Culture.* New York: Columbia University Press, 1993.

Creech, James. *Closet Writing, Gay Reading.* Chicago: University of Chicago Press, 1993.

Cunningham, Michael. *The Hours.* New York: Farrar, Straus, and Giroux, 1998.

Decarnin, Camilla, Eric Garber, and Lyn Paleo, eds. *Worlds Apart: An Anthology of Lesbian and Gay Science Fiction and Fantasy.* Boston: Alyson, 1986.

DeCrecenszo, Teresa. "The Night Watch." *Lesbian News 31* (2006): 33.

Defense of Marriage Act. [Online, January 2007]. Wikipedia, The Free Encyclopedia website <en.wikipedia.org>.

Doty, Alexander. *Making Things Perfectly Queer: Interpreting Mass Culture.* Minneapolis: University of Minnesota Press, 1992.

Ebershoff, David. *The Danish Girl.* New York: Viking, 2000.

———. *The Rose City.* New York: Viking, 2000.

Ehrhardt, Michael. "A Man's Own Story." *The Gay and Lesbian Review 13* (2006): 27–29.

Fone, Byrne R.S., ed. *The Columbia Anthology of Gay Literature: Readings from Western Antiquity to the Present Day.* New York: Columbia University Press, 1998.

Forrest, Simon, Grant Biddle, and Stephen Clift. *Talking about Homosexuality in Secondary School.* 3rd ed. West Sussex, England: AVERT, 2006.

Freeman, Chris. "Bla, bla, blah. But heartfelt." *The Harvard Gay and Lesbian Review 5* (1998): 48–49.

Garber, Eric, and Lyn Paleo, eds. *Uranian Worlds: A Guide to Alternative Sexuality in Science Fiction, Fantasy, and Horror.* 2nd ed. Boston: G.K. Hall, 1990.

Gurganus, Allan. "Dispatch from the Front." *Advocate 750/751* (1998).

———. *Oldest Living Confederate Widow Tells All.* New York: Knopf, 1989.

———. *Plays Well With Others.* New York: Alfred A. Knopf, 1997.

———. *The Practical Heart.* New York: Alfred A. Knopf, 2001.

Hinds, Hilary. "Oranges Are Not the Only Fruit: Reaching Audiences Other Lesbian Texts Cannot Reach." *New Lesbian Criticism: Literary and Cultural Readings.* Sally Munt, ed. New York: Columbia University Press, 1992; 153–172.

Hix, Charles. "A New Generation Has Arrived." *Publishers Weekly 248* (2001): 19.

Jagose, Annemarie. *Queer Theory: An Introduction.* New York: New York University Press, 1996.

Jay, Karla, and Joanne Glasgow, eds. *Lesbian Texts and Contexts: Radical Revisions.* New York: New York University Press, 1990.

Jeffreys, Joe E. "What a Novelist Believes." *The Gay and Lesbian Review 8* (2001): 43–44.

Kaczorowki, Craig. "Allan Gurganus." [Online, June 2005]. GLBTQ: An Encyclopedia of Gay, Lesbian, Bisexual, Transgender, and Queer Culture website <www.GLBTQ.com/social-sciences/gurganus_a.html>.

Krause, Charles. "Every Good Boy Does Fine." *Lambda Book Report 6* (1998): 48.

"Lawrence and Garner v. State of Texas." [Online, April 2006]. Sodomy laws website <www.sodomylaws.org>.

Lambda Literary Foundation. 2006. <http://www.lambdaliterary.org/>.

Lee, Ryan. "Edmund White's 'Changing Lives.'" *Houston Voice:* 13.

Macedo, Stephan, and Iris Marion Young, eds. *Child, Family, State.* New York: New York University Press, 2003.

Matzner, Andrew. "Stonewall Riots." [Online, October 2006]. LGBTQ: An Encyclopedia of Gay, Lesbian, Bisexual, Transgender, and Queer culture website <http://www.GLBTQ.com/social-sciences/stonewall_riots.html>.

Meyerowitz, Joanne. *How Sex Changed: A History of Transsexuality in the United States.* Cambridge: Harvard University Press, 2002.

Miller, Tim. "Heart Specialist." *Advocate 847* (2001).

Picano, Eelice. "The Art of Gender Bending." *Gay and Lesbian Review Worldwide 7* (2000): 60–61.

Poubelle, Blanche. "Tom Foolery." *The Guide 26* (2006): 8.

Proulx, E. Annie. *Brokeback Mountain.* New York: Scribner, 2005.

"Queercore." *i-D magazine 110* (1992).

Quinn, Vincent. "Literary Criticism." *Lesbian and Gay Studies* (1997): 39–52.

Rich, Adrienne. "Compulsory Heterosexuality and Lesbian Experience." *Signs* 5 (1980): 631–660.

Stone, Martha E. "Sketches from Memory." *Gay and Lesbian Worldwide Review I7* (2000): 53.

Summers, Claude J. "Gay Voices, Gay Genealogies." *American Literary History* 5 (1993): 147–158.

———. *Gay Fictions: Wilde to Stonewall.* New York: Continuum, 1990.

The Hours. [Online, January 2007]. Wikipedia website <en.wikipedia.org>.

Waters, Sarah. *Affinity.* London: Penguin, 2002.

———. *Fingersmith.* London: Riverhead, 2002.

———. *The Night Watch.* London: Riverhead, 2006.

———. *Tipping the Velvet.* London: Riverhead, 1999.

White, Hilary. "US Bishops' Organization Gives Glowing Review of Homosexual-Sex Propaganda Film." [Online, December 2005]. LifeSite website <www.lifesite.net>.

White, Edmund. "'I See My Life as a Novel as I'm Leading It.'" *Gay and Lesbian Review Worldwide* 7 (2000): 26–31.

———. *The Beautiful Room is Empty.* New York: Knopf, 1998.

———. *The Married Man.* New York: Knopf, 2000.

Woelz, Karl. "Tales of the Unnoticed." *The Gay and Lesbian Review* 8 (2002): 40.

Woodland, Randall. "Edmund White." [Online, December 2004]. GLBTQ: An Encyclopedia of Gay, Lesbian, Bisexual, Transgender, and Queer Culture website <www.GLBTQ.com/literature/white_e.html>.

Woods, Gregory. *A History of Gay Literature: The Male Tradition.* New Haven: Yale University Press, 1998.

Zebrun, Gary. "Edmund White, Outcast Survivor." *The Gay and Lesbian Review* 11 (2004): 28–30.

Zimmerman, Bonnie. *The Safe Sea of Women: Lesbian Fiction 1969–1989.* Boston: Beacon, 1990.

Further Reading

Beemyn, Brett, and Eliason, Mickey, eds. *Queer Studies: A Lesbian, Gay, Bisexual, and Transgender Anthology.* New York: New York University Press, 1996; Bergman, David. *Gaiety Transfigured: Gay Self-Representation in American Literature.* Madison: University of Wisconsin Press, 1991; Castle, Terry. *The Apparitional Lesbian: Female Homosexuality and Modern Culture.* New York: Columbia University Press, 1993; Creech, James. *Closet Writing, Gay Reading.* Chicago: University of Chicago Press, 1993; Decarnin, Camilla, Eric Garber, and Lyn Paleo, eds. *Worlds Apart: An Anthology of Lesbian and Gay Science Fiction and Fantasy.* Boston: Alyson, 1986; Doty, Alexander. *Making Things Perfectly Queer: Interpreting Mass Culture.* Minneapolis: University of Minnesota Press, 1992; Garber, Eric, and Lyn Paleo, eds. *Uranian Worlds: A Guide to Alternative Sexuality in Science Fiction, Fantasy, and Horror.* 2nd ed. Boston: G.K. Hall, 1990; Hinds, Hilary. "Oranges Are Not the Only Fruit: Reaching Audiences Other Lesbian Texts Cannot Reach." *New Lesbian Criticism: Literary and Cultural Readings.* Sally Munt, ed. New York: Columbia University Press, 1992. 153–172; Jay, Karla and Joanne Glasgow, eds. *Lesbian Texts and Contexts: Radical Revisions.* New York: New York University Press, 1990; Meyerowitz, Joanne. *How Sex Changed: A History of Transsexuality in the United States.* Cambridge: Harvard University Press, 2002; Quinn, Vincent. "Literary Criticism." *Lesbian and Gay Studies* (1997): 39–52; Summers, Claude J. *Gay Fictions: Wilde to Stonewall.* New York: Continuum, 1990; Woods, Gregory. *A History of Gay Literature: The Male Tradition.* New Haven: Yale University Press, 1998; Zimmerman, Bonnie. *The Safe Sea of Women: Lesbian Fiction 1969–1989.* Boston: Beacon, 1990.

JENNIFER M. DE COSTE

GRAPHIC NOVELS

Definition. Graphic novels are often considered a subgenre of comic books. The definition of the term *graphic novel* is determined by the way the piece of work under consideration was originally produced. A graphic novel may consist of a collection of comic strips that has been published as a volume of work. A graphic novel might also be a collection of short stories that deal with the same subject matter or that are created by the same author. One overriding factor in defining a graphic novel is its length. Graphic novels are longer, more complex, and ambitious stories, which are shown through the graphic visual elements as well as told by text that supports the visual. A graphic novel is a "novel in comic form" (Kaplan 2006, 14). A present trend in the industry involves previously published works, such as publication of Eoin Colfer's *Artemis Fowl* in graphic novel form as *Artemis Fowl: The Graphic Novel.* Such adaptations further complicate any attempt at stabilizing a set definition for graphic novels. The graphic novel must also be considered a format, rather than a genre. To define a format, we must first consider its development.

It is commonly but wrongly believed that the term *graphic novel* was invented by Will Eisner in 1978 when Eisner's *A Contract with God* was first published. The term actually had been coined in a Comic Amateur Press Alliance's Newsletter, *Capa-Alpha* #2, in 1964 by Richard Kyle. The term first appeared on the title page of George Metzger's *Beyond Time and Again* in 1976, which was published by none other than Richard Kyle.

Eisner's usage of the term in connection with the recognition *A Contract with God* received from critics and fans alike popularized the term. "Graphic novel" appeared on the front cover, and because of the seriousness of the content, this signaled a new direction for future authors. Will Eisner (2008) has been quoted as saying, "It was intended as a departure from the standard, what we call 'comic book format.' I sat down and tried to do a book that would physically look like a 'legitimate' book and at the same time write about a subject matter that would never have been addressed in comic form, which is man's relationship with God."

History. The history of the graphic novel begins with the history of the comic book. There is no separation from comic book history because the graphic novel is an offshoot of comics in general.

With the popularized usage of the term in 1978 with Eisner's *A Contract with God,* the graphic novel began to develop and expand uses of various genres within comic formats. The time and space of a graphic novel allowed for the deeper development of plotlines and social commentary. Early on, authors of comic books were

---

TRENDS AND THEMES

Origin of *Graphic Novel*

Will Eisner maintained that his use of the term *graphic novel* was independent of other influences. He used the term in order to ensure publication of the book. Eisner said, "[The phrase] 'graphic novel' was kind of accidental . . . a little voice inside me said, 'Hey stupid, don't tell him it's a comic or he'll hang up on you.' So I said, 'It's a graphic novel'" (Olson 2005, 7). The term was "permanently cemented into the lexicon" when the book was eventually published by Baronet Books, who was responsible for the inclusion of the phrase "A Graphic Novel" on the cover of *A Contract with God.*

not allowed to explore deep psychological issues. Art Spiegelman notes, "Cartoonists were actually expected to keep a lid on their psyches and personal histories, or at least disguise and sublimate them into diverting entertainments" (1995, 4).

The freedom from social barriers in the late 1960s and early 1970s also marked a freedom of exploration for cartoonists. The underground comics movement established a genre in which taboos could be broken and psychological breaks could be explored. Because these comics were intended for adult audiences, with low print runs and high cover prices, the publishers were able to sidestep the Comic Code Authority, which was established in 1955 to censor anything that might possibly corrupt younger readers.

Context and Issues

Confessional Autobiography. Justin Green's *Binky Brown Meets The Holy Virgin Mary* was the first comic to explore the darker recesses of memory and autobiography. Spiegelman praises Green's work, noting, "What the Bronte sisters did for Gothic romance, what Tolkien did for sword-and-sorcery, Justin Green did for confessional autobiographical comix" (1995, 4).

"Confessional autobiographical" graphic novels were not always factual graphic novels. Neil Gaiman's *Violent Cases* is clearly designed to give the reader ambiguity regarding the elements of truth in memory and recall. Chris Ware's *Jimmy Corrigan* is a mix of both autobiographical aspects and purely fictional elements; in Ware's dedication to his mother, he clarifies that the mother in his book bears no resemblance to his real mother. This fusion of fact and fiction is called "autobifiction-alography" by cartoonist Lynda Barry. Whether these stories are true or fabricated is unimportant; these stories ring emotionally true to both the creator and the consumer. Craig Thompson's *Blankets* recalls his repressive upbringing and his sexual revolution to that upbringing.

Representing the Historical. Art Spiegelman's *Maus* consists of a mix of the autobiographical and the historical. *Maus* tells the story of Spiegelman's father, Vladek, and his mother, Anja. *Maus* was originally written as a three-page strip for a 1972 comics anthology called *Funny Aminals* [*sic*]. Spiegelman's first idea was to write about race relations, with mice being African Americans and cats representing white supremacists. He abandoned this idea because he felt the story would be lacking in authenticity. Instead he chose to display the bedtime stories his father told his as a child—the story of his parents' life in Poland as the Nazis took over and of his parents' life in Auschwitz.

There are two tales told in *Maus*. Both tales are equally important but for very different reasons. There is the story of Vladek Spiegelman, Art's father, who is successful both in business and in love. In this past story, it is clear that Vladek marries Art's mother Anja for her money; he comments that they learned to love each other. The Nazis invade, and Vladek's world comes to an end. It is replaced with fear and hiding, the death of their young son Richu, and finally, Auschwitz. Through Vladek's story, the reader is provided with an excuse to pardon the twisted, bitter man who appears in the second story, told simultaneously with the first story.

The second story is also the story of Vladek, but it is the story of Art as well. This tale details the relationship of the Auschwitz survivor and widower Vladek with his adult son Art. The relationship is fraught with misunderstandings and

Art's depression and angst as he comes to terms with the history of his father (and his mother, who committed suicide) as his father "bleeds history," the subtitle of the second book.

The biographic and autobiographic aspects of this graphic novel are clearly seen in both visual and textual ways. Art remains in mouse character through the entire piece, even when referring to himself and the difficulties he is experiencing in dealing with his father. When Art experiences writer's block early in the second book, he depicts himself as a mouse in present-day clothing surrounded by the corpses of Jews/mice from concentration camps. This visual experience combines the past and the present as well as juxtaposes the shared Holocaust history with the personal history of Art and his father.

The attacks on September 11, 2001, caused Spiegelman to return to the graphic novel, and in 2004 Pantheon published Spiegelman's *In the Shadow of No Towers*. Spiegelman had spent the previous 10 years away from graphic novels and comics, choosing instead to work for *The New Yorker*. During this 10-year period (1992–2002), Spiegelman wrote a number of essays and produced 21 covers, including on September 24, 2001, the first cover after the attacks. Both personal and political, Spiegelman's *In the Shadow of No Towers* focuses on generational relationships, echoing previous themes seen in his earlier work; this time it is Spiegelman the father who needs to rescue his daughter from her school at the foot of the Twin Towers after the attacks. The cover of *In the Shadow of No Towers* reiterates the cover Spiegelman produced for *The New Yorker*. The covers are black, as are the towers illustrated on the page.

The book itself consists of a personal catharsis for Spiegelman. In the 10 pages displayed as broad sheets of newspaper, Spiegelman expresses his fears and anger about how September 11 was handled and about the political situation in which Americans now find themselves. Spiegelman wrote in his introduction to *In the Shadow of No Towers,*

> I hadn't anticipated that the hijackings of September 11 would themselves be hijacked by the Bush cabal that reduced it all to a war recruitment poster . . . . When the government began to move into full dystopian Big Brother mode and hurtle America into a colonialist adventure in Iraq—while doing very little to make America genuinely safer beyond confiscating nail clippers at airports—all the rage I'd suppressed after the 2000 election, all the paranoia I'd barely managed to squelch immediately after 9/11, returned with a vengeance.

The anger and outrage provide a springboard for Spiegelman's political attacks while including homage to famous comics Spiegelman grew up with, such as *Yellow Kid, Katzenjammer Kids,* and *Krazy Kat.* Spiegelman refers to his own book *Maus,* and in one example, Art says that the smoke in Manhattan smelled just like Vladek said the smoke in the concentration camps smelled. He even draws himself as he did in *Maus.* Not near the critical success of *Maus, In The Shower of No Towers* represents an interesting bookend in Spiegelman's work.

Selected Authors. The American comic book industry today includes many successful writers and artists such as Geoff Johns, Jim Lee, Alex Ross, Jessica Abel, Devin Grayson, Gail Simone (the previous three being among a growing number of women creators), and particularly Brian Michael Bendis. Yet some of today's most influential writers are native to England and Scotland, such as Warren Ellis and

Mark Millar. Bendis, Ellis, and Millar are known particularly for their carefully developed characters and storylines, dynamic dialogue, and attention to and commentary on political and global issues and for vastly redefining and reenvisioning American superheroes.

Brian Michael Bendis (b. 1967). Following art school, well-known comic book writer and occasional artist Brian Michael Bendis emerged in the comic book world in the 1990s with independent, creator-owned series and later began working with Image Comics, where he developed *Torso,* about the hunt for the Cleveland Torso Murderer. Well known for his dialogue style and story arc pace, Bendis's transition from crime and noir stories to superhero noir stories began in 2000 when Marvel asked him to revitalize Spider-Man for their Ultimate line.

Bendis embraced the opportunity and was largely successful in revamping the popular superhero and appeased even hard-core fans. In *Ultimate Spider-Man* Bendis brought Peter Parker into the new century and created a story about a kid who gets powers during modern times as opposed to the Peter Parker of 1962. Instead of getting bitten by a radioactive spider as in the original, Bendis's Parker gets bitten by Osborn Industries' genetically engineered spider that has been subject to drug tests. Rather than working at the *Daily Bugle* print newspaper office, the new Parker is employed at the *eBugle,* an online newspaper. Parker's Aunt May and Uncle Ben are younger than in previous iterations, and his love interest, Mary Jane, has more intellectual interests than her 1960s predecessor.

Bendis's Spider-Man remains a human being underneath the costume and has more problems than powers. Spider-Man is strong, but he can also be hurt physically and emotionally, just like anyone else, and Parker has everyday tasks and problems like the rest of us: laundry, money worries, and deadlines at work. Bendis's leisurely pace allows readers to better know Spider-Man and his supporting cast, rendering more depth of character, a major point of praise for Bendis's reworking of this title. *Ultimate Spider-Man* was generally well received by old and new fans alike. A best seller its first month in publication and later a successful feature film, it still faced criticism from some fans, but most fans were pleased Bendis did not mess with the essentials of Stan Lee and Steve Ditko's original character. In fact, many argue Bendis improved on the original by creating a more enriched Spider-Man mythos through his fleshed-out characters and dialogue.

Bendis contributed another groundbreaking title to the American comic book scene with *Alias.* In 2001 *Alias* was the debut title in Marvel's new "MAX Comics," a mature-themed line aimed at adult readers, often depicting scenes of sex and violence. Bendis was prepared to tone down the sex and violence when he pitched *Alias* to Marvel, but instead they decided to bypass the irrelevant Comics Code Authority and released their own rating system, one demonstration of Bendis's influence on today's comic book industry.

Blending crime and superhero genres, *Alias* focuses on Jessica Jones, a former superheroine turned private investigator. Through Jessica Jones and the MAX Comics line, Bendis was able to explore typically taboo aspects of superheroes' lives, such as their moral principles, decisions, and humanity. Jones, a self-declared failed superheroine, is self-destructive and has quite an inferiority complex because of her lack of acceptance within the superhero loop. When a routine missing persons case not only reveals but even video records the secret identity of Captain Marvel, Jones finds herself in a dilemma, calling into question Jones's principles and the power dynamics of her former and current relationship to the superhero world. She is faced not only with outing one of the most well-known heroes, but also with the decision to render him powerless by exposing his true identity. In essence, Jessica realizes absolute power can inflict powerlessness and loss of will on others, and she wrestles over which side of this power dynamic she belongs on. Readers experience her struggle through her self-destructive behavior, including excessive drinking, foul-mouthed blowups, and promiscuity. Moral and ethical decisions are not typically fleshed out for comic book characters, especially superheroes, but Bendis shows readers explicitly how Jessica battles her dilemma and her self-worth through her reckless actions, ultimately rendering her more human and relatable.

Alias illustrates Bendis's knack for creating natural, engaging dialogue and for altering the Marvel universe to influence the comic book industry one character at a time. Within the first two months on the stands, *Alias* sold out despite its graphic scenes of violent or sexual nature inappropriate for younger audiences.

Warren Ellis (b. 1968). British writer Warren Ellis has played a prominent role in today's American comic books as a prolific creator displaying breadth and diversity of subjects, genres, and forms. He is known for his approachable and consistent Internet presence through various comics and culture message boards, forums, and blogs he hosts online, creating a strong connection with his fans. A writer of comic books since 1994, when he began working for Marvel, Ellis has been key in redefining and ushering the superhero into the twenty-first century. Ellis's work often displays grim worldviews and frequently explores various futures rather than pasts while also addressing current issues around popular culture, technology, gender roles, global politics, and human rights. In 1999 Ellis and artist Bryan Hitch collaborated on one of his most highlighted titles, *The Authority,* featuring a team of superheroes striving to change the world for the better rather than merely maintain the status quo. Critics and readers alike responded positively to Ellis's treatment of the superhero in *The Authority.* Ellis avoided stereotypical superpowers and personalities by developing human characters who happen to have superpowers and who display a sense of humor regarding their overblown celebrity status, demonstrating their ability to deconstruct their roles within society and explicitly recognize and comment on the importance of world peace and human rights over their own notoriety.

Rather than traditional powers such as flying or superhuman strength, Ellis's *Authority* heroes display more advanced and unique powers. Jack Hawksmoor, "King of the Cities," demonstrates superhuman agility and strength and has the capability to "read" and control urban environments through telepathy, allowing him to link into and control any city through such means as the animation and possession of architecture and infrastructure. Meanwhile, Angie Spica distilled numerous intelligent technological devices into nine pints of liquid machinery to replace her blood and became "The Engineer," with nanotechnology flowing through her body and offering infinite mechanical abilities, such as tapping into technological infrastructures or creating weapons.

The Authority was also groundbreaking in its positive portrayal of a homosexual couple on the team. Apollo and Midnighter at first glance seem to be stereotypical muscle-ridden, masculine heroes yet are romantic partners in a caring, monogamous relationship. While homosexual characters are not new to comic books, positive and prominent portrayals of homosexual characters are. Ellis's readers see the tender, intimate side of their relationship several times without being distracted from the main plot. Ellis illustrates a healthy rather than dysfunctional homosexual relationship between essential characters when typically homosexual comic book characters are portrayed in poor light or end up being killed off.

Apollo and Midnighter's groundbreaking relationship in *The Authority* generally garnered positive responses from readers. There was some controversy regarding a panel illustrating a kiss between the two men, and Ellis was asked to alter it to show Apollo kissing Midnighter on the cheek instead. Readers responded indignantly to DC Comics editors, questioning why a series regularly depicting murder, genocide, and events of mass destruction should warrant censoring an innocuous kiss between a homosexual couple.

Aside from pushing the boundaries of the superhero and gender roles, *The Authority* also speaks volumes to current world issues such as global politics and human rights. At the turn of the millennium, the team encounters global political and economic superpowers such as Europe and Japan, as well as terrorist-prone and vulnerable cities such as London, Los Angeles, and New York. Fighting to protect inhabitants of planet Earth, the team fights colonization by other planets and protects human rights by punishing those committing genocide and political corruption in their nations.

Ellis's more recent collaboration with artist Ben Templesmith on *Fell* is another series widely recognized for its dense storytelling and experimentation with comic book forms and models of production. In *Fell,* Detective Richard Fell has been transferred "from over the bridge" to Snowtown, a resident-described "feral city" that is run-down, decayed, and plagued with poverty and crime. An illustration of Ellis's grim worldview, Snowtown offers an anonymous depiction of a mixture of many existing urban contexts and problems, and Templesmith's gloomy colors and gritty illustrations enhance that feeling.

Detective Fell goes about his work trying to make sense of this city whose desperate citizens have given up on it yet spray paint the city's tag everywhere as a form of protective magic, in hopes the city will not destroy what has already been labeled its own. Fell goes about solving unique and bizarre crimes in each issue, but citizens question his practices. Because crime is such a prevalent part of daily life in Snowtown, they do not understand Fell's motivations for solving crimes that will just occur again the very next day—or hour, for that matter. It seems as if Fell wants to change Snowtown for the better rather than maintain the status quo, sentiments Ellis's characters in *The Authority* also exhibit.

Aside from the dense and meaningful stories, Ellis's experimentation with the form of *Fell* is perhaps the comic's greatest contribution to modern American comic books. Creator-owned, *Fell* was conceived by Ellis and designed to be accessible to readers financially and contextually. With the comic priced at $1.99 per issue (well under the usual price of today's comics, between $2.50 and $3.99), readers could enter a comic shop with pocket change and leave with a self-contained story in one issue rather than longer story arcs requiring the purchase of multiple issues. Undertaking a comic sticking to this price point meant both Ellis and artist Templesmith remained uncompensated until issues were printed and actually sold.

Ellis's low-cost model required compressed stories with shorter page counts but was supplemented with "back material," including unfinished artwork, author notes expanding on the story, and reader responses. Still in production, *Fell* has been positively received by readers and critics alike for both its form and its content and has garnered several comic book award nominations. Readers have shown gratitude to Ellis and Image Comics for developing a low-cost pricing model and appreciate Ellis's full use of the shorter page count through carefully developed, dense, and full storylines in each issue.

Mark Millar (b. 1969). Scottish comic book writer Mark Millar began writing comics as a college student. Initially his work was submitted to and published by British comic book presses, like the popular *Saviour,* which Trident Comics published in the early 1990s. DC Comics brought Millar into the mainstream American comics scene, where he immediately established a high profile by taking over Warren Ellis's *The Authority* in 2000. However, scheduling, artist, and censorship problems with editors and competing lucrative offers from publishers caused Millar to move to Marvel in 2001, where he began working on their Ultimate line of comics.

Marvel's Ultimate line aimed to increase readership by revamping popular Marvel Universe characters to make them accessible and attractive to new readers. Millar played a seminal role in rewriting the Marvel character histories through his work on *Ultimate X-Men, Ultimate Fantastic Four,* and most notably *The Ultimates.* In the Ultimate Marvel Universe, the Ultimates (known as the Avengers in previous Marvel Universes) are a team of superheroes banded together to fend off supervillains and other superhuman threats. Millar's task was not to merely provide a face-lift to these Marvel Universe characters, but to start from scratch and rebuild them anew.

The Ultimates included core members from the Avengers, including Captain America, Iron Man, Thor, Wasp, Giant Man, and The Hulk, with a handful of others. The Ultimates team is funded by the U.S. military through S.H.I.E.L.D. (Strategic Hazard Intervention, Espionage and Logistics Directorate), a counterterrorism intelligence unit directed by Nick Fury, former U.S. Army hero and spy. Fury, with the backing of the U.S. government, hopes to reinvigorate the super-soldier program that originally spawned Captain America and also recruits the Ultimates to fight against increasingly threatening global meta-human and mutant activity.

Emergent themes in Millar's *The Ultimates* series reflect current global and domestic issues such as homeland security, colonization and genocide, and the United States' motives and involvement with the Middle East. Early on, the Ultimates face protecting homeland security and the challenge of controlling their own member, the Hulk, as he rampages New York City while going after his ex-girlfriend's date in a jealous rage, killing over 800 civilians. Millar carefully develops his characters before moving on to his next story arc where the Ultimates protect the Earth from colonization and possible extinction, reflecting current genocide crimes and the imperialistic global climate. Millar wanted his superheroes to be working and fighting relevant and meaningful battles rather than chasing down supervillains, and this is apparent in the sequel, *The Ultimates 2,* where the team begins to face potential involvement in U.S. foreign relations in the Middle East. Pressured by the White House to work with European Union super-soldiers, members of the Ultimates begin to question their role in helping the United States push for increasing global power and control of oil resources. Climatically, the group faces off against the Liberators, a superhero force made up of recruits from enemy nations in the series, including Iran, North Korea, China, Russia, and Syria, reflecting the recent threat of attacks on American land. Battling the Liberator's invasion on U.S. soil, the Ultimates organize a counteroffensive and successfully defeat the invaders one-by-one.

Throughout the larger obstacles facing the Ultimates, Millar weaves subplots and themes allowing for character development, such as Janet (the Wasp) and Hank Pym's (Giant Man) marital issues, Bruce Banner's (the Hulk) internal struggles over his abilities as a research scientist trying to reformulate the super-soldier serum, and Steve Rogers's (Captain America) adjustments to living in the modern world after being resurrected from a World War II incident in 1945. The rich subplots also reveal tensions within the group. Some members distrust Bruce Banner because of his volatility and perceived lack of mental stability, while Hank Pym is jealous of the attention Steve Rogers has been paying his wife, Janet. Other tensions relate to the goals and mission of their team. Thor, in particular, feels they should not be used as a tool for the United States to establish its power with preemptive strikes, and he is quite vocal about his opinions, causing some to question his loyalty to the group. Meanwhile, their celebrity status causes other tensions. Some team members share snide remarks regarding Tony Stark's (Iron Man) numerous television news talk-show appearances and romantic trysts with leading ladies of Hollywood or demonstrate jealousy about Captain America's potential movie deal.

Readers familiar with the Marvel Universe were likely skeptical about Millar's ability to successfully rewrite decades-old mythology without alienating fans and characters or destroying the continuity of the existing Marvel Universe, but responses to *The Ultimates* were mostly favorable, especially among reviewers and critics. Some hard-core fans blasted Millar and his work on various comic book message boards and blogs, but the soaring sales figures spoke to the success of Millar's undertaking.

Millar's exploration of American domestic issues continued in his much anticipated seven-part *Civil War* series published by Marvel Comics in 2006 and 2007. Considered a "Marvel Comics Event," the storyline included superheroes fighting against one another in an ideological battle that could forever change the Marvel Universe. The basis of the conflict regarded the Superhuman Registration Act, a law passed by the U.S. government requiring all superhumans to register their powers and identities with the government or be persecuted by S.H.I.E.L.D. (the government-funded superhuman counterterrorism and intelligence unit), registered superhumans, and nongovernment enforcers such as civilian supporters. Reaction to the policy among superheroes was mixed, creating a divide between former allies, with the pro-registration camp led by Iron Man and the anti-registration camp led by Captain America.

Millar uses this conflict as a basis to explore many current domestic issues facing the United States, such as the immigration reform debate, the politically and ideologically divided climate of the nation, and the erosion of civil liberties. The Superhuman Registration Act and the superhumans' reactions to it reflect some of the debates surrounding the United States' immigration reform issue. Some heroes feel they should not have to register with the government because they already positively contribute to society by capturing supervillains or protecting the public. On the other hand, the pro-registration camp recognizes the value of standardized training for superhumans and feels the registration process would allow for more legitimacy and respect from the American public.

Millar's political allegory continues with the divided superhero community replicating the currently divided political ideologies of the American public under the current administration. The philosophical war the superheroes are experiencing brings up issues of government oversight and involvement in the private lives of its citizens, including the erosion of civil liberties. The anti-registration camp feels being forced to work for the government renders them lackeys of the government and takes their freedom to perform their work as they choose. They also feel their civil liberties are threatened because if they register and reveal their true identities, their privacy and safety are at risk, and they will be subject to heavy surveillance by registration enforcers or S.H.I.E.L.D. whether they register or not.

Millar's *Civil War* was highly anticipated, and sales soared, though reader response remained mixed, as is normal with a major comic book event such as this. Millar's undertaking changed the Marvel Universe in a big way, and readers will continue to learn to what extent the future Marvel storylines involving *Civil War* characters will develop from the outcome of the war. Even *Civil War*'s numerous "crossovers" or "tie-ins" (stories that combine two or more otherwise separated characters, stories, settings, or universes that meet and interact with each other) demonstrated the degree to which this conflict altered and influenced the mythology of the Marvel Universe. While crossovers and tie-ins are normal in the comic book industry, Millar's *Civil War* spawned over 100 comic book issues under 20-plus titles, demonstrating the impact of *Civil War* on the Marvel Universe and the comic book industry. Numerous new titles were also developed from the plotlines in *Civil War* that illustrate and unfold the results of the war in the entire Marvel Universe.

Women in Today's Comic Book Industry. Because of the prominent number of males in the field, some criticize the comic book industry for remaining a "boys club," yet female editors, writers, and artists are becoming more common and gaining more recognition for their work in the medium. American writer Devin Grayson's (b. 1971) *Batman: Gothic Knights* emerged in 2000, making her the first woman to have a regular ongoing writing assignment on the Batman title, and she has garnered distinction and recognition among the industry and from fans. Grayson's Batman marked a new direction in that she brought a concern for relationships to the character, something her male contemporaries did not display as well in their stories. Nominated in 1999 and 2000 for the Comics Buyer's Guide Award for Favorite Writer, Grayson is still an active comic book writer today. In 2005 she wrapped up a five-year run on *Nightwing* and wrote the creator-owned *Matador* for DC Comics' Wildstorm imprint, and in 2006 published *DC Universe: Inheritance,* a novel about fathers and sons starring Batman, Nightwing, Green Arrow, Arsenal, Aquaman, and Tempest.

Jessica Abel (b. 1969) is another American comic book writer and artist gaining recognition; her work leans more toward the independent or alternative genre of comic books. In the early 1990s, Abel self-published her embellished hand-bound comic book *Artbabe,* which was eventually picked up by Fantagraphics for publication. Abel delved into longer comic books in 2000 when she started *La Perdida,* originally a five-part series and later reissued as a single volume in 2005. Receiving positive critical response, *La Perdida* featured a Mexican American woman, Carla, venturing into Mexico City in search of her identity after being raised by only her white American mother. Abel's work often includes the experiences of Generation X characters and demonstrates careful attention to communicating her characters' gestures and facial expressions. Recently Abel has worked on *Carmina,* a prose novel for teens; *Life Sucks,* a new graphic novel; and a textbook about making comics.

Gail Simone is yet another prominent woman writer in today's comic book industry. Simone first entered mainstream comics with her work on *Deadpool* (later relaunched as *Agent X*) in 2002 but had previously been noticed by comic book fans through her *Women in Refrigerators* Web site cataloging the many instances in which female comic book characters were victimized in plot devices for male protagonists. Simone took over DC Comics' *Birds of Prey,* featuring an all-female cast of characters. Her work on this title has garnered credit for her balance of suspenseful action, thoughtful character development, and humor. Simone also contributed to DC Comics' 2006 "Infinite Crisis" event through the *Villains United* series, in which she revitalized the Catwoman character. She has remained active in the online comic book community through her "You'll All Be Sorry" weekly column on the Comic Book Resources Web site and through *Bloodstains on the Looking Glass,* her blog. She continues to write and recently has worked on a series for *Gen 13* as well as *Welcome to Tranquility,* a creator-owned project for Wildstorm.

Bibliography

Abel, Jessica. *Artbabe* [Issues 1–5]. Self-published, 1992–1996.
———. *Artbabe* [Vol. 2, Issues 1–4]. Seattle, WA: Fantagraphics, 1997–1999.
———. *Carmina.* New York: HarperCollins, 2007.
———. *Life Sucks.* New York: First Second, 2007.
———. *La Perdida.* New York: Pantheon Books, 2006.
Batman. Directed by Tim Burton. Warner Home Video, 1989.
Batman and Robin. Directed by Joel Schumacher. Warner Home Video, 1997.
Alien. Directed by Ridley Scott. Twentieth Century Fox Home Entertainment, 1984.
Bendis, Brian Michael. *Alias.* New York: Marvel Comics, 2002.
———. *Torso.* Orange, CA: Image Comics, 2001.
———. *Ultimate Spider-Man: Power and Responsibility* [Vol. 1]. New York: Marvel Comics, 2001.
———. *Ultimate Spider-Man: Learning Curve* [Vol. 2]. New York: Marvel Comics, 2001.
Benton, Mike. *The Comic Book in America: An Illustrated History.* Dallas, TX: Taylor Publications, 1989.
Eisner, Will. 2008. http://www.time.com/time/columnist/arnold/article/0,9565,542579,00.html.
Ellis, Warren. *The Authority: Relentless* [Vol. 1]. LaJolla, CA: Wildstorm/DC Comics, 2000.
———. *The Authority: Under New Management* [Vol. 2]. LaJolla, CA: Wildstorm/DC Comics, 2000.
———. *Fell* [Issues 1, 2, 4, 5]. Orange, CA: Image Comics, 2006.
Gaiman, Neil. *The Sandman* [Issues 1–75]. New York: Vertigo, 1989–1996.
Grayson, Devin. *Batman: Gothic Knights* [Issues 1–32]. New York: DC Comics, 2000–2002.
———. *DC Universe: Inheritance.* New York: Warner Books, 2006.
———. *Matador* [Issues 1–6]. LaJolla, CA: Wildstorm/DC Comics, 2005.
———. *Nightwing* [Issues 53, 71–100, 108–117]. New York: DC Comics, 2000–2005.
Jones, Gerard. *Men of Tomorrow: Geeks, Gangsters, and the Birth of the Comic Book.* New York: Basic Books, 2004.
Justice League Unlimited. 2001–2007. Created by Gardner Fox. Warner Brothers Entertainment.
Kaplan, Arie. *Masters of the Comic Book Universe Revealed!: Will Eisner, Stan Lee, Neil Gaiman, and More.* Chicago: Chicago Review Press, 2006.
McFarlane, Todd. *Spawn* [Issues 1–73]. Orange, CA: Image Comics, 1992–1998.
Millar, Mark. *Civil War* [Issues 1–3, 5, 6]. New York: Marvel Comics, 2006–2007.
———. *Saviour* [Issues 1–5]. Leicester, UK: Trident Comics, 1990.
———. *Ultimate Fantastic Four* [Issues 1–6]. New York: Marvel Comics, 2003–2004.
———. *Ultimate X-Men* [Issues 1–12, 15–33]. New York: Marvel Comics, 2000–2003.

———. *The Ultimates, Vol. 1: Superhuman.* New York: Marvel Comics, 2002.

———. *The Ultimates, Vol. 2: Homeland Security.* New York: Marvel Comics, 2004.

———. *The Ultimates 2: Gods and Monsters* [Vol. 1]. New York: Marvel Comics, 2005.

Miller, Frank. *Batman: The Dark Knight Returns* [Issues 1–4]. New York: DC Comics, 1986.

———. *Daredevil* [Issues 168–191]. New York: Marvel Comics, 1981–1983.

———. *Sin City* [Issues 1–13]. Dark Horse Comics, 1991–1992.

Olson, Stephen P. *Neil Gaiman.* New York: Rosen, 2005.

Raiders of the Lost Ark. Directed by Steven Spielberg, produced by George Lucas. Paramount Home Video, 1981.

Simone, Gail. *Agent X* [Issues 1–15]. New York: Marvel Comics, 2002–2003.

———. *Birds of Prey* [Issues 56–102]. New York: DC Comics, 2003–2007.

———. *Bloodstains on the Looking Glass* [Online January 2007]. http://happystains.blogspot.com

———. *Deadpool* [Issues 65–69]. New York: Marvel Comics, 2002.

———. *Gen 13* [Vol. 4] [Issues 1–4]. LaJolla, CA: Wildstorm/DC Comics, 2006–2007.

———. *Villains United* [Issues 1–6]. New York: DC Comics, 2005.

———. *Welcome to Tranquility* [Issues 1–6]. LaJolla, CA: Wildstorm/DC Comics, 2006–2007.

———. *Women in Refrigerators.* Accessed January 2007 at http://www.unheardtaunts.com/wir.

———. "You'll All Be Sorry" [Weekly column]. http://www.comicbookresources.com/columns

Smallville. Created by Alfred Gough and Miles Millar. Warner Brothers Entertainment, 2001–2007.

Spiegelman, Art. "Foreword: Symptoms of Disorder, Signs of Genius." In *Justin Green's Binky Brown Sampler,* by Justin Green. San Francisco: Last Gasp, 1995. 4–7.

———. *In the Shadow of No Towers.* Self-published, 2004.

———. *Maus.* New York: Pantheon, 1991.

Star Trek. Directed by Robert Wise. Paramount Home Video, 1980.

Superman. Directed by Richard Donner. Warner Home Video, 1978.

Ware, Chris. *Acme Novelty Library.* New York: Pantheon, 2005.

Wertham, Fredric. *Seduction of the Innocent.* New York: Rinehart, 1954.

Further Reading

Benton, Mike. *The Comic Book in America: An Illustrated History.* Dallas, TX: Taylor Publications, 1989; Klock, Geoff. *How to Read Superhero Comics and Why.* New York: Continuum, 2002; McCloud, Scott. *Reinventing Comics: How Imagination and Technology Are Revolutionizing an Art Form.* New York: Perennial, 2000; McCloud, Scott. *Understanding Comics.* New York: HarperPerennial, 1994; Wright, Bradford. *Comic Book Nation: The Transformation of Youth Culture in America.* Baltimore, MD: Johns Hopkins University Press, 2001.

TAMMY MIELKE

H

HISTORICAL FANTASY

Definition. To the extent that inner and outer are separable, history forms the surface of the past: chronology, geography, economics, sociology, technology, and politics. In contrast, fantasy conveys the internal past—the emotions and the dreams hidden beneath them. Whereas **historical fiction** stays closer to the surface (by avoiding the supernatural) and high fantasy has a generic, medieval setting in some invented country, historical fantasy depicts reality comprehensively, combining actual history with dreamlike depths. As such, it makes unusually great demands both on the research time and creativity of its authors and on the erudition and imagination of its readers.

It uses a factual and fantastic past to address the authors' present (the time of composition) in preparation for their future. Consider, for instance, Neil Gaiman's historical fantasy series for Vertigo **comic books**, ending with a conversation between William Shakespeare and the Sandman (1996). Not only was Gaiman's career changing from comic books to other projects, but his close connection to America was also drawing him there; Gaiman therefore named that episode after Shakespeare's comedy *The Tempest,* a drama often deemed to be that playwright's farewell to his art and also Shakespeare's response to the New World. In the Sandman series, this episode culminates parallels between the two authors, such as Gaiman's attributing the same complaint to both his daughter Holly and Shakespeare's daughter Judith: each writer's existence consists of either composing lies or stealing them from previous books (Kwitney 2003, 61). At the end of the series, Gaiman has Shakespeare himself express this as a regret, adding that it has kept him from ever truly living. Given Gaiman's situation (ending his most famous series), this problem might sound autobiographical entirely, except that it comes through the mouth of Shakespeare and is itself indebted to Jorge Luis Borges's parable *Everything and Nothing,* where Shakespeare says it to God (Borges 1962, 248–249). Through this intertwining of personal and literary allusions with the exploits of the supernatural Sandman, Gaiman suggests that his portrait of personal remorse on concluding the series belongs to some larger pattern—the nature of writing historical fantasy. This genre inevitably borrows from the past, sometimes staying close to sources but otherwise sidestepping the ordinary version of reality in order to reassess its norms, often controversially. The context of this episode was Gaiman's struggle for comic books' First Amendment rights, which brought him America's Comic Book Legal Defense Fund's Defender of Liberty Award the next year (1997).

History. Because the very nature of historical fantasy concerns the past, it often involves rewriting ancient epics and legends—for example, Stephan Grundy's *Gilgamesh* (2000), which re-imagines the heterosexual descriptions of the ancient epic with bisexual ones. Why do old sources seem so outmoded as to require rewriting? Predating science, ancient epics presented myths as fact rather than fiction and thus were not designed to be historical fantasy per se. For instance, when around 1300 B.C.E. the exorcist priest Sin-Leqi-Unninni produced the best-preserved version of the Gilgamesh legend, he added an appendix in which a dead character appears as a ghost, appropriate to the editor's professional concern with such beings. In doing this, he violated the sequence of the narrative, which itself is patched together from previous accounts with so little care for consistency that he could not decide whether the central character should be spelled "Gilgamesh" or "Bilgamesh" (Maier 1984, 1–50). In other words, like Grundy's, his *Gilgamesh* is a magical version of the past reshaped for his own needs, but unlike current historical fantasists, he did not live in an age that distinguished skillfully between history and fantasy.

That distinction became a shade clearer during the Protestant Reformation in Europe and America (sixteenth to seventeenth centuries C.E.), with its contrasting what it called "scripture" (the Protestant section of the Bible) to "apocrypha" (the rest of the Catholic Bible, deemed historically inaccurate by Protestants). The emphasis of the time, however, was in purifying faith rather than in writing historical scholarship per se. From that period, Edmund Spenser's *Faerie Queene* (1590–1596) recognizes that it is not literally true, but an allegory of Spenser's own Elizabethan Britain, set in the legendary Arthurian period. His concern, though, is denouncing vice rather than portraying historical detail. Shying from such preaching, L. Sprague de Camp and Fletcher Pratt parodied it in their *The Incomplete Enchanter* (1940)—a humor already nascent in the *Faerie Queene* becomes more playful and detailed after book one, as if evolving toward modern historical fantasy.

Perhaps coincidentally, at approximately the same time as Spenser but in China, the *Journey to the West* (*Hsi Yu Chi*, attributed to Wu Ch'eng-en) turns a historical event (Hsuan Tsang's bringing Buddhist scriptures from India) into an enormous amalgam of legends, humor, and allegory, comparable to Spenser's. Admittedly, the *Hsi Yu Chi* has inspired some American historical fantasy (e.g., Mark Salzman's *The Laughing Sutra*, 1991, and Gerald Vizenor's *Griever: An American Monkey King in China*, 1987), but the primary influence on American historical fantasy has not been from the East or even from the West in general but has been specifically British. This dependence has been both a way for America to reimagine its roots and a way for American writers to learn a genre pioneered by English fascination with the past.

From such British Gothic historical fantasies as William Beckford's *Vathek* (French 1782; English 1786) or Matthew Lewis's *The Monk* (1796) later comes American Gothicism, for example, Edgar Allan Poe's "Masque of the Red Death" (1842). All of these use history as an excuse for eroticism (to the extent that Beckford first had to publish in France), yet ultimately they denounce the old, adopting and adapting the model of confessional literature. This dissatisfaction with the past was not confined to the Gothic. Despite substituting humor for the *frissons* of Beckford, Lewis, and Poe, Mark Twain's (Samuel Langhorne Clemens's) historical fantasy *A Connecticut Yankee in King Arthur's Court* (1889), for instance, makes even more explicit the superiority of the present over the past, while implicitly criticizing even his age as not sufficiently modernized.

Enough appreciation of the past for a richer historical fantasy again comes from England: Rudyard Kipling's *Puck of Pook's Hill* (1906), composed after globe-trotting, including years in the United States, evidences a new perspective on his British heritage. Kipling's own childhood was divided between an idyllic, multicultural Indian period with his art-historian father and a hellish British period with an anti-artistic evangelical. *Puck of Pook's Hill* exorcizes that trauma by imagining an alternative: the multiculturalism and tolerance of his India brought home to England in a way that would make it more like the United States. By way of artifacts, comparable to those in the museum in which Kipling's father was curator, a fairy introduces children to previous local cultures, pagan included. As Donald Mackenzie remarks in a preface to *Puck of Pook's Hill*, the artifacts embody Victorian fact-based history, what he calls the "archaeological imagination" (Mackenzie 1993, xiv)—a past that remains visible, unlike the invisible realm of merely oral legends.

Puck of Pook's Hill inspired many children's books designed to teach history through fantasy. Because of a need to redefine national identity during and directly after the chaos wrought by World War II, that period was particularly open to these. For instance, Alison Uttley's *A Traveler in Time* (1939) and Phillippa Pearce's *Tom's Midnight Garden* (1958) tour history via a temporal slip. One notable series from the period was Mary Norton's *The Magic Bed-Knob* (1943) and *Bonfires and Broomsticks* (1947), later collected together as *Bedknob and Broomstick* (1957) and made eventually into a Disney movie (1971). The books (with far more historical connection than the film) reflect the war period's mood of precarious hope via an incompetent witch who just barely manages to take a family of children to more promising times (e.g., the seventeenth century). Equally notable, beginning in 1954 with *Half Magic*, Edward Eager's tales of magic series (*Knight's Castle*, 1956; *Magic by the Lake*, 1957; and *The Time Garden*, 1958) fit Britain's slow recovery from the wartime economy by giving children only "half magic"; nonetheless, it reaffirms British tradition. By the early 1960s, a Cold War paranoia underlay the "wolves series" by Conrad Aiken's daughter Joan Aiken. Beginning with *The Wolves of Willoughby Chase* (1962), the series tells of continental werewolves invading eighteenth-century England.

This was a period when America was following the patriotic British trend, though in a less distinguished way—for example, Carley Dawson's now-out-of-print colonial magic series (*Mr. Wicker's Window*, 1952; *The Sign of the Seven Seas*, 1954; and *Dragon Run*, 1955). With a depiction of racial relations that today seems embarrassingly conservative, these show a twentieth-century magician's apprentice time-traveling to help save eighteenth-century America from foreign influences.

These series are relatively conventional compared to a trend in historical fantasy that came to the United States first via the works of Jorge Luis Borges. A translator of Kipling into Spanish, Borges began his highly metaphysical version of the genre in 1935 with his *Universal History of Infamy* (*Historia universal de la infamia*). Particularly in the 1940s, his short stories often juxtaposed historical settings with some temporal paradox, for example, a subjective year sandwiched within an objective instant, or a labyrinth of time, or the same work changing its meaning over the centuries, or immortals devolving into troglodytes. His essay "A New Refutation of Time" ("Nueva refutación del tiempo," 1952) explains this fascination with temporal paradox as a futile desire to nullify time and thus deny death, despite his recognizing himself as being composed of time (Borges 1962, 234). Learning from Borges the complex interweaving of fantasy and history but remaining political, a **magical realism** movement developed in Latin American from the 1960s onward. Among its first masterpieces was Gabriel García Márquez's *One Hundred Years of Solitude* (*Cien años de soledad,* 1967), which interconnects the story of a village with the history of the world and mixes verisimilitude with fantasies, freeing the unconscious as part of an agenda of liberating the repressed and oppressed.

As an influence on historical fantasy in the United States, this engagé yet speculative metaphysical current blended eventually with the more staid British one—the latter represented particularly by the American fad for J.R.R. Tolkien's high fantasy *Lord of the Rings,* written 1937–1949, published 1953–1954. The American blending started in the late 1960s, when Tolkien's combat between clearly defined good and evil no longer matched the more complex moral questions raised by the Vietnam War and the youth revolution, which had affinities with the liberalism of magic realism. Typical of the period in America were Roger Zelazny's Amber books, commencing with *Nine Princes in Amber* (1970), and Anne Rice's Vampire Chronicles, starting with *Interview with the Vampire* (1976). Both form larger-than-life anatomies of dysfunctional societies and their histories, with the protagonist poised between traditional action and metaphysical rumination. Anne Rice recovered from the alcoholic despair flowing from her daughter's demise by writing *Interview with the Vampire* (1976), in which a girl survives death as a monster among the undead—Rice's imagining something worse than the loss of her daughter and thus reconciling herself to it. Whereas Rice had become morbid and nocturnal in her alcoholic phase, the vampire society offered an exaggerated version of that condition that helped her recognize and move beyond her addiction. The scenes with that society, however, exist in their own lyrical sense of time, like Borges's "A Secret Miracle" ("El Milagro secreto," 1945).

During the 1970s, American blending of the British conservative and the Hispanic liberal currents remained tentative; in contrast, during the 1980s, America dominated the genre. After almost a decade of silence, in 1985 Anne Rice produced a radically new, second Vampire volume, *The Vampire L'Estat.* Pervaded by the whining of its protagonist, Louis (i.e., by remnants of Rice's own depression), *Interview* had peered at the dark places of the psyche myopically. The more mature second volume retold and expanded the previous adventure from the perspective of L'Estat, wolf-killer, actor, and existentialist. Viewed through Louis's eyes, the first volume's character L'Estat was a pathetic parasite. The retelling and its sequels made him a multimillionaire playboy, whose exuberance testified that an extended lifetime need not decrease humanity's energy, even in an absurd universe.

Like *The Vampire L'Estat,* many other historical fantasies of the 1980s in America culminated themes developed in the 1970s. Although feminist **Arthurian literature** had been published throughout that decade (e.g., in Britain, Vera Chapman's *The Green Knight,* 1975; *The King's Damosel,* 1976; *King Arthur's Daughter,* 1976), the year 1982 brought Marion Zimmer Bradley's enormously popular American tome *The Mists of Avalon,* about the women of Camelot. Its very length and amount of historical detail granted it opulence and verisimilitude.

Within her own **science fiction** Darkover series, Bradley had pioneered the use of bisexual personae in formulaic adventure plots. Set, however, on another planet in a distant future with the characters part-alien, Darkover was a heavily disguised comment on human nature. Slightly bolder, *The Mists of Avalon* posits that here on earth, in one of the founding Anglo myths, Camelot did not fall because of

Lancelot's adultery with Guinevere. Instead, Bradley's King Arthur forms a three-some with them, in which the only sexual tension comes from the two men's being more interested in one another than in the woman. For Bradley, the major cause of Camelot's decline is Christian intolerance. Such a liberal rewriting of legends had been extremely rare in historical fiction, but the fantasy elements in *The Mists of Avalon* gave just enough distancing so that readers of the 1980s found it tolerable. By the 1980s the British begin to follow the American lead, an example being the bisexuality of Peter Vansittart's *Parsifal,* where the Arthurian grail knight falls in love with both the goddess-like Kundry and Sir Gawain.

Historical romance, previously one of the most traditional genres, thus found fantasy as a means of expanding its scope. The Vampire Chronicles eroticized blood-sucking between bisexuals whose very mode of being Rice described as a magical sensuous and sensual ecstasy. Comparably provocative, Judith Tarr's Hound and Falcon trilogy (*The Isle of Glass,* 1985; *The Golden Horn,* 1985; and *The Hounds of God,* 1987) reflects 1980s sexual liberalism with a relatively sympathetic homosexual character (King Richard the Lionhearted) and a denunciation of Roman Catholic celibacy. Despite being a monk, the protagonist is also an elf who resembles a pretty, lusty boy and who nonetheless keeps his monastic vows for longer than a human being could live. Eventually, he falls in love with a shape-shifting elf, who spends long periods as a dog at his feet, from where she sends him tempting thoughts telepathically. R.A. Macavoy's Damiano series (*Damiano,* 1983; *Damiano's Flute,* 1984; and *Raphael,* 1984) also contains a human/canine, the protagonist's talking dog. The two end up playing naked together in heaven where the dog has acquired a human soul and form.

Another of the themes in the Damiano series as well as in many other historical fantasies of the period is conflict between Christianity and wizardry. Katherine Kurz's Deryny series (1970–2002), despite her MA in Medieval English history, cast that enmity in another world, where the religion was just different enough from Christianity so that Christian readers might not be offended. By bringing it into our world, Tarr, Bradley, and Macavoy removed the disguise, using Christian history to indict that faith. Tarr's Hound and Falcon trilogy delivered a passionate denunciation of the Fourth Crusade, much of which was spent with Christians killing one another, when Europeans attacked Constantinople, capital of Eastern Christendom. Although Tarr's and Macavoy's satires of Christianity seem to come from outside that faith, Rice's years of researching Church history for her books has been radically ambivalent, compounding Roman Catholic devotion and existential atheism in shifting combinations ranging from blasphemy to piety.

In the 1980s, Orson Scott Card's first three volumes of his Alvin Maker series (*Seventh Son,* 1987; *Red Prophet,* 1988; and *Prentice Alvin,* 1989,) ridiculed various Christian denominations, but did so from his perspective as a dedicated member of the Church of Latter Days Saints. The primary model for Alvin's life was Joseph Smith, though in miracle-working powers, Alvin resembles Jesus. Despite satirizing some organized religions and excusing the practice of magic, the series is very Christian in its presentation of each person's spiritual gift (or, in frontier parlance, "knack"). What was new for historical fantasy in the Alvin Maker series was Card's large-scale interweaving of American frontier superstitions of the uneducated with actual history. This makes it (among other things) magical realism, even to its sympathy for the oppressed. The series is a monumental redoing of American history, so that the Native Americans retain a large territory, slavery is combated by magic, and the early American dream of founding a New Jerusalem is almost achieved. Although some other books during the 1980s, such as Mark Helprin's *Winter's Tale* (1982), a magical history of New York, or S.P. Somtow's *Moon Dance* (1989), a history of werewolves on a Native American reservation, play with portions of American history, the Alvin Maker series constitutes one of the grandest revisions.

The 1980s achieved so much in historical fantasy that its authors tended to extend their series thereafter, not always with much new. In **fantasy literature**, the great development of the 1990s and early twenty-first century was again British: the worldwide fad of Harry Potter, beginning with *Harry Potter and the Philosopher's* [or, in American editions, *Sorcerer's*] *Stone* (1997). That series, however, ridicules history (the class so dull that only hyper-intellectual Hermione Granger stays awake in it). One source of most characters' antipathy to the past may be its having been traumatic for them, as in Harry's literal scar, Ron's spider phobia, the effects of Lucius's bullying on his son Draco, Sirius's dreadful childhood memories, young Lupin's being bitten by a werewolf, the abandonment of Tom Riddle, and the commission of Neville's parents to an asylum. In book three (*Harry Potter and the Prisoner of Azkaban*, 1999), Lupin gives the children a charm to combat their phobias, by reimagining and deriding the feared person or animal. One exception to the unpopularity of history at Hogwarts is Kennilworthy Whisp's *Quidditch through the Ages* (published by Rowling in 2001 as part of Comic Relief) because it substitutes sports for the agonizing struggles of real history. In it, Rowling demonstrates through her parodies that she is a real student of history, but that is not quite the same as infusing her series with actual events and dates. Spurred by the popularity of Harry Potter, publishers promoted what seemed to them like it; thus, the resulting boom in fantasy literature did little to nurture the historical variety.

Trends and Themes. The chief legacy of Harry Potter has been an emphasis on children's literature, often in very extended series. Before Rowling, the only well-known heptalogy (seven-volume work) was C.S. Lewis's Narnia; today, more and more fantasies stretch themselves into vast sagas. Whereas the 1980s somewhat matured fantasy, the 1990s and early twenty-first century inspired more young people and adults to read children's books, which were admittedly becoming quite long, challenging, and complex but which were exempted by their primary audience from such subjects as explicit sexuality. Rather, the principal Harry Potter–like theme has been magical education, as in Patricia Wrede's Mairelon series (*Mairelon the Magician*, 1991; and *Magician's Ward*, 1997), where a nineteenth-century street waif rises to a position in the magical community. Libba Bray's *A Great and Terrible Beauty* (2005) and *Rebel Angels* (2005) have a 16-year-old psychic from India secretly learning to master her powers in a Victorian girl's school designed to teach propriety.

Advertised as "Harry Potter for adults," Susanna Clarke's *Jonathan Strange & Mr. Norrell* (2004) has also become a best seller in the United States. It presents magical education with enough real history to have taken her 10 years of research and enough invented history to fill notes that often occupy as much space as the main text. The book's central theme is a history simultaneously copious and parsimonious, analogous to modern Britain, preserving a rich past without quite managing prosperity. For Jonathan Strange, that situation occurs both with his miser father and with his mentor, Mr. Norrell, owner of most books on magic ever written yet reluctant to loan Strange any of them.

Whereas magical education and hyperrealism are trends particularly associated with the early twenty-first century, the themes of historical fantasy continue to be very traditional (usually more than one per volume): (1) the preternaturally old, (2) time slips (i.e., time travel by magic), (3) reincarnation, (4) old magical objects, and (5) secret histories. If there is any change in these themes, the difference is in an ever-increasing simplification of them to resemble popular formulae.

Even further in magical education from Harry Potter is Philip Pullman's His Dark Material series (*Northern Lights* [British edition] or *The Golden Compass* [American edition], 1995; *The Subtle Knife*, 1997; *The Amber Spyglass*, 2000). In this nineteenth-century-like England, each person's unconscious is imaged as an accompanying animal, which, according to Pullman's Web site, "is that part of you that helps you grow towards wisdom." In other words, the means of education is fantastic (a metaphor depicted as literal), but the result is ordinary. Not recognizing that such depiction is the norm in fantasy—historical or otherwise—Pullman has tended to deny that the series is "fantasy." Comparably, J.R.R. Tolkien and C.S. Lewis tended to deny that their Christian allegories were "allegories." Such a denial simply meant that, for their period, they were infusing the fantasy with more verisimilitude, as, with even higher standards, Pullman is doing now. Such an increasing emphasis on real details is a trend in every kind of fantasy and leads to expanding research in the historical variety.

For centuries, miraculously long-lived beings entered historical fantasy so that the author could philosophize on the human condition and give congruity to a vast stretch of time, as in George Sylvester Viereck's and Paul Eldridge's *My First Two Thousand Years: The Autobiography of the Wandering Jew* (1928). Now, more common is Karen Marie Moning's historical fantasy/romance *Kiss of the Highlander* (2001), where an American tourist awakens a handsome Scottish laird after his 500-year slumber and then takes him back to his century via a time slip (and not for philosophizing). Today, immortals commonly come in teams competing with one another to fit the adventure formula, as in Mercedes Lackey and Roberta Gellis's *This Scepter'd Isle* (2004), where elves fight over who will be the heir to Henry VIII. Last century, reincarnation was an uncommon idea in the West, requiring slow explanation, as in Rider Haggard's *She* (1887), but lately it not only is common in Western popular culture but also is reintroduced by Asian historical fantasy, such as Rumiko Takahashi's typical *manga Inu-Yasha* (2003–), where a teenage reincarnation of an ancient priestess takes a time slip to antiquity to team with an immortal demon in battles with other immortals. An archaeology of magical objects goes back at least to *Puck of Pook's Hill* but now is likely to come redolent of Indiana Jones, as with Alex Archer's Rogue Angel series (*Destiny*, 2006; *Solomon's,* 2006) and Kate Mosse's *Labyrinth* (2006). Alternatively, a magical object can link romances spread through centuries, as in Shana Abe's *The Last Mermaid* (2004). Traditionally, an author of a secret history had to remain mysterious about whether presumably skeptical readers should take supernatural events seriously, for example, Paul Féval's *The Vampire Countess* (1856). Today, conspiracy theories belong to genres of both factual and fictional literature; thus, in Archer's *Destiny* (2006) a field reporter for the cable series *Chasing History's Monsters* encounters the kind of religious conspiracy that has become a cliché, particularly since Dan Brown's extraordinarily popular **historical fiction**, *The Da Vinci Code* (2004).

Context and Issues. Particularly in the United States and Britain, the legacy of twenty-first-century terrorist attacks and wars in the Middle East has been a traumatized public, like Rowling's wizards under attack by Voldemort's death-eater terrorists. In direct response to the falling World Trade Towers, the historian Don LoCicero wrote *If Animals Could Speak: A 21st Century Fable Inspired by 9/11/2001* (2004). With the help of an actor pursued as a terrorist by the misguided American government, talking farm animals defend their home against developers.

Comparably, though for older readers, Brian K. Vaughan and Niko Henrichon's **comic book** *Pride of Baghdad* (2006) transforms the real escape of four zoo lions during the 2003 American-Iraqi war into a vehicle for discussing whether liberation can be forced on people or whether they must cooperate. The male lion's having two wives mirrors one Near Eastern tradition, while the lions' conversations with a tortoise occasion a long perspective on war in the region.

More commonly, however, authors have simply skewed their material slightly to reflect recent East–West relations, as with Kevin Crossley-Holland's Arthur trilogy (*The Seeing Stone*, 2001; *At the Crossing Places*, 2004; and *King of the Middle March*, 2006). Advertised for the Harry Potter market, the books likewise form a coming-of-age series—the first volume written before September 11, 2001. In it, the twelfth-century, teenage protagonist receives from Merlin a magic stone, which permits the boy to watch the adventures of his namesake King Arthur as a model while the lad traverses the "crossing place" of adolescence. In subsequent volumes, however, the disastrous Fourth Crusade looms more prominently, so that the protagonist must consider a question very prominent after 9/11: why Muslims and Christians fight one another.

Similarly, Elizabeth Kostova spent 10 years researching her best seller *The Historian* (2005), linked to even earlier memories of European jaunting with her raconteur father. Nonetheless, the finished version begins with a note remarking, "The glimpses of religious and territorial conflict between an Islamic East and a Judeo-Christian West will be painfully familiar to a modern reader" (xvi). Whereas this theme was common in the 1980s, it then usually occasioned a neo-pagan attack on Christianity. Probably because of 9/11, Crossley-Holland and Kostova handle the topic more evenly and gingerly, neither East nor West wholly to blame. With rich historical detail, Kostova portrays present (associated with the West) and past (associated with the East) as symbols for conscious and unconscious states of mind. Their relationship is either loving or sadomasochistic (i.e., based on either equality or dominance). Dracula, who learned evil from both East and West, personifies such sadomasochistic dominance, particularly in his lust for impaling and vampirism. This is to say he personifies a Western (conscious) mind fighting against the Eastern (unconscious), which seduces him into imitating it; he thus exemplifies self-division. All of the major characters are historians, whose potentially pure love for the past risks deterioration into a perversion. The way to escape this fall is a willingness to change and mature (contrasted with the seemingly immutable Dracula, given that his warping occurred before the narrative began). As Kostova reveals in an interview appended to the novel, she deliberately begins the book in the voice of a sheltered 16-year-old, so that her maturing (and that of the older but reclusive other voices) comes "through exposure to evil" (3). As a repository of foul memories, history therefore holds the place it has since 9/11: a guide away from childish naivety and thus, potentially, a teacher of mature love.

The Australian author of children's books Gillian Rubinstein (writing as Lian Hearn) addresses an equally disturbing 9/11 question: what if one is raised by terrorists? In her Otori series (*Across the Nightingale Floor,* 2002; *Grass for his Pillow,* 2003; *Brilliance of the Moon,* 2004; *Cry of the Heron,* 2006), young Takeo, despite his moral qualms, is expected to use such magical powers as invisibility for the profession of the "Tribe," a ninja-like group of spies and assassins. Rubinstein's pseudonym, Hearn, recalls the late-nineteenth-century essayist Lafcadio Hearn, whose works did much to introduce Japanese culture to America, but in a mannered, not entirely authentic manner. Consequently, her choice of the name is inherently apologetic, a recognition that Western appropriation of the East is controversial. Indeed, Near Eastern terrorists have presented themselves as defenders of Asia against various forms of appropriation.

Reception. Although "historical fantasy" is a marketing category briefly glossed in such works as Brian Stableford's *Historical Dictionary of Fantasy Literature* (2005), it is not a genre that has received much scholarly attention as such. Perhaps because major authors tend to wander in and out of its boundaries, it tends to be clumped with genres tangential to it: historical fiction, high fantasy, horror, or **romance novels.** This, however, does not mean that it is either rare or unrewarded.

Like those genres that border it, historical fantasy books often have screen versions, such as *Interview with the Vampire* (1994), a large-budget production that offers a somewhat moralistic simplification of the far-more amoral book. Rubinstein has received millions from Universal for the film rights to her Otori series. According to Borys Kit (*The Reporter,* September 12, 2006), Peter Jackson has optioned Naomi Novik's Temeraire series, which begins with *His Majesty's Dragon* (2006), about a corps of talking dragons during the Napoleonic wars. Naturally, many of the cinematic adaptations of historical fantasy are made for television, such as the 2001 miniseries of *The Mists of Avalon* on TNT.

Typical of historical fantasies adapted into films, Alan Moore and Kevin O'Neill's comic book series *The League of Extraordinary Gentlemen* (2000) was simplified significantly to become the 2003 movie of the same name. The original abounds in jokes about the lives of Moore and O'Neill, both shown in nineteenth-century garb on the back cover, the latter as an unconscious drunk. Stereotypically, the movie begins with the League run by a gallant Alan Quartermain. In humorous contrast to its title, the original series begins with the League run by its one woman member, whereas its Quartermain is almost completely incapacitated by opium addiction. In other words, the balance between conservative and liberal, though common in written historical fantasy, tends to tip toward the conservative in cinematic adaptations.

Selected Authors. Aside from those formulaic writers not worth treating anywhere, the authors of historical fantasy tend to be as original as erudite and move from genre to genre, and thus many are found in other sections of this encyclopedia as well. Although obviously there is not room to treat all historical fantasists here, six may stand as representatives of the various types: Orson Scott Card, Stephen King, Neil Gaiman, Anne Rice, Diana Paxson, and Judith Tarr.

A major figure with a largely American focus, Orson Scott Card has through his Alvin Maker series provided a major rethinking of Joseph Smith's nineteenth century, a world of angels and other supernatural forces, where Card can play out the tensions between his conservative politics and his imaginative empathy with people of all sorts. One of the primary voices in the series is the real British poet William Blake, an extreme liberal (if not radical) and thus a challenge for Card to integrate into his conservative worldview, which he does with his own version of Blake as an American. In addition to the Alvin Maker series, Card has also contributed to historical fantasy through his *Enchantment* (1999), a retelling of Sleeping Beauty in a relatively realistic, tenth-century Russian setting. A modern, American Jewish graduate student finds himself in the middle ages, when Christianity and paganism warred. Naturally, Card is more sympathetic to the Christian side than are neopagan authors, but he also includes virtuous Jewish characters, just as his Alvin Maker series evidences religious sympathy for Native Americans (perhaps because the Book of Mormon alleges their descent from various peoples mentioned in the Bible). Critical studies of Card include Michael Collings's *In the Image of God: Theme, Characterization, and Landscape in the Fiction of Orson Scott Card* (1990), Collings's *Storyteller: The Official Orson Scott Card Bibliography and Guide* (2001), and Edith Tyson's *Orson Scott Card: Writer of the Terrible Choice* (2003). Often compared to C.S. Lewis as a Christian apologist and to Stephen King as a depicter of gritty reality, Card has been a teacher of creative writing whose own *How to Write Science Fiction and Fantasy* (1990) is also useful as a guide to his work.

Although Stephen King writes primarily within the horror genre, his most important work to date, the seven-volume Dark Tower series, takes places in multiple universes, including ours. The real-world setting includes so many historical allusions that Robin Furth's concordance to the series devotes four pages of continuous type just to listing those allusions in volumes 5 through 7 (Furth 2005, vol. 2, 433–436). This large real history interweaves with the vast history of other worlds and characters from several of King's best-known novels. In its final form, the series is King's attempt to pull his life together after a hit-and-run accident almost destroyed it. Based on a long interview with King when he was just beginning his Dark Tower series, Douglas Winter's *Stephen King: The Art of Darkness* (1986) offers a meticulous, uncontroversial presentation of facts up to that time. For discussion of the later part of King's career, see Furth's *Stephen King's The Dark Tower: A Concordance* (2003–2005) and Michael Collings's *Stephen King Is Richard Bachman* (2007).

Although Card, King, and Gaiman all depict the graphically repugnant and teach comparable morals, Gaiman—a secularized Jewish, British American—is even more of an outsider than the others and perhaps thus less prone to stereotypes. For King, the unconscious, imaged usually as some horror working its way throughout history, tends to be a place of barely repressed violence and guilt. For Card, the unconscious can connect one to either the diabolical or the divine. For Gaiman, conscious and unconscious form a continuum, shading one into another, frightening and beautiful at once. His Sandman series was his training in historical fantasy, which has since assumed various forms, notably the subterranean London detritus of *Neverwhere* (1998), the melting pot of mythologies in *American Gods* (2002) and *Anansi Boys* (2006), and the fairy-tale, nineteenth-century ambience of *Stardust* (2001). Studies of his work include Stephen Rauch's *Neil Gaiman's "The Sandman" and Joseph Campbell: In Search of the Modern Myth* (2003) and Joe Sanders's *The Sandman Papers: An Exploration of the Sandman Mythology* (2006).

Even further from traditional morality than Gaiman (despite her loudly announced return to Christianity), Anne Rice's books are the antithesis of King's tendency to frighten people into principles. For her supernaturals, evil is an unavoidable and therefore forgivable sadomasochism, often with blasphemous associations, as when the pharaoh usually considered the villain of Exodus is treated as a hero (in *The Mummy or Ramses the Damned*, 1991), when Lestat drinks blood flowing from the crucified Christ (in *Memnoch the Devil,* 1997), or when the young Jesus finds himself miraculously murdering his playmates at the opening of *Christ the Lord: Out of Egypt* (2005). Lushly described and often well researched, exotic historical settings are her ways of evoking erotic aspects of the unconscious. Written in close cooperation with Rice, three particularly useful books on her are Katherine Ramsland's *Prism of the Night: A Biography of Anne Rice* (1994), *The Vampire Companion* (1995), and *The Witches' Companion* (1996), treating the Mayfair witches, whose saga interweaves with the Vampire Chronicles.

Diana Paxson deserves mention as one of the most prominent voices of neo-paganism in historical fantasy. Whereas Paxson's friend Marion Zimmer Bradley was a priest of a Pre-Nicene Catholic Church (which presented a common ground between Christianity and paganism), Paxson has been more closely connected to Norse pagan traditions, as with her how-to book *Taking Up the Runes: A Complete Guide to Using Runes in Spells, Rituals, Divination, and Magic* (2005). Perhaps best known for her postapocalyptic Westria series of high fantasy, she is also prolific in historical fantasy, with series on the Nibelungen and Arthurian legends, the latter close enough to *Mists of Avalon* so that she collaborated with Bradley in writing the prequel to it, *Priestess of Avalon* (2001), which Paxson finished after Bradley's death in 1999. Since then, Paxson has continued the series. According to a 1989 interview with Raymond H. Thompson, Paxson saw her Arthuriana as more historically accurate than Bradley's, in that Paxson has been researching tirelessly since her graduate-school days in order to combine high verisimilitude with occult theories. For further information on her life and writings, see the Gale Reference Team's online biography of her, and for Paxson's cultural context, see Eric Davis's and Michael Rauner's *The Visionary State: A Journey Through California's Spiritual Landscape* (2006).

To date, Judith Tarr has found time amid her output in other genres (some under such pseudonyms as Caitlin Brennan) for 13 historical fantasies. The quality of her writing ranges from excellent to formulaic, and she is better at characterization than plotting. At her best, however, she has helped to shape the genre, by finding new ways to reconcile fantasy with history. Her Hound and Falcon series demonstrated how invented, magical characters could be interpolated into famous events as alleged advisors to the great. Her Norman series (beginning with *Rite of Conquest,* 2004) showed how to make the famous themselves wizards—what she does to William the Conqueror and his wife Matilda. According to Tarr's Web site, her primary interest seems to be raising Lipizzans, with prolific authorship paying the bills. In a posting on Amazon.com, she has explained that she writes under various names because bookstores stock fewer and fewer of her works, given that their sales are average rather than outstanding. Thomson Gale has a biography of her, and she is mentioned from time to time in such journals as *Mythlore* (e.g., Kondratiev 1989, 53, 57). At her less spectacular, however, her situation resembles that of those countless historical fantasists who rewrite the past prolifically without astronomical remuneration.

Bibliography

Abé, Shana. *The Last Mermaid.* New York: Bantam, 2004.
Aiken, Joan. *The Wolves of Willoughby Chase.* Garden City, NY: Doubleday, 1962.
Archer, Alex. *Destiny.* Pahrump, NV: Golden Eagle, 2006.
———. *Solomon's Jar.* Pahrump, NV: Golden Eagle, 2006.

Beckford, William. *Vathek*. Dublin: Nonsuch, 2006. Originally published 1786.

Borges, Jorge Louis. *Historia universal de la infamia*. Buenos Aires: Emece Editores, 2005. Originally published 1935.

————. *Labyrinths: Selected Stories and Other Writings*. Donald A. Yates and James E. Irby, eds. New York: New Directions, 1962.

Bryson, Bernarda. *Gilgamesh*. New York: Henry Holt, 1967.

Card, Orson Scott. *Alvin Journeyman*. New York: Tor, 1995 [Alvin Maker 4].

————. *Crystal City*. New York: Tor, 2003 [Alvin Maker 6].

————. *Enchantment*. New York: Del Rey, 1999.

————. *Heartfire*. New York: Tor, 1998 [Alvin Maker 5].

————. *How to Write Science Fiction and Fantasy*. Cincinnati, OH: Writers' Digest, 1990.

————. *Prentice Alvin*. New York: Tor, 1989 [Alvin Maker 3].

————. *Red Prophet*. New York: Tor, 1988 [Alvin Maker 2].

————. *Seventh Son*. New York: Tor, 1987 [Alvin Maker 1].

Chapman, Vera. *Arthur's Daughter*. New York: Avon, 1978.

————. *The Green Knight*. New York: Avon, 1975.

————. *The King's Damosel*. London: Avon, 1978.

Clarke, Susanna. *Jonathan Strange & Mr. Norrell*. New York: Bloomsbury, 2004.

Collings, Michael. *In the Image of God: Theme, Characterization, and Landscape in the Fiction of Orson Scott Card*. Contributions to the Study of Science Fiction and Fantasy. Westport, CT: Greenwood, 1990.

————. *Stephen King Is Richard Bachman*. Hiram, GA: Overlook Connections, 2007.

Davis, Eric, and Michael Rauner. *The Visionary State: A Journey through California's Spiritual Landscape*. San Francisco: Chronicle, 2006.

Dawson, Carley. *Dragon Run*. New York: Houghton Mifflin, 1955.

————. *Mr. Wicker's Window*. New York: Houghton Mifflin, 1952.

————. *Sign of the Seven Seas*. New York: Houghton Mifflin, 1954.

Eager, Edward. *Half Magic*. New York: Harcourt, Brace, 1954.

————. *Knight's Castle*. New York: Harcourt, Brace, 1956.

————. *Magic by the Lake*. New York: Harcourt, Brace, 1957.

————. *The Time Garden*. San Diego, CA: Harcourt Brace, 1999. Originally published 1958.

Féval, Paul. *The Vampire Countess*. Translated by Brian Stableford. Sherman Oaks, CA: Black Coat Press, 2003.

Frost, Lauri. *Elements of His Dark Material*. New York: Fell, 2006.

Furth, Robin. *Stephen King's The Dark Tower: A Concordance*. 2 Vols. New York: Scribner, 2003–2005.

Gaiman, Neil, Michal Zull, Jon J. Muth, and Charles Vess. *The Wake*. Sandman, Book 10. New York: Vertigo, 1999.

Gale Reference Team. "Tarr, Judith (1955–)." *Contemporary Authors Online*. December 2007. http://www.amazon.com/Biography-Judith-1955-Contemporary-Authors/dp/B0007SFN98/sr=8-26/qid=1168054089/ref=sr_1_26/002-3699287-7913633?ie=UTF8&s=books.

————. "Paxson, Diana Lucile (1943–)." *Contemporary Authors Online*. December 2007. http://www.amazon.com/Biography-Paxson-Diana-Contemporary-Authors/dp/B0007SHLB6/sr=1-8/qid=1166315377/ref=sr_1_8/104-6733110-3468700?ie=UTF8&s=books.

Garcia Marquez, Gabriel. *Cien años de soledad*. Buenos Aires: Editorial Sudamericana, 1967.

Grundy, Stephan. *Gilgamesh*. New York: William Morrow, 2000.

Haggard, Rider. *She*. Oxford: Oxford University Press, 1998. Originally published 1887.

Helprin, Mark. *Winter's Tale*. New York: Harvest, 1982.

King, Stephen. *The Dark Tower*. New Hampshire: Donald M. Grant/Scribner, 2004 [Dark Tower VII].

————. *The Drawing of the Three*. New York: Plume-Penguin, 1989 [Dark Tower 2].

————. *The Gunslinger.* New York: Plume-Penguin, 2003, rev. ed. Originally published 1987 [Dark Tower I].

————. *Song of Susannah.* New Hampshire: Donald M. Grant/ Scribner, 2004 [Dark Tower 6].

————. *The Waste-Lands.* New York: Plume Penguin, 1993 [Dark Tower 3].

————. *Wizard and Glass.* New York: Plume-Penguin, 1997 [Dark Tower 4].

————. *Wolves of the Calla.* New Hampshire: Donald M. Grant/Scribner, 2003 [Dark Tower 5].

Kit, Borys. "Lord of Fantasy: Jackson Eyeing 'Temeraire.'" *Hollywood Reporter,* September 2006. http://www.hollywoodreporter.com/hr/search/article_display.jsp?vnu_content_id=1003120747.

Kondratiev, Alexei. "Tales Newly Told: A Column on Current Fantasy." *Mythlore: A Journal of J.R.R. Tolkien, C.S. Lewis, Charles Williams, and the Genres of Myth and Fantasy Studies* 16.1 (1989): 53, 57.

Kostova, Elizabeth. *The Historian.* New York: Little, Brown, 2005.

Kwitney, Alisa. *The Sandman: King of Dreams.* San Francisco: Chronicle, 2003.

Lackey, Mercedes, and Roberta Gellis. *This Scepter'd Isle.* New York: Baen, 2004.

Lewis, Matthew. *The Monk.* Oxford: Oxford University Press, 2002. Originally published 1796.

Macavoy, R.A. *Damiano.* New York: Bantam, 1983.

————. *Damiano's Flute.* New York: Bantam, 1984.

————. *Raphael.* New York: Bantam, 1984.

Mackenzie, Donald. "Introduction." *Puck of Pook's Hill and Rewards and Fairies,* by Rudyard Kipling. Donald Mackenzie, ed. Oxford: Oxford University Press, 1993.

Maier, John. "Introduction." *Gilgamesh.* Translated from the Sin-leqi-unninni version by John Gardner and John Maier, with the assistance of Richard A. Henshaw. New York: Vintage Books, 1984.

Moning, Karen Marie. *Beyond the Highland Mist.* New York: Dell, 1999.

————. *Kiss of the Highlander.* New York: Dell, 2001.

Norton, Mary. *Bedknob and Broomstick: A Combined Edition of "The Magic Bed-Knob" and "Bonfires and Broomsticks."* New York: Harcourt, Brace, 1957.

Pearce, Phillippa. *Tom's Midnight Garden.* Oxford: Oxford University Press, 1998.

Pratt, Fletcher, and L. Sprague de Camp. *The Incomplete Enchanter.* New York: Prime, 1940; HarperCollins, 1958.

Pullman, Philip. "About the Writing." Philip Pullman's Web site. Retrieved December 2006 from http://www.philip-pullman.com/about_the_writing.asp.

————. *The Amber Spyglass.* New York: Scholastic, 2000 [His Dark Materials 3].

————. *The Golden Compass.* New York: Scholastic, 1995 [His Dark Materials 1].

————. *The Subtle Knife.* New York: Scholastic, 1997 [His Dark Materials 2].

Ramsland, Katherine. *Prism of the Night: A Biography of Anne Rice.* New York: Plume, 1994, rev. ed.

————. *The Vampire Companion.* New York: Ballantine, 1995.

————. *The Witches' Companion.* New York: Ballantine, 1996.

Rauch, Stephen. *Neil Gaiman's "The Sandman" and Joseph Campbell: In Search of the Modern Myth.* Rockville, MD: Wildside Press, 2003.

Rice, Anne. *Christ the Lord: Out of Egypt.* New York: Fawcett, 2006.

————. *Complete Vampire Chronicles (Interview with the Vampire, The Vampire L'Estat, The Queen of the Damned, The Tale of the Body Thief).* New York: Ballantine, 1993.

————. *The Anne Rice Collection: The Mayfair Witches—3 Titles—Witching Hour—Lasher—Taltos.* New York: Ballantine, 2001.

————. *Memnoch the Devil.* New York: Ballantine, 1997 [Vampire Chronicles 5].

————. *The Mummy.* New York: Ballantine, 1991.

Rowling, J.K. (writing as Kennilworthy Whisp). *Quidditch through the Ages.* New York: Scholastic, 2001.

Saltzman, Mark. *The Laughing Sutra.* New York: Vintage, 1991.

Sanders, Joe. *The Sandman Papers: An Exploration of the Sandman Mythology.* Seattle, WA: Fantagraphics, 2006.

Somtow, S.P. *Moon Dance.* New York: Tor, 1989.

Spenser, Edmund. *The Fairie Queene.* New York: Penguin, 1979. Originally published 1590–1609.

Stableford, Brian. *Historical Dictionary of Fantasy Literature.* New York: Scarecrow, 2005.

Takahashi, Rumiko. *Inu-Yasha.* Vol. 1. San Francisco: Viz Media, 2003.

Tarr, Judith. *The Golden Horn.* New York: Bluejay, 1985.

———. *The Hounds of God.* New York: Bluejay, 1986.

———. *The Isle of Glass.* New York: Bluejay, 1985.

———. *Judith Tarr's Brand New Shiny Home Page.* Accessed February 2006 at http://www.sff.net/people/judith-tarr.

———. Posting on Amazon.com. Retrieved December 2006 from http://www.amazon.com/Rite-Conquest-Judith-Tarr/dp/B000BTH508/sr=1-1/qid=1167168206/ref=pd_bbs_sr_1/002-3699287-7913633?ie=UTF8&s=books.

———. *Rite of Conquest.* New York: Bluejay, 2004.

Thompson, Raymond H. "Interview with Diana Paxson." *Interviews with Authors of Modern Arthurian Literature.* July 1989. http://www.lib.rochester.edu/camelot/intrvws/paxson.htm.

Twain, Mark. *A Connecticut Yankee in King Arthur's Court.* Berkeley: University of California Press, 2002. Originally published 1886.

Tyson, Edith. *Orson Scott Card: Writer of the Terrible Choice.* Scarecrow Studies in Young Adult Literature, 10. Lanham, MD: Scarecrow, 2003.

Uttley, Alison. *A Traveler in Time.* London: Faber and Faber, 1939.

Vansittart, Peter. *Parsifal: A Novel.* London: Peter Owen, 1988.

Vaughan, Brian K., and Niko Henrichon. *Pride of Baghdad.* New York: Vertigo, 2006.

Viereck, George Sylvester, and Paul Eldridge. *My First Two Thousand Years: The Autobiography of the Wandering Jew.* New York: Sheridan House, 2001. Originally published 1928.

Vizenor, Gerald. *Griever: An American Monkey in China.* Minneapolis: University of Minnesota Press, 1987.

Wrede, Patricia. *Magician's Ward.* New York: Tor, 1997.

———. *Mairelon the Magician.* New York: Tor, 1991.

Wu, Ch'eng-en [attributed]. *Journey to the West.* 4 vols. Translated by Anthony Yu. Chicago: University of Chicago Press, 1952–1983.

Zelazny, Roger. *Nine Princes in Amber.* New York: Avon, 1970.

JAMES WHITLARK

HISTORICAL FICTION

Definition. Historical fiction is fiction that is set, completely or in large part, in the past. The past in question must be historical from the author's point of view—that is, a novel written during the 1930s about the Great Depression is not historical; one written in the twenty-first century is. There is no universal agreement on how far in the past a novel's setting must be to be considered historical, but common usage of the term suggests a gap of several decades. The Historical Novel Society, for instance, defines historical fiction as being at least 50 years in the past and specifies that the work be done from research, not from the memory of the author.

The term *historical fiction* is most often used for works where the historical setting is crucial to the action, not simply incidental. Some historical fiction is concerned with famous people and events, and many works incorporate real historical figures as characters. Other works focus on more ordinary people and purely fictional characters. Most writers of historical fiction try to portray history accurately,

As fiction closely related to reality, historical fiction is sometimes associated with documentary fiction and the nonfiction novel. As narrative about the past, historical fiction shares characteristics with **historical nonfiction, biography**, and **autobiography and memoir**. And because almost any genre can be set in the past, historical fiction overlaps with many other kinds of fiction: **romance novels, science fiction, time travel fiction, mystery fiction**, thrillers, **western literature, adventure fiction, Christian fiction**, and **fantasy literature**. Historical fiction is a thriving area in **children's** and **young adult literature** and a small but growing subset of **graphic novels**.

incorporating factual information about known people and events and creating fictional characters who live plausibly in the era they inhabit. Still, historical fiction, like all fiction, requires invention. Writers of historical fiction frequently extrapolate from what is known, invent inner lives and daily details for historical figures, imaginatively fill in gaps in the historical record, and illuminate what might have been.

Some historical fiction intentionally alters or plays with history. Postmodern historical fiction questions the notions of historical truth and linear narrative. Alternate histories present a counterfactual world: what might have happened if some event in history had been different. Another form of historical fiction closely related to science fiction is the time-slip or time travel fiction, in which characters—by accident or design—find themselves transported to another historical time. Other historical novels revise or reimagine previous literary works—altering endings, creating sequels, or inventing lives for previously minor characters.

Historical fiction often connects the present and past or links historical periods, sometimes by including multiple times in different threads of the narrative. Historical novels frequently suggest ideas about the importance of the past, the effect of the past on the present, and the nature of history itself.

History. The first wildly successful and popular historical novels read by Americans were written by the British writer Sir Walter Scott (1771–1832), whose 1814 novel *Waverly* inspired generations of readers and historical novelists. Year after year, Scott's historical romances were among the best-selling books in the United States. By the 1820s and 1830s, with Scott's great popularity, a proliferation of American historical societies, and talk swirling of American literary independence, it is not surprising that there was demand to "let us have our own *Waverly*" (Hart 1950, 79). One of the first novelists to apply was James Fenimore Cooper (1789–1851), whose book *The Spy* (1821) was set during the American Revolution. Cooper followed with a series of five historical frontier novels, entitled *The Leatherstocking Tales* featuring Natty Bumppo—*The Pioneers* (1823), *The Last of the Mohicans* (1826), *The Prairie* (1827), *The Pathfinder* (1840), and *The Deerslayer* (1841)—and did indeed join Scott on the best-seller lists.

Cooper's historical themes—the American fight for independence, the rugged outdoorsman in the wilderness, and the encounter of settlers with Native Americans—also preoccupied other historical novelists of the early nineteenth century. According to James Hart, in the 1820s "almost a third of the novels written by Americans dealt with the colonial period or the Revolution" (1950, 80). Among the novels exploring contact between colonists and Native Americans were *Hope Leslie* (1827) by Catherine Maria Sedgwick (1789–1867) and *Hobomok* (1824) by Lydia Maria Child (1802–1880). Some of the most popular historical novels of the 1830s were the American Revolution novel *Horse-Shoe Robinson* (1835) by John Pendleton Kennedy (1795–1870); *The Yemassee* (1835) by William Gilmore Simms (1806–1870), an account of Native American wars in colonial South Carolina; *The Green Mountain Boys* (1839) by Daniel Pierce Thompson (1795–1868), a novel of colonial Vermont and the American Revolution; and the wilderness romance *Nick of the Woods* (1837) by Robert Montgomery Bird (1806–1854).

Some of the most respected authors of the middle and late nineteenth century wrote historical novels. Nathaniel Hawthorne's (1804–1864) *The Scarlet Letter* (1850) is set two centuries in the past, examining Puritan society and the relationship of the past to the present. Harriet Beecher Stowe (1811–1896), while most famous for her contemporary work *Uncle Tom's Cabin* (1852), also wrote an historical novel set in the eighteenth century, *The Minister's Wooing* (1859). Herman Melville (1819–1891), author of *Moby-Dick* (1851), wrote an historical novel about an American Revolution hero, *Israel Potter: His Fifty Years of Exile* (1855).

Mark Twain's (1835–1910) best-known book, *Huckleberry Finn* (1884), is a prime example of a work that challenges the definition of historical fiction. While the setting is within Twain's lifetime, the novel is set several decades in the past during a very different historical time, and the historical setting is integral to the plot and meaning of the novel. Twain's novel, *A Connecticut Yankee in King Arthur's Court* (1889), is an early example of both time slip and alternate history fiction, as the protagonist, a contemporary man, mysteriously finds himself in sixth-century England and immediately begins changing history. And a lesser-known work by Twain, *Personal Recollections of Joan of Arc* (1896), is a forerunner of a popular contemporary trend: a novel presented as memoir or biography—in this case a fictional "translation" of a nonexistent account by Joan of Arc's secretary.

The most popular historical novel of the late nineteenth century was *Ben-Hur* (1880), written by Lew Wallace (1807–1905), a politician and former Union Army general. Set in Palestine and Rome during the time of Christ, the book became one of the great best sellers in American history and a cultural phenomenon: "an edition was issued under the sponsorship of the Holy See and another was put out in a printing of a million copies by Sears, Roebuck. Probably no other American novel has had either of these distinctions; certainly none has had both" (Hart 1950, 164).

The Civil War inspired a new generation of historical fiction in the late nineteenth and early twentieth centuries, and Civil War fiction has been one of the predominant forms of American historical fiction ever since. *The Red Badge of Courage* (1895) by Stephen Crane (1871–1900) presents the war from the point of view of a new recruit seeing battles and death for the first time. The early twentieth century saw Civil War and Reconstruction novels by a wide range of writers, including Thomas Dixon (1864–1946), Ellen Glasgow (1873–1945), and William Faulkner (1897–1962). Regional historical fiction was also popular around the turn of the century, especially novels of the Old South and of the West. Owen Wister's (1860–1938) *The Virginian* (1901) became a best seller and set the model for many western historical novels to come, and throughout the first third of the century, Zane Grey (1872–1939) published one western after another, remaining almost continuously on the best-seller lists.

In the first half of the twentieth century, historical fiction was both popular and critically acclaimed. Thornton Wilder (1897–1975) published *The Bridge of San Luis Rey* (1927), the story of the community affected by a bridge disaster in eighteenth-century Peru. The most popular book of 1928, *The Bridge of San Luis*

Rey won the 1928 Pulitzer Prize for Fiction. *Anthony Adverse,* the sprawling pica-resque tale of a hero wandering through Europe, was published by Hervey Allen (1889–1949) in 1933. Margaret Mitchell (1900–1949) created even more of a cul-tural phenomenon with her Civil War saga *Gone with the Wind* (1936), which became one of the all-time best sellers and won the 1937 Pulitzer Prize for Fiction. Kathleen Winsor (1919–2003) also created a sensation with her 1944 historical romance of Restoration England, *Forever Amber,* which was widely popular in spite of, or perhaps because of, its racy reputation.

In the second half of the twentieth century, several novelists achieved popular suc-cess with wide-ranging historical epics or family sagas. James Michener (1907–1997) published many best-selling historical novels, often covering hundreds or even thou-sands of years and usually focused on a particular place. *Hawaii* (1958); *The Source* (1965), spanning 12,000 years of Middle East history; *Centennial* (1974), on the his-tory of Colorado; *Chesapeake* (1978); *The Covenant* (1980), covering 15 centuries in South Africa; *Poland* (1983); *Texas* (1985); *Alaska* (1988); *Caribbean* (1989); and *Mexico* (1992) all follow this approach. Howard Fast (1914–2003) wrote several novels about the American Revolution, including *Citizen Tom Paine* (1943), and was the author of *Spartacus* (1950), the novel about a Roman slave rebellion that became the basis of the acclaimed 1960 film. Fast also completed a six-volume saga titled *The Immigrants,* which follows one family through most of the twentieth century. John Jakes (1932–) has published several series of historical novels, frequently centered on a particular family. The Kent Family Chronicles, eight novels published from 1974 to 1980, trace one family's adventures from the American Revolution through the nineteenth century. The North and South trilogy—*North and South* (1982), *Love and War* (1984), and *Heaven and Hell* (1987)—follows two families through several gen-erations, culminating with the Civil War and Reconstruction. Among his many other books, Jakes has also published a two-volume saga of an immigrant family, *Homeland* (1993) and *American Dreams* (1998); *California Gold* (1989), set in the late nineteenth century; and *Charleston* (2002), a work spanning several generations in South Carolina.

Gore Vidal (1925–), a significant late twentieth-century writer, is best known as an historical novelist for his seven-volume American Chronicles series, beginning with *Washington D.C.* (1967), which covers 1937 to 1952. Vidal followed with *Burr* (1973), presenting an alternate view of the founding fathers; *1876* (1976); *Lincoln* (1984); *Empire* (1987) and *Hollywood* (1990), both set in the early twentieth century; and *The Golden Age* (2000), completing the narrative from 1939 to the present. Among his many other novels, Vidal has written two historical novels set in the ancient world, *Julian* (1964) and *Creation* (1981), and a time-travel historical novel, *The Smithsonian Institution* (1998), based in 1939.

The authors of **African American literature** figures prominently in late twentieth-cen-tury historical fiction. As Keith Byerman notes, "while there has been an interest in his-torical narrative as long as blacks have been writing fiction, this is the first generation to make it the dominant mode" (2005, 1). *Jubilee* (1966) by Margaret Walker (1915–1998) was one of the first and best novels to tell the story of slavery and eman-cipation from a female point of view. Alice Walker (1944–) focused on the lives and voices of black women in the early twentieth century in her Pulitzer Prize–winning *The Color Purple* (1982). Portraying two historical women, one black and one white, *Dessa Rose* (1986), by Sherley Anne Williams (1944–1999), is frequently seen as a response to *The Confessions of Nat Turner* (1968) by William Styron (1925–2006).

David Bradley (1950–) based *The Chaneysville Incident* (1981), winner of the PEN/Faulkner Award, on a historian's quest to document a tragedy. In his 1982 novel, *Oxherding Tale,* Charles Johnson (1948–) combines new versions of slave narrative and picaresque adventure; in his 1990 novel *Middle Passage,* he uses a similar melding of genres to tell the story of a stowaway on an 1830 slave ship; in *Dreamer* (1998), Johnson imagines a double for Martin Luther King Jr. All three novels mix fact and fiction, storytelling and philosophy. Nobel Prize winner Toni Morrison (1931–) has written several historical novels, including *Beloved* (1987), *Jazz* (1992), and *Paradise* (1998). *Beloved,* set after the Civil War but entwined with prewar memories and the nature of memory itself, won the Pulitzer Prize; in 2006 the *New York Times* named it the best novel of the last 25 years.

Several novelists associated with the late twentieth century's postmodern movement have written historical novels that challenge the notion of a firm boundary— or perhaps any boundary at all—between fact and fiction. Postmodern writers express skepticism about the possibility of stable knowledge or representation, frequently using techniques such as self-referentiality, unconventional narrative structure, and mixtures of genres, pastiche, and parody. *The Sot-Weed Factor* (1960) by John Barth (1930–) is a metafictional mock epic of the founding of Maryland, a work purportedly written by Ebenezer Cook—the name of a real poet who did write a poem called "The Sot-Weed Factor." In *Gravity's Rainbow* (1973), Thomas Pynchon (1937–) uses the historical moment of World War II to build a complex allusive narrative that has challenged a generation of readers. His 1997 novel *Mason & Dixon* is a saga dense with allusions, anachronism, and complexity, as the two surveyors journey through eighteenth-century America. In *Against the Day* (2006), Pynchon turns to the late nineteenth and early twentieth centuries, again marshalling a wide array of characters, ideas, and moments. Among Don DeLillo's (1936–) many novels, two stand out for their use of history and interweaving of fact and fiction: *Libra* (1988), an alternate version of President Kennedy's assassination, centered on Lee Harvey Oswald, and *Underworld* (1997), a novel of the Cold War, baseball, and the threat of nuclear war.

In his essay "False Documents," E.L. Doctorow (1931–) contends that "there is no fiction or non-fiction as we commonly understand the distinction: there is only narrative" (1983, 26). Whether considered postmodern or not, much historical fiction of the late twentieth and early twenty-first centuries blends fact and fiction, interweaves multiple narratives, and challenges conventional notions of time, memory, and truth.

Trends and Themes (Since 2000). In the twenty-first century, while historical fiction has covered a wide range of focuses and approaches, certain trends are notable.

Historical fiction is frequently set in periods of tumult, such as wars and disasters, or in a time period one or two generations before the author's life. Many recent historical novels are set during the Civil War or World War II, with a smaller number set in the American Revolution and World War I.

Jeff Shaara (1952–) covers the span of the American Revolutionary period from 1770 to its conclusion in two best-selling novels, *Rise to Rebellion* (2001) and *The Glorious Cause* (2002). Former President Jimmy Carter (1924–) published an historical novel, *The Hornet's Nest* (2003), focusing on the American Revolution in 1770s Georgia, and Robert Morgan (1944–) sets *Brave Enemies* (2003), with its runaway cross-dressing heroine, in North Carolina in the same era.

In three Civil War novels—*The Black Flower* (1997), *The Year of Jubilo* (2000), and *The Judas Field* (2006)—Howard Bahr (1946–) describes the experience of ordinary soldiers in Mississippi and Tennessee. Also focusing on the South is James Lee Burke (1936–) in his Louisiana novel *White Doves at Morning* (2002). Charles Frazier uses the Odyssey as his model for portraying a soldier's journey home in *Cold Mountain* (1997), a phenomenal best seller and winner of the National Book Award. *In the Fall* (2000) by Jeffrey Lent, *The Night Inspector* (1999) by Frederick Busch (1941–2006), and *Paradise Alley* (2002) by Kevin Baker (1958–) all focus on the war's effect on ordinary people. The Pulitzer Prize winner *March* (2005) by Geraldine Brooks (1955–) and the PEN/Faulkner winner *The March* (2005) by E.L. Doctorow each follow one famous person, the fictional Mr. March of *Little Women* and the historical General Sherman, respectively. Jeff Shaara's *Gods and Generals* (1996) and *The Last Full Measure* (1998) paint a broad, action-filled picture of the war before and after Gettysburg—together with *The Killer Angels* (1974) by Shaara's father Michael Shaara (1928–88), these novels form a Civil War trilogy.

Two notable World War I novels are Jeff Shaara's *To the Last Man: A Novel of the First World War* (2004) and John Rolfe Gardiner's epistolary tale of an American doctor, *Somewhere in France* (1999). Many more recent historical novels have focused on World War II, either the war itself or its effects on the home front. *A World Away* (1998) by Stewart O'Nan (1961–), the alternate history *The Plot Against America* (2004) by Philip Roth (1933–), and Gore Vidal's *The Golden Age* are all set in the United States, depicting the war's effects on families as well as its effects on national politics. *When the Emperor Was Divine* (2002) by Julie Otsuka (1962–) follows the lives of a family in a Japanese American internment camp. Novels by Leslie Epstein (1938–), including *Pandaemonium* (1997) and *The Eighth Wonder of the World* (2006), mix fictional and real characters, Hollywood and the Holocaust, architecture and Mussolini. Centered on the fighting of the war itself are *Europe Central* (2005) by William T. Vollmann, winner of the National Book Award; *Cryptonomicon* (1999) by Neal Stephenson (1959–); and the more conventional narrative *The Rising Tide: A Novel of World War II* (2006) by Jeff Shaara.

These works illuminate the idea that "by choosing a setting half a century or so before the present, the creative writer can capture the elusive relationship between the individual and society at a moment when a particular fragment of the past is slipping over the horizon from memory into history" (Morris-Suzuki 2005, 44–45). In addition to World War II, this time frame now includes the civil rights movement. Two notable recent novels are the aforementioned *Dreamer* by Johnson and *Four Spirits* (2003) by Sena Jeter Naslund (1942–), a novel of the Birmingham church bombing in 1963.

In addition to common time periods, contemporary historical novels share several common approaches to storytelling. These approaches include the following: centering the narrative on one historical person, sometimes in the form of a journal, letters, or pseudo-memoir; creating a mix of real and fictional characters; using multiple threads, storylines, or time periods; mixing or crossing boundaries between different genres; and creating alternate history or literature.

A large number of twenty-first century historical novels center on one historical figure and sometimes take the form of a purported memoir, biography, or autobiography. The range of figures is a microcosm of the topics and themes of recent historical fiction. Some are American presidents or national figures, as in *Abe* (2000) by Richard Slotkin (1942–); *Scandalmonger* (2000), about Alexander Hamilton and

Thomas Jefferson, by William Safire (1929–); and *Lucy* (2003) by Ellen Feldman, a novel about Lucy Mercer's affair with Franklin Delano Roosevelt. Novels about American civil rights leaders include *Cloudsplitter* (1998) by Russell Banks (1940–), about John Brown; Johnson's *Dreamer* (1998), about Martin Luther King; and *Strivers Row* (2006) by Kevin Baker about Malcolm Little, later Malcolm X. Several novels involve other world leaders, including two first-person novels about Marie Antoinette, Sena Jeter Naslund's *Abundance* (2006) and Kathryn Davis's (1946–) *Versailles* (2002); Karen Essex's *Kleopatra* (2001); Brooks Hansen's (1965–) *The Monsters of St. Helena* (2003) about Napoleon writing his memoirs; and Lily Tuck's *The News from Paraguay* (2004), on the dictator Francisco Lopez. Norman Mailer's (1923–) novel *The Castle in the Forest* (2007) follows this pattern with a twist, telling Adolf Hitler's story from the point of view of the devil.

Novels centered on a scholar, scientist, or doctor include two by T. Coraghessan Boyle (1948–)—*The Road to Wellville* (1993) about Dr. John Harvey Kellogg, inventor of corn flakes, and *The Inner Circle* (2004) about sex researcher Alfred Kinsey— as well as *Freud's "Megalomania"* (2000) by Israel Rosenfield (1939–). Writers, musicians, and artists featured in historical fiction include Virginia Woolf in *The Hours* (1998) by Michael Cunningham (1952–); Gertrude Stein and Alice B. Toklas in *The Book of Salt* (2003) by Monique Truong (1968–); composer Gustav Mahler in *The Artist's Wife* (2001) by Max Phillips, narrated by Alma Mahler; composer Robert Schumann in *Longing* (2000), a fictional biography, by J.D. Landis; and the architect of Paris in *Hausmann, or The Distinction* (2001) by Paul LaFarge (1970–).

Whether featuring actual historical figures or purely fictional characters, many recent novels are told in the form of letters, journals, or memoir, including, for example, the Pulitzer Prize winner *Gilead* (2004) by Marilynne Robinson (1943–) and *One Last Look* (2003) by Susanna Moore (1947–). Many novels, such as Charles Frazier's *Thirteen Moons* (2006), combine fictional characters with historical figures. Other important trends include using multiple points of view, as in *Master of the Crossroads* (2000) by Madison Smartt Bell (1957–); multiple narratives, generations, and locations as in *The Bonesetter's Daughter* (2001) by Amy Tan (1952–); and multiple genres, such as the mix of historical fiction and science fiction in *Specimen Days* (2005) by Michael Cunningham. Ivan Doig's (1939–) works, such as *Prairie Nocturne* (2003) and *The Whistling Season* (2006), belong to both western literature and historical fiction. Diana Gabaldon's (1952–) Outlander series mixes historical fiction, romance novel, and science fiction, defying genre classification.

One intriguing and genre-mixing branch of historical fiction is alternate (or alternative) history, "the branch of literature that concerns itself with history's turning out differently than what we know to be true" (Hellekson 2001, 1). One of the earliest American novels that can be considered alternate history is Mark Twain's *A Connecticut Yankee in King Arthur's Court*. Alternate history is related to science fiction in its consideration of other worlds that in some sense reflect our own; some critics, in fact, consider it a branch of science fiction, and some of its well-known practitioners are classified as science fiction authors, including Philip Dick (1928–82), Harry Turtledove (1949–), Orson Scott Card (1951–), and Connie Willis (1945–). A prominent recent example of alternate history is Philip Roth's *The Plot Against America*, in which Charles Lindbergh is elected president in 1940. Other recent novels that change or invent history are Don DeLillo's *Libra*, Thomas Pynchon's *Mason & Dixon*, Charles Johnson's *Dreamer*, William Safire's *Scandalmonger*, and Michael Chabon's (1963–) *The Yiddish Policeman's Union* (2007).

Even more than other forms of historical fiction, alternate history examines not just historical events but the significance of history itself. According to Karen Hellekson, "alternate history as a genre speculates about such topics as the nature of time and linearity, the past's link to the present, the present's link to the future, and the role of individuals in the history-making process" (2001, 4). Still there is debate over whether alternate histories are really historical fiction because they assume facts contrary to historical knowledge, and they are sometimes set in the present or in an altered future. Another form of historical fiction often categorized as science fiction is the time-slip or time travel fiction, in which characters find themselves transported to another historical time. Examples of time-slip historical fiction include *Kindred* (1979) by Octavia Butler (1947–2006), *Timeline* (1999) by Michael Crichton (1942–), and *The Doomsday Book* (1992), *To Say Nothing of the Dog* (1997), and *Lincoln's Dreams* (1988) by Connie Willis (1945–).

Other historical novels reinvent, revise, borrow characters from, or pay homage to a previous literary work. Recent examples include *The Hours* by Michael Cunningham, inspired by Virginia Woolf's *Mrs. Dalloway; Ahab's Wife* (1999) by Sena Jeter Naslund, an exploration of the world left behind in *Moby-Dick;* and *March* by Geraldine Brooks, a Civil War novel that focused on the father from Louisa May Alcott's *Little Women.*

Context and Issues. Contemporary historical fiction, not surprisingly, reflects many problems and concerns of the twenty-first century, including war, disaster, disease, discrimination, and scandals in politics and business. Many historical novels involve the popular contemporary topics of science, technology, and invention. Others center on the world of entertainment and sports. Historical fiction also reflects growing cultural diversity in authors and subjects as well as concern with issues of gender and sexuality.

Twenty-first century America is living in the aftermath of September 11, 2001, in the midst of the Iraq war, and in the third decade of the AIDS struggle. One of the first historical novels to include September 11 is *Forever* (2003) by Pete Hamill (1935–), a New York City epic that begins in 1740. Other novels that confront disaster and disease are *In Sunlight, in a Beautiful Garden* (2001) by Kathleen Cambor (1948–) on the Johnstown flood of 1889; *The Gates of the Alamo* (2000) by Stephen Harrigan (1948–); *The Great Fire* (2003) by the Australian American writer Shirley Hazzard (1931–); *Year of Wonders* (2001), a novel of the bubonic plague by another Australian American, Geraldine Brooks; *A Prayer for the Dying* (1999) by O'Nan; and Sheri Holman's *The Dress Lodger* (2000), set in London during a cholera epidemic.

As Americans continue to wrestle with discrimination and debate topics such as affirmative action, slavery has continued to be a compelling theme in historical novels, including Banks's *Cloudsplitter;* Bell's Haitian trilogy; the Pulitzer Prize winner *The Known World* (2003) by Edward P. Jones (1951–); *Property* (2003) by Valerie Martin; and *Walk through Darkness* (2002) by David Anthony Durham (1969–). Durham is also the author of *Gabriel's Story* (2001), set in the aftermath of slavery as settlers move west.

Political sexual scandals—a topic that led to the impeachment trial of President Clinton in 1999—are featured in Feldman's *Lucy* and Safire's *Scandalmonger.* Business scandals and mysteries—also much in the news—are at the center of David Liss's (1966–) novels set in the seventeenth and eighteenth centuries: *A Conspiracy of Paper* (2000), *The Coffee Trader* (2003), and *A Spectacle of Corruption* (2004).

As the pace of scientific and technological innovation accelerates, writers of historical fiction focus on the discoveries and inventions of the past. Andrea Barrett (1954–) examines scientific exploration and conflicts in the National Book Award winner *Ship Fever and Other Stories* (1996), *The Voyage of the Narwhal* (1998), and *Servants of the Map* (2002). Scientific and mathematical conflicts and rivalries of the seventeenth and eighteenth centuries are crucial to the novels of Stephenson's Baroque Cycle: *Quicksilver* (2003), *The Confusion* (2004), and *The System of the World* (2004), and code-making and breaking is at the heart of *Cryptonomicon* (1999). Emily Barton (1969–) and Thomas Kelly (1961–) have each created novels that look back on invention and building: a harness inventor in Barton's *The Testament of Yves Gundron* (2000), the dream of building a bridge to Manhattan in Barton's *Brookland* (2006), and the construction of the Empire State Building in Kelly's *Empire Rising* (2005).

Many recent historical novels have focused on the entertainment world, often mixing entertainment with politics, war, or scandals—perhaps not surprising in an era when baseball players testify before Congress and political leaders make documentary films. DeLillo's *Underworld* uses the story of a renowned baseball to frame a postmodern narrative about the Cold War; Chabon creates comic book artists who battle Nazism in the Pulitzer Prize winner *The Amazing Adventures of Kavalier & Clay* (2000); Glen David Gold (1964–) follows the aftermath of President Harding's participation in a magic show in *Carter Beats the Devil* (2001); Susan Sontag (1933–2004) depicts a Polish actress who forms a utopian community in California in *In America* (2000), winner of the National Book Award. Charley Rosen tackles basketball and discrimination in *The House of Moses All-Stars* (1997) and basketball and scandal in *Barney Polan's Game* (1998), while Darin Strauss (1970–) interweaves boxing, entertainment, and impersonation in *The Real McCoy* (2002).

As the United States has become more diverse, so have the authors of historical fiction. Over the last several decades, African American authors, including the Nobel Prize winner Toni Morrison, have been prominent in historical fiction. Edward P. Jones, Jewell Parker Rhodes (1954–), and David Anthony Durham are just a few of the African American authors who have published historical novels in the twenty-first century. Asian American writers of historical fiction include Ha Jin (1956–), Otsuka, Tan, and Truong. Hispanic American writers include Julia Alvarez (1950–), author of *In the Name of Salome* (2000), and Sandra Cisneros (1954–), author of *Caramelo* (2002).

Contemporary issues of gender, gender identity, sexual orientation, and family are reflected in several recent historical works. Interest runs high in the life and work of sex researcher Alfred Kinsey, as evidenced by the 2004 film and by Boyle's historical novel titled *The Inner Circle*. Transgender issues are reflected in David Eibershoff's (1969–) *The Danish Girl* (2000), an account of the transgendered artist who underwent the first sex change operation in 1931, and in Jeffrey Eugenides's (1960–) *Middlesex* (2002), the Pulitzer Prize–winning novel depicting the history and life of an intersexed protagonist.

Reception (and Adaptation). Historical fiction has been a popular American literary genre since the early nineteenth century. While every generation witnesses declarations that the historical novel is pedestrian, obsolete, or even dead, historical novels have continued to thrive, among both literary authors and mass-market publishers. Some writers, readers, and critics avoid the term "historical fiction," claiming, in effect, that a work is not an historical novel, but rather a novel about history. As Sarah Johnson has noted of late twentieth-century historical fiction, "Historical fiction was everywhere, but nowhere. It had become the genre that dared not speak its name" (2005, 3). Many reviews of historical novels omit the term entirely, characterizing the work as a novel about memory, about the meaning of the past, about time, but not as historical. Nevertheless, authors continue to write historical novels, many are very popular, and a significant number receive critical acclaim.

One measure of the acclaim received by writers of historical fiction is the number of major prizes won by their books, and there is good evidence that we are in the midst of an historical fiction renaissance. In the 10 years from 1997 to 2006, historical novels (or novels about history) won 6 of the 10 Pulitzer Prizes for fiction; indeed, two of the three 2006 finalists, the coincidentally named *The March* by E.L. Doctorow and *March* by Geraldine Brooks, were historical. (Even the third finalist was set a few decades in the past.) Over the same period, both the National Book Award for fiction and the National Book Critics Circle Award for fiction were awarded to historical novels at least half of the time.

In the twenty-first century, historical fiction is intertwined with a range of print, film, broadcast, and electronic media. As Tessa Morris-Suzuki notes, "As the media of historical expression multiply, so they increasingly interact with one another. Historical novels are made into films and TV mini-series; historical dramas on television generate accompanying museum displays; Internet web sites are developed to accompany historical documentaries" (2005, 16). Historical novels are frequently adapted into other media, particularly film and television. At the same time, historical novels compete with original films, documentaries, graphic novels, Web sites, and even games.

Film is especially well suited for historical narrative, sharing with the novel "the ability to reconstruct the past in ways that engage the empathy of the audience" (Morris-Suzuki 2005, 127). Historical novels have been popular material for **film adaptations of books** from the early days of Hollywood. *Ben-Hur,* which inspired a Broadway stage version in 1899, has been adapted on film four times (so far), beginning with an unauthorized silent version in 1907 and including the Academy Award-winning 1959 version. The D.W. Griffith silent classic *Birth of a Nation* (1915), "a film whose brilliance of cinematic technique is exceeded only by the grotesqueness of its racist message" (Morris-Suzuki, 127) was based on Thomas Dixon's *The Clansman: An Historical Romance of the Ku Klux Klan* (1905). Owen Wister's *The Virginian* was first adapted as a silent film in 1914 by Cecil B. DeMille; it has since been readapted as a film in 1923, 1929 (with Gary Cooper), and 1946 and in 2000 as a television movie.

Most of the blockbuster historical novels of the early twentieth century have been adapted at least once into equally successful films. Wilder's *The Bridge of San Luis Rey* has been made into films in 1929, 1944, and 2004. The 1936 film version of *Anthony Adverse* won four Academy Awards and was nominated for Best Picture. The film version of *Gone with the Wind,* based on Mitchell's novel, won 10 Academy Awards, including Best Picture. *Forever Amber,* the literary sensation of the 1940s, also became a popular 1947 film.

The multigenerational sagas published during the late twentieth century were especially well suited to the development of a new form of television programming: the miniseries. Alex Haley's (1921–92) historical novel *Roots: The Saga of an American Family* (1976) was transformed into a 1977 miniseries—critically acclaimed and one of the highest-rated programs ever. Byerman notes that by "creating a saga of a black family with a heroic ancestor, Alex Haley brought African American experience within the framework of mass culture" (2005, 16). Michener's *Centennial* was produced as a popular television miniseries that aired in 1978 and 1979. The television miniseries *The Bastard* (1978) was based on the first volume in Jakes's Kent Family Chronicles, and each book in Jakes's North and South trilogy became a television miniseries, in 1985, 1986, and 1994, respectively. The later twentieth century also saw a resurgence of successful films based on American historical novels, including *Ragtime* in 1981, *The Color Purple* in 1982, *Gettysburg* in 1993 (based on Michael Shaara's *The Killer Angels*), *The Road to Wellville* in 1994, and *Beloved* in 1998.

In the twenty-first century, interest in historical feature films—adaptations of historical novels, original features, and documentaries—continues. Recent adaptations of historical novels include *The Hours* (2002), nominated for an Academy Award for best picture; *Cold Mountain* (2003), based on the Frazier novel; and *Memoirs of a Geisha* (2005), based on the 1997 Arthur Golden (1956–) novel. These adaptations fit into a larger trend of historically based films ranging from the Academy Award–winning *Titanic* (1997) to the documentary miniseries *Band of Brothers* (2001), based on Stephen Ambrose's nonfiction book.

Selected Authors. Among the many fine writers of historical fiction in the twenty-first century, several merit particular attention for their accomplishments in the field and their ongoing work.

Kevin Baker (1958–) is the author of four well-received historical novels, two since the turn of the century. His first, *Sometimes You See It Coming* (1993), is

---

THE GRAPHIC HISTORICAL NOVEL AND MEMOIR

The graphic novel is a vibrant and growing form of popular literature, blending text and art. While most people are familiar with superhero comics, historical topics have been treated since at least the mid-twentieth century, beginning with short vignettes of heroes in history and developing, by the late twentieth century, into full-fledged graphic novels, documentaries, and memoirs. "Comic books are a very important medium of historical communication in many parts of the world, and, despite growing competition from electronic media, continue to play a vital role in shaping popular images of the past. The comic also reaches audiences who may seldom read academic history texts or historical novels" (Morris-Suzuki 2005, 204). In the late twentieth century, some of the most acclaimed historical graphic novels were *Maus* (1986) by Art Spiegelman (1948–), the Pulitzer Prize-winning Holocaust narrative; *Kings in Disguise* by James Vance (1953–) and Dan Burr (1951–), set amid riots in 1932 Detroit; *Stuck Rubber Baby* (1995) by Howard Cruse (1944–), exploring the 1960s civil rights movements for African Americans and gay people; *The Jew of New York* (1999) by Ben Katchor (1951–), set in 1830; and *300* (1999) by Frank Miller (1957–), an account of the Battle of Thermopylae in ancient Greece. Noteworthy twenty-first century historical graphic novels include both fiction and memoir: *Berlin: City of Stones* (2000) by Jason Lutes (1967–), set in Weimar Berlin; *The Golem's Mighty Swing* (2002) by James Sturm (1965–), about a Jewish barnstorming baseball team in the 1920s; *The Boulevard of Broken Dreams* (2002) by Kim Deitch (1944–), about an animator in the 1930s; *Palomar: The Heartbreak Soup Stories* (2003) by Gilbert Hernandez (1957–), a multigenerational saga set in Latin America; *Fun Home: A Family Tragicomic* (2006) by Alison Bechdel (1960–), on growing up gay in the 1960s and 1970s; and *We Are on Our Own* (2006) by Miriam Katin (1942–), an autobiographically based account of a woman hiding with her daughter in Nazi-occupied Hungary.

steeped in baseball history, with many of the characters based on real players. In *Dreamland* (1999), Baker combines fictional characters and historical figures in a panorama of life and corruption in early twentieth-century New York City. Delving further into the city's past, Baker sets *Paradise Alley* during New York City's 1863 draft riots, as Irish residents violently protested a war they feared would lead to the loss of their jobs to freed slaves. Further exploring the themes of race and violence, *Strivers Row* (2006) is set in 1943 Harlem and features as a character the young Malcolm Little who would become Malcolm X. Baker creates vivid characters, entertaining stories, and themes—race, immigration, violence, corruption—that resonate in the twenty-first century. Critics—sometimes comparing his work to Doctorow's—praise his novels for their intelligence, imagination, and historical detail.

Andrea Barrett (1954–) has combined her expertise in biology and history to create several works of historical fiction related to science and exploration. After writing several novels centered on contemporary families, Barrett's first historical work was *Ship Fever and Other Stories* (1996), a collection of short fiction revolving around nineteenth-century science and medicine. Continuing that focus, *The Voyage of the Narwhal* (1998), narrated by a cousin of Charles Darwin, tells the story of a fictional expedition to the Arctic from 1845 to 1847. Another collection of short fiction, *Servants of the Map* (2002), ranges widely through history and geography and features the reappearance of several characters, and relatives of characters, from the previous works. Barrett's scientific historical fiction has been widely acclaimed, including a National Book Award for *Ship Fever*. According to Michiko Kakutani (2002), she writes "as persuasively about the mysteries of science as she does about the mysteries of the human heart."

Barrett has spoken about the need for thorough research, noting that the writer, like the explorer, does not know at the outset what the final route will be: "I could never know beforehand what might be useful, or where the things I found might lead me" (Barrett 2001, 508).

Madison Smartt Bell (1957–), before turning to historical fiction, had established a reputation as a talented novelist portraying complex relationships and characters in contemporary, often urban, settings. His breakthrough as a novelist, and as a writer of historical fiction, came with *All Souls' Rising* (1995), a rich, complex, violent work about the slave rebellion in Haiti that began in 1791. One historical figure in that novel, the leader Touissaint L'Ouverture, becomes the central character in the book that continues the story, *Master of the Crossroads* (2000). Bell completes the trilogy with *The Stone That the Builder Refused* (2004), following the revolution to its inevitable conclusion. Bell's work has been praised for thorough research, rich detail, and his use of multiple voices and perspectives; included in the rich detail is horrifying violence, too much for some readers. Bell has criticized minimalist fiction and has been praised by John Vernon (1995) for being "refreshingly ambitious and maximalist," meaning not just that his work is big, but that it is detailed, vivid, and complex.

T. Coraghessan Boyle (1948–) is the author of a wide range of novels and short fiction, including five historical novels; he has said, "Moving back and forth keeps me alive" (Ermelino 2006, 25). Boyle's first novel, *Water Music* (1981), involves two explorers, one historical and one fictional, at the turn of the nineteenth century. *World's End* (1988), winner of the PEN/Faulkner Award, follows three families through multiple time frames from the seventeenth through the twentieth centuries. His next three historical novels all feature a mixture of historical figures and invented characters. *The Road to Wellville* (1993) satirizes contemporary health and self-improvement crazes with a fictionalized version of the early twentieth-century sanitarium run by Dr. John Kellogg, inventor of Corn Flakes. Another novel set in the early twentieth century, *Riven Rock* (1998), is based on a real married couple, Stanley McCormick, son of the inventor, and Katherine Dexter, a women's rights activist. *The Inner Circle* (2004) tells the story of sex researcher Alfred Kinsey's research and relationships from the perspective of one of his assistants. While critics differ on whether his characters are fully realized, Boyle is universally praised for his invention, humor, and deft use of language. He has been one of the most significant writers of twenty-first century historical fiction.

E.L. Doctorow (1931–) has been one of the most prolific, influential, and controversial historical novelists of the late twentieth and early twenty-first centuries. Doctorow first showed his affinity for history in the western *Welcome to Hard Times* (1960) and his variation on the Rosenberg executions, *The Book of Daniel* (1971). But it was *Ragtime,* the best-selling novel of 1975, that solidified both his popular reputation and his influence. *Ragtime* broke new ground in the postmodern historical novel by interweaving multiple plots and featuring a mix of fictional and historical characters—including Emma Goldman, Harry Houdini, Sigmund Freud, Carl Jung, and Henry Ford. Doctorow, always concerned with economic and political issues, followed *Ragtime* with three novels set during the Great Depression: *Loon Lake* (1980); *World's Fair* (1985), winner of the National Book Award; and *Billy Bathgate* (1989), winner of the PEN/Faulkner Award and the National Book Critics Circle Award. Several of Doctorow's works are set in and around New York City, including *Billy Bathgate* and *The Waterworks* (1994), a sort of gothic nineteenth-century mystery. In his widely acclaimed *The March* (2005), winner of the PEN/Faulkner Award, Doctorow applies his creative imagination and interweaving of narratives to an iconic American episode, General Sherman's march through Georgia during the Civil War.

Doctorow has been both praised and criticized for his postmodern approach to historical fiction, an approach that blurs the distinction between fact and fiction. According to Doctorow, "History is a kind of fiction in which we live and hope to survive, and fiction is a kind of speculative history, perhaps a superhistory, by which the available data for the composition is seen to be greater and more various in its sources than the historian supposes" (1983, 25). Where the historical record is incomplete, Doctorow imaginatively fills in the gaps in ways that challenge the reader's assumptions.

David Anthony Durham (1969–) is an African American writer whose three historical novels have won him wide acclaim. His first published novel, *Gabriel's Story* (2001), is set in the period after the Civil War as his teenage protagonist makes his way west, eventually joining a group of cowboys. Set before the Civil War, *Walk through Darkness* (2002) also traces a journey, this time of a fugitive slave and the man hired to pursue him. Durham's third novel, *Pride of Carthage* (2005), tells the story of Hannibal's march on Rome in the Second Punic War. Durham's novels have all been well received, with critics praising his perceptiveness and imagination and noting his ability to range from quiet reflection to dramatic storytelling. Janet Maslin (2002) writes, "Durham ultimately combines history and morality with a dynamic intelligence." Durham's works raise complex issues. As he stated in an interview with the *Historical Novels Review,* "the best works of historical fiction—

Toni Morrison's *Beloved,* for example—are not so much about providing answers as they are about asking questions."

Thomas Mallon (1951–) is the author of five historical novels and a critic and theorist of historical fiction. Mallon is known for the depth of his research and the breadth of his subjects, which have taken him across centuries and from earth to space. His first historical novel, *Aurora 7* (1991), is an account of Scott Carpenter's space mission interwoven with the tale of a missing boy. The next two novels, *Henry and Clara* (1994), a narrative of the couple who witnessed Lincoln's assassination, and *Dewey Defeats Truman* (1997), both connect political and personal worlds. *Two Moons* (2000) is a nineteenth-century romance set at the United States Naval Observatory, while *Bandbox* (2004) turns to a magazine rivalry in 1920s New York City.

Mallon is widely praised for his storytelling ability and historical accuracy; as Jay Parini notes about *Dewey Defeats Truman,* he "always uses his research cleverly, and the novel effortlessly summons the feel of a bygone era" (1997, 13). In "Writing Historical Fiction," Mallon stresses, "Getting things to look right is the historical novelist's paramount task" (2001, 288). Mallon sees the twenty-first century as the age of historical fiction; as technology brings us closer together, perhaps uncomfortably so, Mallon writes in "The Historical Novelist's Burden of Truth," the "past is the only place to which we can get away, and if I had one prediction for the millennium it would be that all of us, including novelists, shall be spending a lot of time—more than ever before—looking backward" (2001, 295).

Robert Morgan (1944–) has published five historical novels, all set in his native state of North Carolina. Known primarily as a poet for the first two decades of his career, Morgan began writing historical fiction with *The Hinterlands: A Mountain Tale in Three Parts* (1994), a story of pioneer life over three generations in the late eighteenth and early nineteenth centuries. He followed with *The Truest Pleasure* (1998), the story of a nineteenth-century marriage, and *Gap Creek* (1999), the novel about turn-of-the-century farming life that greatly expanded Morgan's popularity when it was selected by Oprah Winfrey for her book club. *This Rock* (2001), set in the 1920s, is a sequel to *The Truest Pleasure,* focusing on the next generation of the Powell family. With *Brave Enemies* (2003), Morgan returns to the eighteenth century with a creative narrative about a husband and wife who find themselves on opposite sides of the American Revolution. Morgan has been praised for his storytelling ability, his attention to detail, and his particular skill in creating the voices of strong women. While ranging widely in time, he has concentrated on evoking a sense of place and a respect for rural life. In his essay "Writing the Mountains," Morgan notes that the focus of his writing "has been on one particular place, not even a county, just a community, part of the Green River valley in Western North Carolina. And really not even the whole community, but about a square mile of land on the banks of Green River bought by my great-great-grandfather Daniel Pace in 1840." In the same essay, he notes that "the more we study a place, the longer we know a place, the more mysterious it becomes." Morgan's historical fiction is based on that sense of mystery connecting place, family, and the past.

Bibliography

Barrett, Andrea. "Four Voyages." *Michigan Quarterly Review* 40.3 (2001): 507–517.
Boyle, T.C. *The Inner Circle.* New York: Viking, 2004.
Brooks, Geraldine. *March.* New York: Viking, 2005.

Byerman, Keith. *Remembering the Past in Contemporary African American Fiction.* Chapel Hill: University of North Carolina Press, 2005.

Cunningham, Michael. *The Hours.* New York: Farrar, Straus, and Giroux, 1998.

Doctorow, E.L. *Billy Bathgate.* New York: Random House, 1998.

——. "False Documents." In *E.L. Doctorow, Essays and Conversations.* Richard Trenner, ed. Princeton: Ontario Review Press, 1983.

——. *Ragtime.* New York: Random House, 1975.

Durham, David Anthony. *Gabriel's Story.* New York: Doubleday, 2001.

Ermelino, Louisa. "According to Boyle." *Publishers Weekly* 253.25 (2006): 24–25.

Frazier, Charles. *Cold Mountain.* New York: Atlantic Monthly, 1997.

Hart, James D. *The Popular Book: A History of America's Literary Taste.* Berkeley: University of California Press, 1950.

Hellekson, Karen. *The Alternate History: Refiguring Historical Time.* Kent, OH: Kent State University Press, 2001.

Historical Novels Review. Interview with David Durham. Retrieved January 2007 from the David Durham Web site, http://www.fantasybookspot.com/node/1763.

Historical Novel Society Web site. Accessed January 2007 at http://www.historicalnovel society.org.

DeLillo, Don. *Libra.* New York: Viking, 1988.

Johnson, Charles. *Dreamer.* New York: Scribner, 1998.

Johnson, Sarah L. *Historical Fiction: A Guide to the Genre.* Westport, CT: Libraries Unlimited, 2005.

Kakutani, Michiko. "Scientists Plumb Life's Mysteries with Minds and Hearts." *New York Times* 11 January 2002. http://query.nytimes.com/gst/fullpage.html?res= 9B0CEFDE1139F932A25752C0A9649C8B63&fta=y.

Mallon, Thomas. *Dewey Defeats Truman.* New York: Pantheon, 1997.

——. "The Historical Novelist's Burden of Truth." *In Fact* 291–295.

——. *In Fact: Essays on Writers and Writing.* New York: Pantheon, 2001.

——. "Writing Historical Fiction." *In Fact* 279–290.

Maslin, Janet. "A Fugitive Slave's Quest for Freedom and Family." *New York Times* 16 May 2002. http://query.nytimes.com/gst/fullpage.html?res=9F03E4DC1039F935A25756C0A9649 C8B63&sec=&spon=&pagewanted=all.

Morgan, Robert. "Writing the Mountains." Retrieved March 2008 from Robert Morgan Web site, http://www.robert-morgan.com/default.aspx?c=10.

Morris-Suzuki, Tessa. *The Past within Us: Media, Memory, History.* New York: Verso, 2005.

Parini, Jay. "Everything Up to Date in 1948." *New York Times Book Review* 2 February 1997: 13.

Pynchon, Thomas. *Mason & Dixon.* New York: Henry Holt, 1997.

Roth, Phillip. *The Plot Against America.* Boston: Houghton Mifflin, 2004.

Safire, William. *Scandalmonger.* New York: Simon & Schuster, 2000.

Vernon, John. "The Black Face of Freedom." *New York Times* 29 October 1995. http://query.nytimes.com/gst/fullpage.html?res=990CE3DB1F3FF93AA15753C1A96 3958260&sec=&spon=&pagewanted=1.

Further Reading

Carnes, Mark C., ed. *Novel History.* New York: Simon & Schuster, 2001; Hellekson, Karen. *The Alternate History: Refiguring Historical Time.* Kent, OH: Kent State University Press, 2001; HistFiction.net, accessed January 2007 at http://www.histfiction.net; Historical Novel Society Web site, accessed January 2007 at http://www.historicalnovelsociety.org; Johnson, Sarah L. *Historical Fiction: A Guide to the Genre.* Westport, CT: Libraries Unlimited, 2005; Lukács, George. *The Historical Novel.* Trans. Hannah and Stanley Mitchell. Lincoln: University of Nebraska Press, 1983. Originally published 1937; Madden, David, and Peggy Bach, eds. *Classics of Civil*

War Fiction. Jackson: University Press of Mississippi, 1991; Mallon, Thomas. *In Fact: Essays on Writers and Writing.* New York: Pantheon, 2001; Morris-Suzuki, Tessa. *The Past within Us: Media, Memory, History.* New York: Verso, 2005; Simmons, Philip E. *Deep Surfaces: Mass Culture & History in Postmodern American Fiction.* Athens: University of Georgia Press, 1997.

CAROLYN KYLER

HISTORICAL MYSTERIES

Definition. Historical Mysteries are stories featuring a crime that occurred and was investigated in the past. The point at which the "past" begins, to distinguish it from "contemporary," is rather fluid. When the Crime Writers Association established the Ellis Peters Historical Dagger award in 1999 for the year's best historical mystery, it defined the category as "any period up to the 1960s." Mike Ashley in his volume *The Mammoth Book of Historical Whodunnits* (1993) defined it as a time before the author's birth, whereas Michael Burgess and Jill H. Vassilakos in *Murder in Retrospect* (2005) defined it as taking place at least fifty years before the story's composition. If there is any common ground between these definitions, it would seem to be not later than the early 1950s.

Hovering on the border of the historical mystery are those stories set in the present day that seek to solve an historical crime, the best known being *The Daughter of Time* (1952) by Josephine Tey, and, more recently, *The Wench is Dead* (1989) an Inspector Morse novel by Colin Dexter. Though they appeal to the same readership, strictly speaking they are not historical mysteries because of the contemporary element and are not covered in this chapter. There are also those that start in the present day but through some device, such as a time-slip, the protagonist ends up in the past. John Dickson Carr used this approach in several novels, including *The Devil in Velvet* (1951) and *Fire, Burn* (1957), where present-day characters move back in time and become involved in solving a mystery. The crime and investigation are both set in the past, therefore these technically qualify.

History. The historical mystery as a distinct publishing niche emerged following the popularity of the Brother Cadfael books by Edith Pargeter (1913–1995) writing as Ellis Peters. These books are set in England and Wales in the twelfth century during the civil war between King Stephen and the Empress Matilda and take place primarily at the Abbey in Shrewsbury. Pargeter had already earned a reputation as an author of both detective novels and historical novels. In 1976, she was musing over an actual historical event in which the Brothers at Shrewsbury ventured into North Wales in 1137 to collect the relics of Saint Winifred and bring them to the Abbey. Pargeter realized this would provide an excellent way to conceal a body and so wrote *A Morbid Taste for Bones* (1977). This introduced Brother Cadfael as the world-wise monk who had previously served as a soldier in the Crusades but had now settled at the Abbey as its herbalist. Pargeter had not intended to start a series but a couple of years later another idea occurred to her relating to the Battle of Shrewsbury in 1138 and *One Corpse Too Many* (1979) became the second Cadfael book. Their popularity led Pargeter to produce one or two books a year for the rest of her life, resulting in twenty novels and three short stories. With their appearance in paperback in 1984, a new commercial genre was created.

There had been historical mysteries before Cadfael but they were neither enough nor of sufficient prominence to create a distinct category. There had, for example, been many Sherlock Holmes pastiches written after Conan Doyle's death in 1930, and most of these stories were set in the period 1890–1920 and qualify as historical mysteries, but they are usually regarded as a category in their own right.

The existing genres of historical and crime fiction, although both popular in the late Victorian and Edwardian periods, remained separate. There were occasional items involving crimes set in periods earlier than the story's composition, such as *Barnaby Rudge* (1841) by Charles Dickens (1812–1870) or *The Other Side of the Door* (1909) by Lucia Chamberlain (1882–1978), but there is minimal detection in either book.

The usual starting place for the historical mystery is the Uncle Abner stories by Melville Davisson Post (1871–1930), which began with "The Broken Stirrup Leather" (1911). These are set in the hills of Virginia at the start of the nineteenth century and feature Uncle Abner, a god-fearing elder of the community who roots out wrong-doers by a combination of psychological awareness and skilful deduction. Early stories were collected as *Uncle Abner, Master of Mysteries* (1918) with later stories uncollected until *The Methods of Uncle Abner* (1974).

At the same time British writer Jeffery Farnol (1878–1952), who had established a reputation for his Regency adventures, introduced the character of Bow Street detective Jasper Shrig in *An Amateur Gentleman* (1913). Low key at first, Shrig moved center stage with *The Loring Mystery* (1925). Of special interest is *Murder by Nail* (1942), in which Shrig becomes obsessed by a case that happened seventy years earlier, making it a historical within a historical.

One writer who was fascinated with real-life historical mysteries was American lecturer Lillian de la Torre (1902–1993). She used several as the basis for stories featuring Dr Samuel Johnson, with Boswell serving as his Dr. Watson. The series started in *Ellery Queen's Mystery Magazine* in November 1943, and the first collection appeared as *Dr. Sam: Johnson, Detector* (1946). Four more volumes followed up to *The Exploits of Dr. Sam: Johnson* (1987). De la Torre is the real grand dame of the historical detective story and yet is woefully neglected.

Another Grand-Dame, Agatha Christie (1890–1976), turned her hand only once to the historical mystery—surprising for someone who, through her husband, became so involved in archaeology. *Death Comes at the End* (1945) is set in ancient Egypt, though it is perhaps otherwise a little too like St. Mary Mead.

Rather more unusual are the Judge Dee stories by Robert Van Gulik (1910–1967). He was the Dutch ambassador to Japan and became fascinated with the real-life stories about Dee, a seventh-century Chinese magistrate. He translated an ancient collection as *Dee Goong An,* which he had privately printed in 1949, and then created new stories about Dee, some based on real events, starting with *The Chinese Bell Murders* (1956). Sixteen more books followed.

The floodgates really opened with the success of the Brother Cadfael novels, but Pargeter was not alone in producing such works at that time. Peter Lovesey (1936–) established his reputation with a series featuring Victorian detective Sergeant Cribb, starting with *Wobble to Death* (1970). Lovesey also developed a series based around the life of the Prince of Wales (the future Edward VII) starting with *Bertie and the Tinman* (1987).

Barbara Mertz (1927–), writing as Elizabeth Peters, launched her first Amelia Peabody archaeological detective novel set in the late Victorian period with *Crocodile on the Sandbank* (1975). Jeremy Potter (1922–1997) wrote several novels re-evaluating noted historical mysteries, including *A Trail of Blood* (1970) about the Princes in the Tower, and *Death in the Forest* (1977) about the death of William II. But if there was one single work that established the historical mystery beyond doubt, it was *The Name of the Rose* (1980) by Umberto Eco (1932–). This atmospheric novel, set in a monastery in Italy and involving bizarre deaths, ciphers, and ancient manuscripts, became an international bestseller, and with it the new genre was confirmed.

Trends and Themes. Because the Brother Cadfael books and *The Name of the Rose* were set in the Middle Ages, the first flurry of interest from publishers was for more medieval mysteries. It was not long before most periods were being covered, but three stood out as the most popular, the Victorian and Elizabethan periods and ancient Rome; more recently, ancient Egypt and the early twentieth century have also emerged. The oldest setting used is almost certainly Pleistocene France some 37,000 years ago, in *Hyenas* (1998) by Sandy Dengler (1939–).

It has also become common to use real historical characters, often as the investigator. Charles Dickens and Wilkie Collins appear in a series of books by William J. Palmer (1943–); Benjamin Franklin is in a series by Robert Lee Hall (1941–); Jane Austen in a series by Stephanie Barron (1963–); and Dashiell Hammett is not only in *Hammett* (1975) by Joe Gores (1931–) but also in a series along with Raymond Chandler and Erle Stanley Gardner by William F. Nolan (1928–).

Selected Authors. With over five hundred authors active in this area in recent years, coverage here can only be selective. The authors discussed here are those who have produced significant work over the last decade and whose work is of both literary merit and historical interest. They are discussed in order of the time periods covered by their work.

Ancient Egypt. Two authors have established themselves as the primary writers of mysteries set in ancient Egypt: Lauren Haney (Betty Winkelman, 1936–) and Lynda S. Robinson (1951–). Robinson's series is set in the fourteenth century B.C.E., at the time of the Pharaoh Tutankhamun. It features Lord Meren, the Pharaoh's Chief Investigator, and concentrates on court life and intrigue. Robinson's research is impeccable and she has the advantage of depicting one of the best known of Egypt's pharaohs at a time when the ruling house was in turmoil following the heretical reign of Akhenaten. The series is so far six books from *Murder in the Place of Anubis* (1994) to *Slayer of Gods* (2001). Haney's series is set a century earlier, at the time of the 18th Dynasty Pharaoh, Queen Hatshepsut. It features Lieutenant Bak, Head of the Medjay Police who administers a chain of forts along the Nile, many miles south of Egypt's capital. The series began with *The Right Hand of Amon* (1997) and has continued through eight books so far to *A Path of Shadows* (2003). Bak invariably is given charge of a project that leads to the discovery not only of a murder but also potentially empire-threatening plots. Paul Doherty (1946–) has also written a series set at the time of Hatshepsut, whom he calls Hatusu. These series feature Lord Amerotke, the Chief Judge in Thebes, who works alongside the Queen to strengthen the kingdom. This series has reached seven volumes from *The Mask of Ra* (1998) to *The Poisoner of Ptah* (2007) and is notable for its attention to detail. Both Doherty and Haney delight in the minutiae of everyday life, making ancient Egypt more accessible, but whereas Doherty and Robinson explore the lives of royalty and court officials, Haney follows the lives of the common people.

Ancient Greece. Despite the popularity of ancient Greek history and mythology, it has not featured prominently in historical mysteries, though as far back as 1978 Canadian writer Margaret Doody (1939–) produced a one-off novel *Aristotle Detective*. The great philosopher plays the role of an "armchair" detective helping another save his cousin who has been accused of murder. The book was critically well received at the time but then vanished almost without trace until an Italian translation in 1999 revived interest. Since then Doody has completed further novels, *Aristotle and Poetic Justice* (2002), *Aristotle and the Secrets of Life* (2003), *Poison in Athens* (2004) and *Mysteries of Eleusis* (2005). Aristotle's friend, Stephanos, does most of the legwork with Aristotle serving as the focal point to explore Greek beliefs and customs. Although Doody brings considerable academic knowledge to the series, using it, for example, to explore her theories about the origin of the novel, it is also relatively light-hearted.

Paul Doherty has also set two series in ancient Greece, or more accurately Macedonia, at the time of Alexander the Great. The first two books appeared under the alias Anna Apostolou, *A Murder in Macedon* (1997) and *A Murder in Thebes* (1998), and featured twin detectives, Jewish by birth. Raised at the court of Alexander and serving as clerks they are taken into Alexander's confidence after the death of his father, whose murder they must solve. The idea of the twin detectives was clever but Doherty dropped that series for another featuring a physician, Telamon, also at the court of Alexander, who accompanies him on his conquests. The series began with *The House of Death* (2001) and continued through *The Godless Man* (2002) and *The Gates of Hell* (2003). Although as colourful as the original two books, the new series lacks that spark of ingenuity.

Ancient Rome. Rome has been a setting for a number of series, including those by Rosemary Rowe, David Wishart, John Maddox Roberts, and Marilyn Todd, but two authors dominate the market, Lindsey Davis (1949–) and Steven Saylor (1956–).

Davis rapidly earned an enviable but justified reputation with her novels featuring the "informer" Marcus Didius Falco. The first, *The Silver Pigs* (1989) starts in 70 C.E. during the reign of the Emperor Vespasian and takes place, for the most part, in Britain, but thereafter the novels take Falco to many parts of the Empire. *The Times* called her books "models of the genre." The series appeals on several levels. Davis succeeds in recreating Rome in a seemingly effortless way, the places, particularly the seedier sides of Rome, coming alive through comments by the characters rather than by detailed description. All the characters are well drawn, especially Falco and his wife Helena, the real power behind the man. Most noticeable, though, is the humor. Falco is a typical lovable rogue, with all the panache of a Chandleresque private eye transplanted to the ancient world. He is streetwise, quick witted, and able to fend for himself. He is also fallible, and in her portrayal of cases Davis is realistic and not averse to leaving some crimes unsolved. Falco, though, makes steady progress, even rising to the rank of Procurator in *One Virgin Too Many* (2000). Her books won Davis the CWA's Dagger in the Library award in 1995 as the author who has given most pleasure to readers, and *Two for the Lions* (1999) won the inaugural Ellis Peters Historical Dagger. Recent novels include *Ode to a Banker* (2000), *A Body in the Bathhouse* (2001), *The Jupiter Myth* (2002), *The Accusers* (2003), *Scandal Takes a Holiday* (2004), *See Delphi and Die* (2005), and *Saturnalia* (2007).

Saylor's novels are set over a century earlier during the days of Cicero and Julius Caesar. They feature Gordianus the Finder, who is from a more privileged family than Falco, though like Falco he is married with children. In the first book, *Roman Blood* (1991), Gordianus helps Cicero solve a case the orator is defending, and thereafter Gordianus has Cicero's patronage, at least for as long as Cicero remained in favor with the Republic. Most of the novels are set against major historical events, such as the slave rebellion of Spartacus (*Arms of Nemesis*, 1992) or

Catilina's revolt (*Catilina's Riddle*, 1993). The novels from *A Murder on the Appian Way* (1996) take place against the civil war between Caesar and Pompey, and thereafter the paths of Gordianus and Caesar cross several times. The most recent novels have been *A Mist of Prophecies* (2002) and *The Judgment of Caesar* (2004) plus two collections of short stories set in Gordianus's early days.

Both Davis and Saylor are thorough in their depiction of Roman life, and whereas Davis's work has the advantage in humor and character, Saylor's series is more realistic in its action and atmosphere.

Medieval Period. The medieval period, especially the years from the Norman Conquest to the death of Richard III (1066–1483) has been the one most plundered by writers, in the wake of the popularity of the Brother Cadfael books.

One of the earliest, and still the most prolific, authors was Paul Doherty, who originally produced a one-off novel, *Death of a King* (1985), about an investigation into the death of Edward II and then launched into what would be the first of his many series with *Satan in St. Mary's* (1986) featuring Sir Hugh Corbett, who conducts investigations on behalf of King Edward I. This remains Doherty's longest running series, with the fifteenth title, *The Waxman Murders,* published in 2006, and one of his best realized, chiefly because the period is the one in which Doherty is most expert—his doctorate was on the reign of Edward II.

Other authors whose series cover this period include Edward Marston, Sharan Newman, Sharon Penman, Bernard Knight, Ian Morson, Candace Robb, Susanna Gregory (Liz Cruwys, 1958–), Michael Jecks (1960–), and Margaret Frazer. The works of these authors, although showing individualistic traits, are broadly in a similar mood to the Cadfael books. Their market overlaps, so much so that Jecks, Knight, Morson, and Gregory have teamed up with Philip Gooden as "The Medieval Murderers" and have produced a couple of books where the storyline is connected by a common theme. Each author contributes a self-contained chapter set in a specific time period.

Susanna Gregory's primary historical series features Matthew Bartholomew, a teacher of medicine at Michaelhouse, part of the fledgling University of Cambridge in the mid-fourteenth century. The first book, *A Plague on Both Your Houses* (1996), is set at the time when the Black Death is ravaging Europe and threatening Cambridge, though Bartholomew has other deaths on his mind. The series has reached twelve books with *The Tarnished Chalice* (2006), though in time-span they have covered only eight years.

Gregory has written two other series. Under the alias Simon Beaufort, she created the Crusader Knight Sir Geoffrey Mappestone. In *Murder in the Holy City* (1998) he has to solve a series of murders in Jerusalem in the year 1100. The second book, *A Head for Poisoning* (1999), brought Mappestone back to England, and thereafter he finds himself serving as an agent for King Henry II in various trouble spots around Henry's empire.

Gregory's books are known for her meticulous attention to historical detail and frequently contain notes on historical sources relative to the plot. All of Gregory's series have in common a turbulent society coming to terms with significant changes that have disrupted the social order, be it the Black Death, the aftermath of the Norman Conquest, or, in her latest series featuring Sir Thomas Chaloner, the years after the execution of Charles I and the Restoration of Charles II. Gregory explores how the truth is often the first victim in such difficult times.

Michael Jecks has concentrated on only one series, known generally as the West Country mysteries, starting with *The Last Templar* in 1995. The twenty-second volume, *The Malice of Unnatural Death,* appeared in 2006. The books are set chiefly in Devon and Cornwall, and primarily around Dartmoor. They feature Simon Puttock, the bailiff of Lydford Castle—Lydford was then the main administrative center for Devon and Dartmoor—and Sir Baldwin Furnshill, a former Templar knight now dispossessed of his lands, who has become the Keeper of the King's Peace in Crediton. The stories are sequential, starting in 1316. Jecks has firmly embedded the series in the historical climate, with the background of the weak reign of Edward II and the consequent civil unrest, but what makes the series of special interest is Jecks's use of the local laws and rights relating to Dartmoor and the stannaries. Jecks's detailed research allows one to step straight into the past, and Jecks writes with a pace and enthusiasm that injects life and action into the characters.

Tudor and Elizabethan. As with other periods, two authors dominate the Elizabethan scene. Valerie Anand (1937–) is a British author of historical fiction who uses the alias Fiona Buckley for a series set in Elizabethan England. Her lead character is Ursula Blanchard, widowed with a young child and shunned by the court. She is an illegitimate child of Henry VIII and thus Queen Elizabeth's half-sister. In the first novel, *The Robsart Mystery* (1997; U.S. as *To Shield the Queen*) Blanchard becomes involved in the historical scandal of the death of Amy Robsart. As a consequence of her actions the Queen believes she can trust Ursula, who becomes one of the Queen's spies. The novels are set in the 1560s against the background of Elizabeth's tenuous hold on the throne and the threat from Mary, Queen of Scots. All of the books tie in to real historical events. Other recent titles include *Queen's Ransom* (2000), *To Ruin a Queen* (2000), *Queen of Ambition* (2002), *A Pawn for a Queen* (2002), *The Fugitive Queen* (2003), and *The Siren Queen* (2004).

Under her own name, Patricia Finney (1958–) has written both a series of historical mystery stories for younger readers and a trilogy that might be defined as Elizabethan thrillers and that caused Ruth Rendell to dub her "The Le Carré of the 16th Century." The trilogy is *Firedrake's Eye* (1992), *Unicorn's Blood* (1998), and *Gloriana's Torch* (2003), featuring the escapades of Elizabeth I's loyal courtier Simon Ames and his dubious friend, the soldier David Becket. In the first volume they thwart a plot to assassinate Elizabeth, whereas the second book sees them trying to thwart another plot, this time to murder Mary, Queen of Scots. By the third book Ames has been captured while spying for the Queen in Spain, and Becket, who is head of the Queen's Ordnance, has to rescue him while also infiltrating the Spanish fleet. The books are a mixture of historical drama and spy thriller and Finney succeeds admirably in capturing the spirit of the age and distilling that essence that distinguished the Elizabethan age. This mood carries across into her historical mystery series written under the alias P.F. Chisholm, which began with *A Famine of Horses* (1994). It features the historical character of Sir Robert Carey, who was a cousin of Elizabeth I. He was a loyal servant to the Queen, renowned not only for his enforcement of the law but also for his understanding and interpretation of legal matters. He served both as a soldier and in various roles in governing the Scottish borders before becoming Lord Warden of the Marches in 1596. Drawing upon Carey's own memoirs, Finney has produced a series that works both as historical mysteries and as authentic recreations of life around Elizabeth's domain. The series has continued with *A Season of Knives* (1995), *A Surfeit of Guns* (1996), and *A Plague of Angels* (1998), with more planned. Finney has also contributed to a series for young readers (aged 9 to 12) that purports to be the accounts related by 13-year-old Lady

Grace Cavendish, Elizabeth's favorite Maid of Honor, who becomes involved in various court intrigues and mysteries. The series began with *Assassin* (2004), in which she investigates the murder of one of her own suitors, and continued with *Betrayal* (2004) and *Conspiracy* (2005). Jan Burchett and Sara Vogler continued the series with *Deception* (2005), *Exile* (2005), and *Gold* (2006), with Finney contributing the sixth book, *Feud* (2005). The series introduces younger readers to the historical mystery and helps them appreciate the political intrigue of the Elizabethan age.

Victorian/Edwardian Age. The Victorian period, especially the gaslight era, is synonymous with Sherlock Holmes, and so many Holmesian pastiches have been produced that they restricted the market for anything else. That dam was eventually breached by Anne Perry (1938–), who over the last twenty years has become the undisputed master of the Victorian detective story. In recent years she has become remarkably prolific, developing several series, but her major Victorian work falls into two series of equal merit. The first features Thomas Pitt, an Inspector (later Superintendent) with the Bow Street Police, and has currently reached 24 volumes. At the start in *The Cater Street Hangman* (1979), set in 1881, he is investigating a series of murders that brings him into contact with the upper-class Ellison family. Pitt himself is middle class, his family having suffered from strife, and Perry uses the class system with its blinkered attitudes toward the murders, to highlight Victorian prejudices and social divides. To the Ellison household, crime emanates from the lower classes, and it is only when the truth comes closer to home that they are forced to recognize the undercurrents of Victorian society. At the end of the first book Pitt proposes to Charlotte Ellison, whose role was key to Pitt solving the case, and he is reluctantly admitted into the Ellison family. Charlotte Pitt plays an important part in all of the novels, her understanding of Victorian society helping open doors for an otherwise often restricted and bewildered Pitt. The books have explored many of the problems that Victorian society tried to ignore, including illegitimacy (*Callander Square,* 1980), male prostitution (*Bluegate Fields,* 1984), homosexuality (*Belgrave Square,* 1992), and pornography (*Half Moon Street,* 2000). In *The Whitechapel Conspiracy* (2001), which draws upon the Jack the Ripper murders, Pitt falls foul of a clique of influential men known as the Inner Circle and as a consequence is fired as Superintendent at Bow Street and is forced to work in the newly created Special Branch, pursuing anarchists. This allowed Perry to expand Pitt's world into one of espionage and political intrigue, with the Inner Circle forever thwarting his plans. Recent titles are *Southampton Row* (2002), *Seven Dials* (2003), and *Long Spoon Lane* (2005).

Perry's other main series is set in the 1850s and 1860s and features William Monk and Hester Latterly. Monk is a police inspector who has an accident in the first novel, *The Face of a Stranger* (1990), and loses his memory. It is only gradually that he recalls flashes of his past, but with Hester's help he starts to rebuild his life. Monk finds it difficult to continue in his role as a policeman, and in *Dangerous Mourning* (1991) he is dismissed and becomes a private investigator. The Monk series is bleaker than the Pitt books, as Monk struggles to recover his identity while investigating crimes that frequently place him in situations reminiscent of his former life. This works especially well in *Death of a Stranger* (2002) where Monk's investigations into possible corruption in a railway company bring him head on with his past. His investigations occasionally take him outside England, including America at the start of the Civil War in *Slaves of Obsession* (2000). Monk and Latterly are married in *The Twisted Root* (1999), and Hester subsequently opens a clinic catering to the health of London's prostitutes. In *The Shifting Tide* (2004) Monk becomes involved with London's River Police and enters their employ in *Dark Assassin* (2006), providing further potential for the series. Whereas the Pitt series explores the relationship between crime and the upper crust of society, the Monk books look into the darker corners of all strands of society.

In recent years the Victorian setting, not solely in Britain, has provided an opportunity to explore factors that contributed to the modern world. Caleb Carr (1955–) is both a novelist and a military historian, and the majority of his books have been nonfiction, unrelated to his few fictional outings. *The Alienist* (1994), which was on the *New York Times* bestseller list for many months, is set in New York in 1896 where there has been a series of violent murders of young boy prostitutes. Theodore Roosevelt, then the Police Commissioner, gathers together a team of experts to help solve the crime. The team is headed by Dr. Laszlo Kreisler, a criminal psychologist, here called an "alienist." The story is narrated by another of the team, reporter John Moore, who recalls the events years later. By introducing criminal profiling at such a period, Carr is able to analyze not just the psychology of the criminal but the psychology of a city that could produce such a killer. Carr had planned a series of books each narrated by a different member of the team but so far only one has appeared, *The Angel of Darkness* (1997), which looks again at child abuse and killings. The first novel stands out as one of the most profound of recent historical crime novels, almost on a par with *The Name of the Rose*.

The work of Matthew Pearl (1976–) has been likened to that of Carr's. He has written two literary mysteries, which he regards as "intellectual thrillers," drawing upon his profound knowledge of both Dante and American nineteenth-century literature. *The Dante Club* (2003) depicts a serial killer on the loose in Boston in 1865. His methods of murder resemble those inflicted upon sinners as described in Dante's *Inferno*. This comes to the attention of the Dante Club, a group of literati that includes Henry Wadsworth Longfellow, Oliver Wendell Holmes, James Russell Lowell, and James Thomas Fields, who formed the Club out of their interest in Dante and their desire to protect his work. Their deep understanding of Dante helps them gain an insight into the criminal's mind. *The Dante Club*, which went on to become a major bestseller, has been compared to Caleb Carr's *The Alienist*, though the similarities are chiefly in the descriptions of nineteenth-century American city life and the exploration of a criminal's motivation. Pearl draws his inspiration from the aftermath of the American Civil War and its impact upon a generation. Pearl's second novel, *The Poe Shadow* (2006), is another atmospheric study, this time into the facts behind the death of Edgar Allan Poe. In both volumes Pearl brings considerable literary knowledge and analysis to the detective genre.

Boris Akunun (Grigory Chkhartishvili, 1956–) is a Russian author and translator whose novels about the detective Erast Fandorin, set at the end of the nineteenth century in Imperial Russia, have become international bestsellers. Fandorin is at the outset a young police detective but in later novels becomes a private investigator. He is intelligent but vain and his rakish style of dress more than once saves his life. The novels are a mixture of styles assembled in a rather cavalier fashion intended as much to amuse as entertain and aimed at a broad readership who want both popular and literary escapism. Each book has followed a different crime sub-genre. The first volume, *Azazel* (1998; translated as *The Winter Queen*, 2003), set in 1876, in which a young Fandorin, only recently recruited to the police force, finds himself involved with a group of anarchists, is written like a Ruritanian adventure with Fandorin described as "our hero." *The Turkish Gambit* (1998; translated 2005) is a spy thriller, whereas *Leviathan* (1998; translated as *Murder on the Leviathan*, 2004), set on a cruise ship, is imitation Agatha Christie. The books abound with literary references and Akunin clearly enjoys creating each new style. He has identified sixteen different sub-genres and plans sixteen books in the Fandorin cycle, eleven of which have so far appeared in Russia with five translated into English. When *The Winter Queen* was translated, the *New York Times* (13 July 2003) likened Akunin to Alexander Pushkin. He has a broad cosmopolitan style that succeeds in depicting Tsarist Russia's place in the world in such a way as to highlight parallels with present-day Russia.

Akunin, who has also written a trilogy set in Russia in the 1890s about a nun, Pelagiya, who, like Cadfael, has a talent for solving mysteries, has demonstrated that having fun with old stereotypes recast in new packages can prove successful.

The dawn of the twentieth century was a time of change but one that still clung to the past. These conflicts are evident in several series taking place between 1900 and 1914.

Gillian Linscott (1944–) has written several historical mysteries, but she is best known for her series about British suffragette Nell Bray in the years before the First World War. When the series starts, in *Sister Beneath the Sheet* (1991), Bray has just been released from prison after throwing a brick through a window at 10 Downing Street, and she soon finds herself embroiled in a possible murder investigation. The series follows the suffragette movement over the next decade. *Absent Friends* (1999), which takes place after women have received the vote, has Bray standing as a parliamentary candidate. The volume won Linscott both the Ellis Peters Historical Dagger and the Herodotus Award as that year's best historical mystery. Recent books in the series, set in earlier years, include *The Perfect Daughter* (2000), *Dead Man Riding* (2002), and *Blood on the Wood* (2004). Linscott's creation of the period is both intelligent and forceful but is written with a wry sense of humor sufficient to deflate Edwardian pomposity and provide the reader with an understanding of the prejudices of the age.

The United States was also witnessing changes at this time. David Fulmer (1950–), already known as a jazz critic and journalist, caused a stir with his first novel, *Chasing the Devil's Tail* (2001). Set in New Orleans in 1907 it features Valentine St. Cyr, a Creole former police detective who is employed by Tom Anderson, the unofficial mayor of the Storyville district, to investigate the murder of prostitutes. The book is far more than a detective story because Fulmer recreates the atmosphere of Storyville with the emergence of "jass" and the early days of formative musicians Jelly Roll Morton and "King" Buddy Bolden. The book won Fulmer the Shamus Award as that year's Best First Private Eye Novel and was nominated for the *Los Angeles Times* book award and the Barry Award. The next two books in the series are *Jass* (2005), which won the Georgia Author of the Year award, and *Rampart Street* (2006), both of which add depth to the setting—the "palpable ambience" as *Booklist* described it. Fulmer also wrote *The Dying Crapshooter's Blues* (2007) set in his native Atlanta in the 1920s amidst racial and social division when a mixed-race thief determines to get to the bottom of a racial shooting. In all of his books Fulmer treats the past with respect and allows us to pass cautiously through the portals.

Michael Pearce (1933–) was raised in what was then the Anglo-Egyptian Sudan, which has given him an understanding of the culture, mores, and attitudes of the various nationalities embroiled in the region. He has used this to considerable effect in his series of books featuring Gareth Owen, the Mamur Zapt, or Head of the Secret Police in Egypt in the years before and during the First World War. The series began with *The Mamur Zapt and the Return of the Carpet* (1988) and has currently reached fifteen volumes with *The Mamur Zapt and the Point in the Market* (2005). Throughout each book the Mamur Zapt often serves as an observer, only becoming involved when he has to, though also manipulating events behind the scenes when he can. As a consequence the reader feels they are being taken into his confidence, seeing events as a secret witness, a mood strengthened by Pearce's lean style, which speaks directly to the reader. He is also frequently very humorous, with a wry observation on attempts by various factions to gain the upper hand. Pearce's books have become timely in the light of the current relationship between the West and the Arab world, and his commentary provides a shrewd insight into diplomacy.

Pearce has written two other historical series in similar style. There were only two volumes about Dmitri Kameron, a Russo-Scottish lawyer living in Tsarist Russia in the 1890s (*Dmitri and the Milk-Drinkers*, 1997, and *Dmitri and the One-Legged Lady,* 1999). With *A Dead Man in Trieste* (2004), set in 1910, Pearce began a new series featuring the exploits of Sandor Seymour, a British Special Branch officer whose expertise takes him to various European embassies and consulates, describing a world inexorably spiralling toward war. The series allows Pearce a broader canvas than the Mamur Zapt books, though he brings to it the same humor and perception. Read from the advantage of a further century of conflict it is easy to see how the same mistakes continue to be made and lessons remain unlearned.

Twentieth Century. The First World War destroyed the old order and brought the twentieth century of age. There are several profound series that use the experiences and aftermath of the Great War to good effect.

Rennie Airth (1935–) scored a critical success with *River of Darkness* (1999), which was short-listed for several major awards. It was a dark, brooding novel set in the aftermath of World War I. Inspector Madden, already psychologically scarred by the harrowing experiences in the War has also lost his wife and daughter in the flu epidemic. He investigates the slaughter of a family in a quiet Surrey village. Airth succeeds in blending the traditional country-house mystery with the concept of psychological profiling, producing a powerful but rather solemn evocation of post-war Britain blighted by tragedy. It was five years before Airth completed the second book, *The Blood-Dimmed Tide,* set a decade later in 1932. Madden is retired, living on a farm in Surrey, but gets drawn into the murder of a young, local girl. Madden's insight links this crime to others and a picture emerges of dark deeds in a Britain gripped by the Depression and coping with the rise of Nazism. A third and final volume is planned.

Ploughing similar territory was Charles Todd, the pen name for American mother-and-son writing team, Carolyn and David Watjen. Their series features Inspector Rutledge, a detective who is nearly killed during the War and suffers from shell shock, haunted by the voice of a companion who was killed alongside him. Originally a highly intuitive detective, he now fears his inner voice, uncertain how to react. The crimes that Rutledge investigates, starting with *A Test of Wills* (1996), bring him into contact with others scarred by the War, both physically and spiritually. The books atmospherically depict a shell-shocked post-War Britain, and Rutledge's determination to seek justice for the murder victims is seen as part of a wider justice for all the dead, a mood especially poignant in *A Long Shadow* (2006). The series reached nine volumes with *A False Mirror* (2007).

The immediate post-War period soon gave way to the Roaring Twenties. British writer and former teacher Barbara Cleverly has rapidly risen to the front rank of historical mystery writers with her series set in colonial India in the early 1920s. It features Scotland Yard detective Joe Sandilands who has been seconded to the Bengal Police and becomes involved in a connected series of murders at a local army regiment. Cleverly brings India alive not only with considerable local color and an atmosphere of a lost world but also with believable characters and an intriguing plot. The book won the author the Crime Writers' Association Debut Dagger and was listed by the *New York Times* as one of the year's best books. Cleverly continued to develop both the characters and the local atmosphere in *Ragtime in Simla* (2003); *The Damascened Blade* (2004), which won the CWA's Ellis Peters Historical Dagger Award; and *The Palace Tiger* (2004). With the fifth book, *The Bee's Kiss* (2005), she brought Sandilands back to England at the time of social unrest and the General Strike, whereas in *Tug of War* (2006) he is in France in an unusual case of trying to identify a shell-shocked soldier. Cleverly's books are all ingeniously plotted and move at a relentless pace.

Max Allan Collins (1948–) is a prolific writer of hardboiled crime fiction who has turned his talents to writing a number of novels set in the first half of the twentieth century. He is perhaps best known for his graphic novel *Road to Perdition* (1998), set in the heart of organized crime in America in 1930 and made into the critically acclaimed film in 2002. Collins is noted for his historical gangster series featuring Nate Heller, a Chicago ex-cop turned private detective and a friend of Eliot Ness. In the early novels, Collins recreated the real-life gangsters of the period, including Al Capone in *True Detective* (1983) and John Dillinger in *True Crime* (1984). Later novels explored the kidnapping of Charles Lindbergh's baby in *Stolen Away* (1991), the murder of Sir Harry Oakes in 1943 in *Carnal Hours* (1994), and, in *Angel in Black* (2001), the still unsolved murder of Hollywood starlet Elizabeth Short in 1947 (also the subject of James Ellroy's first best-seller, *The Black Dahlia*, 1987). *Chicago Confidential* (2002), set at the dawn of the McCarthy era, has Heller trying to protect himself from both the FBI and organized crime, because of his knowledge of "where the bodies are buried." Most of the novels in this series have been nominated for the Shamus Award presented by the Private Eye Writers of America with *True Detective* and *Stolen Away* winning. Collins is known for his gritty realism, presenting the past as it was, violent, corrupt, and dangerous. Neither is Heller any shining knight, frequently protecting his own interests.

Collins is immensely prolific, despite the detailed research he undertakes. His other major historical mystery work is the Disaster series. In each novel a well known author becomes involved in solving a crime that happened during a major disaster. For *The Titanic Murders* (1999) Collins uses the fact that Jacques Futrelle, the author of the "Thinking Machine" stories, was on the *Titanic* and has him investigate two murders before he goes down with the ship. In *The Hindenberg Murders* (2000), Leslie Charteris, creator of The Saint, is directly involved in the fate of the eponymous airship. Edgar Rice Burroughs turns detective in *The Pearl Harbor Murders* (2001), S.S. Van Dine in *The Lusitania Murders* (2002), Agatha Christie in *The London Blitz Murder* (2004), and Orson Welles in *The War of the Worlds Murder* (2005). Although these are obvious gimmick novels and lack the violent realism of the Heller series, they are still as faithful to the facts as a work of fiction can be and are highly entertaining. J. Kingston

Pierce, writing in *January Magazine,* said of Collins that he is "certainly today's foremost expert at concocting credible criminal scenarios within the turbulent timeline of history" (April 1999).

The shift in mood from the 1920s to the 1930s and that uneasy transition between the wars is captured in David Roberts's series featuring Lord Corinth and Verity Browne. Corinth and his brother, the Duke of Mersham, are in positions of influence, working behind the scenes to stave off a second world war. The series, which began with *Sweet Poison* (2001), explores the rise of fascism and Communism throughout Europe, including Britain, and explores events related to the Spanish Civil War. In *The Hollow Crown* (2002), Roberts covers the abdication crisis of Edward VIII in 1936. The seventh book, *The Quality of Mercy* (2006), takes place against the backdrop of Hitler's invasion of Austria. The books not only present intriguing murder mysteries but also set them within the ever increasing atmosphere of dread that presaged the Second World War, an intriguing contrast with the attitude prior to the First World War depicted in Michael Pearce's books.

The 1940s and 1950s may seem recent, but even these periods can be seen in a new perspective. The modern master of the near contemporary historical whodunit is Andrew Taylor (1951–), whose books, especially the Roth trilogy, bridge the gap between the historical and the present. The Roth trilogy works in reverse, each book taking us further back in time to understand the source of later criminal action. The third book, *The Office of the Dead* (2000), which won the Ellis Peters Historical Dagger and which is set in the 1950s, reveals the key events that became the root of subsequent evil. Taylor's primary series is set in the decade after the Second World War in the fictional town of Lydmouth on the Anglo-Welsh border, near the Forest of Dean. It began with *An Air That Kills* (1994) with the eighth volume, *Naked to the Hangman,* appearing in 2006. Although the books are told through various viewpoints, the chief protagonists are both strangers to the area, Detective Inspector Thornhill, who had served in the War, and journalist Jill Francis. Their growing relationship forms the backbone to the series in

---

WHY ARE HISTORICAL MYSTERIES SO POPULAR?

The reasons for the popularity of historical mysteries have yet to be fully assessed. Although they bring together two existing popular genres, the books remain primarily crime novels. They may alienate devotees of both genres because they are genuine hybrids, but there is no denying their popularity. Nickianne Moody in her paper "Everyday Life in the Medieval Whodunnit" saw part of the appeal as relating to the cyclical nature of British experience, in effect "what goes around come around," revealing that the problems we experience today have much in common with those of past generations, though they may have been dealt with entirely differently. Moody also believed, at least in regard to Ellis Peters's books, that there was an appeal to a romanticized past, and this is true of many historical mysteries. It is not so much that the murders are glamorized but that there is huge potential for selecting favorite periods of history and populating them with popular characters. The more successful of the novels are those that can capture the mood of the past but relate it to the present.

Jean Mason writing in *The Mystery Reader* (25 March 2001) believed that the appeal of historical mysteries resided in the ability of the author to recreate the past and to create a "police procedural" that fit the time.

which the crimes are implanted in the social fabric. Taylor's intent was to explore a social and moral climate near to us in time and yet strangely different, a world in the process of reluctant change. The books are steeped in the atmosphere of the age from which the characters and stories condense and there is a strong impression that what ought to be the present is becoming the past before our eyes. Taylor's work thus stands at the portals of the historical mystery, like sands in an hourglass, ushering the reader into the past.

There is thus a challenge to authors to create a believable scenario where someone may investigate a crime in the past in accordance with the laws, procedures, and social climate of the day, and the degree to which they succeed adds to the pleasure of the story beyond a basic historical premise. The end result tells us much about how crime was viewed and dealt with at different times, and it may be reassuring to learn just how civilized, or otherwise, different cultures and ages have been.

Bibliography

Airth, Rennie. *River of Darkness*. New York: Viking, 1999.

Akunin, Boris. *The Winter Queen*. Trans. Andrew Bromfield. New York: Random House, 2003.

Anand, Valerie. *The Robsart Mystery*. New York: Orion, 1997.

Ashley, Mike. *The Mammoth Book of Historical Whodunnits*. London: Constable and New York: Carroll & Graf, 1993.

Burgess, Michael, and Jill H. Vassilakos. *Murder in Retrospect*. Westport, CT: Libraries Unlimited, 2005.

Carr, Caleb. *The Alienist*. New York: Random House, 1994.

Chisholm, P.F. *A Famine of Horses*. New York: Walker and Co., 1995.

Collins, Max Allan, and Richard Payner. *Road to Perdition*. New York: Pocket Books, 2002.

Davis, Lindsey. *The Silver Pigs*. New York: Crown, 1989.

de la Torre, Lillian. *The Exploits of Dr. Sam Johnson*. New York: International Polygonics, 1987.

Dexter, Colin. *The Wench is Dead*. New York: St. Martin's, 1990.

Doherty, Paul. *Death of a King*. New York: St. Martin's, 1985.

———. *The Mask of Ra*. New York: St. Martin's, 1998.

———. *The Poisoner of Ptah*. London: Headline, 2007.

Doody, Margaret. *Aristotle Detective*. New York: Harper and Row, 1978.

Finney, Patricia. *Firedrake's Eye*. New York: Picador, 1992.

———. *Gloriana's Torch*. New York: St. Martin's, 2003.

———. *Unicorn's Blood*. New York: Picador, 1998.

Fulmer, David. *Chasing the Devil's Tail*. Scottsdale, AZ: Poisoned Pen Press, 2001.

Gregory, Susanna. *A Plague on Both Your Houses*. New York: St. Martin's, 1996.

Haney, Lauren. *The Right Hand of Amon*. New York: Avon Books, 1997.

Jecks, Michael. *The Last Templar*. New York: Avon Books, 1995.

Linscott, Gillian. *Sister Beneath the Sheet*. New York: St. Martin's, 1991.

Lovesey, Peter. *Bertie and the Tinman*. New York: Mysterious Press, 1987.

Moody, Nickianne. "Everyday Life in the Medieval Whodunnit: The Popularity of Ellis Peters in the 1980s." Paper produced for Media & Cultural Studies, Liverpool University, 1996.

Pearl, Matthew. *The Dante Club*. New York: Random House, 2003.

Perry, Anne. *The Cater Street Hangman*. New York: St. Martin's, 1979.

Pierce, J. Kingston. "A Case to Remember." *January Magazine*. 1999. http://januarymagazine.com/crfiction/titanic.html.

Robinson, Lynda S. *Murder in the Place of Anubis.* New York: Walker, 1994.

———. *Slayer of Gods.* New York: Mysterious Press, 2001.

Saylor, Steven. *Roman Blood.* New York: St. Martin's, 1991.

Taylor, Andrew. *The Office of the Dead.* New York: St. Martin's, 2000.

Todd, Charles. *A Test of Wills.* New York: St. Martin's, 1996.

Further Reading

Browne, Ray Broadus, and Kreiser, Lawrence A., eds. *The Detective as Historian: History and Art in Historical Crime Fiction.* Bowling Green University, Popular Press, 2001; Johnsen, Rosemary Erickson. *Contemporary Feminist Historical Crime Fiction.* London: Palgrave Macmillan, 2006; Onotade, Ayo, "Courts, Knights and Treachery," *Crime Spree Magazine* #6, 2005, at <http://www.crimespreemag.com/MedievalCrimeFictionPaper.pdf>.

Websites

Bishop, Alan J. "Criminal History," <http://www.criminal-history.co.uk/>

Crime Thru Time, <http://www.crimethrutime.com/index.htm>

Heli, Richard M. "The Detective and the Toga," Roman Mysteries, <http://histmyst.org/>

Hurt, N.S. "Historical Mystery Fiction," <http://members.tripod.com/~BrerFox/historicalmystery.html>

Swank, Kris. "The Sybil and Sleuth," Ancient Greek Mysteries, <http://personal.riverusers.com/~swanky/greece.htm>.

MIKE ASHLEY

HISTORICAL WRITING (NONFICTION)

Definition. From Daniel Defoe's *Robinson Crusoe* (1719) to James Frey's *A Million Little Pieces* (2006), many famous works of fiction have first presented themselves as fact. Consequently the claim to be nonfiction may be controversial, particularly in a very skeptical, postmodern age. That claim, nonetheless, is inherent to historical writing, which is real, although not necessarily an entirely objective account of data. In partial contrast to **autobiography and memoir**, and **biography**, centered on a single life, collective history needs some shaping purpose to focus the material—a purpose that drives the historian yet can be shared by the reader.

Consider, for instance, the historian Aby Warburg. After admission to an asylum, he managed to restore his sanity through a "cultural-historical" study of Pueblo Indian myths and rituals for the way they helped their society to represent and thus control primal fears; this then taught him to do the same for his own fears (Mali 2003, 134). His case exemplifies one common function of history writing: historians may begin with a trauma that is both personal and collective—in Warburg's case, paranoia occasioned by World War I. The historian then seeks a solution from the past—sometimes a very different past, as with Warburg's countering the lack of collective, therapeutic ritual in modern Europe with its presence in early America.

History. Although oral histories may have existed from the beginning of humanity—and written ones from the origin of writing—Herodotus (c. 484–c. 424 B.C.E.) was one of the first to engage in a large-scale form of what he called "demonstration of research" (*apodexis histories*) (Hughes-Warrington 157). From this phrase near the beginning of his *Histories,* our word "history" may derive. Writing during the Peloponnesian War, but about the earlier Persian one, his stated purpose was to show the source of people's coming into conflict (Herodotus 1). Greek by culture but Asian by birth, Herodotus was fascinated with the war between Persia and Greece, which mirrored the tensions within his own origins. Despite admitting that all of the tales he recounted were not equally credible, he did not rudely label legends as lies but, as if with a reconciling purpose, used them to introduce readers to diverse cultures. He set a paradigm for this, which continues to be appreciated in such books as François Hartog's *The Mirror of Herodotus* (1988), Aubrey de Selincourt's *The World of Herodotus* (2001), and Carolyn Dewald and John Marincola's *The Cambridge Companion to Herodotus* (2006).

This tolerant laxity contrasts with the next great Greek historian, Thucydides (460–400 B.C.E.), who was careful to maintain the appearance of credibility. If one judges by the mines he owned in Thrace and by his father's Thracian name (Olorus), his ancestors may have been from that land, but he was for much of his life Athenian, engaged in its politics and strategies during the Peloponnesian War, which was the subject of his history (Hughes-Warrington 319). His appearance of objectivity therein is itself an important technique for arguing the reader into his conclusions, such as his decision after the Athenians exiled him that their expansionism was largely to blame for the war. Thucydides provided the pattern for history as a record of conscious policies, unlike Herodotus's fascination with legends that function as a people's collective dreams, set in some antique, unverifiable time. Although the dominant pattern of historiography in the nineteenth century, Thucydides's ostensible objectivity now seems outdated to such revisionists as Marshall Sahlins in his *Apologies to Thucydides: Understanding History as Culture and Vice Versa* (2004)

Another pioneer, the Roman historian Livy (c. 64 B.C.E.–c. 12 C.E.) was the author of a 142-book history of Rome; only 35 volumes of it remain along with ancient summaries of the rest. His original intention was for it to span from the founding of that city to the murder of Cicero (42 B.C.E.), but according to the elder Pliny, Livy extended beyond that because "his restless spirit thrived on hard work" (Pliny 1958, 16). Although earlier historians, Herodotus among them, had discussed how a country's moral degeneration may lead to its political decline, Livy added to this the notion that degeneration sprang from foreign ideas (Hughes-Warrington 205). As T.J. Luce and P.A. Stadter have demonstrated, Livy's hunger for order caused him to reorganize his sources with a major event at the beginning, middle, and end of each book and the treatment of intervening material being extended or compacted to make the book completely fill a papyrus scroll (Luce 1977, 6; Stadter 2007, 287–307).

Naturally, foreign influences, against which he wrote obsessively, could not be excluded, and the attempt to do so may even have decreased Rome's ability to grow and adapt. During the final wars and the ensuing chaos, European history writing largely halted. It returned in the hands of such monks as Bede (c. 673–735), who spent his life in a monastery from the age of seven. Typical of medieval historiography, he credits miracles and shapes the material in a religiously edifying manner— history writing as defense of the pious order as compared to Livy's of the moral and political. Outside Europe, of course, events continued to be recorded, particularly in China, which had a long tradition of annals, some of which turned into subjects for state examinations. Like the Western tradition from Herodotus to Bede, Chinese history was a way to exemplify moral norms. For the West, the historical classic was the Bible, which became a model; for instance, Sir Thomas Malory's *Morte D'Arthur* (1485) likens the immoral anarchy before Arthur's coming to that throughout the Book of Judges and patterns Merlin's vision of dragons on that in the Vulgate's Book of Esther. This is to say that during and before) the Middle Ages, history was largely normative, affirming traditional patterns and showing the disasters that resulted from the breach of them.

However, as early as the fourteenth century Ibn Khaldun (1332–1406) was using history to question traditional norms in much the manner of Niccolo Machiavelli (1469–1527), both of them to further their political agendas. Thereafter, conservative and revisionist versions of the past warred against one another, at first to establish one norm or another. With the nineteenth century came an amplified professionalism through the example of Leopold von Ranke (1795–1886), who, in *History of the Latin and Teutonic Nations* (1824), used it to make his argument for the unity of Europe seem an objective reflection of the people's origins.

Such professionalism, with its careful assessment of sources, limning of causation, and focus on political and military leadership, constituted a conscious history: the deliberate choices made by officials and the lives of everyone else repressed from public awareness. It presents the slow, linear skeleton of verifiable events while refraining from fleshing them with speculative details. In the twentieth and twenty-first centuries, however, a growing number of historians have emphasized instead the sensuous and sensual texture of common lives and emotions as well as the popularly held myths and metaphors that gave them meaning. The change has occurred gradually. A founder of the famous journal *Annales d'Histoire Economique et Sociale* (1929), Marc Bloch (1886–1944), for example, began his career in reaction against the Dreyfus Affair (the French government's complicity with anti-Semitism). To undermine the prestige and power of rulers, he showed medieval governments advancing human freedom through confusion and weakness rather than intent. Today, though, Bloc's version of the Middle Ages sounds very old-fashioned in its assumption of politics as the shaper of life (albeit sometimes accidentally). Since then history has uncovered a far more diverse, self-contradictory, visionary Middle Ages, such as in Carolly Erickson's *The Medieval Vision: Essays in History and Perception* (1976), where she demonstrates that those desiring a return to medieval simplicity, uniformity, and order have missed that period's true interest, its expression of the unconscious—although staying within the facts, she, nonetheless, evokes a world almost as strange as **historical fantasy.**

Trends and Themes. The increased desire to make history psychologically appealing often brings at least some deviation from dull linearity, as with Michael Brown's *The Wars of Scotland, 1214–1371,* which interrupts the flow of text with magazinelike boxes, singling out stimulating remarks. In other books, advances in printing make possible lavish illustrations, such as Douglas Brinkley's *National Geographic Visual History of the World* (2005) with timelines on each page and color-coded sidebars, so that readers may flip at random. A step beyond this are such tomes as Felipe Fernandez-Arnesto's two volume *The World: A History* with interactive CD-Roms (2006) or Jane Bingham's *The Usborne Internet-Linked Encyclopedia of World History* (2001).

Availability of illustration not only embellishes traditional historical subjects but inspires ones built around pictures, for example, Jack Larkin's *Where We Lived* (2006). By combining photographs from the Historic American Buildings Survey with travelers' diary entries, he recreates the experience of the past. Project director for "Back to Our Roots," Larkin makes material remains fulfill a common function of myth, a sense of restored origin. Finally, Larry Gonick's *The Cartoon History of the Modern World* (2006) and similar books allow for a commingling of fact and fantasy, where the two remain sufficiently separable so that a careful reader can learn history from the former and be amused by the latter without necessarily confusing the two.

Some history books share much with cinema (the most popular amalgam of picture and condensation). This connection is occasionally literal, such as the flood of film histories, for example, Robert A. Rosenstone's *History on Film/Film on History* (2006) or Robert Niemi's *History in the Media: Film and Television* (2006). So far, though, the more common tendency is to share with the popular media sensational topics, especially sex. Such histories focus on erotic situations (e.g., Antonia Fraser's *Love and Louis XIV: The Women in the Life of the Sun King*, 2006) or embrace a broader scope as with Stephen Chippenham's *Histories of Sexuality* (2004), Kim Phillips's *Sexualities in History* (2001), and Elizabeth Reis's *American Sexual Histories* (2001).

One of the fascinations of pictures comes from their suggesting understanding at a glance, an effect also of condensation, a process like dreams, which tell whole stories in moments of Rapid-Eye-Movement sleep. Working as well (or badly) as other labor-saving devices, literary condensation (or the promise of it) has become a publishing staple, such as E.H. Gombrich's *A Little History of the World* (2005), Bill Bryson's *A Short History of Nearly Everything* (2005), and Ken Wilber's new age *A Brief History of Everything* (1996). Gombrich's title perhaps best exemplifies this tendency because the book was first published in German in 1936 as *World History from the Beginning to the Present* (*Weltgeschichte von der Urzeit bis zur Gegenwart*) and then in 1985 as *A Short World History for Young Readers* (*Eine kurze Weltgeschichte für junge Leser*). The earliest title presupposes readers desirous of much for their money, the second is a concession to the short attention span of children, and the third suggests that everyone may share this trait. Given the vogue of promised condensation, when David Harvey decided to employ such a jawbreaker as "neoliberalism" in a title, he felt obliged to soften it by calling the book *A Brief History of Neoliberalism* (2005). After the success of Stephen Hawking's *A Brief History of Time* (1988) came *The Illustrated Brief History of Time* (1996) and then *A Briefer History of Time* (2005).

To the extent that technological developments affect the trend, these are also chronicled, for example, in Joan Meyerowitz's *How Sex Changed: A History of Transsexuality in the United States* (2002). Ranging from Marilyn Yalom's *History of the Breast* (1998) to David Friedman's *A Mind of Its Own: A Cultural History of the Penis* (2001), every part of the subject is exposed repeatedly and treated directly, indirectly, or even by its absence, as with Gary Taylor's *Castration: An Abbreviated History of Western Manhood* (2000) or Piotr O. Scholtz's and John A. Broadwin's *Eunuchs and Castrati: A Cultural History* (2000)—both probably stemming from a curiosity whetted by the movie *Farinelli* (1994).

Freudian analysts began with a historiography that Richard H. Armstrong titled *A Compulsion for Antiquity* (2005) and continue to publish that the past is an expression of subconscious sexual impulses. In such books as Robert B. Clarke's *An Order Outside Time: A Jungian View of the Higher Self from Egypt to Christ* (2005), Jungian psychologists chronicle spiritual history. Although relatively old-fashioned ecclesiastical histories (the conscious side of religion) continue to be published, newer publications examine trancelike, spiritual experiences that contradict orthodoxy. For years, there was one voluminous tome on that subject, Evelyn Underhill's *Mysticism: A Study of the Nature and Development of Spiritual Consciousness* (1911), but its examples, largely from the lives of the saints, were only a mild challenge to the Christian church because Underhill was a devout Anglo-Catholic.

However, the poet and former college professor Nicholas Hagger has been publishing one massive compendium on the history of mysticism after another, among them *The Light of Civilization: How the Vision of God has Inspired All the Great Civilizations* (2006). What is remarkable, however, is their unparalleled mix of real scholarship and amateurish reliance on very questionable sources. Even the latter constitute a quarry of information about new-age groups. Admittedly, there has been a tradition of idiosyncratic religious historiography among some British poets since Robert Graves's *The White Goddess: A Historical Grammar of Poetic Myth* (1948). Nicholas Hagger's accomplishment, however, is to be one of the first to publish the kind of unselective information accumulation that the Internet has made available, which is many students' experience of history—a flood of data that once (for both good and ill) was prevented by academic prejudices and standards. The twenty-first century, of course, also issues more restrained and limited treatments of his subject (e.g., Roy Anker's *Catching Light: Looking for God in the Movies*, 2004; or Eva Parinou's *The Light of the Gods: The Role of Light in Archaic and Classical Greek Cult*, 2000). Hagger, though, is one of the most conspicuous examples of writers whose very personal spiritual search expresses itself through historical research; other examples are Layne Redmond's *When the Drummers Were Women: A Spiritual History of Rhythm* (1997) or Nevil Drury's *The History of Magic in the Modern Age: A Quest for Personal Transformation* (2000).

As Amy Hollywood has demonstrated in her *Sensible Ecstasy* (2002), during the latter twentieth century, many French intellectuals, even atheists, wrote sympathetically about past mystics, especially if they were women, because the intellectuals favored the emergence of the repressed and suppressed (including feminism). Twenty-first-century feminism is not only exhuming women's history but also giving voice to the emotions and spiritualities once dismissed by academic historians. Bonnie Smith's *The Gender of History* (1998), for instance, recovers a time when women historians, condemned as amateurs, were dealing conspicuously with the emotional and spiritual traumas that underlie history being the realm of the dead. In addition to pursuing the theoretical issues of a feminist historiography, as in Sherna Berger Gluck and Daphne Patai's *Women's Words* (1991) and Sue Morgan's *The Feminist History Reader* (2006), feminist historians have been rethinking religious traditions, for example, Luise Schottroff, Barbara Rumscheidt, and Martin Rumscheidt's *Lydia's Impatient Sisters: A Feminist Social History of Early Christianity* and Rita Gross's *Buddhism After Patriarchy; A Feminist History, Analysis and Reconstruction of Buddhism* (1995).

Other formerly suppressed voices finding their histories include sexual and racial minorities. African American history is epic celebrated in such major works as Taylor Branch's three-volume chronicle of the King years: *Parting the Waters* (1988); *Pillar of Fire* (1998); and *At Canaan's Edge: American in the King Years, 1965–1968* (2004). Also notable are African American contributions to world culture, as with Leland's *Hip: The History* (2004). Particularly since Martin Bernal's *Black Athena: The Afroasiatic Roots of Classical Civilization* (1988; rev. ed. 2006) and Chancellor Williams's *Destruction of Black Civilization: Great Issues of a Race from 4500 B.C. to 2000 A.D.* (1971), black history has challenged traditional versions of the past and served as a model for recollections of other suppressed minorities, for example, Melissa Wender's *Lamentations as History: Narratives by Koreans in Japan, 1965–2000* (2005). At least since Edward Said's *Orientalism* (1979), the Occident's projection of its own unconscious on Asia has been a recognized problem, studied, for instance, in Robert Markley's *The Far East and the English Imagination, 1600–1730* (2006). Ruth MacKay's *"Lazy, Improvident People": Myth and Reality in the Writing of Spanish History* (2006) exemplifies a related kind of book, the defense of a slandered nation; the diasporas of so many states' citizens almost guarantees that they will form minority groups somewhere with reason to question the dominant group's version of history.

Comparably, twenty-first century historians are likely to focus on people outside the dominant culture, including the feral children of Michael Newton's *Savage Girls and Wild Boys* (2002), the loafers in Tom Lutz's *Doing Nothing* (2006), or even the obnoxious in Mark Caldwell's *A Short History of Rudeness* (2000). Of course, this trend encompasses recollections of the American counterculture in Robert Stone's *Prime Green: Remembering the Sixties,* (2007), and Marc Fisher's *Something in the Air: Radio, Rock, and the Revolution That Shaped a Generation* (2007) as well as a much longer span of pleasure seeking in Barbara Ehrenreich's *Dancing in the Streets* (2007). Given the success of the *Pirates of the Caribbean* movies (2003 and 2006), books on sea rovers proliferated in time for the films and their CD and television re-release, for example, Gail Sellinger's and W. Thomas Smith's *The Complete Idiot's Guide to Pirates* (2006) and John Matthews's *Pirates* (2006). Typical of much American history writing, Hampton Sides's *Blood and Thunder: An Epic of the American West* (2006) stresses the wilds and their inhabitants in the United States adventure.

This chronicling of what and whomever lies beyond the pales of propriety, civilization, and conscious control already constitutes a history of the unconscious's imagery. Histories of the unconscious itself may include such post-Freudian research as is summarized in Frank Tallis's *Hidden Minds: A History of the Unconscious* (2002) and Guy Claxton's *Wayward Mind: An Intimate History of the Unconscious* (2006). Given the growing prominence of "dissociation" and the continuing importance of myth in psychological theory, the subject also includes Robert Rieber's *The Bifurcation of the Self: The History and Theory of Dissociation and Its Disorders* (2006) and Karen Armstrong's *A Short History of Myth* (2002). The idea of the unconscious explicitly figures in Jenni Hellwarth's *The Reproductive Unconscious in Late Medieval and Early Modern England* (2002), Lesslie Hossfeld's *Narrative, Political Unconscious and Racial Violence in Wilmington, North Carolina* (2004), and Elizabeth Ezra's *The Colonial Unconscious: Race and Culture in Interwar France* (2000).

One of the most prominent ways that authors serve a public desire for representations of the unconscious, however, is to take a metaphor for it and build a history around it associatively. Consider, for instance, Victoria Finlay's *Color: A Natural History of the Palette* (2002), which commences with images of her tumbling somewhat like Alice in Wonderland, but through a "paintbox," into the imagination, which is inhabited by a "rainbow serpent" (ix). She writes "I dreamed of a mountain with veins of blue, inhabited by men with wild eyes and black turbans, and when I woke up I knew that one day I would go there" (281). Her journey for pigments brings her to the Afghanistan of her dream and to Australia, where she contemplates how sacred ochres lead the aborigines into dreamtime: "Dreamtime—a dream in the sense that it is not set in the past, but in a kind of parallel present universe, rather like the one we operate in while we are asleep" (35–36). As for

Hagger, light represents a reality both internal and transpersonal, so for Finlay do the colors of light. What makes her book much more popular than Hagger's, however, is that she manages to integrate her subject as symbol with its very physical manifestations.

Comparable books treat the histories of specific colors, such as the synthesizing of royal purple: Simon Garfield's *Mauve: How One Man Invented a Color that Changed the World* (2000). They easily focus on light solidified—some shiny object as with Eric Wilson's *The Spiritual History of Ice: Romanticism, Science, and the Imagination* (2003) or Mark Kurlansky's *Salt: A World History* (2002), which begins with a mysterious, luminous, icelike saline mass that the author bought. Given, for instance, Chinese use of gardens as spiritual microcosms of the world, Tom Turner's *Garden History: Philosophy and Design 2000 B.C.–2000 AD* (2005) belongs here as well. Related to these single fetish books are ones that bring together many treasures from the past and the search for them, as in Frank Pope's *Dragon Sea: A True Tale of Treasure, Archeology, and Greed off the Coast of Vietnam* (2007) and in Josh Bernstein's *Digging for the Truth: One Man's Epic Adventure Exploring the World's Greatest Archaeological Mysteries* (2006). They follow the very gradual shift in history writing from finished record to search in progress—a search as much internal as external.

Context and Issues. The approach of the year 2000 inspired apocalyptic speculations, which did not entirely disappear when the first few years of the twenty-first century brought September 11, 2001, a variety of wars, including the American invasions of Afghanistan and Iraq, and natural disasters, notably a 2004 tsunami in the Pacific and a 2005 inundating hurricane in New Orleans. Perhaps coincidentally, books on past disasters that might have seemed like academic exercises began to sound like precursors of the present, for example, Willam Wayne Farris's *Japan's Medieval Population: Famine, Fertility, and Warfare in a Transformative Age* (2006). Naturally, people wondered what might be done. The biologist Jared Diamond had written two, very fatalistic, previous books, with humans as chimpanzees controlled by their environments: the Pulitzer-Prize-winning *Guns, Germs, and Steel: The Fates of Human Societies* (1999) and *The Third Chimpanzee: The Evolution and Future of the Human Animal* (1992). His twenty-first-century book was *Collapse: How Societies Choose to Fail or Succeed* (2004)—still portraying history as a response to weather and geography but with a greater recognition that people could adapt to adverse conditions.

In order to adapt, however, people had to decide what had happened, beginning with 9/11, and publishers were very obliging in this regard: Mitchell Fink's *Never Forget: An Oral History of September 11, 2001* (2002), Damon DiMarco's *Tower Stories: An Oral History of 9/11* (2007), Lawrence Wright's *The Looming Tower: Al-Qaeda and the Road to 9/11* (2006), and so on. The larger questions about the Middle East reaped a comparable harvest: F.E. Peters's *The Monotheists: Jews, Christians, and Muslims in Conflict and Competition* (2005), Andrew Wheatcroft's *Infidels: A History of the Conflict Between Christendom and Islam* (2004), Bernard Lewis's *The Middle East: 2000 years of History from the Rise of Christianity to the Present Day* (1996; rev. ed. 2000), Michael Oren's *Power, Faith, and Fantasy: America in the Middle East: 1776 to the Present* (2007), and so on. Such books as *American Fascists: The Christian Right and the War On America* (Hedges, 2007) have argued that government measures to defend America against terrorism have helped a larger conservative agenda. A few books themselves became foci of

"BASED ON A TRUE STORY"

At a time when fictions like to advertise themselves as "based on a true story," history constitutes a very marketable commodity. A revelation about organized crime, such as Nicholas Pileggi's *Wiseguy* (1985), is very likely to be filmed—in this case, becoming *Goodfellas* (1990). Sports are another photogenic activity, as with Laura Hillenbrand's *Seabiscuit* (2001) adapted into a major movie (2003). Mark Bowden's military thriller *Blackhawk Down* (2000) evoked the moment by moment panic of combat in Mogadishu so powerfully that it easily flowed into Ridley Scott's riveting cinema of it (2001). George Jonas's *Vengeance: The True Story of an Israeli Counter-Terrorist Team (1984)* first inspired the 1986 TV movie *Sword of Gideon* and then Steven Spielberg's *Munich* (2005).

controversy—somewhat the case with Jimmy Carter's *Palestine: Peace Not Apartheid* (2006), accused of being pro-Arab, and more obviously with Bob Woodward's *State of Denial* (2006), which played a part in President Bush's declining popularity. The title of Woodward's book well captures the mood of the time with its suggestion that the real situation was being politically suppressed and/or psychologically repressed by those in power. In more questionable books, extreme speculations flourished about the United States causing the attack on the twin towers. These theories were opposed in *Debunking 9/11 Myths: Why Conspiracy Theories Can't Stand Up to the Facts* by the Editors of Popular Mechanics with an "Introduction" by John McCain (2006).

Reception. When one includes the "History Channel" on American cable television, historiography seems very much alive. Consequently, Francis Fukuyama caused a stir in 1992 when he expanded his 1989 article "The End of History? After the Battle of Jena" into the book *The End of History and the Last Man.* He was writing about Immanuel Kant's notion that, in large terms, historical writing narrates the long development from prehistory to modern liberal democracy, so that readers can see the goal of history and participate in it (Fukuyama 1992, 57). George W. Hegel concluded that with Napoleon's victory over the Prussian monarchy in 1806, the idea of liberty had materialized, so that further history writing was pointless. This, of course, ignores the value of limited historiography, designed to help a specific society become more democratic, but it raises interesting questions about "Universal History." At the end of his book, Fukuyama wonders if we are in the age of (what the philosopher Friedrich Nietzsche called) "the Last Man," who contents himself with creature comforts because there is no longer any great purpose to be achieved.

The basic problem with Fukuyama's premises is that they come from Kant and Hegel, who assumed "history" meant (as it did in their day) a chronological account of changing political structures. The history writing of the twentieth and early twenty-first century, however, has not been limited to the external shape of events but has suggested the internal: how impulses, impressions, and intuitions contribute. Because of Hegel's influence on Marx, communism was a fossil preserving the old history to inspire the struggle toward utopia. After the fall of communism, though, the function of history has tended to be an enlargement of awareness and (whether or not this leads to structured political and economic changes) its goal is achieved as reading history opens the minds of the readers to greater complexity. The continuing struggle, of course, is that such complexity is initially frightening. Consequently, histories are most widely received if they include elements of the familiar—the degree of reassurance needed, of course, being related both to the fearsomeness of each age described and each age in which the describing occurs.

Selected Authors. During an economic boom, when the government was lavishly funding social and educational projects, the "New Left" of the 1960s was attracted to Herbert Marcuse's *Eros and Civilization* (1955), which viewed the past as a record of unnecessary repression and championed unconscious impulses. The "New New Left" of the 1970s and 1980s reveled in such philosophical historiography as Michel Foucault's *Discipline and Punish: the Birth of the Prison* (*Surveiller et Punir: Naissance de la Prison*, French 1975; English 1977)—a strident condemnation of enforcing norms. Naturally, even then there was a growing neo-conservative movement in reaction against the proposed anarchy. Near the ominous year 2000, the most prominent interpreters of history tended to be far from the radicalism of Marcuse or Foucault. This is not to say that history writing went back entirely to the old mode, but it often mixed the new impressionistic approach with a relatively conservative nostalgia, as with Thomas Cahill, Felipe Fernandez-Armesto, Eric Larson, and Thomas Friedman.

Author of *Jesus' Little Instruction Book* (1994), Thomas Cahill is publishing a multi-volume "Hinges of History" series, mostly Christian apologetic. Back in 1936, C.S. Lewis argued in his *Allegory of Love* that Christianity had raised the status of women through courtly love, which he traced to Christian roots (thereby, perhaps, underplaying the importance of Arab sources). Cahill's *Mysteries of the Middle Ages: The Rise of Feminism, Science, and Art from the Cults of Catholic Europe* (2006) functions in a similar way, focusing almost exclusively on possible Christian influences. Even though many patriarchal cultures have had idealized images of the feminine (e.g., Kuanyin in China or the goddesses of Greece), Cahill presumes that the Catholic version of these led to feminism. Even though alchemy flourished in China with no connection to the transubstantiation allegedly occurring in the Christian mass, Cahill presumes such a connection instrumental in Western alchemy and that alchemy was the source of science. Another way feminism and science might be explained is quite the opposite: the breakdown in Christian orthodoxy that allowed people to deviate from tradition.

Cahill's other "Hinges of History" also emphasize the possible contributions of Christian tradition. Although the copying of manuscripts in Irish monasteries during the Dark Ages has been a given in many studies of world history, Cahill titles the first volume in this series *How the Irish Saved Civilization: The Untold Story of Ireland's Heroic Role from the Fall of Rome to the Rise of Medieval Europe* (1995). Obviously, the Greco-Roman civilization therein preserved was not the only one in the world, and the preservation of its books owes at least as much to the Byzantines and Arabs as to the Irish, but *How the Irish Saved Civilization* spent over two years on the New York Times bestseller list. Winner of a Christopher award, Cahill's next book *The Gifts of the Jews: How a Tribe of Desert Nomads Changed the Way Everyone Thinks and Feels* (1998) makes what Christians call the "Old Testament" the foundation of civilization. The third volume, *Desire of the Everlasting Hills: The World Before and After Jesus* (1999) interprets Jesus as the shaper of civilization. The fourth volume, *Sailing the Wine-Dark Sea: Why the Greeks Matter* (2003) comes closest to diverging from Christian apologetic, but functions to introduce Greek culture as a component of early Christianity and thence an influence today.

Although lacking that kind of tunnel vision, the erudite, multi-cultural Felipe Fernandez-Armesto is in his own way even more conservative. He grew up as part of a Hispanic minority in Britain, and his *The Spanish Armada: The Experience of War in 1588* (1988) mocks the Britains' notion that their victory over Spain showed the superiority of liberty over despotism. A Roman Catholic, his *Reformations: A Radical Interpretation of Christianity and the World, 1500–2000* (written with Derek Wilson, 1997) argues that the Protestant Reformation was not a major event but merely one of many reform movements. In this and as a refrain through many of his works, he argues that, given history as a whole, change is a relatively rare aberration, likely to go away (see his Internet interview, "Back to the "Future"). His *So You Think You're Human?* (2005) portrays people as a species of chimpanzee. With nostalgia for the jungle, his 2001 *Civilizations* considers civilization to be a mistake. In an age when postmodernism makes many historians skeptical about the existence of objective truth, he not only believes in it but has written *Truth* (2001) to defend the comforting idea that history can be objective truth.

The former Wall Street Journal reporter Erik Larson began with standard liberal notions but has been following an ever darker skepticism about progress, which is taking him in the direction of Fernandez-Armesto. Larson's reporting career led him to write *Naked Consumer: How Our Private Lives Become Public Commodities* (1993) in reaction against the rise of invasive technologies. With *Lethal Passage: The Story of a Gun* (1994), he was, of course, advocating gun control to preserve us from a murdering sixteen-year-old with an M–11/9. His swerve from liberal reportage was *Isaac's Storm: The Drowning of Galveston, 8 September 1900* (2001). The villain is no standard target of liberals, such as prying censors or gun manufacturers, but nature aided by a meteorologist's naïve trust in an imperfect technology. The swerve from liberalism continues in *The Devil in the White City* (2006). Larson contrasts the World's Fair—embodying the age's optimism about technology—with a serial killer, employing his own technology for homicide. In *Thunderstruck* (2006), Larson again contrasts an image of technological progress, Guglielmo Marcone, inventor of the wireless, with a murderer, this time H.H. Crippen. Repeatedly, Larson makes the point that public acceptance of the new technology was spurred by the hunt for Crippen, so that homicide and problematic advance become conflated, as with his previous book. Both volumes are rather like the movie *Forbidden Planet*, where progress runs up against monsters from the unconscious.

Although initially a fairly liberal reporter, Thomas Friedman's long support for the Iraq war and for capitalist expansion aligned him with President Bush's neo-conservative government. Eventually, Friedman condemned the war, but by then so did a number of conservatives. Winner of three Pulitzer Prizes for reporting, he brought first-hand experience to his *From Beirut to Jerusalem* (1989), in some ways a moderate and conciliatory survey of the Middle East, but sufficiently appreciative of force so that the book's prestige may have helped to steer America in that direction. His angry reaction to 9/11, *Longitudes and Attitudes: Exploring the World After September 11* (2002) was distinctly hawkish. His encomiums to the Internet, *The Lexus and the Olive Tree* (1999) and *The World is Flat: A Brief History of the Twenty-First Century* (2005) recognize some dangers of globalization but focus more on the boons to the privileged than on the banes to those not in a position to profit.

THE PULITZER PRIZES FOR HISTORY

Recent Pulitzer Prizes for history writing have included these:

2007	*The Race Beat: The Press, the Civil Rights Struggle, and the Awakening of a Nation* by Gene Roberts and Hank Klibanoff (Alfred A. Knopf)
2006	*Polio: An American Story* by David M. Oshinsky (Oxford University Press)
2005	*Washington's Crossing* by David Hackett Fischer (Oxford University Press)
2004	*A Nation Under Our Feet: Black Political Struggles in the Rural South from Slavery to the Great Migration* by Steven Hahn (The Belknap Press of Harvard University Press)
2003	*An Army at Dawn: The War in North Africa, 1942–1943* by Rick Atkinson (Henry Holt and Company)
2002	*The Metaphysical Club: A Story of Ideas in America* by Louis Menand (Farrar, Straus and Giroux)
2001	*Founding Brothers: The Revolutionary Generation* by Joseph J. Ellis (Alfred A. Knopf)
2000	*Freedom From Fear: The American People in Depression and War, 1929–1945* by David M. Kennedy (Oxford University Press)

Source: Pulitzer Prize Web site. http://www.pulitzer.org/

Like other such great popularizers of history, such as Barbara Tuchman with her *A Distant Mirror* (1978), Cahill, Fernandez-Armesto, Larson, and Friedman have helped bridge past and present. In a world of rapid, seemingly chaotic change, Cahill has given modern Christian readers a sense of some design, working throughout the centuries to unfold their values, and Fernandez-Armesto has presented such a great span of time and space that the disturbing changes almost seem to disappear. Larson has dramatized the current disenchantment with technology, projecting it backward a hundred years, and Friedman has produced the opposite, but also reassuring, *A Brief History of the Twenty-First Century,* where he manages to be nostalgic for traditional communities, which he hopes to preserve, yet also optimistic about a global one to come.

Bibliography

Anker, Roy. *Catching Light: Looking For God in The Movies.* Grand Rapids, Michigan: Eerdman's, 2004.

Armstrong, Karen. *A Short History of Myth.* Edinburgh: Canongate, 2005.

Armstrong, Richard H. *A Compulsion for Antiquity: Freud and the Ancient World.* Ithaca, New York: Cornell University Press, 2005.

Bernal, Martin. *Black Athena: The Afroasiatic Roots of Classical Civilization. The Fabrication of Ancient Greece 1785–1985, Volume 1.* Piscataway, New Jersey: Rutgers University Press, 1988, Rev. Ed. 2006.

Bernstein, Josh. *Digging for the Truth: One Man's Epic Adventure Exploring the World's Greatest Archaeological Mysteries.* New York: Gotham, 2006.

Bingham, Jane. *The Usborne Internet-Linked Encyclopedia of World History.* Tulsa, OK: Usborne, 2001.

Bowden, Mark. *Blackhawk Down: An American War Story.* Philadelphia: Philadelphia Inquirer, 1997.

Branch, Taylor. *At Canaan's Edge: American in the King Years, 1965–1968.* New York: Simon and Schuster, 2007.

———. *Parting the Waters: America in the King Years, 1954–1963.* New York: Simon and Schuster, 1988.

————. *Pillar of Fire: American in the King Years, 1963–1965.* New York: Simon and Schuster, 1998.

Brinkley, Douglas. *National Geographic Visual History of the World.* New York: National Geographic, 2005.

Brown, Michael. *The Wars of Scotland, 1214–1371.* Edinburgh: Edinburgh University Press, 2004.

Bryson, Bill. *A Short History of Nearly Everything.* New York: Broadway, 2005.

Cahill, Thomas. *Desire of the Everlasting Hills: The World Before and After Jesus.* New York: Random House, 1999.

————. *The Gifts of the Jews: How a Tribe of Desert Nomads Changed the Way Everyone Thinks and Feels.* New York: Anchor Books, 1998.

————. *How the Irish Saved Civilization: The Untold Story of Ireland's Heroic Role from the Fall of Rome to the Rise of Medieval Europe.* New York: Doubleday, 1995.

————. *Mysteries of the Middle Ages: The Rise of Feminism, Science, and Art from the Cults of Catholic Europe.* New York: Nan A. Talese, 2006.

————. *Sailing the Wine-Dark Sea: Why the Greeks Matter.* New York: Doubleday, 2003.

Caldwell, Mark. *A Short History of Rudeness: Manners, Morals, and Misbehavior in Modern America.* New York: Picador, 2000.

Carter, Jimmy. *Palestine: Peace Not Apartheid.* New York: Simon and Schuster, 2006.

Chippenham, Stephen Garton. *Histories of Sexuality.* Wiltshire: Routledge, 2004.

Clarke, Rohert B. *An Order Outside Time: A Jungian View of the Higher Self from Egypt to Christ.* London: Hampton Roads, 2005.

Claxton, Guy. *Wayward Mind: An Intimate History of the Unconscious.* New York: Little, Brown, and Co., 2006.

Dewald, Carolyn, and John Marincola. *The Cambridge Companion to Herodotus.* Cambridge: Cambridge University Press, 2006.

Diamond, Jared. *Collapse: How Societies Choose to Fail or Succeed.* New York: Viking, 2004.

————. *Guns, Germs, and Steel: The Fates of Human Societies.* New York: Norton, 1999.

————. *The Third Chimpanzee: The Evolution and Future of the Human Animal.* New York: Harper, 1992.

DiMarco, Damon. *Tower Stories: An Oral History of 9/11.* 1. Santa Monica: Santa Monica Press, 2007.

Drury, Nevill. *The History of Magic in the Modern Ages: A Quest for Personal Transformation.* London: Carroll and Graff, 2000.

Ehrenreich, Barbara. *Dancing in the Streets: A History of Collective Joy.* New York: Metropolitan, 2007.

Erickson, Carolly. *The Medieval Vision: Essays in History and Perception.* New York: Oxford University Press, 1976.

Ezra, Elizbeth. *The Colonial Unconscious: Race and Culture in Interwar France.* Ithaca, New York: Cornell University Press, 2000.

Farris, William Wayne. *Japan's Medieval Population: Famine, Fertility, and Warfare in a Transformative Age.* Honolulu: University of Hawaii Press, 2006.

Fernandez-Armesto, Felipe. "Back to the Future." [Online, January 1999] BBC News. <http://news.bbc.co.uk/hi/english/static/special_report/1999/12/99/back_to_the_future/felipe_armesto.stm>.

————. *The Spanish Armada: The Experience of War in 1588.* Oxford: Oxford University Press, 1988.

————. *Reformations: A Radical Interpretation of Christianity and the World, 1500–2000.* New York: Scribner, 1997.

————. *Truth: A History and a Guide for the Perplexed.* New York: St. Martin's Griffin, 2001.

————. *So You Think You're Human?* Oxford: Oxford University Press, 2005.

————. *Civilizations.* Elgin Illinois: Pan, 2001.

_____. *The World: A History, Volume 1, From 1000 to 1800*. New York: Prentice Hall, 2006.

_____.*The World: A History, Since 1300, Volume Two*. New York: Prentice Hall, 2006 [Bk & CD-ROM edition].

Fink, Mitchell. *Never Forget: An Oral History of September 11, 2001*. New York: Regan, 2002.

Finlay, Victoria. *Color: A Natural History of the Palette*. New York: Ballantine Books, 2002.

Fisher, Marc. *Something in the Air: Radio, Rock, and the Revolution That Shaped a Generation*. New York: Random House, 2007.

Foucault, Michel. *Discipline and Punish: The Birth of the Prison*. London: Penguin, 1977.

Fraser, Antonia. *Love and Louis XIV: The Women in the Life of the Sun King*. New York: Doubleday, 2006.

Friedman, David. *A Mind of Its Own: A Cultural History of the Penis*. New York: Free Press, 2001.

Friedman, Thomas. *From Beirut to Jerusalem*. New York: Anchor, 1990.

———. *The Lexus and the Olive Tree*. New York: Anchor, 1999.

———. *Longitudes and Attitudes: Exploring the World After September 11*. New York: Farrar, Straus, and Giroux, 2002.

_____. *The World is Flat: A Brief History of the Twenty-first Century*. New York: Farrar, Straus, and Giroux, 2005.

Fukuyama, Francis. "The End of History? After the Battle of Jena." *The National Interest* 16 (1989): 3–18.

_____. *The End of History and the Last Man*. New York: Free Press, 1992.

Garfield, Simon. *Mauve: How One Man Invented a Color That Changed the World*. London: Faber & Faber, 2000.

Gluck, Sherna Berger, and Daphne Patai. *Women's Words: The Feminist Practice of Oral History*. London: Routledge, 1991.

Gombrich, E.H. *A Little History of the World*. Translated by Caroline Mustill. New Haven: Yale University Press, 2005.

Gonick, Larry. *The Cartoon History of the Modern World Part 1: From Columbus to the U.S. Constitution*. West Link, Ireland: Collins, 2006.

Graves, Robert. *The White Goddess: A Historical Grammar of Poetic Myth*. London: Farrar, Straus, Giroux, 1948.

Gross, Rita. *Buddhism After Patriarchy: A Feminist History, Analysis and Reconstruction of Buddhism*. Albany: SUNY Press, 1995.

Hagger, Nicholas. *The Light of Civilization: How the Vision of God has Inspired All the Great Civilizations*. New York: O Books, 2006.

Hartog, François. *The Mirror of Herodotus: The Representation of the Other in the Writing of History*. The New Historicism: Studies in Cultural Poetics, 5. Berkeley: University of California, 1988.

Harvey, David. *A Brief History of Neoliberalism*. New York: Oxford University Press, 2005.

Hawking, David. *A Brief History of Time*. New York: Bantam, 1988.

_____. *The Illustrated Brief History of Time*. New York: Bantam, 1996.

Hawking, Stephen, and Leonard Miodinow. *A Briefer History of Time*. New York: Bantam, 2005.

Hedges, Chris. *American Fascists: The Christian Right and the War On America*. New York: Free Press, 2007.

Herodotus: The Histories. 4 vols, trans. A. D. Godley, Loeb Classical Series. London: W. Heinemann, 1926. Online at <http://www.perseus.tufts.edu/Texts.html>.

Hellenbrand, Laura. *Seabiscuit: An American Legend*. New York: Ballantine, 2001.

Hellwarth, Jenni. *The Reproductive Unconscious in Late Medieval and Early Modern England*. Studies in Medieval History and Culture, V. 13. London: Routledge, 2002.

Hollywood, Amy. *Sensible Ecstasy: Mysticism, Sexual Difference, and the Demands of History*. Chicago: University of Chicago, 2002.

Hossfeld, Leslie. *Narrative, Political Unconscious and Racial Violence in Wilmington, North Carolina*. Studies in American Popular History and Culture. London: Routledge, 2004.

Hughes-Warrington, Marnie. *Fifty Key Thinkers in History*. London: Routledge, 2000.

Jonas, George. *Vengeance: The True Story of an Israeli Counter Terrorist Team*. New York: Simon and Schuster, 1984.

Kurlansky, Mark. *Salt: A World History*. New York: Penguin, 2002.

Larkin, Jack. *Where We Lived: Discovering the Places We Once Called Home*. Washington: Taunton, 2006.

Larson, Eric. *The Devil in the White City*. New York: Bantam, 2006.

———. *Isaac's Storm: The Drowning of Galveston, 8 September 1900*. Darby, Pennsylvania: Diane, 2001.

_____. *Lethal Passage: The Story of a Gun*. New York: Vintage, 1994.

_____. *Thunderstruck*. Phoenix, Arizona: Crown, 2006.

Leland, John. *Hip: The History*. New York: HarperCollins, 2004.

Lewis, Bernard. *The Middle East*. New York: Weidenfeld, 1996; rev. ed. 2000.

Lewis, C.S. *The Allegory of Love: A Study in Medieval Tradition*. Oxford: Oxford University Press, 1936.

Lutz, Tom. *Doing Nothing: A History of Loafers, Loungers, Slackers, and Bums in America*. London: Farrar, Straus, Giroux, 2006.

MacKay, Ruth. *"Lazy, Improvident People": Myth and Reality in the Writing of Spanish History*. Ithaca: Cornell University Press, 2006.

Mali, Joseph. *Mythistory: The Making of a Modern Historiography*. Chicago: University of Chicago Press, 2003.

Marcuse, Herbert. *Eros and Civilization: A Philosophical Inquiry into Freud*. Boston: Beacon Press, 1955.

Markley, Robert. *The Far East and the English Imagination, 1600–1730*. Cambridge: Cambridge University Press, 2006.

Matthews, John. *Pirates*. Boston: Athenaeum, 2006.

Meyerowitz, Joanne. *How Sex Changed: A History of Transsexuality in the United States*. Cambridge, Massachusetts: Harvard University Press, 2002.

Morgan, Sue. *The Feminist History Reader*. London: Routledge, 2006.

Newton, Michael. *Savage Girls and Wild Boys: A History of Feral Children*. London: Faber & Faber, 2002.

Niemi, Robert. *History in the Meida: Film and Television*. Santa Barbara: ABC-CLIO, 2006.

Oren, Michael B. *Power, Faith, and Fantasy: America in the Middle East: 1776 to the Present*. New York: Norton, 2007.

Parsinau, Eva. *The Light of the Gods: The Role of Light in Archaic and Classical Greek Cult*. London: Duckworth, 2000.

Peters, F.E. *The Monotheists: Jews, Christians, and Muslims in Conflict and Competition*. Two Vols. Princeton: Princeton University Press, 2005.

Phillips, Kim. *Sexualities in History*. London: Routledge, 2001.

Pliny, the elder. *Natural History*. Translated by H. Rackham. Loeb Classical Library. Vol. 1. London: Heinemann, 1958.

Pileggi, Nicholas. *Wiseguy*. New York: Pocket, 1984.

Pope, Frank. *Dragon Sea: A True Tale of Treasure, Archeology, and Greed off the Coast of Vietnam*. New York: Harcourt, 2007.

Popular Mechanics Editors with "Introduction" by John McCain. *Debunking 9/11 Myths: Why Conspiracy Theories Can't Stand Up to the Facts*. New York: Hears, 2006.

Redmond, Layne. *When the Drummers Were Women: A Spiritual History of Rhythm*. New York: Three Rivers, 1997.

Reis, Elizabeth. *American Sexual Histories*. Blackwell Readers in American Sociala and Cultural History. Oxford: Blackwell, 2001.

Rieber, Robert. *The Bifurcation of the Self: The History and Theory of Dissociation and Its Disorders.* New York: Springer, 2006.

Rosenston, Robert A. *History on Film/Film on History.* New York: Longman, 2006.

Said, Edward W. *Orientalism.* New York: Vintage, 1979.

Sahlins, Marshall. *Apologies to Thucydides: Understanding History as Culture and Vice Versa.* Chicago: University of Chicago Press, 2004.

Schottroff, Luise, Barbara Rumscheidt, and Martin Rumscheid. *Lydia's Impatient Sisters: A Feminist Social History of Early Christianity.* Louisville: Westminster John Knox Press, 1995.

Selincourt, Aubrey de. *The World of Herodotus.* New York: Phoenix, 2001.

Scholz, Piotr O. *Eunuchs and Castrati: A Cultural History.* Translated by John A. Broadwin. Princeton: Markus Wiener, 2001.

Sellinger, Gail, Jr., and W. Thomas Smith. *The Complete Idiot's Guide to Pirates.* New York: Alpha, 2006.

Sides, Hampton. *Blood and Thunder: An Epic of the American West.* New York: Doubleday, 2006.

Stadter, P.A. "The Structure of Livy's History," *Historia,* 21.2 (1972): 287–307.

Stone, Robert. *Prime Green: Remembering the Sixties.* Hopewell, New Jersey: Ecco, 2007.

Tallis, Frank. *Hidden Minds: A History of the Unconscious.* New York: Arcade, 2002.

Taylor, Gary. *Castration: An Abbreviated History of Western Manhood.* London: Routledge, 2000.

Turner, Tom. *Garden History: Philosophy and Design 2000 BC–2000 AD.* Abingdon: Spon, 2005.

Tuchman, Barbara. *A Distant Mirror: The Calamitous 14th Century.* New York: Alfred A. Knopf, 1978.

Wender, Melissa. *Lamentation as History: Narratives by Koreans in Japan, 1965–2000.* Stanford: Stanford University Press, 2005.

Wheatcroft, Andrew. *Infidels: A History of the Conflict Between Christendom and Islam.* New York: Random House, 2004.

Wilbur, Ken. *A Brief History of Everything.* Boston: Shambhala, 1996.

Williams, Chancellor. *The Destruction of Black Civilization: Great Issues of a Race from 4500 B.C. to 2000 A.D.* Dubuque: Kendall/Hunt, 1971.

Wilson, Eric G. *The Spiritual History of Ice: Romanticism, Science, and the Imagination.* New York: Macmillan, 2003.

Woodward, Bob. *State of Denial: Bush at War, Part III.* New York: Simon and Schuster, 2006.

Wright, Lawrence. *The Looming Tower: Al-Qaeda and the Road to 9/11.* New York: Knopf, 2006.

Yalom, Mailyn. *History of the Breast.* New York: Ballantine, 1998.

Further Reading

Crosby, Alfred W. *Ecological Imperialism: The Biological Expansion of Europe, 900–1900* (Studies in Environment and History). London: Cambridge University Press, 1986; Gaddis, Lewis, John. *The Cold War: A New History.* New York: Penguin, 2006; Harrison, Thomas. *Divinity and History: The Religion of Herodotus.* Oxford: Oxford University Press, 2005; Kelley, Donald R. *Frontiers of History: Historical Inquiry in the Twentieth Century.* New Haven: Yale UP, 2006; Lee, Nancy, Lonnie Schlein and Mitchell Levitas, eds. *A Nation Challenged: A Visual History of 9/11 and Its Aftermath.* New York: The New York Times, 2002; Luce, T.J. *Livy: the Composition of his History.* Princeton: Princeton University Press, 1977; Rabasa, Angel M., Cheryl Bernard, Peter Chalk, C. Christine Fair, Theodore Karasik, Rollie Lal, Ian Lesser, and David Thaler. *The Muslim World after 9/11.* Santa Monica: Rand, 2004; Ranke, Leopold von. *History of the Latin and Teutonic Nations, 1494–1514.* Translated by

G.R. Dennis. Houston: Kessinger, 2004; Ricks, Thomas E. *Fiasco: The American Military Adventure in Iraq.* New York: Penguin, 2006; Selincourt, Aubrey de. The *History.* New York: Longman, 2006.

JAMES WHITLARK

HOLOCAUST LITERATURE

Definition. The Holocaust was a series of events between 1933 and 1945 that included the attempted genocide of the Jewish people by the Nazi forces of Germany. More than six million Jews were murdered in this period, a large proportion in specially designed concentration camps (Kremer 2003, xxi).

In his seminal anthology of Holocaust literature, *Art from the Ashes* (1995), Lawrence Langer remarks that "we may never know what the Holocaust *was* for those who endured it, but we do know what has been said about it and . . . the varied ways writers have chosen to say it" (Langer 1995, 3). Thus, Langer distinguishes between the Holocaust as an event—which we can never know—and the Holocaust as a theme for literature, which, as he puts it, changes "the route by which we approach it" (Langer 1995, 3). Yet what does it mean to transform the deaths of millions into a literary theme for a work of fiction? If this is a worrying question for those of us who have no experience of the Holocaust, we can barely imagine how troubling a question it might be for the survivors of the camps, who display both an overwhelming necessity to turn their experiences into words and, at the same time, apprehend that words may be incommensurate with the task.

The Holocaust memoirist Elie Wiesel (1928–) expressed suspicion of the genre when he remarked that "a novel about Treblinka is either not a novel or not about Treblinka" (Wiesel 1990, 7). Wiesel is suggesting that works about the Holocaust can only be factual and, therefore, that fiction cannot be about the Holocaust.

Yet there is such a genre as Holocaust literature. Novels by survivors, their descendents, and others are read, reviewed, and taught on a regular basis. Further, one might venture a straightforward definition of Holocaust literature as simply literature "about the Holocaust" (Eaglestone 2004, 102). This is not quite as clear as it first appears, however, because much late twentieth-century American fiction has been concerned with the Holocaust even when the Holocaust has not been its explicit theme. For example, Philip K. Dick's *Do Androids Dream of Electric Sheep?* (1968) is thematically "about the Holocaust," even though not overtly concerned with Nazis and European Jews (Sammon 1996, 16–17). A similar observation might be made, for example, of Bernard Malamud's *The Fixer* (1966), Thomas Pynchon's *Gravity's Rainbow* (1973) and Don DeLillo's *White Noise* (1984). Indeed, "one might even be tempted to ask what it means when a novel or poem

CAN THE HOLOCAUST BE RESPONDED TO CREATIVELY?

The philosopher Theodor Adorno famously proposed that "to write poetry after Auschwitz is barbaric" (Langer 1975, 1). The same might be said of fiction. How can one derive aesthetic pleasure from contemporary novels after this supreme manifestation of human wickedness? Adorno was particularly suspicious of Holocaust literature precisely because it might provide readers with such aesthetic pleasure. He wrote, "The so-called artistic rendering of the naked bodily pain of those who were beaten down by rifle butts contains, however distantly, the possibility that pleasure can be squeezed from it" (Adorno 1993, 88).

written after 1945 in Europe or America *did not* engage with the issue" (Eaglestone 2004, 106).

For the sake of clarity, we will confine ourselves in this essay to a discussion of canonical Holocaust literature written by survivors to bear witness to the experience of the events and to recent American novels concerned with the Holocaust and its aftermath in the United States.

Trends and Themes

> Auschwitz defies imagination and perception; it submits only to memory. . . . Between the dead and the rest of us there exists an abyss that no talent can comprehend.
>
> I write to denounce writing. I tell of the impossibility one stumbles upon in trying to tell the tale. (Wiesel 1983, 1)

According to Elie Wiesel, if Holocaust literature must be attempted it should be written solely by witnesses of the events. Only those who submit to "memory" can be trusted "to tell the tale" of the disaster. Yet even survivor-writers are confronted with "the impossibility" of conveying their ghastly experiences in the necropolis of the Nazi death camps. Thus, Wiesel recommends silence: "As the ancients said: 'Those who know do not speak; those who speak do not know'" (Wiesel 1967, 152). Throughout the 1960s, the critic George Steiner was similarly recommending "only silence or the Kadish for the unnumbered dead" (Steiner 1967, 168).

Despite such objections, Holocaust literature was written. To trace its development, one must look first to European novelists, including Wiesel. Other important authors to consider are Primo Levi (1919–1987) and Charlotte Delbo (1913–1985). We now turn to the principal texts by these influential writers.

Elie Wiesel's Night (1958). Elie Wiesel was born in the Transylvanian town of Sighet in 1928. When he was fifteen years old, he was deported with his family to Auschwitz. At the end of the war, his parents and younger sister were dead. In 1963 he moved to New York and assumed American citizenship. Since 1976 he has taught at Boston University, and in 1986 he was awarded the Nobel Peace Prize.

Night, Wiesel's account of his time in Auschwitz and deportation to Buchenwald, was published in French in 1958 and English in 1960. The original version of this novelistic memoir, written in Yiddish, was titled *And the World Remained Silent* (1956). Given the importance of silence in all of Wiesel's writings, this title is significant. Indeed, *Night* is concerned with at least four types of silence: the mystery of God's silence in the face of evil, the muteness of the dead, the inadequacy of language in relation to the events of the Holocaust, and the proper awed stance of the reader in the face of Holocaust testimony.

Firstly, there is the mystery of God's silence in the face of evil. This question is theological and concerns theodicy, or whether one can have faith in omnipotent divine providence that, by definition, oversees suffering in the world. The question of theodicy, or of God's silence, is not new. Indeed, it goes back to the biblical Book of Job and the issue of Job's suffering. Much of Wiesel's writing after *Night* approaches such theological issues as a way of indirectly asking the question: Where was God during the Holocaust? Wiesel moves in *Night,* and subsequent books such as *Dawn* (1961) and *The Jews of Silence* (1966), from the immediate terrors that he experienced to a larger cosmic drama; he moves, in other words, from stunned realism to theology: in the absence of divine justice or compassion, silence is the only possible response to this mysterious absence of God. In a key passage from *Night* (which has been published elsewhere as a poem (Schiff 1995, 42)), Wiesel moves from the death of children in the first night of the camp to the death of God inside him:

> Never shall I forget the nocturnal silence which deprived me, for all eternity, of the desire to live. Never shall I forget those moments which murdered my God and soul and turned my dreams to dust. Never shall I forget these things, even if I am condemned to live as long as God Himself. Never. (Wiesel 1981, 45)

Wiesel's second kind of silence is the muteness or silence of the dead. In his essay "A Plea for the Dead" (1967), Wiesel remarks:

> I cannot believe that an entire generation of fathers and sons could vanish into the abyss without creating, by their very disappearance, a mystery which exceeds and overwhelms us . . . All the words in all the mouths of the philosophers and psychologists are not worth the silent tears of that child and his mother. (Wiesel 1967, 143)

Thus, he urges readers to respect the silence of the dead and not to try to speak for them. The essay is an exhortation to "learn to be silent" (Wiesel 1967, 152). In these terms, no writer can speak for the dead.

The third kind of silence derives from the sense that language and our systems of representation cannot do justice to the enormity of the Holocaust. Wiesel, in his essays and criticism, writes of the sheer inadequacy of language to depict the events of the Holocaust. In other words, Wiesel names the enormity of the Holocaust as something that is unnameable, and he calls for silence as the only possible response to these events. He epigrammatically states: "I write to denounce writing." This goes some way to explaining why Wiesel's writing also incorporates the idea of silence.

The final kind of silence is the awed response of the reader in response to these events. For the reader of Holocaust memoirs, silence is supposed to equal a kind of muteness in response to the sacredness of the dead. Gillian Rose, in *Mourning Becomes the Law* (1996), has controversially characterized such sanctification of the Holocaust as "Holocaust piety" (Rose 1996, 43). For Primo Levi, too, the Holocaust takes on something of the sacred in *If This Is a Man*.

Primo Levi's If This Is a Man *(1958).* If This Is a Man was only accepted by a small, short-lived publishing house, De Silvo, in 1947, after being rejected by several major publishers, and so it made little impact until it was republished by Einaudi in 1958 (Kremer 2003, 750). It is now universally acknowledged to be one of the essential Holocaust memoirs.

Following a biblical theme, Levi describes Auschwitz inmates' stories as "simple and incomprehensible like the stories in the Bible" and asks, "But are they not themselves stories of a new Bible?" (Levi 1987, 72). Yet in almost every other way, Levi's novelistic memoir differs from Wiesel's *Night*.

The American Holocaust novelist Cynthia Ozick is not alone in admiring Levi for his "lucid calm," "magisterial equanimity," and "unaroused detachment" (Ozick 1989, 46). Certainly Levi attempts to frame the narrative of his 11 months in Auschwitz-Birkenau within the language of reason. In *If This Is a Man* he writes as a "European" and a secular Jew rather than a religious Jew whose faith has been shaken to its foundations (Levi 1987, 125, 136).

Further, Levi writes as a scientist. He was a twenty-four-year-old chemistry graduate of Turin University, Italy, when he was deported to Auschwitz in 1944. Indeed, he survived mainly due to his chemistry skills being exploited in a rubber factory at the sub-camp of Monowitz-Buna. Thus, it is unsurprising on one level that Levi writes the following of the concentration camp: "We would like to consider that the Lager was pre-eminently a gigantic biological and social *experiment*" (Levi 1987, 93) [my italics]. However, it *is* surprising to encounter such apparently dispassionate "equanimity" from a former inmate of the world's most infamous death camp.

In the Afterword to *If This Is a Man*, Levi attempts to justify the calm tone of his narrative:

> I have deliberately assumed the calm, sober language of the witness, neither the lamenting tones of the victim nor the irate voice of someone who seeks revenge. I thought my account would be all the more credible . . . the more it appeared objective . . . only in this way does a witness in matters of justice perform his task, which is preparing the ground for the judge. The judges are my readers. (Levi 1987: 382)

Here, Levi deploys the rhetoric of law and reason. However, we may ask whether Levi's horrendous experiences can be contained and recounted in this objective narrative voice. How far can a survivor write about himself, as it were, from the outside? What makes *If This Is a Man* especially interesting are the points in Levi's memoir when the language of law and reason proves no longer adequate to the task of narrating his experiences.

Levi's memoir relies heavily on poetry. Indeed, the passionate poem that precedes the prose of *If This Is a Man* reveals the author to be far from objective and detached. The last eight lines of Levi's poem read:

> I commend these words to you. Carve them in your hearts
> At home, in the street,
> Going to bed, rising;
> Repeat them to your children,
>   Or may your house fall apart,
>   May illness impede you,
>   May your children turn their faces from you.

What then of Levi the scientific investigator and the language of law and reason? What then of Levi's humane restraint? References to the Italian poet Dante Alighieri's *Divine Comedy* (1307–21) which pepper the text, serve a similar function in foregrounding poetry, passion, and a sense of rupture in Western culture.

If This Is a Man also features nonscientific anger and frustration. When a religious Jew, Kuhn, thanks "God because he has not been chosen" for the "gas chamber," the narrator is outraged:

> Kuhn is out of his senses. Does he not see Beppo the Greek in the bunk next to him, Beppo who is twenty years old and is going to the gas chamber the day after tomorrow and knows it . . . Does Kuhn not understand that what has happened today is an abomination, which no propitiatory prayer, no pardon, no expiation by the guilty, which nothing at all in the power of man can ever clean again?
> If I was God, I would spit at Kuhn's prayer. (Levi 1987, 135–136)

Again, Levi's frustration is evident when he speaks of the inadequacy of language: "for the first time we became aware that our language lacks words to express this offence, this demolition of man" (Levi 1987, 32). Further, an impersonal, scientific explanation of his experience fails to do justice to the horrendously isolated individuals whom Levi encounters in the camp:

> He told me his story, and today I have forgotten it, but it was certainly a sorrowful, cruel and moving story; because so are all our stories, hundreds of thousands of stories, all different and all full of a tragic disturbing necessity. (Levi 1987, 71–72)

One of the key problems confronting Levi is how to square such "tragic" experience with the collective Western vision of a scientific and rational culture.

Charlotte Delbo's Auschwitz and After *(1946–1971)*. Charlotte Delbo's trilogy *Auschwitz and After* consists of three volumes published between 1946 and 1971: *None of Us Will Return* (1946), *Useless Knowledge* (1970), and *The Measure of Our Days* (1971). They detail the experiences of Delbo and her French Resistance comrades both during and after their traumatic incarceration in Auschwitz. Unlike Wiesel and Levi, Delbo was a non-Jewish political prisoner. Therefore, her time at Auschwitz was not subject to the same degree of lethal threat. Indeed, measures of everyday existence continued to exist side-by-side with the extremities of the concentration camp world for Delbo, as for other political prisoners. It is this relationship between the everyday—for example, domesticity, friendship and romance—and the extreme—traumatic, unrepresentable horror—in Delbo's trilogy that makes it so powerful. Further, such juxtapositions anticipate novels by the American children of survivors such as Thane Rosenbaum (1960–) and Melvin Jules Bukiet (1953–), the so-called "second generation" of Holocaust survivors. ("The 'second generation' is a term used by clinical psychologists and therapists for the children of Holocaust survivors who have in various ways been affected by the after-effects of their parents' experience" (Sicher 2005, 133).) (See later.)

Delbo's project is not simply to document her time in Auschwitz. Her texts also bear witness to what Shoshana Felman and Dori Laub have called a "crisis in truth" (Felman and Laub 1992, 5–6). According to Felman and Laub, testimonial Holocaust "texts do not simply *report facts* but . . . encounter—and make us encounter—*strangeness*" (Felman and Laub 1992, 7). Delbo leads us into such an encounter with strangeness, but her texts also present a version of documentary realism in their reportage of everyday events. Indeed, Delbo's testimony manages to perform a double function. It reveals how the radically strange world of Auschwitz has marked similarities with our everyday world; and, at the same time, it demonstrates that the familiar categories and frameworks of everyday life need to be estranged through a text that forces us to recognize that a complete witnessing by readers of the experiences of the Holocaust is impossible. Both functions correspond to an attempt to narrate the everyday nature of an event in Auschwitz in its historical context and in its extremity as traumatic experience. Delbo manages such a double task precisely by her recourse to literature, a place where historical facts can interact with intense personal memories.

For example, Delbo disrupts her testimony of everyday reality in Auschwitz by introducing *excessive* objects such as teddy bears (Delbo 1995, 162–166) and love letters (Delbo 1995, 155–161). Her fragmented narratives are haunted by such unintegrated details. Indeed, details such as the teddy bear transform her *personal* testimony into a *collective* project. Holocaust literature becomes a recording of trauma in which the ruins of civilian life are assembled in order to disrupt any neat separation between the individual and history; then and now.

"The Teddy Bear" episode begins, innocuously enough, with the description of a Christmas spent in the laboratory of Raisko, a satellite camp of Auschwitz. Though melancholy, this episode seems to represent one of those "moments of reprieve" (Levi 1981) during which privileged prisoners are almost able to obtain an experience of normality in the camps. The festivities reach their climax with the exchange of token gifts, one of which is a small teddy bear for a little girl. This most innocent of presents turns out to have a ghastly origin which, recounted by the narrator, shatters the apparent normality of the scene:

> I stared at the teddy bear. It was a terrifying sight.
>
> One morning, as we passed near the railway station on our way to the fields, our column was stopped by the arrival of a Jewish convoy. People were stepping down from the cattle cars, lining up on the platform in response to the shouted orders of the SS. Women and children first. In the front row, a little girl held her mother by the hand. She had kept her doll tightly squeezed against her body.
>
> This is how a doll, a teddy bear, arrives in Auschwitz. In the arms of a little girl who will leave her toy with her clothing, carefully folded, at the entrance to "the showers." A prisoner from the "heaven commando," as they called those who worked in the crematoria, had found it among the objects piled up in the showers' antechamber and exchanged it for a couple of onions. (Delbo 1995, 166)

This short anecdote establishes a chain of contamination in the camps, connecting the murder of a Jewish girl with the celebration of a Christian holiday, the crematoria and machinery of death to the commerce of the concentration camp. The same process that facilitates Nazi genocide is shown here to enhance an ordinary celebration at the privileged end of the camp hierarchy. In its circulation from one little girl to another, the teddy bear is the bearer of a *double* heritage. Yet it is by no means clear that the Christmas party has been spoiled by the teddy's origins. Only the narrator knows about the bear's original owner—a fact that ensures the chain of evidence leading from murder to celebration will survive. Still, the party goes on despite the murder of the teddy bear's previous owner. From the narrator's chance witness comes this testimony that in turn contaminates the receiver—ultimately, the reader—with *useless knowledge*.

Delbo's elucidation of the teddy bear's progress from arrival to circulation in the camp economy is typical of her use of metonymy. As a poet, she uses the teddy bear to represent something larger: the toy stands for the child who owned it and was murdered. Thus, Delbo reveals the relationship between the everyday world of work and play and the death factory reality of the concentration camp (Rothberg 2000, 152–153).

Contexts and Issues. Since the late 1950s, many American novelists have dealt thematically with the Holocaust. Survivor experience has been conveyed, for example, in Philip Roth's "Eli the Fanatic" (1959) and *The Ghost Writer* (1979); Edward Wallant's *The Pawnbroker* (1961); Isaac Bashevis Singer's *Enemies, A Love Story* (1966); Saul Bellow's *Mr Sammler's Planet* (1972); William Styron's *Sophie's Choice* (1979); Cynthia Ozick's *Cannibal Galaxy* (1983), *The Messiah of Stockholm* (1985), and *The Shawl* (1989); Louis Begley's *Wartime Lies* (1991); Melvin Jules Bukiet's *Stories of an Imaginary Childhood* (1992) and *After* (1996); Anne Michaels' *Fugitive Pieces* (1996); Thane Rosenbaum's *Elijah Visible* (1996), *Second*

Hand Smoke (1999), and *The Golems of Gotham* (2002); Jonathan Safran Foer's *Everything is Illuminated* (2002); and Michael Chabon's *The Amazing Adventures of Kavalier & Clay* (2000) and *The Final Solution* (2005). Between 1978 and 1991, Art Spiegelman drew a Pulitzer Prize-winning graphic novel about the Holocaust, *Maus: A Survivor's Tale* (1992).

> At least since the 1990s, these literary works have shared the perspective of "postmemory." According to the critic Marianne Hirsch, who coined the term, postmemory characterizes the experience of those who grow up dominated by narratives that preceded their birth, whose own belated stories are evacuated by the stories of the previous generation shaped by traumatic events that can be neither understood nor recreated. (Hirsch 1997, 22)

We turn now to contemporary American texts that exemplify this phenomenon of "postmemory" Holocaust literature.

Selected Authors

Art Spiegelman (1948–). Art Spiegelman's *Maus: A Survivor's Tale* shows just how "postmemory should reflect back on memory, revealing it as equally constructed, equally mediated by the processes of narration and imagination . . . Post-memory is anything but absent or evacuated: It is as full and as empty as memory itself" (Young 2000, 15).

Indeed, *Maus: A Survivor's Tale* is not so much about the Holocaust as about the survivor's story and the artist-son's recovery of it. In Spiegelman's own words: "*Maus* is not what happened in the past, but rather what the son understands of the father's story . . . It is an autobiographical history of my relationship with my father, a survivor of the death camps, cast with cartoon animals" (Young 2000, 15).

As the Holocaust survivor Vladek recalls what happened to him at the hands of the Nazis, so his son Artie recalls what happened to *him* at the hands of his father and his father's Holocaust narratives. Much as his father related his experiences to Artie in all their painful immediacy, so Artie tells his experiences of interviews with his father and the painful father-son relationship they reveal. Artie's relationship with Vladek is intimately connected to a past that continues to overwhelm both of them. Thus, Spiegelman's subtitle—*A Survivor's Tale*—may well refer as much to Artie as to his father. In this, it is typical of second-generation American Holocaust literature.

Maus is analyzed in several academic studies, most notably Michael Rothberg's *Traumatic Realism: The Demands of Holocaust Representation* (2000) and James E. Young's *At Memory's Edge: After-Images of the Holocaust* (2000). Young stresses the surprising appropriateness of the graphic novel form to this genre, a "comixture" of words and images [which] generates a triangulation of meaning—a kind of three-dimensional narrative—in the movement among words, images, and the reader's eye (Young 2000, 18).

Similarly, Rothberg praises *Maus* for encouraging "everyone interested in the Holocaust to reflect on how we approach the events of the genocide and how we represent them to ourselves and to others" (Rothberg 2000, 2).

Anne Michaels (1958–). Anne Michaels's *Fugitive Pieces* (1996) concerns the aftermath of the Holocaust. This Canadian novel explores precisely the ways that one remembers an event *not* experienced. The critic Henri Raczymow has characterized such recall as "memory shot through with holes" or absent memory (Raczymow 1994, 98). Michaels is interested less in the clarity and authenticity of testimony than her protagonists' complex relationship to the traumatic past, and its fragmentary traces in the lives of those born too late to remember the *Shoah* (Hebrew for the Holocaust, literally meaning "catastrophe").

The novel is divided into two parts, the first of which concerns a Polish Jewish child (Jakob) who is brought to Greece by an archaeologist (Athos) and so survives the Holocaust. Jakob is haunted by the deaths he did not witness of his parents and sister (Bella). He becomes a poet in order to assert love and a faith in language after the Nazi violence visited upon his family. Part II shifts to Ben, the son of Holocaust survivors, who displays many of the problems experienced by second-generation children. After Jakob and his wife (Michaela) die, Ben travels to Greece in search of Jakob's memoirs. When he finds a note indicating that Michaela was pregnant at her death, Ben takes on the mantle of surrogate child. Thus, the theme of reconciliation through language and love is reasserted. At the same time, the novel resists any comforting resolution of the past. "No act of violence is ever resolved," Michaels writes. "When the one who can forgive can no longer speak, there is only silence" (Michaels 1997, 161).

Fugitive Pieces has provoked much debate about the role of lyricism in portraying the Holocaust. Some reviewers have praised its project of bringing beauty into the equation of post-Holocaust survival. Robert Eaglestone notes the novel's "fugue"-like quality and the exploration of "postmemory through recurring tropes and themes of . . . love, and music" (Eaglestone 2004, 117). By contrast, critics such as Adrienne Kertzer question Michaels's aestheticization of the Shoah in a skeptical stance reminiscent of Adorno's warning about squeezing "pleasure" from the "bodily pain of those who were beaten down by rifle butts" (Adorno 1993, 88).

Melvin Jules Bukiet (1953–). Melvin Jules Bukiet draws on Jewish literary antecedents, including Isaac Bashevis Singer (1904–1991), Bruno Schulz (1892–1942), and Isaac Babel (1894–1940), to create a phantasmagorical world in his collection *Stories of an Imaginary Childhood* (1992). Here, he reinvents a Jewish childhood between the wars in Proszowice, a Polish *shtetl* (Yiddish for "village") unaware of the forthcoming *Churban* (another Hebrew term for the Holocaust, literally meaning "destruction"). Allusively, these stories alert the reader to the fate of the unnamed narrator. Seemingly innocuous descriptions evoke the Holocaust. For example the opening story, "The Virtuoso," introduces an "iron-maiden-shaped box" that holds a violin but resembles an instrument of torture; melodies which "flew like a fireplace cinder to the winds;" and a failed musician's reflection that "burning was too cruel a fate for the creator of beauty" (Bukiet 1992, 3, 6, 11).

In "The Quilt and the Bicycle," the 12-year-old narrator's quilt displays key metonymical signs of the Shoah: "a yellow star and menorahs and bunnies and trains" (Bukiet 1992, 45). Thus, readers are reminded of the Jewish children forced to wear yellow Stars of David before being taken by train to their deaths in concentration camps. Such children were dehumanized by the Nazis, with anti-Semitism preparing the ground for such dehumanization. Here the narrator notes, "I was treated as the creature I had heard called 'Jew'" (Bukiet 1992, 55). Further, Bukiet's text yokes together Christianity and chimneys to subtly suggest that the common denominator in the Church and Auschwitz was anti-Semitism: "I passed the church spire and the Proszoworks smokestack; I forgot where I was going" (Bukiet 1992, 90–91).

Following the success of *Stories of an Imaginary Childhood*, which won the Edward Lewis Wallant Award and was a finalist for the National Jewish Book Award, Bukiet went on to write the Holocaust-related *While the Messiah Tarries* (1995), *After* (1996), and *Signs and Wonders* (1999).

While the Messiah Tarries is mainly relevant for the light it sheds on those who record and archive Holocaust testimony. In "The Library of Moloch," for instance, Bukiet suggests that his American protagonist, Dr. Arthur Ricardo, approaches Holocaust survivors in order to "preserve their suffering, to remit immortality in return for the chronicle of their woe" (Bukiet 1995, 185). Although this may be an ethical ambition, one of Ricardo's interviewees implies that an unacknowledged victim-envy taints such American labors.

After is a picaresque comedy that opens with Isaac Kaufman's liberation from Aspenfeld, a sub-camp of Buchenwald. In tone, it could not differ more from the somber melancholia found, for example, in Cynthia Ozick's *The Shawl* or Saul Bellow's *Mr. Sammler's Planet*. At times the dialogue is zanily reminiscent of a Marx Brothers sketch: "'I like a girl with spirit.' 'I like a man who likes a girl with spirit.' 'I like spirits'"(Bukiet 1996, 124); whereas the comedic narrative recalls Mel Brooks's satirical movie about Nazism, *The Producers* (1968):

> Then the War travelled east and Spain was forgotten in the twentieth-century totalitarian extravaganza, a roadshow complete with posters, banners, songs, salutes, and armies. Madrid was the introductory act; and Berlin was the main event. (Bukiet 1996: 130)

This is clearly the opposite of "Holocaust piety." Rather than fixing its attention on the horrific and incomprehensible past, *After* sets its sights firmly on the future and the American Dream of creating oneself "anew" through enterprise and hard work (Bukiet 1996, 83). Only in this case, Isaac and his friends—principally, a forger, Marcus Morgenstern, and a devout scholar, Fishl—display such American virtues by making money on the black market.

Still, *After* raises important issues. Notably, it asks what values can be redeemed in the aftermath of the Holocaust amidst anarchic free enterprise and amoral commercialism ("Screw the pain. Think of the money" (Bukiet 1996: 102).). In a sense, it reframes Primo Levi's question of what constitutes humanity (*If This Is a Man*) in a post-Holocaust American context. What is morality and who is a Jew after the Holocaust? To some extent, a hopeful riposte is offered in Isaac's mercy toward the son of a Nazi. Isaac decides not to kill the boy, so that he can leave Aspenfeld with "a perfect emptiness . . . create himself anew" (Bukiet 1996, 83). By eschewing ruthless murder, Isaac suggests a humane alternative to nihilism.

Bukiet presents the Holocaust less directly in *Signs and Wonders*. This novel concerns a messianic sect that sweeps Germany on the eve of the new millennium. Considering themselves "New Jews," the so-called Alefites victimize "old Jews" in an eerie echo of *Kristallnacht* ("the night of broken glass" on 9–10 November 1938, when much Jewish property was destroyed by German Nazis):

> The message was redemption. Absolved of all sins, the New Jews no longer had to mortify their own flesh. Instead, they struck outward, and the old Jews, that stubborn, stiff-necked people who refused to accede to the right world order, were the first to feel the sting of the lash of salvation. . . . Windows were smashed and fires were lit elsewhere in the city, wherever a store front had the gall or ill-fate to bear a Jewish surname. (Bukiet 1999, 263)

This is satire of the type found in *After,* though it appears to offer a bleaker vision of violence persisting beyond the Holocaust into the twenty-first century.

Critical responses to Bukiet's work have tended to be favorable. For example, in "Dares, Double-Dares, and the Jewish-American Writer," Sanford Pinsker praises Bukiet's "tone of deliberately disconcerting humor" (Pinsker 1997, 285). He maintains that Bukiet's outrageous narratives serve to "re-humanize Holocaust survivors by allowing them to make jokes, make love, and, yes, connive for money just like other human beings" (Pinsker 1997, 285). However, other critics have found fault in the humor. Deborah H. Sussman, for instance, remarks of *After* that Bukiet fails to achieve "perfect pitch and perfect balance . . . to sustain the tension on the tightrope between hilarity and utter despair" (Sussman 1996).

Thane Rosenbaum (1960–). Thane Rosenbaum has written a trilogy of critically acclaimed Holocaust literature: the short story collection *Elijah Visible* (1996) and the novels *Second Hand Smoke* (1999) and *The Golems of Gotham* (2002). The first of these won the Edward Lewis Wallant Award for the best work of Jewish-American fiction, whereas *Second Hand Smoke* was a National Book Award Finalist. Like Spiegelman and Bukiet, Rosenbaum is a second-generation Holocaust writer: his mother was imprisoned in Maidanek and his father survived Bergen-Belsen.

The stories in *Elijah Visible* are linked by their protagonist Adam Posner. Depicted in Miami, New York, and Atlantic City, Adam comes to represent a *composite* second-generation survivor in America. The collection opens with "Cattle Car Complex," where a New York lawyer gets trapped inside an elevator. Adam's psychological kinship with the Holocaust—"the legacy that flowed through his veins" (Rosenbaum 1996, 5)—leads him to imagine that he is in a cattle car on the train journey to a concentration camp. However, Adam is not a Holocaust survivor. Like other second generation writers, he is burdened by *imagination* of his parents' horrors rather than *memories* of them. The fact that Adam cannot *know* the details of the Holocaust generally, and his parents' experiences specifically, leads to a nebulous terror accompanying a failure of inter-generational understanding. Such failure is depicted, for example, in "The Pants in the Family," where Adam recalls "an impenetrable secret—my parents speaking in code, changing the passwords repeatedly" (Rosenbaum 1996, 48). Only when his father makes some effort to explain the "silence" surrounding the Holocaust in their home is Adam able to make a connection with him (Rosenbaum 1996, 51).

Connecting with the generation of Holocaust survivors is also a central theme of the title story. In "Elijah Visible," Adam and his cousins receive a letter from Artur, a survivor cousin in Antwerp. Artur wants to meet his American relatives in order to recount their family's history in Europe. Although Elijah does not arrive in this story—an arrival which in Judaism would presage the coming of the Messiah—by the conclusion Artur is "on his way" to offer peace and reconciliation to the second generation (Rosenbaum 1996, 103).

As its title suggests, *Second Hand Smoke* explores the Holocaust legacy that survivors pass down to their children. The novel relates the life of Duncan Katz, a Nazi hunter for the Operation of Special Investigations, and the son of survivors. As a boy, he is deprived of parental love. *Second Hand Smoke* opens with the lines: "He was a child of trauma. Not of love, or happiness, or exceptional wealth. Just trauma. And nightmare too" (Rosenbaum 1999, 1). Rather than despair or melancholy, Duncan feels rage. His mother, Mila, encourages his belligerence. After the vulnerability she and her husband Yankee (nee Herschel) experienced in Europe, "what his mother really wanted was not a son, but a comic-book superhero" (Rosenbaum 1999, 32). (Michael Chabon also addresses the theme of a Jewish comic-book "Superman" in *The Amazing Adventures of Kavalier & Clay* (Chabon 2000, 585). See later.)

In order to calm his rage and find restored faith in a changed but viable Jewish continuity, Duncan visits his Zen-master brother Isaac in Warsaw. Isaac offers Duncan the vision to be "kind" to himself and connect without anger to "the murdered ones" of the Shoah (Rosenbaum 1999, 215).

Surprisingly perhaps, *Second Hand Smoke* is also a very funny novel. It affirms post-Holocaust optimism through transgressive comedy. At one stage, Duncan and Isaac appear to be locked overnight in Birkenau by neo-Nazis, although this episode may be dreamt by Duncan. Isaac remarks, "I think what you're talking about is what they call gallows humor, but gallows and gas chambers don't make me laugh. After Auschwitz, nothing is funny" (Rosenbaum 1999, 209). Demonstrating the contrary, *Second Hand Smoke* asserts survival in the same breath as comedy. In this, it resembles Roberto Benigni's Academy Award-winning concentration camp comedy *Life is Beautiful* (1997).

The Golems of Gotham (2002) concludes Rosenbaum's Holocaust trilogy by graphically detailing how the second generation is haunted by the Shoah: "the Holocaust is . . . not in the past" (Rosenbaum 2002, 42). Decades earlier, Philip Roth had imagined the survival of Anne Frank in *The Ghost Writer* (1979) and suggested in *Reading Myself and Others* (1975) that the Holocaust haunted "most reflective American Jews" (Roth 1975, 130). Rosenbaum rhetorically wonders whether "all writers of atrocity are essentially ghostwriters" (Rosenbaum 2002, 61). In *The Golems of Gotham*, such metaphorical haunting becomes literal as the ghosts of six Holocaust literature writers—Primo Levi, Jerzy Kosinski (1933–1991), Paul Celan (1920–1970), Jean Améry (1912–1978), Tadeusz Borowski (1922–1951), and Piotr Rawicz (1919–1982)—are summoned as golems to contemporary New York by Ariel, the granddaughter of survivors. Like her father's parents, who also return as golems, all six writers committed suicide after surviving the Shoah.

Once in New York, the golems attack anything associated with the Holocaust, including tattoos, trains, and showers. As a result, Gotham becomes "suffused with warmth and connection" (Rosenbaum 2002, 103). Ironically perhaps, the golems also express their horror at the humor of *Life is Beautiful*—"a movie made by an Italian clown in which Auschwitz was depicted as no more threatening than a circus"—and the "good-guy-triumphs-over-bad-guy sanctimony" of Steven Spielberg's Holocaust movie *Schindler's List* (1993) (Rosenbaum 2002, 292–293). Unlike this funny and frequently sanctimonious novel, such movies apparently trivialize the Shoah.

Critical reception of Rosenbaum's novels has been enthusiastic. Reviewing *Second Hand Smoke* in the *New York Times Book Review*, Richard Lourie remarked:

> The overheated atmosphere of the novel reminds one of Isaac Babel's *Tales of Odessa* . . . and the film *Life is Beautiful*. But in a style very much his own Rosenbaum depicts the painful comedy of being a regular American kid raised to be an angel of retribution (Lourie 1999, 7).

Sanford Pinsker, the reviewer for the *Wall Street Journal*, lauded *Second Hand Smoke* as "superb, if deeply disturbing, writing" (Pinsker 1999). Academic studies of American Holocaust writers by Alan Berger (*Children of Job: American Second-*

Generation Witnesses to the Holocaust (1997)) and Andrew Furman (*Contemporary Jewish-American Writers and the Multicultural Dilemma: The Return of the Exiled* (2000)) have also praised Rosenbaum's contribution to this genre.

Jonathan Safran Foer (1977–). Like *The Golems of Gotham,* Jonathan Safran Foer's *Everything is Illuminated* (2002) might be described as a postmodern novel insofar as it foregrounds the process of writing rather than the events of the Holocaust. Moreover, it concerns the grandchildren of survivors and bystanders, and is thus also a *third-generation* Holocaust novel (Eaglestone 2004, 128).

One strand of the narrative features the story of Trachimbrod, a *shtetl* on the Ukrainian-Polish border. The author of these sections is introduced as "Jonathan Safran Foer," a young American-Jewish writer who is visiting the Ukraine to explore the history and remnants of the community that his grandfather escaped. The story begins in 1791 and continues until 1942 when "1204 Trachimbroders [are] killed at the Hand of German Fascism" (Foer 2002, 189). Foer's postmodern style focuses on dreams and quirky, marginal moments, mixing comedy, satire, and tragedy.

The second strand of the novel is narrated by Alexander Perchov, son of the Ukrainian owner of "Heritage Touring," which is taking "Foer" in search of Trachimbrod. Alex speaks a self-conscious English of endearing solecisms that foregrounds the postmodern constructedness of this text; for example

> I undertook to input the things you counselled me to, and I fatigued the thesaurus you presented me, as you counselled me to, when my words appeared too petite, or not befitting. (Foer 2002: 23)

Together "Foer," Alex, and his grandfather drive to a house that is all that remains of Trachimbrod. Here the "illumination" occurs, when the grandfather's involvement in the massacre at Trachimbrod is revealed. Threatened with execution, he betrayed his Jewish best friend to the Nazis.

Both these strands form part of an epistolary novel, with monthly letters from Alex to "Jonathan" commenting on the "heritage tour" and the Ukrainian-Jewish past. Foer appears to offer some form of reconciliation, so far as this is possible, between the grandchildren of survivors and bystanders. He optimistically suggests that they share "the same story . . . I am Alex and you are you, and that I am you and you are me? Do you not comprehend that we can bring each other safety and peace? (Foer 2002, 214).

Writing in the *New York Times Book Review,* Francine Prose characterized "this wonderful first novel" as "endearing, accomplished and (to quote Alex one last time) definitely premium." The "assured, hilarious prose," she continued, manages to carry "themes so weighty that any one of them would be enough to give considerable heft to an ordinary novel" (Prose 2002, 8). Henry Hitchings, the reviewer for the *Times Literary Supplement,* was similarly impressed. He noted

> The opening chapters of Jonathan Safran Foer's fictional debut are so vibrant and playful that they succeed in calling to mind not only Philip Roth and Isaac Bashevis Singer, but also James Joyce, Laurence Sterne and Milan Kundera (Hitchings 2002, 21).

However, Hitchings also found Foer's "authorial prestidigitation" occasionally "irritating" and bearing some marks of "a flashy apprentice piece" (Hitchings 2002, 21).

In 2005, *Everything is Illuminated* became a film directed by Liev Schreiber, starring Eugene Hutz as Alex and Elijah Wood as "Jonathan Safran Foer."

Michael Chabon (1963–). Both *The Amazing Adventures of Kavalier & Clay* (2000) and *The Final Solution* (2005) are Holocaust novels with a difference. The former relates the lives of two comic-book artists, one of whom, Josef Kavalier, is a refugee from Nazi-occupied Czechoslovakia. The latter concerns a mute young refugee from Nazi Germany, his parrot, and a plot in the tradition of Sherlock Holmes detective stories.

The Amazing Adventures of Kavalier & Clay won the Pulitzer Prize for fiction. It begins in 1939 as Josef escapes Prague by hiding in the coffin that holds the clay of the golem, Rabbi Loew's seventeenth-century superhero created to protect the Jewish ghetto of the city. Much as the golem becomes the means for Josef's literal escape to America, comic-books subsequently facilitate his imaginary escape from the European past. Josef and his American cousin Sam are clearly based on Jerry Siegel and Joe Schuster, the Jewish creators of Superman. As Sam remarks

> What, they're all Jewish superheroes. Superman, you don't think he's Jewish? Coming over from the old country, changing his name like that. Clark Kent, only a Jew would pick a name like that for himself. (Chabon 2000, 585)

Yet fantasy figures of power cannot save Josef's family from murder at the hands of Nazis. Kavalier and Clay's comic-book hero "The Escapist" frees no European Jews from Auschwitz.

Near the end of the novel, Josef is working on a comic book that resembles Spiegelman's *Maus* insofar as it offers a narrative response to the Holocaust in a traditionally unserious medium. Ultimately, his 2,256-page graphic novel *The Golem* (like Rosenbaum's *The Golems of Gotham*) signifies "a gesture of hope, offered against hope, in a time of desperation" (Chabon 2000, 582). Perhaps like all art, Josef's story is "the voicing of a vain wish, when you got down to it, to escape" (Chabon 2000, 582).

The title of *The Final Solution* calls to mind the Nazi decision at the Wannsee Conference to exterminate all the Jews (Roseman 2003) as well as a Sherlock Holmes short story called "The Final Problem" (Doyle 1984, 469–480). Startlingly, Chabon has produced a homage to Sherlock Holmes that alludes to the Holocaust.

The Final Solution is set in 1944, when a mute German-Jewish boy, Linus Steinman, arrives in Sussex with a talking parrot, Bruno. He is taken into care by a retired Sherlock Holmes, referred to only as the "old man." The parrot, meanwhile, repeats a list of numbers. When it is stolen, the "old man" sets off for London to solve the mystery of the numbers and the theft. However, this particular mystery has no "final solution." Though the numbers may "represent numbered Swiss bank accounts," this is by no means certain (Chabon 2005, 125). Consequently, the "old man" revises his faith in "final" solutions and comes to "perhaps, conclude"

> that meaning dwelled solely in the mind of the analyst. That it was the insoluble problems—the false leads and the cold cases—that reflected the true nature of things. That all the significance and pattern had no more intricate sense than the chatter of an African grey parrot. (Chabon 2005, 125)

This is the opposite of Nazi ideology, and rounds off a novella written in the "spirit of play and of experimentation" that is central to both "storytelling" and freedom (Chabon 2005, 8).

Critics have generally been impressed by Chabon's Holocaust novels. Several have lauded *Kavalier & Clay* for its "big historical relevance without strain" (Maslin 2000) and even judged it a candidate for the title of "Great American Novel." On the other hand, a *Commentary* review by John Podhoretz criticized Chabon's use of the golem as "a symbol of the murdered European diaspora," and the inappropriate mysticism suggested by such a symbol (Podhoretz 2001).

The Final Solution has also won plaudits. Sam Thompson, writing in *The Guardian,* had the following remarks:

> The novella gives us the delights of suspense and resolution, puzzle and solution, but the vast crime that hovers behind the story is a mystery too great for even Holmes to make sense of. (Thompson 2005)

Andrew Lewis Conn, the reviewer for *The Village Voice,* was enthusiastic:

> At once an ingenious, fully imagined work, an expert piece of literary ventriloquism, and a mash note to the beloved boys' tales of Chabon's youth, *The Final Solution* is a major minor work that will come to be seen as a hinge piece in the development of Chabon's art. (Conn 2004)

However, Marco Roth in the *Times Literary Supplement* was uncomfortable with the "grandiosity and poor taste" of the title and concluded that *The Final Solution* was little more than "a lightweight caprice" (Roth 2005, 22).

Bibliography

Adorno, Theodor. Commitment. In *Notes to Literature, II.* Rolf Tiedemann, ed., translated by Shierry Weber Nicholson. New York: Columbia University Press, 2004.

Berger, Alan. *Children of Job: American Second-Generation Witnesses to the Holocaust.* Albany, NY: State University of New York Press, 1997.

Bukiet, Melvin Jules. *Stories of an Imaginary Childhood.* Evanston, IL: Northwestern University Press, 1992.

———. *While the Messiah Tarries.* New York: Harcourt Brace, 1995.

———. *After.* New York: St. Martin's Press, 1996.

———. *Signs and Wonders.* New York: Picador, 1999.

Chabon, Michael. *The Amazing Adventures of Kavalier & Clay.* London: Fourth Estate, 2000.

———. *The Final Solution.* London: HarperCollins, 2005.

Conn, Andrew Lewis. What Up [sic], Holmes? *The Village Voice,* 9 November 2004.

Delbo, Charlotte. *Auschwitz and After.* London: Yale University Press, 1995.

DeLillo, Don. *White Noise.* London: Picador, 1985.

Dick, Philip K. *Do Androids Dream of Electric Sheep?* London: Orion, 1968.

Doyle, Sir Arthur Conan. *The Penguin Complete Adventures of Sherlock Holmes.* Harmondsworth: Penguin, 1984.

Eaglestone, Robert. *The Holocaust and the Postmodern.* Oxford: Oxford University Press, 2004.

Felman, Shoshana and Dori Laub. *Testimony: Crises of Witnessing in Literature, Psychoanalysis, and History.* London: Routledge, 1992.

Foer, Jonathan Safran. *Everything is Illuminated.* London: Penguin, 2003.

Furman, Andrew. *Contemporary Jewish-American Writers and the Multicultural Dilemma: The Return of the Exiled*. Syracuse, NY: Syracuse University Press, 2000.

Hirsch, Marianne. *Family Frames: Photographs, Narrative and Postmemory*. London: Harvard University Press, 1997.

Hitchings, Henry. Elliptical Ideolects. *Times Literary Supplement*, 14 June 2002.

Kertzer, Adrienne. *Fugitive Pieces:* Listening as a Holocaust Survivor's Child. *English Studies in Canada* 26, 22 (22) (2000): 193–217.

Kremer, Lillian, ed. *Holocaust Literature*. New York: Routledge, 2003.

Langer, Lawrence. *The Holocaust and the Literary Imagination*. New Haven, CT: Yale University Press, 1975.

———, ed. *Art from the Ashes: A Holocaust Anthology*. New York: Oxford University Press, 1995.

Levi, Primo. *Moments of Reprieve*. London: Abacus, 1981.

———. *If This is a Man/ The Truce*. London: Abacus, 1987.

Lourie, Richard. Rev. of *Second Hand Smoke*, by Thane Rosenbaum. *New York Time Book Review* 1999. http://www.nytimes.com/books/99/04/11/reviews/990411.11louriet.html?_r=1&oref=slogin

Malamud, Bernard. *The Fixer*. Harmondsworth: Penguin, 1969.

Maslin, Janet. A Life and Death Story Set in Comic Book Land. *New York Times*, 21 September 2000.

Michaels, Anne. *Fugitive Pieces*. London: Bloomsbury, 1997.

Ozick, Cynthia. Primo Levi's Suicide Note. In *Metaphor and Memory*. New York: Alfred A. Knopf, 1989.

Pinsker, Sanford. Dares, Double-Dares, and the Jewish-American Writer. *Prairie Schooner* 71 (1) (1997): 278–285.

———. Review of *Second Hand Smoke*. *Wall Street Journal:* W10, 9 April 1999.

Podhoretz, John. Escapists. *Commentary* 111 (6) (2001): 68–72.

Prose, Francine. Back in the Totally Awesome U.S.S.R. *New York Times Book Review,* 14 April 2002.

Pynchon, Thomas. *Gravity's Rainbow*. 1973. New York: Penguin, 1987.

Raczymow, Henri. Memory Shot through with Holes. *Yale French Studies* 85 (1994): 98–105.

Rose, Gillian. *Mourning Becomes the Law*. Cambridge: Cambridge University Press, 1996.

Rosenbaum, Thane. *Elijah Visible*. New York: St. Martin's Griffin, 1996.

———. *Second Hand Smoke*. New York: St. Martin's Griffin, 1999.

———. *The Golems of Gotham*. New York: HarperCollins, 2002.

Roth, Marco. Pass the Aspergillum. *Times Literary Supplement,* 28 January 2005: 22.

Roth, Philip. *Reading Myself and Others*. New York: Farrar, Straus, & Giroux, 1975.

———. *The Ghost Writer*. London: Jonathan Cape, 1979.

Rothberg, Michael. *Traumatic Realism*. London: University of Minnesota Press, 2000.

Sammon, Paul M. *Future Noir: The Making of Blade Runner*. London: Orion, 1996.

Schiff, Hilda, ed. *Holocaust Poetry*. London: HarperCollins, 1995.

Sicher, Efraim. *The Holocaust Novel*. London: Routledge, 2005.

Steiner, George. *Language and Silence: Essays 1958–1966*. London: Faber, 1967.

Sussman, Deborah H. From Horror to Humor: Review of *After*. *Washington Post* C2, 21 Nov. 1996.

Thompson, Sam. Lost in the Broken World. *The Guardian,* 26 Feb. 2005.

Wiesel, Elie. A Plea for the Dead. In *Art from the Ashes: A Holocaust Anthology*. New York: Oxford University Press, 1967.

———. *Night*. London: Penguin, 1981.

———. Does the Holocaust Lie Beyond the Reach of Art? *New York Times*, 17 April 1983: sec 2, p. 1.

———. The Holocaust as Literary Inspiration. In *Dimensions of the Holocaust*. Evanston, IL: Northwestern University Press, 1990.

Young, James E. *At Memory's Edge: After-Images of the Holocaust in Contemporary Art and Architecture*. London: Yale University Press, 2000.

Further Reading

Berger, Alan. *Children of Job: American Second-Generation Witnesses to the Holocaust.* Albany, NY: State University of New York Press, 1997; Budick, Emily Miller. The Holocaust in the Jewish American Literary Imagination. In *The Cambridge Companion to Jewish American Literature*, edited by Michael P. Kramer and Hana Wirth-Nesher. Cambridge: Cambridge University Press, 2003; Eaglestone, Robert. *The Holocaust and the Postmodern.* Oxford: Oxford University Press, 2004; LaCapra, Dominic. *Representing the Holocaust: History, Theory, Trauma.* Ithaca: Cornell University Press, 1994; Langer, Lawrence. *The Holocaust and the Literary Imagination.* New Haven, CT: Yale University Press, 1975; Langer, Lawrence. *Art from the Ashes: A Holocaust Anthology.* New York: Oxford University Press, 1995; Langer, Lawrence. *Preempting the Holocaust.* New Haven: Yale University Press, 1998; Rothberg, Michael. *Traumatic Realism.* London: University of Minnesota Press, 2000; Schiff, Hilda, ed. *Holocaust Poetry.* London: HarperCollins, 1995; Sicher, Efraim. *The Holocaust Novel.* London: Routledge, 2005; Vice, Sue. *Holocaust Fiction.* London: Routledge, 2000; Wollaston, Isabel. *A War Against Memory?* London: Society for Promoting Christian Knowledge, 1996; Young, James E. *At Memory's Edge: After-Images of the Holocaust in Contemporary Art and Architecture.* London: Yale University Press, 2000.

PETER LAWSON

HUMOR

Definition. Defining humor has proven slippery over the centuries, but that difficulty has not stopped philosophers, scholars, and critics from trying, in a long line from Aristotle (384–322 B.C.E.) to Sigmund Freud (1856–1939) to more current thinkers. A simple dictionary definition—"the quality of being amusing or comic"—might suffice as a beginning, but even such a simple definition depends on two other slippery terms: "amusing" and "comic." The dictionary further complicates matters by referring not to a quality one can perceive, but to a "state of mind; mood; disposition" ("Humor" 1982). Add the equally slippery term "literary" to the mix, and one quickly sees the trouble that lies in definition. A common sense definition might call literary humor writing intended to amuse or to provoke laughter, writing focused on the comic as opposed to the serious. Such a loose definition embraces a multitude of forms, from slapstick to light verse to satire. In the end, "humor" is as variable as each individual because all people do not laugh at the same things; what Bill finds humorous might mortally offend Mary, and vice versa.

Three main theories of humor, or more properly, theories of laughter, have emerged over time: the superiority theory, the relief theory, and the incongruity theory. Each attempts to explain why we laugh and thus explain what we perceive as humorous and why. The superiority theory, associated most closely with Thomas Hobbes (1588–1679), who used ideas dating back to Plato (427–347 B.C.E.) and Aristotle, states that we find humor in the perception that we are superior to others. As Hobbes writes, "the passion of laughter is nothing else but sudden glory arising from some sudden conception of some eminency in ourselves, by comparison with the infirmity of others, or with our own formerly" (qtd. in Morreal 1987, 20). Such a theory explains why we laugh at a person slipping on a banana peel or why we laugh at ourselves when we think back to some stupid act we performed in the past. But as many have shown, such a theory cannot account for all humorous situations, as Hobbes claimed.

The relief theory takes two general forms, the first from Herbert Spencer (1820–1903), who saw laughter as a release of nervous energy, release that occurs after we build up energy because of the tension of a situation or joke and then release the energy when we recognize that the situation is comic rather than serious—thus bringing about relief. To return to the slipping on a banana peel example, we build up nervous tension as we think the person is in dire trouble, and then we release that energy when we recognize that the person is not in any real danger. Freud used Spencer's ideas to postulate a second, more psychological, form of relief: psychic relief. In *Jokes and Their Relation to the Unconscious* (1905), Freud saw laughter arising from a release of repressed desires, emotions, and thoughts. In this way, Freud saw jokes (and other forms of humor) as ways to reveal the unconscious, just as he had done earlier for dreams. Like the superiority theory, the relief theory can explain much humor, but certainly not all.

The last theory, the incongruity theory, can again be traced back to Aristotle but is most associated with Immanuel Kant (1724–1804) and Arthur Schopenhauer (1788–1860). In its simplest form, we may say that laughter arises from our sudden perception of a mismatch between what we expect in our usually ordered world and the incongruity we perceive when that order is overturned. In Kant's terms, "Laughter is an affectation arising from the sudden transformation of a strained expectation into nothing" (qtd. in Morreal 1987, 47). The incongruity theory proves more satisfactory than the other theories in explaining most humor: it explains the banana peel situation, as well as jokes, riddles, and puns. We laugh at a joke because it sets up an expectation, based on our past experience, and then suddenly reverses that expectation with an incongruous and well-timed punch line (hence the importance of "*sudden* recognition of incongruity" in the definition). Although the incongruity theory does not explain all laughter, it does explain much humor and can serve as a good way for us to distinguish and identify literary humor. Actually, all three theories, taken together, are useful in helping us define and understand literary humor. These theories from the seventeenth through twentieth centuries are being supplemented by more recent scientific research into the brain and cognitive function, and the twenty-first century will surely bring greater understanding of what causes laughter and thus help explain what we perceive as humorous.

But to turn to a much older definition, Horace's ideas about art can be used in formulating a definition of literary humor. The purpose of art, Horace (65–8 B.C.E.) wrote in "The Art of Poetry," is "to delight and instruct" (Richter 2007, 91), and thinking of literary humor in these terms will be helpful. Surely literary humor delights, but it can also, to varying extents, instruct. For example, Mark Twain (1835–1910) claimed in a letter that his humor will last because, as he says, he has "always preached" (Twain 1906, 202). Actually, much of his humor is intended merely "to delight," but his "preaching," or "instructing," truly is one of the reasons he has endured. American literary humor certainly contains much of both, one of the reasons it has always been so important, and one of the reasons it remains so.

Literary humor can be found in all the major literary genres: fiction, poetry, drama, and non-fiction. Satire and parody are important characteristics of much literary humor, with examples in all the previously mentioned genres.

History. American literary humor can be traced back to the beginnings of European settlement in the New World, and even before that if we look to the oral tradition of Native American trickster tales, which used humor to delight and instruct. Among the English settlers, John Smith (1580–1631) used humor, consciously or unconsciously, to recount his adventures and to advertise the New World; Thomas Morton (c. 1579–1647) used humor as a weapon against his Puritan tormentors; William Byrd (1674–1744) used humor in both his public and secret histories of the dividing line between Virginia and North Carolina. But a convenient starting point for a history of American humor would be Benjamin Franklin (1706–1790), most notably *Poor Richard's Almanac,* which first appeared in 1773. Franklin's creation of comic personas such as Silence Dogood and Poor Richard put a particularly American stamp on a long line of English humor, and his aphorisms used humor to define American characteristics, humor whose delight helps deliver the moral, capitalistic instruction that was to help found the new country. Franklin's "Rules by Which a Great Empire May be Reduced to a Small One" (1773) is one of the first examples of humorous political satire, an important kind of American literature that continues today.

Humor was an essential ingredient in the work of Washington Irving (1783–1859), the first American literary artist to be fully recognized by the English literati. The popularity of his Knickerbocker Tales and *The Sketch Book* (1819–20) owed as much to their humor as to their borrowing from a European folktale tradition. We can see the beginnings of the American short story in such comic tales as "Rip Van Winkle" and "The Legend of Sleepy Hollow." From the start, American literature was founded on a firm bed of humor.

The canonical writers of the American Renaissance, although more noted for their serious, philosophical ideas, often employed humor at the heart of their works. Nathaniel Hawthorne (1804–1864) and Herman Melville (1819–1891) are comic writers despite their darker themes; Edgar Allan Poe's (1809–1849) humor shines through in some of his most macabre tales; and Henry David Thoreau (1817–1862), with a Yankee persona of dour stoicism, was an inveterate punster and wit. But much of American humor in the nineteenth century appeared in newspapers and periodicals, and much of it was regionally localized. In New England, Down East humor produced such characters as Jack Downing, Sam Slick, Widow Bedott, and Mrs. Partington in tales and sketches that used dialect and local color to comment satirically on Jacksonian democracy, the Mexican War, and other political matters, but even more importantly they served to cement for the American consciousness a vision of New England.

In what were then the frontier regions of the young country, Southwestern humor also used dialect and local color, less for overt political commentary and more for an exploration of the comic possibilities inherent in the clash between the educated and the untutored. The chief Southwestern humorists were Augustus Baldwin Longstreet (1790–1870), *Georgia Scenes* (1835); Joseph G. Baldwin (1815–1863), *The Flush Times of Alabama and Mississippi* (1853); Johnson J. Hooper (1815–1863), *Some Adventures of Simon Suggs* (1845); Thomas Bangs Thorpe (1815–1878), "The Big Bear of Arkansas" (1854); and George Washington Harris (1814–1869), *Sut Lovingood* (1867). Common in many of these tales and sketches is the use of a frame narrative, with an educated, genteel narrator introducing an uneducated narrator who recounts his story in often raw vernacular language. The stories of the Southwestern humorists capture for us a part of the nation in the midst of transformation, with rollicking and often violent humor that greatly influenced Mark Twain later in the century and William Faulkner (1897–1962) in the next.

After the Civil War, the Literary Comedians were the most important American humorists. Also called the "Phunny Phellows" for their use of comic misspelling, the Literary Comedians included Petrolem V. Nasby (1833–1888), Orpheus C. Kerr (1836–1901), Josh Billings (1818–1885), Artemus Ward (1834–1867), and Mark Twain. Almost always under pseudonyms, they wrote newspaper and magazine sketches, published books, and traveled the country giving lectures. They were a nineteenth-century version of standup comedians, although their strong tie to printed humor made them different from what we think of today as standup comedy.

Another important development in the post-Civil War era was local color, an attempt in various regions of the country to capture local speech and manners, almost always through humor. Harriet Beecher Stowe (1811–1896) and Sarah Orne Jewett (1849–1909) in New England, Joel Chandler Harris (1848–1908) in the south, and Bret Harte (1836–1902) and Mark Twain in the west are examples of writers who used humor to capture and preserve for the nation pockets of local national life that were undergoing rapid change. The local colorists were influential in the rise of American literary realism, the dominant literary movement of the second half of the nineteenth century.

In many ways, Mark Twain was the culmination of the historical trends of nineteenth-century American humor. An heir of the Southwestern tradition and a "member" of the Literary Comedians and the local colorists, he burst on the national scene with "Jim Smiley and His Jumping Frog" in 1865, and then solidified his fame with a bestseller that lampooned travel books and helped change travel for Americans, *The Innocents Abroad* (1869). Twain used humor in nearly everything he wrote, but he also used humor as a device and a weapon to tackle serious issues such as racism, hypocrisy, and colonialism. Even as he claimed for himself an iconic position as America's beloved cracker-barrel philosopher and humorist, he increasingly turned his sardonic wit to the darker side of human behavior. His stature grew even more after his death in 1910, with his masterpiece *Adventures of Huckleberry Finn* (1885) outgrowing its boy-book status to become recognized as one of the great works of American (and world) literature. Mark Twain has long claimed the title of America's greatest comic writer and indeed used his humor to be counted among the great writers of any kind.

In the twentieth century, humor became increasingly urban as the population shifted to cities. Newspaper columns and magazines were the major sites for humor. Finley Peter Dunne (1867–1936), George Eugene Field (1850–1895), Damon Runyon (1884–1946), H.L. Mencken (1880–1956), Will Rogers (1879–1935), and Ring Lardner (1885–1933) were first known to a national reading audience from their newspaper columns. But perhaps the central event for American humor in the first half of the century was the founding of *The New Yorker* in 1925. The writers associated with the Algonquin Roundtable—Dorothy Parker (1893–1967), George S. Kaufman (1889–1961), Robert Benchley (1889–1945), and Alexander Woolcott (1887–1943)—were soon all writing for the new sophisticated humor magazine, as well as S.J. Perelman (1904–1979) and James Thurber (1894–1961). The fiction,

---

BLACK HUMOR

In the post–World War II era, the most important trend in American humor was what has been labeled (or mis-labeled) "black humor." Referring not to race but to a bleak existentialist, post-apocalyptic vision, black humor describes an impulse to laugh at that which should more properly invoke tears or horror. As Brom Weber notes, "Black humor disturbs because it is not necessarily nor always light-hearted funny, amusing, laughter-arousing. Furthermore, black humor seems to have little respect for the values and patterns of thought, feeling, and behavior that have kept Anglo-American culture stable and effective, have provided a basis of equilibrium for society and the individual" (Weber 1973, 362).

A list of so-called "black humorists" shows how loose the term is: John Barth (1930–), Kurt Vonnegut, Jr. (1922–2007), Thomas Berger (1924–), Joseph Heller (1923–1999), Thomas Pynchon (1937–), J.P. Donleavy (1926–), Ken Kesey (1935–2001), William Gaddis (1922–1998), Terry Southern (1924–1995), and Vladimir Nabokov (1899–1977).

---

short sketches, and above all the cartoons of *The New Yorker* were a driving force in American humor until well after World War II.

Humor was also central to the important novelists of the first half of the century. F. Scott Fitzgerald (1896–1940), Ernest Hemingway (1899–1961), and John Steinbeck (1902–1968), although certainly not considered "humorists," nonetheless all possessed great comic gifts. William Faulkner is clearly an heir of the Southwestern humor that pervaded his region in the previous century, with humor an integral part of his best work, including *The Sound and the Fury* (1929), *As I Lay Dying* (1930), and *The Hamlet* (1940). Southern writers such as Flannery O'Connor (1925–1964) and Eudora Welty (1909-2001) effectively used humor, often combined with a sense of the grotesque and with what has been called "Southern gothic," in their short stories and novels.

Just as black humor was a response to the political realities of the postwar world, other dominant developments in humorous fiction arose from the new world order that began in 1945. In response to political movements involving ethnicity, race, and gender, numerous comic writers explored their group identities and emerged as major voices. After the war, Jewish writers gained a national readership far beyond what they had ever achieved before in America, and the most notable—Saul Bellow (1915–2005), Norman Mailer (1923–2007), Bernard Malamud (1914–1986), and Philip Roth (1933–)—all used humor as a central element in their work to explore the Jewish experience in a predominantly Christian culture. The Civil Rights Movement opened white society to African Americans, and African American writers Ralph Ellison (1913–1994), James Baldwin (1924–1987), Ishmael Reed (1938–), Alice Walker (1944–), Toni Morrison (1931–), Rita Mae Brown (1944–), and Toni Cade Bambara (1939–1995) used humor as an artistic and political tool, the emergence of what could *properly* be called "black humor." Similarly, from the women's movement of the 1960s and 1970s emerged many female comic writers: Judith Viorst (1931–), Nora Ephron (1941–), Gail Parent (1940–), Erica Jong (1942–), and Fran Lebowitz (1950–), to name only a few. The rise of various ethnic and subgroup literatures—Asian American, Latino American, Native American, and gay—also brought forth writers who used humor to explore the conflicts within their groups and with the dominant culture. In *Cracking Up*, Paul Lewis poses several conflicted comic scenarios that help us understand recent developments in humor:

> The paradox of American humor since 1980 appears in just such moments of conflict or perplexity: during years in which the country has been drawn together in ever larger audiences via new technologies of communication, the jokes we've told and our responses to them suggest that we are deeply divided. We think about humor in contradictory ways. Split into subgroups, we are delighted and outraged by the comic treatment of different ideas. (Lewis 2006, 2)

In the first half of the twentieth century, pioneering humor scholars such as Constance Rourke and Walter Blair posited unifying concepts like "the American comic spirit"; as we move into the twenty-first century, we had best make that "spirit" plural.

The groupings in this survey are somewhat arbitrary, and they omit perhaps the greatest comic novel of the twentieth century, J.D. Salinger's (1919–) *The Catcher in the Rye* (1951). They also focus almost exclusively on fiction, overlooking the rich comic history of American poetry, drama, and nonfiction. The sheer breadth of the field makes cogent and comprehensive summary nearly impossible, but that breadth is testimony to the enduring richness of the comic imagination in America. The comic spirit lies deep in the heart of the American experience, a nation that has always joked about itself, a nation that has produced a long line of artists who use humor not just to delight, but also to instruct; when the ideals of a nation do not match up with its practices, as is so often the case, the weapon of choice, more often than lofty speeches, is the pomposity-deflating joke, the hypocrisy-exposing satire. In an introduction to a study of American humor, Nancy A. Walker makes this concluding point:

> While the concept of a single "national character" has been wisely abandoned, it is nonetheless true that certain widely shared values, such as the freedoms put forth in the Bill of Rights, stand in contrast to our many differences, and this leads to a final conclusion about American humor: the paradox that while humor declares nothing to be sacred, Americans have used it to press for those ideals of equality, opportunity, and freedom that often seem to gleam elusively in the distance. (Walker 1998, 64)

Or as Mark Twain wrote near the end of his career, "Against the assault of laughter nothing can stand" (Twain 1900, 166).

Context and Issues. The year 2000 (or more properly by the calendar, 2001) ushered in a new millennium, which in itself would be an auspicious marker, a cusp in time sure to bring recognition and reflection. But the events of September 11, 2001, overshadow and color contemporary times as markedly as the events of December 7, 1941, marked an earlier era. The attacks on the World Trade Center and the Pentagon stopped humor for a time, just as the planes all over America were grounded until the threat was understood. A comic mainstay like *The David Letterman Show* became for a time a solemn gathering of stunned witnesses; *Saturday Night Live* began its first show after the attacks with a permission-granting request from then-New York City mayor Rudy Giuliani: "It's time to be funny again." Although respectfully silent for a time, American humor resurged in the troubled aftermath of 9/11, with humor taking a stronger political edge than it had for many years. The contested Bush presidency, decided not by American voters but by a 5-4 vote of the Supreme Court, presided over a deeply divided nation, and humor has proven to be both a weapon and comfort in troubled times. As the war in Iraq moved from an apparently swift victory to a protracted quagmire, world events and America's unpopularity in the world have been reflected and sharpened in the nation's literary humor of the first decade of a new century.

In the contest for American minds that has followed 9/11, humor has been used by both sides to make their arguments. Some who support Bush's version of a war on terror have often used ridicule to make their points. Those who oppose Bush's handling of the war and its aftermath have used polemic, but they have also effectively used humor as a weapon. The rise of sharpened political humor has mirrored the split in American politics and society.

The other strains that have dominated American humor in the last years of the twentieth century have also remained: racial, ethnic, and gender humor, as well as the continuing presence of post-modernism, a humor that calls attention to itself as humor.

Perhaps above all else, the persistence of humor in a troubled and divided time, rather than merely reflecting contemporary issues, also shows something about the human spirit. As humans, we need to laugh, to be amused, even if that laughter is something bitter and sardonic. In its own way, as it has done in other dark passages of history, American humor has helped us survive.

Trends and Themes. Literary humor has always been used, as Horace said of art in general, to delight and instruct; in most eras, humor focuses more on amusement than teaching. But events since 2000 have caused a shift in American humor: although the commitment to amusement remains strong, much recent humor has taken on a more didactic and politically engaged edge. The most important trend in American literary humor since 2000 has been the resurgence of political humor. In many ways, humor had become, by the end of the twentieth century, largely disengaged from the events of the world. The black humor of the 1950s and 1960s, which rebelled against the horrors of the Holocaust and impending nuclear disaster, had given way to a humor that more often turned on its own existence, a postmodern, cynical, detached humor about humor. The stunning political events of the new millennium partially recalled humor to its didactic uses, although the comic force can never be wholly contained within the serious. Although the world situation caused this general shift in both fictional and non-fictional humor, many of the trends of the last quarter century continued, including the changes in ethnic, gender, and sexual orientation issues.

In perhaps a counter-trend, a turning in toward the self and the world, the memoir has become increasingly important in the American literary scene, with humor playing a central role in some of the most popular recent autobiographical works.

Finally, humor for the sake of amusement (or even escapism) has remained strong, partly perhaps in reaction to the serious turn of our age but mainly because that has always been the case with the comic spirit.

Reception. Serious critical study of American humor began in the 1930s, with pioneering scholars Constance Rourke (1885–1941) and Walter Blair (1900–1992). Rourke's *American Humor: A Study of the National Character* (1931) laid the groundwork analysis of American humor, followed later in the decade by Blair's *Native American Humor* (1937). Both Rourke and Blair argued that America's humor tradition was evidence of a "national comic spirit"—although their studies excluded many Americans, focusing almost exclusively on the work of white males.

As the literary canon was opened to include works by women, African Americans, and other ethnicities and nationalities, humor studies began to address works that had been forgotten or ignored. One highly influential study was Nancy Walker, *The Tradition of Women's Humor in America* (1984), which helped reclaim women's status in the humor tradition. Pioneering studies of African American humor include Roger Abrahams, *Deep Down in the Jungle* (1964) and William Schecter, *The History of Negro Humor in America* (1970). Those interested in keeping up with developing trends in American humor should consult the annual overview article "Year's Work in American Humor Studies" by Judith Yaross Lee in the academic journal *Studies in American Humor.*

Selected Authors. A good place to begin a survey of humorous literature since 2000 is Philip Roth's *The Human Stain* (2000). Set in 1998, the novel captures the moment in America when the Clinton-Lewinsky scandal broke, not by focusing on the president's misdeeds but on a classics professor resigning from his job for saying the word "spooks" in class. Ironies abound in this comic tale that ultimately turns tragic: the professor intends no racism with his use of the term, not even knowing that the missing students he is referring to are black, and the professor, it turns out, is himself black, having spent most of his life passing as Jewish. The novel is narrated by Nathan Zuckerman and is the eighth of Roth's Zuckerman novels. *The Human Stain* shows academe (and America) confronted with issues of multiculturalism, sexism, classism, and political correctness, issues that dominated American culture in the 1990s and continued into the new century. *The Human Stain* completes a recent trilogy of Zuckerman novels, the first two works being *American Pastoral* (1997) and *I Married a Communist* (1998). Roth's burst of creativity late in a career that has already been monumental cements his position as one of the great comic writers of the last half century.

Thomas Berger (1924–) is best known for his comic novel *Little Big Man* (1964), but like Roth, he continues to publish into the new century. His novel *Adventures of the Artificial Woman* (2004), an updating of the Pygmalion myth, contains witty, dark comedy. Another novelist with a large body of comic work, John Irving (1942–), published *The Fourth Hand* in 2001. Like Irving's best and most-read novels, *The World According to Garp* (1978) and *The Hotel New Hampshire* (1981), *The Fourth Hand* revolves around macabre, grotesque events: a man's loss of his left hand and his subsequent hand transplant. The novel was widely praised for its satire of TV news.

Jane Smiley's (1949–) *Good Faith* (2003), further establishes her status as the most important and prolific comic woman novelist. Smiley won the Pulitzer Prize for fiction with *A Thousand Acres* (1991), and her novel *Moo* (1995) is a comic parody of academia. In *Good Faith,* she examines the real estate boom of the 1980s, with an ethical small-town real estate agent lured into a Faustian bargain of quick riches and sleazy dealings. In *Ten Days in the Hills* (2007), she uses Boccaccio's *Decameron* as a literary subtext, with a group of Hollywood actors and executives telling stories (many of them luridly sexual) in the Hollywood Hills.

The September 11, 2001, attacks on the World Trade Center are imaginatively prefigured by Don DeLillo (1936–) in *Cosmopolis* (2003). DeLillo has used dark, disturbing humor in important works such as *White Noise* (1985) and *Underworld* (1997); in *Cosmopolis,* he traces one day in 2000, a limousine ride that moves from the comic to the apocalyptic. His novel catches the end of one era—the self-indulgent 1990s—from the perspective of post-9/11 America.

The most direct literary influence of the 9/11 attacks, the Bush presidency, and the Iraq war has been an increase in political humor, particularly from those opposed to Bush and his policies. Al Franken (1951–) had a big bestseller with *Rush Limbaugh Is a Big Fat Idiot* (1996), success continued with *Lies and the Lying Liars Who Tell Them* (2003), a scathingly humorous attack on George Bush, Dick Cheney, and conservative media commentators Bill O'Reilly and Ann Coulter, among others. His most recent book is *The Truth: With Jokes* (2005). Franken is now running for the U.S. Senate in his native Minnesota, a state that could move from electing a pro wrestler as governor to a *Saturday Night Live* writer/comedian as senator. Television has also given a comedy/satiric political pulpit to Bill Maher (1956–) and Jon Stewart (1956–), both of whom have published books of political humor and commentary since 2000. Maher, who lost a television job for comments he made about the 9/11 hijackers in the immediate aftermath of the attacks, a time when any remarks about the events were closely scrutinized, published *When You Ride Alone, You Ride With Bin Laden* (2002), a wry updating of World War II propaganda posters, and then *Keep the Statue of Liberty Closed: The New Rules* (2004) and *New Rules: Polite Musings from a Timid Observer* (2005). Jon Stewart's *America (The Book): A Citizen's Guide to Democracy Inaction* (2004), a mock high school history textbook, was a number one bestseller, following on the heels of his Comedy Central spoof news program, *The Daily Show,* from which many people, especially the young, now get their main dose of news. Stephen Colbert, a *Daily Show* alumnus, whose own show, *The Colbert Report,* is also a popular satiric look at the news, had his own bestseller in 2007 and 2008: *I Am America and So Can You,* a compendium of goof-ball tips on how to be more patriotic.

Humor has become one of the main ways many people try to make sense of an increasingly crazy world. Comedian George Carlin (1937–) also had a big bestseller with *When Will Jesus Bring the Pork Chops?* (2004), a collection of his characteristic observations on religion, politics, and other contemporary topics.

The political right has its own humorists, notably P.J. O'Rourke (1947–), who made his mark with books in the 1980s and 1990s, such as *Republican Party Reptile* (1987), *Parliament of Whores* (1991), and *Give War a Chance* (1992). *The CEO of the Sofa* (2001) skewers corporate ethics scandals of the late 1990s and the young new century. He examines America at war with the sardonically titled *Peace Kills: America's Fun New Imperialism* (2004). More recently, he has trained his satiric skills on capitalism with *The Wealth of Nations* (2007). Christopher Buckley (1952–), son of noted conservative spokesman and writer William F. Buckley, has had great success with several satirical political novels. His *Thank You For Smoking* (1994) looks satirically at the tobacco lobby and was made into an acclaimed film in 2006. In *No Way to Treat a First Lady* (2002), Buckley recounts the murder trial of a first lady who kills her husband, with blazing satire of the Lewinsky scandal and its treatment in the media. Post-9/11 he turned his attention to the Middle East with *Florence of Arabia* (2004), in which a female State Department worker crusades for women's rights in a fictional Muslim country. His most recent work is *Boomsday* (2007), a comic novel about, of all things, social security reform.

Perhaps the prevailing literary trend of the new century is the memoir, especially autobiographical accounts of childhood abuse and substance addiction. Despite such somber themes, the memoir has become an important trend among humorous writers. Most notable and successful is David Sedaris (1956–), whose autobiographical humorous essays explore his family life, his Greek background, his North

Carolina upbringing, his homosexuality, and his childhood speech impediments, among many other topics. *Me Talk Pretty One Day* (2000) and *Dress Your Family in Corduroy and Denim* (2004) collect his essays from magazines and public radio. Bill Bryson (1951–), a travel writer who often employs humor in his work, including the science book *A Short History of Nearly Everything* (2003), nostalgically and comically remembers his 1950s childhood in *The Life and Times of the Thunderbolt Kid* (2006). Completing a trilogy, Frank McCourt's (1930–) *Teacher Man* (2005) employs the same bittersweet Irish humor as in his earlier *Angela's Ashes* (1996) and *'Tis* (1999). The novelist Pat Conroy (1945–) effectively uses humor to tell the story of his basketball career at The Citadel in the 1960s, *My Losing Season* (2002).

Humor remains a mainstay among younger novelists, promising that the new century, no matter how bleak its start, will continue the long tradition of American humor. Some notable recent novels include *Indecision* (2005) by Benjamin Kunkel (1972–), in which a 28-year-old man tries to banish his indecision with an experimental pill; *All Is Vanity* (2002) by Christina Schwarz, a humorous novel about aspiring novelists; *John Henry Days* (2001) by Colson Whitehead (1969–), an African American writer whose novel concerns the unveiling of a postage stamp and the folk hero of the title; *You Suck: A Love Story* (2007) by Christopher Moore (1957–), who uses goth-horror-humor in a postmodern Dracula love story; and *The Locklear Letters* (2003) by Michael Kun (1962–), whose epistolary novel about a software salesman writing letters to Heather Locklear has been called by several on-line book reviewers for sites such as Amazon.com "the funniest novel ever written." Such praise for a very funny and clever novel is hyperbole, of course, but the sentiment attests to the vitality and endurance of the comic spirit as we move our way into a new millennium.

Bibliography

Abrahams, Roger. *Deep Down in the Jungle.* Hatboro, PA: Folklore Associates, 1964.
Berger, Thomas. *Adventures of the Artificial Woman.* New York: Simon and Schuster, 2004.
Blair, Walter. *Native American Humor.* New York: American Book Company, 1937.
Bryson, Bill. *The Life and Times of the Thunderbolt Kid.* New York: Random House, 2006.
———. *A Short History of Nearly Everything.* New York: Random House, 2003.
Buckley, Christopher. *No Way to Treat a First Lady.* New York: Random House, 2002.
———. *Florence of Arabia.* New York: Random House, 2004.
———. *Boomsday.* New York: Twelve, 2007.
Carlin, George. *When Will Jesus Bring the Pork Chops?* New York: Hyperion, 2004.
Colbert, Stephen. *I Am America and So Can You.* New York: Grand Central Publishing, 2007.
Conroy, Pat. *My Losing Season.* New York: Doubleday, 2002.
DeLillo, Don. *Cosmopolis.* New York: Scribner, 2003.
Franken, Al. *Lies and the Lying Liars Who Tell Them.* New York: Dutton Books, 2003.
———. *The Truth (With Jokes).* New York: Dutton Books, 2005.
Franklin, Benjamin. "Rules by Which a Great Empire May be Reduced to a Small One." London, 1773.
Freud, Sigmund. *Jokes and Their Relation to the Unconscious.* 1905. Trans. James Strachey. New York: Norton, 1960.
Horace. "The Art of Poetry." David H. Richter, ed. *The Critical Tradition: Classic Texts and Contemporary Trends.* 3rd ed. Boston: Bedford/St. Martin's, 2007.
"Humor." *The American Heritage Dictionary, Second College Edition.* Boston, MA: Houghton-Mifflin, 1982.

Irving, John. *The Fourth Hand*. New York: Random House, 2001.

Kun, Michael. *The Locklear Letters*. New York: MacAdam/Cage, 2003.

Kunkel, Benjamin. *Indecision*. New York: Random House, 2005.

Lewis, Paul. *Cracking Up: American Humor in a Time of Conflict*. Chicago, IL: University of Chicago Press, 2006.

Maher, Bill. *When You Ride Alone, You Ride With Bin Laden*. New York: Ingram Publishing Services, 2002.

———. *Keep the Statue of Liberty Closed: The New Rules*. New York: New Millennium, 2004.

———. *New Rules: Polite Musings From a Timid Observer*. New York: St. Martin's Press, 2005.

McCourt, Frank. *Teacher Man*. New York: Scribner, 2005.

Moore, Christopher. *You Suck: A Love Story*. New York: William Morrow, 2007.

Morreal, John, ed. *The Philosophy of Laughter and Humor*. Albany, NY: State University of New York Press, 1987.

O'Rourke, P.J. *The CEO of the Sofa*. New York: Grove/Atlantic, 2001.

———. *Peace Kills: America's Fun New Imperialism*. New York: Grove/Atlantic, 2004.

———. *The Wealth of Nations*. New York: Grove/Atlantic, 2007.

Roth, Philip. *The Human Stain*. New York: Houghton Mifflin, 2000.

Rourke, Constance. *American Humor: A Study of the National Character*. New York: Harcourt, Brace, and Company, 1931.

Schecter, William. *The History of Negro Humor in America*. New York: Fleet Press Corporation, 1970.

Schwarz, Christina. *All is Vanity*. New York: Doubleday, 2002.

Sedaris, David. *Me Talk Pretty One Day*. New York: Little, Brown and Company, 2000.

Smiley, Jane. *Good Faith*. New York: Alfred A. Knopf, 2003.

———. *Dress Your Family in Corduroy and Denim*. Boston, MA: Little, Brown and Company, 2004.

———. *Ten Days in the Hills*. New York: Alfred A. Knopf, 2007.

Stewart, Jon. *America (The Book): A Citizen's Guide to Democracy Inaction*. New York: Warner Books, 2004.

Twain, Mark. "The Chronicle of Young Satan." *The Mysterious Stranger Manuscripts*. 1900. William M. Gibson, ed. Berkeley, CA: University of California Press, 1969; 35–174.

Twain, Mark. *Mark Twain in Eruption*. 1906. Bernard DeVoto, ed. New York: Grosset and Dunlap, 1922,

Walker, Nancy A. *The Tradition of Women's Humor in America*. Huntington Beach, CA: American Studies Publishing, 1984.

———, ed. *What's So Funny?: Humor in American Culture*. Wilmington, DE: Scholarly Resources, Inc, 1998.

Weber, Brom. "The Mode of 'Black Humor.'" *The Comic Imagination in American Literature*. Louis D. Rubin, Jr., ed. New Brunswick, NJ: Rutgers University Press, 1973.

Whitehead, Colson. *John Henry Days*. New York: Anchor Books, 2001.

Further Reading

Blair, Walter, and Hamlin Hill. *America's Humor: From Poor Richard to Doonesbury*. New York: Oxford University Press, 1978; Cohen, Sarah Blacher. *Comic Relief: Humor in Contemporary American Literature*. Urbana, IL: University of Illinois Press, 1978; Michelson, Bruce. *Literary Wit*. Amherst, MA: University of Massachusetts Press, 2000; Mintz, Lawrence E. *Humor in America: A Research Guide to Genres and Topics*. Westport, CT: Greenwood, 1988; Morreal, John. *Taking Laughter Seriously*. Albany, NY: State University of New York, 1983; Morris, Linda A., ed. *American Women Humorists: Critical Essays*. New

York: Garland, 1994; Oring, Elliott. *Engaging Humor.* Urbana, IL: University of Illinois Press, 2003; Sloane, David E.E., ed. *New Directions in American Humor.* Tuscaloosa, AL: The University of Alabama Press, 1998; Wallace, Ronald. *God Be With the Clown.* Columbia, MO: University of Missouri Press, 1984.

JOHN BIRD

INSPIRATIONAL LITERATURE (NONFICTION)

Definition. Inspirational literature is a large genre that consists of easily understood rhetoric and personal stories designed to appeal to the emotions and spirituality of the reader. This type of literature attempts to uplift readers and encourages them to be hopeful and optimistic about their lives. The inspirational genre does not use complicated philosophies or in-depth doctrine, relying instead on anecdotal stories and simple instructions to accomplish its goals.

Because inspirational literature tends to emphasize spiritual topics, the genre is dominated by evangelical Christian authors and readers. The pastor of the evangelical Saddleback Church, Rick Warren (1954–), is the author of *The Purpose Driven Life* (2002), which has recently sold over 25 million copies, making it the biggest selling hardcover book in American history (*Financial Times* 2006) and a *New York Times* bestseller. Joel Osteen (1963–) and Max Lucado (1955–) join Warren as evangelical authors whose writings currently dominate the inspirational literature market. Even the secular inspirational series *Chicken Soup for the Soul* aims at the evangelical reading base with entries such as *Chicken Soup for the Christian Soul* (1997) and *Chicken Soup for the Christian Soul II* (2006).

Philip Yancey conveys the spirit and intent of inspirational literature in the introduction to *What's so Amazing about Grace* (1997), saying, "I will rely more on stories than on syllogisms. In sum, I would far rather convey grace than explain it" (Yancey 1997, 16). Joel Osteen's introduction to his book *Daily Readings from Your Best Life Now* (2005) likewise claims that inspirational passages are "not meant to be an exhaustive treatment of a particular passage of Scripture; instead, it is intended to inspire ardent love and worship of God" (Osteen 2005, vi). Therein is the essence of inspirational literature: convey easy concepts with stories in order to inspire rather than explain difficult ones with dogma.

History

Types of Inspirational Literature. Both past and current authors have chosen three main ways of writing within the genre. A staple of inspirational literature is true and personal stories that are used in an attempt to relate to the audience. These stories are collected in book form and often appeal to a particular kind of readership. Entries are short and several can be read in one sitting.

The second type of writing found in the genre is more of an instructional type of writing that uses short chapters and simple language in order to present guidance to the readership. Instead of organization based on individual stories, these books often base chapters on specific simple points, with personal stories woven in at various points.

The third major type of inspirational literature corresponds a particular entry with a specific date. The goal of these collections is to provide a brief, uplifting selection to be read in order on a specific set of days. These entries are often a combination of true, personal stories and moralizing prose that attempts to encourage the reader into a specific action or state of mind. Warren's *The Purpose Driven Life* is meant to be read on forty consecutive days because, according to Warren, "Studies have shown that something doesn't become a habit until you have done it . . . every day for six weeks" (*Philippine Daily Inquirer* 2006).

True Inspirational Stories. Inspirational collections based on the short true story format generally have some characteristics in common. Often, the stories are written recordings of stories people have told orally. These collections tend to organize the stories topically, and they tend to include many different contributors. Usually, these books leave the readers to their own thoughts on the story and tend to leave moralizing out of the prose of the story itself.

In the Chicken Soup series, the original book, *Chicken Soup for the Soul,* is organized into sections such as "On Love" or "Overcoming Obstacles," with each short story in each section designed to encourage the reader about that particular topic. For instance, the section "On Learning" contains a four-page story told by Sister Helen P. Mrosla about a student she taught in elementary and high school and the lesson she learned from her student (Canfield 1993, 125–28). Thus, contributors are matched with topics in which they have some experience or degree of authority.

Expanding on this principle of organization, later books in the series focus on a particular niche and employ contributors specialized in that field. *Chicken Soup for the Pet Lover's Soul* contains entries by veterinarians such as George Baker, D.V.M.; the president of The Squirrel Lover's Club, Gregg Bassett; and various other pet owners and enthusiasts. Even these books are divided into sections, and many of the books, whether written for general or niche audiences, typically start with "On Love" as the first section.

Many other books of inspirational literature follow this pattern. *Apples and Chalkdust* (1998) is compiled by Vicki Caruana, a professional teacher and curriculum

---

CHICKEN SOUP FOR EVERYONE

Perhaps the most popular example of book collections of inspirational true life stories is the *Chicken Soup for the Soul* series. Originally written and compiled by Jack Canfield and Mark Victor Hansen, this series boasts over one hundred books. The series attempts to appeal to audiences of all kinds, from the general *Chicken Soup for the Soul* (1993) and *A 2nd Helping of Chicken Soup for the Soul* (1995) to *Chicken Soup for the Pet Lover's Soul* (1998) and *Chicken Soup for the College Soul* (1999).

designer. Each story is introduced by a quotation of a famous person. The stories are very short and designed to provide encouragement to primary and secondary educators by sharing true stories from other teachers. *God's Little Devotional Book for Couples* aims at "sharing 'moments of the soul' with a spouse" (1995, 9) and includes stories from the lives of other married couples.

Evangelist Joel Osteen recently published *Daily Readings from Your Best Life Now* (2005) using a similar template. Each entry is introduced by a Bible verse that corresponds to it, and many of the entries contain brief personal references or stories from Osteen's life. Osteen, however, goes on to provide the moral or the point he wants the reader to glean from his experiences. Also, unlike many other collections of the genre that use this template, Osteen is the exclusive author for this particular book.

Inspirational Instructionals. Although this second type of inspirational literature may include true stories to illustrate different points, it relies on a book format with basic chapters and non-fiction prose that is intended to persuade the reader toward a certain action or particular way of thinking. The amount of literature that falls into this category is vast and is dominated to a great degree by authors who are evangelical pastors.

These books attempt to tackle a specific subject audiences may struggle with. Max Lucado's *It's Not about Me* begins with the premise that "trying to make life 'all about us' pushes happiness further out of reach" (Lucado 2004, xiii), and he attempts to inspire the reader to move "from me-focus to God-focus by pondering him" (9). John Eldredge's *Wild at Heart* (2001) attempts to provide a different view of a man's soul and challenges the emasculation of males in today's culture. Philip Yancey's *What's so Amazing about Grace* (1997) focuses on the Christian concept of grace. Anne Graham Lotz's *Just Give Me Jesus* (2000) focuses on the role of Jesus in inspiring people. She writes, "[W]e would be desperate for the simplicity and the purity, the freedom and the fulfillment, of 'life in his name'" (Lotz 2000, x). Such is the nature of inspirational books designed to promote feelings of well-being and encouragement about specific topics and situations.

Calendar Readings. The third major type of inspirational literature resembles the first in structure, but uses both personal stories and instructional prose to inspire the reader. The entries are short and meant to be read in one sitting, and like Osteen the authors have a specific purpose for each entry, which they reveal to the reader. What makes this third type unique is that the readings are set up to correspond with particular days, either general numbered days or specific calendar days of the year.

The two seminal publications of inspirational literature represent the two subtypes of this category of the genre. *My Utmost for His Highest* (1992) is a compilation of lessons given by Oswald Chambers (1874–1917). Originally published in 1935, the book has enjoyed an amazing run, with several reprints, including an updated 2006 edition. Each entry is one page long and corresponds with a specific date on the calendar. The format is very similar to the format of the true inspirational stories. Each entry starts with a Bible verse and includes the date it should be read (i.e., January 1). However, the entries are instructional in nature rather than contemporary true personal stories.

The other seminal work is Warren's *The Purpose Driven Life*. Warren's book is meant to be read one chapter per day on any forty consecutive days. Like Chambers' book, each entry begins with a Bible verse but also adds a quote from a famous person that relates to the topic of the chapter. Also like *My Utmost for His Highest*,

Warren's book relies mostly on instructional prose, only occasionally inserting true stories, such as his conversation with Bill Bright, founder of Campus Crusade for Christ, on the topic of writing out physical contracts to God (Warren 2002, 106).

Many other works of inspirational literature follow the template laid out by Chambers. Charles Stanley's *On Holy Ground* (1999), Norman Vincent Peale's *Positive Living Day by Day* (2003), and Dennis and Barbara Rainey's *Moments Together for Couples* (1995) have page-long readings for a specific calendar day. Selwyn Hughes and Thomas Kinkade's *Every Day Light* (1997), like Warren, have ordered readings for general, nonspecific days. Besides this unique feature of calendar readings, these works are not compilations of various authors; rather, the same author typically writes all of the entries. Also, instructions or advice replaces the true stories found in other works in the inspirational genre.

Other Forms of Inspirational Literature. Another form in which inspirational literature frequently comes is periodical publications. These publications have the same traits as other forms of the genre: personal true stories, instruction or advice on a particular topic, dates with entries to read. One such magazine is *Guideposts,* which includes true stories about a variety of people and issues. Often, celebrities are featured on the cover and provide stories from their own lives. Other magazines such as *Our Daily Bread, Homelife, Journey,* and *Stand Firm* provide inspiration to different readerships and on different topics.

The utilitarian nature of inspirational literature allows it to show up in many other forms of literature as well. Inspirational stories are frequently included in literature falling outside the genre. For example, financial advisor and radio talk-show host Dave Ramsey (1960–) inserts inspirational literature into his best-selling *The Total Money Makeover* (2003). The book contains over thirty true stories strategically placed to illustrate Ramsey's financial plans and to encourage the readers to put them into practice by revealing how other people with similar struggles have done so successfully. These stories help readers identify with the material. Local print advertisement papers, such as *Harvest Weekly* from Sylvester, Georgia, also often contain columns that are inspirational literature. A particular issue from December 2006 included a column titled "Switch Seats" that tells a true story about a company that makes spiritually themed t-shirts. The purpose, in this case, is to encourage *Harvest Weekly* readers to follow God, a theme often found in the genre.

Trends and Themes. Although the formats used for inspirational literature have changed little since Oswald Chambers's seminal *My Utmost for His Highest,* content has clearly shifted. Contemporary inspirational writers tend toward simplistic writing, refer to looser translations of the Bible, such as *The Message,* when it is used, and eliminate exclusive or judgmental doctrine from their work. Current writers want to make their inspirational message universal.

Besides the major shift in content, other trends have emerged to prominent places within the genre. Many authors have large followings and thus a built-in audience for their work. Many recent works of inspirational literature have quickly risen to best-selling prominence. There is a current movement of sophisticated marketing of the books and the concepts they teach. Technology has also become an important tool that has impacted the genre by providing an additional outlet by which authors of inspirational texts can reach massive audiences and achieve notoriety quickly.

Contemporary Content. Chambers's work did not shy away from complex thoughts, taking on sanctification (Chambers 1992, 15), personal responsibility (Chambers

1992, 74), and self-denial, with entries that read, "Sorrow removes a great deal of a person's shallowness. . . . But if a person has not been through the fires of sorrow, he is apt to be contemptuous, having no respect or time for you" (Chambers 1992, 177). The current trend in the literature, however, is away from difficult concepts and toward attempts to eliminate personal challenges. Osteen, who wrote the *New York Times* bestselling book *Your Best Life Now* (2004), provides a stark counterpoint to Chambers. Osteen's devotional topics include entries such as "Having a Positive Vision," which persuades people to visualize success (Osteen 2005, 7–10), and "God is a Giver" (Osteen 2005: 253–5). Sanctification is not a concept that shows up.

Rick Warren has been described by *The Wall Street Journal* in similar fashion: "His sermons rarely linger on self-denial and fighting sin, instead focusing on healing modern American angst, such as troubled marriages and stress" (Sataline 2006). Like Chambers, the literature is representative of what the author preaches from the pulpit. *The Purpose Driven Life* is made of the same substance as Warren's sermons. A section in the book for thinking about life's purpose reads, "Life is all about love" for a "point to ponder," and, "Honestly, are relationships my first priority?" for a "question to consider" (Warren 2002: 161). Warren attributes his book's success to its universal appeal and simplicity. "It deals with a universal subject. Everybody's interested in 'What am I here for?' . . . I intentionally made it extremely simple to read" (*Philippine Daily Inquirer* 2006). He sums up the biggest trend in content succinctly: "It's a universal question; it's not a religious question" (*Philippine Daily Inquirer* 2006). Warren has also ventured into political and economic territory by teaching others to apply his principles in those areas as well as the area of spirituality.

Max Lucado is one of the few major inspirational writers who, to some extent, does not fit completely into this current trend. Like Warren and Osteen, he frequently quotes Bible verses from *The Message* translation. Also like other writers in his field, he uses simple language and short, catchy sentences: "Lesser orbs, that's us. Appreciated. Valued. Loved dearly. But central? Essential? Pivotal? Nope. Sorry . . . Our comfort is not God's priority" (Lucado 2004, 5). However, in this passage, self-denial and discomfort are prevalent themes. Even the title of this recent book, *It's not about Me* (2004), brings to mind Oswald Chambers and sets Lucado apart from the current positivism found in so much contemporary inspirational literature.

Context and Issues

Popularity and Influence. Of Americans surveyed in a recent Gallup poll, 91.8 percent said they believed in God or a higher power (Grossman 2006), and over 50 million are evangelicals (Sataline 2006). Much of the current inspirational literature plays on that belief. Current authors also tend to have large built-in audiences for their work. Many authors are already pastors of churches with thousands of members and the ability to network. Warren's Saddleback Church has 100,000 registrants (*Philippine Daily Inquirer* 2006). Osteen preaches multiple sermons in a weekend to crowds as large as 16,000 per service (*St. Petersburg Times* 2006). Lucado is also the pastor of a large church. Even authors who are not pastors already have large followings when their inspirational books are published. Canfield had a strong reputation as a "success coach" (www.jackcanfield.com) well before the first *Chicken Soup for the Soul* book was published. Often, these authors become celebrities, thus fueling the popularity of their works. Osteen was featured on "Barbara Walter's Presents: The 10 Most Fascinating People of 2006," the first pastor to be featured on that show (*Christian Newswire* 2006). Warren has speaking engagements all over the world, including a tour of Asia and even a visit to Syria. Jack Canfield has appeared on more than 1,000 radio and television shows, including Oprah, 20/20, Larry King Live (who has also hosted Warren and Osteen), and others (www.jackcanfield.com).

The best gauge of the popularity and influence of these writers is the sale of their works. Currently, sales are record setting. Canfield's *Chicken Soup for the Soul* franchise has sold over 100 million books, and he holds the *Guinness* world record for having seven books on *The New York Times* bestseller list simultaneously (www.jackcanfield.com). Warren's *The Purpose Driven Life,* with 25 million copies sold, is the best selling hardcover book in American history and has been translated into 56 languages (*Philippine Daily Inquirer* 2006). Max Lucado has sold over 33 million copies of 20 different inspirational books (www.christnotes.org), and Osteen's *Your Best Life Now* has been a *New York Times* bestseller. *Guideposts,* the popular inspirational magazine, has over 2.3 million paid subscribers and a 71% renewal rate (www.guidepostsmedia.com).

Marketing and Technology. Perhaps the most interesting trend in contemporary inspirational literature is how well and how hard the literature is marketed and how cutting edge technological trends are incorporated into the marketing. Rick Warren, whose trendy book currently dominates the genre, has been a lead innovator in this area. Warren has created a marketing campaign called "Forty Days of Purpose," based around *The Purpose Driven Life* and the forty consecutive days recommend for the reading of it. Through this campaign, Warren has trained 400,000 pastors and priests around the world (Sataline 2006). He is attempting to tap into the Roman Catholic market as well, compiling a Catholic workbook for *The Purpose Driven Life* with American priests (*Philippine Daily Inquirer* 2006).

What Warren has done more effectively than any of his predecessors in the inspirational genre is, through training of pastors, get his book into many churches as the curriculum from which sermons and Sunday school lessons are drawn. Often, church leaders adopt "a strategic plan built around Warren's five fundamental purposes: worship, fellowship, discipleship, ministry, and evangelism" (Sataline 2006). Warren has also created acronyms to market new programs based on his inspirational text. One such acronym is P.E.A.C.E., which stands for partner with or plant a congregation, equip servant leaders, assist the poor, care for the sick, and educate the next generation (Lawton 2006).

While Warren works to bring attention back to *The Purpose Driven Life,* other authors capitalize on their publishing success by marketing support material or new material based on the same formula. Joel Osteen published *Daily Readings from Your Best Life Now* as a companion to his bestseller *Your Best Life Now.* Canfield and Hanson used the same formula and almost the same title to market 100 new variations of *Chicken Soup for the Soul* after the first one's initial success.

Technology has also become a big part of the marketing scheme. Warren's church does pod casting, and a social networking site based on *The Purpose Driven Life* has popped up (*Christian Newswire* 2006). Many inspirational authors, including most of the major ones, have Web sites, and some e-mail inspirational texts to those who have signed up. *Guideposts* has such a site with thoughts and devotionals updated daily at www.guidepostsmag.com/.

Reception. Inspirational literature is not prominently studied in an academic setting, and because of this lack of interest, academic criticism of the field in general and works in particular is muted. However, contemporary culture does have many people critical of the content, rather than literary quality, of these works.

Despite the widespread popularity and bestseller status of many inspirational books, critics of the works in the evangelically dominated genre have been harsh. The contemporary content, with its simplistic ideas and unwillingness to tackle divisive topics, has drawn especially heated criticism. Joel Osteen is criticized as a "cotton-candy preacher who specializes in Christianity lite" (Day 2006). Rick Warren is accused of encouraging simplistic Bible teaching, and *The Purpose Driven Life* is described as "a slogan-filled view of faith" (Lawton 2006). This kind of criticism of these two leaders of the genre is typical of the reaction many inspirational authors receive.

Ole Anthony, president of Trinity Foundation in Dallas, says Osteen's popularity is "a testimony of the spiritual infantilism of American culture. . . . He's qualified to be an excellent spiritual kindergarten teacher" (Day 2006). A contributing factor is Osteen's lack of an academic background: he never went to seminary. As the most popular contemporary writer of inspirational literature, Warren receives the harshest criticism, as well as blame, for dividing evangelical churches with *The Purpose Driven Life* curriculum. Churches such as Iuka Baptist in Mississippi have split because of dissent over the curriculum's management tactics, such as writing mission statements to increase membership and viewing the church as a market (Sataline 2006).

Selected Authors. The major contemporary authors and works in the inspirational genre are Jack Canfield and Mark Victor Hansen's *Chicken Soup for the Soul* series, Joel Osteen's *Your Best Life Now*, Max Lucado, the *Guideposts* inspirational monthly magazine, and Rick Warren's *Purpose Driven Life*.

Jack Canfield's Web site, www.jackcanfield.com, claims he "fostered the emergence of inspirational anthologies as a genre." Both Canfield and Hansen have extensive backgrounds as motivational speakers and make presentations in areas such as sales strategies and personal success. Certainly, the popularity of the *Chicken Soup for the Soul* "anthologies" has made it a major force within the inspirational genre. The first book was published in 1993, and over 100 entries later, the *Chicken Soup* books have sold over 100 million copies. Each book contains 101 true stories. Although the first few books were marketed for a general audience (*Chicken Soup for the Soul* and *A 2nd Helping of Chicken Soup for the Soul*), the more recent trend has been to publish books marketed toward a particular subsection of inspirational literature readers, as well as spin series off of the main anthologies. Recent books geared toward specific audiences include *Chicken Soup for the Entrepreneur's Soul, Breast Cancer Survivor's Soul,* and *Dieter's Soul* among others. Currently, the series also publishes cookbooks and a healthy living series spin-off. Still, the mainstay of the collection is the general *Chicken Soup* books, with its "6th bowl" published in 1999.

Joel Osteen's *Your Best Life Now* has been a *New York Times* number one bestseller, and as a pastor, Osteen represents part of the large inspirational segment that is evangelical Christian. Osteen has capitalized off of the success of *Your Best Life Now* with a second book, *Daily Readings from Your Best Life Now,* a calendar, audio compact discs, and a journal. Osteen is also representative of the genre's distance from academia: he has no advanced degrees in higher education or seminary training. He is currently the pastor at Lakewood Church, which draws 42,000 people to weekly services.

Max Lucado, like Osteen, is an evangelical pastor of Oak Hills Church. However, Lucado is one of the most prolific writers of the contemporary inspirational genre. According to his Web site, "In 1994, he became the only author to have eleven of his twelve books in print simultaneously appear on paperback, hardcover, and children's CBA (Christian Book Association) bestseller lists." Also, he "set a new industry record by concurrently placing nine different world publishing titles on the CBA hardcover bestseller list in both March and April 1997" (www.maxlucado.com). As of February 2007, Lucado's *Cure for the Common Life* was ranked second on the CBA inspirational bestseller list. He has published 21 inspirational titles to date.

Guideposts is a magazine of "true stories of hope and inspiration." Published monthly, the magazine often features true stories from celebrities, such as model Niki Taylor (May 2006) and country singer Martina McBride (November 2006). *Guideposts* was founded in 1945 by Dr. Norman Vincent Peale, who wrote *The Power of Positive Living*, a forerunner of much of the contemporary inspirational literature. The magazine's mission is to help "people from all walks of life achieve their maximum personal and spiritual potential" (www.dailyguideposts.com). *Guideposts* even featured inspirational literature heavyweight Rick Warren on the cover of its October 2006 magazine.

Perhaps the most prominent, recognizable, and influential contemporary inspirational writer is Rick Warren. His bestselling *The Purpose Driven Life* has garnered the most popularity and drawn the most criticism. Like Osteen and Lucado, Warren is an evangelical pastor. His Saddleback Church is one of the biggest churches in the United States, and he has trained hundreds of thousands of clergy around the world with his *Purpose Driven* curriculum. Also like Osteen, Warren's *The Purpose Driven Life* has become something of a franchise, with journals, additional readings, and audio compact discs based on the material for sale. In fact, *The Purpose Driven Life* is itself a spin-off of Warren's *The Purpose Driven Church* (1995). Originally, this book was written for pastors and contains a five-part growth strategy.

The Purpose Driven Life illustrates the philosophical simplicity of much of the inspirational genre in a section titled "The Reason for Everything." Warren writes, "Wherever you are reading this, I invite you to bow your head and quietly whisper the prayer that will change your eternity: 'Jesus, I believe in you and I receive you.' Go ahead. If you sincerely meant that prayer, congratulations! Welcome to the family of God" (Warren 2002, 74).

Bibliography

Canfield, Jack, and Mark Victor Hansen, eds. *Chicken Soup for the Soul.* Deerfield Beach, FL: Health Communications, Inc., 1993.
Caruana, Vicki. *Apples and Chalkdust.* Tulsa, OK: Honor, 1998.
Chambers, Oswald. *My Utmost for His Highest.* Grand Rapids, MI: Discovery House, 1992.
Day, Sherri. "God's Cheerleader." *St. Petersburg Times* 26 Nov. 2006.
Eldredge, John. *Wild at Heart.* Nashville, TN: Thomas Nelson, 2001.
God's Little Devotional Book for Couples. Tulsa, OK: Honor, 1995.
Grinnan, Edward, ed. *Guideposts.* (2006) http://www.guidepostsmag.com/.
Grossman, Cathy Lynn. "View of God Can Predict Values, Politics." *USA Today* 12 Sept. 2006.

Hughes, Selwyn, and Thomas Kinkade. *Every Day Light.* Nashville, TN: Broadman, 1997.

"Joel Olsteen to be Featured on Barbara Walters' '10 Most Fascinating People.'" *Christian Newswire* 4 Dec. 2006.

Lawton, Kim. "Purpose Driven Pastor Rick Warren Goes Global." *Religion News Service* 8 Sept. 2006.

Lotz, Annie Graham. *Just Give Me Jesus.* Nashville, TN: Word Publishing, 2000.

Lucado, Max. *Come Thirsty.* Nashville, TN: Word Publishing, 2004.

———. *It's not about Me.* Nashville, TN: Integrity, 2004.

Osteen, Joel. *Daily Readings from Your Best Life Now.* New York: Warner Faith, 2005.

———. *Your Best Life Now.* New York: Faith Words, 2004.

Peale, Norman Vincent. *Positive Living Day by Day.* Nashville, TN: Ideals, 2003.

Sataline, Suzanne. "Strategy for Church Growth Splits Congregation." *The Wall Street Journal* 5 Sept. 2006.

Stanley, Charles. *On Holy Ground.* Nashville, TN: Thomas Nelson, 1999.

"The Purpose Driven Rick Warren." *Philippine Daily Inquirer* 30 July 2006.

Warren, Rick. *The Purpose Driven Life.* Grand Rapids, MI: Zondervan, 2002.

Yancey, Philip. *What's so Amazing about Grace?* Grand Rapids, MI: Zondervan, 1997.

CHAD R. HOWELL

J

JEWISH AMERICAN LITERATURE

Definition. The Jewish American literary genre first developed in the late-nineteenth and early-twentieth centuries as a literature that was linked inextricably to a particular place, time, and social state—primarily the impoverished urban immigrant communities of Chicago and New York's Lower East Side. Of course, this is not at all surprising considering the fact that Jews, since the inception of their history, have consistently written with a very acute awareness of place, of where they were physically at a given point in time. This awareness defines both their collective and individual identities and the place of such identities in a world of non-Jews. Even in the biblical era, writing by Jews sought to define their existence in very concrete terms, and in the context of their surrounding environment, as destabilized as it might be. Throughout history, Jews have had a way of not only making themselves at home wherever they are, but also of redefining themselves according to that geographical place in a manner that perhaps challenges the traditional belief that Jews are a diasporic community of people whose roots are in a Jewish homeland. In an examination of the evolution of literature by Jews and American Jews, it seems that this tendency has not changed. Place often defines the people, and if it doesn't, at the very least it forces them into a constant examination of both collective and individual identities.

In a landmark book entitled *New Jews: The End of the Jewish Diaspora* (2005), David Shneer and Caryn Aviv argue provocatively that the new generation of Jews has liberated itself from older and more traditional ideologies and is instead committed to creating homes and communities wherever they live. Jewish unity, they implicitly argue, is grounded not in the shared (and, in their opinion, all but obsolete) longing for a Jewish homeland, but in the common search for new identities. Shneer and Aviv find, further, that in this contemporary era, the focus shifts from Jewish unity to Jewish diversity. The point being that Jews and various manifestations of Jewish life are thriving in all sorts of places—a global community of multiple networks comprised by a diversity of Jewish languages, cultures, and concerns that are each distinctively Jewish in their own ways. Contemporary Jews, they argue, particularly the younger generation, are deeply concerned with Jewish culture and its various expressions, but they are also less religious than their parents and grandparents, and still less interested in Israel and the Holocaust as markers of their Jewish identity.

History. The notion that Israel and an image of Jewish life that perceives the state as the primary homeland need not remain a defining facet of Jewish identity for those Jews who live outside of the state is perhaps nowhere more evident than in the diversity of Jewish American literary expressions of the past decade. Jewish American writing began as the first manifestation of immigrant writing in the United States, and later transitioned into what we might call the literature of assimilated Jews in the middle and later part of the twentieth century. The writing of the last decade is unique in that a single unifying characteristic is lacking from the body of work as a whole. The most recent writing of American Jews depicts a diverse community of people who are at home in America. These are people whose concerns about Judaism or Jewishness—although it should be noted that a number of the more recent American Jewish writers, Paul Auster for instance, seem not to be overly concerned with this at all—have more to do with what it means to be an American who also happens to be a Jew.

Sometimes—as in the case of writers like Shalom Auslander (*Beware of God,* 2005), Pearl Abraham (*The Romance Reader,* 1996), Tova Mirvis (*The Ladies Auxiliary,* 2000), and even Allegra Goodman (*Kaaterskill Falls,* 1998)—this means responding directly to Jewish rituals and traditions, whether through critiquing, rejecting, or redefining them. It is interesting to note, however, that the books that follow in many of these writers' repertoires often move completely away from such concerns. Judaism and Jewish community, for example, which dominate the concerns of the religious enclave in Goodman's *Kaaterskill Falls,* could not be farther from the minds of the characters in Goodman's *Intuition* (Goodman 2006), who are comprised primarily of postdoctoral researchers in a scientific laboratory. The characters remain deeply complex and brilliantly developed, but it is as if they inhabit a world not accustomed to the religious concerns of her previous novel.

In other instances, it manifests itself in a critique of the tendency of an older generation of Jews to see their identity as connected primarily to the events of the Holocaust. As in Tova Reich's provocative *My Holocaust,* which satirizes the way in which the Holocaust has become not just a marker of Jewish identity, but a commodity or industry to be exploited. Reich's novel attacks not just the abuse and misuse of the Holocaust, but also the tendency of a previous generation of Jews to define themselves in the shadow of the Holocaust. Indeed, a number of Jewish American writers—including Jonathan Safran Foer and even Art Spiegelman, the creator of the infamous graphic narrative Holocaust memoir entitled *Maus*—have shifted their focus from the Holocaust as a Jewish tragedy, to the events of 9/11 as an American tragedy. This, of course, is not to say that the Holocaust is not addressed in contemporary Jewish American literature—quite the contrary. Michael Chabon's *The Final Solution* (2004), Cynthia Ozick's *Heir to the Glimmering World* (2005), and E.L. Doctorow's *City of God* (2000), for example, do not address the events of the Holocaust directly, but depict a world over which its dark shadow looms largely, haunting us from the margins and backdrops of the stories.

We have now seen the Jewish American literary tradition progress in three main waves: immigrant writing (Gold, Henry Roth, Yezierska, Cahan), assimilationist literature (Philip Roth, Saul Bellow, Bernard Malamud, E.L. Doctorow, Nathaniel West, Norman Mailer), and the literature of the past two decades, which often returns to the cultural and religious themes of the Jewish tradition (Allegra Goodman, Tova Mirvis, Steve Stern, Nathan Englander, Pearl Abraham), sometimes dealing simultaneously with complex issues of gender and sexual orientation. The 1980s saw the emergence of many new Jewish American voices, and on the heels of these new voices followed an increased interest in Orthodox Judaism and Hasidism, feminism, post-Holocaust issues, and Jewishness as an ethnic manifestation. The product of these new and revived curiosities is a multiplicity of Jewish American voices that together represent a complex contemporary Jewish American literary identity—one that flirts with memory and history while exploring both the sacred and secular as equally important veins of a new Jewish American literary canon. At the same time, some of the most significant writers of the Jewish American literary field (and, arguably, of the American literary canon in general) continue to forge novelistic expressions of American concerns and multi-cultural identities. Philip Roth, for example, has published five novels since 2000, including *The Human Stain* (2000), which deals with American racism and the feasibility of passing in American culture; and *The Plot Against America*, which is set in 1940s America and creates an alternate American history that includes the election of Charles Lindbergh to the American presidency—what follows in this chilling historical revision is the rise of anti-Semitism in America.

Over the past decade we have also begun to see the emergence of a fourth wave of Jewish American writing. Since the collapse of the Soviet Union there has been a substantial influx of Russian-Jewish immigrants. Many of these immigrants and their children have begun to write fiction, and they write with new, compelling voices, sometimes evocative of the prose of famed modern Russian-Jewish writer Isaac Babel, carefully revealing the interior life of the Jewish underworld. In other instances, these post-Soviet voices are sharp with the cynical wit and insight possessed only by those who have experienced both the scarcity of Soviet life and the excess of American life. Writers in this wave include Gary Shteyngart (*The Russian Debutante's Handbook* [2002] and *Absurdistan* [2006]), Lara Vapnyar *(There Are Jews in My House,* 2003), David Bezmozgis (*Natasha,* 2004), Anya Ulinich (*Petropolis,* 2007), Sana Krasikov (*One More Year,* 2008), and even Jonathan Safran-Foer, among others.

Trends and Themes. In his now infamous introduction to *Jewish American Stories* (1977), Irving Howe insisted upon the imminent demise of the Jewish American literary canon, a genre that would certainly dissipate with the passing of its major voices—Bernard Malamud, Saul Bellow, and Philip Roth—and the scattering of Jewish distinctiveness among the milieu of mainstream American culture. In Howe's assessment of the Jewish American literary world, which according to his estimation had already moved past its high point once it climaxed with Bellow, the key figures were those writers upon whom the mark of immigrant life and the distinctive experience of Jewishness was ineradicably placed.

Indeed, what we now know as Jewish American literature began as the efforts of Jewish (primarily Russian and Polish) immigrants and their children to grapple with the pervasive feelings of alienation and conflict that characterized their experience in the new world. Works such as Abraham Cahan's *The Rise of David Levinsky* (1917), Anzia Yezierska's *Bread Givers* (1925), Michael Gold's *Jews Without Money* (1930), and Henry Roth's *Call It Sleep* (1934)—all written by immigrants or children of immigrants—focused on the trials and tribulations of immigrant life in New York's Lower East Side or Chicago. They provided the starting point for a literary genre that would continue to flourish and evolve over the next century and beyond. Such writers had barely shaken the *shtetl* mud from the soles of their feet when they found themselves plagued not by the pogroms and raging Cossacks from which they and their traditions had narrowly escaped, but by the insular world of tenement life that was colored by greed, poverty, and even ethnic persecution. (*Shtetl* is Yiddish. A *shtetl* was typically a small village with a predominately Jewish population in pre-Holocaust Eastern Europe. The notion of *shtetl* culture is often used as a metaphor for the traditional way of life of 19th-century Eastern European Jews. *Shtetl* communities were characterized by their adherence to Orthodox Judaism, and members of the community lived under constant threat of pogroms— large-scale, violent anti-Semitic rioting thought by many historians to be advocated by Tsarist Russian secret police in many cases. The events of the Holocaust culminated in the disappearance of most *shtetls*, through both extermination and mass exodus to the United States and eventually the State of Israel.)

One need look no farther than little David Schearl of Roth's *Call it Sleep* for a vivid account of the difficulties faced by immigrants and their young children, eager to escape the tell-tale Yiddishisms of their family lives, but unable to hide them from the leering (or, so it seemed) faces of other—primarily Irish and Italian—immigrant communities who were faced with some of the same struggles as Jewish immigrants, namely, how best to assimilate quickly into mainstream American culture. It is as if Roth means to say that, as immigrant Jews, we are not free from threat and persecution here in America—it may not be the Cossacks and pogroms, but the threat is just as real as it was in the Eastern European communities from which we came; we have not yet escaped such terrors. To be sure, as part of the first wave of Jewish American writing, the work of such writers is characterized by the influence of the immigrant world, a world dominated by *shtetl* sensibilities, Yiddish accents, and a certain tentativeness when it came to the perception of America as the land of opportunity.

In many respects, however, the immigrant communities of Roth's, Cahan's, Gold's, and Yezierska's worlds were much different from the European *shtetls* from which they had fled. The new immigrant living conditions forcibly pushed immigrants into living nearly on top of one another, in such close proximity that it was virtually impossible to have a life of one's own—this compared to the Russian and Polish *shtetls*, where people lived apart from one another and enjoyed a certain level of privacy and autonomy. Such, however, was the life of the new American Jew—destined to live, at least during this period, confined by language, unfamiliar customs, cultural idiosyncrasies, and the difficulty of finding suitable jobs and a dignified manner of living. They were, like many other immigrant communities, set apart from the American society to which they could only dream of belonging. Clearly, the work of Cahan, Roth, Gold, and Yezierska depicts a portrait of Jewish life that is quite different from the earlier depictions of writers such as Sholem Aleichem and Isaac Babel, whose sensibilities were generated through imaginative depictions of European *shtetls* and the perpetual threat of pogroms. The modern Jewish immigrant writers relate to us the stories of a people who have truly immigrated, and who find themselves in the squalor and impoverishment of the "land of opportunity."

Life in the "New World," of course, was clearly not as glorious and rewarding as the first Jewish American writers had hoped it would be. In fact, the new surroundings delivered many new hardships and a great deal of suffering for hopeful

European Jewish families who tried to create fresh lives in America, hoping to leave their suffering in Europe behind them. Perhaps it was this disappointment that compelled many Jewish American writers to look toward Socialist philosophies and leftist impulses as a means of escaping from the impoverishment—an impulse that would characterize the work many Jewish American writers, beginning with those of the turn-of-the-century period and progressing into the work of more contemporary writers like E.L. Doctorow (see, for example, *The Book of Daniel*).

It is a sense of uneasiness that dominates the Jewish American literature between 1900 and 1945, and much of this can be attributed to language. This era of literature acts as a bridge between the Yiddish literature of the late-nineteenth century and the literature of the second wave of Jewish American writing—primarily the work of Philip Roth, Saul Bellow, and even Bernard Malamud and Cynthia Ozick, whose characters personified the new American Jew who was better educated and had a better grasp of the English language. The literature generated by American Jews in the first half of the twentieth century is in effect a literature of transformation, for in it we witness the often difficult transition from Yiddish to English, as characterized especially by Nobel prize-winning novelist Isaac Bashevis Singer, one of very few Yiddish writers whose work was translated into English. But, it is a transformation that will not be fully developed for at least another twenty years or so. Yiddish is depicted as the language of kings in *Call It Sleep*, for instance. Set against the backdrop of the fragmented, halting, and frequently mispronounced English of the little immigrant street urchins, the Yiddish that is spoken in the homes of Jewish immigrants takes on a regal, almost Shakespearean quality. For, Yiddish was life—it was the gateway to knowledge of just about everything.

And for this reason, Abraham Cahan, the founder and editor of the *Daily Yiddish Forward*, is a particularly important figure in this era of Jewish American literature. The *Forward* was the only means by which the immigrant Jews learned about the world around them—the crux of knowledge for Jewish immigrants at the turn of the century. This, of course, is not directly evident in the works of writers like Yezierska, Gold, and Roth, but the fact that Yiddish figures so largely into the experience of the immigrant world reinforces its significance. These writers may have written in English, which sets them apart from an earlier generation of Jewish writers such as Singer, Aleichem, Chaim Grade, and I.L. Peretz, but Yezierska and Roth clearly imagined in Yiddish, creating an alliance between parallel communities, separated by an ocean, but conjoined by similar problems—one foot in Europe, and one foot in America.

Context and Issues. All in all, Jewish American writers from 1900 to 1945 introduced a literary genre that was entirely their own—infused with new voices, dialects, and rhythms that allowed it to be viewed as the first form of multi-ethnic literature in the United States, arriving earlier than most to the identity politics party that would surface much later in the century within English departments and literary circles. Moving up in the twentieth century, Chaim Potok introduced a new form of the Jewish—though not immigrant—community in *The Chosen* (1967). This novel begins during World War II and ends with the founding of Israel, and it is important to note that, at this time, most writers were not focused on religion or on maintaining the homogeneity of a Jewish community. Instead, the focus of American Jews seemed fixed on the goal of assimilation. But with Potok, we get an undiluted look at the Jewish Orthodox community—an unfiltered view of Lee Avenue of Williamsburg, essentially a *shtetl*-like community of ultra-Orthodox Jews and Modern Orthodox Jews (as it still is today), neither of whom aspire to assimilate or blend in too closely with mainstream American community.

Nearly thirty-five years after Roth introduced us to the world of the Jewish American immigrant community, Potok retains the concept of an insular Jewish community, but doesn't extract from it the religious impulses. One contrast, however, resides in the fact that while earlier Jewish writers conveyed a sense of longing to escape from the immigrant community and move up in American society, Potok depicts a group of American Jews who actually want to live in a close, tightly knit Jewish community, set apart from mainstream American culture and all of its influences—a depiction that would remain remarkably rare in Jewish American literature. Yet, at the same time, these Jews are beset by the same problems experienced by secular Americans, Jewish and Gentile: the relationships between fathers and sons and whether or not to continue to embrace the ways of their fathers. *The Chosen*'s Danny, for example, a great Talmudic genius, doesn't follow his father, but falls in love with Freud—in Freud's very early stages of popularity—who is the embodiment of the new secular world, and goes to graduate school to study rather than a rabbinic school.

What Yezierska, Roth, Potok, and others all have in common is the *shtetl*-like community—totally transported and re-positioned in America. Yet, unlike Yezierska and Roth, who, in their socialist and leftist leanings become nearly anti-religious, Potok presents us with the image of a group of people who, essentially, say no to assimilation. They metaphorically proclaim, "We don't have to give up the Torah, the Talmud, and Ultra-Orthodoxy in order to be American." This really is a critical point because early Jewish American fiction, by definition, was laced with Yiddishisms and Jewish cultural quirks, but implicit in the literature was a tacit understanding that they wanted to be as American as possible—and we see this beginning with the earliest Jewish American writers and culminating in the mid to late-twentieth century writers like Saul Bellow, Bernard Malamud, and Philip Roth. But, an aggressive impulse toward assimilation does not seem to be a problem in Potok's Williamsburg *shtetl*; rather, the issue becomes a divisiveness that exists between religious groups: the Hasidic Jews and the Modern Orthodox Jews. In contrast to the early twentieth-century immigrant community, so religiously entrenched are the Jews of this new community that the issue shifts from being at odds with American culture, to being at odds with the other religious Jews who live just on the other side of Lee Avenue. The Hasidic Jews see the Modern Orthodox Jews as disgraceful, but the genius of this lies in the way in which Potok chooses to open *The Chosen*—with a baseball game, one in which all the boys, both Hasidic and Orthodox, play together a very American game.

The irony, of course, lies in the fact that Potok depicts a religious community, eager to retain and embrace its religious identity in a way that challenges the impulse of most Jews and Jewish writers in America during this time to blend in with mainstream American culture. Even Saul Bellow's first novel, *Dangling Man* (1944), addressed not the issues one imagines would grace the pages of a first novel from a child of immigrants, but the issues that colored the minds and concerns of most Americans during this time, regardless of ethnic or religious descent: war and the draft. Bellow's work, though it often contained Jewish characters and concerns, would continue to focus primarily on the shared issues of mid-twentieth-century mainstream Americans. Bernard Malamud's *The Natural* (1952), of course, utilizes the setting of the baseball field to explore, not the nuances and complexities of religious life in America, but the challenges of isolation and dashed dreams for—true to the American individualist impulse—one man. This very same baseball setting, both the game and the field, will later be used by Ehud Havazelet (*Like Never Before*, 1998) to explore the tension between an older, more religious generation, and a younger, secular generation. Regardless, work by Jewish American writers including Grace Paley, Tillie Olsen, Nathanael West, Joseph Heller, and later Norman Mailer would continue to haunt the mid-twentieth-century era with its striking absence of Jewish characters or concerns, rituals or traditions.

Reception. Though Howe believed staunchly that the era that hailed Jewish American literature, a force with which to be reckoned was drawing to a close, evidence of a newly revived Jewish American literary canon suggests that not only is Jewish American literature alive and well, but also that it is larger than the confines of Howe's imagination could bear. It is perhaps even bigger—in terms of sheer breadth and the variety of its range— than it was during the advent of writers such as Philip Roth and Bernard Malamud. Although much of this has to do with the multiplicity of Jewish voices that have burst onto the literary scene in the past twenty years—from feminist writers, to those writing about neo-orthodoxy and Hasidic communities, to gay writers, and to post-Holocaust voices—one strong element of this literary persistence has to do with the newest generation of Russian Jews who have immigrated to the United States. Once again, the *shtetl*-like communities—though not impoverished and miserable anymore—play a central role in the fiction of Jewish American literature. The storytelling of this new generation of Jewish American writers is infused with both the memories of prior immigrant experiences and the experiences of new ones, and yet it is simultaneously innovative in its tendency to reconcile—or at least draw our attention to—disparate parts of the Jewish American identity. In an essay called "Against Logic," that was part of a 1997 issue of *Tikkun* devoted to the explosion of new Jewish American literary voices, novelist Rebecca Goldstein (*Mazel*, 1995; *The Mind-Body Problem*, 1992) ponders the persistence of a collective Jewish literary imagination despite generations of assimilation into mainstream American culture. She writes:

> Yet here I am . . . dreaming Jewish dreams. Deep down in the regions of psyche where fiction is born, regions supremely indifferent to criteria of rationality, being Jewish seems to matter to me quite a lot; and in this way my own small and personal story might be offered up as a metaphor for the very re-awakening in Jewish American letters . . . For here we all of us are, after several generations that have tried their damnedest to shrug off the accidents of our shared precedents; here we all are, having sufficiently assimilated the culture at large to be able to inhabit, should we so choose, the inner worlds of characters to whom Jewishness is nothingness; here we all are, against logic, dreaming Jewish dreams. (Goldstein 1997, 43)

Yet, perhaps this logic-defying phenomenon has as much to do with a shared history, as it does with the ability of American Jews to thrive in and adapt to the places in which they find themselves, rather than lament the loss of a shared Jewish homeland.

The ghettos may be far behind them, but they are not long forgotten—they continue to appear, albeit in newer and less miserable forms; Brooklyn's Brighton Beach is a prime example of this new phenomenon of Jewish Russian immigrant communities. Moreover, Henry Roth's attempt to reconcile the vulgarity of the English spoken by little immigrant street urchins with the Yiddish of an almost Shakespearean quality spoken in the home is mirrored by new sets of cultural discrepancies in the newest wave of Jewish immigrant literature. It turns out that, in terms of part of his prediction, Howe was right; he just didn't know exactly how right he was. Much like the Jewish people and the collective history that is so much a part of the burden that compels them to satisfy, even fulfill, the literary imagination, their literature tracks the experiences of its people.

Selected Authors. The novelist who, in many ways, both reinforces and transcends many of these boundaries is Philip Roth; an examination of Jewish American literature would not be complete without an extended discussion of his work. Philip Roth's work is particularly interesting and unarguably important to the Jewish American literary genre as a whole in that it spans two different waves of Jewish American writing (In an article published in *The Nation* in 2001, it was suggested by Morris Dickstein that *The Ghost Writer* actually launches and propels us into the next wave of Jewish American writing.) and offers readers a lasting glimpse into the making of the so-called American Jew. Through the trajectory of Roth's novels, we have the rare opportunity to observe the continually evolving identity of the American Jewish male. However, because Roth so obviously, and purposely, plays with both real and fictional depictions of the Jewish American identity (and perhaps his own evolving identity), frequently melting and molding them into undistinguishable personae, we are often unable to identify concretely what is Roth's own perception of the Jewish American identity that he seems continually to mock through morphing representations of it. A man whose closest friends are "sheer playfulness and deadly seriousness," through his explorations of Jewish, particularly male identities, Roth both entertains and educates his readers. Nevertheless, the ever-transforming protagonist of Roth's work is typically seen in the context of—and habitually in opposition to—the Jewish family and community.

Two of Roth's earliest constructions of personae designed to explore the complexities of Jewish and Jewish American identity include *Goodbye, Columbus* (1959) and *Portnoy's Complaint* (1969). In both of these seminal works, the protagonist is utterly self-conscious, narcissistic, and consumed by sexual neuroses. Clearly this description is more characteristic of Alexander Portnoy than it is of Neil Klugman, who is, after all, supposed to be an Orthodox Jew, but in Neil we see the beginnings of Alexander Portnoy, even if only tentatively. In the ten-year period between the constructions of Neil Klugman and Alexander Portnoy, there was ample time for the faltering Neil to evolve into the notoriously obsessive and sexually perverted Portnoy. Through both characters, Roth begins to unleash his literary voice—an ironic one that contains a real sense of the inner city, stickball-playing boy turned misogynistic assimilated American, consumed by his own narcissism and inferiority complexes. Albeit at different levels, both Neil and Portnoy emerge as somehow suspended between Jewishness and an assimilated American identity—both seem at once within reach and just out of grasp. Just as Portnoy seems unable to fit himself solidly into one identity or another, he is also unable to achieve sexual satisfaction and fulfillment, and his readers are sure to find him either compulsively masturbating or simulating sex with a piece of liver. Whereas Neil Klugman is fixated on Brenda Patimkin, a Jewish girl from a wealthy and assimilated family, Portnoy finds pleasure in taking out his anger and psychological confusion on unwitting *shiksas*. Moreover, Neil's conflicts, of course, are mostly external—with family and community—while Portnoy's conflicts involve everyone around him, including himself. Perhaps Portnoy is Portnoy's own most worthy adversary.

Although they share some similar characteristics, Portnoy is in many cases the polar opposite of Neil. While Portnoy is clearly a much more aggressively liberated individual—an intelligent, high powered government official who seems to be on a mission to copulate with every woman possible—Neil cannot quite get past the allure of Brenda Patimkin, and all that her wealthy, assimilated family represents. Roth's depiction of Neil's fascination with the wealthy Patimkins, Jews who could afford to keep a separate refrigerator for only fruit, provides a kind of anti-thesis to Henry Roth's immigrant world. We cannot quite tell if Neil admires or is repelled by the Patimkins' ability to become successful and to pass. Similarly, while many of Portnoy's hang-ups stem from his relationship with his obsessive mother, Neil's mother is not present in the story. Though both Neil and Portnoy are engaged in a battle with their Jewishness and their ambivalent connection to both their biblical and recent Jewish American past, it manifests itself in much different forms. One cannot help but see in Portnoy the implicit comparison to the good yeshiva boy—deemed the productive, prize-winning student as depicted by Isaac Babel in "Story of my Dovecote," as well as by other Jewish writers, American and European, in the ultimate trajectory of Jewish literature—who would probably never lower himself to attempting to copulate with a piece of liver or even a *shiksa* for that matter. Portnoy, however, though he is prone to frequent Yiddishisms, is anything but the stereotypically good Jewish boy. He is the epitome of someone who knows no boundaries, someone who has spun out of control, who is eternally engaged in a battle against himself. Tellingly, Portnoy recalls that in school he

> chanted, along with [his] teacher "I am the Captain of my fate, I am the Master of my soul," and meanwhile within my own body, an anarchic insurrection had been launched by one of my privates—which I was helpless to put down! (Roth 1969, 38)

His sexual neuroses, ambiguities, and dissatisfactions become a metaphor for the ways in which he deals with his Jewish identity. We see, also, his inability to function sexually even when he is in Israel, at what should be the height of his exploration of his Jewish identity.

As shocking, even disturbing, as some of his characterizations of Jewish identity might be, Roth was very much a man of his day—something that is reflected in not just the early novels, but many of his middle and later works as well. His protagonists are typically unusual characters who are living in the sexual politics of the era, bringing hedonism and bachelorhood to the forefront of Jewish American fiction. In a sense, Philip Roth did for literature what Woody Allen did for film—neurotic, sexually obsessed, self-referential, and imbued with a ferocious sense of artistic entitlement. In *The Breast* (1972), *The Professor of Desire* (1977), and *The Dying Animal* (2001), for instance, we are introduced to David Kepesh, a fully assimilated, graduate school educated Jewish man, who is perhaps a milder, more mature version of Portnoy, living in a state of what he terms "emancipated manhood." The radical individualism of America lays claim to each of Roth's fictional characters, but despite their predisposition toward success, these self-conscious overachievers rarely make for a flattering picture of the American Jew. Instead, they become perhaps pivotal examples of the consequences of too much assimilation, some have argued. As Jewish American identities, they are both alluring and revolting to American Jews living in the real world.

It would be an understatement to suggest that Roth's work abounds in contradictions, and it often seems meant to inspire confusion, especially when it comes to deciphering which are the fictional impulses and which ideas spring directly from autobiographical instances. Critics who have attempted to make such distinctions have often been attacked for taking his work as autobiographical, yet he clearly insists on drawing repeatedly from the commonly known facts of his life in forming many of his protagonists. In keeping with this idea, many of Roth's later works deal specifically with writers and the act of writing—in some cases becoming quite metafictional, as elements of the writer are infused into the text—and *The Ghost Writer* begins this new focus in his work. One of the most interesting aspects of this novel is that it pays homage to two other writers with whom Roth was consistently identified: Bernard Malamud and Saul Bellow. The character of I.E. Lonoff, who the Zuckerman character seems to emulate, is a stand in for Malamud, while the Abravanel character represents Bellow, even down to the multiple marriages. Nathan Zuckerman, the young character who has just published a very controversial set of stories, of course, is clearly indicative of Roth himself when he was that age.

While *The Ghost Writer* seems to be a transitional piece in both Roth's fiction and the wave of Jewish American literature in general, as Roth's work progresses his protagonists become less self-conscious and less self-referential. The Nathan Zuckerman of *The Ghost Writer* is still the same character—still embarrassing to the Jewish community; he has assimilated a bit too well—but the later depictions of Zuckerman are less humiliating, though he is still well assimilated into mainstream American culture. In later works, Roth's emphases are broader and more diverse, ranging from friendly, even loving, father-son relationships (*Patrimony*) to political issues (*The Counterlife*). Morris Dickstein suggests that this phase in Roth's writing reflects the vengeful return of the Jewishness "that once seemed to be disappearing." "In this phase," he asserts, "the inevitability of assimilation gives way to the work of memory." Character construction becomes, it seems, less of a burden—less a reflection of a disjointed self and fractured identity. Similarly, rather than depicting Zuckerman as a protagonist, Roth begins to employ Zuckerman as a narrator, the lens through which other people's stories are told—as in *The Human Stain* (2000) and *American Pastoral* (1997). Since the 1990s, Roth's fiction has often fused autobiographical components with retrospective dramatizations of postwar American life. A sense of frustration with social and political developments in the United States since the 1940s, and with the perpetual collapse of the American dream, is apparent in the American trilogy and his most recent novel *Exit Ghost* (2007), though it was evident in much earlier works that flaunted political and social satire.

But as important as Philip Roth is to the Jewish American literary field and to American literature as a whole, neither his voice nor his concerns reflect those of the majority of Jewish American writers. Of course, it is impossible to conceive of mid to late-twentieth-century Jewish American writing without invoking the name of Cynthia Ozick, who continues to be a major writer in the field, but whose work, though generated in the same time period as Philip Roth's, addresses entirely different concerns. She has characterized her work as being focused primarily on issues that are "centrally Jewish"—that is, Judaism and the history of liturgical issues, in addition to the notion of idolatry. Individual distinctiveness, it seems, is as much a hallmark of Jewish American literature as it is of the Jewish religion and ritual that the literature confronts, embraces, challenges, or repels. And while Roth seems, over the the duration of the twentieth century, to have dealt with his own issues regarding

Jewish identity in America, a growing number of Jewish American writers are grappling with these issues in new ways. Margot Singer's literary debut, *The Pale of Settlement* (2007), amounts to a sustained negotiation on the role of Israel in Jewish American identity today. The linked stories follow Susan from her home in New York across borders into Israel, Germany, and beyond. The transnational focus decenters Israel as the signifier of her Jewish identity and allows for complex dynamics to take shape. The stories are fragmented both geographically and historically, jumping between Palestine pre-1948, Israel in both the present and tumultuous past, and her home in New York where Susan is firmly rooted. The complex influence of Israel as the Jewish homeland is not lost on Susan, but the idea that it supersedes her American or global sensibility is lost. The relationship with history remains important but in the past as it is realized in the stories Susan's mother tells her.

> The places her mother talked about had vanished into a pink blotch that spread across the top of the map that pulled down over the blackboard in Susan's classroom like a window shade. Vilna, Lwow, Bessarabia, Belarus. The Pale of Settlement. You couldn't go to those parts of the world any longer. They were gone. (Singer 2007, 188)

There is a clear sense that return is not possible. The only places in the world that are closed off to Susan are these locations of historical significance to the way Jewish identity has been formulated in the past. Now, she feels part of a networked and interconnected culture that does not rely on a sense of home being the ancient center. The idea is clearly demarcated in the inaccessibility of historical locales. Susan "has the feeling that she could live anywhere in the world, even though New York is the place she's always been" (Singer 2007, 200). The Diaspora is part of history, not the present. It plays a role in defining her cosmopolitan nature but does not pull her toward a homeland or a particular version of what is means to be Jewish in today's global culture.

As much as place has played a major role in defining Jewish American identity, the role of the Holocaust in tying American Jews to Israel throughout the twentieth century cannot be underestimated. Tova Reich takes issue with that role in *My Holocaust* (2007) and confronts the ethics of relying on a historical trauma for contemporary identity. Her primary concern is the commodification of the event and the subsequent foreclosure of meaning for those generations to follow. She clearly delineates how the contemporary generation is supposed to be that of "continuity," the "designated Kaddish," or the "living memorial candle" (Reich 2007, 19). This third generation is intended to carry-on the memory of the Holocaust in exactly the way previous generations have done, reaping the political and financial benefits of doing so. Tova Reich resists such a direct connection and problematizes how prior generations have created a cultural industry that defines the historical trauma. She takes issue with the idea that previous generations should define what the Holocaust means to Jews of the future. She satirizes the way Auschwitz has become a tourist attraction and how the Holocaust Museum on the Washington Mall amounts to a definitive source of cultural memory. Hers is a more complexly-formed idea of the Holocaust and what the trauma means to contemporary Jews. Just like the idea of Israel is dissipating as the definitive homeland of Jewish identity, she discards prescriptive ideas of what the Holocaust represents. Her emphasis on humor and satire and farcical characters drives the point that to define the event to the extent that previous generations have attempted to do is not possible. Contemporary generations need to negotiate with the past on their own terms in order to reside in the present.

Other more recent Jewish American writers have relinquished the idea of the Holocaust as the definitive event and have focused attention on the tragedy of 9/11. The transition can be seen in the graphic novels of Art Spiegelman. His groundbreaking work on the Holocaust in *Maus I* and *II* has given way to an examination of 9/11. In *In the Shadow of No Towers*, he at first portrays himself, in a metafictional moment, as a personified mouse, the legacy of his original graphic narratives where the Jews are mice and the Germans cats. In the role of a mouse/Jew, he insists on putting the events of 9/11 in the context of the Holocaust and his father, a survivor of Auschwitz: "I remember my father trying to describe what the smoke in Auschwitz smelled like . . . That's exactly what the air in lower Manhattan smelled like after Sept. 11!" (Spiegelman 2004, 3). This scene is where the trauma of the Holocaust and being a second generation survivor gives way to being a New Yorker and the eyewitness to a personal trauma. The human depictions shift to being human forms in varied guises to the point where the artist renders himself falling from the tower. He places himself in the tragedy as the narrative moves to the aftermath of the terrorist attack and how the event shifted the political landscape of the United States. Spiegelman depicts himself in a domestic setting, reading *The New York Times* in a nostalgic American living room scene, to drive home the point that he is at home in New York and was personally attacked on 9/11. The comic book frames depict him morphing from his own human form back to that of a mouse as if terrorism and trauma return him to his Jewish identity while at home in New York.

Ken Kalfus picks up Spiegelman's train of thought in *A Disorder Peculiar to the Country* (2006), but with one exception, his Jewish identity is never mentioned. He has the political climate of the United States squarely in view as he depicts how an unhappily married couple experiences the terrorist attack and its aftermath. The focus on the domestic grounds the situation in a decidedly American context, separating the global context of the attack from the way it takes place as a personal event. It forms a dichotomy that poses the broad context of geopolitics against private life. Marshall, the husband, envisions the dichotomy as a personal dilemma,

> Everyone was dating everything now from September 11, regardless of whether they or anyone they knew had been at Ground Zero—when was that going to stop? . . . "I was there. In the World Trade Center. I escaped." (Kalfus 2006, 58)

The event has, as it did for Spiegelman, added a personal experience that heightened the feeling of being a New Yorker. Even in its global implications, the individuals that experienced New York on the day of the trauma take a personal stake in the event. Kalfus portrays this in the marital dispute of the couple. Each thought the other was killed in that attack and instead of mourning the loss was overjoyed at the thought of their spouse's death. The terrorist attack had personal implications for them and the effect had nothing to do with the politics that take place around the world and everything to do with their domestic situation. The divorce turns out to be even "more painful to speak about than September 11" (Kalfus 2006, 59).

Jonathan Safran Foer brings the domestic context of 9/11 to light through the eyes of a child. Oskar Schell lost his father in the World Trade Center and embarks on a journey to find a lock that fits the key he finds in his father's belongings. Ultimately, it is a process of making meaning out of the "worst day" (Foer 2005, 11). It is unclear whether it is the worst day because the towers fell and many lives were lost or simply because Oskar lost his father. Either way, the day is a definitive split in which belief, faith, and all sense of place in the world are questioned. Safran Foer depicts all of the questions through the eyes of a child to contradict the set meanings of what the events meant to the world, the United States, and New York. The places are interrelated, contradicting at times, and ultimately more complex and ambiguous than imagined. The conversation between Oskar and his mother depict this sentiment:

"What do you mean I sound just like Dad?"
"He used to say things like that."
"Like what?"
"Oh, like nothing is so-and-so. Or everything is so-and-so. Or obviously." She laughed.
"He was always very definitive."
"What's 'definitive'?"
"It means certain. It comes from 'definite.'"
"What's wrong with definitivity?"
"Dad sometimes missed the forest for the trees."
"What forest?"
"Nothing." (Foer 2005, 43)

The child begins to learn that what was killed in 9/11 was a sense of center that provided definitive ideas about who people are or where they are going. The uncertainty and complexity brought to light in 9/11 and highlighted by Safran Foer and others shows the place of identity in the contemporary world. It is not tied to a sense of history or a single conception of what it means to be Jewish; identity forms based on events and interactions that occur in the contingent environment of a place.

Paul Auster's entire body of work has followed this same theme. A New Yorker himself, he has avoided direct discussion of 9/11 in his novels since the event. However, his questioning of freedom, America, and terrorism's political goal lead into the same questions other have asked and provide a local, contingently constructed context for identity. *Leviathan*, although published before 9/11, remains his best meditation on the question. Ben Sachs, a writer and New York Jew, takes it upon himself to bomb replicas of the Statue of Liberty around the country in order to get his message about freedom to the public. He decides upon this course of action while writing an extended novel upon the subject, but he knows his writing will never have the political impact of the bombings. It is important to note that Auster depicts the Statue of Liberty as the target of the bombings, meaning the statue is the ultimate referent of freedom. It also appears on the cover of Sachs's book in a blurry photograph, an apt metaphor for both the meaning of freedom and the blurring of the center of identity. As the referent gets lost in the shuffle of a global culture that is endlessly interconnected and complex, the center is lost and fixed meanings are thrown into question.

Though Howe believed staunchly that the era that hailed Jewish American literature a force with which to be reckoned was drawing to a close, evidence of a newly revived Jewish American literary canon suggests that not only is Jewish American literature alive and well, but also that it is larger than the confines of Howe's imagination could bear, perhaps even bigger—in terms of sheer breadth and the variety of its range—than it was during the advent of writers such as Philip Roth and Bernard Malamud. Although much of this has to do with the multiplicity of Jewish voices that have burst onto the literary scene in the past twenty years—from feminist writers, to those writing about neo-orthodoxy and Hasidic communities, to gay writers, and to post-Holocaust voices—one strong element of this literary persistence has to do with the newest generation of Russian Jews who have immigrated to the United States. Once again, the *shtetl*-like communities—though not impoverished and miserable anymore—play a central role in the fiction of Jewish American literature. The storytelling of this new generation of Jewish American writers is infused with both the memories of prior immigrant experiences and the experiences of new ones, and yet it is simultaneously innovative in its tendency to reconcile—or at least draw our attention to—disparate parts of the Jewish American identity. In an essay called "Against Logic," which was part of a 1997 issue of Tikkun devoted to the explosion of new Jewish American literary voices, novelist Rebecca Goldstein (*Mazel*, 1995; *The Mind-Body Problem*, 1992) ponders the persistence of a collective Jewish literary imagination despite generations of assimilation into mainstream American culture. She writes:

> Yet here I am . . . dreaming Jewish dreams. Deep down in the regions of psyche where fiction is born, regions supremely indifferent to criteria of rationality, being Jewish seems to matter to me quite a lot; and in this way my own small and personal story might be offered up as a metaphor for the very re-awakening in Jewish American letters . . . For here we all of us are, after several generations that have tried their damnedest to shrug off the accidents of our shared precedents; here we all are, having sufficiently assimilated the culture at large to be able to inhabit, should we so choose, the inner worlds of characters to whom Jewishness is nothingness; here we all are, against logic, dreaming Jewish dreams.

And yet perhaps this logic-defying phenomenon has as much to do with a shared history, as it does with the ability of American Jews to thrive in and adapt to the places in which they find themselves, rather than lament the loss of a shared Jewish homeland.

The ghettos may be far behind them, but they are not long forgotten—they continue to appear, albeit in newer and less miserable forms; Brooklyn's Brighton Beach is a prime example of this new phenomenon of Jewish Russian immigrant communities. Moreover, Henry Roth's attempt to reconcile the vulgarity of the English spoken by little immigrant street urchins with the Yiddish of an almost Shakespearean quality spoken in the home is mirrored by new sets of cultural discrepancies in the newest wave of Jewish immigrant literature. It turns out that, in terms of part of his prediction, Howe was right; he just didn't know exactly how right he was. Much like the Jewish people and the collective history that is so much a part of the burden that compels them to satisfy, even fulfill, the literary imagination, their literature tracks the experiences of its people.

Bibliography

Abraham, Pearl. *The Romance Reader*. New York: Riverhead Books, 1996.
Auslander, Shalom. *Beware of God*. New York: Simon and Schuster, 2005.
Auster, Paul. *Leviathan*. New York: Penguin, 1992.
Bellow, Saul. *Dangling Man*. 1944. New York: Penguin, 1996.
Bezmozgis, David. *Natasha*. New York: Farrar, Straus and Giroux, 2004.
Cahan, Abraham. *The Rise of David Levinsky*. 1917. New York: Modern Library, 2001.
Chabon, Michael. *The Final Solution*. New York: Harper, 2004.
Doctorow, E. L. *The Book of Daniel*. New York: Plume, 1971.
———. *City of God*. New York: Plume, 2001.
Englander, Nathan. *For the Relief of Unbearable Urges*. New York: Vintage, 1999.

Foer, Jonathan Safran. *Extremely Loud and Incredibly Close*. New York: Mariner Books, 2005.

Gold, Michael. *Jews Without Money*. 1930. New York: Carroll & Graff, 2004.

Goldstein, Rebecca. "Against Logic." *Tikkun* 12.6 (1997): 43.

———. *Mazel*. New York: Penguin, 1995.

———. *The Mind-Body Problem*. New York: Penguin, 1983.

Goodman, Allegra. *Intuition*. New York: Dial Press, 2006.

———. *Kaaterskill Falls*. New York: Dell, 1998.

Havazelet, Ehud. *Like Never Before*. New York: Farrar, Straus and Giroux, 1998.

Howe, Irving. *Jewish American Stories*. New York: New American Library, 1977.

Kalfus, Ken. *A Disorder Peculiar to the Country*. New York: Harper Collins, 2006.

Krasikov, Sana. *One More Year*. New York: Spiegel & Grau, 2008.

Malamud, Bernard. *The Natural*. New York: Farrar, Straus and Giroux, 1952.

Mirvis, Tova. *The Ladies Auxiliary*. New York: Ballantine, 2000.

Ozick, Cynthia. *Heir to the Glimmering World*. Boston, MA: Houghton Mifflin, 2004.

Potok, Chaim. *The Chosen*. New York: Ballantine, 1967.

Reich, Tova. *My Holocaust*. New York: Harper Collins, 2007.

Roth, Henry. *Call it Sleep*. 1934. New York: Farrar, Straus and Giroux, 1996.

Roth, Philip. *American Pastoral*. New York: Vintage, 1997.

———. *The Breast*. New York: Holt, Rinehart and Winston, 1972.

———. *The Counterlife*. New York: Farrar, Straus and Giroux, 1987.

———. *The Dying Animal*. New York: Houghton Mifflin, 2001.

———. *Exit Ghost*. New York: Houghton Mifflin, 2007.

———. *The Ghost Writer*. New York: Farrar, Straus and Giroux, 1979.

———. *Goodbye, Columbus*. New York: The Modern Library, 1959.

———. *The Human Stain*. New York: Houghton Mifflin, 2000

———. *Patrimony*. New York: Simon and Schuster, 1991.

———. *The Plot Against America*. New York: Vintage, 2004

———. *Portnoy's Complaint*. New York: Random House, 1969.

———. *The Professor of Desire*. New York: Farrar, Straus and Giroux, 1977.

Shneer, David and Caryn Aviv. *New Jews: The End of the Jewish Diaspora*. New York: New York Univeristy Press, 2005.

Shteyngart, Gary. *Absurdistan*. New York: Random House, 2006.

———. *The Russian Debutante's Handbook*. New York: Riverhead, 2002

Singer, Margot. *The Pale of Settlement*. Athens, GA: University of Georgia Press, 2007.

Spiegelman, Art. *In the Shadow of No Towers*. New York: Pantheon Books, 2004.

———. *Maus: A Survivor's Tale*. New York: Penguin, 2003.

Ulinich, Anya. *Petropolis*. New York: Viking, 2007.

Vapnyar, Lara. *There are Jews in My House*. New York: Pantheon, 2003.

Yezierzka, Anya. *Bread Givers*. 1925. New York: Persea Books, 2003.

Further Reading

Aleichem, Sholem. *Tevye the Dairyman*. Trans. Hillel Halkin. New York: Schocken, 1987; Babel, Isaac. *The Collected Stories of Isaac Babel*. Nathalie Babel, ed. Translated by Peter Constantine. New York: W.W. Norton, 2002; Bellow, Saul. *Seize the Day*. New York: Viking Press, 1956; Bukiet, Melvin Jules, ed. *Neurotica: Jewish Writers on Sex*. New York: Norton, 1999; Chabon, Michael. *The Yiddish Policemen's Union*. New York: Harper-Collins, 1997; Diamant, Anita. *The Red Tent*. New York: Picador, 1997; Eisner, Will. *The Plot: The Secret Story of the Protocols of the Elders of Zion*. New York: W.W. Norton, 2005; Eve, Nomi. *The Family Orchard*. New York: Alfred A. Knopf, 2000; Foer, Jonathan Safran. *Everything is Illuminated*. New York: HarperCollins, 2002; Goldberg, Myla. *Bee Season*. New York: Anchor, 2000; Horn, Dara. *In the Image*. New York: W.W. Norton, 2002; Kushner, Tony. *Angels in America*. New York: Theatre Communications Group,

1992; Olsen, Tillie. *Yonnondio: From the Thirties*. Lincoln, NE: University of Nebraska Press, 1974; Ozick, Cynthia. "The Pagan Rabbi." *The Pagan Rabbi and Other Stories*. Syracuse, NY: Syracuse University Press, 1995. 1–38; Rosen, Jonathan. *The Talmud and the Internet*. New York: Farrar, Straus and Giroux, 2000; Stern, Steve. *The Angel of Forgetfulness*. New York: Viking, 2005; Stern, Steve. *The Wedding Jester*. St. Paul, MN: Graywolf Press, 1999; Stollman, Aryeh Lev. *The Far Euphrates*. New York: Riverhead, 1997; West, Nathanael. *The Day of the Locust*. New York: Buccaneer Books, 1981; Wiesel, Elie. *The Time of the Uprooted*. Trans. David Hapgood. New York: Alfred A. Knopf, 2005.

MONICA OSBORNE AND DAVID COCKLEY

L

LANGUAGE POETRY

Definition. Language poetry has its roots in the social upheavals of the 1970s. American poetry was a prominent voice in the cultural revolution of the 1960s and 1970s that saw protests against the Vietnam War, the beginning of the Free Speech Movement, and the coming of Second Wave Feminism. With the advent of protest poetry, some writers viewed with dissatisfaction what they considered the artificial constructs of ego in the lyrical conventions of American poetry, particularly those well-grounded in the post-Romantic tradition and Modernism's predilection for lyric and narrative verse forms, styles that came to prominence with the acceptance of "free verse" in the early years of the century.

Language poets reject the Modernist assumption that language is a "transparent" medium that accurately captures the essence of the things described. Instead, they challenge what Bernstein calls "official verse culture," the dominant use of lyric forms in academic writing programs (Bernstein 1986, 246). In his collected essays, *Content's Dream: Essays 1975–1984* (1986), Bernstein's assessment hints at the confrontational nature of the early exchanges between traditional publications and the magazines supporting Language poetry. The acrimonious debates underlined the radical nature of Language poets' challenge to representational structures. In *The Marginalization of Poetry* (1996), an essay collection by another leading poet from this period, Bob Perelman complained that in traditional poetry "sensibility and intuition reigned supreme," and even if "craft and literary knowledge" were still evident, contemporary poetry had become simply "conversational" (Perelman 1996, 12).

The techniques of the Language poets vary as much as the works themselves, but there are certain salient features. One of the leading critics in support of Language poets has been Marjorie Perloff. Her estimation of the poetry of Bruce Andrews, another prominent member of the early group, suggests many of the features found among its practitioners: "The poetic devices you use tend to be rhetorical figures rather than tropes—the pun, the neologism, the portmanteau word—and of course a great deal of sound-play rather than metaphor, simile, symbol" (Andrews 1996, 80). In

---

THE BEGINNINGS OF LANGUAGE POETRY

In the main, Language poets began to explore language as construction, not as a representational medium used to describe experience but as a set of relationships and signifying structures relevant to themselves. Charles Bernstein, a leading theorist and practitioner of the movement, has said, "We were interested in poetry that did not assume a syntax, a subject matter, a vocabulary, a structure, a form, or a style but where all these were at issue, all these were explored in the writing of the poem" (Senning 2005). The subject of Language poetry is often language itself, not its meanings or its message but the particulars of its formal structure and how it creates, and is created by, social and political ideas.

---

similar fashion, Perelman has argued that there are really many different "Language poetries," and yet certain trends are common among the group: "breaking the automatism of the poetic 'I' and its naturalized voice; foregrounding textuality and formal device; using or alluding to Marxist or poststructuralist theory in order to open the present to critique and change"; and "the aggressive dismissals of self-expressive mainstream poetics as politically reactionary" (1996, 13). In her piece, "Experiments," for the seminal anthology, *The L=A=N=G=U=A=G=E Book* (1984), Bernadette Mayer gives a list of exercises for writing poems that reflect the group's understanding: "Systematically eliminate the use of certain kinds of words or phrases from a piece of writing, either your own or someone else's, for example, eliminate all adjectives from a poem of your own, or take out all words beginning with 's' in Shakespeare's sonnets"; and again: "Get a group of words (make a list or select at random); then form these words (only) into a piece of writing—whatever the words allow. Let them demand their own form" (1984, 80). Such arbitrary conditions identify the formal nature of the works.

The Marxist leanings of many of the Language poets in the 1970s made it clear that the normative relationships in language were not innocent correspondences but rather strictures created over time through the process of cultural production. Language, they realized, carried all the imprints of the society against which they had been struggling. The writers' distrust of the poetic tradition was based on its fundamental correspondence with capitalism. But they were also aware of a parallel tradition, what they took as a subversive one composed of writers who had not followed the Modernist dictates of realism, naturalism, and symbolism. Among these were Gertrude Stein with her verbal repetitions, Louis Zukofsky with his musical analogies, and Ezra Pound (although associated with the mainstream tradition as well) with his demands that language must be rewritten to fit the age. Two of these, Zukofsky and Pound, were associated briefly by sympathies with the "Objectivist" movement, often cited as a precursor to the Language poets with its treatment of the poem as object. All Language poets were not, of course, Marxists, and some even found themselves in opposition to Marxism's hegemony in academia in the 1970s (Hartley 1989). Initially, however, the Language writers turned to both Marxist and poststructural ideologies to inform their poetry (Perelman 1996, 13).

These differences within the Language movement are partly responsible for the controversy over its definition. Many rejected the label of "Language Poets" on the grounds that such an attempt to unify the movement undermined the diversity of their approaches and concerns and was, in effect, a way of annexing their efforts. The movement wanted to maintain their marginality as a sign of the challenge to the historicizing process. This ahistorical position was not simply a refusal to accept recognition, Eleana Kim points out, but an effort to place themselves beyond socializing forces that had assimilated earlier avant-garde groups:

> An equally important consideration in any definition of Language poetry is the degree to which it was a self-identifying group. The group's identity is, in many ways, a product of critics and scholars interested in establishing it as the latest in avant-garde formations, and the poets themselves demonstrated deep ambivalences as the tendency began to gain currency under the Language moniker. The poets often resisted a unified identity even as their public manifestations exhibited a more or less stable core to the movement. (1994)

The problem underlines their eventual acceptance into academic institutions, a move that both legitimized and historicized the movement in the 1980s. The desire to retain their individuality was tantamount to a statement rejecting the tradition, particularly aspects associated with old avant-garde poets represented in Donald Allen's anthology, *The New American Poetry* (1960). Allen had broken with New Critical traditions and gathered together elements of the Black Mountain school, the Beats, the New York school, and others in a wide-ranging, avant-garde collection. But the poets in this anthology soon found themselves at the center of a new poetic mainstream (Holcombe n.d.). The Language poets were intent on distinguishing themselves through an even newer understanding of "poetic inheritance, tradition, and the role of literary theory" (Kim 1994). Yet, even among Language poets there were difficulties on how to define the movement, as is evident in the organizing principles in two prominent anthologies: Ron Silliman's *In the American Tree* (1986) and Douglas Messerli's *"Language" Poetries* (1987). Silliman's introduction to his anthology already warns of the "reductive assumptions" of the label "Language Poets," and Messerli uses the plural, "poetries," to show an inclusive factor in the movement (ibid). The main import of these moves to solidify the group was to show the ideological associations rather than the differences in poetries. Silliman suggests that no less was at stake than "The nature of reality. The nature of the individual. The function of language in the constitution of either realm," and "The shape and value of literature itself" (1986, xix).

History. Language poetry begins with a number of small magazines in the early 1970s, corresponding to groups in San Francisco, New York, and the Washington, D.C., area (Perelman 1996, 11). Some argue that it was really the first issue of *This* magazine in 1971 that started the phenomenon (Silliman 1986, xvi). The zenith of the early period is surely the publication of $L=A=N=G=U=A=G=E$ magazine (1978–1982) in San Francisco. $L=A=N=G=U=A=G=E$ created a forum for the discussion of contemporary poetics that helped define the group's distinctions from the lyric tradition (Perelman 1996, 16). The movement grew in the 1970s with the publication of other little magazines, including *Tottel's, Hills, Roof, Miam, Qu, The Difficulties, A Hundred Posters, Sink, Tramen,* and *Tremblor* (Kim 1994; Hartley 1989; Kinsella 2007). Associated primarily with $L=A=N=G=U=A=G=E$ after 1978, it was referred to in various ways as the Language movement, Language poetry, the Language group and as the $L=A=N=G=U=A=G=E$ poets (Perelman 1996, 18; Izenberg 2003). By the late 1970s, a number of anthologies and journal special editions featured the group, adding to its critical legitimacy: *Lisbon & the Orcas Islands* (1973), *Alcheringa* (1975), *Open Letter* (1977), *Hills* (1980), *Ironwood* (1982), *Paris Review* (1982), *The $L=A=N=G=U=A=G=E$ Book* (1984), *Change* (1985), *Writing/Talks* (1985), and *boundary 2* (1986) (Hartley 1989). During this period, a number of poets were identified specifically with the movement, including Bruce Andrews, Rae Armantrout, Steve

Benson, Charles Bernstein, David Bromige, Clark Coolidge, Alan Davies, Ray DiPalma, Robert Grenier, Carla Harryman, Lyn Hejinian, Susan Howe, Steve McCaffery, Michael Palmer, Bob Perelman, Kit Robinson, Peter Seaton, James Sherry, Ron Silliman, Diane Ward, Barrett Watten, and Hannah Weiner (Hartley 1989).

But these experimental publications were the result of changes that had been building for some time. By the early 1970s the lyric trend in American poetry, sustained throughout much of the mid-century under the prominence of the confessional school of poets and their successors were under attack for what a new generation saw as self-centered emotionalism. The confessional school had refined the lyric as a mode of self-examination and personal experience, often dealing with human alienation. Perpetuated during the middle years by powerful influences such as Robert Lowell, Anne Sexton, John Berryman, and Sylvia Plath, it was not until the protest poetry of the 1960s that political and social problems became a general focus of the poetry. A new social awareness brought with it a questioning of language itself as the medium for social and political change, even in the arts.

Although to write the history of Language poetry proves as controversial an act as trying to define what it is, there are definite antecedents to the kind of experimentation that was attracting young poets in the 1970s. In *The Poetics of Indeterminacy* (1981), Perloff delineates a marginalized tradition within 20th-century poetry, and draws a line from Arthur Rimbaud and Gertrude Stein to contemporary postmodernist poets such as John Ashbery. She was one of the first to link the critical theorists of the French and Geneva schools to an understanding of the poetic tradition. By citing Gertrude Stein, and seeing in her word experiments an awareness that language is a material medium, like paint is for the painter, and that it can therefore be manipulated to expose social assumptions, Perloff helped create a critical space for the later understanding of Language poetry.

Other predecessors can be found in the early-twentieth-century Dadaists, who reacted against the "idea of art" in much the way Language poetry would criticize the romanticized tradition. Tristan Tzara's ideas could easily be read in a contemporary context: "It seemed to us that the world was losing itself in idle babbling, that literature and art had become institutions located on the margin of life, that instead of serving man they had become the instruments of an outmoded society" (Kinsella 1996). Perloff makes the connection that Dada was a community effort, not one focused on the individual, and that political action was a primary component of the movement (Perloff 1999). The "anti-art" stance was a political statement about the social constrictions of "high" art, and one that parallels Language poetry's rejection of the Modernist tradition in poetry. Other influences were surely Concrete poetry, a form that took the material nature of letters and words to an extreme and constructed non-linear typographical images. Further connections have been suggested with Charles Olson and the Black Mountain school, William Carlos Williams, the Russian Formalists, the Surrealists, and the OULIPO group in the early 1960s (Kinsella 1996; Hartley 1989; Gelpi 1990; Perelman 1996). It may be indicative of the controversies surrounding its history that its efforts to avoid classification as yet another avant-garde group somehow ensured its place as an avant-garde group in literary history. Kim cautions, however, that the act of historicizing the group carries its own implications: "The connections between the movement and the European avant-gardes of the 1920s have been examined by academics who promote its formal innovations and political interventions, as well as frame it within a narrative of American transavantgardism or postmodernism" (Kim 1994).

Trends and Themes. After a period of wider academic acceptance in the late 1980s and 1990s, the original Marxist components of the movement and the predominance of male writers in the original groups faced challenges from poets who demanded a greater awareness of gender and ethnic concerns. Consequently, many today have come to refer to the "Language Poets" as an historical movement dating to the early 1980s. Some of the earliest poets themselves now "refer to language poetry in the past tense" (Lilley 1997). But it is possible to see a continuance of concerns in what some today call the "postlanguage" poets (Wallace 1998). It might even be said that the "post" state of Language poetry is a necessary development in a poetics that rejected its own historical definition. At the same time, postlanguage poets are disclaiming aspects of the early coalition, and reformulating new positions.

The movement existed on the fringe of American poetry until the mid-1980s, but its early uses of critical theory and poststructural ideas ensured its entrance into academic literary circles just then exploring these fields. Language poetry "enjoyed a privileged status among high-brow academics who had found an art form particularly suited, indeed, symptomatic, of the very forces engendering the rise of postmodern cultural and post-structuralist theories" (Kim 1994). But this also created a dichotomy in that it had "secured an institutional foothold which brokers against our usual notion of the avant-garde" (Reddy n.d.). Presently, theory is one of the critical points of difference, with some postlanguage poets critical of the dominant theoretical focus of the earlier poets (Wallace 1998). In the 1970s, theory was not just a concern but a cohesive element in the movement. *L=A=N=G=U=A=G=E* magazine, for instance, was composed almost exclusively of "critical essays" not "poetry" (Watten 2003, 51). And even "genres" such as these were destabilized whenever possible. The postlanguage poets, however, have retained the intrinsic concern with language and its relationship to power (Wallace 1998). The preeminent role of critical theory in early Language poetry was due, in part, to its marginality within the academic community. Postlanguage poets have rather grown up in an environment accepting critical theory as part of the necessary dialogue of the times. But conceptualizing has become less important:

> Postlanguage poets often feel that theorizing their practice is a burden. Literary theory has often seemed to them something that the dominant power structures of the academy and their elders in avant-garde poetry have demanded that they create in order to justify their practice as poets. Literary theory does continue to be a central part of the practice of many postlanguage poets, yet they tend to undertake it with an ambivalent and often wearied eye. (Wallace 1998)

With greater visibility has come an increased awareness of Language writing in areas outside the two coasts, with poets now writing from regions as diverse as Oklahoma and Hawaii, with international groups in Europe and Australia (Wallace 1998).

Whereas the first poets defined their work in an atmosphere of 1970s cultural revolution, newer members have moved beyond this "militant phase" associated with "manifestos" and turned "toward other, more meditative forms of literary inquiry" (Reddy n.d.). Some have even returned to specific aspects of poetry that were once disapproved of, including "narrative, lyric, spirituality, and a poetics of the every day" (Wallace 1998). Most now see a "growing array of hybridizing writing practices that make use of visual, sound, performance, and cyber media in order to bring the materiality of language (and thus the reader) into a more activist position"

(Osman 2001). Consequently, today "the detached eye of the 'language poem' must share the textual stage with connective, collective, and absorptive forms" (Osman 2001).

The influence of feminism has had the greatest effect on today's Language poetry. Although poets Carla Harryman, Rae Armantrout, Lyn Hejinian, Hannah Weiner, Susan Howe, and Bernadette Mayer were all early members of the movement, much of the early critical theory was written by men, Charles Bernstein, Bob Perelman, and Ron Silliman (Perloff n.d.). The movement, in some ways, reflected the masculine nature of the New Left politics out of which it had grown. It was not until the mid-1980s, and the realization of Second Wave feminism, that women's interests were addressed. Some argue that in the 1980s the movement represented women better than other disciplines, at least in the area of small magazine publication (Vickery 2000, 99). Today, the importance of cultural studies in academia has increased the awareness of gender and ethnic concerns. Postlanguage writers often "highlight problems of identity politics from specific cultural positions," and "critique the limits of identity politics" by crossing "cultural boundaries" (Wallace 1998). Harryette Mullen, Tan Lin, Susan Schultz, Rodrigo Toscano, Myung Mi Kim, and Bob Harrison are writers who "have explored the complex ways that problems of cultural identity interact with poetic practice" (Wallace 1998). In the 1990s two anthologies were published that reflected these changes: *Out of Everywhere: Linguistically Innovative Poetry by Women in North American & the UK* (1996), edited by Maggie O'Sullivan, and *Moving Borders: Three Decades of Innovative Writing by Women* (1998), edited by Mary Margaret Sloan (Retallack 2003, 251). These were complimented by a number of critical studies, including *Translating the Unspeakable: Poetry and the Innovative Necessity,* by Kathleen Fraser (2000); *Lyric Interventions: Feminism, Experimental Poetry, and Contemporary Discourse,* by Linda Kinnahan (2004); and *Women Poets in the 21st Century,* edited by Claudia Rankine and Juliana Spahr (2002) (Ashton 2006).

Early Language Poets conflicted with certain groups due to their denial of the validity of the "subject" in writing. "Since one of its early premises was the critique of 'identity,'" Brian Kim Stefans observes, the movement "never had the language for dealing with minority issues that attempted to legitimize 'identity' as a central subject of discourse" (2001). Similarly, popular women writers of the 1970s, by choosing "traditional lyric forms" were participating in "an unwitting acquiescence to centuries of male dominance in the art of poetry" (Ashton 2006). Citing Rachel DuPlessis's 1985 essay, "Otherhow," Jennifer Ashton points out that "it is not sufficient to write lyric poems in which a woman's experiences are the main subject matter of the song, for the very forms of the lyric—including even basic grammatical forms used to represent the presence of a speaker—are themselves indices of a history of male domination" (Ashton 2006). Finally, "The literary feminism that emerged in the 1980s thus transformed the attack on women's underrepresentation into an attack on representation as such, and it did so by way of the avant-garde requirement of formal innovation," insisting as it did "on an even more literal connection between the text and the body" (Ashton 2006). Others warn that the return to the "subject" risks an acquiescence to socially restrictive language, and writers need to keep the "systemic" nature of language in mind (Spahr 2001).

Contexts and Issues. The critique of the "subject" was at the center of the Language movement's argument with poetic tradition. According to Language poets, modern poetry had prioritized the speaker of the poem in such a way as to perpetuate the "illusion" that the poem simply expressed the truth of psychological states. As the editors of the journal *Rethinking Marxism* explain in "On Language Poetry": "If language is historically changing and constitutive of subjectivity, making us as we make and use it, then it neither reveals nor represses some inner self, some 'species being,' that exists before the fact of its use" (1988). Modernism had lionized the subject and its psychological effects as the domain of the poem. The society within which the individual lives, however, is hegemonic, that is, it rules through official concepts and ideas. As Bernstein writes, "a poem exists in a matrix of social and historical relationships that are more significant to the formulation of an individual text than any personal qualities of the life or voice of an author" (Bernstein 1986, 408). Perloff calls this the "cardinal principle" of the Language group: the "dismissal of 'voice' as the foundational principle of lyric poetry" (Perloff 1998). The realities of the postmodern world are not centered on the individual but on the production of meanings generated by historical, social, and political forces. Writing therefore becomes a dynamic process of exchange. As Andrews writes in "Code Words," "The subject loses authority, disappears, is *unmade* into a network of relationships, stretching indefinitely" (Andrews 1996, 190).

In order to escape this constructed subjectivity poets explore nonreferential language, or words and phrases in other than traditional contexts, such as normative syntax or spelling. These are the semiotic and structural aspects of the language that allow for the free play of malapropos, solecisms, parataxis, and other syntactical experiments. The poetic techniques all attempt to dismantle the poem's dependence on the individual's intention or expression. "All writing is a demonstration of method," Bernstein says, "it can assume a method or investigate it. In this sense, style and mode are always at issue, for all styles are socially mediated conventions open to reconvening at any time" (Bernstein 1986, 226). Henry Sussman argues that this opens the poem to new meanings: "The concrete handling of words and word fragments thus resides at the extreme of language's generative capabilities" (Sussman 2005, 42). A brief example will help clarify: Andrews's piece, "LETTERS" begins "THEIR midst mix power to crystallize with connected the next room hope openings bent her white fragments effusive neck smoked verge of recognition's to hold fast as if unwittingly even to the fissures looming sight shadow surprises stays at home her words for the feeling to arrow soothed" (Silliman 1986, 315). The capitals of the title alert us to the fact that these are both "letters" as separate signs and "letters" such as one writes in correspondence. On the printed page the words are justified and also spaced just a little extra between each, so that each stands out as separate signs. It is possible to sense, rather than strictly "read" a context here, with words such as "crystallize," "connected," "white fragments," "fissures," and "stays at home." These are all things that both kinds of letters do or suggest. Andrews is playing on the multiple sense of how signs both identify a social function, letter writing, and yet can be broken down to signify writing as a momentary act. The idea of nonreferentiality means that words relate to each other in more ways than through normative syntax, such as we are taught in school, or, the poets might say, as we are socialized to believe. The poem is not nonsense, but a disruption of normal reading processes to produce new effects. As Bernstein admits:

> Words are almost always referential, but what many of us were interested in exploring were nonconventional forms, allowing the expressive (and nonexpressive) features of language to roam in different territory than possible with tamer verse forms. So what

you get might better be called polyreferential in that the poems do not necessarily mean one fixed, definable, paraphrasable thing. (Senning 1999)

A key work for the early Language poets was Roland Barthes's essays, "The Death of the Author" (1968). Steven McCaffery, a Canadian member of the Language group, made the connection clear by titling his own essay, "The Death of the Subject" (1976). Andrews also wrote of the essay in his note "Code Words" for the magazine *L=A=N=G=U=A=G=E*. Barthes argues that "Writing is that neutral, composite, oblique space where our subject slips away, the negative where all identity is lost, starting with the very identity of the body writing" (Perloff 1998). His critique of the "subject" was a pivotal moment in the poststructural assessment of authorship. With Barthes's lead, then, Language poetry became involved on an ever-increasing level with critical theory, even as it developed as part of curriculums across the country.

Much has now been made of the "issue of careerism" among early participants in the movement (Stefans 1999). Although at the start it could be said that "despite their general obsession with theory and critical practice, the Language poets tend to be anti-Academic" (Kinsella n.d.), many have now taken academic positions at schools, including the University of California Berkeley, SUNY Buffalo, and the University of Pennsylvania. Kate Lilley points out a crucial aspects of this change:

> The point at which the means of production and distribution passed out of the hands of the original editors and contributors marked an historic juncture in the commodification of language writing as a school, with a reasonably secure curriculum and membership. It also signaled the beginning of the movement's wider dissemination qua movement in a variety of prestigious literary and academic venues. (Lilley 1997)

The effect has been to change the nature of the original experiment: "Along with the assimilation of the group's basic tenets and political strategies into a welcoming leftist academic agenda, the group's deformation has left many of the major participants (most of whom are still writing and publishing) refining their initial positions" (Kim 1994). As Language poetry's importance has grown in influence to compete with traditional poetics, it finds itself in a position not far from the establishment it originally set out to criticize for its dominance of the field: "A few minutes with the Arts and Humanities Citation Index confirms that, during 1994–1997, the number of academic citations for Bernstein's work doubled those for [Anthony] Hecht's" (Caplan 1997). By the 1990s, Language poetry was often talked about in the past tense, as if its new academic standing had somehow compromised its critical position (Kim 1994).

Reception. Although initially accused of "elitism" and "a sense of haughtiness" in refusing to address ethnic or gender questions, there have been noticeable changes in the original makeup of the generally "white" male movement (Gelpi 1990; Stefans 2001). Much of the initial reception was antagonistic: "The negative polemics raised against the Language school project ranged from invocations of McCarthyism and corporate juntas . . . to dismissals of their so-called avant-gardism at a time in which the term itself had been evacuated of its historical or political effect" (Kim 1994). The sense that the new poetics might allow for a "co-opting" by reactionary political forces was extreme (Kovacik 2001). For although Language theorists would continually speak of social advocacy, there was an inherent conflict between hermetic experimentation and social relevance. The fact that all philosophy was now presented as a set of linguistic constructs "is not that the world is just codes and as a result presence is to be ruled out as anything more than nostalgia, but that we can have presence, insofar as we are able, only through a shared grammar" (Andrews and Bernstein 1984, 61). But in contrast, postlanguage poets were looking to reassert the importance of disenfranchised groups, whose identities might continue to be displaced by the theoretical focus on "authorless texts." The practical reality was that authors still created texts: "[I]n practice, we do take signatures seriously as markers of a particular individual, a cultural practice, an historical period, a national formation, a convention, and so on" (Perloff 1998).

Its reception today reflects specific changes that have allowed Language poets a more prominent place in contemporary poetry. Perloff argues for changes in three areas in particular: the early concern with demonstrating "referentiality" has become a more "nuanced emphasis on the how of poetic language rather than the what"; the condemnation of tradition poetic language as a "commodity fetish" has been criticized when poets realized that any language, even Language poetry, can become "fetischized"; and the efforts to give readers a role in the sense-making process of the poem has been seen as merely a shifting of authority from the author to the reader (n.d.). These factors have given today's poets an historical vantage point. Postlanguage poets now incorporate what early groups omitted: "sound poetry, visual and concrete poetry, fluxus, conceptual art, appropriative strategies, oulipian process-oriented writing, a focus on the more performative aspects of poetry, not to mention technological innovations which weren't available then" (Goldsmith 2001).

Some of the strongest early criticism was from Marxist theorists such as Fredric Jameson. Jameson's famous reading of Perelman's poem, "China," in *Postmodernism, or the Cultural Logic of Late Capitalism* (1991), saw the poem as an example of "schizophrenic language" (Hartley 1989, 42). Jameson's position suggests a general attack on the idea of nonreferential language: "these sentences are free floating material signifiers whose signifieds have evaporated" (Jameson n.d.). For the Marxists, reference was grounded in a historical moment that cannot be escaped by poetic innovation. The real complaint, however, was aimed at the more extreme forms of theory: "Theory swallowed all: poetry submerged into criticism and linguistics, words about words; even Marxism exercised itself not in political action but academic analysis" (Gelpi 1990). The fact that postmodern poetry would deny its efficacy as political action was the key, and this difference has remained at the center of the ongoing argument. Kristin Prevallet summarizes an exemplary debate between poets Barrett Watten and Amiri Baraka:

> Watten embraced a poetics of alienation that matched the rupture between speech and society that he had witnessed during the Free Speech Movement and the Vietnam War. In his writing he seeks to reveal the material power of language in order to expose very real divisions between oppressive structures and the language used to maintain them. Baraka also writes to expose power structures, but uses poetry as a lived embodiment of intricately experienced intellectual, emotional, and musical realities. (Prevallet 2000)

The problem also goes to the heart of the question about poetry as an elitist endeavor. Language poetry has adjusted to the new social consciousness, but its initial position remains problematic for many: "Language poetry *was* a self-conscious avant-garde group," Kim points out, "whose poetic and historical distinctions were articulated across of broad set of concerns. . . . It *is* a writing practice that started as a collective belief of a new generation of poets which became an actual shift in the consideration of poetry" (Kim 1994). More recently, Bernstein admits: "Poetry may not be able to redistribute the wealth, but it can open up a way of—again to say—representing the issues that can change how we respond, indeed keep us responding. For the political question is never just what is to be done but also the formulating and reformulating of the issues" (Senning 1999).

Today, Language poets are a general influence in American poetry, not only felt among traditional poets who have adopted certain Language techniques but also by way of early Language poets who have begun to return to traditional forms and even the authorial voice. In addition, a number of early members of the movement:

> have been incorporating elements that might be thought of as postlanguage, including European forms and rhyme schemes, representation and narrative, and social constructions of cultural identity and subjectivity, although they use such elements in ways that expand possibilities for innovation, and critique and expose received notions of tradition and form. (Wallace 1998)

Poets have also revised early theoretical positions in order to accommodate a growing range of contemporary issues, including the realization that all art is not of the same value, whatever the "value" is determined to be (Perloff 1998).

Selected Authors. Harryette Mullen (1953–) has come to the attention of critics particularly because she attempts to bridge certain contemporary concerns of the Language poets with an ethnic and gender focus. One of her most recent collections, *Sleeping with the Dictionary* (2002), although not as sustained in its effort as her earlier, *Muse & Drudge* (1995), which Perloff has called a "pseudo-ballad . . . written, seemingly against the 'Language' grain" (Perloff n.d.), nonetheless questions ethnic roles in postlanguage terms. Many of the poems are "prose" poems, or sections of writing that follow declarative statement form. In "Once Ever After," the mythic echoes are restructured under a feminist sensibility. The "princess" who "wet the bed through many mattresses" is yet "attuned," although she "was born on a chessboard" and seems destined in some ways to struggle against an identity imposed upon her classic role (Mullen 2002, 53). The postlanguage elements include the suspended sentence fragments, "Her lips were. Her hair was. Her complexion was," which go to anticipate the stereotypical phrases as descriptive limits to her identity, and yet by not completing such fragments, Mullen exposes the presuppositions in the mythic construction (Mullen 2002, 53). She does not limit herself to ethnic concerns, however, and can be read in a Language context in her efforts to "disable corporate jargon and political doublespeak" (Thomas 2002). Again, in "All She Wrote," Mullen presents ironic contrasts that mean and do not mean what they say: "Forgive me, I'm no good at this. I can't write back" (Mullen 2002, 3). And yet the collection is itself a "writing back" both against racial and gender stereotypes and against the idea of language as a simple, intentional act. Going beyond the deconstructive assumption that all oppositional terms are prejudiced in favor of one side or the other, a notion critiqued by both Language poets and poststructural theorists, Mullen re-imagines new configurations, including "a resistance to traditional dialectics," by which she "disorganizes this pattern by imagining other ways of being opposite" (Hume 2003). Ultimately, the poetry addresses oppositions that "cannot be read in terms of dualities, the world according to binary oppositions which privilege one side of the equation (rational or emotional, public or private, white or black, male or female) over the other" (Hume 2003).

Rae Armantrout's (1947–) first collections, *Extremities* (1978) and *The Invention of Hunger* (1979), helped define what Silliman calls the "anti-lyric" challenge of the original movement (2004). In *Up to Speed* (2004), the poet moves into more subtle areas of experimentation, arranging her line fragments in three and four stanza groups so that they lend a secondary structure to the book. Armantrout addresses the once taboo subject of domestic angst, a familiar topic for lyric poets. But she does so in a fashion that challenges the reader's notion of the domestic. She builds her poems on absences, but rather than avoiding the moment, each fulfills the collection's sense of a deeper betrayal: "she calls to our attention the overlooked chinks and fissures in the linguistic exoskeleton that stands between us and the experiences it envelops" (Muratori 2002). There are the normal poststructural references in *Up to Speed,* but what has changed for Armantrout of late is that these seems less urgent: "I could handle symbols," she writes, "without being manipulated by them" (Armantrout 2004, 3). Like others, she has moved away from the constant pronouncements of Language poetics, and focused more on human exchanges. At its best, the new work reflects a consciousness where both non-referentiality and humanity coexist. "One's a connoisseur of vacancies," she writes, "loud silences/surrounding human artifacts" (Armantrout 2004, 26). The humanistic concerns of Modernist poetry, which were first rejected wholesale by the Language poets in their efforts to destabilize the traditional emotionalism of the poem, return now with a certain casualness in moments of individualistic clarity: "She's concerned with the rhythm/of her own sequence of events" (Armantrout 2004, 26). There is a sense in Armantrout's recent work that the fragmentary impulses that sustain her early experiments are now coalescing more into questions of recurrent human values.

Myung Mi Kim (1957–) was born in Seoul, Korea, and moved as a child to the United States, a fact that informs her use of poetic structures. For Kim, the experience of the immigrant is one where language always represents multiple voices. Kim seems to be more aware than most that poststructuralism is not simply an aesthetic preference but a natural attribute of growing up divided between cultural identities. Her first work, *Under Flag* (1991) was an important effort to bridge Language experiments with new ethnic concerns. Her most recent work, *Commons* (2002), moves into the area of transliteration, where Kim explores the difficulties of adapting one language to another, in this case her native Hangul alphabet to English. She asks: "Whose ears are at work? Where does the authority of romanizing reside?" (Kim 2002, 110). The questions are not just about the dissemination of meaning through the transliterative act but also about who has the authority to Romanize a language. The nuances of the Hangul are not lost so much as reinterpreted into something else in the standardization of English. Kim's poetry breaks up the standards by fragmenting the impressions and scrambling the process of logical sequence in order to make plain the process hidden in cultural acquisition. Here the Language movement's concern with process seems most clear but has been taken further toward an awareness of how acculturation itself works. About the poem, "Siege Document," Jeon Joseph Jonghyun points out: "the primary audience for this poem is the reader who does not speak or read the Korean language and that knowledge of Hangul does not dramatically change one's reading experience because the author's central preoccupation is with sound; transliteration takes precedence over translation" (Jonghyun 2004). In the end, this is not a process of supplanting one language with another, but an interaction of two in the possibilities of an exchange (Jonghyun 2004).

Lyn Hejinian (1941–) is one of the original west coast members of the Language movement. Her seminal work, *My Life* (1980), remains a major influence on writers. Instrumental in the ongoing critique of "autobiography," it continues the questioning of subjectivity. Hejinian's collected essays, *The Language of Inquiry* (2000), which includes the much cited "Two Stein Talks" on Gertrude Stein, makes clear her prominence among theorists. There is often a direct correspondence between Hejinian's Russian ancestry and her formal tendencies, apparent in her writings on the Russian Formalists, particularly Viktor Schlovsky. Most important among her recent works is the long poem of narrative fragments, *Happily* (2000), which Perloff calls "a Steinian work" for its use of juxtaposed sentence fragments and stanzas. Although Stein's own repetitions are a continual "insistence" of salient features rising to the surface of her prose, Hejinian's fragments work more toward their own autonomous display, weaving a logic of prosaic inclusion rather than repetition. Hejinian has often worked with longer, open lines, with a tendency toward ideation that underlines her exploration into feminist differences. She creates a logic and sequence: "Now is a noted conjunction" she writes, moving to emphasize the immediate "place in place" (Hejinian 2000, 27, 3) that is yet a separation of the act and the moment that inspires it: "States of intuition may be only sudden / *Now* is a blinding instant . . ." (Hejinian 2000, 27). This fluid exchange within "a carefully plotted set of synonyms" plays on the contrasts in words like "happily" and "happen" (Perloff 2000). Hejinian's use of "happily" as opposed to "happiness" is a way of denying the reduction of being to language or language to being: "the adverbial form [*happily*] is preferable to the noun *happiness,* since modification is much more likely to produce contingency than is nominalization, which suggests a state of being" (Perloff 2000). Hejinian's sense of continuance, a Steinian feature in her works, adds to both the book's coherence and its subtle rhythms, reinforcing the poet's primary concern: "Perhaps it is the role of art to put us in complicity with things as they happen" (Hejinian 2000, 13).

Others have moved into different areas of the Internet and electronic media. Silliman has his own blog, where he continues to engage poetic and political matters, and he has published recent reprints and compilations of works, including *Under Albany* (2004), an autobiographical "back story" that informs his earlier poem, "Albany" (*ABC* 1983). This autobiographical work contextualizes the original poem, at the same time that it explores Silliman's own relationship to the "author" as historical sign. Another poet, Bernstein, recently published *Girly Man* (2006). Here he moves further into his familiar sense of parody and self-parody. "This is a totally / accessible poem," he writes. If the work retains a political edge, it is through a renewed attack on governing authority. The poems continue a tradition of the "exploded cliché or the dislocated fragment of conventional unwisdom" (Kaufmann 2007). Bernstein has also written a libretto for an opera, *Shadowtime* (2005), with music by Brian Ferneyhough. Other divergent forms include Andrews's interactive collage with Dirk Rowntree titled *Prehab* (2005) on UbuWeb.com., a leading avant-garde poetry Web site, and various examples of internet cyberspace experiments using flash technology. More centrally, there are increasing numbers of writers who incorporate Language concepts with traditional first-person and third-person voices. The most prominent among these are Juliana Spahr's *Fuck You—Aloha—I Love You* (2001), Fanny Howe's *Gone* (2003), Mei-Mei Berssenbrugge's *Nest* (2003), Lucie Brock-Broido's, *Trouble in Mind* (2004), and Michael Palmer's *A Company of Moths* (2005).

Bibliography

Allen, Donald, ed. *The New American Poetry.* New York: Grove Press, 1960.
Ashton, Jennifer. Our Bodies, Our Poems. *American Literary History.* December 8, 2006. Oxford University Press, 2006. Web Site http://alh.oxfordjournals.org/cgi/content/full/ajl039v1.
Andrews, Bruce. *Paradise and Method.* Evanston, IL: Northwestern University Press, 1996.
———. *Prehab* (with Dirk Rowntree), 2005. UbuWeb.com. Web Site http://www.ubu.com/contemp//andrews/a–ndrews.html.
Andrews, Bruce, and Charles Bernstein, eds. *The L=A=N=G=U=A=G=E Book.* Carbondale, IL: Southern Illinois University Press, 1984.
Armantrout, Rae. Why Don't Women Do Language-Oriented Writing? In *In the American Tree.* Ron Silliman, ed. Orono: National Poetry Foundation, 1986; 544–546.
———. *Up to Speed.* Middletown: Wesleyan University Press, 2004.
———. *Veil: New and Selected Poems.* Middletown: Wesleyan University Press, 2001.
———. *Extremities.* Berkeley, CA: The Figures, 1978.
Bernstein, Charles. *Girly Man.* Chicago, IL: University of Chicago Press, 2006.
———. *Shadowtime.* Libretto for an opera with music by Brian Ferneyhough. Los Angeles, CA: Green Integer, 2005.
———. *Content's Dream: Essays 1975–1984.* Los Angeles, CA: Sun & Moon Press, 1986.
Berssenbrugge, Mei-Mei. *Nest.* Berkeley, CA: Kelsey Street, 2003.
Brock-Broido, Lucie. *Trouble in Mind.* New York: Knopf, 2004.
Caplan, David. Who's Zoomin' Who?: The Poetics of www.poets.org and wings.buffalo.edu/epc. *Postmodern Culture* Vol. 8.1 (1997). [Online January 2007]. Web Site http://muse.jhu.edu/journals/postmodern_culture/v008/8.1r_caplan.html.
Gelpi, Albert. The Genealogy of Postmodernism: Contemporary American Poetry. *The Southern Review,* Summer 1990. [Online December 2006]. Web Site http://www.english.upenn.edu/~afilreis/88/gelpi.html.
Goldsmith, Kenneth. After Language Poetry. Reprint of *OEI* 7-8 2001 (Sweden). Anders Lundgerg, Jonas (J) Magnusson, and Jesper Olsson, eds. UbuWeb.com. [Online October 2006]. Web Site http://www.ubu.com/papers/oei/index.html.
Hartley, George. *Textual Politics and the Language Poets.* Bloomington, IN: Indiana University Press, 1989.
Hejinian, Lyn. *Happily.* Sausalito: Post-Apollo Press, 2000.
———, *My Life.* Providence, RI: Burning Deck, 1980.
Howe, Fanny. *Gone.* New California Poetry, 7. Berkeley, CA: University of California Press, 2003.
Hume, Christine. Review of *Sleeping with the Dictionary* by Harryette Mullen. *The Constant Critic.* [Online January 2007]. Web Site http://www.constantcritic.com/archive.
Izenberg, Oren. "Language Poetry and Collective Life." *Critical Inquiry,* Vol. 30 Number 1, Fall (2003).
Jameson, Fredric. Postmodernism and Consumer Society. *Athenaeum Reading Room.* [Online December 2006]. Web Site http://evans-experientialism.freewebspace.com/jameson.htm.
Jonghyun, Jeon Joseph. Speaking In Tongues: Myung Mi Kim's Stylized Mouths. *Studies in the Literary Imagination,* Spring (2004). [Online December 2006]. Web Site http://findarticles.com/p/articles/mi_qa3822/is_200404/ai_n9471130/print.
Kaufmann, David. Rattling The Chains Of American Poetry: Charles Bernstein's Unique Blend of Polemic, Parody and Just Plain Invention. *The Jewish Daily Forward,* Jan 12

(2007). [Online January 2007]. Web Site http://www.forward.com/articles/rattling-the-chains-of-american-poetry.

Kim, Eleana. Language Poetry: Dissident Practices and the Makings of a Movement (1994). *ReadMe,* Issue #4, Spring/Summer (2001). [Online October 2006]. Web Site http://home.jps.net/~nada/language1.htm.

Kim, Myung Mi. *Commons.* Berkeley: University of California Press, 2002.

———. *Under Flag.* Berkeley, CA: Kelsey St. Press, 1991.

Kinsella, John. C-O-M-M-U-N-I-C-A-T-I-N-G An Ad-Hoc Introduction To American Language Poetry (1996). *Fremantle Arts Review.* Jane Cousins, ed. JohnKinsella.org. [Online October 2006]. Web Site http://www.johnkinsella.org/essays/communicating.html.

Kovacik, Karen. Between L=A=N=G=U=A=G=E and Lyric: The Poetry of Pink-Collar Resistance. *National Women's Studies Association Journal,* 13.1 (2001): 22–39. [Online December 2006]. Web Site http://muse.jhu.edu/journals/nwsa_journal/v013/13.1kovacik.html.

Lilley Kate. This L=A=N=G=U=A=G=E. Pamphlet in *The Impercipient Lecture Series.* Steve Evans and Jennifer Moxley, eds. Vol. 1 No. 4 May (1997). Reprinted in *Jacket* #2. [Online December 2006]. Web Site http://jacketmagazine.com/02/lilley02.html.

McCaffery, Steve. *North of Intention: Critical Writings 1973–1986.* New York: Roof Books, 1986.

Messerli, Douglas. *"Language" Poetries.* New York: New Directions, 1987.

Mullen, Harryette. *Sleeping with the Dictionary.* Berkeley, CA: University of California Press, 2002.

———. *Muse & Drudge.* Philadelphia, PA: Singing Horse Press, 1995.

Muratori, Fred. Seeming is Believing. *Electronic Poetry Review.* Review of Rae Armantrout's *Veil: New and Selected Poems.* [Online December 2006]. Web Site http://www.epoetry.org/issues/issue4/text/prose/muratori1rev.htm.

"On Language Poetry." The Editors. *Rethinking Marxism* 1, 4 (Winter 1988).

Osman, Jena. After Language Poetry. Reprint of *OEI* 7-8 2001 (Sweden). Anders Lundgerg, Jonas (J) Magnusson, and Jesper Olsson, eds. UbuWeb.com. [Online November 2006]. Web Site http://www.ubu.com/papers/oei/index.html.

Palmer, Michael. *Company of Moths.* New York: New Directions, 2005.

Perelman, Bob. *The Marginalization of Poetry: Language Writing and Literary History.* Princeton, NJ: Princeton University Press, 1996.

Perloff, Marjorie. Language Poetry And The Lyric Subject: Ron Silliman's *Albany,* Susan Howe's *Buffalo* (1998). *Electronic Poetry Center (EPC).* [Online December 2006]. Web Site http://epc.buffalo.edu/.

———. After Language Poetry: Innovation And Its Theoretical Discontents (n.d.). *Electronic Poetry Center (EPC).* [Online November 2006]. Web Site http://epc.buffalo.edu/.

———. Dada Without Duchamp/Duchamp Without Dada: Avant-Garde Tradition and the Individual Talent. *Stanford Humanities Review* Volume 7.1 (1999). [Online December 2006]. http://www.stanford.edu/group/SHR/7-1/html/perloff.html.

———. Happy World: What Lyn Hejinian's Poetry Tells Us About Chance, Fortune and Pleasure. *The Boston Review,* February/March (2000). [Online December 2006]. Web Site http://epc.buffalo.edu/authors/perloff/articles/hejinian.html.

———. *The Poetics of Indeterminacy.* Evanston, IL: Northwestern University Press, 1999.

Prevallet, Kristin. The Exquisite Extremes of Poetry (Watten and Baraka on the Brink). *Jacket* #12, July (2000). [Online October 2006]. Web Site http://jacketmagazine.com/12/prevallet-orono.html.

Reddy, Srikanth. Beyond the Manifesto: Language Poetry and Lyn Hejinian's *The Language of Inquiry.* Poets.org. [Online December 2006]. Web Site http://www.poets.org/viewmedia.php/prmMID/5895.

Senning, Bradford. Charles Bernstein Interview. *ReadMe*, Issue #1, Fall (1999). [Online November 2006]. Web Site http://home.jps.net/~nada/bernstein.htm.

Silliman, Ron. Forward to *Veil: New and Selected Poems* by Rae Armantrout. Middletown, CT: Wesleyan University Press, 2001.

———. *The New Sentence*. New York: Roof Books, 1995.

———, ed. *In the American Tree*. Orono: National Poetry Foundation, 1986.

———. *ABC*. Berkeley, CA: Tuumba Press, 1983.

Sloan, Mary Margaret. *Moving Borders: Three Decades of Innovative Writing by Women*. Jersey City, NJ: Talisman House, 1998.

Spahr, Juliana. After Language Poetry. Reprint of *OEI* 7-8 2001 (Sweden). Anders Lundgerg, Jonas (J) Magnusson, and Jesper Olsson, eds. UbuWeb.com. [Online October 2006]. Web Site http://www.ubu.com/papers/oei/index.html.

———. *Fuck You—Aloha—I Love You*. Wesleyan Poetry Series. Middletown, CT: Wesleyan University Press, 2001.

Stefans, Brian Kim. After Language Poetry. Reprint of *OEI* 7-8 2001 (Sweden). Anders Lundgerg, Jonas (J) Magnusson, and Jesper Olsson, eds. UbuWeb.com. [Online October 2006]. Web Site http://www.ubu.com/papers/oei/index.html.

———. Subject: BK Stefans on Standard Schaefer Date: Wed, 19 May 1999 08:13:45 -0400 (EDT). [Online December 2006]. Web Site http://www.writing.upenn.edu/~afilreis/88/stefans-institutionalization.html.

Sussman, Henry. *The Task of the Critic: Poetics, Philosophy, and Religion*. New York: Fordham University Press, 2005.

Thomas, Lorenzo. Review of *Sleeping with the Dictionary* by Harryette Mullen. *African American Review*, Winter (2002). [Online December 2006]. Web Site http://findarticles.com/p/articles/mi_m2838/is_4_36/ai_97515904.

Vickery, Ann. *Leaving Lines of Gender: A Feminist Genealogy of Language Writing*. Hanover: Wesleyan University Press, 2000.

Wallace, Mark. Definitions In Process, Definitions As Process/Uneasy Collaborations: Language And Postlanguage Poetries. *Flashpoint* Spring 1998, Web Issue 2. v [Online December 2006]. Web Site http://www.flashpointmag.com/postlang.htm.

Watten, Barrett. The Secret History of the Equal Sign: L=A=N=G=U=A=G=E between Discourse and Text. *Poetics Today* 20.4 (1999) 581–627. Reprint Porter Institute for Poetics and Semiotics (2000). [Online December 2006]. Web Site http://muse.jhu.edu/journals/poetics_today/v020/20.4watten.html.

Further Reading

Bartlett, Lee. "What Is 'Language Poetry.'" *Critical Inquiry* 12 (1986); Bernstein, Charles, ed. *The Politics of Poetic Form: Poetry and Public Policy*. New York: Roof, 1990; Hejinian, Lyn. *The Language of Inquiry*. Berkeley, CA: University of California Press, 2000; Howe, Susan. *My Emily Dickinson*. Berkeley, CA: North Atlantic Books, 1988; Huk, Romana, ed. *Assembling Alternatives: Reading Postmodern Poetries Transnationally*. Middletown, CT: Wesleyan University Press, 2003; McCaffery, Steve. *Prior to Meaning: The Protosemantic and Poetics*. Evanston, IL: Northwestern University Press, 2001; Jerome McGann. "Contemporary Poetry, Alternate Routes." *Critical Inquiry* 13 (Spring 1987): 624–47; Perelman, Bob. *Virtual Reality*. New York: Roof, 1993; Rasula, Jed. *Syncopations: The Stress of Innovation in Contemporary American Poetry*. Tuscaloosa, AL: University of Alabama Press, 2004; Watten, Barrett. *The Constructivist Moment: From Material Text to Cultural Poetics*. Middletown, CT: Wesleyan University Press, 2003.

GEORGE B. MOORE

LATINO AMERICAN LITERATURE

Definition. Terms of identity are particularly important in a review of Latino American literature, since there has been a tendency to lump all Latinos into one homogeneous group. The result of this has been an undifferentiated mixture of Latinos from Latin America and Latinos who are of the United States (citizens) all classified as one group. This has led to including Latinos from Latin America in anthologies of American (U.S.) literature as if they were Latino writers from the United States. For example, Isabel Allende is a Latina writer from Chile. Including her in *The American Tradition in Literature* (Norton 2002) as a representative of U.S. Latino writers is like including Chinua Achebe, an African writer, as a representative of African American writers. But the fact that she now lives and works in the United States makes her part of that diasporic group of Latino writers contributing to Latino American literature.

Latinos in the United States fall into four broad categories:

- Mexican Americans (many of whom identify themselves with the self-affirming term of "Chicanos") constituting about two-thirds (30 million) of the 45 million Latinos counted in the U.S. Census and concentrated mainly in the American southwest states of Texas, New Mexico, Colorado, Arizona, Nevada, Utah, and California
- Puerto Ricans (many of whom identify themselves with the self-affirming term of "Boricuas"—from Borinquen, the original name of the island by the Taino Indians—to distinguish themselves from the four million Puerto Ricans from the island and not counted in the U.S. Census) numbering about four million in the Continental United States and concentrated in New York, New Jersey, Massachusetts, and Illinois
- Cuban Americans numbering about two million, concentrated principally in Florida and
- about nine million "other" Latinos from Argentina, Bolivia, Chile, Colombia, Costa Rica, Dominican Republic, Ecuador, El Salvador, Guatemala, Honduras, Nicaragua, Panama, Paraguay, Peru, Uruguay, and Venezuela.

Spaniards are not considered in the Latino mix. For example, during the Spanish Civil War (and the period following during which Franco was consolidating the gains of his "revolution"), Federico Garcia Lorca, the Spanish playwright and poet, spent some time living and writing in New York. Some of his major works were written during this time. However, he is not considered a Latino.

It is important to point out, however, that demographically Latinos in the United States are growing exponentially; they are everywhere in the United States. There are large enclaves of Dominicans in New York City and the District of Columbia. More than four million Mexican Americans are spread across the Ohio Valley Crescent from Northfield, Minnesota, to Johnstown, Pennsylvania. The distribution of Latinos in the United States is phenomenal.

History. Many Latinos in the United States have their origins in Spanish settlements dating back to the Sephardic (Spanish) Jews of New Amsterdam, the Spanish communities that were part of the Louisiana Purchase in 1803 especially in New Orleans, and the Spanish communities like St Augustine that were part of the Florida acquisition by the United States in 1819. Countless Latinos immigrated to the United States from the founding of the nation to the present. The Cuban American community of Yuba City, Florida, dates from the early twentieth century, long before the mass exodus of Cubans to the United States after 1959.

In the United States today there are two categories of Latino writers each with a considerably wide latitude in definition. The first group includes Latino writers from the Latin American countries previously mentioned with the exception of Puerto Rico (since all Puerto Ricans are considered U.S. citizens). For the most part, these Latino writers are still citizens of their countries, and their literary and social orientation are generally congruent with the literary and social orientations of their homelands. Many are in the United States as political refugees or exiles, although many more are in the United States because they are simply at odds with the ideological trends in their countries. The Cuban poet Valladares is a good case in point of a Latino writer living and writing in the United States because of political differences with the ruling group of his country. For the most part, this group of Latino writers deals with themes and conventions traditionally part of the literary orientation of their homelands, not with themes pertinent to Latino struggles in the United States. Their works are therefore not classified as Latino literature. In this regard, the works of the Russian writer Solzenitzen's written while he lived (in exile) in the United States are not considered American literature.

The second group of Latino writers is essentially indigenous to the United States, that is, Latinos who are citizens of the United States and identified as members of a Latino group like Mexican Americans, Puerto Ricans, etc.

Like the British roots in the new American soil, U.S. Latino literary roots have yielded a vigorous and dynamic body of literature, which, unfortunately, has been studied historically as part of a foreign enterprise rather then as part and parcel of our American literary heritage. If one were looking for U.S. Latino writers in the libraries of the 1960s, one would not have found them since the Library of Congress and the Dewey System did not have that classification. For example, if one were looking for Mexican American writers, then one would have found them under the classification of "Mexicans in the United States." Asking a librarian for the location of Latino writers would have yielded the names of Octavio Paz, Julio Cortazar, Gabriel García Márquez, Gabriela Mistral, and Miguel Angel Asturias, all in the card catalogs. These are Latino writers, but not Latino American writers.

The point is that the term "Latino Writers" most often directs inquiries to Latin American writers. The unfortunate truth of the matter is that few Americans outside of literary specialists know very much about U.S. Latino Literature today. To be sure, there are successful U.S. Latino writers like Sandra Cisneros (Mexican American), Rudolfo Anaya (Mexican American), Denise Chavez (Mexican American), Piri Thomas (Puerto Rican), Miguel Algarin (Puerto Rican), Nicolasa Mohr (Puerto Rican), Achy Abejas (Cuban American), and Angel Castro (Cuban American). In the main, however, when pressed, uninitiated Americans will ask quizzically: Are there U.S. Latino writers? (Ortego 1983). Who are they? What this points to is the woeful ignorance of most Americans about U.S. Latino writers.

Spaniards are not Latinos; and Latinos are not Spaniards. Though by and large, with the exception of the indigenous peoples of Latin America still there today, Latinos are a product of the historical "blending" (a euphemism for cohabitation) between Spanish males and indigenous women—a process commonly labeled as *mestizaje*, a term from which the word *mestizo/a* (the noun identifying the product of that process) derives.

While the current perspective about U.S. Latinos is that they are recently arrived, Latinos have been markedly part of the American demographic landscape since 1848 when the United States annexed more than half of Mexico's territory as a prize of war with Mexico (1846–1848). No one is sure just how many Mexicans came with the dismembered territory. Puerto Ricans became Americans with the

U.S.-Spanish War of 1898. Cuban Americans began their Americanization process with Fidel Castro's "liberation" of Cuba in 1959. The historical ingress of other Latino groups into the United States is hard to determine.

Mexican American writers have been part of the United States since 1848, some 50 years before the acquisition of Puerto Rico and over a century before the arrival of Cubans in the United States. For more than a century, Mexican American writers produced their works mostly outside the U.S. literary mainstream. There were occasional Mexican American writers whose works were published by major U.S. publishers, but by and large Mexican American writers were known chiefly by Mexican American readers, their works circulating in books with modest runs or in manuscript form like the works of many Cuban American writers today. By the first half of the twentieth century notable Mexican American writers like Aurelio Espinoza, Nina Otero, Aurora Lucero, Arturo Campa, and Fray Angelico Chavez were being published by English-language periodicals, and their works were seriously acclaimed by non-Hispanic readers.

While the boom (the Chicano Renaissance) in Mexican American Literature in 1966 established the primacy of English as the literary language for Chicanos (Ortego 1971) a number of Chicano writers like Alejandro Morales continue to produce works in Spanish.

By and large, Boricua and Nuyorican writers, like most Chicano writers, direct their works toward English language audiences. Some Boricua and Nuyorican writers like Piri Thomas (*Down These Mean Streets*) and Nicholasa Mohr (*El Bronx Remembered*) are published by mainstream U.S. presses. However, most Boricua writers are published by "small" U.S. Hispanic presses like Arte Publico Press in Houston.

Yet, there is really no significant number of American-born Cuban American writers, owing mostly to the recency of the Cuban influx into the United States. This is not to say there is not a large group of Cuban (now American) writers. On the contrary, large numbers of Cuban writers have fled to the United States since 1960. The literary production of Cuban writers in the United States (many, if not most, of them now citizens) may be described as "exilic." Much of their writing is in Spanish and their aims by and large, have been to keep the Cuban American community aware of the state of affairs in Cuba while at the same time creating a positive image of the Cuban diaspora in the United States.

As a group, Latino Americans who are not Mexican Americans, Puerto Ricans, or Cuban Americans is considerably small, although as a group it is the third largest group of U.S. Latinos, numbering some eight million. However, this group is not a coherent group, although there are large pockets of Dominicans, Salvadoreños, Guatemalans, and Peruvians throughout the United States. Until recently this group was identified as "Latinos," rounding out the lexicon of labels that identified U.S. Hispanics: Mexican Americans, Puerto Ricans, Cubans, and Latinos.

Trends and Themes. The early works in English by Mexican Americans focused mostly on the folkloric traditions of Mexico as they existed in the Hispanic Southwest or as they were brought north from Mexico in the peregrinations of Mexicans and Mexican Americans crossing back and forth across the ephemeral U.S.-Mexico border. Until about the First World War, Mexican American literature was written primarily in Spanish and mirrored the themes and conventions of the Hispanic literary tradition as practiced in Mexico.

For the period representing the start of the Chicano movement, 1848 to 1960, less than a dozen novels have been attributed so far to Mexican Americans. However, the project at the University of Houston on Recovering the Hispanic Literature of the United States is hopeful of finding more. The contemporary Chicano novel has its beginnings with publication of *Pocho* in 1959 by Jose Antonio Villarreal, followed in the 1960s with a pittance of novels by a handful of Chicano writers, among them John Rechy (*City of Night*, 1963) and Floyd Salas (*Tattoo the Wicked Cross*, 1967).

There were a number of Chicano practitioners of the short story between 1848 and 1960, the most prominent of whom were Arturo Campa (1934) and Mario Suárez (1947), identified as "the most important short story writer of Mexican descent from the mid-twentieth century" (Suárez 2004, 1).

From 1898 to 1960, there was scant production of fiction by Puerto Ricans in the continental United States. On the island, however, Puerto Rican writers produced a prodigious amount of fiction in novels and short stories (*cuentos*) in the continuing Spanish literary tradition as it had evolved there. What most characterizes Boricua and Nuyorican literature is its discontinuity from the literature of Puerto Rico (the island). The communicative context of each literature is different. Although some roots of Boricua and Nuyorican literature spring from the Puerto Rican literary tradition, Boricua and Nuyorican literature have sprouted other roots intertwined with the roots of mainstream American literature.

Contexts and Issues. The most important issue to consider in surveying the conspectus of Latino American Literature today is that not all Latinos are immigrants in the United States. For example, Puerto Ricans are not immigrants: they are American citizens per their commonwealth status in the American hegemony. As Latinos, Mexican Americans pose a particular consideration. When the United States annexed more than half of Mexico's territory per the Treaty of Guadalupe Hidalgo (February 2, 1848), the Mexicans who came with the land (a territory larger than Spain, France, and Italy combined) became Americans by fiat. There is no accurate number of how many Mexicans came with the dismembered territory. Estimates range variously from a low of 75,000 to a high of 300,000. The land of the Mexican Cession was not an empty wasteland. It included established cities like San Antonio, El Paso, Albuquerque, Santa Fe, Tucson, San Diego, Los Angeles, Santa Barbara, Monterrey, and San Francisco as well as hundreds of smaller communities across the Hispanic landscape from south Texas to northern California. The San Luis Valley of southern Colorado was teeming with Hispanic villages and towns. In Mexican American history, this group of Mexican Americans is referred to as the "conquest generation." Though their numbers were augmented by the ingress of subsequent immigrants from Mexico, this group of Latinos—most of whom eschew the term "Latino," preferring instead to be identified as *mejicanos* (lower case m) or Mexican Americans or Chicanos (an ideological term)—remains steadfast in its avowal that the United States came to them and not the other way around.

Unfortunately, one of the most difficult barriers for Latino American Literature has been the Spanish language. For the most part, Latino Americans wrote in Spanish, continuing in the literary tradition of the countries they came from. In other words, Cuban American literature reflects the themes and traditions of Cuba. So too, Puerto Rican writers on the mainland (Continental Puerto Ricans: those who were born or were raised in the continental United States) wrote employing the literary strictures of the island of Puerto Rico. The same is true for Mexican American writers who in the period of transition (1848–1912) maintained a literary tradition consonant with the literary traditions of Mexico. However, these extensions were short-lived. Within a generation Latino American writers with origins in Cuba, Puerto Rico, and Mexico (as well as the other Latin American countries) were writing in English, probing into their experiences in the United States, and emulating distinctively American themes as they evolved into Americans. This is not to say they were assimilated in the metonymical "melting pot." On the contrary, in the contact zones of culture and language they were "sprouting up" as a bilingual and bicultural people, pushing the envelope of literary creativity to include both Spanish and English in unique binary productions, sometimes disparagingly called "Spanglish" or Tex-Mex in the Mexican American Southwest. This is the phenomenon of languages and cultures in contact: like consenting adults, their issue was innovative and startling. An aspect of this phenomenon blends English and Spanish in the same sentences (intrasententially).

Other Latino American poets like the Chicano Tino Villanueva created poems with more emphatic code switching (alternating Spanish and English words more repeatedly in a sentence):

> always had a movida chueca somewhere up town.

Of course, not all Latino American writers code switch. In the main, though, Mexican Americans, Puerto Ricans, and Cuban Americans code switch the most. Poetry is the genre in which code switching occurs most often among Latino writers. It occurs far less in fiction, and when it does, the Latino writers provide some help in deciphering the Spanish words or expressions by follow-up translations in English that are not intrusive. For example, in Philip D. Ortego's story "The Coming of Zamora," Alarcón is shooing away a stray dog, saying "Vete" followed immediately with "Go," translation of the Spanish word "Vete" (Simmen 1971, 297).

Like the Mexican Americans, Puerto Rican writers reflect the dual circumstances of their presence in the United States. On the one hand, Puerto Rico is still essentially a Hispanic "country" despite its commonwealth status with the United States. Perhaps better said, it is a "Hispanic state." Unlike the Hispanic states of California, Arizona, Texas, New Mexico, and Colorado, whose Hispanicity has diminished over time, the Hispanicity of Puerto Rico is still as strong as ever. The relevance of this fact is manifest in Puerto Rican literature, which is still essentially a Spanish-language literature.

However, there is another Puerto Rican literature that is more akin to the literature of Chicanos. This is the literature of Puerto Ricans in the United States proper, sometimes called "Nuyorican" literature. The tag would be appropriate except for the fact that Puerto Ricans in the United States are found everywhere, not just in New York. To distinguish themselves from Puerto Ricans from the island, many continental Puerto Ricans use the label "Boricuas" to identify themselves, just as some Mexican Americans choose to distinguish themselves from Mexicans by calling themselves "Chicanos." No such term has surfaced for Cuban Americans, although the term "Cubano" is popular among them and issued much the way Mexican Americans use the term "mejicano" [lower case "m"] to identify themselves.

Selected Authors. The most important Nuyorican writer of this period writing in Spanish and English was Jesús Colón, labor activist and polemicist, who paved the way for further Nuyorican literary production (*Herencia: The Anthology of*

Hispanic Literature of the United States, edited by Nicolás Kanellos, Oxford, 2002, 12). Fiction was slow in gaining ascendancy among Puerto Rico writers who until mid-twentieth century were concerned with existential problems of freedom from Spain, then nationhood as a territory of the United States after the U.S. war with Spain in 1898. The most widely recognized Puerto Rican writer in the period extending to the post–World War II era was Enrique Laguerre, a Nobel Prize nominee. A remarkable Puerto Rican female storyteller publishing Puerto Rican folktales in the 1930s and 1940s was Pura Belpré, a librarian with the New York Public Library. Today, REFORMA (the National Association for Library Services to Hispanics, an ALA affiliate), honors her annually with its Pura Belpré prize for Children's Literature.

Of the Continental Puerto Rican writers (Boricuas), Piri Thomas's autobiographical novel *Down These Mean Streets* published in 1967 heralded a wave of Boricua fiction that has not realized its premises nor its promises. Published in 1973, Nicholasa Mohr's novel *Nilda* became a "touchstone" work in Puerto Rican fiction. Nilda is "a classic novel of a Puerto Rican girl coming of age in New York City during World War II" (Extracted from http://biography.jrank.org/pages/3407/Mohr-Nicholasa-1938-Writer.html). Though principally a poet, Judith Ortiz Cofer published the novel *Line of Sight* in 1989 (University of Georgia Press). In the vein of Piri Thomas's street esthetic, Abraham Rodriguez's *Spidertown* (1994) lays out the gritty life of dope and hope in the South Bronx. Focusing on the seamy side of drugs in Spanish Harlem, Ernesto Quiñones's *Bodega Dreams* (2000) serves up a story of hope gone awry by ignorance and romanticism. Since the year 2000, López Nieves has scored with a run of books including *El Corazon de Voltaire* (Voltaire's Heart), winner of the 2000 *Premio Nacional de Literatura* (National Literary Prize) and again in 2006 with *La verdadera muerte de Juan Ponce de León* (The True Death of Juan Ponce de León). In 2003 he authored the historical novel *Seva* (Editorial Cordillera).

Like the themes of Mexican American/Chicano writers of fiction, Puerto Rican novelists focus on self-identity, their cultural and racial identities, and the diasporic problems of life in the United States viewed as neocolonialism. By and large Boricua and Nuyorican writers, like most Mexican American/Chicano writers, direct their works toward English language audiences. Magazines like *The Rican* in Chicago sought to publish the splay of creative efforts by continental Puerto Ricans across the country. Puerto Ricans are well aware that the continental Puerto Rican experience is different from the island Puerto Rican experience. In Puerto Rico, there are still thoughts of independence. In the continental United States, Puerto Ricans are reaching for the "independence" of the mainstream. Their literary works reflect that outreach. Much Boricua literature may reflect anger, just as some black literature of the 1960s and 1970s reflected anger. But most of that anger deals with coming to terms with the facts of American life, not life in Puerto Rico, coming to terms with where "home" is and "what" home is. Piri Thomas' protagonist in *Down These Mean Streets* is trying to carve out the sense of home in East Harlem just as Antonio Mares, Rudy Anaya's protagonist in *Bless Me, Ultima* is trying to carve out the sense of "home" in northern New Mexico.

The English language literary boom of the Chicano Movement does not appear until after World War II. "The Chicano Renaissance" is a product of that movement. Realizing they could expect little recognition by U.S. mainstream publishers, a group of Mexican American writers, led by Octavio Romano, launched a small journal of Mexican American thought appropriately called *El Grito* (The Cry). The first issue appeared in the Spring of 1967, and with its publication the "Quinto Sol" (Fifth Sun) writers (identified with the name of the press) announced their literary independence. Their goals were to praise the people, identify the enemy, and promote the revolution, the Chicano Movement being the revolution. Brown became beautiful and Mexican American writers (now Chicanos) set out like embattled visionaries to make a place for themselves in the American literary sun.

The list of Chicano writers grew rapidly in all genres. Chicano writers won national and international literary prizes. Tomás Rivera won the coveted *Quinto Sol Prize* for literature for his episodic novel *Y no se lo trago la tierra* (And the Earth did not Part), 1971; and Rolando Hinojosa won the Cuban *Premio Casa las Americas* for his work *Klail City y sus alrededores*, 1976. Alejandro Morales had his works published in Mexico (*Caras Viejas, Vino Nuevo*, Old Faces, New Wine), Moritz 1975; and Jose Antonio Villarreal (*Pocho*, 1959), Richard Vasquez (*Chicano*, 1970), and Raymond Barrio (*The Plum Plum Pickers*, 1969) had their works published by mainstream presses.

As a part of Latino American literature, modern Chicano literature exhibits unique characteristics in responses to the particular conditions of contemporary life. Tomás Rivera once called Chicano literature "life in search of form." Indeed, much of contemporary Chicano literature addresses itself to the search for form, a linguistic fit to accommodate the lexical and cultural realities of Chicano life.

Like Puerto Rican and Boricua writers, Cuban American writers have focused on the diasporic condition of Cubans in the United States, many of them now Americans as second generation Cubans in the United States. Their literary production as Latinos in the United States, while still scant, is experiencing a "boom" much like the Chicano Renaissance of the 1960s and 1970s, in English rather than Spanish. The most renowned Cuban American writers is Jose Yglesias, (seven novels) often referred to as the father of Cuban American fiction in English. In 1963, Holt Rinehart published Yglesias's *A Wake in Ybor City* about Cuban immigration to Florida and their experiences as a cultural minority in the United States.

For the most part, Cuban American writers in general, and writers of fiction specifically, have dedicated themselves to the preservation of cultural memory, the loss of *patria* (homeland) caused by the mass exodus of Cubans after 1960 bringing more than 700,000 of them to the United States. Like Chicano writers, Cuban American writers are *vates* (selected ones) in reinventing Cuban Americans in their search for fixity following political turmoil, a place from which to glance back at the "golden age" of their existence and also a place from which to determine their future. Relatively recent Cuban American writers like Oscar Hijuelos (*The Mambo Kings Play Songs of Love*, 1989, Pulitzer Prize) and Cristina Garcia (*Dreaming in Cuban*, 1992, and *A Handbook to Luck*, 2007) have spotlighted the fertility of the Cuban American literary imagination. In 1999, Hijuelos published *Empress of the Splendid Season* (Harper Perennial) the story of a search for roots. While not extensive, the list of Cuban American writers is growing substantially with voices like Elías Miguel Muñoz (*Viajes Fantasticos*, 1999), Gustavo Perez Firmat (*Anything but Love*, 2000), the satirist Roberto G. Fernández (*En la ocho y la doce*, 2001), Achy Obejas (*Days of Awe*, 2001), and Pablo Medina (*The Cigar Roller*, 2005).

Latino American literature is rich in literary diversity with voices from many of the Latin American countries. This includes Dominican American writers like Julia Alvarez with *How The Garcia Girls Lost Their Accents* (1991), *In the Time of the*

Butterflies (1994), and *In the Name of Salomé,* (2000); Junot Diaz *Drown* (1996) with *The Brief Wondrous Life of Oscar Wao* (2007), which won the Pulitzer Prize for fiction in 2008; the Colombian American Jaime Manriquez with *Twilight at the Equator* (2003); the Guatemalan American writer Francisco Goldman with *The Long Night of the White Chickens* (1992) and his most recent work, which is non-fiction, *The Art of Political Murder: Who Killed the Bishop* (2008); and the Chilean (now American writer) Isabel Allende with *House of the Spirits* (1985). Chicanas have outdistanced their Chicano counterparts in the Chicano literary arena since the 1990s, creating a second-wave of the Chicano renaissance. This second wave actually started with Cherrie Moraga and Gloria Anzaldua's *This Bridge Called my Back* (1981). It was followed up by *Intaglio* (1990) by Roberta Fernandez; *Eulogy for a Brown Angel* (2002) by Lucha Corpi; *So Far from God* (1992) by Ana Castillo; *The Candy Vendor's Boy* (1993) by Beatriz de la Garza; *The Memories of Ana Calderón* (1994) by Graciela Limón; *Mother Tongue* (1994) by Demetria Martinez; *Under the Feet of Jesus* (1995) by Helena Maria Viramontes; *Loving Pedro Infante* (2001) by Denise Chavez; *Let Their Spirits Dance* (2002) by Stella Pope Duarte; and *Playing With Boys* (2004) by Alisa Valdes-Rodriguez.

The canon of Latino American literature is beset by a division of nomenclature between Latinos who are residents of the United States (that is, born here), and Latinos who are immigrants. The outcome will depend on "mainstream" publishers—who they favor to publish, how they read the runes of canon formation in the Latino literary galaxy of the United States. Because of their numbers and historical priority, Chicano literary production has defined the parameters of the Latino literary canon, but their presence in that canon has diminished in the lexicon of Latinismo.

Bibliography

Allende, Isabel. *House of the Spirits*. New York: Knopf, 1985.
Alvarez, Julia. *How the Garcia Girls Lost Their Accents*. New York: Penguin Group, 1992.
———. *In the Time of the Butterflies*. New York: Penguin, 1994.
———. *In the Name of Salomé*. New York: Algonquin Books, 2000.
Anaya, Rudolfo. *Bless Me, Ultima*. New York: Grand Central Publishing, 1994.
Barrio, Raymond. *The Plum Plum Pickers*. San Francisco, CA: Canfield Colophon, 1971.
Campa, Arturo. "The Cell of Heavenly Justice," *New Mexico Quarterly* (August 1934): 219–230.
Castillo, Ana. *So Far From God*. New York: Plume Penguin, 1992.
Chavez, Denise. *Loving Pedro Infante*. New York: Washington Square Press, 2002.
Cofer, Judith Ortiz. *Line of Sight*. Athens, GA: University of Georgia Press, 1989.
Corpi, Lucha. *Eulogy for a Brown Angel*. Houston, TX: Arte Publico Press, 2002.
Diaz, Junot. *Drown*. New York: Riverhead Books, 1996.
———. *The Brief Wondrous Life of Oscar Wao*. New York: Putnam, 2008.
Duarte, Stella Pope. *Let Their Spirits Soar*. New York: Harper Collins, 2003.
Fernandez, Roberta. *Intaglio*. Houston, TX: Arte Publico Press, 1990.
Fernandez, Roberto G. *En la ocho y la doce (At 8th and 12th)*. Boston, MA: Houghton Mifflin, 2001.
Firmat, Gustavo Perez. *Anything but Love*. Houston, TX: Arte Publico Press, 2000.
Garcia, Cristina. *Dreaming in Cuban*. New York: Ballantine, 1993.
———. *A Handbook to Luck*. New York: Knopf, 2007.
Goldman, Francisco. *The Long Night of White Chickens*. New York: Atlantic Monthly Press, 1992.
———. *The Art of Political Murder: Who Killed the Bishop*. New York: Grove Press, 2008.

Hijuelos, Oscar. *The Mambo Kings Play Songs of Love*. New York: Harper Collins, 1989.
———. *Empress of the Splendid Season*. New York: Harper Perennial, 1999.
Hinojosa, Rolando. *Klail City y sus alrededores (Klail City and its Environs)*. Havana: Casa de las Americas, 1976.
Limón, Graciela. *The Memories of Ana Calderón*. Houston, TX: Arte Publico Press, 2001.
Manriquez, Jaime. *Twilight at the Equator*. Madison, WI: University of Wisconsin Press, 2003.
Martinez, Demetria. *Mother Tongue*. Tempe, AZ: Bilingual Press, 1994.
Medina, Pablo. *The Cigar Roller*. New York: Grove Atlantic, 2005.
Mohr, Nocholasa. *El Bronx Remembered*. New York: Harper Collins, 1993.
———. *Nilda*. New York: Harper & Row, 1974.
Moraga, Cherrie, and Gloria Anzaldua. *This Bridge Called my Back*. New York: Kitchen Table/Women of Color Press, 1981.
Morales, Alejandro. *Caras Viejas y Vino Nuevo (Old Faces and New Wine)*. DF, Mexico: Moritz, 1975. Published as *Barrio on the Edge/Caras Viejas y Vino Nuevo*. Translated by Francisco Lomelí, Phoenix, AZ: Bilingual Review Press, 1997.
Muñoz, Elías Miguel. *Viajes Fantasticos*. New York: McGraw Hill, 2000.
Nieves, Lopez. *El Corazon de Voltaire (Voltaire's Heart)*. San Juan, Puerto Rico: Editorial Norma, 2006.
———. *La Verdadera Muerte de Juan Ponce (The True Death of Juan Ponce)*. Hato Rey, Puerto Rico: Editorial Cordillera, 2000.
———. *Seva*. Hato Rey, Puerto Rico: Editorial Cordillera, 2003.
Obejas, Achy. *Days of Awe*. New York: Ballantine/Random House, 2001.
Ortego, Philip D. "The Coming of Zamora." In *The Chicano: From Caricature to Self Portrait*. Edward Simmen, ed. New York: New American Library, 1971.
Ortego y Gasca, Felipe de. "Mexican American Literature: Reflections and a Critical Guide." In *Chicana/o Studies: Survey and Analysis*. Dennis Bixler-Marquez, et al., eds. Dubuque, IA: Kendall/Hunt, 2007.
———. "Chicano Poetry." In *The Greenwood Encyclopedia of American Poets and Poetry*. Westport, CT: Greenwood Press, 2006.
———. "Mexicans and Mexican Americans: Prolegomenon to a Literary Perspective." *Journal of South Texas* 18.1 (2005): 71–90.
———. "The Minotaur and the Labyrinth: Chicano Literature and Critical Theory." In *Aztlan: A Journal of Chicano Studies* (Spring 2001). http://www.hispanicvista.com/HVC/Opinion/Guest_Columns/032805ortego.htm.
———. "Twentieth Century Hispanics in Texas Letters." In *Journal of South Texas* 14.1 (2001): 5–21.
———. "Towards a Cultural Interpretation of Literature." In *ViAztlan: International Journal of Chicano Arts and Letters* April–May 4.4 (1986): 10–13.
———. "Chicano Literature: From 1942 to the Present." In *Chicano Literature: A Reference Guide*. Westport, CT: Greenwood Press, 1985.
———. "American Hispanic Literature: A Brief Commentary." *ViAztlan: International Journal of Chicano Arts and Letters* Part I, January–February 1985: 11–13; Part II, March 1985: 8-11; Part III, May 1985: 4–7.
———. *The Cross and the Pen: Spanish Colonial and Mexican Periods of Texas Letters* (Monograph). Washington, DC: The Hispanic Foundation, 1985.
———. "Are There U.S. Hispanic Writers?" *Nosotros Magazine* April (1983): 20–21, 60.
———. "An Introduction to Chicano Poetry." In *Modern Chicano Writers: Twentieth Century Views*. New York: Prentice Hall, 1979.
———, with Jose Carrasco. "Chicanos and American Literature." In *The Wiley Reader: Designs for Writing*. New York: John Wiley & Sons, 1976.
———, ed. *We Are Chicanos: An Anthology of Mexican American Literature*. New York: Washington Square Press, 1973.

————. "Chicano Poetry: Roots and Writers." In *Southwestern American Literature*. 2.1 (1972): 8–24.

————. *Backgrounds of Mexican American Literature*. Albuquerque: University of New Mexico Press, 1971.

————. "The Chicano Renaissance," *Journal of Social Casework* 52.5 (1971): 294–307.

————. "Which Southwestern Literature and Culture in the English Classroom?" *Arizona English Bulletin* 13.3 (1971): 15–17.

————. "Mexican American Literature," *The Nation* 15 Sept. 1969: 258–259.

Quiñones, Ernesto. *Bodega Dreams*. New York: Vintage, 2000.

Rechy, John. *City of Night*. New York: Grove Press, 1963.

Rivera, Tomás. *Y no se lo trago la tierra (And the Earth did not Part)*. Berkeley: Quinto Sol Publications, 1971.

Rodriguez, Abraham. *Spidertown*. New York: Viking Penguin, 1994.

Salas, Floyd. *Tattoo the Wicked Cross*. New York: Grove Press, 1967.

Suarez, Mario. "Señor Garza." *Arizona Quarterly* 3 (1947): 112–115.

Suarez, Mario. *Chicano Sketches: Short Stories by Mario Suarez*. Francisco A. Lomeli, Cecilia Cota-Robles Suárez, and Juan José Casillas-Nuñez, eds. Tucson, AZ: University of Arizona Press, 2004.

Thomas, Piri. *Down These Mean Streets*. New York: Knopf, 1997.

Urista, Alberto, in *El Espejo—The Mirror*. Berkeley: Quinto Sol Publications, 1967.

Valdes-Rodriguez, Alisa. *Playing With Boys*. New York: Macmillan, 2004.

Vasquez, Richard. *Chicano*. New York: Harper Perennial, 1970.

Villanueva, Tino. *Hay Otra Voz Poems*. Staten Island, NY: Editorial Mansaje, 1972.

Villarreal, Jose Antonio. *Pocho*. New York: Random House, 1970.

Viramontes, Helena Maria. *Under the Feet of Jesus*. New York: Penguin, 1995.

Yglesias, Jose. *A Wake in Ybor City*. New York: Holt Rinehart, 1963.

Further Reading

Kanellos, Nicolás. Herencia. *The Anthology of Hispanic Literature of the United States*. Oxford: Oxford University Press, 2002; Ortego, Philip D. *Backgrounds of Mexican American Literature*. Albuquerque: University of New Mexico Press, 1971.

FELIPE DE ORTEGO Y GASCA

LEGAL THRILLERS

Definition. Legal thrillers constitute a crime fiction subspecies focusing on the legal procedures in connection with crime. American writers John Grisham and Scott Turow are contemporary writers central to both form and concerns of the legal thriller. In countries adhering to the tradition of Roman law, the bench has a role during investigations prior to trial and the passing of sentence, for example, Georges Simenon's Paris-based police investigator Maigret, whose life with "juges d'instruction" is seldom easy. In countries building on the Anglo-Saxon tradition of jurisprudence and law enforcement, the court machinery is usually involved only after the police have handed over a case for trial (except for judges' authorizations of search warrants, etc.). Nonetheless, in legal thrillers, the questioning of police procedures and the call for additional or revised investigative procedures take the drama of full-scale crime detection into the courtroom. In the United States especially the genre has found fertile soil, an effect no doubt of the conspicuous role played by law at every level in society.

History. Ancient sources are often, and then mostly facetiously, referred to as the forerunners of present-day popular literature. But it is hardly helpful to look back too far for generic models because the form obviously is dependent on modern print and distribution technology and cultural institutions and lifestyles of comparatively recent standing for its mode of being. It is true that Old Testament King Solomon did act in the capacity of investigative judge, and it is true that the old Chinese tales about investigative judges Dee Jendijeh and Pao Cheng show proto elements of the later full-grown genres. It is also true that lawyers have appeared regularly in literature in English since Chaucer. But to talk generally of generic fiction as such, or specifically of the legal thriller in the contemporary sense of the genre designation, as much older than the twentieth century would be misleading.

The genre of the legal thriller grew out of the crime story adapting itself to the demands of a mass market audience fully ripe only in the second and third decades of the twentieth century. Throughout the nineteenth century court reports had been popular reading, as exemplified by the early career of British novelist Charles Dickens, who as a young man reported cases from the London courts. Dickens showed an interest in courts and lawyers in his later novelistic work but as part of a broader social critique not hinged particularly on this aspect of society adminis-tration. In terms of literary history, the investigator in public employ, as in the case of E.A. Poe's Inspector Dupin, or in self-employ, as in the case of Arthur Conan Doyle's Sherlock Holmes, is more of a generalist than a legalist. Although Holmes had a more than working knowledge of jurisprudence, as he had of an astounding number of other things, fictional investigators of fictional crime typically celebrate their triumphs before the court machinery takes over, only to affirm by sentencing that which detectives have already brought out in the open. The courtroom, how-ever, is where legal thrillers make their distinctive generic mark. It is within the fixed framework of court proceedings that criminal cases are not only wrapped up but also, and more importantly, looked into, frequently to the effect of completely upsetting expectations of routine business.

In British crime fiction the bench was introduced by Gerald Bullett (1893–1958) and Cyril Hare, pseudonym of Arthur Alexander Gordon Clark (1900–1958).

Bullett was a very versatile writer practicing a great variety of literary genres. Working for the BBC during and continuing work in broadcasting after World War II, Bullett wrote regular fiction, crime fiction, children's fiction, and supernatural fiction and did translations. His poems were collected and published by the distin-guished English philologist E.M.W. Tillyard in 1959. Bullett's venture into legal fiction was with the aptly entitled *The Jury* in 1935. Belonging to the literary end of crime fiction with in-depth and sophisticatedly interlocking study of characters and their backgrounds, both of those centrally involved in the murder trial and of those on the jury, Bullett's description of the court procedure reads deliberately like an unedited transcription.

Hare drew on his background as a barrister for many of his nine novels and thirty-eight stories, which he started writing in the thirties. In 1950, he was appointed county court judge in Surrey after having done war-time service in vari-ous legal capacities. One of his most admired novels is *Tragedy at Law* from 1942, introducing barrister Francis Pettigrew, and, arguably, consolidating the legal thriller as a viable genre in England.

Perhaps the all-time best-known fictional English lawyer is Horace Rumpole, who, despite his getting on in years and his gaining of experience by force of his con-troversial views, his preference for seedy clients, and his lack of ambition, remains a junior counsel in his London firm of barristers. The creator of hen-pecked, plonk-swilling, literature-loving Rumpole, who applies his legal competence entirely within the short-story format, and who was so brilliantly TV-cast by Australian actor Leo McKern, was John Mortimer, himself a barrister noted for his freedom of speech cases and as a highly successful writer of novels and stage and TV drama.

Among recent additions to the English variety of the legal thriller are the novels of Frances Fyfield. She worked for the London Metropolitan Police (Scotland Yard) and as a public prosecutor in the employ of the British Crime Prosecution Service. Her work and private-life experiences found their way into her first crime novel, *A Question of Guilt* (1988), featuring Crown Prosecutor Helen West in problematic professional and amorous intercourse with Detective Superintendent Geoffrey Bailey. Fyfield has introduced the feminist agenda, already a stock element in the contemporary private-investigator and police-procedural whodunit, to the English legal profession in its parallel fictional world.

Fictional lawyers, seedy representatives of the profession more often than not, made their appearance in American pulp-fiction crime stories as part of the crime/law set-up but then most frequently as part of the backdrop, not upstage with the main action.

Erle Stanley Gardner, himself a member of the Californian legal profession, supplemented his meager income by writing for the pulp magazines and struck a rich vein when in 1933 he introduced Perry Mason as a very outgoing lawyer. He succeeded in alerting the reading public interested in crime stories to the drama of lawyers' offices and court rooms as being an eventful universe just as exciting as the mean streets stalked by private investigators.

Complementing the new development in the east, Eleazar Lipsky (1911–1993) focused on small-time criminals and their legal handlers in stories from the New York criminal underworld (*Kiss of Death,* 1948), based on his own experience as a Manhattan public prosecutor, whereas in Kentucky the father of pioneer feminist-whodunit writer Sue Grafton, Cornelius Grafton (1909–1982), undertook fictional forays into the legal side of criminal events in the South just before the war (*The Rat Began to Gnaw the Rope,* 1944).

Apart from Erle Stanley Gardner's courtroom dramas sprouting film and TV versions in the post-war period, and apart from the isolated appearances of court-room activities in Herman Wouk's *The Caine Mutiny* (1951), Ben Traver's *Anatomy of a Murder* (1958), and Harper Lee's *To Kill a Mockingbird* (1960), the legal thriller had to wait until the 1980s for its massive break-through.

No doubt the flooding of the literary market with legal thrillers in the 1980s was due to a close watch of the legal profession from outside as well as inside. With the economic boom the spotlight was on the legal profession as the brokers of the golden times. Coinciding with offering assistance to the fast-track economy, lawyers were also busy in the fields of civil and human rights, areas by then recognized as part of the legal business, although usually not very remunerative but good for publicity. Also, the current and highly profiled discussion of the death penalty involved attention on the American way of handling justice. All in all these factors put the legal profession right in the middle of the public gaze.

The practicing of law, being such a diverse field, attracted varied talents, among them lawyers also able to make up exciting stories from the corridors of the law firms and to put them over in compelling prose. It is a quite unique characteristic of the legal thriller, and not only in the United States, that its practitioners more often than not have a solid professional background in their chosen fictional field. Generally, writers of whodunits are professional writers, such as journalists, professional writers of fiction with a creative-writing or self-taught background, or academics in diverse fields, whereas very few writers of private-eye stories are private investigators or policemen who write police procedurals.

Among the most commercially successful types of genre fiction, the legal thriller has been constantly on the bestseller lists since the mid-1980s. Outstanding authors such as John Grisham, Scott Turow, and Brad Meltzer are certain to attract huge interest when they use the court room or the lawyers' offices not only as exciting settings for events where life and property are at stake but also, and certainly not to be ignored, as catalysts for casting critical glances at society at large. The breadth of the genre of the legal thriller in a perspective of issues adopted and positions taken is demonstrated by the gendered approach of such writers as Lia Matera, who presented her heroine Willa Jansson first in *Where Lawyers fear to Tread* in 1987. African American perspectives are provided by writers such as Jay Brandon, Christopher Darden, and Lee Gruenfeld. Issues of American multiculturalism, minority, and gender are not in themselves particularly suited for legal action but often appear as strong determinants when cases are taken to court. The legal thriller, like other varieties of the whodunit, has the capacity for reflecting and modeling the structure and substance of clashes and crises that the particular nature of American society presents.

Trends and Themes. The extent of the scope for investigative action on the part of legal personnel—lawyers in most cases, seldom judges and jurors—depends entirely on national characteristics of the court system. In European countries bordering on the Mediterranean and in Latin America, all relying on the tradition of Roman Law, the use of investigative judges gives such functionaries a chance to complement—or compete with—the police from a point early on in an investigative procedure. In Great Britain, and with it in many countries formerly part of her empire, the traditional system with brief-commissioned barristers acting on behalf of defendants/accused directly represented by solicitors and with barristers commissioned by the state on behalf of the Crown as prosecutors is being increasingly supplemented with a system of state-employed public prosecutors under the judiciary, such as is the case in Germany and Scandinavia. The legal system of the United States is characterized by an extended democratic or popular element reflected in the foregrounding of trials by jury, also in cases of civil litigation, and in both bench and prosecution at the local level being elective offices.

In a legal thriller, when the authorial sympathy is with the district attorney's (DA) office, the antagonist is often organized crime or points of weakness on the public

---

COURTROOM THRILLERS COME FROM THE UNITES STATES

The majority by far of contemporary legal thrillers, printed or screened, originate in the United States. Due no doubt to a mixture of a much more ingrained sense of law as society dynamic and the histrionic opportunities offered by jury trial, the drama of crime and its investigation has in large measure been taken into the courtroom. There can hardly be any doubt that the law—state and federal—is the glue that binds together the otherwise extremely heterogeneous nation. From the constitution and its interpretation by law panels over business law putting a brake on the potential running amok of private enterprise to the safeguarding of individuals, the law looms large in the American awareness, both public and private.

side. Here the law and the courtroom guarantee society's order against lawlessness. When the sympathy is with the defense, focus is often on the carelessness or the cynicism of the publicly employed officers of justice or on the willingness to sacrifice the individual accused of a crime for better statistics or re-election. But the genre is used as the platform for a great many different issues, all with a bearing on the law. Grisham, for instance, generally has a sharp eye for the greediness of the legal profession. Michael Crichton, in *Disclosure* (1994), deals with the issue of political correctness in terms of a case of sexual harassment. He demonstrates the potential damage of legislation well intentioned in its outset, but perhaps having uncalculated effects, as also showcased in the mainstream, but nonetheless legally concerned and focused, novels *Bonfire of the Vanities* (1987) by Tom Wolfe or *A Human Stain* (2000) by Philip Roth.

Contexts and Issues. Marlyn Robinson's opening of her short account of the history of legal thrillers points to the proceedings of the court room and the nature of narrative:

> "Whoever tells the best story, wins the case." To many Americans, this modern maxim embodies the pivotal role of the lawyer: control of the narrative. Whether drafting a contract or laying out evidence in a courtroom, the lawyer's ability to manipulate language determines the outcome of the client's case. Many would argue that the law's language, arcane procedures, rules and conventions are purposely made mysterious by its practitioners. What could be more natural than for lawyers and legal stories to have been instrumental in the creation of the mystery novel, and particularly, the subgenre legal thriller? (Robinson 1998)

By centering on courtroom procedures the legal thriller puts the emphasis of crime and its processing from the events of detection, which constitute whodunits relying on investigators, private or public, to the circumstances under which justice is meted out. It also shifts the perspective from the nonprofessional environment of investigators to the legal profession with its specialized personnel of judges and lawyers. Not of the least importance from a literary perspective, it replaces the action of pre-court investigation with rhetoric. But, in most cases, the plot of a legal thriller is pivoted on the sudden and surprising turn that parallels the investigator's breakthrough in the field.

Since the legal thriller relies on the dialectics of court procedure for its narrative progression, focus is naturally on the verbal presentation of cases, involving witnesses, evidence rendered verbally, and argumentation. The detection of crime is either finalized and has been put into reports, or, insofar as it is still going on, it has to pass into the court room via the counsel for the prosecution or defense. The courtroom and its conventions constitute the narrative bottleneck through which everything must pass.

Related structurally to the legal thriller is the police procedural. This subspecies of crime fiction is concerned only eventually with putting a case into the words of the report. The business is with the crime and all sorts of material evidence. But it shares with the legal thriller the dealing with crime in a publicly sanctioned institutionalized context and also the reliance on a collective effort within a pre-established paradigm of detection, which parallels the gradual unveiling and documentation of crime in the court room. The progression of detection in the police procedural, like the proceedings in court, lends patterns easily transformed into narrative structures with, admittedly, much more room for discourse maneuver in the police procedural, which, in turn, is less free than the private-eye subspecies, where the protagonist often makes a point of his acting with no strings attached whatsoever.

Another sibling of the legal thriller is the political thriller, in its manifestation of "muckraking" domestic politics critique rather than dealing with international political relations. This is a thematic, not a structural sharing, as the critique may be contained within the structural conventions of the legal thriller. Since the law is the common ground of American civic life, it is the natural field for presenting social problems made visible by the crises implied by lawsuits and criminal cases.

The narrative format and conventions of the legal thriller lend themselves readily to film and TV. Here known as courtroom drama, the intermedial dynamics of book-screen tie-in has been cultivated extensively, but many films and TV shows have also been based on scripts originally for the screen. Among extremely popular TV shows based on legal thrillers in book format the Perry Mason series stands out, whereas the intricate problems of a diversity of legal branches and specializations are presented in *L.A. Law* and *Law and Order*. The potential for integrating with the staple diets of soap opera and situation comedy are exploited in series such as *Ally McBeal* and *Judging Amy*. A counter-crossing infotainment phenomenon symptomatic of both the pervasiveness of the sense of the law and its reflection in the more or less fictionalizing formats of the media was *The People's Court* running from 1981 to 1993, featuring the retired judge Joseph A. Wapner. Dealing with real cases presented voluntarily by litigants before his fictional but nonetheless efficacious court, the syndicated TV series reveals, as Helle Porsdam observes, that the "subtext of *The People's Court* was a highly interesting discussion about the role of the legal system, moral values, and preferred behaviour in modern, pluralistic, and law-permeated America" (Porsdam 1999, 91).

Reception. The huge sales figures of legal thrillers tell their own story about the popularity among readers of the genre. The community standing of a writer such as John Grisham, with his committee work for Washington, also tells us a good deal about the public esteem enjoyed by an outstanding practitioner of the genre.

Verisimilitude and authenticity are mandatory in crime fiction, to a far greater extent than in the average realist piece of prose fiction. Even though elements may be spurious, great pains are taken by the author to persuade the reader of the real-world validity of such elements. Courtroom proceedings in themselves constitute drama and suspense, so there is no need to interfere with the plot progression. Staple devices for the creator of legal thrillers, when the action is taken inside the court, are the breaking down of the evidence presented by the opposition and the introduction of startling new evidence. Against that background it cannot surprise that critical interest has primarily been on the extent to which the genre can be said to simulate real court proceedings: in how far does this or that story reflect this or that real trial. Similarly, from the angle of the fiction, the closeness of the made-up train of events is often used to criticize current court principles and practices. In particular, writers of legal thrillers have been interested in the differences between the technicalities of the practice of law and its effects on the individual, whether guilty or not guilty. When capital punishment is involved, with the irreversibility of the sentence after having been carried out, the court with its many fine points of law and the reliance on the varied talents of its officers may sometimes find itself in the dock.

That there is an energetic and very varied interest in not only the legal thriller but also all possible combinations of law and literature in the media and culture generally

---

THE LAWYER IN POP CULTURE

The University of Texas's Tarlton Law Library in Austin, Texas, has an excellent popular collection and Web site, "The Law in Popular Culture Collection." http://tarlton.law. utexas.edu/lpop/index.html. It features lists of legal thrillers, links to old novels that are available online, access to the list of materials included in its library collection, lists of films and posters, quotations about lawyers, and links to other related legal topics.

---

is in ample evidence from the very comprehensive bibliography, including legal poetry, at http://tarlton.law.utexas.edu/lpop/etext/. A comprehensive list of publications on law and the legal thriller, compiled by Marlyn Robinson, may be found at http://tarlton.law.utexas.edu/lpop/lpopbib2.html.

Selected Authors. The following list, ordered chronologically by date of birth of authors, aims at pointing to some important pioneers of the legal thrillers and at demonstrating the scope of the genre. It is by no means meant as exhaustive but is suggestive. It can be supplemented by consulting the bibliographical material in the reference section. Erle Stanley Gardner (1889–1970) must be thought of as the writer who pioneered the American legal thriller and probably set the pattern for the genre worldwide. Self-educated in jurisprudence he passed the Californian Bar Exam in 1911 and started to practice law. To compensate for lack of work and the trivia of the legal business he began to contribute whodunits to pulp magazines. Under various pen names—A.A. Fair, Kyle Corning, Charles M. Green, Carleton Kendrake, Charles J. Kenny, Les Tillray, and Robert Parr—his output of stories was prodigious from the start. What put Gardner on the map was the series of more than eighty titles with the defense lawyer Perry Mason in the lead, which started in 1933 with *The Case of the Velvet Claws* and *The Case of the Sulky Girl.* The Perry Mason stories, resulting in hugely successful cinema films and a TV series, are based on legal action in and out of the courtroom, centering on murder and reported in dialogue with only spare, and then uninventive, description. Mason is regularly helped by his faithful secretary Della Street and cunning private investigator Paul Drake and is always hard up against various representatives from the DA's office. Retiring from law practice in 1933, Gardner retained a link with actual cases by his charitable initiative, "The Court of Last Resort," which looked into alleged miscarriages of justice.

Robert Traver is the pseudonym of John D. Voelker (1903–1991), a former judge of the Michigan Supreme Court. His *Anatomy of a Murder,* published in 1958, is a court room drama classic. Released in 1959 as a film by Otto Preminger with James Stewart in the lead, the novel is based on an actual crime in upper Michigan. The case seems straightforward, as Lieutenant Frederick Manion confesses to the deliberate killing of the man who raped his wife. Defense attorney Paul Biegler seems landed with the comparatively simple job of finding mitigating circumstances to partly exonerate the killer, whose crime was witnessed by several people. But as the case proceeds, there turns out to be more to it than meets the eye.

Robert Traver's legal thriller adheres to the pattern of balancing courtroom procedures with life outside the austere premises, but its high points occur before the jury. With the court technicalities in perfect order and the legal rhetoric in full flourish, the story unfolds against a background of harmonious, provincial America, as the opening paragraph testifies. Against this pastoral background the crime is a most unwelcome disturbance, but the judicial system is up to handling it.

Herman Wouk (1915–) in 1951 published a novel first and foremost addressing the trauma of the Second World War in terms of a moral dilemma: whether to follow the leader under all circumstances. *The Caine Mutiny* was not written as a legal thriller, but to all practical purposes Caine avails himself of the genre format. The first part dramatizes mutiny on board a naval ship in the thick of war. To the fellow officers the behavior of the captain during a crisis seems irresponsible and possibly explainable as determined by incapacitating stress, which to them justifies their relieving him of his duties by force. When the case subsequently is given over to the court martial, what seemed a natural decision under pressure gets enmeshed in considerations that involve legal niceties and court room histrionics.

The Caine Mutiny demonstrates with almost pedagogical clarity how what starts out as the processing (in the context of a court martial) of an allegedly criminal act soon entails deliberations to do with the rights and obligations of the individual. In this way Wouk's novel puts focus on core values in American society.

Nelle Harper Lee (1926–) made one of the most important literary contributions to the civil rights movement in her *To Kill a Mockingbird* (1960; filmed 1962). The novel deals with racial relations in the South during the Depression. The function of the court proceedings is to highlight the discrepancy between the ideals of American law and the realities of a society weighed down by history and prejudice. The court, though, is where all the unspoken is made to come out. Tragically, the ideal notion of equal justice for all is not allowed to triumph, but attention is called to the American legal machinery as a construction never any stronger than the people elected or appointed to serve it.

William J. Coughlin (1929–1992) applied his experience as a defense counsel and judge in Detroit to the writing of fiction, starting with *The Widow Wondered Why* in 1966. Coughlin is especially known for his series hero Charley Sloan in *Shadow of a Doubt* in 1991. Sloan is on the verge of total disintegration from alcohol when an apparently impossible case requires his dormant talents.

George Vincent Higgins (1939–1999) combined careers as journalist, writer, lawyer, and college academic at Boston College and Boston University. Having received his law degree from Boston College in 1967, he worked for the prosecution in Massachusetts, and later, in 1973, he went into private practice. He was counsel for Eldrige Cleaver. In his deliberately rough-hewn-style fiction, Higgins liked to see a case from the perspective of the accused, such as in *The Friends of Eddie Coyle* (1972), *The Digger's Game* (1973), and *Cogan's Trade* (1974). In his stories about the Boston criminal lawyer, Jerry Kennedy, he adopted the more conventional legal-thriller format: *Kennedy for the Defense* (1980), *Penance for Jerry Kennedy* (1985), and *Defending Billy Ryan* (1992).

Dudley W. Buffa's (1940–) working experience came from his teaching of sociology (*Union Power and American Democracy: The UAW and the Democratic Party, 1935–72*, University of Michigan Press, 1984) and practice of law in Oregon. His legal crusader is Portland-based defense attorney Joseph Antonelli, who first appeared in *The Defense* (1998). Further legal thrillers, all with series hero Joe Antonelli, are *The Prosecution* (1999), *The Legacy* (2003), *The Judgment* (2002), *Star Witness* (2004), *Breach of Trust* (2004), and *Trial by Fire* (2005).

Phillip Margolin (1944–) practiced criminal law in Portland, Oregon, and was defense counsel in a number of high-profiled murder cases, from 1972 to 1996, when he retired from the bar to become a full-time writer of legal thrillers. Having grown up in New York and been a Peace Corps volunteer in Liberia in West Africa, he received his degree from New York University School of Law. Margolin's *Proof Positive* (2006) is the fourth novel about defense lawyer Amanda Jaffe, who appeared earlier in *Wild Justice* (2000), *The Associate* (2002), and *Ties That Bind* (2003). Margolin's thrillers are not strictly court-room affairs, but tend to entangle those from the legal profession in often gorily dramatic off-bench goings on.

Steve (Steven Paul) Martini (1946–) introduced his series hero Paul Madriani in *Compelling Evidence* in 1992. At that time he had already tried his hand at fiction with *Simeon's Chamber* in 1987. Martini has a background as both a journalist specializing in legal affairs and, after having completed his law degree, an attorney in private law practice and in various legal capacities in the Californian judiciary. Martini is one of those writers of legal thrillers who make the most of the technicalities and fine points of law, something obviously appealing to the audience as his string of bestselling novel demonstrates.

Scott Turow (1949–) sets an ideal pattern for a writer of legal thrillers, combining an active career in law practice and legal-committee work with his writing, which is always quite close to the legal problems of the contemporary United States. A graduate from Amherst College and having been a lecturer at Stanford in creative writing, he entered Harvard Law School, from which he received his Juris Doctor degree in 1978. At that time he had written and published his first book, about first-year law students, *one L* (1977), and had gained employment with the U.S. Attorney's office in Chicago. With *Presumed Innocent* in 1987, Turow placed the legal thriller firmly on the literary map, following up with *The Burden of Proof* (1990), *Pleading Guilty* (1993), *The Laws of Our Fathers* (1996), *Personal Injuries* (1999), *Reversible Errors* (2002), and *Limitations* (2006). *Ordinary Heroes* (2005) takes us back to a mysterious World War II court martial case. *Ultimate Punishment: A Lawyer's Reflections on Dealing with the Death Penalty* (2003) has a bearing on Turow's committee work for the Governor of Illinois. As an active lawyer in a Chicago law firm, Turow conducts pro-bono cases at the same time as he is committed on behalf of the writing profession.

Michael A. Kahn (1952–) is a busy St. Louis-based practicing lawyer who also has found time to transfer his legal competence into a series of legal thrillers featuring attorney Rachel Gold. Introduced in *Grave Designs* in 1988, she quickly tired of the large law firm and set up her own office, the base of law practice that frequently takes her right into the centers of dramatic action.

Michael Nava (1954–) is a Californian lawyer with roots in the gay community, a circumstance he has turned into his legal-thriller series of seven novels centered on gay lawyer Henry Rios, who made his appearance in *The Little Death* in 1986 and bowed out in *Rag and Bone* in 2001. Sharing atmosphere with the hardboiled whodunit, Nava's Henry Rios stories constitute an increasingly complex character exploration of the protagonist set on taking upon himself the defense of underprivileged people from the edges of society.

Since his breakthrough with *The Firm* in 1991, John Grisham (1955–) has delivered a book with clockwork regularity once a year, most of them legal thrillers. *The Firm* was his second novel. The first one, *A Time to Kill,* was published in 1988. The story about an outraged father's retaliation against his daughter's rapists was written when Grisham, after graduating from University of Mississippi School of Law in 1981, was working in a general law practice, as well as between 1983 and 1990 also being a representative in the state legislature. John Grisham's legal thrillers have enjoyed massive popularity, in both book and movie formats. His distinction as a writer rests on a firm sense of community, which comes out in his thrillers in the form of lawyers caught between conscience and the more or less cynical demands of the law/politics complex combined with personal greed and other human vices. Memorable titles in his literary output, which also includes non-generic fiction (*A Painted House*, 2001) and non-fiction (*The Innocent Man*, 2006) about the South, where Grisham has homes in both Oxford, Mississippi, and Charlottesville, are *The Pelican Brief* (1992), *The Client* (1993), *The Street Lawyer* (1998), and *The Last Juror* (2004).

Christopher Darden (1956–) was with the DA's office during the trial of O.J. Simpson. He left in 1995 to teach law at various Californian universities until in 1999 he established his own firm of attorneys. With his *In Contempt* (co-written by Jess Walter) he in 1996 offered his version of the (in)famous trial of the football player. From 1999 he has collaborated with mystery writer and critic Dick Lochte in authentic fictional legal thrillers beginning with *The Trials of Nikki Hill* in 1999, and continuing with *L.A. Justice* (2001), *The Last Defense* (2002), and *Lawless* (2004).

Brad Meltzer (1970–) is a versatile writer with both TV and graphic-book experience. He graduated from Columbia Law School and his jurisprudence shows clearly in his first legal thrillers, *The Tenth Justice* (1998) and *Dead Even* (1999). From *The First Counsel* (2001) Meltzer has veered away from the beaten path of the legal thriller and moved into the field of the political thriller, a genre he is familiar with from his work for TV.

Alphabetical list of other American legal-thriller writers: David Baldacci, William Bernardt, Michael Bihl, Sallie Bissell, Bill Blum, Jay Brandon, Alafair Burke, David Compton, Rose Connors, Ellis Cose, Rankin Davis, Terry Devane, Dexter Dias, William Diehl, Richard Doolig, Linda A. Fairstein, Joseph Finder, J.F. Freedman, Pat Frieda, Philip Friedman, Lee Gruenfeld, Jeremiah Healy, Tami Hoag, Stephen Horn, Clifford Irving, Jonnie Jacobs, Michael Kahn, Lisa Kelly, John Hanff Korelitz, Carroll Lachnit, William Lashner, Stan Latreille, Mimi Latt, John T. Lescroant, Paul Levine, Harry Levy, Bonnie MacDougal, Christine McGuire, Malcolm MacPherson, John Martel, Penny Mickelburg, Peiri O'Shaughnessy, Barbara Parker, Richard Parris, Richard North Patterson, John A. Peak, Barry Reed, Nancy Taylor Rosenberg, Lisa Scottoline, Barry Siegel, Sheldon Siegel, Grif Stockley, Silliam G. Tapply, Robert K. Tannenbaum, Edwin Torres, Laura Var Wormer, Gallatin Warfield, Marianne Wesson, Carolyn Wheat, Kate Wilhelm, Sabin Willett.

Bibliography

Buffa, Dudley W. *The Defense*. New York: Henry Holt, 1997.
Crichton, Michael. *Disclosure*. New York: A.A. Knopf, 1994.
Coughlin, William J. *Shadow of a Doubt*. New York: St. Martin's, 1991.
Darden, Christopher, and Jess Walter. *In Contempt*. New York: ReganBooks, 1996.
Grisham, John. *A Time to Kill*. New York: Wynwood Press, 1989.
———. *The Firm*. New York: Doubleday, 1991.
The Lawyer's Story: Legal Narrative e-Texts. 2008. http://tarlton.law.utexas.edu/lpop/etext/.
Lee, Harper. *To Kill a Mockingbird*. Philadelphia, PA: Lippincott, 1960.
Margolin, Phillip. *Proof Positive*. New York: HarperCollins, 2006.
Martini, Steve. *Compelling Evidence*. New York: Putnam's, 1992.

Meltzer, Brad. *The Tenth Justice*. New York: Rob Weisbach Books, 1997.

Nava, Michael. *The Little Death*. Boston, MA: Alyson, 1986.

Porsdam, Helle. *Legally Speaking: Contemporary American Culture and the Law*. Amherst, MA: Massachusetts University Press, 1999.

Robinson, Marlyn. "Collins to Grisham: A Brief History of the Legal Thriller." *Legal Studies Forum*, 21, 1998, accessible at http://tarlton.law.utexas.edu/lpop/legstud.html.

Robinson, Marlyn. http://tarlton.law.utexas.edu/lpop/lpopbib2.html.

Traver, Robert. *Anatomy of a Murder*. New York: St. Martin's, 1958.

Turow, Scott. *Presumed Innocent*. New York: Farrar, Straus, and Giroux, 1987.

Further Reading

Ashley, Mike. *The Mammoth Encyclopedia of Modern Crime Fiction*. New York: Carroll and Graf, 2002; Bergman, Paul, and Michael Asimow. *Reel Justice: The Courtroom Goes to the Movies*. Kansas City: Andrews McMeel Publishing, 2006; Bounds, J. Dennis. *Perry Mason: The Authorship and Reproduction of a Popular Hero*. Westport, CT: Greenwood, 1996; DeAndrea, William L. *Encyclopedia Mysteriosa: A Comprehensive Guide to the Art of Detection in Print, Film, Radio, and Television*. New York: Prentice Hall, 1994; Herbert, Rosemary. *Whodunit? A Who's Who in Crime and Mystery Writing*. New York: Oxford University Press, 2003; Herbert, Rosemary, Catherine Aird, John M. Reilly, Susan Oleksiw (eds.), *The Oxford Companion to Crime and Mystery Writing*. Oxford and New York, 1999; Kahn, Michael A. *Grave Designs*. New York: Signet, 1992; Keating, H.R.F. ed. *Whodunit? A Guide to Crime, Suspense & Spy Fiction*. London: Windward, 1982; Lord, Graham. *John Mortimer: The Devil's Advocate*. London: Orion Books, 2005; Murphy, Bruce F. *The Encyclopedia of Murder and Mystery*. New York: Palgrave, 1999; Porsdam, Helle. *Legally Speaking: Contemporary American Culture and the Law*. Amherst, MA: Massachusetts University Press, 1999; Van Dover, J. Kenneth. *Murder in the Millions*. New York: Ungar, 1984.

LARS OLE SAUERBERG

LITERARY JOURNALISM

Definition. Literary journalism has been defined as journalism that reads like a novel or short story. In other words, it tells a story in the conventional sense—starting with a complication that intrigues the reader, proceeding through a series of developmental actions, and concluding with a resolution to the complication. Unlike **autobiography and memoir**, which emphasizes personal revelation, literary journalism emphasizes cultural revelation. The experiences and individuals described in literary journalism are or were real. Literary journalism is not fiction in the sense of the conventional fictional novel or short story. It is not "made up." Ultimately, literary journalism is part of a larger very fluid category of documentary prose, prose that claims to reflect or "document" our world of phenomenon.

The name for the genre begs whether the conventional journalistic essay, such as a newspaper editorial or a think-piece in, say, *The Atlantic Monthly*, could be considered a kind of "literary" journalism, given that in the history of nonfiction forms the essay has been considered to have literary merit. In principle, yes—curiously, however, "literary journalism," during the century in which the term has been used, has usually been applied to those true-life texts of journalism that read like a novel or short story. That may now be changing.

Contexts and Issues. Historically, the term "literary" has been applied to "journalism" either because such work was perceived as reflecting the kind of universal values associated with *belles-lettres* or because the techniques used, those of artful description, were perceived as "literary."

THE MANY NAMES FOR LITERARY JOURNALISM

The genre has had many names. In the 1960s it was called *new journalism,* and in the case of Hunter S. Thompson's work, the subset was *gonzo journalism.* It is classified as *reportage literature* by the Library of Congress, although the latter is rarely used in the United States beyond the Library. It has also been characterized as the *nonfiction novel* and *literary nonfiction,* and more recently as *nonfiction narrative, narrative journalism,* and *narrative serial* in newspapers. Sometimes it has been called *creative nonfiction,* although this last tends to take in a broader range of belletristic nonfiction prose such as memoir and the personal essay. In Europe literary journalism is often called *literary reportage* and has a long tradition there. Today it continues to be known in the United States most commonly as *literary journalism.*

An alternative that has arisen in recent years is "narrative journalism." Some authors prefer that term because they are uncomfortable and consider it presumptuous to characterize their work as "literary." But "narrative journalism" poses problems of its own because it remains unclear if it is the same as literary journalism or whether it is a broader category of journalism (similarly with the aim of cultural revelation written fundamentally in a narrative mode) of which literary journalism is part. If it is a broader category, it can include more extended expository or argumentative discussion of the kind found in sophisticated feature writing (such as in *The Atlantic Monthly*), or it can include more narrative summary combined with analysis of the kind found in history writing. Although literary journalism is also "narrative" in the conventional sense of being a representation of an event or sequence of events, what has distinguished it in the past from such related forms is that it is also fundamentally and broadly descriptive in the attempt to portray people's lives, the descriptive details framed by what Tom Wolfe, one of the eminent literary journalists of the 1960s, described as "scene-by-scene construction" (Wolfe 1973, 31–32). Thus, it is defined primarily by means of two modalities, narrative and descriptive, and for that reason has been characterized in the more rarefied air of academic research as a narra-descriptive journalism in order to differentiate it from a broader category of narrative journalism.

Given that literary journalism is composed primarily of narrative and descriptive modes, this does not mean that the exposition or narrative summary are excluded. Rather, the emphasis in literary journalism is on narrative and descriptive modes synthesized "scene by scene," with the expository and persuasive modes, along with narrative summary, playing tangential and supporting roles, if any.

Contemporary writers of narrative journalism may indulge solely in literary journalism or move among the different modalities according to what they perceive as appropriate to their needs.

Another issue that arises in distinguishing the boundaries of literary journalism, boundaries that are, to be sure, not hard and fast, is how literary journalism differs from and is similar to such forms as **travel writing, true crime literature,** and sports journalism that read like a novel or short story, among some of the more prominently delineated forms defined by their subject matter. What separates literary journalism from, say, travel writing is not that each is a discrete category of journalism, but rather that each is a different genre determined by the critical perspective brought to bear on them. Travel writing is a topical genre. Literary journalism is a modal genre, as determined by its dominant narrative and descriptive modalities.

There is no reason why travel writing, for example, cannot be viewed as both a modal genre and as a topical genre. Thus they are not mutually exclusive. At the same time, not all travel writing need be literary journalism—or a journalism that emphasizes narra-descriptive modalities. That said there may be good reason for setting travel writing aside as a separate grouping if only because in literary history the sheer volume of travel writing could overwhelm considerations of literary journalism. That is the approach taken here.

History

Emergence of modern literary journalism. Literary journalism has a much longer history than generally acknowledged. The emergence of literary journalism in the United States as a modern genre can be traced to after the American Civil War. Three major periods have been identified for when it thrived—the 1890s, the 1930s, and the 1960s and early 1970s. However, it never really disappeared after each of the periods, and after the 1970s it has evolved increasingly into a mainstream literary and journalistic genre. It very much has an ongoing presence today and continues to be practiced for much the same reasons as it was after the Civil War.

There are at least two related reasons for why a modern literary journalism emerged when it did. First, the post–Civil War period was a time of tremendous social and economic change and turmoil in the United States, when different sectors of society found themselves at odds with each other, laborers and capitalists serving as one example, native born and newly arrived immigrants serving as another. Second, this was the period when the concept of "objective" journalism began to emerge (or what at the time was called "factual" journalism). In what has proved a cultural irony, the highly distilled, abstract style of such journalism tended to alienate readers from what they most wanted to comprehend: the economic and social turmoil around them, or, in sum, the distress of society.

In objective journalism, the personal voice of the reporter is viewed as a liability, one that interferes with presenting the news as "factually" or as "objectively" as possible. What practitioners of literary journalism understood then is that the personal voice is more honest in its relationship to the reader, based on the premise that there can be no absolute "objectivity." As we well understand today, all discourse reflects to some degree the inherent personal taste, views, values, mores, and biases of a reporter—in short, what we often call "subjectivity" as opposed to objectivity. For example, the selection of the concrete descriptive details in the scene-by-scene construction by what has been characterized as the literary journalist's "shaping consciousness" (Weber 1974, 20) appeals to what all of us at some level can concretely comprehend with our different senses of sight, touch, hearing, smell, and taste. To read and perceive with one's senses a scene described in a piece of literary journalism is to vicariously "feel" it. Herein lies an important virtue of the form—one lacking in the abstraction of "objective" journalism—a virtue realized by means of a reporter's individual (and subjective) choices in the creation of the text.

The conditions that gave rise to literary journalism's modern manifestation during the post–Civil War period are still very much with us today: As long as there is cultural distress and alienation such journalism remains a viable discourse for trying to understand those who are different from us. As Lincoln Steffens, an editor and advocate of the genre during the 1890s, noted, the purpose of literary journalism is "to get the news so completely and to report it so humanly that the reader will see himself in the other fellow's place"—even if that place is occupied by a murderer awaiting execution (Steffens 1931, 317). Literary journalism, then, requires the subjectivity of a reporter to try to empathically understand the subjectivities of *others,* or what is frequently called the cultural "Other."

To be sure, practitioners of the form have been very much a minority in the journalism establishment, especially in the early years. Among some of those early literary journalists, Lafcadio Hearn stands out as an exemplar who foresaw the promise of the form in the 1870s. Shortly after he arrived in the United States from Ireland, he embarked on a remarkable career as a newspaper reporter. He brought to his work a Chekhovian realism and poignancy as reflected in such stories as "Dolly" and "A Child of the Levee." In Cincinnati, one city where he worked as a reporter, his most common subject was the African American community, a marginalized group largely ignored by polite, genteel white Cincinnatians and, by extension, white Americans in general. Hearn's focus, then, was on the cultural "Other," and the attempt to understand the cultural Other remains a hallmark of literary journalism to this day.

The 1890s remain the first significant period when narrative literary journalism thrived in the United States, and among some of its more noteworthy practitioners we find Hutchins Hapgood, Richard Harding Davis, Ambrose Bierce, George Ade, Nelly Bly, Abraham Cahan, Theodore Dreiser, and Stephen Crane. Bierce, Dreiser, Twain, Cahan, and Crane remain better known as literary fictionists. Others, such as Davis and Bly, remained active as literary journalists well into the twentieth century.

Shortly after the turn of the century, in 1907, we see the as yet earliest instance of the term "literary journalist" applied as a name for writers of this kind of work. This came after a considerable debate in journals of literature and ideas on whether journalism could be literature.

A lull in the practice of narrative literary journalism had set in by the First World War and lasted through the 1920s. One reason is that this was a period when the concept of "objective" journalism was theorized and ascendant. Nonetheless, the form never entirely disappeared, and Ernest Hemingway was one of its practitioners during this period.

By the 1930s literary journalism thrived again for similar reasons as it had in the 1890s. This was the period of the Great Depression and once again Americans were trying to understand the social and economic dislocation around them. Not only was objective journalism not suited for understanding the subjectivities of Americans caught up in the adversity of the times, but the newspaper, the foremost venue for objective journalism, largely ignored the human or empathic element except in the highly personal writing of newspaper columnists. Instead, it fell mostly to magazines, especially Progressive magazines such as *The New Republic* and *New Masses,* to try to examine the cultural upheaval through literary journalism. Often such writing, because it strongly invoked the voice of the writer and thus the feelings of the writer, reflected leftist political sympathies. Two writers who fall into this group are Edmund Wilson and Erskine Caldwell. Yet there were still others who tried to avoid outright political posturing in their writing even as they maintained their personal voice as a means for engaging readers' empathy. These include Sherwood Anderson (better known as a short story writer), Joseph Mitchell at the *New Yorker,* Martha Gellhorn, and, again, Ernest Hemingway (by this point also an established novelist and short story writer).

Mitchell's *New Yorker*, where he worked for more than 30 years, has been a mainstay of the genre since shortly after the publication's founding by Harold Ross in 1925. Moreover, the magazine eschewed the Progressive and leftist sympathies of the other publications noted previously.

Although the end of the Great Depression would result in less literary journalism, the 1940s are important because of what are considered two seminal works of modern American literary journalism, James Agee's *Let Us Now Praise Famous Men*, published in 1941, and John Hersey's *Hiroshima*, published in 1946. What separates them, of course, is a World War. But what they have in common is that they were both major influences on the third period of literary journalism during the 1960s and early 1970s, or what was called the "new" journalism. One measure of how compelling *Hiroshima* has proved in the American cultural experience is that in 1999 a distinguished panel of 36 journalists and academics at New York University ranked it as the most important work of American journalism in the twentieth century.

The 1950s mark another lull in the fortunes of narrative literary journalism, although, as in the 1920s, it never entirely disappeared and *The New Yorker* and *Esquire* magazines were two of its most important venues at this time. Among the form's practitioners during this period were Lillian Ross, A.J. Liebling, Mary McCarthy, Meyer Berger, and, again, Joseph Mitchell.

The "New" Journalism. The 1960s usher in the third most important period of the form since it emerged after the Civil War, the century in between serving then as a kind of incubation period for the genre's maturation. As perhaps the most memorable period, it continues to cast a long shadow over contemporary practice, which to some extent is still judged according to the "new" journalism.

The genre would be called the "new" journalism because its earlier history was largely forgotten, and to many it did indeed seem new. The origin of the expression "new" journalist as applied to this period is not entirely clear. It has been attributed to Pete Hamill, a sometime "new" journalist and part of the movement, who attempted in the mid-1960s to characterize the journalistic trend. Once again, it appeared at a time of considerable social turmoil in the United States, although not necessarily economic as was true of the earlier periods. This was the time of the Cold War, fear of nuclear annihilation, political assassinations, racial strife, increased illicit drug use, changing sexual mores, and the Vietnam War and the mass protests it prompted. Once again "objective" journalism proved inadequate for trying to fathom the complexity of—and the humanity caught up in—those events. Gay Talese, one of the first of the "new" journalists and sometimes considered its godfather, detected this when he observed, "The New Journalism, though often reading like fiction, is not fiction. It is, or should be, as reliable as the most reliable reportage although it seeks a larger truth than is possible through the mere compilation of verifiable facts" (Talese [1970] 1993, xii). Thus he took aim at the inadequacies of a strictly "factual" journalism. So did Michael Herr, whose *Dispatches* is a collection of articles he wrote on the Vietnam War. He observed of that war, "The press got all the facts (more or less): it got too many of them. But it never found a way to report meaningfully about death, which of course was really what it was all about" (Herr 1991, 214–15).

Besides Talese and Herr, some of the major writers of literary journalism during this period were Tom Wolfe, Truman Capote, Hunter S. Thompson, Joan Didion, Norman Mailer, John McPhee, Richard Rhodes, Joe Eszterhas, and Sara Davidson.

Unlike the 1930s, however, much of their work appeared in mainstream magazines and increasingly in book form, reflecting the genre's greater cultural acceptance. Magazines included, among others, the *New Yorker* and *Esquire* again, the *Village Voice, Rolling Stone, New York, Playboy,* and the *Saturday Evening Post.*

Among watershed book-length efforts are Truman Capote's *In Cold Blood* (1966) and Tom Wolfe's *The Electric Acid Kool-Aid Test* (1968). What we detect in them are challenges to societal assumptions in order to understand the cultural "other." Capote engaged in an assault on the American Dream by attempting to empathetically understand the psychologies of two killers who murdered the archetypal white American family. The book appeared to considerable critical acclaim, in part because Capote claimed he had invented a new genre, the "nonfiction novel." As we understand now, he did not, but at the time it did seem new because of the lack of recognition of the genre earlier in the century. Although *In Cold Blood* is still considered a classic, it is a flawed one because evidence has emerged that some scenes in the book were invented. In other words, they are fiction. Still, the volume is considered fundamentally true and factual in the sense that the characters and experiences portrayed once existed.

Wolfe's *Electric Acid Kool-Aid Test* takes as its theme the counterculture of the 1960s. He accompanies the novelist Ken Kesey and a group of friends called the Merry Pranksters on a journey across the country in an old school bus painted colorfully in psychedelic designs. Often, they are smoking marijuana and tripping on LSD and other hallucinogenic drugs on their journey. To staid, white middle-class Americans, the book served as a similar challenge to the shibboleth of the American Dream.

Wolfe has been characterized as the journalist most completely identified with the "new" journalism. In part this is because he created a critical furor with his linguistic pyrotechnics that seemed to pose a taunt to advocates of standard English usage, over-using, for example, expressive punctuation and onomatopoeia, such as the vocal imitation of a speeding car: "Ggghhzzzzzzzhhhhhhggggggzzzzzzzeeeeong!" (Wolfe 1965, 129) The result is baroque in its exaggeration. What also attracted attention to Wolfe was his eye for phenomena that reflected and marked the tensions, ironies, and existence of subcultures, characteristics described as "status details" or "symbolic details." These could include an individual's gestures, as well as styles of furniture and clothing, and were often used for satiric effect. In 1973 Wolfe also published *The New Journalism,* an anthology of examples from the period. Aside from the examples, the work is perhaps more important because it included an essay of the same name, "The New Journalism," by Wolfe that became a kind of coda for the genre for many of the aspiring literary journalists of the period.

Thompson deserves to be singled out because he was a practitioner of what came to be called "gonzo" journalism, or a journalism that consistently challenged taken-for-granted assumptions about what constitutes "reality" by engaging in outrage. He did Wolfe one better because his journalism often was drug induced and he irreverently challenged many sacred American cultural themes, thus infuriating the cultural status quo. One example is Thompson's *Fear and Loathing in Las Vegas,* which appeared in 1971. The term "gonzo" was coined by journalist Bill Cardoso in 1970, who characterized Thompson's notorious and over-the-top journalism as "pure gonzo" (Weingarten 2006, 235).

After the "New" Journalism. By the mid-1970s the "new" journalism no longer seemed so new and was entering a more stable middle age. It was also less noticed, perhaps, and as a result it would be easy to conclude that it had waned as it had in the 1920s and 1950s. This would be a mistake, however, and an understandable one because what had changed was that much of the social turmoil subsided after the end of the Vietnam War. What was gone by the late 1970s was the edge that whetted the social appetite for trying to better understand cultural "others" in a turbulent world.

Another reason why it appeared to wane is that until very recently literary journalism remained largely unstudied by the academy: It was not considered politically correct either as journalism or literature. Except for a small group of pioneering scholars of the genre located in the journalism, literature, and American studies disciplines, it was largely ignored because of the difficulty of negotiating the divides between those disciplines, particularly between journalism and English.

Nonetheless, literary journalism continued to be practiced and the "new" journalism served as an important inspiration for younger generations of writers. Among them was Jon Franklin. Franklin is notable because he was one of the few newspaper journalists to see the potential of publishing the form in the daily report. In 1979, writing for the Baltimore *Evening Sun,* he won a Pulitzer Prize for his series "Frightening Journey Through the Tunnels of the Brain," an account of a risky brain operation in which Franklin witnesses the patient dying on the operating table. Eventually, and prompted in part by his public advocacy, daily newspapers would, by the 1990s, take an increasing interest in publishing a narra-descriptive journalism, a subject to be explored later.

Another who saw the potential of literary journalism in newspapers is Barry Newman, who joined *The Wall Street Journal* in the 1970s and carved out a niche for himself as a narrativist who had to limit his stories to no more than 2,000 words. As a roving foreign correspondent for the *Journal,* he wrote on subjects as varied as maggot farmers and bullfighters.

Although the seeds had been planted, then, for newspapers to publish more such work, literary journalists continued to publish books as well as articles in magazines. Tracy Kidder, who is still publishing today, first achieved considerable national recognition when he won the Pulitzer Prize for his book, *The Soul of a New Machine.* Published in 1981, his is an account of engineers engaged in inventing a new computer. Since then Kidder has published a number of critically acclaimed books of literary journalism, including *House* (1985), *Among Schoolchildren* (1989), *Old Friends* (1993), and *Home Town* (1999). To demonstrate the eclectic nature of his work, they are, briefly, and in the same order, accounts of building a house, the daily lives of elementary school children in the classroom, life in a nursing home, and life in a small town. As much of Kidder's work demonstrates, the ordinary and prosaic can be just as promising as topics for literary journalism as the extraordinary and unusual.

Other notable literary journalists during this period are Mark Kramer, Mark Singer, Jane Kramer, Richard West, Ron Rosenbaum, Ted Conover, and Bill Barich.

Trends and Themes. The work of the current generation has been characterized as "the new new journalism" from a book of the same name by Robert Boynton who suggests that such writing differs today from the earlier "new" journalism because the contemporary "movement's achievements are more reportorial than literary. . . . The days in which nonfiction writers test the limits of language and form have largely passed" (Boynton 2005, vii). The emphasis, then, is more on "how" such practitioners get the story, not on linguistic style as exemplified by such "new" journalists as Wolfe, Didion, and Thompson.

But if the current generation is less inclined to literary flourish, one issue that has emerged is how "literary" such works are and the corollary of how memorable they will prove to be. A criticism that has been raised about such work is that it tends to be more ethnographic, sociological, or anthropological than such work in the past, which is not entirely surprising given literary journalism's intent is to examine the cultural "other," no matter how problematic that may prove as an act of linguistic representation. That social scientific ambition is, moreover, not surprising when one considers that in the formative years of a "factual" journalism (the 1890s), and in the formative years of "objective" journalism (the 1920s), the journalism community viewed itself as engaged in a scientific profession. That legacy still influences journalism today, including literary journalism.

One example of a work perceived as having social scientific attributes is Conover's *Newjack*. Conover is described as possessing "a sociologist's eye for detail" by the publisher on the back of the book's dust jacket. Similarly, a *Newsweek* reviewer characterized LeBlanc's 2003 *Random Family* as "literary anthropology" (Agovino 2003, 68). Elsewhere the book has been characterized as "ethnographic" (Hartsock 2004, 193–194). By comparing their works to the social sciences, in other words investing them with the scientific ambition to eliminate ambiguity in meaning, the issue remains as to what may be lost in terms of literary qualities, given that literature is about the possibilities of meaning and not just about locking up meaning with the kind of unambiguous scientific precision associated with, say, a sociological text. To utilize one common definition of the literary, what about such work will "tease us out of thought"—this because of a deliberate linguistic ambiguity or resonance to suggest possibilities of meaning, much as one would find, say, in Shakespeare. Only time will tell if such recent works are as memorable as those of the period of the "new"journalism, when there was considerably more experimentation with language.

Another consequence has been to further blur the already blurred boundaries between literary journalism in which the narrative and descriptive modalities predominate, on the one hand, and, on the other, the broader "narrative journalism" discussed earlier. That's because many of the authors characterized as "new new" journalists, even as the moniker betrays they are part of the "new" journalism legacy, also engage in writing that is more expository at the expense of dominating "narra-descriptive" modalities. In other words, the writing tends to engage more in narrative summary and explication to make for a kind of "journalism-history," or it simply tends to be more expository in the tradition of conventional feature writing.

An example is Lawrence Wright's 2006 *The Looming Tower: Al-Qaeda and the Road to 9/11*. It is largely a summary narrative on the rise of Islamic terrorism and is integrated with essaylike analysis, much like a conventional history. Except for the chapter on the Boeing 747s crashing into the World Trade Center, the book for the most part lacks the sustained scene-by-scene descriptive construction to which Wolfe alluded. Such a "journalism-history" does not attempt to demarcate where journalism leaves off and history begins given the inherently problematic and ambiguous nature of such boundaries as reflected in the old adage that "journalism is the first draft of history."

The other variation can be found in the sophisticated and complex feature writing often found in *The New Yorker* or *The Atlantic Monthly* that may make a more limited use of the descriptive techniques associated with literary journalism. An example is Ron Rosenbaum's *Explaining Hitler: The Search for the Origins of His Evil* (1998). Occasionally, the book engages in the kind of scenic description associated with literary journalism, but it is not sustained, which is the hallmark of literary journalism at least as the term has been applied in the past. Instead, the expository mode predominates. Similarly, conventional feature writing is written largely in an expository mode framed by narrative elements. Often, it drafts brief descriptive sketches (presented sequentially in narrative form) to illustrate the expository point. Description then becomes only a handmaiden in support of exposition, the latter of which remains the dominant mode for such a discourse.

But this is why the boundaries of literary journalism are not fixed and may indeed be shifting. Either they are enlarging to include such variations, or the narrative "journalism-histories" and the narrative-expository emphasis in complex and sophisticated feature writing are close siblings to a narra-descriptive literary journalism within a larger "narrative journalism." Only time and cultural usage will tell.

But even if it continues to be viewed as a form of journalism that reads like a novel or short story, literary journalism is a practice that is likely to endure for the foreseeable future. This is because the genre tells a story in the conventional sense—starting with a complication that intrigues the reader, proceeding through a series of developmental actions, and concluding with a resolution to the complication (although not necessarily a happy ending). Thus literary journalism helps us to understand, if only vicariously, how others live, think, and die in the real world of phenomenon, this in a way that "objective" journalism cannot. Whether it is in times of cultural turmoil or cultural peace, there will always be a need to better understand the nature of those who are different from us.

Selected Authors

Magazines and Books. The contemporary period of literary journalism finds practitioners continuing to ply their art in books and magazines. One signal event in the improving fortunes of literary journalism is that the venerable *Atlantic Monthly* magazine announced in 2005 that it would cease to publish fiction (an area in which it had excelled for more than 150 years) on a regular basis. In its place, it promised to publish more "long-form narrative reporting," its term for a broad narrative journalism that includes literary journalism (Wyatt 2005). Today *The Atlantic Monthly* is one of the standard bearers among magazines to publish literary journalism,

In addition to *The Atlantic Monthly,* other magazines that publish such writing include the perennial *New Yorker, Outside,* and *GQ.* Writers for magazines often expand their short-form literary journalism into books. For example, Susan Orlean's *The Orchid Thief* (1998), an account of an obsessed lover (and thief) of rare orchids in Florida, first appeared as an article in the *New Yorker.* Similarly, Jon Krakauer's *Into the Wild* (1996) and *Into Thin Air* (1997) initially appeared as articles in the magazine *Outside.* The first is about a young man who starves to death when his efforts to live in the wilderness of Alaska go awry. The second is about an expedition to climb Mt. Everest that results in death during a horrific snow storm on the slopes.

But another development has also emerged. As often as not, authors now write books from the outset and not initially magazine pieces. As the books near completion they may then be excerpted in magazines. For example, Adrian Nicole LeBlanc is the author of *Random Family* (2003), which is an account of uneducated and unemployed Latinas and Latinos attempting to survive in New York City's barrios. The book was excerpted in *The New Yorker* and *The New York Times Magazine.* Still another work conceived first as a book and not as a magazine article is Jonathan Harr's *A Civil Action* (1995), an account of a lawsuit against chemical companies who were sued on civil charges that their toxic wastes poisoned children in the community of Woburn, Massachusetts.

Among other contemporary exemplars of the form is Alex Kotlowitz, the author of *There Are No Children Here* (1991), which is an account of two African American brothers growing up—and surviving—in the housing projects of Chicago. He followed this in 1998 with *The Other Side of the River,* an account of two neighboring Michigan towns divided by a river, the death of a black teenager, and how long-held misperceptions and attitudes undermine race relations. Another author is Lawrence Weschler, who has published several collections of magazine pieces, as well as *Mr. Wilson's Cabinet of Wonder* (1995), which is an account of scientific oddities at the storefront "Museum of Jurassic Oddities" in Los Angeles.

Since the advent of 2000 notable examples of literary journalism—or a "narra-descriptive" journalism—include the following publications.

Ted Conover published *Newjack: Guarding Sing Sing* in 2000. Conover, who had already established his credentials as a literary journalist with *Rolling Nowhere: a Young Man's Adventures Riding the Rails with America's Hoboes* (1984) and *Coyotes: A Journey Through the World of America's Illegal Aliens* (1989), demonstrates the extent to which literary journalists will immerse themselves in their material in order to write authoritatively about it. In *Newjack* he takes a job as a prison guard at the infamous maximum-security Sing Sing prison on the banks of the Hudson River above New York City in order to provide a cultural portrait about life on the inside, both for prisoners and their guards.

In 2001 Michael Lewis published *Next: The Future Just Happened,* which is an account of how the Internet has challenged the hierarchical world of top-down knowledge. He tells his narrative with extensively developed sketches of individuals, such as 15-year-old Jonathan Lebed, who figured out how to hack into the stock markets online to engage in stock fraud. Although the volume is largely composed of such descriptive sketches, it also engages in some extended expository examinations of the issue, illustrating just how fragile the boundaries are between literary journalism and related narrative journalistic forms. Since *Next,* Lewis, who usually writes about the financial world and sports, published *Moneyball: The Art of Winnng an Unfair Game* (2003), which recounts how the Oakland Athletics defy the conventional business wisdom by winning games without paying astronomical star-athlete salaries.

Richard Preston first gained national fame with *The Hot Zone,* published in 1994. The book, developed from one of his *New Yorker* articles, recounts an outbreak of the Ebola virus among monkeys in a laboratory in Reston, Virginia, and how it was contained from becoming an infectious disease crisis. He has continued to write about scientific topics, and in 2002 published *The Demon in the Freezer,* an account focusing on smallpox. Despite official pronouncements that smallpox had been eradicated in 1979, Preston relates how frozen specimens in a laboratory in Siberia remain unaccounted for and could be used as a weapon against humans who no longer receive smallpox vaccinations.

Jane Kramer's *Lone Patriot: The Short Career of an American Militiaman* (2002) recounts the life of a white supremacist who lives in the Pacific Northwest. Kramer is remarkable because her publication credits go back to the "new" journalism of the 1960s. In 1963 she published her first book, a collection of her stories from the *Village Voice* called *Off Washington Square: A Reporter Looks at Greenwich Village.* Thus she has been contributing to the genre for half a century.

Still other examples include works by Richard Ben Cramer, William Langewiesche, Daniel Bergner, and, once again, Kidder and Kotlowitz. Cramer published *Joe Dimaggio: The Hero's Life* in 2000. Aside from being an account of the baseball star written largely in the form of narra-descriptive journalism, it also illustrates once again how documentary genres can overlap. In this case the account is also an example of two topical genres, sports journalism and **biography**, thus serving as a cautionary lesson about trying to insist too strongly that documentary genres can be clearly delineated.

Langewiesche is the author of, among other books, *American Ground: Unbuilding the World Trade Center* (2002), an account, as the title suggests, of those who responded to the attack on and collapse of the World Trade Center in New York on September 11, 2001, and then had the grisly task of removing the remains. In 2003, Bergner published *In the Land of Magic Soldiers,* which recounts the savagery of civil war in the West African country of Sierra Leone. Also in 2003, Kidder published *Mountains Beyond Mountains,* an account of an American doctor's efforts to provide medical care for AIDS patients in Haiti. Meanwhile, Kotlowitz published *Never a City So Real* (2004), a personal account, or series of accounts, of everyday ordinary people who are representative of the Chicago not normally seen by outsiders.

As these examples illustrate, the subject matter is eclectic, and indeed covers the range of human experience.

Newspapers. Perhaps the most remarkable contemporary development in the area of literary journalism has been that since the 1990s daily newspapers have become more receptive to publication of the form. Except in individual newspaper columns, narrative literary journalism appears to have been largely (although not entirely) absent from newspapers through the course of much of the twentieth century. One notable exception was the old New York *Herald-Tribune,* which had encouraged the form in the 1920s and 1930s, and again in the 1960s. Also, its Sunday magazine, *New York* (not to be confused with the *New Yorker*) survived the newspaper's bankruptcy and demise in 1967 to become a showplace in its own right for the form. But as noted, it was in the 1970s that Barry Newman and Jon Franklin began publishing literary journalism in their respective newspapers. Thus, in the aftermath of the "new" journalism, some editors and reporters at newspapers sensed the possibilities of the form for the daily report.

This has important consequences for where we are today because the most dramatic growth for this kind of "story" journalism appears to be in newspapers. Just how much will stand the test of time as "literary" remains to be seen. But certainly what we can detect are ambitious efforts to write journalism that are narrative and descriptive in their modalities.

The reasons for why newspapers are turning to this form are not difficult to understand. Increasingly since the 1920s, newspapers have had to share the media market with newer forms of media, starting with cinema, radio, and recorded music and then broadcast television, cable TV, and most recently the Worldwide Web. This has meant a decreasing portion of media market for newspapers. When one considers the inherently alienating nature of "objective" news reporting, one can see the attraction of a more "reader-friendly" literary journalism that elicits empathy from the reader and thus engages the reader on a more personal level.

Moreover, a small group of practicing journalists has taken the lead in promoting publication of narrative literary journalism in newspapers. Perhaps most notable are Franklin; Managing Editor Jack Hart of the Portland *Oregonian*; Roy Peter Clark of the Poynter Institute; The Associated Press's features editor, Bruce DeSilva; and Mark Kramer of the Nieman Foundation at Harvard University.

Aside from winning a Pulitzer Prize in 1979 for his literary journalism, Franklin founded Writer-L in the 1990s, which is an online paid chat group that discusses literary journalism and has included Pulitzer Prize winners among its participants. Moreover, he is the author of *Writing for Story: Craft Secrets of Dramatic Nonfiction by a Two-Time Pulitzer Prize Winner*, which has been characterized as "iconic" and a "bible" for aspiring narrative literary journalists (Hartsock 2007).

Hart of the *Oregonian* has nurtured his reporters to win Pulitzer Prizes for their narratives and since the 1990s has been one of the most vocal advocates of such work, writing frequently in trade journals about how newspapers could benefit from the genre, which he prefers to call simply "narrative journalism." Clark, vice president of the Poynter Institute in St. Petersburg, Florida, which is dedicated to providing ongoing professional education to journalists, published a manifesto in *The Quill*, the journal of the Society of Professional Journalists, in the mid-1990s calling for more such writing in newspapers, and he continues to actively promote the genre to this day. DeSilva was hired by The Associated Press for the express purpose of encouraging this kind of writing at the wire service. Finally, Mark Kramer, whose publication history is in magazines and books, established the annual Narrative Conference at the Nieman Foundation for Journalism at Harvard. The conference has provided an important venue attended largely by newspaper reporters and editors to learn how to write narrative journalism, again, his preferred usage for the form.

The results are that since the millennium newspapers around the country have been publishing more "story" journalism on a scale not seen since the beginning of the twentieth century. This is not to suggest that all newspapers are doing so. But that some are is still remarkable considering how absent traditional narrative storytelling had been from newspapers. A sampling of papers includes the *St. Petersburg (Florida) Times*, the Norfolk *Virginian-Pilot*, the Pittsburgh *Post-Gazette*, The Boston *Globe*, the Asheville *Times-Citizen*, the Raleigh *News and Observer*, the Des Moines *Register*, the Baltimore *Sun*, the Arkansas *Democrat-Gazette*, and the *Seattle Times*.

To be sure, newspapers with national reputations also publish examples of narrative literary journalism, namely, *The New York Times*, the *Washington Post*, and the *Los Angeles Times*. With their extensive resources, this is perhaps to be expected. But that newspapers without national readerships give reporters the time and other resources to write narratives reflects the value increasingly placed on publication of the form.

One of the most notable examples was Mark Bowden's *Black Hawk Down*. Bowden initially wrote it as a series that was published in 1997 in the *Philadelphia Inquirer*, where he was a reporter. Eventually it was expanded into a book as well as made into a feature-length movie.

Among other exemplars in newspapers can be included Tom Hallman Jr., of the Portland *Oregonian*. His series, "The Boy Behind the Mask," published in 2000, won the Pulitzer Prize. The series is about a boy who suffers from a disfiguring facial abnormality and requires a risky operation. Hallman's relationship with Jack Hart, who was his coach on the story at the *Oregonian*, has been characterized "as the most innovative editor/writer team in America, which is why journalists everywhere should pay close attention to their work" (Clark 2003).

Another exemplar of the form in the newspaper field is Thomas French of the *St. Petersburg Times* in Florida, who won a Pulitzer Prize in 1998 for his "Angels & Demons" series about how authorities tracked down the murderer of an Ohio mother and her two teenaged daughters in the Tampa Bay area.

Still another is Sonia Nazario of the *Los Angeles Times*. Her *Enrique's Journey* series reveals the lengths, once again, to which literary journalists will go to attempt to reconstruct a story. The Pulitzer Prize-winning series, published in the *Times* in 2002 and later published as a book, recounts the eight attempts by "Enrique," a 17-year-old Honduran, to travel illegally to the United States to be reunited with his mother, a passage that an unusually high number of Central American children and teenagers make to be reunited with parents who immigrate illegally to the United States. She left him when he was 5 to find work in the United States so that she could send back money to support him and his sister. Enrique rides freight trains through Mexico to get to the American border. Seven times he was caught, arrested, and returned to Honduras by Mexican police. At one point he was nearly beaten to death by gang members who prey on illegal migrants traveling through Mexico. Finally, on his eighth attempt, he succeeds in crossing the Rio Gande illegally and eventually reunites with his mother. In reconstructing the story, Nazario took the same route as Enrique and rode atop freight trains herself along with a photographer from the *Los Angeles Times,* doing so at no small personal risk.

Even The Associated Press has been encouraging reporters to engage in journalistic "storytelling," their preferred term for literary journalism. Among them, Helen O'Neill has carved out a niche as a narrativist and in 2005 won an American Society of Newspaper Editors award for excellence in journalism with her 2004 series "The Kidnapping of Grandma Braun." The story recounts the kidnapping and rescue of an elderly grandmother in Wisconsin. What makes The Associated Press's encouragement of narrative literary journalism so remarkable is that the world's largest wire service and news gathering organization has long been viewed as "the bastion of hard news leads and for-the-record coverage" (Grimes 1997, 28). Clearly that bastion has been breached.

Some of the other accomplished newspaper reporters who write in the form are Bob Batz, Paula Bock, Anne Hull, Lisa Pollack, and Mary Miller. Medical topics—a patient, for example, who needs a rare surgical operation—seem to be one common theme, thus following in a tradition established by Jon Franklin. Other topics include murder (again), as well as homelessness, high school marching bands, adolescence, and mine disasters—in effect the vast experience of life in its many different shades and colors.

Bibliography

Agovino, Michael J. "I Wanted to be Here All of the Time." *Newsweek* (10 February 2003): 68.

Bergner, Daniel. *In the Land of Magic Soldiers*. New York: Picador, 2003.

Boynton, Robert S. *The New New Journalism*. New York: Vintage, 2005.

Clark, Roy Peter. "Tell Me a Story." Poynter Online (12 December 2003). Available from: http://www.poynter org/content/content_view.asp?id=51437.

Cramer, Richard Ben. *Joe DiMaggio: The Hero's Life*. New York: Simon and Schuster, 2000.

Grimes, Charlotte. "Rewired." *American Journalism Review* (October 1997): 28.

Harr, John. *A Civil Action*. New York: Random House, 1995.

Hartsock, John C. "Caught Between the Rhetoric of the Scene and the Rhetoric of the Polemic: A Review of *Random Family*." *Points of Entry* 2.1 (2004): 192–195.

———. "It Was a Dark and Stormy Night: Newspaper Reporters Rediscover the Art of Narrative Literary Journalism and Their Own Epistemological Heritage." *Prose Studies* (2007).

Herr, Michael. *Dispatches*. New York: Vintage, 1991.

Kidder, Tracy. *Among Schoolchildren*. New York: Harper Perennial, 1990.

———. *Home Town*. New York: Pocket, 1999.

———. *House*. New York: Mariner, 1999.

———. *Mountains Beyond Mountains*. New York: Random House, 2003.

———. *Old Friends*. Boston, MA: Houghton Mifflin, 1993.

Kotlowitz, Alex. *Never a City So Real*. New York: Crown, 2004.

———. *The Other Side of the River*. New York: Nan A. Talese, 1998.

Krakauer, John. *Into the Wild*. New York: Villard, 1996.

———. *Into Thin Air*. New York: Villard, 1997.

Kramer, Jane. *Lone Patriot: The Short Career of an American Militiaman*. New York: Pantheon, 2002.

Langewiesche, William. *American Ground: Unbuilding the World Trade Center*. New York: North Point Press, 2002.

LeBlanc, Adrian Nicole. *Random Family*. New York: Scribner, 2003.

Lewis, Michael. *Next: The Future Just Happened*. New York: Norton, 2001.

Nazario, Sonia. *Enrique's Journey*. New York: Random House, 2006.

Orlean, Susan. *The Orchid Thief*. New York: Random House, 1998.

Preston, Richard. *The Hot Zone*. New York: Random House, 1994.

Rosenbaum, Ron. *Explaining Hitler: The Search for the Origins of His Evil*. New York: Random House, 1998.

Steffens, Lincoln. *The Autobiography of Lincoln Steffens*. New York: Harcourt, 1931.

Talese, Gay. [1970] *Fame and Obscurity*. New York: Ivy Books, 1993.

Weber, Ronald. Some Sort of Artistic Excitement. In *The Reporter as Artist: A Look at the New Journalism Controversy*. Ronald Weber, ed. New York: Hastings House, 1974.

Weingarten, Marc. *The Gang That Wouldn't Write Straight*. New York: Crown, 2006.

Weschler, Lawrence. *Mr. Wilson's Cabinet of Wonder*. New York: Pantheon, 1995.

Wolfe, Tom. Last American Hero. In *The Kandy-Kolored Tangerine-Flake Streamline Baby*. New York: Farrar, 1965.

———. The New Journalism. In *The New Journalism: With an Anthology*. Tom Wolfe and E.W. Johnson, eds. New York: Harper, 1973.

Wright, Lawrence. *The Looming Tower: Al-Qaeda and the Road to 9/11*. New York: Knopf, 2006.

Wyatt, Edward. "The Atlantic Monthly Cuts Back on Fiction." *New York Times* (6 April 2005): late edition, E2.

Further Reading

Barringer, Felicity. "Journalism's Greatest Hits." *New York Times* (1 March 1999): C1; Connery, Thomas B., ed. *A Sourcebook of American Literary Journalism: Representative Writers in an Emerging Genre*. Westport, CT: Greenwood, 1992; Hartsock, John C. *A History of American Literary Journalism: The Emergence of a Modern Narrative Form*. Amherst, MA: University of Massachusetts Press, 2000; Sims, Norman, ed. *Literary Journalism in the Twentieth Century*. New York: Oxford University Press, 1990.

JOHN C. HARTSOCK

M

MAGICAL REALISM

The contemporary reader of magical realism by American authors—here meaning authors writing and/or originating from the United States—may not anticipate such an encounter or, indeed, recognize the experience for what it is. Although the United States shares in common with Latin America many of the seeds from which the literary mode sprang, critics and readers alike still ascribe to magical realism a decidedly Latin American sensibility. Yet contemporary American authors use the mode as a means of addressing such issues as consumerism and popular culture, as well as for challenging the veracity of history and revising notions of truth.

Definition. Most readers approaching a novel or short fiction described as "magic realism" anticipate the presence of something "unnatural" or magical, but evidence of the supernatural in and of itself does not constitute magical realism. In magical realism, neither the natural nor the supernatural is compromised. The author creates a supernatural as ordinary or normal as the everyday, a supernatural that ultimately does not stand out for the reader. Critic Amaryll Chanady works toward a concrete and applicable rubric against which texts can be evaluated as magical realism. Chanady offers the following criteria for magical realism. First, it is characterized by two perspectives, one based on a "rational view of reality and the other on the acceptance of the supernatural as part of everyday life" (Chanady 1985, 21). Next is the fact that "the supernatural is not presented as problematic"; characters and narration alike perceive it as normal (Chanady 1985, 23). Finally, Chanady argues, magical realism lacks "judgments about the veracity of the events and the authenticity of the world view expressed in the text," so that the supernatural world as the author presents it is not subordinate or the "real" world privileged (Chanady 1985, 29–30). The magical realist text makes no attempt to invoke the uncertainty that would challenge a reader's decision to believe or not believe in the world described as it is in the text. Thus, the supernatural cannot be explained away—as a miracle, for example, or a possible illusion—or the equality between the natural and unnatural would be imbalanced. A final required aspect is that in order for the supernatural and the real to coexist without hierarchy or questions, they must be in balance. A magical moment in a text—even one that conforms to Chanady's criteria—cannot be enough to warrant the text's classification as magical realism.

Franz Roh first coined "magic realism" in 1925 for post-expressionist art, but by the late 1920s the term had already crossed over into literature. Authors Alejo Carpentier, Arturo Uslar Pietri, and Miguel Angel Asturias and critics Angel Flores and Luis Leal were among those responsible for labeling magical realism as a distinctly Latin American phenomenon. Carpentier coined the phrase *lo real maravilloso* in the preface to *The Kingdom of This World* (1949), privileging a Latin American (or Caribbean or even Cuban) sensibility he believed unduplicated elsewhere in the world. Yet only after the 1960s literary event known as the "Boom," when Latin American literature exploded onto the world scene, would magical realism become a marketable literary commodity—a simultaneous Latin American and literary happening. The text most influential both in the Boom and in Latin American magical realism, *One Hundred Years of Solitude,* brought Gabriel García Márquez international fame. At the same time, the literary mode's sudden popularity and Latin America's seemingly exclusive claims gave rise to broad generalizations that still threaten the term's denotation and application.

Perhaps the greatest threat to magical realist criticism in the years since critics such as Leal and Flores first borrowed it for literary applications—even greater a risk than the threat of reductive geographic constraints—is this tendency to misappropriate the term for contemporary literature without first establishing a decisive and applicable denotation. One failing of critics and publishers alike has been to use the term loosely—begging the question as they market texts or even label entire collections "magical realism"—and so inaccurately that other modes, genres, and even religious beliefs are subsumed under the heading. To this day, "magical realism" appears on book jackets to connote Latin American origins or to "explain" the inclusion of the supernatural or miraculous rather than to categorize a text that creates what critic Joe Benevento describes as a "hybrid" of the everyday with the supernatural. The end result has been that many scholars and readers fail to recognize the mode or, worse, begin assigning it with impunity to fantasy and folklore, myth and science fiction, and blurring the lines in between.

Although the supernatural in literature rarely defies description, both magical realism and any number of other modes or sub-genres suffer when this literary mode is misidentified. Inevitably, other supernatural texts privilege either the real or magical worlds they create. Fairy tale, science fiction, horror, and fantasy, for example, create imaginary places—physical spaces defined not by the rules of the natural world as we know it—and conform to often rigid conventions or to explanations that explain away the supernatural altogether. Fairy tales, for example, often begin with the formulaic "Once upon a time," letting readers know that the rules of reality no longer apply to the actions of the text. Legends and lore function as sites of communal knowledge or superstition and operate under similar systems of order. For instance, stories of vampires or of other supernatural creatures generally abide by a set of rules for the supernatural: we *know* that a silver bullet kills a werewolf and thus we can often explain away or mediate for the supernatural events in works with werewolves.

In literary terms, magical realism's closest European relatives are perhaps surrealism and the fantastic. Surrealism has no interest in portraying a realistic world; that divorce from reality is made manifest in an exploration of the workings of the mind and, in particular, the subconscious. Like surrealism, the fantastic avoids or distances reality altogether, though Roger Caillois claims that the fantastic "presupposes the solidity of the world but only to ruin it more radically" (qtd. in Durix 1998, 82). The fantastic requires what Tzvetan Todorov describes as "hesitation" on the part of the reader or characters. Unlike magical realism, the fantastic, because it does not establish that the supernatural events have or have not taken place, calls into question whether or not the reader should believe in them.

History. As if magical realism's bonds with postmodernism and American Romanticism were not enough to ensure that magical realism could hold its own in North America, our shared history and postcolonial status with Latin America and the changing face of the American reading public has augmented its appeal. Magical realism is a catalyst "for the development of new national and regional literatures" (Zamora and Faris 1995, 2), a development perhaps best understood by nations with relatively young literary traditions. The Americas, in sharing a certain cultural indebtedness to the historical and literary traditions of Europe, also have in common the goal of independence and distinction from those traditions. Arriving white Europeans brought much of that unrest upon our "historical selves" by attempting to superimpose European culture onto the indigenous races they found in or brought to the Americas. To some extent, though, the U.S. subjugation of the natives was unusual in that it largely displaced and marginalized indigenous peoples, pushing them ever westward and away from the center, or, in an even more radical displacement, introduced marginalized groups, such as during slavery. The Spanish, unlike the Protestants settling on the Eastern shores of the United States, were more concerned with the inclusive civilizing and conversion of native peoples.

The make-up of the New World, largely through the colonizers' own doing, is heterogeneous rather than homogenous. Of course, not all marginalized groups are brought to or made out of nations against their wills, as illustrated by the tremendous influx of Latino/a people into the United States. These new arrivals carry with them their traditions, whether historical, religious, or cultural; in addition, they transport their language and their literary legacies. As marginalized groups, natives and immigrants create only slight tremors in the structure of the nations they call home. Still, together they challenge ideas of national language and culture; out of their oppression and misfortune spring the tools of change—such as multicultural and bilingual education, affirmative action, and political correctness. And the features of their literary consciousness are slowly being woven together with the traditional strands of the majority.

Just as the Americas are refining questions of "nation," they are also either forming or redefining questions of national identity. Literary modes such as magical realism play an important role in the reviewing and revision of self; literature is the means by which assimilation of different influences is reflected. Because assimilation can sometimes mean the loss of culture, narrative modes such as magical realism also constitute a reaction to such potential loss. And because magical realism juxtaposes the reality of America with other options, it provides an excellent forum for the marginalized voices in the Americas.

Latin American magical realism began as an outgrowth of and reaction against Latin American political upheaval and socioeconomic distress. Although the United States shares at least some of those socioeconomic concerns, the magical realism of the United States is necessarily something quite different. A relatively stable nation, with no major overturning of its *system* of government in the past 230 years, the

United States reflects a facade of stability, yet magical realism still allows mainstream and marginalized communities alike to express discontent with oppressive situations, the political rhetoric of capitalism, and the consumer culture. Such American magical realist writers as Laurie Foos, Ana Castillo, and Marie Arana challenge the rhetoric that equates the consumer society with cultural norms by infusing the consumptions of goods with supernatural qualities. The magical realism of U.S. writers also frequently manifests itself as an extension of the marginalized, the "Other" of Western culture and society, as illustrated by the revision of accepted religious, historical, and even supernatural beliefs by such marginalized authors as Louise Erdrich, Toni Morrison, Ana Castillo, and Jonathan Safran Foer. As such, magical realist literature ultimately makes powerful statements about America as both a consumer culture and the Other in North Atlantic society, but the foundation of its assertions is primarily social or cultural rather than predominantly political. If the Boom privileged the white male center of Latin American culture, the North American counterpart has set out to dethrone the center.

Magical realist authors—and American magical realist authors in particular—are not writing constantly in the mode. Jeanne Delbaere notes, "Writers do not as a rule think of themselves as magic realists or write exclusively magic realist works; if the label fits some of their novels or stories it is usually because what they had to say in them required that particular form of expression" (Delbaere 1992, 98). Some texts incorporate particular elements of magical realism but may ultimately fail to sustain the supernatural in juxtaposition with the real across the whole of the text; other works provide the acceptable rationale of religious beliefs, counteracting the possibility that the text can be read as magical realism. Yet those who draw upon magical realism for their short fiction and novels often employ supernatural effects. Thus, Laurie Foos's *Ex Utero*, a feminist take on magical realism, is the only one of her novels to date that would classify as such. *Twinship*, her most recent work, is closer to the surreal, with characters and readers alike questioning the impossible notion of a woman giving birth to herself, her mother having planted the suggestion in her desire for a child just like the perfect daughter to whom she gave birth.

Steven Millhauser's short story "Flying Carpets" (surrounded as it is by a collection of works closer to the fantastic than to any other mode or genre) seems to call into question whether or not it could be magical realism. It is, after all, a story about the sort of "magic" readers expect in fairy tales. Yet Millhauser's matter-of-fact description of the narrator's first maneuvers on the carpet treats the title objects as little more than glorified go-carts for the boys in his neighborhood. And these details are balanced against the narration's skeptical imaginings of anything "out of this world": "My father had taught me not to believe stories about Martians and spaceships, and these tales [about cities in the clouds] were like those stories: even as you refused to believe them, you saw them, as if the sheer effort of not believing them made them glow in your mind" (Millhauser 1999, 72). Millhauser lulls his reader into an easy belief in the most supernatural effect in the story, a "toy" that bores its young owner when it promises the moon but seems instead to make his world shrink and that ultimately goes missing, neglected in the attic. The story both calls into question and romanticizes stories of Martians and floating cities and, in so doing, leaves us unguarded against flying carpets.

Some North American texts lend themselves easily to a discussion of the magically real, upholding the precepts for magical realism set forth by Chanady. For example, such contemporary American texts as *Ex Utero, Beloved, Everything Is Illuminated,* and *Cellophane*—despite drastic differences among their authors, tones, settings, and purposes—provide clearly definable instances of magical realism by writers practicing in the United States. Other works, perhaps even those frequently described as magically real, require more extensive justification in order to be considered as such, particularly texts such as *Tropic of Orange* and *Everything Is Illuminated,* with their very postmodern approaches to storytelling.

Trends and Themes

Consumerism. In a capitalist, consumer culture, the "have-nots" do not live in remote villages where little interaction between the upper and lower classes takes place. Instead, daily life continuously emphasizes the differences between the two, and the popular culture is largely responsible for highlighting for the less-fortunate the paradox of living in America without living "the American dream." William Leach explains that the separation of customer from goods on display behind glass contributed to the increasingly obscured "difference between the real and the unreal" in consumerism (Leach 1993, 189). Because even the language Leach uses to describe the consumer culture is rich with the same rhetoric of magical realism (where "the difference between the real and the unreal" is blurred), it stands to reason that the narrative mode is appropriated as an effective means for discussing socioeconomic conditions in the United States. Thus, the American brand of magical realism dramatizes both the popular culture and the consumer culture in all their manifestations; in doing so, it challenges the authority of those cultures and their effects on the American population.

Dreaming in Cuban's questionable magical realist status results from Garcia's almost hesitant use of the supernatural. The fact that, generally, only one or two characters experience the supernatural at any one time might compromise the novel's status as magical realism were it not for Garcia's intentionally nonlinear storyline. Certainly, some events also can be accounted for by religion: Felicia's dependence on the very traditional, Caribbean spiritual medium of Yoruba offers several moments that, though supernatural in tone, cannot be considered magical realism, even when her reliance on the occult fails her. But Garcia also incorporates other indefinable elements into *Dreaming in Cuban,* redeeming the magical realism by interspersing these examples throughout the text: the emotional bond between Pilar in the United States and her grandmother Celia in Cuba, Jorge's visits to both daughter and wife after his death, Celia's ability to transfer her son's cancer to her own breast.

In Cristina Garcia's novel, even the most culturally marginalized characters rarely seem at risk of becoming consumed; instead their appetites as U.S. consumers are perpetually fed, both literally and figuratively. Consider, for example, Lourdes's massive consumption of baked goods. Her appetite in the kitchen translates into a sexual appetite; and the "heavier she got, the more supple she became" (Garcia 1992, 21). Yet because she equates her dieting (during which she eats no solid foods whatsoever) with transparency, "as if the hard lines of her hulking form were disintegrating," she loses interest in sex. Only when her "metamorphosis is complete," when she can fit into a size-six designer suit, does she begin to eat again. "On Fifth Avenue, Lourdes stops to buy hot dogs (with mustard, relish, sauerkraut, fried onions, and ketchup), two chocolate cream sodas, a potato knish, lamb shish kebabs with more onions, a soft pretzel, and a cup of San Marino cherry ice. Lourdes eats,

eats, eats, like a Hindu goddess with eight arms, eats, eats, eats, as if famine were imminent" (Garcia 1992, 174).

As opposed to the literal consumption in Garcia's text, *Ex Utero* transforms the consumer culture into the impetus for (and a menace against) the magical realism of the text. Foos refigures the shopping mall as the site of loss of womanhood for the main character. "Somehow, in her quest to achieve a versatile wardrobe, she'd lost her womb, the way some people misplace car keys or a pair of sunglasses" (Foos 1995, 2). Rita's pursuit at the mall symbolizes the stereotypical female desire in our consumer shopper, the desire to "shop 'til you drop"—only in this instance the "dropping" refers to Rita's uterus rather than to Rita herself. Shopping, the consumption of goods, and consumers themselves all play important roles in the creation and perpetuation of the consumer cycle.

Popular Culture. Garcia's *Dreaming in Cuban* illustrates ways in which the consumer culture and the popular culture commingle. For Garcia, *what* Cubans import from the United States is as important as *that* they import. Cuban characters eat, drink, wear, and play the United States, even if they are unable or unwilling to live there. From Jorge's and Lourdes's love of baseball to the Coca-Cola they keep in their fridge, the del Pinos in *Dreaming in Cuban* are shaped by the popular culture of the United States as much as they are by their own. But when Jorge and Lourdes embrace this foreign element, it inspires them to move away from Cuba. Celia, by choosing to place her loyalty in El Lider, champions Cuba; her country is her spirituality.

Of the many messages that Foos advances in *Ex Utero,* the most significant in terms of popular culture is her indictment of the talk show genre. After she loses her womb, Rita makes the round of the syndicated talk shows, finally ending up on *The Nodderman Show.* Rod Nodderman is the quintessential talk show host, and Rita finds herself in *TV Guide,* along with Nodderman, whose Nielson ratings skyrocket after her appearance. One character and fan of the show, Adele,

> likes to make love with her boyfriend Leonard while watching talk shows. There is something about the distant murmur of voices, she says, that never fails to propel her to orgasm. Some of the syndicated shows do the trick, but it is *The Nodderman Show* that drives her into a frenzy. Certain shows have sent her tearing at Leonard's hair and begging for commercials. She has been known to scream with pleasure at the opening strains of game show theme songs, writhing on the bed from the spinning of the Wheel of Fortune. (Foos 1995, 33)

But her sympathy for Rita's plight causes Adele's vagina literally to seal shut, and not even Leonard's hammering, drilling, and chiseling can reopen it. A third central figure in the text, Lucy, expresses her sympathy for Rita through constant menstruation. When reporters follow her trail of blood to her apartment, they pass unanswered notes under the door: "*We just want a few shots of you bleeding,* the notes say, *or a couple of quotes about menstruation. Why won't you give us that much?*" (Foos 1995, 101). Women are not the only casualties of the media frenzy. Marty, a shoe salesman who cannot keep red pumps in stock after Rita's appearance on the talk show, thinks "perhaps it is the constant bombardment of wombs by the media that has driven him to [an] insatiable lust" (Foos 1995, 75). *Ex Utero* equates popular culture or "the boob tube" with both the female reproductive system and sexual excitement; the novel's supernatural elements become a pawn in the production and reproduction of mass media, daytime television, and femininity.

The women in *Ex Utero* (whose bodies have rebelled against them) and in *So Far From God* (who gravitate toward rebellion) become media icons in what has become an all-too-familiar response to tragedy and personal misfortune. Castillo's characters experience a very traditional set of supernatural occurrences in extremely unconventional ways. Castillo references resurrection, saints, *curanderas,* and even La Llorona in such original ways that the supernatural can no longer be explained away by the religion that supposedly produces it. Foos insists that the reader not only accept that her main characters' sexual organs have "closed up shop," but also that the corresponding effects on the male characters are immediate and drastic. Drawing upon the everyday settings of the television studio and the shopping mall, Foos directly implants the supernatural into the ideological constraints of North America, restrictions that typically guard against the representation of the supernatural as anything other than a ghost story.

The temptation for some readers of magical realist fiction is to rely on more traditional or popular claims to explain away the supernatural elements in the texts. One popular attempt at contextualizing Morrison's novel *Beloved* has been to refigure it as a ghost story; in her own discussions of the work, Morrison herself describes it as such. Yet *Beloved's* continual presence, along with the other supernatural events in the novel, bumps up against but does not consume the natural aspects of the story. Her return encompasses many possibilities, and her primary effect on both the implied reader and the characters in the story is not to elicit horror or suspense. Beloved functions as the site for many histories, rather than just one; ultimately, she embodies magical realism.

Truth and History. Returning to the origin of things, finding the "true" history and making meaning of it, seems a constant task for American magical realism. Because it delves into the historical, social, mythical, individual, and collective levels of human reality (Hancock 1986, 47), magical realism offers new ways of exploring literature, but it also offers a space where truth can be confronted, challenged, or even changed. *Beloved* is perhaps the best example of such revisions. *Beloved's* recollections of the "other side" are the supernatural reflection of the South (and of the Middle Passage spawned by the South's commodification of black flesh) in the text. Sethe's house on Bluestone Road is the middle ground, the only place in the text where the two realms meet. The specter of Beloved seducing Paul D and torturing Sethe pale in comparison to Paul D's earlier subjugation or Sethe's victimization at the hands of the young white boys who steal her milk. Because we see slavery in such a light, because Morrison forces us to deal with hatred and racism and evil, two things happen for the reader: we can forgive Sethe's actions, and we can accept Beloved's presence as easily as the main characters do. After all, this spirit plaguing the text, comparatively, is neither fantastic *nor* terrifying. If history is the privilege of the oppressor, then *revision* of history, Morrison suggests, is the purview of the oppressed.

The plague of truth in *Cellophane* recalls the insomnia plague in *One Hundred Years of Solitude* and demonstrates one of the ways in which Marie Arana manipulates what is "true" through magical realism. Even before the plague, Arana's characters seek truths about the world—Tía Esther's stories for Victor, Victor's unwillingness to remember his past and his obsession with paper, Belén's escape from reality into the library housing her books, and Elsa's wishful translation of the note she believes the general has given her all conspire to create individual truths for characters surrounded by the unsympathetic and oftentimes hostile rainforest. And because Victor, an engineer, constantly looks for how reality works, he discovers that technology is a bigger joke on humanity than on nature. In the window of a shop in Lima, Victor both finds his calling (in a poster of the Peruvian rainforest) and learns to regard technology and the supernatural on equal footing. "Perhaps, as with Señor Urrutia's perpetual-motion machine, an explanation [for the medicine man's abilities in delivering Victor's children or for other rain forest magic] lurked in the wings. Events only seemed miraculous—one had to look for the science behind them. . . . Someday he would trace all these circuits and see the truth of the world clearly" (Arana 2006, 10). Later, his spiritual guide and friend Yorumba tells him, "There is a difference between the truth of the world and the world as a person sees it. We cannot know the truth" (Arana 2006, 134). Technology fails to protect Victor's fanciful and unnatural desire to produce cellophane out of the rainforest. Victor loses the war against nature and the people living in (rather than in conflict with) nature; the natives disassemble the machinery and return Floralinda to the land.

Context and Issues. Critics such as Lois Parkinson Zamora and Wayne Ude contend that the United States, by looking "to the south," is actually rediscovering its own influences on the Latin American magical realist tradition. Both Zamora and Ude cite the American Romantic tradition as a precursor, arguing that Latin American authors borrowed heavily from romanticism, which freed itself from the moral and realistic requirements of traditional forms. Ude suggests that the frontier myth plays a part in the emergence of the North American strain of magical realism and extends the mode's family tree to include the Gothic and folklore traditions as well.

Magical realism has even closer familial ties with postmodernism, another critical term with Latin American roots. Indeed, innovative postmodern features—including awareness of the work as a text, or metafiction; multiplicity; discontinuity; and the erasure of boundaries—are the frequent tools of magical realists. And both magical realism and postmodernism blur the lines between popular or mass culture and "high" or literary arts. Still, Romanticism and postmodernism do share their counter-realism with magical realism. Romanticism created readers who were ready for something new, for authors and texts that would counter scientific reason. Postmodernism discarded our conventional definitions of reality and challenged the literary techniques constrained by that reality. Both paved the way for magical realism's journey north and, in doing so, prepared readers for the "new" mode.

IS MAGICAL REALISM FOUND ONLY IN LATIN AMERICAN LITERATURE?

Until recently, magical realism has been such a geographically bound commodity that it was difficult to imagine it in terms of literature outside Latin America, much less to apply the phrase in scholarly criticism of other literatures or, more specifically, to consider American texts through a magical realist lens. Yet the very features that distinguish magical realism as an historically situated mode—its postcolonial nature, its shared history with postmodernism—also keep it from such proprietary claims. Magical realism, as Argentinean author Jorge Luis Borges suggests, may have germinated in, rather than been imported into, the United States.

Reception. The many thematic capabilities of magical realism converge for the marginalized text. Issues of consumerism, popular culture, identity, history, revision, and truth intersect within the worlds of marginalized authors, where the magical realist mode allows writers to uncover inconsistencies of an American life. As such writers challenge the terms "mass" or "popular culture," "identity," and "history"—and because majority rules tend not to apply to predominantly diversified areas such as the Los Angeles of *Tropic of Orange*—marginalized authors relocate the mainstream and the margin to a more unified center.

When critic Debra Spark laments the paucity of magical realist works in the United States, her own difficulties as a writer attempting the mode on American soil may ultimately hinge on a personal rather than communal difficulty. The American magical realist author does not work in the mode exclusively, and yet the breadth of offerings provide rich and convincing truth that the literary mode deserves careful and continued critical attention.

Selected Authors. In Jonathan Safran Foer's novel *Everything Is Illuminated,* the magical realism revolves around the act of telling truths—whether those events are factual or not. Chronologically, the tale begins with the discovery that a wagon has overturned in the river Brod. The location—Trachimbrod—is named for an event that may not even have caused the death of Trachim, who is merely the rumored occupant of the wagon. The current-day setting for the work is no less interested in truthfulness: in the letters Alexander Perchov writes to the character Jonathan Safran Foer, Alexi weaves a series of not-truths into language that relies on a thesaurus to present a more engaging—though less, or at least alternately, meaningful—version of Alexi's own words. He tells Jonathan, "In Russian my ideas are asserted abnormally well, but my second tongue is not so premium. . . . I fatigued the thesaurus you presented me, as you counseled me to, when my words appeared too petite, or not befitting" (Foer 2002, 23).

As Jonathan and Alexi reconstruct the story of Jonathan's European roots, crafting the novel together, Alexi's letters reveal that fiction could tell the better story: "I could hate you! Why will you not permit your grandfather to be in love with the Gypsy girl, and show her his love? Who is ordering you to write in such a manner? We have such chances to do good, and yet again and again you insist on evil" (Foer 2002, 240). Soon after, in the same letter, Alexi contends, "I would never command you to write a story that is as it occurred in the actual, but I would command you to make your story faithful" (Foer 2002, 240). Alexi's complaint comes full circle as he realizes that Jonathan's narrative will also incorporate a more "actual" version of his own grandfather's tale, the horrific version in which Grandfather is accomplice to his Jewish friend Hershel's death in order to save his own family. Alexi's preference for the "good" versions of these stories, where the Gypsy girl finds love with Safran and where Grandfather risks his family's wellbeing to keep Hershel's secret, might ironically create a world in which neither Alexi nor Jonathan was alive to tell *any* tale.

Such attempts at revision comprise an equally important theme in contemporary magical realism. Morrison re-envisions the legacy of slavery incarnate in *Beloved.* Alexi actively participates in the process of revising the family history in the Jewish novel Jonathan is writing. American-Canadian writer Thomas King revises Native American creation myths, history, and even a classic John Wayne movie in *Green Grass, Running Water.* When the Indian characters (already in the act of revising the white Western canon by taking on iconographic names) Lone Ranger, Hawkeye,

Robinson Crusoe, and Ishmael view a store owner's favorite Western, they find mistakes in the production.

> "The next scene," said Bursum, "used over six hundred extras, Indians and whites. And five cameras. The director spent almost a month on this one scene before he felt it was right."
> "He didn't get it right the first time," said the Long Ranger.
> "But we fixed it for him," said Hawkeye. (King 1994, 351–352)

These four new "directors" of the movie colorize their version and remove the cavalry that charges in to save John Wayne. "There at full charge, hundreds of soldiers in bright blue uniforms with gold buttons and sashes and stripes, blue-eyed and rosy-cheeked, came over the last rise./And disappeared [. . .]. 'What the hell,' said Bursum" (King 1994, 357). Those in the store watch as John Wayne and Richard Widmark "[pull] the trigger on empty cartridges" and the tide of the battle turns to favor the Indians. John Wayne looked down and stared stupidly at the arrow in his thigh, shaking his head in amazement and disbelief as two bullets ripped through his chest and out the back of his jacket" (King 1994, 358). Bursum's response is to stab at the remote in an attempt to stop the revision, but Charlie— the son of Portland, an actor not "Indian" enough to portray himself until he dons a prosthetic nose—hisses "Get 'em, Dad" (King 1994, 358). King, whose text rewrites multiple histories, reverses the cultural impact intended by the movie. His Indians refigure the popular genre of the Western into a new space where the Portlands and not the John Waynes save the day. In doing so, King and his team of revisionists return to Charlie a father, as well as a culture and a history, of which he can be proud.

Magical realism allows for supernatural blendings of history and identity, one of its most important benefits to authors searching for what makes the historic *real* for readers and characters. In *Cellophane*, Victor's identity is defined by his actions; locals call him "the shapeshifter" for what he creates (cellophane, paper) out of nature (hemp, cotton). Jonathan's grandfather is "Shalom-then-Kolker-now Safran" and then a statue known as the Dial in *Everything Is Illuminated*; his journey through the text is a constant attempt to find an identity that will allow him to fit into Trachimbrod. And Morrison's Beloved encompasses any number of possible existences, including the "crawling-already?" baby, the young escaped woman from Deer Creek, and the Middle Passage personified. Using magical realism to negotiate the often merciless histories of contemporary existence, authors such as King, Foer, Arana, and Morrison rescue identities worth more than those allowed by outsider's accounts.

Humor. Magical realist texts make for some of the most haunting and brutal writing imaginable. Yet several contemporary writers use the mode to great comedic affect, even as those authors juxtapose playful rhetoric against the horrors of daily life. In *Everything Is Illuminated*, Alexi's malapropisms and jokes are at the expense of the character and "author," Jonathan Safran Foer, who is searching for the woman who saved his family from the Holocaust. Alexi's first letter to Jonathan includes a scene where his father describes Jonathan to Alexi and his grandfather: "'He desires to write a book about his grandfather's village.' 'Oh,' I said, 'so he is intelligent?' 'No,' Father corrected. 'He has low-grade brains. The American office informs me that he telephones them every day and manufactures numerous half-witted queries about finding suitable food.' . . . Here," Alexi inserts, well aware of Jonathan as his audience, "I will repeat that the hero is a very ingenious Jew," but he immediate quotes his Grandfather's lament that he does "not want to drive ten hours to an ugly city to attend to a very spoiled Jew" (Foer 2002, 6–7).

Joe Hill's "Pop Art," with its easy and simple beginning—"My best friend when I was twelve was inflatable" (Hill 2001, 85)—uses humor as a mediator between reader and text, allowing the magical realist text to speak to injustice while still taking delight in the circumstances that would make Art easy prey. Hill's text could thwart the reader's efforts to accept its premise as a reality were it not for the author's liberal use of practical concerns for a character weighing only eight ounces. The narrator describes Art early in the story: "Also, I can say truthfully, he was the most completely harmless person I've ever known. Not only would he not hurt a fly, he *couldn't* hurt a fly. If he slapped one and lifted his hand, it would buzz off undisturbed" (Hill 2001, 87). Art writes with a crayon to avoid the danger of pencils and is kicked around, literally, on the playground for being different: "There was something special about Art, an invisible special something that just made other kids naturally want to kick his ass" (Hill 2001, 87). When another kid "held Art down during recess and wrote KOLLOSTIMY BAG with indelible ink," Art writes on his pad that "[t]he worst thing was my mom saw. Bad enough she has to know I get beat up on a daily basis. But she was really upset it was spelled wrong" (Hill 2001, 89).

The Native American experience King creates in *Green Grass, Running Water* counteracts its own spiritual origins by humorously reframing the traditional myths. King appropriates and rewrites *The Last of the Mohicans, Robinson Crusoe, Moby Dick*, the Bible, and even a radio-originated television series (*The Lone Ranger*). The four Native Americans—who are the four originary women of the story (First Woman, Changing Woman, Thought Woman, and Old Woman) and who first reject the Christian myths of "Ahdamn" and Eve, Noah and the Flood, Mary's immaculate conception, and Christ (Young Man Walking On Water)—adopt their (male) names from the white Anglo texts and are responsible for establishing the narrative frame around the story. In the tale, then, King also irreverently modifies Native American myths because he uses four cross-dressing, cross-naming women to effect changes in the "present" of the text and because Coyote, the audience for their tale, is traditionally the story-teller.

King's playful irreverence does not stop with Native American mythology or the Western canon. When A.A. Gabriel (whose business card lists him as a Canadian Security and Intelligence Service agent *and* as the Heavenly Host) appears to Thought Woman, the interviewer attempts to rename her Mary, to require "virgin verification," and to take her picture next to a "snake" who is actually Old Coyote. When she refuses him and floats away again on the ocean, A.A. Gabriel shouts after her: "There are lots of Marys in the world. . . . We can always find another one, you know" (King 1994, 301). And one of King's most elaborate jokes unfolds over the course of the novel as he toys with the idea of "discovering" a continent filled with indigenous peoples. Columbus's three ships' journey to the New World is recreated and revised in the destruction of the Parliament Lake Dam by three cars sailing on the lake—"a Nissan, a Pinto, and a Karmann-Ghia" (King 1994, 448). King's magical realism "out-Coyotes" Coyote because it plays tricks on the tricksters.

Coincidence. Because coincidence calls into question the planned nature of human events and our seeming control of the world around us, many magical realists delight in confounding plots with nearly miraculous coincidences. Arana's *Cellophane* is riddled with them. When he mistranslates the Australian's course note, Luis inadvertently sparks love between John Gibbs and Marcela the school teacher, allowing Gibbs to be in the right place at the right time to save the family; Tía Esther arrives on the Australian's boat the very day they will need to escape Floralinda. The *tsantsa*, a shrunken puma head Tía wears as a souvenir from a failed love affair from her youth, warns off the Jivaro; the tribe of Machiguenga inadvertently save Victor from the Jivaro. Most important to Victor's family's fate and yet a matter of coincidence itself, the monkey *La Negrita*'s fortune, suitably vague and drawn at random out of the mini shrine, becomes a self-fulfilling prophecy of the ending of the story. Coincidences conspire by the end of the novel, tying together the realist threads, becoming more than mere conveniences or plot contrivances, and these once random events begin to form a pattern for Victor's life. Though Victor is a man who finds "truth . . . in tangible things" (Arana 2006, 49), as with his cellophane, the *intangibles*—as both the monkey fortune and Yorumbo warn him—force him to let go.

Abby Frucht's *Polly's Ghost* translates coincidence into an extraordinary performance of motherly love. Polly, newly learning her abilities and limitations as a ghost, attempts to bond her youngest son Tip and his new acquaintance Johnny but instead causes the death of the man who will dissolve that bond. "I never intended for Tom Bane's airplane to fall out of the sky," begins Frucht's narrative (Fruchy 2000, 11). Polly spends the novel learning how much she is at the whim of her dance partner, the night. *Polly's Ghost* refuses the confines of a ghost story but also disallows Polly's own need to offer Tip her forgiveness (she dies bearing him) and to have a motherly influence in his life. Instead, she hovers on the fringes, touching Tip's life indirectly through the small influences she has with others; and as the novel winds to a close, that disparate group of individuals forms a protective chain around the now-adult Tip. Frucht literally illustrates how, according to Zamora, "[m]ost contemporary U.S. magical realists find a way to bring their ghosts above ground and integrate them into contemporary U.S. culture in order to enrich or remedy it" (Zamora 1995, 118).

Marginalization. When we categorize a writer's work as marginal, the issue often becomes a question of "nature or nurture"—is the author's natural (biological or geographical) marginality the deciding factor, or does the theme or subject matter "nurtured" in the text determine whether the work is a peripheral one? Criticism that addresses this question generally chooses "natural" marginalization as the more dominant feature. Marginalized writers tend to produce marginalized works, whether they intend to or not, because the very conditions at work on the authors similarly affect judgments of their texts. According to Jean-Pierre Durix, "Through 'marginal modes' of expression, writers [search for their own roots and rediscover] those myths which might help them to transcend this marginal position" (Durix 1998, 148). Magical realism not only challenges the center, it also allows the margins to rediscover their historical and mythical past.

Writers and critics in the United States are redefining our very "Americanness," how we perceive ourselves as parts of a larger whole in the New World—a fluid perception that, for marginalized authors, is predetermined by their peripheral status. Magical realism provides a tool for revision of marginality, perhaps especially for those authors who are themselves bound by geography, by race, by gender, or by other collective categorizations of identity. Magical realism permits the margins more than an entry into the main discourse, it offers the opportunity to reevaluate that central ideological constraint and to challenge the very features of the mainstream that allow for a margin in the first place. And, as the marginalized female magical realists perhaps best illustrate, the revision of the center inevitably requires confronting the margins themselves.

For the marginalized female writer, magical realism proves an optimum mode of choice because if its flexibility and marketability. Magical realism allows women writers who themselves exist on multiple planes to create worlds that can address all of those levels within a single work. Counterbalanced with this marginalization and silencing of the (m)other is the fact that women are cultural impetuses for the supernatural. Women provide magical realism with several things—children, homes, and rebellion being only a few of their offerings—as Morrison, Castillo, Foos, and others detail in their literature.

Frequently, the imposed order of the mainstream needs to be revised in order for mother and daughter characters to survive the margins. Pilar Puente manages to get herself kicked out of the Catholic school to which she refers as "Martyrs and Saints" (Garcia 1992, 58). M.O.M.A.S. (Mothers of Martyrs and Saints) does this for *So Far From God;* for a people "so far" from the God of Catholic religion, the rules of martyrdom are bent in order to honor the children whom the Hispanic mothers are losing. La Loca's death experience and visit to Hell reenvision what the priest understands his religion to be, but her experience grants her mother a privileged position in the community of other marginalized mothers.

Though the Hispanic origins of both the characters and the authors are driving forces behind the magical realism of Castillo's and Garcia's works, these authors, by reveling in (rather than separating themselves from) an admixture of traditionally U.S. popular culture with Hispanic overtones, claim simultaneous places in the Latin American and North American traditions. Several of this chapter's primary texts are set partially or entirely outside the United States, suggesting that a particular categorization such as American literature cannot hope to encapsulate the full landscapes of the text. In the most extreme cases, such as with *Cellophane, Dreaming in Cuban,* or *Everything Is Illuminated,* the supernatural occurrences are often or completely off site. Yet the authors refuse to compartmentalize the magic, to make it "foreign" or exotic and therefore less real.

Bibliography

Arana, Marie. *Cellophane.* New York: Dial, 2006.

Castillo, Ana. *So Far from God.* New York: Plume, 1994.

Chanady, Amaryll. *Magical Realism and the Fantastic: Resolved versus Unresolved Antinomies.* New York: Garland, 1985.

Delbaere, Jeanne. "Magic Realism: The Energy of the Margins." *Postmodern Fiction in Canada.* Theo L. D'haen and Hans Bertens, eds. Amsterdam: Rodopi, 1992.

Durix, Jean-Pierre. *Mimesis, Genres and Post-Colonial Discourse: Deconstructing Magic Realism.* New York: St. Martin's Press, 1998.

Foer, Jonathan Safran. *Everything Is Illuminated.* New York: Harper Perennial, 2003.

Foos, Laurie. *Ex Utero.* Minneapolis, MN: Coffee House Press, 1995.

Frucht, Abby. *Polly's Ghost.* New York: Scribner, 2000.

Garcia, Cristina. *Dreaming in Cuban.* New York: Ballantine Books, 1992.

Hancock, Geoff. "Magic or Realism: The Marvellous in Canadian Fiction." *Magic Realism and Canadian Literature: Essays and Stories.* Peter Hinchcliffe and Ed Jweinski, eds. Ontario, Canada: University of Waterloo Press, 1986.

Hill, Joe. "Pop Art." *With Signs & Wonders: An International Anthology of Jewish Fabulist Fiction.* Daniel M. Jaffe, ed. Montpelier, VT: Invisible Cities Press, 2001, 85–107.

King, Thomas. *Green Grass, Running Water.* New York: Bantam, 1994.

Leach, William. *Land of Desire: Merchants, Power, and the Rise of a New American Culture.* New York: Pantheon, 1993.

Millhauser, Steven. "Flying Carpets." *The Knife Thrower and Other Stories.* London: Phoenix, 1999, 66–75.

Morrison, Toni. *Beloved.* New York: Plume, 1987, 1998.

Yamashita, Karen Tei. *Tropic of Orange.* Minneapolis, MN: Coffee House Press, 1997.

Zamora, Lois Parkinson. *The Usable Past: The Imagination of History in Recent of the Americas.* Cambridge: Cambridge University Press, 1997.

Zamora, Lois Parkinson, and Wendy B. Faris, eds. *Magical Realism: Theory, History, Community.* Durham, NC: Duke University Press, 1995.

SHANNIN SCHROEDER

MANGA AND ANIME

Definition. *Manga* means, simply, "comic books" made for the Japanese market and *anime* is animation made for the Japanese market. In Japan these same terms are used in a general sense to mean works from anywhere in the world. For this essay, however, the narrower definition, which is the dominant one in the English speaking world, shall be used.

Other terms are used to describe types of manga commonly seen. *Shônen* is used to refer to manga for boys from grade school to the late teens. *Shôjo* is manga for girls of roughly the same age. *Seinen* is the kind of managa aimed at young men from late teens through mid twenties, college aged or young working men. *Gekiga* can be translated as "dramatic pictures" and is used for grittier manga stories with a certain hard edge to them. There is no plural ending to Japanese words; thus *manga* can refer to one or many. Generally, in this chapter I list the English title after the Japanese title for the section on Japan and vice versa for the section on the English market; the title used will be for the U.S. commercial release rather than an accurate translation. In some cases, the title is the same in both languages.

Why include animation in a work devoted to reading? Almost all anime available in North America is released subtitled; a format that historically the majority of anime fans have preferred over works being re-dubbed into English. Fans of anime and manga will notice that the historical section is slanted toward works and creators that have had an impact on the North American market.

History

Japan. Observing the history of manga and anime gives us a view on the development of these two forms of entertainment. This essay is far too short to go into much detail; however, this history can be seen as one of increasing sophistication and improvement of craft.

Manga Predecessors. There are many types of works that are considered predecessors of modern manga. These range from graffiti left on ancient temples to the humorous "Animal Scrolls" of Bishop Toba from the twelfth century (Schodt 1986, 28). Later there were the various illustrated books of the Edo Period (1603–1867), some of which, such as the Kibiyôshi, had images taking up much of the page with text for dialog and narration.

Osamu Tezuka (1928–1989) revolutionized the manga and anime industries with his willingness to experiment and innovate. One of his early innovations was to move away from conventional layouts in his manga and to draw his work as if he was using still images from the storyboards of a live action movie. Manga was then, and is still today, almost always black and white.

THE BEGINNINGS OF MANGA

During the Meiji Period (1868–1912) there was a rejection of older illustrated genres that led to the end of publication of these types of works for adults. At the same time the use of illustration in children's magazines became common. After World War II there was a shortage of affordable entertainment so manga rental shops, kashibonya, became common. Several noted manga artists of the late 1940s and the 1950s wrote works intended for sale to these shops. Among these was Osamu Tezuka, a young medical school graduate who found he could make a living as a manga artist rather than as a doctor.

Although manga stories can be short, comparable in length to an American comic book, they commonly are long works with a single story spanning multiple volumes, such as Rumiko Takahashi's *Maison Ikkoku,* which has 15 volumes in the English edition. The same is true of anime television series, which are often adapted from manga; usually television anime series are either 26 episodes or 13 episodes long. In these programs each episode is a chapter in a longer story; when the story is over, the series ends to be replaced by an entire new show. This structure for both anime and manga helps create a great deal of diversity because creators are able to try new ideas, and television time slots are not taken up by shows that last years.

Another type of manga that bears mentioning is *dôjinshi.* These are self-published works and not always manga because they sometimes are text publications, much like zines in America. The dôjinshi scene in Japan is very different than the scene for fan-produced works in the United States. Dôjinshi often use actual characters from manga, anime, video games, movies, or television shows and sometimes even actual people. Who makes and consumes dôjinshi? Fans, often of high school or college age, are often girls. Many professionals in Japan started out publishing dôjinshi and later graduated to professional work. Some professionals still produce dôjinshi as a hobby, occasionally spoofing their own characters. There are even several conventions entirely devoted to creators selling their own dôjinshi; the largest is Tokyo's famous Comic Market, commonly referred to as Comiket or Komiket, which takes place twice a year for three days in August and December drawing about 500,000 attendees. What do the Japanese companies think of this fan activity? They usually look the other way. Japanese trademark law is such that unauthorized use of their characters will not harm a company's rights and the popularity of a series can be measured in a sense by how many dôjinshi there are based on it.

Anime. The oldest commercial anime dates from 1917 when Oten Shimokawa made *Imokawa Mukuzo genkanban no maki* (*Mukuzo Imokawa, the Doorman*), the first of a series of shorts to be shown in movie houses before regular features. Such short works remained the norm until 1945 when the first anime feature length black and white film, *Momotaro Umi no Shinpei* (*Momotaro's Divine Sea Warriors*), was released. This was the longest of a series of anime made for internal propaganda, and it was paid for by the Japanese Imperial Navy. It would not be until 1958 that the next feature, *Hakujaden* (*Panda and the Magic Serpent*), would be released, this time in color.

The 1960s brought a new element to anime in Japan, works made for television. *Otogi Manga Karendâ* (*Otogi Manga Calendar*), made in 1962, was the first made-for-television series. *Otogi Manga Karendâ* consisted of three-minute educational clips discussing history; eventually 312 of these short works were made. The first half-hour children's series firmly establishing anime format in the medium for television in Japan was *Tetsuwan Atom* (*Astro Boy*) in 1963 to be soon followed by *Tetsujin 28-go* (*Gigantor*) and *8 Man* (*8th Man*).

The 1970s saw the number of anime titles for middle school students increase as well as the further development of the "giant robot" genre that started with *Tetsujin 28-go*. The end of the decade saw pivotal titles establish that older viewers could be an audience for anime. *Kido Senshi Gundam* (*Mobile Suit Gundam*) was a giant robot science fiction show about future war. Unlike other giant robot shows, the enemies were not invaders from space or another dimension; they were other humans, rebelling space colonists. The show had a serious element also, including the impact of war on civilians as well as the emotional impact of combat on soldiers. The television series was cut short after the sponsor realized that the toys were not selling well. However, reruns of the show had a high viewership that was proven to be older than the usual giant robot show audience. When *Gundam* model kits were released, they sold very well. This resulted in other *Gundam* anime being made, some that were not set in the same "universe" as the original series. In fact, to differentiate between these "universes," the original series and related works are referred to as belonging to the "Universal Century" *Gundam* shows.

The 1980s brought anime creators a new method of distribution made possible by the VCR. Original Video Animation, usually referred to as OVA by the Japanese and sometimes as OAV by others, were works made for sale directly as videos rather than first shown in theatres or on television. This format allowed creators to experiment and produce works that did not have a clearly defined market or had one that was too small to be profitable with the previous methods of distribution. The first commercial OVA was *Dallos,* directed by Mamoru Oshii and released in 1983. The experimental nature of many of the early OVA is apparent in the variety of works released in this format in the 1980s. Some OVA titles, such as the successful *Patlabor* and *Aa! Megamisama!* (Oh! My Goddess), would later be adapted into television series. Creators of OVA also had an advantage over television series in that OVA did not have the strict deadlines that broadcasting requires. This meant a series episode could be delayed if needed to ensure quality work. The OVA formant also increased the number of erotic works. There had been some relatively tame erotic anime released in theatres in the late 1960s and early 1970s with little financial success. However, erotic anime is still a very small percentage of the market; only a few titles are released each year, compared to the much larger television, movie, and non-erotic OVA markets.

In 1984 Hayao Miyazaki released his first independent animated feature, *Kaze no Tani no Nausicaä* (*Nausicaä of the Valley of the Wind*). A few years later Miyazaki was one of the most noted and internationally famous directors from Japan. In 1985 Miyazaki and fellow director Isao Takahata founded their own studio, Studio Ghibli, to make and release the kinds of anime they wanted to make. Also in 1984 a new company, GAINAX, was founded by a group of science fiction fans in their twenties, some of whom worked professionally in the anime industry. In 1987 GAINAX released *Oritsu Uchuugun—Honneamise no Tsubasa* (*Royal Space Force: The Wings of Honneamise*), one of several anime that raised the standards of quality and sophistication at the end of the 1980s. Other transformative titles of the period were *Akira,* released in 1988 and directed by Katsuhiro Otomo, and *Kidou Keisatsu Patlabor Gekijouban* (*Patlabor: The Movie*) in 1989, directed by Mamoru Oshii.

In the 1990s the anime industry experienced growth with an increasing number of programs on television, both conventional broadcast and cable or satellite. The general quality of the craft of animation increased with many works made for television rivaling feature films and OVA for the quality of their imagery. GAINAX continued to produce critically acclaimed works, and in 1995 it produced a 26-week episode television series that was to become one of the most watched anime series of the period. *Shin Seiki Evangelion (Neon Genesis Evangelion)*, directed by Hideaki Anno, proved highly successful and resulted in two movies, as well as a continuing line of toys and related merchandise. There are still other *Neon Genesis Evangelion* works in production over a decade later.

Miyazaki, Takahata, and Anno were only a few of the directors who attained auteur status in this period. Others include Oshii and Satoshi Kon. Kon, a manga artist, went from relative obscurity to international fame when the first anime he directed, the 1997 feature *Perfect Blue,* premiered at the Berlin International Film Festival. Anno and Oshii have also made award-winning live action films, whereas Kon has steadfastly stuck to doing just animation.

The United States and Canada

1960s. In the United States the history of translated anime began in the 1960s and manga in the 1970s. The earliest anime releases in the United States were three theatrical features, all re-dubbed into English in 1961: *Magic Boy (Shônen Sarutobi Sasuke)*, *Panda and the Magic Serpent (Hakujaden)*, and *Alakazam the Great (Saiyuki)*. Televised anime series were broadcast in the United States beginning in 1963 with *Astro Boy (Tetsuwan Atom)* by Osamu Tezuka. In 1965 the first color anime television series, also based on a Tezuka story, was shown on U.S. television. *Kimba The White Lion (Jungle Taitei)* was a series about an orphaned lion cub who was the ruler of his part of Africa. In fact, it was due to NBC licensing the show ahead of its production that allowed the use of color, which was much more expensive to produce than the various grays of earlier shows. Soon other Japanese shows, such as *Gigantor (Tetsujin 28-go)* and *8th Man (8 Man)*, were broadcast in the United States in edited and redubbed versions. The late 1960s saw another series that attained icon status for American television viewers, *Speed Racer (Mach, Go, Go, Go)*, edited in the U.S. version so no one died.

1970s. The 1970s was an era in which animated shows with even a mild level of violence were removed from network television and relegated to independent stations showing reruns of older programs. Anime, which often was far more serious than American cartoons, was largely not available for television viewers during this time. However, in 1978 the first new anime series to be shown on U.S. television hit the airwaves. *Battle of the Planets* was a heavily rewritten version of *Kagaku Ninjatai Gatchaman*. The story was drastically altered with the intent to capture some of the popularity of the first *Star Wars* movie of the previous year. The original tale was set in Japan with a special force defending the earth; the U.S. script set the tale far away in another part of the galaxy and greatly toned down the seriousness of the original story.

In 1977 there was another development that changed the market for anime and manga in the United States. The first anime and manga fan club, the Cartoon/Fantasy Organization, C/FO for short, held its first meeting in May 1977. Drawing its members heavily from existing science fiction fans, the founding of the C/FO was a significant event that resulted in similar clubs being established across the United

States. These early clubs helped solidify and expand early English-speaking anime and manga fandom by holding regular meetings, screenings of shows in raw Japanese, publishing newsletters, sharing information, and recruiting new fans. These fans provided the foundation for the establishment of a market in North America for anime and manga. In 1978 the first English translated manga was published, the first volume of *Barefoot Gen* (*Hadashi no Gen*)—the autobiographical manga of a Hiroshima survivor.

1980s. In 1983 the Japanese based publisher Kodansha International released the first book on manga in English, *Manga! Manga!*, by Frederik L. Schodt. *Manga! Manga!* quickly became, and remained, an essential reference for anyone interested in the subject.

It was nearly a decade after *Barefoot Gen* was first published in English that new translated manga titles were released. In May 1987 First Comics published its first issue of excerpts from the *Lone Wolf and Cub* (*Kozure Okami*) manga series. In the same month a partnership between Eclipse International and the new, Japanese owned, company Viz Communications released its first joint publications: *Area 88, Legend of Kamui* (*Kamui Gaiden*), and *Mai the Psychic Girl* (*Mai*). These works were not published in book form; rather they were in the usual American pamphlet format of comic books. Manga finally became a regular feature of comic book shops.

The following year was the beginning, by the Epic Comics branch of Marvel Comics, of publication for Katsuhiro Otomo's famous manga *Akira*. This was a project that also involved adding color to the original black and white work and took until 1995 to complete. Also in 1988 was the Eclipse International publication of *Appleseed* by the soon to be famous Masamune Shirow and translated by Studio Proteus, a company founded by Toren Smith in 1986 and dedicated to high quality work in their releases. Many of these early manga were seinen manga aimed at a late teen and early twenties male audience.

In 1989 the feature length version of the *Akira* anime was released redubbed into English to the American art house theatre circuit. It became a landmark film—for many years afterward if anyone had seen only one anime feature, the odds were that it was Otomo's groundbreaking work. Several companies were established in 1987 and 1988 to release anime, such as The Right Stuf, U.S. Renditions, Streamline Pictures, and AnimEigo. All four companies began releasing anime on VHS in 1989 and 1990, including the first subtitled anime releases, which started with AnimEigo's release of *Metal Skin Panic Madox 01*.

North American fans were ready to go beyond club publications and began launching commercial anime magazines, beginning with *Anime-Zine* in April 1986, *Animage* in 1987, and *Protoculture Addicts* in 1988. *Protoculture Addicts,* published in Montreal, was devoted to one show, *Robotech,* until 1990, when it became a general anime, manga, and Japanese culture magazine; it still exists today, making it the longest running anime magazine in North America.

In November 1987 Ann Schubert launched the first Usenet newsgroup devoted to anime, rec.arts.anime, and soon it was not only available through computer BBS networks but also via the Internet. Today it still exists divided into several specialized newsgroups all beginning with rec.arts.anime. In 1988 the Valley of the Wind BBS, the official BBS for *Animag* magazine, started in San Mateo, California. This was perhaps the first anime BBS established in North America.

Another significant development in the late 1980s was the creation, with the use of computers and video editing hardware, of fan subs, that is, noncommercial, and illegal, video releases of anime with subtitles created by fans and distributed for free, mainly to clubs for showings, by networks of volunteers. This was to provide clubs with a greater number of titles to show and help spread anime to more viewers.

College and University based anime clubs also came into existence at this time. Earlier some C/FO chapters used facilities at schools without actually being student organizations, for example the Cartoon/Fantasy Organization of Denver, founded in 1982, met in an available room at the Iliff School of Theology until the club president, Michael Burgess, who was an Iliff student, graduated. In time actual student-run groups began organizing, such as Cal-Animage Alpha, the anime club at the University of California Berkeley, which was founded in January 1989, and MIT Anime, which was founded the following year.

1990s. Dallas, Texas, holds the distinction of being the location of the first U.S. anime convention with three locally advertised conventions, Yamatocon in August 1983 and March 1986 and Animagic in September 1986, and the first nationally advertised general anime convention, Project A-Kon, in July 1990. In 1991 Anime-Con '91 took place in San Jose, California. Organized in part by Toren Smith of Studio Proteus and Toshio Okada of GAINAX, AnimeCon '91 had a large number of Japanese guests and an original opening animation done by U.S. fans. In October U.S. Manga Corps, a division of Central Park Media, released the first tape of their first anime title *Dominion*. After this new anime and manga companies were established every few years.

Viz entered the anime magazine scene with the release of *Animerica* issue 0 in November 1992. The magazine was to run until June 2005 as a newsstand publication and then be transformed into a free quarterly issued largely to publicize Viz products. In the early 1990s Studio Proteus changed publishers and had their seinen manga works handled by Dark Horse.

With organized anime and manga fandom firmly established, AnimEigo released a title in 1993 that shaped fan activities for some time: they did not even bother to translate the title. *Otaku no Video* was another product from GAINAX, which was an OVA playfully mocking both Japanese fandom and their own science fiction fan origins. American fans looked at this work, which is extremely dense with examples of Japanese fan activities, and gleefully took part in many similar activities, even proudly calling themselves otaku. Otaku is a term with mixed origins: originally a word that can be used to address someone in a very polite manner, it became heavily used by polite and shy Japanese fans when speaking to each other. In time it came to be used to refer to obsessed fans and often not in a complimentary manner, much like nerd or geek in English. However, there are Japanese fans who without hesitation use the term to describe themselves. In recent years the term has lost some of its edge in Japan as otaku have come to be seen as important in both the production and consumption of entertainment, not only anime and manga but also live action movies and video games.

The mid-1990s saw the earliest U.S. anime releases of works that were intended for a female audience. Starting in September 1995 *Sailor Moon* hit the television airwaves in a highly edited and redubbed version that quickly drew teenaged and younger girls to anime. This permanently transformed anime fandom; before *Sailor Moon*, fans were mainly male, college age and older. Girls and women now became major players in the fan scene. Partly due to the popularity of *Sailor Moon* bringing in younger fans, High School anime clubs began to spread at this time. The first subtitled video release of a title aimed at a female audience, *Here is Greenwood*, set in a boy's high school dorm, was released in 1996. The following year, 1997, saw the first anime DVD released in the United States, *Battle Arena Toshinden* from Central Park Media.

Given the growth of female fandom, a new company, Mixx Entertainment, began releasing the *Sailor Moon* manga in 1998, with the original characters renamed to match the anglicized names in the U.S. version of the television series. They also published a manga anthology magazine called *MixxZine,* later renamed *TOKYOPOP,* that ran until 2000. Other anthology magazines started at this time, such as the Eisner Award-nominated *Pulp,* aimed at releasing "manga for grownups," *Animerica Extra* for boys and girls, and *Smile,* a girl's magazine that also included manga. Most of these magazines only lasted a few years. However, at the same time, more of the manga publishers were abandoning the releasing of manga in American comic book format and switching to anthologies or directly to the paperback book format, which quickly became the standard way to package most manga.

In July 1998 Viz did something very different—released the first volume of the *Neon Genesis Evangelion* manga in a special collector's edition unflipped. Until this time all manga had been flipped from its original Japanese right-to-left orientation to the Western left-to-right orientation. This involved extra work on the part of the companies to touch up the art that not only increased the cost of production but also took time. Japanese artists also often requested that their design work not be reversed, and some were rumored to refuse to license their works unless they would not be flipped. Readers easily adjusted to the change, and it would not be long before leaving the art unflipped became the norm, even to the point of re-releasing previously flipped volumes in second unflipped editions. A few years later, in January 2002, TOKYOPOP not only announced that all of their manga were going to an unflipped format but they also made this decision a major part of their publicity for that year with their "100% Authentic Manga" advertising campaign.

In the late 1990s there was another significant development—major chain bookstores began selling manga. This opened up the market to a significant segment of the population that would rarely enter comic book shops—girls. For the next several years, manga sales grew at a rate of over 100% per year mainly due to teen-age girls becoming a large segment of the customer base. This also resulted in companies placing more of their resources to serve the needs of this segment of the market

The Internet also played a larger role in communication between fans. In 1995 the Anime Web Turnpike, a large directory of anime and manga related Web sites, was started to help fans locate useful resources online. In 1998 two new anime services were established on the Web, The Anime News Network and Anime on DVD. Both contain archives of press releases from companies, reviews, articles, online forums, reference tools, and the latest news.

2000–. In the early twenty-first century, magazine anthologies are still being released and experimented with in the United States, such as the successful monthly *Shônen Jump* boy's manga anthology from Viz, which began publishing in 2002, and its sister publication, *Shojo Beat,* which began in 2005, serializing manga for girls. Other manga anthologies, such as the seinen and *Raijin Comics* (2003–2004) and the general *Super Manga Blast* (2000–2006), did not do as well.

Trends and Themes. Anime and manga have had an impressive growth in North America over the past few decades; however, they still remain a niche market and have not become part of the mainstream entertainment industry. After all, entertainment news programs on television and columns in the press rarely cover anime or manga. Because of the niche market for these products, fans are a significant percentage of the consumers. Perhaps this will change in the near future—perhaps even by the time these words reach print. However, even now manga and anime are so firmly established that almost all manga is no longer flipped, and it is almost unheard of to release anime unless it is unedited and subtitled. The twenty-first century has also seen the practice of localization, the removal of Japanese elements in anime, and manga translations have almost vanished. Whereas in the past names were changed to American sounding ones, foods were given "familiar" names like pizza or pancakes instead of okonomiyaki, and in extreme cases scenes where people were eating with chopsticks were edited out, today many see the Japanese elements as part of why anime and manga sell. This has reached the point that some works are released under their original Japanese titles, such as *Hikaru no Go, Rurouni Kenshin, Kaze Hikaru, Genshiken, Gokusen, Kaze no Yojimbo,* and *Haibane Renmei.*

Female fandom had changed since 1995 when *Sailor Moon* hit the American airwaves. Many of the earlier fans have grown up, but the girls did not leave their anime and manga interests behind when they became women. Instead they often delved deeper into anime, manga, and fan activities. This was evident in a convention that even five years earlier, before *Sailor Moon,* would not have seemed possible, an entire convention devoted to what is variously called shônen-ai, Boys Love, or BL by the Japanese. YAOI-con 2001 was an entire convention devoted to manga and anime that focus on male-male romance, often with a sexual element to it. Needless to say the convention had, and continues to have, an age requirement of 18 and over for admission. In Japan such male-male love stores have existed in women's manga since the 1970s, the stories and images ranging from Platonic to torrid. The term *yaoi* is a Japanese abbreviation for the phrase yâma-nashi, ochi-nashi, imi-nashi (no climax, no punch line, no meaning). In Japan yaoi is a genre of fan-published manga, often male-male pairing parodies of commercial works, much like Slash fiction in Star Trek and other English language fandoms. English-speaking fans have come to apply the term *yaoi* to all stories involving male-male parings, not just fan produced works. In recent years the number of translated anime and manga that are in this genre have increased to the point that some stores have subsections devoted to these volumes.

The growth of yaoi as a genre shows that adult women are not only consuming manga and anime but also actually becoming active in the translation and release of products, not only product lines of established companies, such as Digital Manga, but also independent companies, such as Blu and DramaQueen. Major players such as Viz and TOKYOPOP have for some time released non-yaoi manga for women.

Adult male, seinen, fans have always had some anime and manga aimed at their interests, especially titles from Studio Proteus and Viz. In 2002 TOKYOPOP published their first manga title aimed at a seinen audience. For a publisher with a reputation for publishing works aimed at teen and pre-teen girls this was quite a step. This title was *GTO: Great Teacher Onizuka* by Tohru Fujisawa, the tale of a former biker turned private schoolteacher. *GTO* was to become very popular with adult fans of both genders as well as older teens; TOKYOPOP later released the *GTO* anime television series on DVD. TOKYOPOP has continued to publish some seinen with works such as *GTO The Early Years* and *Rose Hip Zero,* both also by Fujisawa.

Another trend, reflected in the growing market for yaoi and seinen manga titles is the growing number of adults enjoying these stories—many of whom started out as fans at a younger age. Fans are also becoming much younger with grade school aged kids now wanting to read more manga and watch more anime. Companies now have to take both age ranges into consideration when they shop for new titles to bring out, not just readers in their teens.

Since the turn of the century, a few manga companies began publishing works by North American creators with Asian elements and calling them manga. TOKYOPOP even began an annual contest called the Rising Starts of Manga; the winners have their works published. These have been variously called American-manga, Ameri-manga, Original English Manga, and other names. Some see this as a cynical ploy to simply make more money off the popularity of manga. After all, why refer to a work done by American creators with a Japanese term like *manga* when perfectly good English terms like *comic book* and *graphic novel* already exist?

On the other hand, many American fans of anime, manga, and Japanese video games have begun to create their own comics with Japanese influences, some on the Internet in the form of Web Comics. Publishers in the United States have even commercially released a few of these Web Comics in printed form; popular examples include *Megatokyo* by Fred Gallagher or *Peach Fuzz* by Lindsay Cibos.

The year 2003 brought several interesting developments. Hayao Miyazaki's *Spirited Away* (*Sen to Chihiro no Kamikakushi*) won the Oscar for best-animated feature. Vertical Inc., a respected New York-based publisher of Japanese popular literature, published the first hardcover volume in Osamu Tezuka's *Buddha* eight-volume manga series. *Buddha* received excellent reviews in the regular press and sold well enough that the company started publishing older classic works that were unlikely to come out from other manga publishers. Also in 2003, the Fremont, California,-based manga publisher Comics One, later renamed DR Master, brought out a translation of the *Onegai Teacher* novel, a work related to previously released anime and manga series. Later, other manga publishers began releasing prose works related to manga and anime, such as Dark Horse's release of the *Ghost in the Shell Stand Alone Complex* novels, *The Great Adventure of the Dirty Pair* by noted science fiction writer Haruka Takachiho, as well as ADV Manga's release of GAINAX executive Yasuhiro Takeda's autobiographical work *The Notenki Memoirs*.

We are now also seeing licenses to anime and manga titles lapse, and they may either become available in English or be re-released by other companies. Sometimes after a title has been out of print for some time, another company steps in and picks up the license with the view that the market has changed and the particular work will do better now than in the past. An example of such a title is the manga *Crying Freeman* by Kazuo Koike that was originally licensed by Viz and years later reissued by Dark Horse.

Televised anime have also changed, especially on cable and satellite systems. Whereas the Cartoon Network began regularly broadcasting anime in the late 1990s, other companies have also begun dedicated cable channels for anime. A.D. Vision established the Anime Network in late 2002, and in 2006 the FUNimation Channel was created. Because of its wide distribution throughout the country, The Cartoon Network's two weekly slots, Toonami and Adult Swim, showing anime on a regular basis has had the greatest success in introducing many more viewers to anime and manga. As the other networks expand their market penetration, this could shift.

To some, it appeared that the industry was becoming saturated with large numbers of titles being released, for example 810 different anime DVD releases for 2005 declining to 765 for 2006. For manga, 1,014 volumes were released in 2005 and 1,096 in 2006. In late 2005 the anime and manga industry was hit with a financial blow when Musicland shut down all 61 of the Media Play stores it owned, filed for protection from creditors, and closed many Sam Goody and Suncoast stores. Several anime companies had been selling directly to the Musicland-owned chains and found themselves lacking needed cash. In early 2006, Central Park Media announced that it was in the uncomfortable position of laying off most of its staff as a result of the Musicland bankruptcy. Central Park Media even issued a press release with an email address for prospective employers if they had positions open that former staff could apply for.

In 2004 Toren Smith, citing a saturated manga market, sold Studio Proteus to his publisher Dark Horse Comics after nearly 20 years of producing some of the best manga translation in the industry. Smith continues to do translation work without the grueling schedule he had set for himself while running the company. Dark Horse, on the other hand, has continued to provide manga for the seinen audience, such as many works written by the prolific and popular Kazuo Koike, including a complete edition of the *Lone Wolf and Cub* manga series.

Context and Issues

Different Cultural Perspectives. Anime and manga give those who enjoy such products exposure to several perspectives that are very different from the U.S. and Canadian entertainment industries. On one hand, there is the exposure to Japanese culture and history, such as *Rurouni Kenshin* set in the late nineteenth century, *Maison Ikkoku* set in modern Tokyo, and *Genshiken* with its cast of college student otaku.

On the other hand, there are also stories with different views than those reflected in American works. Relating to the concerns of adolescents, this is especially true for girls, a market largely ignored by American comic book and graphic novel publishers. However, this is also true for boys—for example, the male oriented romance manga, and the anime adapted from them, of Masakazu Katsura and Izumi Matsumoto. Issues of gender identity are also topical in some recent works, aimed at teens but popular with adults, such as *Revolutionary Girl Utena* (*Shoujo Kakumei Utena*), *Day of Revolution* (*Kakumei no Hi*), and *Kashimashi—Girl Meets Girl.*

Geopolitics. Internal and international politics do not escape scrutiny. A recent two-season series *Ghost in the Shell Stand Alone Complex* (*Kokaku Kidotai Stand Alone Complex*) dealt extensively with a near-future Japan that, although neutral, did not escape damage and repercussions of World War III, such as large numbers of refugees afterward. The series also deals with Japan's often-uncomfortable military relationship with the United States and the treaties between the two nations. In fact, one key thread that runs through many anime and manga that deal with war and the aftermath is the impact on the civilian populations. Japan's experience of losing a significant percentage of its young male population and the destruction of its major cities in World War II is only part of what shapes such a view. There is also a considerable body of literature, memoirs, as well as manga and anime based on the experiences of children during war time, the most famous of these are *Barefoot Gen* and Studio Ghibli's anime feature *Grave of the Fireflies* (*Hotaru No Haka*).

Libraries. Libraries have increasingly made manga and anime part of their collections. Workshops on graphic novels, manga, and anime are common at librarian conventions. Articles appear in the professional press and increasingly titles are reviewed to assist in the selection of material for library collections. This is not as easy as selecting books where there have been long established resources for evaluating items to add to collections. Anime and manga have only recently been sufficiently reviewed to enable libraries to make decisions about adding them to library collections. This is especially important with mediums that are visual; local community standards concerning violence, nudity, and sexuality have to be considered in ways that are not a problem with written text. Librarians have a long history of standing up for freedom of access to materials. However, they also do not particularly care for conflict and will pay attention to the community they serve. Sometimes elements in a community will not respect this viewpoint and will seek to impose their will on the local library with the assistance of outside forces such as local politicians. For example, in April 2006 Paul Gravett's book *Manga: Sixty Years of Japanese Comics* was pulled from the libraries of suburban San Bernadino County, California, on orders from Bill Postmus, Chairman of the Board of Supervisors. Why would a scholarly book on manga get pulled? Two pages, 144 and 145, had six small images—pages from adult manga with sexual content. The book was shelved in the adult section of the library, where a teen-age boy found it, checked it out, and showed the two pages to his mother.

Conventions. Conventions continue to play a significant role in fan activities. The number of conventions in the United States and Canada has grown since the first small ones of the early 1990s to well over 100 each year. Many are small local events; some are much larger. The largest are Anime Expo, which in 2006 released attendance figures of over 40,000, and Otakon, which has had to cap attendance at 25,000, as that is what they feel the Baltimore Convention Center can safely handle.

Reception

Exhibits. Two art exhibits focusing on anime and manga were held in 2005. Little Boy: The Arts of Japan's Exploding Subculture, curated by Takashi Murakami, ran from April 8–July 24 at the Japan Society in New York City. Another ran from October 26–December 8 at California State University Chico and was titled Shojo Manga: Girl Power! and curated by associate professor of art education Masami Toku. The Shojo Manga exhibit also toured North America. Both exhibits sought to expose Americans to aspects of Japanese post-World War II entertainment, and both were curated by artists. In 2007 the Asian Art Museum in San Francisco held the first manga and anime exhibit at a major U.S. museum from June 2–September 9. The exhibit, Tezuka: The Marvel of Manga, was devoted entirely to one creator, Osamu Tezuka, whose influence and significance is widely acknowledged in Japan.

Awards. In the U.S. comic book industry, the most prestigious award is the Eisner. Between 1998 and 2006 manga won Eisner awards 7 out of 9 times for the Best U.S. Edition of Foreign Material. Given the high quality of much of the European work released in the United States, these figures are significant.

As was already mentioned, in 2003 Hayao Miyazaki's *Spirited Away* won the Oscar for best animated feature. However, other anime features not made for a child audience that have been submitted for consideration have not been able to reach the ballot. Many of these films have also received notable awards elsewhere, such as *Millennium Actress*, which won both the Best Animation Film and the Fantasia Ground-Breaker Award at the Fant-Asia Film Festival in 2001.

Adaptations. The American movie and television industries have expressed interest in releasing remakes of several titles for the U.S. market. Proposed films include *Neon Genesis Evangelion, Battle Angel Alita, Ghost in the Shell, Speed Racer, Witch Hunter Robin,* and others. However, to date (2007) few have reached the stage of production.

Selected Authors. To North American consumers many works released in Japan before 2000 have only recently become available in English. For this reason, any discussion of contemporary creators has to include some works done before 2000. Also, given the large number of persons and companies whose works are available, the following choices are limited to a few of the better known.

Hayao Miyazaki is perhaps the best-known creator of anime. His *Nausicaa* manga, his only manga series to be translated, is available in a large format duplicating the tones and colors of the original Japanese release. One cannot mention Miyazaki without pointing out the work of his fellow Studio Ghibli cofounder Isao Takahata. Works recently released in North America directed by Takahata include *Pom Poko* and *My Neighbors the Yamadas*.

Another name with both an anime and manga connection is Mamoru Oshii. Oshii has written both novels and manga, some of which have been adapted into anime. One of his most recent anime works, *Ghost in the Shell Innocence*, was funded in part by Studio Ghibli and animated by Production I.G, a well-known company heavily associated with Oshii's projects. Production I.G also released the *Ghost in the Shell Stand Alone Complex* television series, inspired by a manga series by Masamune Shirow. Shirow continues to release manga at a slow pace, as well as work on various video game and animation projects, such as the *Appleseed* movie series. Satoshi Kon continues to be productive with such recent works as *Millenium Actress, Tokyo Godfathers,* the *Paranoia Agent* television series, and his most recent feature, *Paprika*.

For manga, Osamu Tezuka, who died in 1989, has become widely known through recent translations of his works for adult readers, such as the *Ode to Kirihito, Buddha,* and *Phoenix* series. A major factor in the growing awareness of his work is the fact that magazines and newspapers that rarely cover manga have reviewed many of his titles. Writers popular with a younger audience include one of the best known, Rumiko Takahashi, author of large multivolume series such as *Urusei Yatsura, Maison Ikkoku, Ranma ½,* and *Inuyasha*. All of these works and several shorter ones have been adapted to anime and released in the United States. A contrast to Takahashi is a man whose works are very different than her teen and young adult style, a man who was her teacher when she was beginning her career. Kazuo Koike is best known in the United States for his lengthy *Lone Wolf and Cub* manga series. However, several other series of his have been coming out in English in rapid succession—*Lady Snow Blood, Samurai Executioner, Path of the Assassin,* and a new release of his *Crying Freeman* manga. Koike does not do the art; he is a writer and has worked with a variety of artists over the years. His manga have not only been adapted into anime but also into live action movies and television shows. An artist who works with several writers is Takeshi Obata, who illustrated *Hikaru no Go*, the tale of a high school student who discovered the ancient game of Go and struggles to become a professional player. Another work Obata illustrated is *Death*

Note, a suspenseful tale of murder and the supernatural. Both titles are also available as anime in the United States. Reviews are difficult to track down, outside of anime and manga specialty magazines aimed at fans, only professional journals for librarians review such works with any regularity.

One interesting development since 2000 is the increasing number of academics writing about anime and manga. For manga there are such books as *Permitted and Prohibited Desires* by Anne Allison and *Adult Manga* by Sharon Kinsella. Anime books include *Anime From Akira to Princess Mononoke* by Susan Napier released in 2000 and in a later edition titled *Anime From Akira to Howl's Moving Castle,* Brian Ruh's *Stray Dog of Anime: The films of Mamoru Oshii,* and *Cinema Anime,* an anthology of essays edited by Steven T. Brown. There is even an annual scholarly anthology of essays titled *Mechademia* published by the University of Minnesota Press.

Bibliography

Allison, Anne. *Permitted and Prohibited Desires.* Boulder, CO: Westview Press, 1996.
Kinsella, Sharon. *Adult Manga.* Honolulu, HI: University of Hawaii Press, 2000.
Koike, Kazuo. *Path of the Assassin.* Milwaukie, OR: Dark Horse Manga, 2006.
———. *Lady Snow Blood.* Australia: Madmen Entertainment, 2005.
———. *Lone Wolf and Cub.* Tokyo: Futabasha, 1970–1976.
———. *Samurai Executioner.* Milwaukie, OR: Dark Horse Manga, 2004.
Miyazaki, Hayao. *Spirited Away.* San Francisco, CA: Viz Communications, 2002.
Napier, Susan. *Anime From Akira to Princess Mononoke.* New York: Palgrave, 2000.
Obata, Takeshi. *Hikaru No Go.* San Francisco, CA: Viz Communications, 2004.
Ruh, Brian. *Stray Dog of Anime.* New York: Palgrave, 2004.

Further Reading

Anime News Network: http://www.animenewsnetwork.com/; Anime on DVD: http://www.animeondvd.com/; Clements, Jonathan, and Helen McCarthy. *The Anime Encyclopedia: Revised and Expanded Edition.* Berkeley: Stone Bridge Press, 2006; Patten, Fred. *Watching Anime Reading Manga.* Berkeley: Stone Bridge Press, 2004; Schodt, Frederik. *Manga! Manga!* Tôkyô: Kodansha International, 1986; Schodt, Frederik. *Dreamland Japan.* Berkeley: Stone Bridge Press, 1996; Yasuhiro, Takeda. *The Notenki Memoirs.* Houston, TX: ADV Manga, 2005.

GILLES POITRAS

MILITARY LITERATURE

Definition. Stories about soldiers and war have been a staple in American literature. As such, military literature is an extremely expansive, influential genre. Military literature can be broadly defined as any literature that represents one of the many facets of the military. While much military literature is focused on what may be termed *combat literature*—fiction and nonfiction narratives that describe combat—military literature is much more than only stories about combat. As Philip K. Jason and Mark A. Graves write, "The literature of war has a wider arc that takes in presentations of causes and consequences of the battlefield action. It has political, cultural, and psychological dimensions" (Jason and Graves 2001, ix). In this broad scope, military literature portrays life in the military—both during war and times of peace—as well as explores how civilians interact with the military, either completely outside the military looking in or as family and friends of soldiers attempting to deal

ACCLAIMED MILITARY LITERATURE WRITERS WHO NEVER SERVED

Authors of military literature have often had close contact with the military, but service in the armed forces is not a prerequisite for writing military literature. For example, Sabina Murray's *The Caprices* (2002) is written about two soldiers in the Pacific Campaign of World War II and has won many comparisons to military literature icon Stephen Crane's *Red Badge of Courage* for its imaginative power, especially because, like Crane, Murray never actually experienced the battlefield firsthand before writing about war. Likewise, Tom Clancy, usually classified as a techno-thriller writer, deals extensively in military representations and themes but was rejected from military service because of his nearsightedness (Garson 1996, 4). Even though these writers haven't served in the military, their works are still considered military literature because some aspect of the military is focused on in their writing.

with how the military shapes their lives. Military literature is often, but not always, focused on soldiers (traditionally men, but this stereotype is slowly equalizing) who experience combat on the battlefront. Most military literature fiction, poetry, and memoirs tend to describe this aspect of the military and could be aptly called "war stories" for their focus on combat details But there are pieces of military literature that portray other aspects of the military, such as Dale Brown's short story "Leadership Material" (Brown 2001), which describes the process of rank advancement while exploring the strained relationships of those who fight on the frontlines and those who provide the infrastructure necessary for the armed services to function.

One of the most popular military literature genres is the memoir or personal narrative. Since 2000, memoirs on Vietnam and the first Gulf War have been widely published. Works such as Joel Turnipseed's *Baghdad Express* (2003) or Anthony Swofford's *Jarhead* (2003), which became a better-known movie two years after its publication, have held popular attention, especially with their publications coinciding with the beginning of the current war in Iraq. Fictional stories about the military are also extremely popular (just look through any bookstore and see how many tanks, planes, subs, or soldiers are on the covers) and traditionally tend to glorify the armed forces, combat, and undying patriotism toward the United States. Conversely, poetry about the military since Vietnam has been largely protestant. Fluctuating between these apparent polar opposites, memoirs are often a conflation of the two extremes, generally attempting to portray both the dehumanization of military experience while simultaneously describing the camaraderie and personal growth one finds in a military life.

Historical works on past wars have also been extremely prolific, the Gulf War in particular during the buildup to and invasion of Iraq in 2004. Other forms of writing that could possibly be defined as military literature are blogs and letters of soldiers serving in the armed forces, as well as journalistic writing from reporters embedded with active troops. Overall, the defining element of military literature is that the piece of writing is about the military in some way.

Because military literature is any writing that deals with military issues, there are obviously ample opportunities for blurring genre lines. For instance, Tom Clancy and Stephen Coonts, two authors whose works are traditionally labeled as techno-thrillers, could also easily be classified as military literature writers because many of their works focus on the armed forces. Likewise, contemporary military literature is not constricted to contemporary militaries or current conflicts, so one will quickly find multiple science fiction military literatures, such as David Drake's collection *Foreign Legions* (2001) or Dave Grossman and Leo Frankowski's *The Two Space War* (2005). Authors also often reach back in time to portray earlier wars. Jeff Shaara, for instance, wrote his highly acclaimed *Gods and Generals* (1998) about the Civil War, and has since written recently written *To the Last Man* (2004), which takes place during World War I, and *The Rising Tide: A Novel of World War II* (2006), among his many other works. Shaara's and others' works that deal with past events are traditionally labeled historical fiction, but their focus on war or the military of days gone by make these works military literature. While authors such as Shaara create **historical fiction**, the creation of alternate histories has also been a fruitful bed for authors, such as Harry Turtledove in his *American Empire* series, to explore military literature in a world of what might have been if, for instance, the Allies didn't win World War II or if the North didn't force the confederacy back into the Union. Vastly different from the other types of military literature, *Married to the Military: A Survival Guide for Military Wives, Girlfriends, and Women in Uniform* (Leyva 2003) or Shellie Vandevoorde's *Separated By Duty, United In Love* (2006) appeal to an audience with a very different interest in and viewpoint of the military, that of the military wife. These books tend to focus on offering advice over telling a story. James Thomas's *My Dad Is Going Away, but He Will be Back One Day: A Deployment Story* (2004) pushes genre limits even further by creating military literature in children's book form.

Military literature can be anything from techno-thrillers to self-help and relationship books to children stories. From this we see that military literature is a broad, inclusive term applicable to many genres of writing. In this chapter we will examine the most popular forms of military literature—novels and memoirs. This is not to slight other forms of writing dealing with any of the many aspects of the military but to instead focus on the most popular forms of military literature. See FURTHER READINGS at the end of the chapter for information on military poetry.

History. This broad spectrum of possible military literature genres is to be expected. Stephen Coonts, author of countless fictional works, argues in his introduction to *Combat,* a collection of what he calls "techno-thriller novellas," (Coonts 2001, 12) that "armed conflict has been a fertile setting for storytellers since the dawn of the written word, and probably before" (Coonts 2001, 9). Others agree. As John W.I. Lee informs us, the aristocratic Greek soldier, Xenophon, wrote the first soldier's memoir in the fourth century B.C.E. (Lee 2005, 41). *The Iliad,* possibly the best-known example of military literature, is estimated to have been written about four centuries earlier. Every nation since (and most likely before) has had its various military literatures, and while American literature has been no different in writing about war, American literature is unusual because it is relatively modern, without ancient national literatures of its own. The modern war story, then, has undergone vast changes while keeping in touch with traditional military story themes. As we trace the development of military literature in America, it will be helpful to examine a few particular works to illustrate the depth of the genre. The pieces focused on in this chapter are often considered some of the most influential pieces of military literature, and themes we see in them are often returned to in military literature written today. Again, for space constraints we are forced to limit the number of "key" pieces of American military literature over the centuries, but the selected bibliography will offer those interested further readings connected to this issue.

Before beginning this short summary, it is interesting to note that some scholars believe military literature perhaps consciously attempts to erase its literary legacy. According to Samuel Hynes, well known war narrative scholar,

> The stories that men tell of war belong to a curious class of writing. In most war narratives there is nothing to suggest that the author is aware of any previous example: no quotations or allusions or imitations of earlier models, and no evident knowledge of previous wars, or even of other theatres in the war that he is recalling. War writing, it seems, is a genre without a tradition to the men who write it. (Hynes 1997, 4)

This noted, it is interesting that there are still trends and threads of commonality among many military literatures. But Hynes's commentary hinges on the word "seems" in the final sentence. In fact, military literature, as with most literature, in some way responds to the writing of earlier generations. As we will see, there are themes and trends in contemporary military literature that can be traced to literary ancestors since the Civil War.

In this light, many view Stephen Crane's *The Red Badge of Courage* (1895) as the genesis of the modern American war story. Written by a young author who never experienced war before producing the novel, *The Red Badge of Courage* tells the story of a young soldier, Henry Flemming, usually identified as "the youth," who enlists with the Union army; his subsequent fleeing from the battlefield; his attempt at self-justification for his supposed cowardice; and finally his triumphant return to the battle and earned self-respect. While Crane hadn't experienced war personally before writing *Red Badge,* it was immediately hailed as a realistic depiction of the Civil War by veterans who experienced what the story depicts. *Red Badge* deals with, among other things, issues of courage, honor, duty, and the craziness and atrocities of war—themes that many pieces of military literature since have repeated.

For example, note how the following passage describes a charge the main character, Fleming, makes with his company on the opposing army's lines:

> But there was a frenzy made from this furious rush. The men, pitching forward insanely, had burst into cheerings, moblike and barbaric, but tuned in strange keys that can arouse the dullard and the stoic. It made a mad enthusiasm that, it seemed, would be incapable of checking itself before granite and brass. There was the delirium that encounters despair and death, and is heedless and blind to the odds. (Crane 2001, 102).

Crane uses particular words such as "frenzy," "furious," "moblike," and "delirium" to give a feeling of insanity and confusion in the charge, describing what many have called the "fog of war." This craziness of war has been both repeated by many authors and transformed into a humorous theme by displaying just how absurd war is. *Catch-22* (1961) by Joseph Heller, unlike the seriousness of *Red Badge,* turns to humor and absurdity instead of poignancy and realism. In one instance the character Yossarian, a bomber pilot who has decided he doesn't want to fly any more missions, tries to convince a doctor he is crazy, thus forcing the doctor to ground him and not allow Yossarian to fly any more missions. But as Doc Daneeka explains to Yossarian, the only pilots who are truly sane are those who don't want to fly the missions. As Yossarian and Doc Daneeka discuss another "crazy" pilot, the narrator informs us

> There was only one catch and that was Catch-22, which specified that a concern for one's own safety in the face of dangers that were real and immediate was the process of a rational mind. Orr was crazy and could be grounded. All he had to do was ask; and as soon as he did, he would no longer be crazy and would have to fly more missions. Orr would be crazy to fly more missions and sane if he didn't, but if he was sane he had to fly them. If he flew them he was crazy and didn't have to; but if he didn't want to he was sane and had to. Yossarian was moved very deeply by the absolute simplicity of this clause of Catch-22 and let out a respectful whistle. (Heller 1961, 46)

This passage is not only entertaining through its dizzying ridiculousness but also highlights another aspect of the craziness of war—that to desire to go to war is in itself an act of lunacy because it places one's body in harm's way. Both the serious and comic representations of the craziness of war have been underlying themes in many military literatures in American history.

Catch-22 has been praised by many as one of the most influential novels of the twentieth century, and has influenced much subsequent military literature. For example, Turnipseed's *Baghdad Express* also deals with issues of absurdity, in somewhat different fashions. While Turnipseed isn't as out and out funny as Heller, he does use absurdity to add a humorous element to his memoir. For example, his memoir is dotted with homemade comics that break up the narrative tension his story creates. In one instance, a comic portrays soldier responses to an air raid call. Among the jokes in this comic is that the air raid informs soldiers that three enemy planes are en route to attack and that two are intercepted and destroyed, but it forgets to mention the state of the third enemy plane. Instead of mentioning the plane, the voice over the intercom states "the skies are now clear and should continue to clear up" (Turnipseed 2003, 49). The statement is even more absurd because the picture before it indicates the weather is rainy, driving all soldiers inside. Thus the clear skies are false on two levels. While the joke isn't particularly funny, it's medium—a comic in the middle of a memoir—helps to illustrate the absurdity of both the information given to troops as well as the illogical elements of the military itself. From this we see a gradual progression from one century to another where issues of the craziness of war are played out in different ways, and we can expect further representations of the craziness of war in military literature to come.

Tim O'Brien has also held major influence over the military literature genre. His works *Going After Cacciato* (1978) and *The Things They Carried* (1990) have set standards of form and style that many military writers have felt compelled to follow. One of his most popular works, *The Things They Carried* is a series of loosely related stories dealing with issues such as one soldier's contemplated draft-dodging or how soldiers cope with losing friends and fellow soldiers in battle. Like *Catch-22*, O'Brien's narratives question the value of war by portraying the drastic psychological changes and moral dilemmas forced on individuals in wartime, as well as explore the sheer violence and madness of wartime situations. For example, O'Brien tells a story of one soldier, Curt Lemon, who steps on a mine. To drive the point home to an audience that may not be familiar with the effects of a landmine on a soldier, O'Brien writes the following:

> Then he took a particular half step, moving from shade into bright sunlight, and the booby-trapped 105 round blew him into a tree. The parts were just hanging there, so Dave Jensen and I were ordered to shinny up and peel him off. I remember the white bone of an arm. I remember pieces of skin and something wet and yellow that must've been the intestines. The gore was horrible, and stays with me. But what wakes me up twenty years later is Dave Jensen singing "Lemon Tree" as we threw down the parts. (O'Brien 1998, 83)

This passage illustrates aptly the aforementioned absurdity of war and the descriptive power of O'Brien's writing, but it also signifies what other writers have tried to produce. Compare, for instance, Buzz Williams's *Spare Parts: A Marine Reservist's Journey from Campus to Combat in 38 Days* (2004) depiction of a look into the remains of the Iraqi invasion of Kuwait he discovered during his tour during Desert Storm:

> It didn't sink in right away . . . a mattress on the floor . . . bloody undergarments strewn about . . . lengths of rope for binding hands and feet . . . kerchief gags for muffling screams. [. . .] As I walked back to the living room, a toilet caught my attention. What I wanted was to take a leak, but even the bathroom wasn't what it seemed. Electrical wires from a chandelier ran along the ceiling, with bare ends dangling into the bathtub. Next to the tub was a homemade device fashioned with batteries and wires. And more rope [. . .] The washer and dryer showed it had once been a laundry room. The blood splash on the wall, though, showed it had been used for executions. The walls and floor were sticky with innards—blood and guts and brains. The grisly scene drove me out into the alley gagging on the stench of death, spitting to rid my mouth of the taste, and blowing to lose the smell. (Williams 2004, 245)

Graphic violence such as this is intended to shock the reader into a sense of disgust-inspired awe, a feeling to drive home the brutality and depravation of the situation, and is a common trope of much military literature.

O'Brien's work is also interesting due to his narrative structure. Instead of telling a consecutive story, each chapter building from the previous one and into the following one, O'Brien's *The Things They Carried* makes jumps in time and space, going from various locations in the jungles of Vietnam to hometown America before the soldiers left for the war. In addition, instead of following the story of one or two characters, as most novels do, *The Things They Carried* follows the lives of the men in one company, telling incomplete stories for each of them. The final effect of this is to force the reader to be in a constant state of uneasiness, always attempting to understand how one story is placed in connection with another. This uneasiness, though difficult for the reader, is obviously what O'Brien wants his readers to experience. Instead of reading a tidy war story, O'Brien's audience is forced into a new situation, as are the characters in the novel. This adds a greater sense of what a soldier in Vietnam would have faced, giving the reader a closer (though not perfect) connection to the reality of war experience.

In addition to these highly acclaimed war novels, military literature on the popular front has been extremely prolific. One of the best known writers whose works deal with military issues is Tom Clancy. While usually classified as a techno-thriller writer, Clancy's work often involves Special Forces, military weaponry, and even the military's relationship with other branches of the government, therefore qualifying some of his novels as military literature. If we were to consider only the 1.6 million copies of Clancy's *Clear and Present Danger* that sold in 1989 alone and exclude all the novels by other writers such as Stephen Coonts, Dale Turner, and Jeff Shaara, we can still see that military literature is extremely well received, at least in terms of book sales.

Trends and Themes. From this short survey of twentieth century military literature and some of the descendants of these works, we can calculate where military literature in the twenty-first century is going. As we have seen, some but not all military literature is centered on blood, guts, weaponry, and Rambo-esque super soldiers single-handedly eradicating the enemy. While there is this tendency in much of what could be called military thrillers, and even some memoirs, to focus on the Rambo-style characters or small, elite groups of soldiers on secret missions, other genres of military writing offer other focuses. Military thrillers that focus on the technological aspect of the military or their need for the commandos to save the day and become national heroes in the end of the novel tend to be weak in strong character development and complexity, thus weakening the stories' believability and influence over a reader's response. But saying this doesn't mean there aren't many redeeming qualities in the military thriller. Instead of just being tales of suspense and action that are quickly forgotten, military thrillers, like other types of military literature, often deal with contemporary issues in the military and society.

Like in *The Red Badge of Courage, Catch-22,* and *The Things They Carried,* the craziness of war is often portrayed in contemporary military fiction. But, interestingly, this theme has emerged more in the past decade in memoirs and personal narratives than in contemporary fiction. As we have seen, Turnipseed responded to the craziness of war in a quirky way and Pantano reacted to the craziness of war by trying to portray the graphic details of his encounter with the "rape room." But most military fiction, especially the military thrillers, tends to overlook this detail to portray soldiers performing their duties with precision and even flair. The stereotypical military thriller hero is calm, composed, and deadly.

Although different genres in military literature may employ different themes, just as often they share other themes across genre borders. One such shared theme is camaraderie among soldiers. Much military literature draws on the natural bond that is created through training and serving with a group of soldiers. This camaraderie separates soldiers from the rest of society. As Jason and Graves suggest, this theme, once used to exemplify the "melting pot" theory of America—that the United States is a blend of multiple nationalities and ethnicities—and create a greater sense of American nationalism, has been drastically changed to create instead a loyalty among soldiers, separate from the nation. In many ways, the soldiers become outcasts of society, freaks that can only relate to one another after their war experiences (Jason and Graves 2001, xi).

For example, in *Jarhead* a scene takes place in Michigan, where Swofford and five other marines travel to a former comrade's funeral six years after serving in the Gulf War. In describing the experience of mourning the death of his friend from the Marines, Swofford writes, "We were all hurt badly, and ready to die, to join our friend" (Swofford 2003, 76). After the funeral services, Swofford and his friends go to a bar where one of them drinks until he passes out. A local mocks the marine, hits his head against the bar, and a fight between the marines and apparently everyone else in the bar ensues. While Swofford feels he and the marines did their comrade an honor in fighting ("he'd have wanted us spending the evening of his funeral drunk and at combat" (Swofford 2003, 81), the dead marine's mother is upset because she sees the marines' actions as tarnishing her son's memory. Swofford's story illustrates that civilians can't quite understand soldiers, and so soldiers must turn to their own kind for support.

Another theme that is extremely prevalent in contemporary military literature is the individual's growth. This theme is often seen in two forms—either in a character's coming of age or in rehabilitation/healing of former problems. Jason and Graves claim that "the great bulk of war narratives that focus on young men [. . .] are essentially initiation or coming of age stories" (Jason and Graves 2001, xi). While we don't see this as much in military thrillers as we do in memoirs, it is still a common theme. Stephen Coonts's novella, "Al Jihad," likewise implies this same message; the military's tough love, discipline, and second chance on life is symbolically offered through Charlie Dean (retired marine sniper turned gas station owner) giving Candy (a stereotypical multiple-facial pierced, thieving, cowardly punk) a beating for stealing from the station. This, along with Dean's mercy as Candy's plot to rob Dean's filling station fails and Dean keeps Candy from being arrested, helps straighten out the troubled youth and turns him into a hardworking, respectable citizen. If the marine's tough love can do this for Candy, then it can do it for anyone.

Similar to Candy's treatment, another trend in military memoirs is the rehabilitory effects of military service. Many characters are presented as troubled youth who the military straightens out. For example, Joel Turnipseed, in his *Baghdad Express,* describes his less than ideal youth with a father who beat his mother and horrific nightmares that turn out to be memories of a car fire that he barely escaped from as a child (Turnipseed 2003, 26). As Turnipseed states, "This awkwardness, this abruptness, was not new to me: I was born into it [. . .] In all, I went to a different school in a different city every year from kindergarten to tenth grade. It made me a connoisseur of loneliness" (Turnipseed 2003, 25). For Turnipseed and others, life in the military is seen as a step toward stability away from a chaotic family.

Like the broad range of themes, there has also been a trend emerging in military literature to portray previously unheard elements of the military. Two that have been particularly interesting are the infrastructure and politics of the military and the roles of women in war. Neither necessarily focuses on combat, and so were not written about to a great extent in the past. But recently these subjects have seen more publishing. The tendency of the literature to focus on the soldier who has seen fighting creates a largely skewed vision of the military because most individuals who serve in the military do not experience firsthand firefights or modern warfare. From the majority of military literature, then, one forgets the huge infrastructure used to support a nation's war efforts. Resource transportation, training, and paperwork happen away from the battlefront but require as much if not more manpower than troops on the ground. While most military literature is still focused on the men on the frontlines, there is an increasing trend to represent the military superstructure and women's roles in the military in literature. One such example is Dale Brown's "Leadership Material." In this short story, we see the process of rank advancement through committee. In Orson Scott Card's short story "50 WPM" (2002) we see another example of the bureaucratic element of the military. In this story, a young man is trained by his father to be exceptional at typing. The youth's war veteran father chooses to train his son in typing in order to save him from battle in case he is ever drafted into the army, since this skill is a rare commodity and more useful in the general's offices where there is less chance for fighting.

Another realm where we see an expanded interest in non-fighting military stories is in the abundant memoirs about the Gulf War. Turnipseed's *Baghdad Express* is his story of being a convoy driver, a dangerous job but not one that necessarily required him to constantly be on the front lines. From the popularity of these examples, we see a growing interest in not only what a military does on the battlefield but also rather a general interest in the mystery of how the military functions.

Context and Issues. While many critics of military literature claim it is mostly a lot of pulp fiction that offers readers little valuable intellectual work, military literature in general since 2000 has done well responding to current events and debates. The two most obvious contextual issues are the post September 11, 2001, American "War on Terrorism" and its subsequent wars in Iraq and Afghanistan. Each age of military literature has its stereotypical bad guys. In the 1980s and early 1990s it was the Soviet Union and communist countries in general. Today it is the terrorist, and stereotypically the Islamic, usually Middle Eastern or American convert, extremist bent on destroying good Americans wherever they exist, as in Oliver North and Joe Musser's *Mission Compromised* (2003). As one would expect, direct and indirect responses to the September 11th attacks on the World Trade Center and the Pentagon and the failed attack on the White House pepper military literature. This trend is especially strong in military thriller novels, possibly because they are attempting to tap into readers' fear in an attempt to entertain.

The current war in Iraq stoked an already heated debate in the American culture as to what roles the different genders should play in war, especially in battle. Traditionally, women have been able to serve in various positions in the military, from nurses to supply troops, but never in active combat forces. While here is not the place to discuss the many sides of this debate, there are inexhaustible resources for those interested. For example, at http://www.militarywoman.org/reading.htm, one can trace one of these debates as it has evolved over more than ten years. And even the U.S. Army has made it a point to discuss women's roles in fighting units as it has allowed some women to serve as HUMVEE turret gunners in patrol units ("Books about Women in the Military"). This debate was again revived as America invaded Iraq in 2003. Radio talk shows, TV news programs, newspapers, and even online forums discussed the national policy that barred women from combat duty. This debate was in part further ignited by the capture of U.S. convoy soldiers on March 23, 2003, and their subsequent rescue on April 1, 2003, including two female soldiers, Shoshona Johnson and Jessica Lynch. Initial reports (that are still unsubstantiated) that Lynch was repeatedly raped by her captors fueled those who feared this very possibility for servicewomen. Both women were rescued, along with members of their convoy, but media responses to their individual stories appeared biased toward Lynch—a blonde Caucasian—and away from Johnson—an African American, sparking another deeply seeded debate of racism in the military and media. Jessica Lynch's story has continued to make headlines, with occasional updates on her college education and the birth of her daughter, Dakota. Pulitzer Prize winning journalist Rick Bragg even wrote a book on Lynch entitled *I Am a Soldier, Too: The Jessica Lynch Story* (2003).

While the country has argued about women's roles in the military and infantry divisions, military literature writers have taken the opportunity to weigh in on the subject through their writing. For example, Charles W. Sasser's *Detachment Delta: Punitive Strike* (2002) follows in part the story of two fictional soldiers—one a man and the other a woman—who are captured by Islamic terrorists. In Sasser's novel, both the male and female prisoners are beaten, but only the female is assaulted sexually. From this we see military writers responding to current debates and events, possibly to garner an interested readership, but also to make statements on military policy.

Just as headline savvy as those writers who discuss women in the military are the writers who take on issues of interrogation and torture. In Spring 2004 stories broke through *The New Yorker* and *60 Minutes II* on torture and prisoner abuse at the U.S. controlled Iraqi prison, Abu Ghraib. This event called into question the actions of U.S. service men and women while offering fodder for those who criticized U.S. occupation of Iraq. Likewise, reports of U.S. interrogation methods came under fire as reports from Afghanistan and Guantanamo Bay trickled out.

David Alexander, like many other military literature writers, deals with this issue and other contemporary issues and debates directly in his novel *Marine Force One* (2003). As he describes early in his novel, Alexander portrays illegal interrogation by the U.S. government. He writes, "Saxon did not approve of the methodology of interrogation, but it was out of his hands now and in the hands of the spooks. The Geneva Convention (banning torture in interrogation) didn't apply here. Neither did the Constitution or Bill of Rights. The spooks called the shots and they had opted for chemicals" (Alexander 2003, 41). This passage is especially illustrative in that it is shortly followed by the mentioning that the observers of the interrogation include "representatives from the president's small group of advisors and the DOD and NSC deputies groups, as well as lawyers from the JAG and Marine Corps Office of Special Operations" (Alexander 2003, 41). That the narrator informs the audience that the main character openly disapproves of illegal interrogations serves to sway the reader's opinion of events transpiring in the novel, even though we clearly see that the illegal interrogation is sanctioned by both the military and the president. Passages such as this draw the readers with news stories, such as one reported through *Newsweek* that "The Bush administration's emerging approach [. . .] that America's enemies in this war were "unlawful" combatants without rights" (Barry, Hirsh, and Isikoff 1996), thus linking Alexander's novel to current hot debates. Alexander's decision to present prisoner abuse as a negative thing offers his audience an extension of the debate. So from military literature's dealing with women's roles in the military and prisoner abuse and interrogation we see that military literature writers often offer their audiences both fiction dealing with current events and commentary on these debates and current events.

Reception. While military literature has been a staple in the reading public, certain genres garner much more commentary, applause, and criticism than others. In particular, military memoirs are often seen as much more "valuable" literature than military thrillers and have therefore earned more attention. In the ever-expanding field of military literature, there has been a surge of military memoirs since 2000. This has happened in part because of the current war in Iraq, creating a reading audience wanting to experience the previous Gulf War as a means of understanding the current conflict. As a result, memoirs such as *Jarhead* and *Baghdad Express* have seen increased sales. Indeed, the exigency of the issue has spurred the public reception of the works. But even though these works have received a lot of public attention in the form of book reviews, they have not received much critical attention.

Baghdad Express and *Jarhead* have garnered most of the critical attention, but even these two works have been slow to gain academic, or "literary," acceptance. We will focus on the reviews of Anthony Swofford's *Jarhead* because, as the most well-known piece of military literature to be written within the decade, *Jarhead* offers both a continuation of a discussion of the themes and contextual issues in military literature as well as an opportunity to discuss how military literature is translated into major motion pictures.

Jarhead is a contemporary war narrative that has, in good military fashion, stormed the United States, captured popular approval, and earned for its author, Anthony Swofford, all the essential popular literature medals of honor—numberless book reviewer's hearts and praise, television interviews, including *Good Morning America* and *The Daily Show with Jon Stewart,* and the ever-coveted Hollywood blockbuster.

There are generally three focuses reviewers have taken when dealing with *Jarhead*. First, reviewers have read *Jarhead* as a form of protest or antiwar narrative. This form of review is nearly always accompanied by accolades about how well written or how accurately *Jarhead* portrays reality. For example, a 2002 *Publisher's Weekly* anonymous review of *Jarhead* says it "offers . . . an unflinching portrayal of the loneliness and brutality of modern warfare and sophisticated analyses of—and visceral reactions to—its politics" (241). Mark Bowden, author of *Black Hawk Down* (1999), follows form, stating the following:

> *Jarhead* is some kind of classic, a bracing memoir of the 1991 Persian Gulf War that will go down with the best books ever written about military life. It is certainly the most honest memoir I have read from a participant in any war. Swofford writes with humor, anger and great skill. His prose is alive with ideas and feeling, and at times soars like poetry. He captures the hilarity, tedium, horniness and loneliness of the long prewar desert deployment, and then powerfully records the experience of his war. (2003, 8)

With phrases such as "some kind of classic" or "best books ever written about military life," we quickly see Bowden approves of Swofford's work.

Marc Herman agrees with Bowden but expands this praise by lauding the accusational tone of the memoir, stating "*Jarhead* emerges as a scary, detailed, well-written indictment of life in the military" (2003, 76). Like Bowden, Herman uses imagery loaded phrases, "scary" and "well-written indictment," to illicit a particular response from his audience. That this indictment of the military is "detailed" and "well-written" is Herman's rhetorical evidence that not only is Swofford correct because he has offered enough proof through his details but also he has proven he is a trustworthy spokesman because what he has written is executed with skill. Herman also claims the memoir "could hardly be more timely" (2003, 76) by hitting the bookshelves at the start of the current war in Iraq (in fact, it was pushed a couple months ahead of schedule by publishers eyeing a valuable opportunity). The exigency of the issue, along with the message *Jarhead* appears to purport, leads Herman to believe *Jarhead* works as a protest against the current war and U.S. foreign policy.

The second bend reviewers have taken toward *Jarhead* is to examine the work from a cultural perspective. Edward Nowatka believes *Jarhead* catches the incongruence of American feelings about war. In his 2003 article in *Publisher's Weekly* entitled "On the Heals of *Jarhead*," Nowatka, like Bowden and Herman, suggests

Jarhead's popularity comes from its ability to "[capture] the contradictions of modern warfare for the average soldier—the tedious days of waiting punctuated by moments of jolting terror, friendly fire, and surreal encounters with the dead" (2003, 20). This is what makes *Jarhead* so successful as compared to its Gulf War narrative counterparts—it shows not only the fear and surrealism of war, but balances these images with feelings of boredom and monotony, creating a more realistic and trustworthy work instead of works that focus "on the lives of elite warriors and read like thrillers" (2003, 20). Like Nowatka, Justin Ewers finds a rough cultural ambiguity in *Jarhead*, but for Ewers this represents something more than accusations against the military. He writes in *U.S. News and World Report* that "In Swofford's conflicted psyche and lucid prose can be seen the evolution not only of the war memoir but of American attitudes toward war—and war's current place in the American consciousness" (Ewers 2003, 52). Claiming the American war memoir finds its roots in World War II, when more educated servicemen were returning from a grisly war and finding a need to write about their experiences, Ewers places *Jarhead* in a historical context of previous war memoirs. Common themes in these memoirs were often the brutality of war and distrust of officers and authority, while many "still overflowed with pride in the cause and the flag and the uniform" (Ewers 2003, 52). This changed in Vietnam, when, according to Ewers, "memoirs became overtly antiwar" (52). He claims *Jarhead* "combines the anti-authoritarian tone of World War II with the lingering cynicism of Vietnam" (52). *Jarhead*, then, is in many ways a culmination of the twentieth century war narrative, with Swofford's anti-authoritarianism and cynicism oddly mixed with pride to be a marine, making the book reveal Swofford's dysfunctional relationship with the marines.

Margo Jefferson offers another cultural approach by referring to Walter Benjamin, who claims the two oldest forms of storytelling are the historical chronicle and the fairy tale. From this Jefferson decides "when we read a good memoir we know we are reading both history and legend," in this case history and legend about "all male worlds of secrecy and ritual" where "strangers are seen as aliens, inferiors, or enemies" (2004, 27). For Jefferson, *Jarhead* is a peek into a world from which she and women have generally been excluded. Implied in her analysis of *Jarhead* is the suggestion that Swofford claims women are "aliens, inferiors, or enemies," and she is right. There is plenty of male chauvinism in *Jarhead*, with women portrayed as comforting mothers, wives, or girlfriends while simultaneously being unfaithful to their soldier husbands. Few women are portrayed without sexual connotations attached to them, a fact that has garnered little attention from critics.

The third approach reviews have taken to *Jarhead* is to read the personal over the narrative, or to examine the work as more indicative of Swofford's psyche than the actual Gulf War. Edwin B. Burgess's review typifies this approach by stating *Jarhead* "is in no sense a chronicle of the Gulf War but instead an interior monolog reflecting Swofford's inner journey from despised childhood to coming of age as an enlisted marine and finally coming somewhat to terms with the man he has become. For Swafford, warfare was the culmination of everything he had experienced, so that his existential narrative hangs on his pivotal nine-month tour of duty" (Burgess 2003, 126). To Burgess, Swofford's time in Iraq is the turning point in his life, where Swofford finds a greater sense of self through his training and experience than a bad childhood and chemical dependency offered, but at the same time is able to "back away from the total absorption of combat to live in the real world" (126). In this way *Jarhead* isn't so much about the Gulf War as it is about Swofford's personal development. In fact, Swofford, tells us on the second page of his memoir that "my vision was blurred—by wind and sand and distance, by false signals, poor communication, and bad coordinates, by stupidity and fear and ignorance, by valor and false pride. By the mirage. Thus what follows is neither true nor false, but *what I know*" (Swofford 2003, 2). From this early introduction of Swofford's own acknowledgement of his shortcomings in describing his Gulf War experience, Swofford intends for his reader to understand that he is writing about himself.

As we have seen, book reviewers have approached *Jarhead* in various ways, but what have scholars said about the memoir turned movie? Surprising or not, they have said very little. Except for the positive reviews the book has received, few scholars have paid much attention to Swofford's memoir. This seemingly minor interest in *Jarhead* is surprising not only considering the vast amount of commentary it has produced in the public sphere but also that it falls into a natural position in the discussion of war narratives and provides much unbroken ground in war narrative studies. Even with the 2004 film based on the book, there has been relatively little scholarly work published on Swofford's memoir. The fact that *Jarhead* is perhaps the best known, critically acclaimed piece of contemporary military literature that hasn't been taken seriously in the academic world perhaps tells us a little about how military literature is being received generally.

Bibliography

Alexander, David. *Marine Force One: Recon by Fire*. New York: Penguin Putnam, 2003.

Barry, John, Michael Hirsh, and Michael Isikoff. "The Roots of Torture." *Newsweek* 1996. http://www.msnbc.msn.com/id/4989436/site/newsweek/. (accessed Feb 28, 2007).

Bowden, Mark. "The Things They Carried: One Man's Memoir of the 1991 Gulf War and Other Battles." *New York Times Book Review* 2 Mar 2003:8.

———. *Black Hawk Down*. New York: Atlantic Monthly Press, 1999.

Bragg, Rick. *I Am a Soldier, Too: The Jessica Lynch Story*. New York: Knopf, 2000.

Brown, Dale. "Leadership Material." In *Combat*. Stephen Coonts, ed. New York: Tom Doherty, 2001; 73–147.

Burgess, Edwin B. "Rev. of *Jarhead: A Marine's Chronicle of the Gulf War and Other Battles*." *Library Journal* Jan. 2003: 126.

Card, Orson Scott. "50 WPM." In *In the Shadow of the Wall: An Anthology of Vietnam Stories That Might Have Been*. Byron R. Tetrick, ed. Nashville: Cumberland House, 2002.

Crane, Stephen. *The Red Badge of Courage*. 1895. New York: Tor Classics, 2001.

Drake, David. *Foreign Legions*. Riverdale: Baen, 2001.

Ewers, Justin. "Soldiers' Stories: A Marine's Memoir Reflects the Changing Literature of War." *U.S. News and World Report* 24 Mar. 2003: 52.

Garson, Helen S. *Tom Clancy: A Critical Companion*. Westport: Greenwood Press, 1996.

Grossman, Dave, and Leo Frankowski. *The Two Space War*. Riverdale: Baen, 2005.

Herman, Marc. "*Jarhead*." *Mother Jones* 28.1 (2003):76

Heller, Joseph. *Catch-22*. New York: Simon and Schuster, 1961.

Hynes, Samuel. *The Soldier's Tale: Bearing Witness to Modern War*. New York: A. Lane, 1997.

Jason, Philip K., and Mark A. Graves. "Introduction." *Encyclopedia of American War Literature*. Westport: Greenwood Press, 2001.

Jefferson, Margo. "The Stuff of Legend." *New York Times*, 2004.

Lee, John W.I. "Xenophon's *Anabasis* and the Origins of Military Autobiography." In *Arms and the Self: War, Military, and Autobiographical Writing*. Alex Vernon, ed. Kent: Kent State University Press, 41–60.

Leyva, Meredith. *Married to the Military: A Survival Guide for Military Wives, Girlfriends, and Women in Uniform.* New York: Simon and Schuster, 2003.

Murray, Sabina. *The Caprices.* Boston: Houghton Mifflin, 2002.

O'Brien, Tim. *The Things They Carried.* 1990. New York: Broadway, 1998.

Nowatka, Edward. "On the Heels of *Jarhead.*" *Publisher's Weekly* 31 March 2003: 20.

Pantano, Ilario, with Malcolm McConnell. *Warlord: No Better Friend, No Worse Enemy.* New York: Threshold, 2006.

Sasser, Charles W. *Detachment Delta: Punitive Strike.* New York: Avon, 2002.

Shaara, Jeff. *The Rising Tide: A Novel of World War II.* New York: Ballantine, 2006.

———. 2004. *To the Last Man: A Novel of the First World War.* New York: Ballantine, 2004.

———. *Gods and Generals.* New York: Ballantine, 1996.

Swofford, Anthony. *Jarhead: A Marine's Chronicle of the Gulf War and Other Battles.* New York: Scribner, 2003.

Thomas, James, and Melanie Thomas. *My Dad Is Going Away, but He Will Be Back One Day: A Deployment Story.* Victoria: Trafford, 2004.

Turnipseed, Joel. *Baghdad Express: A Gulf War Memoir.* St. Paul, MN: Borealis, 2003.

Turtledove, Harry. *American Empire: Blood and Iron.* New York: Del Rey, 2001.

———. *American Empire: The Center Cannot Hold.* New York: Del Rey, 2002.

Vandevoorde, Shellie. *Separated by Duty, United in Love: A Guide to long-Distance Relationships for Military Couples.* New York: Citadel Press, 2006.

Williams, Buzz. *Spare Parts: A Marine Reservist's Journey from Campus to Combat in 38 Days.* New York: Gotham Books, 2004.

"Books about Women in the Military." http://www.militarywoman.org/reading.htm.

Further Reading

Bates, Milton. *The Wars We Took to Vietnam: Cultural Conflict and Storytelling.* Berkeley: University of California Press, 1996; Benedetto, Christian M. *War Cries: A Collection of Military Poems.* Shelbyville: Wasteland Press, 2005; Carroll, Joseph. "War novel (Representations of war in the novel)." In *Encyclopedia of the Novel.* 2 vols. Chicago: Fitzroy Dearborn, 1998; Gannon, Charles E. *Rumors of War and Infernal Machines: Technomilitary Agenda-Setting in American and British Speculative Fiction.* Lanham: Rowman and Littlefield, 2003; Jason, Philip K. *Acts and Shadows: The Vietnam War in American Literary Culture.* Lanham: Rowman and Littlefield, 2000; Jason, Philip K., and Mark A. Graves. *Encyclopedia of American War Literature.* Westport: Greenwood Press, 2001; Smith, Myron J. *War Story Guide: An Annotated Bibliography of Military Fiction.* Metuchan: Scarecrow Press, 1980; Stallworthy, Jon. *Were You There?: War and Poetry.* Cheltenham: Cyder Press, 2005; Tatum, James. *The Mourner's Song: War and Remembrance from The Iliad to Vietnam.* Chicago: University of Chicago Press, 2003; Vernon, Alex. *Arms and the Self: War, the Military, and Autobiographical Writing.* Kent: Kent State University Press, 2005; "Women in Combat Forces." Military Women. www.militarywoman.org/reading.htm—debate. Acessed Feb 27, 2007; Yuknavitch, Lidia. *Allegories of violence: Tracing the writing of war in Twentieth-Century fiction.* New York: Routledge, 2001.

CHAD MCLANE

MUSICAL THEATRE

Definition. "Musical theatre," like "poetry," might be a term better said to describe the presentation and reception of a work rather than its form or structure. In the last ten years, pieces as diverse as *Contact* (a set of three dramatic sketches set to mostly prerecorded music), *Fosse* (a revue of dances by choreographer-director Bob Fosse), and *Hairspray* (a traditional musical comedy in which the dialogue often gives way to songs sung as an extension of the spoken text) have all been given the "Best Musical" Tony Award. Scholars who attempt to define the genre usually define their boundaries generously. In the introduction to his book *The World of Musical Comedy,* Stanley Green writes that musical theatre "covers operetta, comic opera, musical play (now frequently merely called 'musical'), musical comedy itself, revue, and, in the past, spectacle or extravaganza" (Green 1974, xiii). In his *Encyclopedia of Musical Theater,* published two years later, Green extends his definition to include opera "if offered for a regular commercial run" (Green 1976, v).

In general, then, almost any piece of theatre that uses music in a significant way could be called a musical. In practice, though, the titles usually marketed and studied as musicals can be distinguished from other forms of theatre that use music by three defining characteristics:

1. **Words are important.** Unlike opera, which, in general, privileges music, and ballet, which privileges dance, the musical tends to encourage the audience to attend closely to its text. Sheldon Harnick, lyricist of *Fiddler on the Roof,* writes that the "book" (or unsung text of a musical) is "of primary importance" (Guernsey 1974, 38). This sentiment is echoed by lyricist and composer Stephen Sondheim who claims, "Books are what the musical theater is about" (Guernsey 1974, 91). Operas can be appreciated and understood purely for their music; they are often performed in a language unfamiliar to the majority of their audience. Musicals, as a rule, require the audience to understand what is being said and sung.

2. **Songs are sung in a "popular" style.** Opera and operetta are typically sung in a classical style, a performance practice developed to project the sound of the voice across great distances. In *The Rise and Fall of the Broadway Musical,* Mark Grant contrasts the classical with the "popular" style, which places "more emphasis on consonants and the clarity of the lyrics than on vowels and tonal beauty" (Grant 2004, 17–18). Musicals today are usually sung in a popular style that, arguably, privileges the acting (rather than singing) ability of the performer. "Opera is designed to show off the human voice," says Sondheim, contrasting the form to his *Sweeney Todd,* which he says, "is about telling a story and telling it as swiftly as possible" (Bryer and Davison 2005, 202).

3. *Extra-diegetic* **songs are used.** Although most shows on Broadway use music in some way, songs in nonmusical plays are typically diegetic, that is, the characters in the play recognize these songs as songs. Musicals (and for that matter operas), on other hand, make extensive use of extra-diegetic songs (songs sung by characters who don't realize they are singing). Musicals may, of course, contain diegetic songs—in *The Phantom of the Opera,* Christine sings "Think of Me" and is lauded by other characters for her exceptional performance. However, when she sings "All I Ask of You" to Raoul, there is no indication that the characters realize they are singing rather than speaking. A play that contains only diegetic songs is usually not considered a musical.

A musical may be defined, then, as a piece of theatre that uses both spoken text and extra-diegetic songs sung in the popular style to communicate to its audience. This definition, though, only circumscribes the form and distinguishes it from other, similar, kinds of performances. In the next section we will look further at the parts of the musical, both spoken and sung, to further understand the nature of the form itself.

Parts of a Musical. **The Book:** In the study and practice of musical theatre, the term "book" is used to refer to the part of the musical that is spoken rather than sung. Stephen Sondheim further defines the book as "the scheme of the show, the way the songs and the dialogue work together, the style of the show" (Guernsey 1974, 91). Thus, musicals such as *Les Misérables,* which contain almost no spoken text, may still be said to have a book. The book is sometimes known as the libretto (though, often, this refers to the entire text, both spoken and sung).

The Music: In addition to the songs, which will be discussed shortly, musicals usually include several pieces of instrumental-only music.

- **The Overture:** The overture is the music usually played after the lights are lowered but before the action of the musical begins. It is entirely instrumental (there is no singing), and usually consists of a medley of songs from the show. The overture serves to lead the audience into the world of the musical and to establish the mood of the first scene.

  Since the early 1970s, overtures began to be less frequently used in new musicals. In 1969, the relatively traditional musical *1776* began with a fife and drum medley that transported the audience to the revolutionary congress in Philadelphia. In 1970, the musical *Company* brought the audience into the contemporary world of the musical, no less effectively, with the sound of a telephone busy signal. Since then, there has been an increasing tendency on the part of musical theatre composers to dispense with an overture of any significant length.

- **Underscoring:** The underscore is the music that plays under spoken dialogue. It is common in nonmusical films and plays as well as in musicals and serves to enhance the mood of a scene. In musicals, underscoring often immediately precedes or follows a song and helps to make the transition between speaking and singing.

- **Bows/Exit Music:** The bows and exit music are the counterpart to the overture. As the name suggests, this music plays while the performers bow to the applauding audience and continues while the audience files out of the theatre. The exit music usually consists of the most memorable melodies in the show and works to ensure the audience leaves the theatre with the songs in their head (hopefully predisposed to tell their friends about the show).

Songs: Theatre writer Aaron Frankel credits choreographer Bob Fosse with classifying musical theatre songs into three categories: "I am songs," "I want songs," and "new songs" (95).

- In **"I am"** songs, in Frankel's words, "the character commits himself in some way" (Frankel 2000, 95). This may be as simple as a character introducing himself (the title song in "The Phantom of the Opera") or as complex as a character realizing the reality of her situation ("See I'm Smiling" from *The Last Five Years*).

- **"I want"** songs, on the other hand, express the "need" of a character "to reach" (Frankel 2000, 95). The character may directly express her desires ("The Wizard and I" in *Wicked*) to the audience or may imply them by what he sings to another character (for instance, in a love song like *Rent's* "I'll Cover You").

- **"New"** songs are Fosse's catch-all category for songs that don't exactly fit into either of the other ones. "Masquerade" in *Phantom of the Opera*, for example, serves as a spectacular and colorful opening to Act II and underscores the musical's theme of the masks but does not directly express the needs or nature of any of the characters.

Fosse, as a director, centered his categories on the motivations of characters. A more structural taxonomy is described by musical theatre teacher and writer Lehman Engel in his book, *The American Musical Theatre*. Engel describes the following six types of songs:

- **Opening number:** As the name suggests, this is the song that begins the musical and establishes the world of the piece. The importance of the opening number is illustrated by the familiar story of the development of *A Funny Thing Happened on the Way to the Forum*, which according to those involved, failed to entertain audiences until Sondheim wrote the opening number, "Comedy Tonight," which tells the audience how to respond to the show (Guernsey 1974, 67).

- **Soliloquy:** A soliloquy is a moment in which a single actor expresses his inner thoughts as they move from one state to another. In *Les Misérables,* Jean Valjean sings "Who Am I" to the audience as he thinks through an ethical dilemma. By the end of the song he has made his decision, and he directs his song once more to other characters in the piece.

- **Charm Song:** A charm song, in the words of Engel, "embodies generally delicate, optimistic, and rhythmic music, and lyrics of light though not necessarily comedic subject matter" (Engel 1975, 87). *Rent*'s "Santa Fe," in which the action stops as two characters dream of opening a restaurant in New Mexico, is a recent example.

- **Musical scene:** At the end of Act I of the musical *Wicked,* the two witches from *The Wizard of Oz* are trapped in a broom closet in the Emerald City. A moment of crisis has come, and they must each decide whether to defy the corrupted establishment or serve their own interests by joining it. Throughout the scene, the dialogue moves back and forth between spoken and sung text. This is an example of what Engel calls a musical scene. Other examples include "Light My Candle" in *Rent* and "Chip on My Shoulder" from *Legally Blonde.*

- **Comic song:** Engel observes that the most successful comic song is usually character-driven and "evokes in people the amusement of seeing themselves (or others whom they recognize instantly) and being entertained by the spectacle of their own foibles" (Engel 1975, 104). "Everyone's A Little Bit Racist" and "The Internet is for Porn" from *Avenue Q* both fit into this category.

- **11 o'clock number:** Named for the actual time at which a song of this sort would be sung in an evening, 11 o'clock numbers are usually up-tempo songs close to the end of the final act, which serve to energize the audience for the final few scenes. The song "The American Dream," in *Miss Saigon,* in which the character known as the "Engineer" fantasizes about American life in a spectacular, brassy number just before the action begins its final descent toward the musical's inevitably tragic conclusion, is an example. Others include "What You Own" in *Rent* and "No Good Deed" in *Wicked.*

To Engel's categories, I would add three others (though these are hardly original):

- **Recitative:** Recitative (an Italian term that rhymes with "cassette at Eve"), describes words sung using the normal patterns of speech (usually without rhyme). The answering machine messages in *Rent* (e.g., "That was a very loud beep") are an example.

- **Act I Finale:** The finale of the first act of a musical usually establishes what remains to be accomplished in the next act. "Defying Gravity" in *Wicked* establishes the main character's choice to be "wicked" (that is, opposed to establishment) and ends with her battle cry against anyone who would try to "bring her down." Usually this song is upbeat and memorable so the audience will be likely to have it in their heads during intermission and return to their seats with the action of the first act fresh in their minds.

- **Finale:** The final song of a musical is often a reprise of music that originated earlier in the show, but which is so connected with a major theme of the musical that it deserves repetition at the privileged final position. *Rent*'s finale begins with a reprise of "Without You" and concludes with a reprise of "Seasons of Love," solidly establishing the musicals message about the importance of finding and maintaining loving relationships. *Avenue Q,* on the other hand, introduces a new song "Only for Now," that explicitly expresses a response to the questions about "purpose" that are asked throughout the show.

History. Recent studies of musical theatre have looked into the far past to find the beginning of musical theatre. In *Musical! A Grand Tour,* Denny Martin Flinn traces the beginnings of the musical from Greek theatre through Italian *Commedia Dell'Arte* to operetta. This path reveals a good deal about the sources of musical theatre, and, indeed, along this path one finds shows that meet the definition of a musical as given previously. However, the concept of musical theatre as an art form distinct from other forms of drama and with a corpus of its own only clearly emerged in the late nineteenth century.

Many accounts of the history of musical theatre begin in September of 1866 at the opening of *The Black Crook.* The play, by a virtually unknown writer named Charles M. Barras, tells the story of the titular magician who has promised the demons that he will lead one soul a year to damnation in exchange for infernal powers and his own immortality. It was probably not originally intended to include a great deal of music, but, so legend has it, a fire at the Academy of Music stranded a troupe of French ballet dancers in New York and the producer of both the ballet and *The Black Crook* was inspired to combine them into the extravaganza that would, for many, define the beginning of musical theatre.

The Black Crook has been designated as a milestone in musical theatre history since the form first became a legitimate object of study. Cecil Smith's 1950 work, *Musical Comedy in America,* begins with the claim that the musical stage "reached major dimensions for the first time" when *The Black Crook* opened (Smith 1950, 3), and Lehman Engel dedicates a large portion of the first chapter of his 1967 book, *The American Musical Theater,* to a discussion of the show. Denny Martin Flinn makes a long stop in the sixth chapter of his tour to discuss *The Black Crook* and calls the show "the beginning of a new era in theatre" (Flinn 1997, 87). On the other hand, early musical theatre historian Julian Mates argues "nothing about *The Black Crook* justifies its position as the precursor of our modern lyric stage; all its forms and conventions derive from a long tradition established well before 1866" (Mates 1996, 31–32). Whatever the case, *The Black Crook* was, in many ways, a microcosm of the musical theatre of the next sixty years. It contained a more or less coherent plot told through both words and music, but it was also something of a variety show (later productions employed trapeze artists as well as dancers). This marriage of high art and low, of operetta and variety, represents for many the beginning of musical theatre. *The Black Crook* was followed by many similarly intentioned extravaganzas including *The White Fawn* (1868) and *Evangeline* (1874) (Smith 1950, 22).

By the mid-1870s, the tastes of audience began to shift from spectacle to satire and from melodrama to comedy (a progression that occurred again, as we will see, at the beginning of the twentieth century). From 1871 to 1896, the Englishmen William S. Gilbert (lyricist) and Arthur Sullivan (composer) wrote a series of shows that redefined musical theatre for the remainder of the nineteenth century. Although sometimes called "comic operas," these shows, when sung in the popular style, are barely distinguishable from musical theatre as it is understood today. Gilbert and Sullivan's work, unlike most operas, privilege the libretto to a greater degree even than many of those shows undisputedly classified as musicals today. A better designation for Gilbert and Sullivan's musicals is "operetta." Operetta is not distinct from musical theatre but may be considered a subset of the larger genre. Operettas tend to be light, though not necessarily comic. Although Gilbert and Sullivan's operetta's were primarily satirical, others of the time, such as Sigmond Romberg's *Desert*

Song, were melodramatic with valiant and aristocratic (if one dimensional) heroes and evil villains.

At the same time that Gilbert and Sullivan operettas were entertaining middle and upper class audiences, variety shows continued to combine music, drama, and dance in a form that appealed, in general, to working class audiences (Hamm 1997, 175). Vaudeville shows ("family friendly" versions of the more risqué variety shows of earlier decades) often contained songs sung in character by actors in a short skit. At the turn of the century, vaudeville performers such as George M. Cohan extended Vaudeville-like sketches and songs to create full-length musicals (usually celebrating American patriotism during World War I). The plots of these musicals were, in many ways, just as melodramatic and their characters just as one dimensional as those in operettas, but they tended to tell the stories of "average" people in a musical idiom more like the popular "folk" music of the time than that of European concert hall.

Also during this time Florenz Ziegfeld staged spectacular variety shows, known as the *Follies,* in which songs, dances, and dramatic sketches were stitched together against a backdrop of spectacular scenery and special effects. In the late 1920s Ziegfeld's work took a more serious turn when he joined with writer P.G. Woodhouse, Lyricist Oscar Hammerstein II, and Jerome Kern to produce *Show Boat,* a serious "musical play" that explored thematic elements unknown to either operetta or the Cohan musicals. The musical is now viewed as a milestone in the genre, and Geoffrey Block observed the following: "Beginning in the late 1960s historians would almost invariably emphasize *Show Boat'*s unprecedented integration of music and drama, its three-dimensional characters, and its bold and serious subject matter, including miscegenation [interracial marriage] and unhappy marriages" (Block 2003, 20–21).

Throughout the 1930s, as the country entered the Great Depression, another subgenre, the political musical, emerged. Based in large part on the German works of Kurt Weill (e.g., *Threepenny Opera*), musicals such as Marc Blitzstein's *Cradle Will Rock* and the Gershwins' *Of Thee I Sing* satirized and critiqued the political and economic systems they saw as corrupt. Although Gilbert and Sullivan and other creators of operetta had addressed similar themes with their work, they were usually set in far off times and places. The political musicals of the 1930s were set in contemporary America (or at least an obvious allegorical representation thereof).

Political musicals continued into the 1940s, though a rush of patriotism following the beginning of World War II swept away most of their earlier popularity. The public had also lost patience, however, with the one-dimensional patriotic pageants that had entertained the home front during the First World War. In response, the lyricist of *Show Boat,* Oscar Hammerstein II, and Richard Rodgers, composer of many of the operettas of the previous decades, developed a new form of patriotic musical for the new war. The musicals of Rodgers and Hammerstein, beginning with *Oklahoma* in 1943, told stories that celebrated American ideology with fully developed characters who spoke and sang in the popular language of the time. These musicals distributed the storytelling over dialogue, song, and dance and integrated each into the narrative more fully than most of the work of earlier decades. The Rodgers and Hammerstein model more or less defined musical theatre until the mid-1960s and for many, even today, is what the word "musical" evokes.

The sixties were a time of many changes, however, and musical theatre was not unaffected by them. Patriotism, along with most sorts of institutional fealty, was out of fashion and had been replaced by a new ethos of individualism and institutional defiance. The 1969 musical, *Hair*, with no plot to speak of and songs with titles like "Hashish" and "Sodomy," epitomized these values, but they found quieter expression in more traditionally structured musicals such as *Fiddler on the Roof*, which challenged the supremacy of tradition while at the same time celebrating it.

In the following decade the transformation of the Rodgers and Hammerstein model was effectively completed by composer-lyricist Stephen Sondheim. Sondheim had earned respect as a lyricist in the late 1950s and early 1960s for his work on *West Side Story* and *Gypsy*, but his music and lyrics for *Company* and *Follies* in the early 1970s made him, in the eyes of many, the master of late twentieth century musical theatre. Sondheim broke with the Rodgers and Hammerstein model in both form and content. *Company* and *Follies*, termed "concept musicals" because they were structured, not around a narrative, but by a theme or "concept," explored the often unpleasant realities of marriage and growing old—concepts foreign to the idealistic celebration of love and marriage in *The Sound of Music* or *Oklahoma*. Like many of the artistic revolutions of the 1960s and 1970s, however, what once defied convention was quickly absorbed into the mainstream. By 1982, the two most commercially successful musicals on Broadway, *A Chorus Line* and *Cats*, were concept musicals.

The latter launched a new trend of spectacle-driven, sung-through, mostly British musicals popularly designated "megamusicals" for their scale. These musicals, especially *Phantom of the Opera*, *Les Misérables*, and *Miss Saigon*, were hugely popular with audiences, yet were largely reviled by critics and many in the theatre community who felt the shows promoted an aesthetic of spectacle that worked against the more serious direction the art form had taken in the 1970s. These critics were, to some degree, vindicated in the mid-1990s as the demand for bigger and better spectacles became unsustainable. *Sunset Boulevard*, one of the last of the megamusicals, closed quickly on Broadway and cut short its tour, in large part because the musical required unrealistically high ticket sales to recover its astronomical expenses. The season after *Sunset Boulevard* opened on Broadway, Jonathan Larson's *Rent* announced the death of the megamusical and the beginning of a new era.

Rent, performed on a nearly bare stage by a small cast, was, in its simplicity, a sort of implicit reaction to the excess of the megamusical. In contrast to the soaring ticket prices necessitated by the expense of the megamusicals, top tickets to *Rent* were available for $20 to fans who arrived on the day of the show. *Rent*, which dealt directly with contemporary problems including AIDS and drug addiction, was also as thematically far removed from the megamusical as the political musicals of 1930s were from the operettas that preceded them. Many who watched *Rent's* rise to fame predicted Jonathan Larson would redefine musical theatre for the twenty-first century. Alas, the day before the first preview, Larson died of an aortic aneurysm.

At the same time that *Rent* was working its way from workshop to Off Broadway to Broadway, a titanic machine was gearing up production for a new set of megamusical-like spectacles that would transform not just musical theatre, but the entire New York City Theatre District. Before the 1990s, the Disney Company, although responsible for some of the most successful film musicals of all time, had been content to produce live theatre only within the boundaries of its theme parks. Throughout the 1990s, however, New York City, and the Theatre District in particular, underwent a major urban revitalization project that made Broadway more attractive to tourists (and more acceptable to the clean and safe Disney ethos).

Disney contributed to this revitalization through the purchase and reopening of several defunct theatres. In 1998 Disney reopened the New Amsterdam, the theatre in which Ziegfeld's *Follies* had originally played but which had fallen into disrepair in the following decades, and soon after mounted within it an adaptation of its 1994 animated movie, *The Lion King.*

The last chapter of the history of musical theatre in the twentieth century might end, then, with a newly redecorated Broadway under the new management of multinational corporations. The era of the megamusical had passed and had been replaced, not, as the success of *Rent* might have suggested, by small musicals produced by new, young artists, but by movie adaptations produced by committees rather than by artists. Such a narrative, while true to an extent, would, however, unfairly neglect the important voices that began to be heard from Off Broadway during this period and that, in important ways, laid the foundation for the musical in the beginning of the twenty-first century.

Theatre in New York City is separated into three divisions: Broadway, Off Broadway, and Off Off Broadway. These distinctions are, among other things, used for determining the jurisdiction of the various theatre unions. There are 39 theatres designated by theatre producers and unions as "Broadway" theatres. Off Broadway is limited by the Actor's Equity Association's "Off Broadway Rulebook" to productions "presented in the borough of Manhattan" but not performed in "any theatre located in an area bounded by Fifth and Ninth Avenues from 34th Street to 56th Street and by Fifth Avenue and the Hudson River from 56th Street to 72nd Street" (in general, the area immediately around Broadway, the street) and in "any theatre having a capacity of more than 499" (Actors' Equity Association 2005, 1). The 39 Broadway theatres are, in general, within these geographical boundaries and tend to have more than 500 seats. In their *Seasonal Showcase Code,* Actors' Equity implicitly defines Off Off Broadway by limiting the union's agreements for that "arena" to theatres in New York City with less than 100 seats (Actors' Equity Association 2006, 1).

During the 1990s the Off Broadway work of composers Jason Robert Brown, Michael John LaChiusa, and Adam Guettel provided a thoughtful alternative to the spectacle driven shows that were playing in Broadway theatres. Much like *Rent,* the work of these composers tended to explore nontraditional themes in experimental forms (Guettel's *Floyd Collins,* for instance, uses bluegrass and country music to narrate the last days of a man who slowly dies after an accident traps him in a cave in Kentucky). Few of these artists had produced a commercial hit by the end of the century, but through cast recordings and regional productions, the influence of these composers' shows extended beyond their limited original Off Broadway runs. Their work established a second, parallel stream of musical theatre work that, in the middle of the next decade, would arrive on Broadway.

Trends and Themes. The twenty-first century began with the September 11, 2001, terrorist attacks on New York City and Washington, D.C. Escapist comedies based on popular movies set in what were perceived to be simpler times sprouted up in their wake. *The Producers* (set in the 1950s), *Thoroughly Modern Millie* (set in the 1920s), and *Hairspray* (set in 1962) all allowed audiences to momentarily forget the anxiety they might have felt from being in an area so near the location of the attacks. However, even as big budget musicals produced by big corporations continued to draw big audiences, small, low-budget musicals that, in earlier days, might have had limited runs in not-for-profit theatres also began to make their way to

Broadway where they often were tremendously successful. Just days after September 11, *Urinetown*, a Blitzstein-esque satire of American capitalism opened on Broadway where it ran for three years. In the 2002–2003 season Universal Studios, a company best known for its films, produced the hugely successful, hugely expensive musical *Wicked* (based on Gregory MacGuire's retelling of *The Wizard of Oz*). At the same time, however, the previously mentioned *Avenue Q*, a puppet show with very adult themes, rose quickly from a class project to an Off Broadway show to a Broadway hit that beat *Wicked* in almost every category at the 2003 Tony Awards. The 2002–2003 season demonstrated that there is an audience for both kinds of musical, and both *Wicked* and *Avenue Q* continue to play to packed houses at the time of this writing in December 2007. The success of *Urinetown* and *Avenue Q* paved the way for other, slightly quirky, relatively low budget musicals to come to Broadway. In the following seasons, *The 25th Annual Putnam County Spelling Bee, The Drowsy Chaperone, Grey Gardens,* and *Spring Awakening* all successfully transferred from Off Broadway to Broadway, where they found welcoming audiences and, often, critical acclaim.

Many of these Off Broadway hits originated in the various musical theatre festivals and workshops that were founded in the previous century to promote the development of new musicals. The oldest and most successful of these, the BMI (Broadcast Music, Inc.) Workshop, was founded in 1961 and originally directed by musical conductor Lehman Engel. It was intended to be, in the words of the official Web site, "a setting where new writers for the musical theatre could learn their craft," and, given the names of its alumni, it has succeeded in being exactly that. Bobby Lopez and Jeff Mark, for instance, met and conceived the idea for *Avenue Q* at BMI and speak well of their experience in interviews. More recently, the New York Musical Theater Festival (NYMF), founded in 2005, has provided a venue for new artists to stage their work relatively inexpensively in New York. Over the few years of its existence, the Festival has produced the premieres of many Off Broadway hits, including the acclaimed *Altar Boyz*.

Also during this period the non-animated movie musical became popular once again. The spectacular commercial failures of the 1985 movie version of *A Chorus Line* and the 1992 Disney movie *Newsies* led many in the 1980s and 1990s to believe the movie musical was a defunct form. However, in 2001, director Baz Luhrman's *Moulin Rouge*—an original musical with a score composed mostly of pop songs from the 1980s—earned critical acclaim and surprising commercial profits. Over the next six years the success of the movie adaptations of *Chicago, Dreamgirls,* and *Hairspray* and the phenomenal popularity of the 2006 Disney Channel television movie, *High School Musical,* confirmed that the film musical was, once again, a commercially viable form.

Selected Authors. Musical theatre is clearly alive and well in the twenty-first century. Despite the perennial complaints of cynics who complain musical theatre is a dying art, exciting new works are regularly produced on Broadway, Off Broadway, in workshops and festivals, and on film. The remaining pages of this chapter outline some of the most influential musical theatre authors producing these works in the twenty-first century. Of course, musical theatre is a highly collaborative art and it is not always easy to determine who should be considered the author of a particular show. At times, directors, producers, and even key performers exercise as much authorial power as do those who write the words and music. Still, because of space constraints I will limit this list only to librettists, composers, and lyricists.

Even within these limits, it is impossible to be comprehensive, but I hope this list will give interested readers a sense of the genre in the first decade of the twenty-first century.

Lynn Ahrens (1948–)—*Lyricist & ***Stephen Flaherty** (1960–)—*Composers.* Ahrens and Flaherty are among the few contemporary musical theatre writing teams that work almost exclusively together. They met at the BMI workshop in the 1980s and, soon after, had their New York premiere Off Broadway with *Lucky Stiff* (1988)—a musical about a man who, in order to inherit 6 million dollars, must take his dead uncle's corpse on a gambling vacation. Their next collaboration, *Once on This Island* (1990), a retelling of *The Little Mermaid* set in the Caribbean, transferred from Off Broadway to Broadway and established the team as a thoughtful alternative to the megamusicals that then ruled Broadway. Their epic adaptation of the E.L. Doctorow novel, *Ragtime* (1998), about the maturation of America in the early twentieth century, is considered by many to be their masterpiece and one of the best musicals of the 1990s. Since 2000 the pair have collaborated on the critically and commercially disappointing *Seussical* (based on the children's books of Dr. Seuss); a charming Off Broadway adaptation of the 1994 film *A Man of No Importance* (2002) about a gay bus conductor who longs to stage Oscar Wilde's *Salome* in his conservative Irish community; *Dessa Rose* (2005), from a 1986 Sherley Anne Williams novel about the friendship of a runaway slave and the daughter of her old master; and *The Glorious Ones* (2007) about a troupe of *commedia dell'arte* players struggling to adapt to changes in dramatic taste in the sixteenth century.

Jason Robert Brown (1970–)—*Composer / lyricist.* Jason Robert Brown is perhaps the most popular of the young musical theatre composers who rose to prominence in the 1990s. His first piece, *Songs for a New World* (1995), a song cycle of the his own work (mostly written for other projects), was directed by Daisy Prince and opened Off Broadway at the WPA Theater to critical praise. During rehearsals for the show, Brown was hired by the director's father, Hal Prince, to collaborate on a musical based on the true story of Leo Frank, a Jewish man falsely accused of the murder of a young girl in Atlanta at the turn of the century. The musical, which was eventually titled *Parade,* opened on Broadway at Lincoln Center's Vivian Beaumont Theatre in 1998 and, despite an early closing, earned Brown critical acclaim and a Tony Award. Brown's next piece, *The Last Five Years,* a two-person song cycle about a short-lived marriage between a singer and a writer, opened at the Minetta Lane Theatre in 2002 to mixed reviews but went on to become a staple of regional and amateur theatre seasons. In 2003 Brown was nominated for his second Tony Award for his work as a composer, lyricist, and music director for the short lived and critically despised, *Urban Cowboy.* As of this writing, he is working on two new musicals: *13,* about the quest of a Jewish boy in Indiana to find 13 friends to invite to his Bar Mitzvah, and *Honeymoon in Vegas,* a stage adaptation of the 1992 film of the same name.

Brown's music is a difficult to classify mixture of jazz, rock, and musical theatre ballad. He often cites Billy Joel and Joni Mitchell as major influences on his work, but he is also clearly aware of the traditions of classical music and musical theatre and has consciously and successfully adopted the styles of composers such as Charles Ives and Kurt Weill when a dramatic situation demanded it. The accessibility of his lyrics and music has earned him a large following of fans who celebrate his work on internet discussion forums and on the composer's own blog (http://www.jasonrobertbrown.com).

William Finn (1952–)—*Composer / lyricist.* William Finn has been working in New York theatre since the 1970s, but his contemporary style and subject matter often earn him a place in lists of the "new" musical theatre artists. Best known for his Off Broadway *Falsettos* trilogy about the life of a gay Jewish man named Marvin, Finn's musicals are distinctive for their transparently autobiographical plots and characters. When Finn suffered a brain disease, originally diagnosed as an inoperable brain tumor, he wrote *A New Brain* about a musical theatre composer who survives a near-fatal brain operation. Most recently, though, Finn has branched out from purely autobiographical work and contributed music and lyrics for the 2005 Broadway hit *25th Annual Putnam County Spelling Bee,* for which he earned a Tony nomination for Best Score.

Ricky Ian Gordon (1956–)—*Composer / lyricist / book writer.* Ricky Ian Gordon, now in his forties, is one of the oldest of the "young" new musical theatre artists working in New York. His work, which in musical style tends to resemble opera more than musical theatre, has not yet been on presented Broadway, though his *Only Heaven* (a 1995 song cycle of Langston Hughes poetry), *My Life With Albertine* (2003, based on a novel by Proust), and his 2005 reimagining of the Orpheus myth all received critical praise for their Off Broadway productions and associated cast recordings. His most recent project, an opera adaptation of *The Grapes of Wrath,* opened in Minnesota in February 2007.

Adam Guettel (1965–)—*Composer / lyricist / book writer.* Adam Guettel is the grandson of composer Richard Rodgers and son of composer Mary Rodgers, but Guettel's voice is unquestionably his own. Guettel's Off Broadway musicals *Floyd Collins* (1996), about a man trapped in a Kentucky cave, and *Saturn Returns* (1998), a song cycle of Greek and Christian mythology demonstrated a style far removed from those of his grandfather and mother and established Guettel as an important new voice in musical theatre. Guettel's first commercial success, the 2005 hit *Light in the Piazza* about an American mother and her mentally handicapped daughter's romantic journey to Italy, ran for over a year at the Vivian Beaumont Theatre in Lincoln Center and earned Guettel Tony Awards for best score and best orchestrations. Stephen Sondheim appears to have great respect for Guettel and named "The Riddle Song" from *Floyd Collins* as a "song I wish I'd written" in a list compiled for a concert at the Library of Congress (Horowitz 2003, 171).

Michael John LaChiusa (1962–)—*Composer / lyricist / book writer.* Michael John LaChiusa is perhaps the most prolific musical theatre composer in recent history. A musical featuring the work of LaChiusa has opened each year since 1999, usually to some critical praise but limited commercial success. Like many of the young, critically praised musical theatre composers listed here, LaChiusa's subject matter tends to be unconventional. He has written song cycles about prominent first ladies (*First Lady Suite,* 1993) and sexual intercourse (*Hello Again,* 1993). His Broadway musicals, an updating of the Greek tragedy *Medea* (*Marine Christine,* 1999) set in Louisiana and an adaptation of the 1928 poem *The Wild Party* (unrelated to the Off Broadway adaptation by Andrew Lippa that also opened in 2000), were praised by some music critics but mostly confused audiences and closed quickly. LaChiusa remains an influential voice in the art form and is, in the eyes of many critics, an under-appreciated genius. Musical theatre historian Ethan Mordden expresses a common prediction for the composer in his book, *The Happiest Corpse I've Ever Seen:* "LaChiusa is now where Sondheim was in the early 1970s. But *Marie Christine* was recorded, and discerning ears will hear it. By the next generation or so, it will be in the repertory of every major opera company in the Western world." (Mordden 2004, 153).

Andrew Lippa (1964–)—*Composer / lyricist / book writer.* Andrew Lippa is probably best known for the additional songs he wrote for the 1999 revival of *You're A Good Man, Charlie Brown,* especially "My New Philosophy," which helped launch the career of Broadway and film star Kristin Chenoweth. However, Lippa's other work, including the book, music, and lyrics for the 2000 Off Broadway version of *Wild Party* (unconnected to the Broadway adaptation of the same title by Michael John LaChiusa) and *john & jen* (1995), earned him the respect of critics and fans as one of the important composer-lyricists-book writers of the post-Sondheim generation. Lippa's music tends to be relatively accessible, though he has not yet written a complete score for a commercial Broadway hit. As of this writing, he is working on a musical adaptation of the Addams Family television series (Jones 2007).

Stephen Schwartz (1948–)—*Composer / lyricist.* In the early 1970s Stephen Schwartz had three hit shows running simultaneously on Broadway: *Godspell, Pippin,* and *The Magic Show.* In the next three decades, though, Schwartz struggled to write a musical that would last even a few months on Broadway until his music and lyrics for the 2003 hit, *Wicked,* brought his work to the attention of a new generation of fans.

Schwartz's music is a blend of both rock and traditional Broadway sounds. In an interview for Al Kasha and Joel Hirschhorn's 1985 book, *Notes on Broadway,* Schwartz cites "Rodgers and Hammerstein, Lerner and Lowe, Bock and Harnick, and Stephen Sondheim" as well as "The Mamas and the Papas" and "Jefferson Airplane" as influences on his work (Kasha and Hirschhorn 1987, 267). Thematically, his work is often centered on moral, even religious, questions. Three of his musicals—*Godspell, Children of Eden,* and the animated film *Prince of Egypt*—are adaptations of Biblical stories, and *Mass,* as the title suggests, is an adaptation of a Christian church service. *Wicked* is less obviously religious, though it does explore the nature of good and evil and begins with a main character asking, in a parody of Shakespeare's *Twelfth Night,* whether people are "born wicked" or "have wickedness thrust upon them." As of this writing, Schwartz is working on an opera version of the 1964 film *Séance on a Wet Afternoon,* commissioned by the Opera Santa Barbara, which will premiere in a staged reading at Lincoln Center in January of 2008.

Jeanine Tesori (1961–)—*Composer.* Jeanine Tesori debuted as a New York composer with her 1998 Off Broadway musical *Violet* about a young girl whose face was disfigured by an accident at age 13 and who travels across the country on a bus to be touched by a faith healer. The musical was recorded on CD and was staged in several regional productions, but Tesori's real rise to prominence came in 2002 with her Tony Award nominated score for the stage adaptation of *Thoroughly Modern Millie.* She was further lauded for her work with Tony Kushner on his semi-autobiographical *Caroline, or Change*—about a black washer-woman and the Jewish family who employs her in 1960s Louisiana. She is currently working on a musical adaptation of the Dreamworks animated film, *Shrek* (Gans 2007).

David Yazbek (1960–)—*Composer / Lyricist.* Originally a rock musician whose best known work was, perhaps, the theme song to the 1990s PBS game show "Where in the World is Carmen Sandiego," Yazbek reports having no real interest in theatre music until composer Adam Guettel suggested to producers that Yazbek might be the appropriate composer-lyricist for a stage adaptation of the 1997 movie

The Full Monty (Finn 2001). He was hired and was nominated for a Tony Award for his efforts. Yazbek went on to contribute lyrics to Andrew Lloyd Webber's production of the Bollywood musical *Bombay Dreams* and music and lyrics to the 2005 adaptation of *Dirty Rotten Scoundrels*. Critics praise Yazbek's work as a much needed updating of the somewhat anachronistic Broadway musical style that, at the beginning of the decade, lagged significantly behind the rest of the music culture (Singer 2001).

Bibliography

Actors' Equity Association. *Seasonal Showcase Code.* 2006. <http://www.actorsequity.org/docs/codes/Seasonal_Showcase_06.pdf>. [Accessed December 16, 2007.]

Actors' Equity Association. *Off Broadway Rulebook.* 2005. <http://www.actorsequity.org/docs/rulebooks/OB_Rulebook_05-09.pdf>. [Accessed December 16, 2007.]

"The BMI Lehman Engel Musical Theater Workshop." <http://www.bmi.com/genres/entry/533378>.[Accessed December 16, 2007.]

Block, Geoffrey. *Enchanted Evenings: The Broadway Musical from Show Boat to Sondheim.* Oxford: Oxford University Press, 2003.

Brown, Amanda. *Legally Blonde.* New York: Plume, 2003.

Brown, Jason Robert. *The Last Five Years.* Milwaukee: Hal Leonard, 2002.

———. *Songs for a New World.* Milwaukee: Hal Leonard Corp., 1996.

Bryer, Jackson R., and Richard Allan Davison. *The Art of the American Musical: Conversations with the Creators.* New Brunswick: Rutgers University Press, 2005.

Engel, Lehman. *The American Musical Theater: A Consideration.* New York: Collier, 1975.

Finn, Robin. "'Full Monty' Composer's Tony Anxiety Is Pell-Mel." *New York Times* 31 May 2001: B.2.

Finn, William. *A New Brain.* Miami, Florida: Warner Brothers, 1999.

———. *The 25th Annual Putnam County Spelling Bee.* Van Nuys, California: Alfred, 2005.

Flaherty, Stephen. *Lucky Stiff.* Miami, Florida: Warner Brothers, 1998.

Flaherty, Stephen, and Lynn Ahrens. *The Ahrens and Flaherty Songbook.* Miami, Florida: Warner Brothers, 2001.

Flinn, Denny Martin. *Musical!: A Grand Tour: The Rise, Glory, and Fall of an American Institution.* New York: Schirmer Books, 1997.

Frankel, Aaron. *Writing the Broadway Musical.* Cambridge: Da Capo Press, 2000.

Gans, Andrew. "Keenan-Bolger and Sieber Are Part of Aug. 10 *Shrek* Reading." *Playbill Online.* 10 August 2007. <http://www.playbill.com/news/article/110239.html>. [Accessed December 17, 2007.]

Gordon, Ricky Ian. *Finding Home: The Songs of Ricky Ian Gordon.* Milwaukee: Hal Leonard, 2003.

Grant, Mark N. *The Rise and Fall of the Broadway Musical.* Lebanon: University Press of New England, 2004.

Green, Stanley. *The World of Musical Comedy.* 3rd ed. New York: A.S. Barnes and Company, 1974.

———. *Encyclopedia of the Musical Theatre.* New York: Dodd, Mead and Company, 1976.

Guernsey, Otto L. *Playwrights, Lyricists, Composers on Theater: The Inside Story of a Decade.* New York: Dodd, Mead, and Company, 1974.

Guettel, Adam. *Light in the Piazza.* Milwaukee: Hal Leonard, 2005.

Hamm, Charles. *Irving Berlin: Songs from the Melting Pot: the Formative Years, 1907–1914.* Oxford University Press, 1997.

Hollman, Mark. *Urinetown.* New York: Faber and Faber, 2003.

Horowitz, Mark Eden. *Sondheim on Music: Minor Details and Major Decisions.* Lanham: Scarecrow Press, 2003.

Kasha, Al, and Joel Hirschhorn. *Notes on Broadway: Intimate Conversations with Broadway's Greatest Songwriters*. New York: Simon and Schuster, 1987.

Jones, Kenneth. "Go, Go, Go Gomez! *Addams Family* Musical, by Lippa, Brickman and Elice in Development." *Playbill Online*. 21 May 2007. <http://www.playbill.com/news/article/108236.html>. [Accessed December 16, 2007.]

Larson, Jonathan, et al. *Rent*. New York: Rob Weisbach, 1997.

Mates, Julian. "*The Black Crook* Myth." *Theatre Survey*. 7 (1996): 31–43.

Mordden, Ethan. *The Happiest Corpse I've Ever Seen: The Last 25 Years of the Broadway Musical*. New York: Palgrave Macmillan, 2004.

Schwartz, Stephen. *Wicked*. Milwaukee: Hal Leonard, 2003.

Singer, Barry. "Pop Self-Consciousness Finally Infiltrates Broadway." *New York Times* 26 Aug 2001: 2.3.

Smith, Cecil. *Musical Comedy in America*. New York: Theatre Arts Books, 1950.

Tesori, Jeanine. *Thoroughly Modern Millie*. Milwaukee: Hal Leonard, 2003.

Yazbek, David. *The Full Monty*. Milwaukee: Hal Leonard, 2000.

Further Reading

Block, Geoffrey. *Enchanted Evenings: The Broadway Musical from Show Boat to Sondheim*. Oxford: Oxford University Press, 2003; Bryer, Jackson R., and Richard Allan Davison. *The Art of the American Musical: Conversations with the Creators*. New Brunswick: Rutgers University Press, 2005; Chesterton, G.K. "Introduction." In *Gilbert and Sullivan: A Critical Appreciation of the Savoy Operas*, A.H. Godwin. Port Washington: Kennikat Press, 1926; Ganzl, Kurt. *The Musical: A Concise History*. Boston: University Press of New England, 1997; Hernandez, Ernio. "*Wicked* Creator Schwartz's First Opera, *Séance on a Wet Afternoon*, to Be Presented in January." *Playbill Online*. 14 December 2007; Hibbert, Christopher. *Gilbert and Sullivan and Their Victorian World*. New York: American Heritage Publishing Co., 1976. <http://www.playbill.com/news/article/113565.html>. [Accessed December 16, 2007.]; Perry, George C., et al. *The Complete Phantom of the Opera*. New York: Henry Holt, 1988.

DOUG RESIDE

MYSTERY FICTION

Definition. At its broadest, the definition of mystery fiction is that of a story in which a crime is solved. The popularity of crime fiction in the United States is significant. Over 28,000 fiction titles were released in the United States in 2004 ("U.S. Book Production"). Although it is difficult to pinpoint exactly what percentage of this production is mystery/detective/crime fiction, a recent estimate is that crime fiction grabs approximately 25 percent of the fiction market ("U.S. Book Production"). The subgenres and categories of mystery fiction are seemingly endless. The most influential subgenres, however, have been the cozy, the hard-boiled detective, the police procedural, and most recently the forensic detective.

History. There is scholarly disagreement about which novel is the first true mystery novel, as many early novels contained elements of the mystery genre. Wilkie Collins's *The Moonstone* (1868), Edgar Allan Poe's short stories about C. August Dupin, Anna Katharine Green's *The Leavenworth Affair* (1878), and William Godwin's *Caleb Williams* (1794) have all been put forth as firsts on both sides of the Atlantic. In general, however, the origin of the *detective* story is usually traced to mysteries solved by Poe's Dupin: "The Murders in the Rue Morgue" (1841), "The Mystery of Marie Roget" (1842), and "The Purloined Letter" (1844). In these stories, Poe established some of the conventions of detective fiction, including an eccentric detective, an impossible crime, and the creation of a series character.

In the nineteenth century, dime novels with their sensational and lurid stories proliferated and the detective novel was born. Arthur Conan Doyle, G.K. Chesterton, R. Austin Freeman, Jacques Futrelle, and Anna Katharine Green were major contributors to the field until the 1920s. In 1920, Agatha Christie made her debut with *The Mysterious Affair at Styles*, which was followed soon after by Dorothy Sayers's *Whose Body* in 1923. Together they ushered in what is known as the Golden Age with novels often referred to as cozies. Cozies have low levels of overt violence (the murder takes place off-stage), are solved by an amateur, and are usually set in a narrow environment (a small village, an estate, a train, etc.), which allows the detective to find a motive among a few limited suspects and to concentrate on the victim's relationship to the killer.

The Golden Age belonged to the British. In the United States, the 1920s produced Earl Derr Bigger's Charlie Chan novels and S.S. Van Dine's Philo Vance. The establishment of the magazine *The Black Mask*, co-founded by H.L. Mencken, offered writers like Raymond Chandler, Rex Stout, and Erle Stanley Gardner a place for their more robust stories. The launching of the hard-boiled detective is credited to the writers published in *The Black Mask* between 1926 and 1936. The hard-boiled detective is described as being a loner, a man with values that are laced with moral ambiguity: a man who doesn't shun violence. James M. Cain's *The Postman Always Rings Twice* (1934), Cornell Woolrich's *I Married a Dead Man* (1948), and Jim Thompson's *The Killer Inside Me* (1952) were so dark that their style of writing was dubbed *noir*, a genre upon which Hollywood capitalized.

By the 1960s, Cold War espionage or **spy fiction** had all but ousted the traditional detective and the cozy. Writers like Ian Fleming, John le Carré, and Len Deighton wrote novels set in post World War II Berlin or Moscow. Romantic suspense authors, influenced by the gothic novels of eighteenth-century Horace Walpole and Ann Radcliffe and of the nineteenth-century Charlotte Brontë (particularly *Jane Eyre*, 1847), were immensely popular as well. Victoria Holt, Mary Stewart, and Phyllis A. Whitney penned dozens of romantic suspense novels. (See **Romance Novels**.)

The subgenre of historical mysteries, those set in an historical era, such as the Middle Ages, or the age of Victoria, exploded in the 1970s. Elizabeth Peters's nineteenth-century sleuth Amelia Peabody and Ellis Peters's medieval monk Brother Cadfael were among the popular offerings. Women have always populated the mystery field as heavily as men; however, it wasn't until the 1980s that their work began to receive much critical acclaim. Female sleuths occupied the police force and private eye offices in record numbers. Women's novels frequently commented on social issues. Since then, the mystery genre has seen contributions from increasing numbers of writers from multicultural backgrounds, and the field is dominated by diversity. It is also apparent that while there are still many mysteries that are clearly genre-driven, just as many are blurring the line between mystery and mainstream fiction.

Trends and Themes. There are numerous subgenres within the genre of mystery fiction. Some of the most notable and popular are described below.

The Cozy. A lack of graphic crime scene description is the first indicator that one is reading a cozy. Another is the fact that the mystery takes place in a seemingly ordinary environment where violence is not a common occurrence. The cozy sleuth is an amateur, helped by or a helper of the official investigative force. Cozies, established in the 1920s, dominated the world of fiction for many decades, waning and waxing in popularity. In recent decades, cozies have splintered into dozens of categories. Many readers of this genre are interested in books with a certain type of sleuth: bibliophiles, cooks or gardeners, dog or cat lovers, or practitioners of innumerable hobbies (quilting, for example). Academic and religious mysteries also fall into this category. Teachers, professors, and anthropologists are some of the characters found in academic mysteries; priests, pastors, and other lay people are central to religious mysteries.

Mary Higgins Clark appeared on the mystery scene in 1975 with the publication of her first suspense novel, *Where Are the Children*. Because of the lack of on-stage violence, Clark's books are often categorized as cozies. She has written more suspense novels than true mysteries, basing her plots on current events and newspaper headlines and providing social commentary with her clearly defined good/evil characters. Clark's books have been praised for their fast pace, detailed locations, and breathless action. At the same time her characters and plots have been criticized for being formulaic. However, Clark's formula of rollercoaster storylines and strong heroines have led to the publication of over 20 suspense novels selling 80 million copies worldwide. Her latest, a novel based on telepathy, is *Two Little Girls in Blue* (2006).

Since 2000, she has co-authored three Christmas suspense titles with her daughter Carol Higgins Clark. The younger Clark is best known for her Regan Reilly mysteries, of which *Decked* (1991) was nominated for both the Agatha and Anthony Awards.

Academic Mysteries. Scholarship is the basis of many mystery subgenres. Religious sleuths such as Rabbi Small and Father Koesler delve into Scripture and the Torah to solve crimes. Historians of every ilk, manuscripts in ancient abbeys, archaeological digs, Native American pottery, herbology—any and all subjects lend themselves to scholarship. Mysteries set in academic settings are popular mostly with academics themselves; universities and boarding schools serve as the most popular locations.

The popularity of academic crossover novels is seen by writers such as A. S. Byatt and her novel *Possession* (1990), about the mystery surrounding the letters of a Victorian poet. Dan Brown's successful *Da Vinci Code* (2003), although definitely not a cozy, follows Harvard professor Robert Langdon's scholarly romp through the mysteries of the Holy Grail, indicating that the study of esoteric subjects can have wide appeal.

Carolyn G. Heilbrun, one of the first female professors of literature at Columbia University, created the pseudonym Amanda Cross in the 1960s. Her character professor Kate Fansler served as Cross's alter ego, combating chauvinism in the academic world and overcoming obstacles as Heilbrun herself did. Fansler first appeared in the 1964 *In the Last Analysis*, which received an Edgar nomination, and became an immediate favorite. Cross's academic mysteries are considered the finest of the genre, mixing solid plots with witty satire directed against the university. Often compared to Dorothy Sayers, who Cross admired, her Fansler mysteries are set in a university locale and examine both feminist and academic issues. *The Edge of Doom* (2002) was the last Cross novel before Heilbrun committed suicide in 2003.

Gillian Roberts's character Amanda Pepper is an English teacher in a Philadelphia prep school. Pepper made her debut in the 1988 Anthony-winning *Caught Dead in Philadelphia*. *A Hole in Juan* (2006) and *All's Well That Ends* (2007) are Roberts's most recent installments in the Pepper series. Charlotte Macleod's charming Professor Peter Shandy is introduced in the 1978 *Rest You Merry*. Her series of 10 novels is set at Balaclava Agricultural College headed by college president Thorkjeld Svenson. Macleod's humorous narratives about academic life culminated in her 1996 *Exit the Milkman,* her final Shandy novel. Pamela Thomas-Graham presents a darker look at academia. Harvard University is the location of amateur sleuth Nikki Chase as she struggles to become the first tenured African American woman at the university.

Culinary Mysteries. Nan and Ivan Lyons introduced the combination of food and mysteries with the 1978 *Someone Is Killing the Great Chefs of Europe.* It was food editor Virginia Rich's creation of chef Eugenia Potter in the 1982 *Cooking School Murders,* though, that set the stage for the dozens of culinary mysteries that crowd the mystery shelves in bookstores. Eugenia appeared in three Rich novels until her death in 1985. Nancy Pickard completed Rich's *The 27 Ingredient Chili Con Carne Murders* (1993) and went on to produce several Potter mysteries on her own. In a culinary mystery, the sleuth is usually a food professional of some sort (chef, restaurant or inn owner, caterer, even a restaurant critic), but not a professional detective. The murder is often committed through the food itself, with a kitchen utensil, or in a culinary environment, such as a party, a convention, a kitchen, or even in a cooking school.

Some famous mystery characters have an interest in food, even though they are not professionals. For example, Rex Stout's Nero Wolfe and Patricia Cornwell's Kay Scarpetta are food lovers and have had their recipes collected in cookbooks. A true culinary mystery, however, is one that focuses on the food and its relationship to the murder victim. Culinary mysteries often feature recipes from the characters as well. *Mystery Readers International* devoted two issues to "Culinary Crime" in 2002 by contributors who are mostly gastronomic mystery writers.

Catering seems to be a risky business; several authors have created characters who become involved in murder while catering events. Diane Mott Davidson is one of the foremost names in cooking crimes. Her novels feature Goldy Bear, Colorado owner of Goldilocks Catering, her son Archie, and husband investigator Tom Schulz. The series opener is titled *Catering to Nobody* (1990) and is followed by 12 more Goldy Bear installments, the most recent *Dark Tort* (2006). Katherine Hall Page's character Faith Fairchild, a minister's wife, owns a catering business in Aleford, Massachusetts. Fairchild has starred in 16 mysteries, the most recent *The Body in the Ivy* (2006). Lesbian restaurant owner Jane Lawless stars in over a dozen Ellen Hart mysteries (*Night Vision,* 2006).

Bed and breakfasts, or inns, are often locations of culinary mysteries. Claudia Bishop's Hemlock Falls series features Sarah Quilliam and her sister Meg as owners of the Hemlock Falls Inn in upstate New York. The fourteenth book in the series is *Ground to a Halt* (2007). Like many other culinary mysteries, Bishop's include recipes from the books' storylines. Tamar Myers began her Pennsylvania Dutch Mysteries with Recipes series in 1994 with *Too Many Cooks Spoil the Broth* featuring PennDutch Inn owner Magdalena Yoder. The series has been very popular and Hernia, Pennsylvania has been the setting for 16 Yoder mysteries. Food writers and restaurant critics often appear as main characters. Another Ellen Hart character, Sophie Greenway, is a *Minneapolis Times Register* restaurant reviewer/sleuth (*No Reservations Required,* 2005).

Scores of mystery titles have humorous titles that rely on puns or other wordplay, but culinary mysteries seem to take the art of punning to a higher level. Plays on cooking terms and techniques are seen in such examples as Nancy Fairbanks's

Crime Brulee (2001), Farmer's *Dim Sum Dead* (2001), and Lou Jane Temple's *Red Beans and Vice* (2001). Along with their humorous titles are often hilarious romps featuring irate customers, cooking mishaps, and other kitchen slapstick. Though some culinary mysteries do have serious crimes and themes at the heart of them, most are light cozies penned for sheer enjoyment rather than edification (unless one counts the inclusion of recipes).

Gardening Mysteries. In 1868, Wilkie Collins published *The Moonstone,* one of the all-time great mystery novels. The detective in the novel, Sergeant Cuff, has a passion for rose gardening, and the first connection between gardening and mysteries was established. The most famous detective/plant lover was Nero Wolfe whose love for food was matched only by his passion for orchids. Barbara Michaels, fond of gardening, penned *The Dancing Floor* (1999) in which mazes and country gardens figured.

Gardening mysteries include gardeners, herbalists, and florists. Kate Collins introduced Abby Knight, flower shop owner in *Mum's the Word* (2004). Nursery owner Janis Harrison has created the Gardening Mystery series featuring florist Bretta Solomon. The most popular gardening author is Susan Wittig Albert. Her China Bayles series is set in Pecan Springs, Texas, where Bayles moves to open an herb shop after quitting her law practice. *Spanish Dagger* (2007) is the fifteenth entry in the series. Although not based on a book, a British TV series produced from 2003–2006 called *Rosemary & Thyme* was a popular program, featuring two female landscape design and gardening sleuths.

Religious Mysteries. G.K. Chesterton's Father Brown appeared in 1911 in *The Innocence of Father Brown.* Other notable British authors of religious mysteries are Ellis Peters (Brother Cadfael), Veronica Black (Sister Joan), Margaret Frazer (Dame Frevisse), and Peter Tremayne (Sister Fidelma). There are quite a few sleuths in religious orders on the American side of the Atlantic as well. Religious sleuths are often underestimated by the other characters around them. Chesterton's Father Brown is a stumpy sort of individual, very plain looking and mild seeming, yet he is well versed in the complexities and depravities of the human mind. Religious figures are often privy to times of grief and horror and the events that precipitate them. Their understanding of people and their knowledge of their particular religious order make them useful in solving crimes, often surprising the police with their accurate solutions.

An ordained priest, Andrew Greeley is a prolific author of books on religious and sociological topics. It is for his Father "Blackie" Ryan series, however, that he is best known. Greeley's *The Bishop in the Old Neighborhood* (2005) marks the fifteenth installment in the Father Ryan, or rather the Bishop Ryan series, as he achieves this status midway through the series. Greeley uses his fiction not only to criticize various aspects of the Catholic Church, but to explore matters of Christian living that he feels do not receive enough attention by parish priests.

After leaving the priesthood in 1974, William X. Kienzle combined his journalistic skills with his knowledge of the Church and experience as a Roman Catholic priest to create the popular Father Koesler who debuted in the 1979 *The Rosary Murders.* Detroit and its environs operate as the backdrop for the Koesler mysteries, and Kienzle's familiarity with the city comes through in his detailed descriptions of Detroit's locales and people. Compared to Greeley in his use of the mystery novel to highlight problems in the Church, Kienzle's Koesler series has, however, received the praise for his plots and characters that Greeley's often failed to. Kienzle's final installment in the series, *The Gathering* (2002), was published posthumously.

Harry Kemelman began his writing career contributing stories to *Ellery Queen's Mystery Magazine*. These stories, about a New England English professor were collected in *The Nine Mile Walk* (1967). With a desire to chronicle the lives of suburban Jews, he eventually used his mystery writing talents to create Rabbi Small, an armchair detective who solves crimes in his community using Talmudic logic. The Rabbi Small novels depict a community and its people, not just the character of Small and his family. *Friday the Rabbi Slept Late* (1964) won the Edgar award and Rabbi Small went on to become one of the most famous and loved fictitious rabbis. In the final Rabbi Small mystery, *The Day the Rabbi Left Town* (1996), a retired Small begins teaching at a local college. Kemelman's books have been praised for their intellectualism and depiction of the often-uneasy existence of Jewish communities in a predominantly Gentile culture.

Notre Dame professor Ralph McInerny began his Father Dowling series in 1976 at an agent's suggestion. *Her Death of Cold* (1977) has been followed by 25 more Dowling novels. A teacher of philosophy, McInerny invests his novels with serious considerations of moral issues. Under the pseudonym Monica Quill, McInerny wrote a series of mysteries about Sister Mary Magdalene, a Carmelite nun, which culminated in a collection of stories and novellas in the 2001 *Death Takes the Veil*.

Ministers are not the only religious sleuths popular with mystery writers; nuns have also been successful as amateur detectives. Aimée and David Thurlo are better known for their *Ellah Clah* series (see Native American Mysteries), but Sister Agatha who is an extern nun for a cloister in New Mexico, has proven popular as well. The eighth Sister Agatha mystery is *Prey for a Miracle* (2006). Sister Carol Anne O'Marie introduced Sister Mary Helen in *Novena for Murder* (1984), which she has followed up with 10 more Sister Mary Helen titles. Neither a minister nor a nun, Faith Fairchild is the wife of a minister in Aleford, Massachusetts. Katherine Hall Page's Body series has 16 titles, the latest *The Body in the Ivy* (2006).

Crimes Feline, Canine, and Equine. Beginning with the Depression-era publication of D.B. Olsen's *The Cat Saw Murder* (1939), cats have been featured as detectives in a niche that has turned into a subgenre all its own—that of cat mysteries. Cat mysteries can be defined as mysteries in which a cat either solves a crime or assists its human in doing so. Lilian Jackson Braun is the undisputed queen of cat mysteries: her "Cat Who" series numbers over two dozen titles. Jim Qwilleran, a retired journalist, moves to a small town up North to escape the hectic rush of big city life. He partners with KoKo, a Siamese cat, in his first mystery, *The Cat Who Could Read Backwards* (1966). Along with Yum Yum, another rescued Siamese, Qwill and KoKo have starred in 29 *Cat Who* mysteries, the most recent, *The Cat Who Had Sixty Whiskers* (2007). The series, although always featuring a murder, is loved for Braun's humorous depiction of small town life and lack of overt violence.

Close behind Braun in production is Lydia Adamson, who has published 21 feline mysteries since 1990. Alice Nestleton is an actress/cat sitter who stumbles across crimes while taking care of her feline charges. Lydia Adamson is the *nom de plume* for Frank King who has written both a dog series and a cat series under the Adamson name. Carole Nelson Douglas's feline mysteries revolve around Midnight Louie, who solves crimes in Las Vegas. Unlike the lighthearted *Cat Who* books, Douglas's series has won much praise and a number of awards for its exploration of such serious issues as sexual addiction. To mystery readers, Rita Mae Brown, who achieved critical acclaim with *Rubyfruit Jungle* (1973), is better known for her Mrs. Murphy and Sneaky Pie Brown mysteries. Set in Crozet, Virginia, the animals help their owner, postmaster Harry, solve crimes.

Elizabeth Peters/Barbara Michaels has not written about a feline sleuth, but many of her novels include cats, the most famous being Bastet who appears in the Amelia Peabody books. Other detectives own cats, even though they don't participate in their owners' sleuthing: Sharon McCone, Peter Shandy, Amanda Pepper, and Annie Laurence Darling are all fictional sleuths who own cats.

Although cats are popular as companions to sleuths, dogs are close behind in representation. Susan Conant has won the Maxwell Award for Fiction Writing given by the Dog Writers' Association of America for three of her *Dog Lovers Mysteries* titles. Her detective is Holly Winter, a dog trainer and columnist who owns two Alaskan Malamutes. The novels are humorous and replete with dog information along with the requisite crime solving. *Gaits of Heaven* (2006) is the most recent Malamute and Winter novel. Another author who sets her mysteries in the far North, Sue Henry lives in Alaska, where she teaches writing at The University of Alaska. Her Alaska mystery series featuring musher Jessie Arnold debuted with *Murder on the Iditarod Trail* (1991), which won both the Anthony and the Macavity awards.

Dick Francis is unquestionably the ruler of equine mysteries. A former jockey, Francis used his knowledge of horseracing to write over 40 equine mysteries. Following in his footsteps is Kit Ehrman, whose Steve Kline mysteries are set in the horseracing circuit. Another veterinarian, Gail McCarthy, solves crimes in mysteries related to horses in Laura Crum's series. Quarter horse trainer Michaela Bancroft is the creation of Michele Scott, author of the *Horse Lover's Mystery* series.

Hard-Boiled. It is argued that the hard-boiled detective is a truly American phenomenon that grew out of the disillusionment of the post World War I period. Carroll John Daley's Race Williams is one of the first tough guys of detective fiction. Dashiell Hammet's Continental Op and Sam Spade and Raymond Chandler's Philip Marlowe made the genre memorable, particularly with the help of Humphrey Bogart playing the part of Spade and Marlowe in several Hollywood blockbusters.

A loner, the hard-boiled private eye works on the margins of society, offering a window into both the underworld of criminals and the mainstream world as it appears to the outsider. Often cynical and seemingly callous, the typical hard-boiled detective is no stranger to the meanness in his fellow man, and woman. Women are often portrayed as deceitful and insincere, luring the detective into danger for purposes often nefarious. The detective is tough and inured to violence, but often presents dark gallows humor and a fondness for metaphorical descriptions. Almost disappearing under the onslaught of espionage novels in the 1960s, the hard-boiled detective was revived by Robert B. Parker's Spenser and Bill Pronzini's Nameless Detective. Andrew Vachss's Burke, Loren D. Estleman's Amos Walker, Lawrence Block's Matthew Scudder, and Walter Mosley's Easy Rawlins (see **African American Literature**) are descendants of the hard-boiled tradition.

Set in Northern California, Bill Pronzini's prolific series about the Nameless Detective follows the detective's career through 32 installments in as many years (*The Snatch* was published in 1971 and *Savages* in 2007). Nameless is a detective in the pulp tradition. Overweight, a smoker, he resembles Raymond Chandler's Continental Op. Like the Op, Nameless views the world of San Francisco through the eyes of a working-class stiff who sees the seamier side of both the underbelly of the criminal world and the glitzy neighborhoods of the wealthy.

Unlike Chandler's detective, Pronzini's investigator solves "impossible" or "locked room" crimes. These types of crimes, difficult to solve as it appears impossible for the criminal to have been able to enter or leave the room without being detected, usually belong to the school of ratiocination, where crimes are solved by sheer intellectual genius. Pronzini has created a hard-boiled detective with a brain. *Hoodwink* (1981) features Pronzini's astonishing grasp of the history of mystery fiction. Nameless, a collector of pulp fiction, attends a pulp convention, where he investigates two murders. The novel combines Pronzini's passion for pulp with Nameless's strong detection skills, earning the novel a Private Eye Writers of America Shamus Award for best novel.

Andrew Vachss began his career as a children's rights lawyer among other legal system jobs. He uses his background in many of his novels. Since the publication of his first novel *Flood* (1983), featuring ex-con and private investigator Burke, Vachss has been labeled a writer of "hard-boiled" or "neo-noir" detective stories. His characters, particularly Burke, cross the line of right and wrong easily, resorting to vigilante violence when justice does not seem to be forthcoming through legal channels. In Vachss's 16 Burke novels, the tough investigator is often called upon to find child abusers and killers. Vachss's novels are often brutal, but they are praised for their high quality writing.

Lawrence Block is one of the most respected mystery writers today. The creator of three popular series and dozens of stand-alone titles, Block has become synonymous with successful mystery fiction. His Bernie Rhodenbarr series is written in the tradition of the humorous caper. Novels about Evan Tanner are set squarely in the Cold War years of spy novels. Tanner is a Korean War veteran who becomes involved in international intrigues.

Block's most successful series, however, is the dozen or so novels about former cop and alcoholic Matthew Scudder. After a gunshot goes awry, killing a small girl, Scudder resigns from the police force, drowning his guilt in alcohol and fighting bad guys with the help of his less-than-upright friends. The first novel in the series, *The Sins of the Fathers* (1976), introduces Scudder and reveals his drunken life working out of the hotel room in which he lives for the better part of the series. As morally ambiguous as any hard-boiled detective ever created, Scudder is not above using criminal behavior or relying on the "favors" of criminals to obtain justice for his clients.

A bottle in the desk drawer has been a hard-boiled detective tradition, equating to strength and masculinity. As the series progresses, though, Scudder dries out, but maintains his bachelor lifestyle combing the streets of New York and visiting with his old bar buddies, all of whom live on the seamy side. His sometime girlfriend, the high-priced prostitute Elaine, marries Scudder in a recent installment, and they begin making a life together. Nothing is as it appears in Scudder's world: The good are often evil and the bad guys, although not saints, are often the ones who reclaim a justice that the universe has denied the victims. As Block's characters age, the darker tone of Scudder's nihilistic early appearances recedes; yet the world he and Elaine inhabit is still a rough one.

Michael Connelly's novels are located in the *noir* world of Raymond Chandler's Los Angeles. He exploded onto the mystery landscape with the publication of his first novel, *The Black Echo,* featuring detective Harry Bosch, in 1992. The novel was well received by critics and readers, winning the Edgar Award for Best First Novel by the Mystery Writers of America. Hieronymus (Harry) Bosch is named for the fifteenth-century Dutch painter whose nightmarish canvases were peopled with grotesque figures against the backdrop of violent landscapes. Bosch is a fictional composite of bits from both real detectives and fictional ones: Raymond Chandler's Philip Marlowe and Ross McDonald's Lew Archer, along with film icons Dirty Harry and Frank Bullit are some of the characters who shape Bosch.

In *Echo Park* (2006), Bosch is out of retirement and working cold cases for the Open Unsolved Unit. He is obsessed by a 13-year-old case that he was unable to solve. Bosch's whole career as a cop is thrown into question when a jailed serial killer confesses to the death of the woman whose killer eluded him. In all of Connelly's Bosch novels, he creates a real man performing a real job. The man is flawed and his flaws contribute to his own torturous path through his career and into his own psyche. Bosch must confront his own demons and find a way to make peace with his path to salvage his future.

Robert B. Parker is best known for his Spenser novels, a series that prompted the creation of the television series *Spenser for Hire* (1985–1988), in which Robert Urich played the part of the Boston detective. A prolific author, Parker has written over 30 Spenser novels beginning with *The Godwulf Manuscript* in 1974. Unlike the archetypal private investigator, Spenser does not hold himself apart from the community in which he works. In Spenser, Parker has created a detective whose connection to Boston and its people is strong, and a sense of place is important in the novels. Like his predecessors, Spenser does have an idealistic code that he is unable to carry out in the traditional venue of police work; thus he strikes out on his own. Along with his partner, Hawk, and his lover, Susan Silverman, this college-educated private eye battles stereotypes, all the while upholding his traditional hard-boiled image. In the late 1990s, Parker created two more series characters, former LAPD detective Jesse Stone and another former police officer (a female this time), Sunny Randall.

Another Boston writer is Dennis Lehane, whose series is set in working-class immigrant neighborhoods. The gritty *Mystic River* (2001), bringing together three childhood friends in an investigation of one of the group's murdered daughters, was made into a successful film. Lehane's writing career began with a mystery series featuring Boston detectives Patrick Kenzie and Angela Gennaro. The novels, particularly *Darkness, Take My Hand* (1996), generated praise for their brutally realistic portrayals of Boston and its environs. Both *Mystic River* and *Gone, Baby, Gone,* Lehane's 1998 title featuring Kenzie and Gennaro, have been made into successful and critically acclaimed films.

Hard-boiled detective fiction was long the jurisdiction of male writers. The genre appeared particularly ill suited to women characters. Although historically there have been many female private eyes in mystery fiction (one of the first was Seeley Regester's *Dead Letter: An American Romance*, which appeared in 1864), it wasn't until the 1980s that the female sleuth broke the barrier of the male-dominated private detective and garnered praise for doing so. Sue Grafton, Sara Paretsky, and Marcia Muller are the foremost authors with female private eye protagonists.

Marcia Muller introduced the popular Sharon McCone in the 1977 *Edwin of the Iron Shoes*. Influenced by her husband Bill Pronzini (see Hard-Boiled Detective), Muller created the first female detective to compete in the hard-boiled tradition. McCone begins her career working as a detective for the All-Souls Legal Cooperative.

Unlike most hard-boiled PI's, though, McCone has a circle of friends and family to whom she is close and who she often helps. Female sleuths are rarely portrayed as loners. Muller's earlier titles show McCone as becoming personally invested in her client's problems; in later works, the issues are more social and political in nature. McCone also becomes hardened, particularly after she kills a man in self-defense. Muller's plots involve shady ethics in many industries (dot coms, country music, politics), and she finds in typical hard-boiled fashion, that her own ethics in pursuing justice for her clients become slippery as well.

Sara Paretsky and Sue Grafton both began their publishing careers in 1982 with series characters that became much more commercially successful for them than Sharon McCone did for Marcia Muller. Paretsky and Grafton are consistently on the bestseller lists.

Sara Paretsky founded Sisters in Crime in 1986. The worldwide organization states that its mission is "To combat discrimination against women in the mystery field, educate publishers and the general public as to inequities in the treatment of female authors, raise the level of awareness of their contributions to the field, and promote the professional advancement of women who write mysteries." Paretsky's protagonist, V.I. Warshawski introduced readers to strong, capable female characters who are not victims, but rather the protectors of victims. Playing with the conventions of the hard-boiled genre, Paretsky carves a niche for Warshawski and for other female authors in the male world of hard-boiled private eyes. Warshawski is a fighter for justice, taking on cases where the downtrodden have no other hope. Her cases are often more socially oriented than Chandler's or Hammett's would be. In *Indemnity Only* (1982), Paretsky provides a background for her character that is strengthened as the series continues. Warshawski left the public defender's office jaded with the corrupt nature of the job. Thirteen novels later Paretsky has legions of fans of the feminist ideas imbued in her mystery fiction. Warshawksi is involved with feminist issues, but also with issues of community and social responsibility. Her cases often center on white-collar crime, which defrauds the poor and defenseless. She comes up against, and overcomes, traditional patriarchal objections to her decision to ply a man's trade. Like McCone, Warshawski differs from male hard-boiled detectives in her deep social relationships with families and friends.

Kinsey Millhone is one of the best-recognized female sleuths being published today. She was introduced by Sue Grafton in the 1982 *A is for Alibi. T for Trespass* (2007) is her twentieth Millhone installment. Grafton has created in Millhone a traditional loner of a private eye, one with demons in her past, including a stint as a police officer and two failed marriages. What sets the novels apart from those of her male predecessors is the consistently strong background and personality development of Millhone. Grafton's novels tackle social themes in an effort to understand the "whys" behind the murders investigated.

Police Procedurals. Helen Reilly was a prolific author of mystery novels, whose career stretched from 1930 to 1962. Her books feature New York City Police Inspector Christopher McKee. They were among the first American novels to stress police procedure. Authors of police procedurals strive to create an accurate environment in which their characters respond to crime scenes, perform investigative work, and apprehend criminals. They focus in on the various officers in a force, their relationships with each other, and the development of their characters. Lawrence Treat's *V as in Victim* (1945) is usually acknowledged as the first novel in this genre; however, the television show *Dragnet* (1951–1959) is often credited with jumpstarting the popularity of police procedurals. Unlike the classic hard-boiled private eye or cozy, with its amateur sleuth, the hero of a police procedural is acting as part of a team. The reader of this genre is thrust into a setting where rules (procedures) are followed and the operation of a police force is described in great detail. Ed McBain's 87th Precinct novels are a superb example of this genre.

Ed McBain, pseudonym of Salvatore Albert Lombino (AKA Evan Hunter), was a prolific writer, with over 125 novels published under various names. More than 50 of these titles have been part of the influential and highly regarded 87th Precinct series, which provided the impetus for many police force television series, such as *Hill Street Blues* and *NYPD Blue*. The 1956 *Cop Hater* was the first novel in the 87th Precinct series. McBain's novels stood out from the heroic detective story in that the hero was a collection of police officers, each with his own eccentricities and talents, working together as a team to apprehend criminals. The novels are set in New York and the setting is an important part of the series' success. New York is portrayed through the eyes of those on the streets, walking the beat, knocking on door after door to find witnesses, questioning suspects, gathering evidence bit by bit. The settings are realistic as are the characters, the dialogue, and the crimes. In over 40 years of creating novels for the series, McBain has continued to move forward in time, keeping his characters updated in the latest crime-solving techniques and innovations. His novels have been consistently praised for their strong characters and gritty outlook. The final 87th Precinct novel, *Fiddlers,* was published in 2005, the year McBain died.

Stuart M. Kaminsky, well known for several series characters (see Historical Mysteries), is most celebrated for his series about Russian inspector Porfiry Rostnikov. *Death of a Dissident* (also published as *Rostnikov's Corpse*) was published in 1981 and was praised for both its depiction of police work in a constantly changing Russia and the characterization of Rostnikov himself, a dedicated cop in a corrupt world. Kaminsky's 1989 *Cold Red Sunrise* won an Edgar for best novel.

Pulitzer Prize winning journalist John Camp is better known as John Sandford. Sandford has published 17 novels in his Prey series, beginning with *Rules of Prey* in 1989, setting his Police Lieutenant Lucas Davenport mysteries in Minneapolis.

Capers. A caper is a humorous mystery novel, one in which both felons and law enforcement are equally incompetent. Capers often involve criminals attempting to pull off major heists and usually doing so badly. Donald Westlake's Dortmunder series and the Parker series written under a pseudonym, Richard Stark, are two of the best caper characters. Stark's first Parker installment, *Point Blank* (1962) was made into a film starring Lee Marvin and Angie Dickinson. Parker was such a successful character that Westlake created Dortmunder, a bungling jewel thief, who debuted in the 1970 *The Hot Rock*. There have been over a dozen Dortmunder titles and over 20 Parker titles, all absurdly fast-paced and comic. Bernie Rhodenbarr, created by Lawrence Block, is the proprietor of a used bookstore by day and a thief at night. As humorous as Westlake's Dortmunder series, Rhodenbarr is a far cry from Block's retired cop and reformed alcoholic Matthew Scudder. Block introduced the thief in *Burglars Can't Be Choosers* (1977) and has written almost a dozen more installments in the series.

Forensic Science. The current public fascination with forensic science reaches back to the television series *Quincy, M.E.* (1976–1983), starring Jack Klugman, and is now reflected in dozens of shows, specifically the *CSI* franchise currently on the air. Forensic novels are those that use science to solve crimes: pathology, anthropology, toxicology, and behavioral profiling among many other fields. High-tech investigative techniques are often employed to solve otherwise impossible crimes. The novels are also often gory with descriptions of autopsies and close-up details of the victims' causes of death making for unsettling reading. Kathy Reichs, Patricia Cornwell, and Jeffrey Deaver lead the pack with detectives who use science to solve crimes.

Although preceded by P.D. James's *Death of a Expert Witness* (1977) and Susan Dunlap's *Pious Deception* (1989), both medical detective mysteries, Patricia Cornwell's 1990 *Postmortem* introduced mysteries readers to the world of Kay Scarpetta, Chief Medical Examiner for the State of Virginia, and opened the floodgates to a slew of forensic mysteries. Cornwell's novels employ all of the features of forensic science in her Scarpetta mysteries. Critics praise Cornwell's use of highly detailed forensic techniques, but often criticize the character of Scarpetta as being too introspective, and at times, downright unpleasant. *Postmortem* was followed by over a dozen more Scarpetta novels, following the medical examiner as she moves to several states, working in various capacities to solve crimes.

Kathy Reichs is a forensic anthropologist for Quebec, medical examiner for North Carolina, and anthropology professor at the University of North Carolina, Charlotte. Her experience in the field has helped her books about Temperance "Tempe" Brennan rival those of Cornwell. Brennan debuted in *Deja Dead* (1997) where readers are also introduced to Brennan's archenemy, Montreal Police Inspector Luc Claudel. Grisly forensic details are based on Reich's own examination of bodies too far decomposed to be identified by pathologists. It is Reichs's ability to combine explanations of forensic procedures with strong storylines that have captured an ever-increasing fan base for her novels. The television series, *Bones*, is based on Reichs and her character. The tenth Brennan installment is *Bones to Ashes* (2007).

Jeffery Deaver has introduced a new type of forensic scientist. Injured while working a case, Lincoln Rhyme is now a quadriplegic, able to move only a finger. Equipped with every high-tech gadget known to the world of forensic science, Rhyme works out of his home/lab in New York. A complex man, Rhyme does not endear himself to many, but his intellect is highly sought after. In *The Bone Collector* (1997), made into a 1999 movie starring Denzel Washington and Angelina Jolie, Rhyme begins working with Amelia Sachs. Sachs goes where Rhyme sends her and acts as his eyes and ears as she investigates crime scenes and tracks criminals. Deaver's Lincoln Rhyme series is praised for the books' dizzyingly fast-paced and twisted plot lines.

Nursery rhyme titles catapulted James Patterson into the spotlight. *Along Came a Spider* appeared in 1993, and much to his readers' delight, has been followed by 10 more Alex Cross novels. Cross is a psychologist who works with the police department to track killers. His ability to get inside the mind and psyche of criminals often clashes with his desire to live quietly with his family. Patterson's books are filled with action, and despite his doctoral studies in literature at Vanderbilt, simple in style and language. *Kiss the Girls* starring Morgan Freeman and Ashley Judd was released in 1997, followed by *Along Came a Spider* (2001); *Roses Are Red* is scheduled for release in 2007.

Thomas Harris's novels about FBI agent Clarice Starling and Hannibal Lecter are often categorized as forensic mysteries, and forensic mysteries are often grouped along with those about serial killers. Forensic techniques, particularly psychological profiling of killers, are often employed to track down the criminals. In *Silence of the Lambs* (1988), the second Harris book to include Lecter, Agent Starling must use

Lecter's own psychological insights along with her intuition to track down a serial killer. The book was made into an extremely successful movie (1991) starring Anthony Hopkins and Jodie Foster and has become the definitive serial killer movie, against which all others are evaluated. *Silence* was followed by *Hannibal* (1999, a prequel to *Silence*), and *Hannibal Rising* (2006, a sequel to *Silence*). Both have been made into films along with *Red Dragon* (1981), which was made into the movie *Manhunter* (1986).

Ridley Pearson's police procedurals about serial killers featuring detective Lou Boldt and police psychologist Daphne Matthews are set in Seattle, Washington. Like Reichs and Cornwell, Pearson employs up-to-the-minute forensic techniques in his mysteries. Caleb Carr offers readers a look at forensic science as it "might have been." In *The Alienist* (1994) Laszlo Kreizler, a psychologist (alienist) tracks down a killer in 1896 New York. The characters from *The Alienist* reunite in the 1997 *Angel of Darkness*. Set in future world of 2023, Gideon Wolfe is an expert criminal profiler criminologist living in an apocalyptic New York in *Killing Time* (2000).

Edgar winner Aaron Elkins introduced anthropologist and forensics professor Gideon Oliver, better known as the "Skeleton Doctor" in *Fellowship of Fear* (1982). Oliver travels to various locales worldwide to read the crimes written in the victims' bones in this often-humorous series. Elkins's latest novel is *Unnatural Selection* (2006), which follows Oliver to the Isles of Scilly.

Other sciences prove useful in finding killers as well. Forensic geologist Em Hansen (Sarah Andrews) uses her background to help her dig up criminals in Utah and Montana. *In Cold Pursuit* (2007) is the eleventh Hansen novel. Sarah R. Shaber's Professor Simon Shaw is a forensic historian in North Carolina, solving crimes with southern connections.

Archaeology is a subgenre of forensic mysteries. Sharyn McCrumb has received awards for her contributions to Appalachian literature with such titles as *If I'd Killed Him When I Met Him . . .* (1995). Elizabeth McPherson appears in nine mysteries set in Appalachia. As a forensic anthropologist, McPherson uses her knowledge to solve old crimes that have modern repercussions. (See also Regional Mysteries.) Beverly Connor has created two more bone experts: Lindsay Chamberlain, who divides her time between excavating archaeological sites and solving crimes, and Diane Fallon, who is the director of the RiverTrail Museum of Natural History in Georgia.

Context and Issues

Cultural Diversity in Mysteries. Since the 1980s, the mystery genre has seen an explosion of authors from different cultural backgrounds. Novelists who had been on the publishing fringes were beginning to enter the mainstream mystery market. Multicultural characters as well as those of alternate sexual orientations appeared on the shelves with more regularity.

Gay and Lesbian. Two excellent sources cover the history of gay detective fiction: Drewey Wayne Gunn's *The Gay Male Sleuth in Print and Film* (2005) and Judith Markowitz's *The Gay Detective Novel* (2005). Both investigate the history of this subgenre from the first openly homosexual character, the British psychiatrist Tony Page (*The Heart in Exile* by Rodney Garland, 1953) to Ellen Hart's lesbian restaurant owner, Jane Lawless. They trace the development of gay mystery fiction, at its height until 2000, with several authors contributing to the genre with their series:

Mark Richard Zubro (Paul Turner, a gay Chicago police detective), John Morgan Wilson (journalist Benjamin Justice), Lev Raphael (English professor Nick Hoffman), Dorien Grey (detective Dick Hardesty), and Richard Stevenson (private investigator Donald Strachey).

One of the better-known sleuths is George Baxt's creation, Pharoah Love (deliberately misspelled), a homosexual African American New York detective who makes his first appearance in *A Queer Kind of Death* (1966). The novels have not aged well, and although there is much humor in the adventures and characters surrounding Love, the characters are more stereotypical and campy than modern gay detectives.

Joseph Hansen's Dave Brandstetter novels were a groundbreaking phenomenon in the world of mystery fiction. As tough as traditional mystery protagonists of the late 1960s, Brandstetter was also openly homosexual. Hansen introduced Brandstetter in the 1970 *Fadeout,* a mystery in which the upstanding gay characters are positioned as being extreme opposites of the sleazy heterosexual ones. Hansen's first mystery, *Known Homosexual* (also published as *Stranger to Himself,* 1978, and *Pretty Boy Dead,* 1984) involved a love affair between an African American and his white lover. In a 1991 interview with Peter Burton (collected in *Talking To . . . ,* 1991), Hansen said he wanted to overturn gay stereotypes with his characters. He had not planned on writing so many books about Brandstetter, but mainstream acceptance of the character led him to write 12 mysteries featuring the insurance investigator.

M.F. Beal's *Angel Dance* (1977) broke ground with Latina private eye, Kat Guerrera. From the beginning, lesbian mystery writers have foregrounded serious subjects in their novels, tackling issues of racism, sexism, violence against women, and homophobia. Lesbian mysteries often also have a romantic subplot that is often missing from gay mysteries. The now defunct Naiad Press (it has been incorporated into Bella Books) began publishing lesbian mysteries in the 1980s, featuring the works of Katherine V. Forrest who created the first lesbian police detective. Kate Delafield is a former Marine and first appears in *Amateur City* (1984). Forrest has twice won the Lambda Literary Award for best mystery. The latest Delafield novel *Hancock Park* was published in 2004. Another feminist publisher, Seal Press, brought forth the Pam Nilsen series by Barbara Wilson.

Sandra Scoppettone's lesbian character Lauren Laurano is a private investigator living in Greenwich Village. Very successful, Scoppettone is the first author of a lesbian mystery to be published by a mainstream press. Laurano was a very popular character and when Scoppetone ended the series at number six, *Gonna Take a Homicidal Journey* (1998), her fans begged for her return.

Laurie R. King is best known for her Mary Russell series set in England during World War I. Russell solves mysteries with the retired Sherlock Holmes, whom she marries. Although heterosexual herself, King has also created San Francisco-based Kate Martinelli, a lesbian homicide detective. King's first Martinelli novel, *A Grave Talent* (1993) won the Edgar Award for the best first crime novel of the year.

Jane Lawless is a restaurant owner in Minneapolis. Ellen Hart, Lawless's creator, has been compared to Agatha Christie and Barbara Vine. Extremely popular, the latest Lawless installment, *Night Vision* (2006), numbers the fourteenth in the series.

African American. Before the Continental Op, Philip Marlowe, Lew Archer, and Sam Spade, there was John Edward Bruce's *The Black Sleuth* appearing in *McGirt's*

Magazine in 1907. Bruce's West African protagonist Sadipe Okukenu is one of the earliest known black mystery writers ever published. And then there was Florian Slappey, a black private detective created by Octavus Roy Cohen. Regrettably stereotypical and conceived out of the minstrel show tradition, the Slappey stories achieved great popularity and were published in the "Darktown Birmingham" column in *The Saturday Evening Post*. Rudolph Fisher's 1932 *The Conjure-Man Dies* was a product of the Harlem Renaissance.

Chester Himes was one of the most important African American mystery novelists. His novels introduced Coffin Ed Johnson and Grave Digger Jones in *A Rage in Harlem* (1957) after the publication of several other novels. Himes's mysteries showed the violence of African American lives in Harlem and the racism that kept whites and blacks divided. Highly regarded in France where he moved in the 1950s, Himes won the Grand Prix de Littérature Policiére in 1957.

After Himes there were no African American detective series with much staying power until the Shaft novels appeared in 1970. John Tidyman, the white author of the Shaft novels, was awarded the NAACP Image Award. The Shaft movies were immensely popular, and *Shaft* was remade in 2000 starring Samuel L. Jackson. John Shaft was ranked as one of the toughest hard-boiled detectives of the 1970s. Other African American detectives created between the 1950s and 2000 are Ezell "Easy" Barnes, created by Richard Hilary; and Carver Bascombe, originally created by Kenn Davis and John Stanley.

In 1990 Walter Mosley achieved critical acclaim with his first Easy Rawlins book, *Devil in a Blue Dress*. Rawlins, a war veteran, walks the streets of post World War II Los Angeles. Mosley's novels follow Rawlins through time as he marries and starts a family; the first novel is set in 1948, the most recent, *Cinnamon Kiss* (2005) takes place in 1969. A series featuring Fearless Jones and his sidekick Paris Minton is also set in the Los Angeles of the 1950s. A third series character is Socrates Fortlow (*Walkin' the Dog*, 1999). Through Socrates and Rawlins, Mosley poses hard questions about the nature of race relations and the future of the black man in America of the fifties and sixties and in the Los Angeles of the 1990s. His novels are seen as providing strong social commentary on the life of African Americans in a volatile period that still has repercussions today.

Racial tension and violence are the backdrop for Gary Phillips's Ivan Monk series set in Los Angeles. C.J. Floyd is Robert Greer's Denver-based bail bondsman and private eye. Greer is a professor of Pathology and Medicine at the University of Colorado, and he brings his erudition to the Floyd novels (*The Fourth Perspective*, 2006). Police Commander Larry Cole of the Chicago Police Department is the creation of Hugh Holton. Holton himself was a police detective until his death in 2001.

A scene formerly dominated by male writers has experienced an explosion of female authors. Along with focusing on social issues as their male counterparts do, African American authors often infuse their mysteries with family dynamics as well. Former *Essence* magazine editor Valerie Wilson Wesley's Tamara Hayle is a Newark, New Jersey ex-cop turned private eye. Wesley's novels follow Hayle as she struggles to raise her son. Barbara Neely created Blanche White, a nosy 40-year-old domestic who frequently finds trouble. *Blanche on the Lam* (1992) was her first appearance and won the Agatha, the Macavity, and the Anthony awards. Nikki Chase solves crimes while teaching economics at Harvard (*Orange Crushed*, 2004). Eleanor Taylor Bland's popular series stars Marti McAlister. McAlister is a Chicago cop transplanted to a small town, Lincoln Prairie, Illinois, where fighting crime goes hand in hand with fighting small town attitudes. *Suddenly a Stranger* (2007) is the fourteenth in the series.

Native American. Although not a Native American himself, Tony Hillerman is unquestionably the most popular author to feature Indian characters. Influenced by Arthur W. Upfield's Australian police officer who is part Aborigine, Tony Hillerman created Joe Leaphorn, a member of the Navajo Tribal Police in New Mexico. Leaphorn grew out of an encounter Hillerman had with a Texas sheriff he met while a young reporter. His Leaphorn novels, beginning with *The Blessing Way* (1970), became very popular for their authentic depictions of Navajo life and the Southwest. Leaphorn's partner Jim Chee was introduced with *People of Darkness* (1980), adding a deeper look into the religious beliefs of the Navajo as Chee balances his desire to be both a law officer and a shaman. Based on the students Hillerman taught at the University of New Mexico, Chee is young and idealistic. Although he has written other mysteries and nonfiction titles, the Leaphorn/Chee novels are the most popular; almost 20 have appeared since his 1970 publication of *The Blessing Way*. The most recent title is the 2003 *Sinister Pig*.

The husband and wife team of Aimée and David Thurlo has written two series of books based on Navajo characters. Lee Nez is a nightwalker, the Navajo equivalent of a vampire in the Lee Nez series (*Second Sunrise*, 2002). Nez teams up with an FBI agent to solve crimes both human and supernatural. *Blackening Song* (1995) is the first in the acclaimed Ella Clah series about Clah, a former FBI agent, now a Navajo Police Special Investigator, who combines modern investigative techniques with ancient Navajo tradition as she solves crimes on the reservation. *Turquoise Girl* (2007) is the latest in the series.

Peter Bowen's Gabriel Du Pre, cattle-brand inspector and Toussaint, Montana deputy, makes his first appearance in the 1994 *Cattle Wind*. Bowen's 13 Du Pre mysteries revolve around current events as well as Native American issues. Margaret Coel is an expert on the Arapaho Indians. Her series featuring Father John and Arapaho lawyer Vicky Holden are set on the Wind River Reservation. In the eleventh book of the series, *Eye of the Wolf* (2005), the inhabitants of the Wind River Reservation are on the brink of civil war with the neighboring Shoshone. Award-winning Jean Hager is the author of two series characters: Mitch Bushyhead is a half-Cherokee police chief, and Molly Bearclaw is an investigator for the Cherokee Nation.

Inupiat Police Detective Ray Attla investigates mysteries in Christopher Lane's Inupiat Eskimo series. Like many mysteries featuring Native Americans, Lane's series features the tension of Attla trying to straddle two different cultures. Another Alaskan native, Dana Stabenow, is the author of the Kate Shugak mysteries. *A Cold Day for Murder* (1992), winner of the Edgar Award, introduces Shugak, an Aleut who has left her job with the Anchorage district attorney to live in the Alaskan wilderness. Stabenow's books have been praised for their accurate depictions of Native Alaskan societies, particularly fishing communities.

James D. Doss adds an element of humor to his Southern Ute tribal policeman Charlie Moon series. *Stone Butterfly* (2006) is the eleventh novel to feature Moon and his aunt Daisy Perika, an Ute shaman. FBI special agent Anna Turnipseed, a Modoc Indian, and Bureau of Indian Affairs Investigator Emmett Parker, a Comanche, star in Kirk Mitchell's mysteries. In the 2003 *Sky Woman Falling*, an Oneida creation myth stirs up modern day trouble.

Asian American and Hispanic American. Japanese American gardener Mas Arai becomes involved in unraveling a decades-old mystery in Naomi Hirahara's *Summer of the Big Bachi* (2004). *Bachi* is the Japanese spirit of retribution; Mas's less than pure life after Hiroshima is catching up with him. Sujata Massey has created Japanese American sleuth Rei Shimura, a Japanese American antiques dealer working in Tokyo. The seventh installment, Agatha Award nominee *The Pearl Diver* (2004), finds Shimura making a fresh start in Washington, D.C. New York City detective lieutenant Jimmy Sakura solves crimes in Harker Moore's *Cruel Season for Dying* (2003) and *A Mourning in Autumn* (2004). S.J. Rozan's mystery series featuring Chinese American private investigator Lydia Chin, have garnered many nominations and awards (*Winter and Night*, 2003, won the Edgar and Macavity awards and was nominated for the Shamus and the Anthony).

Sonny Baca appears in Rudolpho Anaya's *Albuquerque Quartet*. Baca is a minor character in *Albuquerque* (1992), but in the next three installments he takes the lead role. Each installment of the quartet is concerned with the Mexican American traditions associated with the seasons. Anaya combines Mexican mythology, history, and legend with current issues, such as drugs and corporate greed. In *Shaman Winter* (1999), Baca fights his nemesis Raven as he travels back in time to 1598 New Mexico. The series has been continued beyond the quartet with *Jemez Spring* (2005).

Critically acclaimed Michael Nava writes mysteries about a gay Chicano character, Henry Rios. Inspired by Joseph Hansen, Nava has created a character who represents a marginalized group within the marginalized Chicano society. Rios is introduced in the 1986 *The Little Death*, in which he resigns from his position in a law firm to start his own business defending society's outcasts. *Rag and Bone* (2007) is the seventh Rios mystery. Like Rios, Luis Montez is a Chicano legal aid attorney helping the down and out. Burned out by his job, Ruiz longs for his activist youth in the series debut, *The Ballad of Rocky Ruiz* (1993).

Rex Burns has written several mysteries featuring introspective Hispanic American Gabe Wager, a homicide detective for the Denver Police Department. Cuban American Lupe Solano is the creation of Carolina Garcia-Aguilera. The Miami private investigator has been featured in six installments (*Bitter Sugar*, 2001). K.J.A. Wishnia's New Yorker Filomena Buscarsela returns to her native Ecuador in *Blood Lake* (2002).

Regional Mysteries. Although many mysteries have strong locales as part of their plots, some mystery writers are inextricably linked to a particular region: the South, the West, and even specific states or cities: New York, Chicago, or Los Angeles. More so than most general fiction, the often-regional nature of many mysteries, especially those written with series characters, appeal to readers in various geographic regions.

New England. Boston figures prominently as a locale for a number of mystery writers. Jane Langton's series about Homer Kelly includes Cape Cod and other Massachusetts environs, while Linda Barnes's Carlotta Carlyle investigates crimes in Boston. Other popular Bostonians are Robert B. Parker and Jeremiah Healey. Dennis Lehane's series featuring private investigators Kenzie and Gennaro is set in his hometown of Dorchester, Massachusetts.

Mid Atlantic. New York City has been cited as the U.S. city most frequently serving as the setting for mystery novels. Ed McBain, Rex Stout, and Donald Westlake have all set mysteries in New York. Lawrence Block lends a strong air of realism to his several series of mysteries, including the popular Matthew Scudder, by evoking New York both pre- and post-9/11. Janet Evanovich sets her wildly popular novels about bond agent Stephanie Plum in New Jersey. Gillian Roberts's Amanda Pepper series is set against the backdrop of Philadelphia as are those of Lisa Scottoline and Jane Haddam. K.C. Constantine created the mythical Rocksburg, Pennsylvania, and Tamara Myer depicts the Pennsylvania Dutch country. Margaret Truman's Capital Crimes series in set in Washington, D.C., as are George P. Pelecanos's Derek Strange novels.

The South. The South is home to many mystery writers. Patricia Houck Sprinkle and Kathy Hogan Trochek both use Atlanta and its environs as settings. Charlotte, North Carolina is the setting for both Kathy Reichs's Temperance Brennan series and for Patricia Cornwell's Kay Scarpetta titles. (See Forensic Mysteries.) Julie Smith sets her novels in New Orleans and Edgar Award-winning James Lee Burke's hard-boiled mysteries about Dave Robicheaux span the area from the Big Easy to the bayous.

There are currently sixteen titles featuring Burke's character Dave Robicheaux, a retired New Orleans police officer who has moved to the small town in New Iberia parish. The setting is intrinsic to a Burke novel. The bayous and their landscapes and wildlife are not just backdrops, they act as characters, often fighting against the same ills faced by many southern locales: increasing development and crime, which decimates the wildlife and the economy of rural areas. Into the mix are thrown felons hiding in the swampy backwoods and the often crime-laced nightlife of the French Quarter.

Florida is the location of Carl Hiaasen's novels, which tackle the multiple issues of theme parks, endangered species, and overdevelopment. *Strip Tease* (1993) was the first of Hiaasen's novels to make the best-seller list. The novel was later adapted for the screen in 1996 with Demi Moore and Burt Reynolds. Readers are introduced to a recurring character in Hiaasen's work: Clinton "Skink" Tyree, a Florida governor who suddenly vacates the office after the corruption around him becomes too much to bear. Tyree ultimately flees into the swamps and becomes something of an ecoterrorist or prankster, a role often taken up by characters in later works, sometimes after direct contact with Skink, who appears to mature into a teacher figure.

Joan Hess's characters live in Farberville, Arkansas and feature bookstore operator Clair Malloy. Hess's 16 novels featuring Malloy present all aspects of southern culture, including family relationships and racism. Hess's other character is Arly Hanks, chief of police in Maggody, Arkansas. Ruby Bee's Bar & Grill and Estelle's Hair Fantasies are the locations Hanks goes to relax, and that provide moments of humor in the midst of sometimes biting social commentary.

The Appalachian Mountains of Eastern Tennessee are the setting of Sharyn McCrumb's extremely popular best sellers. Her Ellen McPherson mysteries are read as social satires of southern life as she works as a forensic anthropologist. McCrumb's novels on the McPherson series provide voluminous information about the history of the South, both its Confederate ancestors and its Native American ones. Her ballad series, beginning with *If Ever I Return, Pretty Peggy-O* (1990) are set in a fictional Tennessee town, and the mysteries are structured like ballads with their stories of passion that have their roots in the past and their violent consequences in the present.

Margaret Maron sets her dozen judge Deborah Knott titles in the South as well. Her characters are representative without being stereotypical, with sharply rendered dialogue and plots played out against the backdrop of a fictionalized North Carolina comparable to William Faulkner's Yoknapatawpha, Mississippi.

One of the most popular mysteries series set in the South has been Carolyn Hart's "Death on Demand" and "Henrie O" novels. Set on a fictional South Carolina resort island, the "Death on Demand" series features an attractive, wealthy couple, Annie and Max Darling. They own a mystery bookshop, and also work together to solve the many real mysteries that come their way. Hart hit on a winning formula with her "Death on Demand" series. The stories combine elements of romance, mystery fiction, and bibliophilia, and have proven tremendously popular with readers. Part of the fun of the series comes from Annie Laurance Darling's devoted customers, all of whom are fanatical mystery readers. The author reveals in the books a familiarity with esoteric mystery fiction that appeals to devotees of the genre.

The Midwest. William Kienzle's Father Koesler mysteries and Loren D. Estleman's Amos Walker novels are both set in Detroit; and Ellen Hart's Jane Lawless and John Sandford's Lucas Davenport both operate in Minnesota as well. Estleman is equally well known and well respected for his westerns as for his mysteries. Amos Walker was created in the tradition of Hammett and Chandler, but the streets he walks are those of Detroit instead of Los Angeles. *Motor City Blue* (1980) is the first Walker novel and shows Estleman's deep research and sharp eye as the characters ply their trades on the often seedy and dangerous streets of the city. A detective with a blue-collar background, Walker takes the reader on location from Detroit's poverty-stricken inner city to the prestigious Grosse Point.

The West and Southwest. Rudolfo Anaya, best known for his coming of age novel *Bless Me, Ultima*, joins the ranks of mystery writers with his series featuring Sonny Baca set in New Mexico. The novels of Susan Wittig Albert are set in Pecan Springs, Texas. Nevada Barr sets her environmental mysteries in various national parks, including those in New Mexico and Texas, among other southwestern locales. Walter Mosley's Easy Rawlins prowls the streets of Los Angeles along with Michael Connolly's Harry Bosch. T. Jefferson Parker has published well-received novels set in 1950s Orange County, California.

Selected Authors

Historical Mysteries. There are dozens of mysteries that feature historical characters, real or imagined, solving crimes in every time period imaginable—from the Paleolithic to World War II. The following discussion focuses on characters created by Americans and writers still producing works in the 2000s.

Robin Paige, the pseudonym of husband-wife team Susan Wittig Albert and Bill Albert, has created a series set in Victorian England and featuring Kate Ardleigh and Sir Charles Sheridan. Susan Wittig Albert, better known for her China Bayles series, has developed a series of mysteries around the children's author, Beatrix Potter. Emily Brightwell introduced Mrs. Jeffries in the 1993 *The Inspector and Mrs. Jeffries.* Mrs. Jeffries keeps house for Scotland Yard Inspector Witherspoon and helps him solve crimes. These historical mysteries are light enough to be considered cozies.

Far from the world of cozies, Caleb Carr is a military historian and novelist who has written thrillers set in the past and future. Reviewers praised *The Alienist* as an engrossing book infused with the authentic atmosphere of turn-of-the-century New York. Some critics, however, found that the story was sometimes overwhelmed by historical detail. A sequel to *The Alienist* is *The Angel of Darkness.* In 2005, Carr published *The Italian Secretary: A Further Adventure of Sherlock Holmes.* There has long been a mania for creating Sherlock Holmes stories to satisfy the detective's legions of fans. In *The Italian Secretary*, Watson and Holmes are joined by Holmes's brother, Mycroft, and the three are drawn into an investigation of the mysterious death of two workers at Queen Victoria's castle in Scotland. Conspiracy theories abound, along with the possibility of supernatural predators hovering in the gloom, but the clues that Holmes discovers lead him in quite a different direction.

Laurie R. King is another author who has created a series based on the further adventures of Sherlock Holmes. King's Mary Russell first appeared in 1994 with *The Beekeeper's Apprentice*. The novel is set in 1914 and Homes takes the 15-year-old Mary under his wing and the two solve crimes; she eventually becomes his wife. Sherlock Holmes purists rejected King's novels, but their inclusion of a female character at the heart of the mysteries have won over many female readers. In the eighth series installment, *Locked Room* (2005), though, Holmes emerges as the lead character.

Barbara Mertz writes under two extraordinarily popular pseudonyms: Elizabeth Peters and Barbara Michaels. Peters has set dozens of books in nineteenth-century Egypt with its many tombs and historical locations described in great detail. Family life may have curbed her archaeological activities, but her vast knowledge of the field lends much background interest and credibility to her Amelia Peabody novels (begun in 1975), which are set against the backdrop of the excavations of Egypt's Valley of Kings. Mertz has continued to publish yearly installments in the Amelia Peabody series. *Tomb of the Golden Bird* (2006) is the eighteenth Peabody novel.

Bruce Alexander's final two installments in the Sir John Fielding series about an eighteenth-century blind London judge are *The Price of Murder* (2003) and *Rules of Engagement* (2005).

Stuart M. Kaminsky is a prolific author of mysteries and creator of several sleuths, one of them the World War II-era Toby Peters. The Peters mysteries feature historical figures, such as Errol Flynn and Emmett Kelly, involved in fictional actions.

Legal Mysteries and Thrillers. Technically speaking, a thriller is a genre that has a plot devoted to the chase or hunt. Thriller subgenres are endless: medical thrillers, techno thrillers, spy novels, and so on. However, **legal thrillers** are popular with mystery readers because the pursuit of justice is usually local and based on a particular crime as is a traditional mystery. John Grisham, a former Mississippi attorney and author of almost 20 best-selling novels, most of which are legal thrillers, has said, "Though Americans distrust the profession as a whole, we have an insatiable appetite for stories about crimes, criminals, trials and all sorts of juicy lawyer stuff" (Grisham).

As early as Charles Dickens and Wilkie Collins, the legal thriller was appearing in the marketplace to great popular success. For example, Collins's *The Moonstone* (1868) and *The Woman in White* (1859) contain elements of a legal thriller: an innocent person, the criminal justice system (legal proceedings and courtroom drama) playing an intrinsic part of the storyline (e.g., Dickens's *Bleak House* [1853]), witness testimony, legal documents (wills, etc.), and lawyers assisting in solving the crime. In the 1930s Erle Stanley Gardner, a practicing attorney, became one of the most prolific and popular authors of courtroom dramas with his creation of Perry Mason.

Many authors of legal thrillers are former attorneys themselves. Grisham, Scott Turow, Richard North Patterson, and Steve Martini are four of the most recognized attorney/authors in the genre. It was Turow's 1987 *Presumed Innocent* that opened the floodgates to modern courtroom dramas.

Turow's first novel, *One-L* (1977), written while Turow was a law student at Harvard, documented the difficulties of law school. *Presumed Innocent* was published while Turow was working as an assistant U.S. district attorney in Chicago. The novel was well received and its publisher, Farrar, Strauss, paid more money for the title than they ever had for a book by a first-time author. Their chance paid off as *Presumed Innocent* hit the best-seller lists. The novel was praised for its insight into the legal system and its refusal to divide the world into simplistic fields of black and white, good and evil. The film, starring Harrison Ford, was released in 1990. Turow's most recent title is *Limitations* (2006), originally published as a weekly serial in the *New York Times Magazine*.

John Grisham's first novel, *A Time to Kill* (1989), was slow to take off in the market, but when it was republished by a major publishing house, he became a household name very quickly. *A Time to Kill* was inspired by a courtroom case, but several of his subsequent novels were criticized as being too formulaic. His 1994 *The Chamber* was written at a much slower pace and garnered more critical acclaim than some of the earlier titles. Grisham's novels, although sometimes criticized for their unrealistic plots, are almost always praised for their characterization and their intense pace. These two elements have led to several of Grisham's titles, among them *A Time to Kill*, *The Firm* (1991), and *The Pelican Brief* (1992), being made into blockbuster films.

Before turning to fiction writing, Richard North Patterson was a successful lawyer who worked for the prosecution on the *Watergate* case of the 1970s. His literary career took off after the publication of his second novel, *Degree of Guilt* (1992) published after an eight-year hiatus from writing. Unlike many other mystery writers, Patterson does not have a series character; each novel is written about a different protagonist, in a different place, with different kinds of crimes. The common thread in Patterson's mysteries is the attention paid to the legal system. In the 2005 *Conviction*, an eleven-year-old conviction is re-investigated; *Balance of Power* (2003) combines politics and law in issues about gun control; and in *Exile* (2007) the Middle East of today's headlines is at the center of attorney David Wolfe's most difficult case.

Steve Martini is a former journalist and attorney. His skills combine to make him one of the foremost authors of courtroom drama. Most of Martini's titles feature attorney Paul Madriani, whose cases are always part of a larger, more corrupt, political scene. He has been praised for his torn-from-the-headlines plots and exceptionally well-drawn and exciting courtroom pyrotechnics. *Double Tap* (2005) is the eighth Madriani installment.

Many people are curious about how the law works and doesn't work, and authors spend a good amount of ink on explaining points of law that make the novels not only entertaining but educational. As in forensic mysteries, the author of legal thrillers must clearly explain the points, in this case legal, upon which a case rests. Legal mysteries often focus on glitches in the justice system or the manipulation of the law by shady attorneys. The protagonists themselves are usually of two types, the idealistic young attorney who is up against a corrupt system, or a jaded lawyer who is closer to the wrong side of the law than to the right. Michael Connelly has created Michael Haller, who is an example of the latter type in *The Lincoln Lawyer* (2005).

THE EDGAR AWARD FOR BEST MYSTERIES

Since 1946, the Mystery Writers of America has annually presented the Edgar awards, named in honor of Edgar Allan Poe, for the best mysteries of the year, although there was no "Best Novel" category until 1954, for fear of alienating key members. (Instead, there was a "Best First Novel," which is still given.) The recent "Best" mystery novel winners have included

2007	*The Janissary Tree* by Jason Goodwin (2007)
2006	*Citizen Vince* by Jess Walter. Regan Books.
2005	*California Girl* by T. Jefferson Parker. William Morrow.
2004	*Resurrection Men* by Ian Rankin. Little, Brown.
2003	*Winter and Night* by S.J. Rozan. St. Martin's Minotaur.
2002	*Silent Joe* by T. Jefferson Parker. Hyperion.
2001	*The Bottoms* by Joe R. Lansdale. Mysterious Press.
2000	*Bones* by Jan Burke. Simon & Schuster.

Source: Mystery Writers of America Web site. http://mysterywriters.org/

Female authors have cornered a large sector of the legal thriller market as well. Lia Matera began publishing fiction after law school, creating the characters Willa Jansson and Laura Di Palma, who have starred in over a dozen titles. Lisa Scottoline is another former lawyer who sets her novels in Philadelphia. Her novels about the all female law firm Rosato and Associates have won her many awards.

Reception

Awards. There are several awards for mystery fiction. The Edgar Allan Poe Awards (The Edgars) were established by the Mystery Writers of America for various categories (best novel, best first novel, etc.). The first award was given in 1953 to Jay Charlotte's *Beat Not the Bones*. The winner of the 2007 award for best novel is *The Janissary Tree* by Jason Goodwin. The Grand Master Award, also presented by the Mystery Writers of America association, recognizes lifetime achievements of nominees. Recent winners have been Stephen King (2007), Stuart Kaminsky (2006), and Marcia Muller (2005). Other awards include the Agatha, which honors the traditional mystery and is awarded by Malice Domestic. The Anthony Awards are named for Anthony Boucher, one of the founders of Mystery Writers of America. And finally, there is the Macavity Award, presented by Mystery Readers International.

Bibliography

Anaya, Rudolpho. *Albuquerque.* Albuquerque: University of New Mexico Press, 1992.

Anderson, Patrick. *The Triumph of the Thriller: How Cops, Crooks, and Cannibals Captured Popular Fiction.* New York: Random House, 2007.

Bailey, Frankie Y. *Out of the Woodpile: Black Characters in Crime and Detective Fiction.* New York: Greenwood Press, 1991.

Beal, M.F. *Angel Dance.* New York: Daughters, 1977.

Bishop, Claudia. *Ground to a Halt.* Waterville, ME: Wheeler, 2007.

Block, Lawrence. *The Sins of the Fathers.* Arlington Heights, IL: Dark Harvest, 1976.

Brown, Dan. *The Da Vinci Code.* New York: Doubleday, 2003.

Browne, Ray B. *Murder on the Reservation: American Indian Crime Fiction, Aims and Achievements.* Madison, WI: University of Wisconsin Press, 2004.

Burke, Jan. *Bones.* New York: Simon & Schuster, 1999.

Burton, Peter. *Talking To . . . Peter Burton in Conversation with Writers Writing on Gay Themes.* Exeter, England: Third House, 1991.

Carr, Caleb. *The Alienist.* New York: Random House, 1994.

Clark, Mary Higgins. *Two Little Girls in Blue.* New York: Simon & Schuster, 2006.

Collins, Max Allan. *The History of Mystery.* Portland, OR: Collectors Press, 2001.

Conant, Susan. *Gaits of Heaven.* New York: Berkeley Prime Crime, 2006.

Connelly, Michael. *Echo Park.* New York: Little, Brown, 2006.

Cross, Amanda. *The Edge of Doom.* New York: Ballantine, 2003.

"Culinary Crime: First Course." *Mystery Readers International* 18.2 (Summer 2002).

"Culinary Crime: Second Seating." *Mystery Readers International* 18.3 (Fall 2002).

Deaver, Jeffrey. *The Bone Collector.* New York: Viking, 1997.

Demko, George J. Crime in Cold Places: A Geographic Review of George J. Demko's Landscapes of Crime. http://www.dartmouth.edu/~gjdemko/toc.htm.

Fischer-Hornung, Dorothea, and Monika Mueller. *Sleuthing Ethnicity: The Detective in Multiethnic Crime Fiction.* Madison: Fairleigh Dickinson University Press; London: Associated University Presses, 2003.

Goodwin, Jason. *The Janissary Tree.* New York: Farrar, Straus and Giroux, 2006.

Gorman, Ed, et al., eds. *The Fine Art of Murder.* New York: Carroll & Graf Publishers, Inc., 1993.

Greeley, Andrew. *The Bishop in the Old Neighborhood.* New York: Forge, 2005.

Grisham, John. "The Rise of the Legal Thriller: Why Lawyers are Throwing the Books at Us." *New York Times,* Book Review Section. 18 October 1992: 33.

Gunn, Drewey. *The Gay Male Sleuth in Print and Film.* Lanham, MD: Scarecrow Press, 2005.

Harris, Thomas. *The Silence of the Lambs.* New York: St. Martin's, 1988.

Helen Windrath, ed. *They Wrote the Book: Thirteen Women Mystery Writers Tell All.* Duluth, MN: Spinsters Ink, 2000.

Hiaasen, Carl. *Strip Tease.* New York: Knopf, 1993.

Johnson, Adrienne Gosselin, ed. *Multicultural Detective Fiction: Murder from the "Other" Side.* New York: Garland Press, 1999.

Kemelman, Harry. *The Day the Rabbi Left Town.* New York: Fawcett Columbine, 1996.

Kienzle, William. *Motor City Blue.* Boston: Houghton Mifflin, 1980.

King, Laurie R. *The Beekeeper's Apprentice.* New York: St. Martin's, 1994.

Klein, Kathleen Gregory, ed. *Diversity and Detective Fiction.* Bowling Green, OH: Bowling Green State University Popular Press, 1999.

Klein, Kathleen Gregory, ed. *Great Women Mystery Writers: Classic to Contemporary.* Westport, CT: Greenwood Press, 1994.

Knight, Stephen. *Crime Fiction, 1800–2000: Detection, Death, Diversity.* Houndmills, Basingstoke, Hampshire; New York: Palgrave Macmillan, 2004.

Lansdale, Joe R. *The Bottoms.* New York: Warner Books, 2000.

Malmgren, Carl Darryl. *Anatomy of Murder: Mystery, Detective, and Crime Fiction.* Bowling Green, OH: Bowling Green State University Popular Press, 2001.

Markowitz, Judith. *The Gay Detective Novel: Gay and Lesbian Characters and Themes in Mystery Fiction.* Jefferson, NC: McFarland & Co., 2004.

McDermid, Val, and Nevada Barr. *A Suitable Job for a Woman: Inside the World of Women Private Eyes.* Scottsdale, AR: Poisoned Pen Press, 1999.

Mizejewski, Linda. *Hardboiled and High Heeled: The Woman Detective in Popular Culture.* New York: Routledge, 2004.

Mosley, Walter. *Devil in a Blue Dress.* New York: Norton, 1990.

Murphy, Bruce F. *The Encyclopedia of Murder and Mystery*. New York: St. Martin's Minotaur Books, 1999.

Panek, Leroy Lad. *New Hard-Boiled Writers, 1970s–1990s*. Bowling Green, OH: Bowling Green State University Popular Press, 2000.

Parker, T. Jefferson. *California Girl*. New York: William Morrow, 2004.

———. *Silent Joe*. New York: Harper Collins, 2003.

Pronzini, Bill. *Savages*. New York: Forge, 2007.

"New York and London Are Most Popular Settings for Novels, According to Newly Released Fiction Statistics Analysis from Bowker." Bowker. http://www.bowker.com/press/bowker/2006_0121_bowker.htm.

Quill, Monica. *Death Takes the Veil*. Waterville, ME: Fiver Star, 2001.

Rankin, Ian. *Resurrection Men*. Boston: Little, Brown, 2003.

Reddy, Maureen. *Traces, Codes, and Clues: Reading Race in Crime Fiction*. New Brunswick, NJ: Rutgers University Press, 2003.

Reynolds, Moira Davison. *Women Authors of Detective Series: Twenty-One American and British Writers, 1900–2000*. Jefferson, NC: McFarland & Co., 2001.

Rich, Virginia. *Cooking School Murders*. New York: Dutton, 1982.

Rippetoe, Rita Elizabeth. *Booze and the Private Eye: Alcohol in the Hard-Boiled Novel*. Jefferson, NC: McFarland & Company, 2004.

Rodriguez, Ralph E. *Brown Gumshoes: Detective Fiction and the Search for Chicana/o Identity*. Austin: University of Texas Press, 2005.

Roth, Laurence. *Inspecting Jews: American Jewish Detective Stories*. Brunswick, NJ: Rutgers University Press, 2004.

Rozan, S.J. *Winter and Night*. New York: St. Martins, 2002.

Schwartz, Richard B. *Nice and Noir: Contemporary American Crime Fiction*. Missouri: University of Missouri Press, 2002.

"U.S. Book Production, 1993–2004." Book Wire. http://www.bookwire.com/bookwire/decadebookproduction.html.

Walter, Jess. *Citizen Vince*. New York: Harper Perennial, 2006.

Watson, Priscilla L. Walton, and Manina Jones. *Detective Agency: Women Rewriting the Hard-Boiled Tradition*. California: University California Press, 1999.

Williams, John. *Back to the Badlands: Crime Writing in the USA*. London: Serpent's Tail, 2007.

Woods, Paula. *Spooks, Spies, and Private Eyes: Black Mystery, Crime and Suspense Fiction*. New York: Doubleday, 1995.

Web Sites

African American Mysteries. http://mystnoir0.tripod.com/MystNoirDir/.

Classic Crime Fiction: The History of and Articles about Detective, Crime, and Mystery Fiction. http://www.classiccrimefiction.com/history-articles.htm.

Crime thru Time: Historical Mysteries. 1999. http://crimethrutime.com/.

"Detective, Mystery, and Suspense Fiction." New York Public Library. 2007. http://www.nypl.org/research/chss/grd/resguides/detective/print.html.

Grost, Michael E. A Guide to Classic Mystery and Detection. 2007. http://members.aol.com/MG4273/classics.htm.

"History, Literary Criticism & Theory and Other Agendas." The Thrilling Detective Web site. 2007. http://www.thrillingdetective.com/trivia/triv257.html.

Malice Domestic. http://www.malicedomestic.org/.

The Mysterious Home Page. 2005. http://www.cluelass.com/MystHome/index. html.

Mystery Writers of America. http://www.mysterywriters.org/.

Sisters in Crime. http://www.sistersincrime.org/.

Ultimate Mystery/Detective Web Guide. 2003. http://www.magicdragon.com/UltimateMystery/.

Further Reading

Anderson, Patrick. *The Triumph of the Thriller: How Cops, Crooks, and Cannibals Captured Popular Fiction.* New York: Random House, 2007; Collins, Max Allan. *The History of Mystery.* Portland, OR: Collectors Press, 2001; Johnson, Adrienne Gosselin, ed. *Multicultural Detective Fiction: Murder from the "Other" Side.* New York: Garland Pr., 1999; Murphy, Bruce F. *The Encyclopedia of Murder and Mystery.* New York: St. Martin's Minotaur Books, 1999; Schwartz, Richard B. *Nice and Noir: Contemporary American Crime Fiction.* Missouri: University of Missouri Press, 2002.

PATRICIA BOSTIAN